WHOLE GREEN CATALOG

WHOLE GREEN CATALOG

1,000 BEST THINGS FOR YOU AND THE EARTH

Edited by **MICHAEL W. ROBBINS** Foreword by **BILL MCKIBBEN** Introduction by **RENÉE LOUX**

Designed by **WENDY PALITZ** Illustrations by **JOEL HOLLAND**

RODALE

Printed in Canada

FSC

Mixed Sources
Product group from well-managed forests, controlled sources and recycled wood or fibre

Cert no. SW-COC-000952
www.fsc.org
© 1996 Forest Stewardship Council

Using Cascade Rolland Enviro100 School book text paper for the first printing of *Whole Green Catalog* reduces the book's ecological footprint by saving:

★ 1,093 trees
★ 69,461 pounds of solid waste
★ 655,604 gallons of water
★ 439 pounds of suspended particles in the water
★ 152,531 pounds of air emissions
★ 158,951 cubic feet of natural gas

Book design by Wendy Palitz
Credits for illustrations and photographs can be found on page 377.

Library of Congress Cataloging-in-Publication Data

Whole green catalog: 1,000 best things for you and the earth / edited by Michael W. Robbins ; foreword by Bill McKibben ; introduction by Renée Loux.
    p. cm.
  Includes index.
  ISBN-13: 978–1–59486–887–0 (pbk.)
  ISBN-10: 1–59486–887–5 (pbk.)
  1. Sustainable living. 2. Green products—Catalogs. 3. Environmentalism. 4. Green movement. I. Robbins, Michael W.
  GE196.W56 2009
  640—dc22

           2009023660

Distributed to the trade by Macmillan
2 4 6 8 10 9 7 5 3 1 paperback

RODALE
LIVE YOUR WHOLE LIFE™

We inspire and enable people to improve their lives and the world around them
For more of our products visit **rodalestore.com** or call 800-848-4735

FOR ROBERT FRENAY (1946–2007)

Good friend, coworker, versatile and valued professional colleague, brilliant author of Pulse, *and the inspirational spark for this book. We miss his understated humor, his relentless curiosity, his ideas, his passion, his determination to get it right. And—at the end—his courage.*

contents

The series of interlocking environmental crises we now face—global warming, water shortage, food supply, peak oil—seem daunting. That's because they *are* daunting, the worst cul-de-sac into which human beings have ever stumbled. It will take every bit of wit and skill we have to chart a course through the next few decades—and it will demand real community and political engagement from everyone who cares.

But of course, that's the view from up high, taking in the whole sprawling mess. It can also be viewed, productively, from down below, where each of us actually lives. Where, a hundred times a day, we make small choices that influence the future, our own and the planet's. That's where this catalog does most of its work, helping us figure out what some of those choices look like—and why far from being grim, they're mostly sweet.

Take your home: Buildings, including homes, are the biggest source of greenhouse gases worldwide, ahead of cars and industry. And hence, they'll need to be a place where change comes quickly. Which it can. I've spent time, for instance, in Chinese cities—cities of a million people—where 98 percent of homes heat their domestic hot water with solar arrays on the roof. It's not because of some government edict; it's because it's cheap. Almost anywhere in the world, the payback time on solar thermal hot water is just a few years. Solar photovoltaic panels to produce electricity are pricier—but many state and local governments now help pay the cost. And the satisfaction of watching your electric meter run backward—of knowing that you're a utility!—can hardly be measured.

New technologies are making all kinds of conservation easier. Google, for instance, has just released free technology to let you monitor how much electricity your house is using at any given moment—it's an enormous incentive to see that when you unplug that flashing phone charger or that unwatched television set, there's a noticeable dip in the current. On the road, there are of course hybrid cars (and soon plug-in hybrids, a really revolutionary technology). But just as important, your iPhone now comes with applications that let you easily arrange to share a ride to the grocery store—remember, half as many car trips is the same as driving twice as efficient a vehicle.

Wherever you look around the house, this guide will help you figure out ways to shave both waste and cost. In fact, now is the perfect moment for its emergence, since the financial crisis makes wasting money almost as painful as the ecological crisis makes wasting carbon. Toaster oven when you don't need to fire up the whole range? That's easy. Solar cooker on the deck on a sunny day, with the sun making your chili for you while you work? That's sweet. Or consider that most useful of all high-tech solar devices, the clothesline: It can save you 6 or 7 percent of the electricity you use each year.

But the clothesline also helps you realize something else: Many of the technologies we can switch to come with advantages far beyond the energy they save. A clothes dryer is basically pretty dull. You load it, push a button, it makes some noise and burns some energy, and eventually a buzzer goes off. A clothesline, by contrast, takes you outdoors for a few minutes into the real world. You feel the sun on your shoulders, you move your body a bit, you hear the birds. And you have to pay some attention to the weather, study the sky to see if you've got an hour before the rain rolls in. It takes a little longer to use, but that extra time is a cost, not a benefit.

Similarly, food. Some years ago, I made sure that everything I fed my family for a whole year came from local farms in our small valley. It had many effects: We ate healthily, since processed food was not an option. We also ate less meat, since raising it locally and responsibly means it costs more than we're used to (and in turn that means that you cook with it the way most people in the world do, as a flavoring). It made me a better cook, since I had to learn many ways to make the same basic items interesting. And it took more time. The question became: Was that time a bonus or a detraction? Bonus, I decided: Before the year was out I'd made many new friends among the region's farmers, and I had a far better idea of how my place worked. It made home seem richer, more interesting.

Something similar happens to most people who start making these switches. The farmers' market is the fastest growing part of our food system in America, with sales rising sharply year after year. It provides better food (think how you feel after you travel 2,000 miles—that's how the supermarket tomato feels, too). And it's environmentally better—our conventional food system uses so much energy that your dinner is essentially marinated in crude oil. But the biggest benefit, I think, is that it changes the feeling of shopping. A few years ago, a pair of sociologists followed shoppers as they did their marketing. First in the supermarket, where everyone falls into a light trance, visits to the stations of the cross around the market, and then exits into the vast parking lot. Next, the farmers' market—where, on average, they found that shoppers were having ten times as many conversations per visit.

Ten times! Shoppers were rebuilding community, which is probably the most crucial environmental task of all. Think about it: Cheap fossil fuel has made us the first people on earth who have essentially no need of our neighbors. We've decided that the American Dream involves larger houses farther away from the neighbors. It's a big reason we're such energy wastrels. But it's also the reason that—get this—fewer Americans say they're very satisfied with their lives than 50 years ago, when our standard of living was a third as high. The data make clear the reason for that creeping unhappiness—we're much lonelier and less connected than the people who came before us. The average American eats meals with friends and family half as often as 50 years ago and has half as many friends. There's not enough stuff on earth to make up for that.

So our best environmental solutions combine things that make ecological sense—locally grown food—with things that make human sense—small-scale farmers' markets, say. If you want to see what this means in practice, take a trip to Europe. The average European lives a life as decent and dignified as the average American—but they use half as much energy per capita. Cities draw people in instead of repelling them out into suburban sprawl. And they've built the kind of communities where it seems completely natural to, say, travel together on the train instead of alone in a car. And what do you know?

Europeans say they're considerably happier with their lives than Americans, and that satisfaction hasn't declined the way ours has.

So there's lots of room for optimism. We have the technologies we need to make real change—the kinds of change that can make us happier. This catalog provides you with ideas that will point the way and fire your imagination. Some of them are for things to buy, but the most important are for things that let you stop buying, that help you see real possibilities for doing things differently. Better.

But I would be negligent if I stopped here. Because, cheerful as the possibilities are, the reality is much darker. It's not just that we need to change—it's that we need to change very, very fast. And not just those of us likely to be holding a book like this one, but everyone. The best science now tells us that we've already overshot the amount of carbon we can safely tolerate in the atmosphere; that that's why the Arctic is melting, the Southwest is caught in epic drought, Australia is burning. To get ahead of those problems, we'll need to move not just one by one but collectively. In other words, you can't actually solve global warming one lightbulb at a time. Not in the few years we have.

So some of our time and effort has to be saved for working jointly to make the kind of systemic change that could yield results on a large enough scale. I've spent much of the last few years organizing some big campaigns—at the moment, something called 350.org (http://350.org), which has turned into the largest global grassroots campaign about climate—in the hope of helping to shape new international treaties. These laws would finally raise the price of carbon to reflect accurately the damage it does on this sweet planet. And when that happens, the market for every item in this book would suddenly increase dramatically. It wouldn't just be environmentalists who wanted hybrid cars or solar hot water or to shop at farmers' markets. It would be everyone with a wallet.

What pleasure to imagine the future, for ourselves and our society—that's what this catalog allows. But what pleasure, too, to shape that future, in time to actually matter.

—*Bill McKibben, Middlebury College*

ACKNOWLEDGMENTS

Robert Frenay, our longtime friend and colleague, envisioned this catalog—"a retail-level" book about all things green—as a follow-up to his dense and brilliant 2006 book, *Pulse*, in which he foresaw "the coming age of systems and machines inspired by living things." While planning a further exploration of that future in a third book, Bob asked us to collaborate on the *Whole Green Catalog*; after some months of working together on the concept, the proposal, and the budget, he fell ill and was diagnosed with inoperable pancreatic cancer. We all continued to work on the book proposal until agent Devin McIntyre took it into the publishing market and Rodale made the winning offer. Bob succumbed to the cancer on January 27, 2007, about two weeks after our last conversation, which was about the potential of the *Whole Green Catalog*. We promised him we would do this book.

Hanya Frenay, whose strength, love, and courage were our inspiration.

Devin McIntyre, our agent at the Mary Evans Agency, whose encouragement, understanding, diplomacy, and negotiating skills carried us all through the daunting process of creating something of value from an idea.

Michael Urban, managing editor, who kept this train running at express speeds while maintaining an inexplicable level of good humor and concentration, day and night.

Vicky Vaughn Shea, layout artist, who brought a marathoner's energy to the huge challenge of getting it all down on coherent pages.

All the chapter contributors brought their experience, expertise, and enthusiasm to bear in finding, evaluating, and writing about the freshest and greenest goods and services that now enhance our marketplace. A special debt of gratitude goes to Renée Loux, who researched and wrote three of the chapters with her unique blend of drive, rigor, and unmistakable style.

Joel Holland, our illustrator, who instantly grasped every challenge and conveyed the essence of each item with his beguiling lines.

Karen Rinaldi, senior vice president and publishing director of Rodale Books, whose energetic enthusiasm and support for the project never wavered.

Shannon Welch, our editor at Rodale, got the whole green picture early on and fought for quality edit and design, pushing for improvements and appreciating the results. With heart and mind in the right places, she was always a pleasure to work with.

A special thanks to the Rodale production/design team for handling all challenges with professional aplomb: Nancy Bailey, senior project editor, Chris Krogermeier, senior managing editor, Chris Gaugler, associate art director, Brooke Myers, director of asset management, and Caroline McCall at Quad Graphics.

Alan Sussman, whose early grasp of the manifold potential of this book idea—and whose understanding of the commercial intricacies—were invaluable from first to last.

Stephen Palitz, whose unflagging attention to legal detail and quest for accuracy and fairness made the whole green agreement possible.

Patrick Robbins, our chief image researcher who pushed fearlessly into many uncharted territories.

Geoffrey Leonard, our night-shift image researcher.

Emily Paine, our permissions researcher who tracked down every supplier and detail.

Paula Brisco, our chief copy editor, who swiftly and successfully scrutinized every line, every word.

Ellen Urban, our proofreader who brought a stylist's eye to an onerous task.

Without the tireless hard work, focus, and enthusiastic cooperation of every one of these contributors, it is difficult to imagine how this complex book could have come together. A glance at any part of the book makes it clear that this was, to an unusual extent, a true team production.

—*Michael W. Robbins and Wendy Palitz*

why green now?

If not now, when? The perfect storm of global climate crisis, dwindling resources, and an unsustainable model of consumer appetite is upon us and growing in urgency. Now is the time for individual action.

Never have everyday choices carried more consequences than right now. Think of the choices we can make—do make—every day as small steps, in either a positive or a negative direction. Each choice can work to benefit you, me, and our whole community—and ultimately, our global environment.

How can we make those right choices? One at a time, with the help of this catalog. We've convened thought leaders in every imaginable category to share with you a wealth of green information and green ideas. Just a few years ago, there were very few "green" products on store shelves and little or no "green" components in many of these categories; they simply didn't exist or couldn't compete in the marketplace. The sheer size of the *Whole Green Catalog* illustrates the diversity of possibility, discovery, and potential. Consider the items reviewed here as the furnishings of one's life, the furnishings for a whole new world that we can all live (better) in.

There is a fundamentally simple idea at play in this publication: We all need things with which to live in the world, and the things we choose (or don't choose) for our own lives can, in the aggregate, have a deep reaching impact and can make a significant contribution to renewing our world.

This catalog is a browser book. Like the original *Whole Earth Catalog*, which helped to define the credo of its age, this is a resource guide to a special kind of life: then, an alternative lifestyle and now, a sustainable one. We don't expect anyone to read it straight through, and we did not structure it that way. It is designed for people to peruse, consult, find, and choose. And it is full of surprises and delights—on every page. Flip through, and you'll find that it opens many doors.

The reviews in this catalog can foster a fresh way of thinking about where we are in time and in our world. Call it life-cycle thinking or thinking about the whole cradle-to-grave arc of the things we live with: where raw materials come from; how they are harvested or obtained; and how they are processed, transported, marketed, and packaged. Then, once their usefulness to you is ended, how are they passed on, reused, or disposed of. This is the "over the horizons" thinking that is fundamental to environmental awareness and action.

So, can we buy our way to sustainability? Probably not, but we can, with our consumer choices, take steps in the direction of solutions rather than continue—again, with our choices—to move along in familiar ways that only contribute to the larger problems.

While the green marketplace is no longer ahead of the curve or at the fringes, it is in process and getting better all the time. And in this new world of green, the same old laws of supply and demand still apply: When we demand greener things, the marketplace supplies them. We've grown in leaps and bounds from the seeds planted by the environmental movement over the last score of years, and this catalog speaks eloquently of that growth.

We have arrived at a point where it is not a personal compromise to make these choices. To live a sustainable life, it's no longer necessary to forfeit comfort, convenience, and luxury or to freeze, drown, and starve in the dark. Today, we can choose to move in the right direction.

—*Renée Loux*

cleaning House

Green housekeeping is contagious! It starts with one thing, which leads to the next, and suddenly green housekeeping is too good to stop because it seems to make everything better.

It wasn't so long ago that housekeeping methods relied on a handful of basic, natural materials and some elbow grease to keep every surface, fabric, nook, and cranny spic-and-span. Materials like plain old soap, vinegar, baking soda, alcohol, and salt are so inherently nontoxic that most do double duty as staples in the kitchen pantry. They get the job done properly without leaving lingering, harmful residues inside the home or running amok on the environment outside.

In recent years, the dizzying array of modern household cleaning products spawned from the marriage of petroleum and chlorine has trumped the tried-and-true methods of yesteryear. Synthetic household cleaners reared in the age of the petrochemical revolution are riddled with unpronounceable chemicals that can literally make your head spin, mess with your hormones, undermine your central nervous system, and contaminate the ecosystem beyond the drain. But that is changing. As people realize that chemical-based housekeeping products can be toxic, more nontoxic products emerge. Today, people are learning that cleaning with chemicals is incongruous when plant-based products can do the job; that one-time disposables made from chlorine-laden virgin tree products are uncouth when oxygen-bleached recycled fibers work just as well; and that green housekeeping is not an alternative or a compromise but is instead how things should be done to enhance health, happiness, and well-being.

As the words *ecology* and *environment* join the common vernacular, a growing standard of eco-friendly products and practices is fueling a new kind of revolution for better living. While vinegar and elbow grease will still do the job, there are now scores of savvy, supereffective, eco-friendly, nontoxic products and tools that champion the power of plants, minerals, and renewable materials to tackle every housekeeping task. Among them: biodegradable cleaning products for every surface and material; absorbent paper products made from recycled fiber; dish and hand soaps based on botanical extracts and vegetable oils; laundry and dish detergents with no chlorine, phosphates, or synthetic surfactants; trash bags made from recycled content and even biodegradable plastics—and much more.

Without exception, green housekeeping enhances your life, home, and well-being. After all, the products we use to wash, wipe, scour, scrub, polish, and deodorize have a tremendous influence on our quality of life at home and in the outside world. Who wants to live or entertain friends and family amid lingering fumes and intractable residues of chemicals? Who wants to dump products down the drain that will harm fish and bees and pollute the water that our children drink? Green housekeeping isn't a privilege or a luxury, and it isn't restricted to a certain ZIP code; it's about being responsible stewards of our beautiful, complex world and of our personal domains by governing our actions with etiquette and accountability. The beauty of being green is that it not only serves the planet, but serves us, too. It fulfills our desire to make this world a better, cleaner, safer place, starting in our own homes.

—Renée Loux

ALL-PURPOSE SURFACE CLEANERS
The Best for the Basics

Method Home All-Surface Cleaner is a biodegradable, nontoxic product that cleans virtually any surface in your home using plant-based surfactants. This all-purpose spray is packaged in a 100 percent recycled plastic trigger-spray bottle that is recognized by Design for the Environment's Cradle to Cradle protocol for environmental design. The cleaner is available in three naturally derived scents and also in unscented. (www.method home.com)

Mrs. Meyer's All-Purpose Cleaner is a nontoxic, concentrated formula in a screw-top bottle and is made from plant-derived surfactants, agents, and extracts. It's good for just about every surface in the home. Mrs. Meyer's Countertop Spray is by no means limited to counter-cleaning might—it's a wonder on all nonporous surfaces. This trigger-spray bot-

tled formula combines the formula of the all-purpose cleaner with a special vegetable protein extract that naturally removes odors. Both formulas are totally biodegradable and available in four scents made from antiseptic essential oils and naturally derived fragrances. (www.mrsmeyers.com)

Seventh Generation Natural All Purpose Cleaner is a green go-to for nontoxic, eco-friendly ceiling-to-floor cleaning. Its biodegradable formula harnesses the multitasking strength of minerals and plants to effectively clean and degrease all types of surfaces and doesn't create harsh fumes or unhealthy residues. It's even excellent for wet mopping, though not recommended for wood floors. (www.seventh generation.com)

METHOD'S CLEANING WIPES: THEY'RE COMPOSTABLE!

Disposable one-use cleaning wipes are certainly handy, but they're wasteful and typically made from petrochemical ingredients, non-biodegradable plastic fibers, and virgin tree paper. There's an alternative. **Method**'s All Surface Wipes are handy, neat, nontoxic wipes made from compostable bamboo fibers that biodegrade safely—keeping the planet every bit as clean as your home. Packaged in a sleek, resealable, recyclable flat-pack film pouch, these multipurpose wipes are available in naturally scented French lavender, pink grapefruit, and Go Naked (unscented). (www.method home.com)

GLASS CLEANERS
Sparkling Green

★ **Biokleen** Ammonia Free Glass Cleaner's vinegar cleaning power and natural soil lifters dissolve dirt, pollution, smoke, and grease from shiny hard surfaces and leave streak-free results. Odorless, free of ammonia, and with no harsh fumes, it's safe to use around plants and pets. (www.biokleenhome.com)

★ **Ecover**'s Glass & Surface Cleaner is formulated with plant-based ingredients that clean, shine, and cut through grease and grime on household surfaces with no-smear results—after which the cleanser quickly and completely biodegrades. Because it's safe around food, this cleaner is particularly suitable for hard surfaces in the kitchen and bathroom, including glass, tile, enamel, acrylic, and chrome. Its fresh fragrance is derived from plant-based sources, and zero colorants are added. (www.ecover.com)

★ **Seventh Generation**'s Natural Glass & Surface Cleaner effectively cleans glass, mirrors, chrome, and other hard, shiny surfaces around the home without leaving streaks or harsh chemicals or ammonia. With full disclosure of ingredients, this entirely plant-based formula harnesses plant-derived cleaning agents for fast, easy cleaning of tough dirt and grime. Available in a couple of scents as well as unscented. (www.seventhgeneration.com)

Important Terms

Several key terms and concepts appear frequently in this chapter. Here are simple definitions of these terms and quick explanations of how they relate to basic household cleaning products (HHCPs).

Biodegradable. Products deemed biodegradable must break down into elements found in nature within a reasonable amount of time. Supposedly, there must be competent and reliable scientific evidence to back up the claim and prove a substance will decompose in a reasonably short period of time after customary disposal, though that period of time is not legally defined. While it's illegal to misrepresent a product as being biodegradable, there's no substantial regulation. Look for products that provide information, specifics, and qualification to back up biodegradable claims, including full disclosure of plant- and mineral-based ingredients.

Plant-based and mineral-based ingredients. Plant-based and mineral-based products are made from renewable resources and, by nature, are biodegradable and generally nontoxic to humans and the environment. Plant-based and mineral-based HHCPs do their jobs efficiently, without human harm during use, and they cause minimal eco-impact during manufacture and after use. HHCPs that are made entirely of plant-based and mineral-based ingredients are free from chemicals such as chlorine, ammonia, synthetic solvents and surfactants, and artificial fragrances and dyes.

Chlorine free. Chlorine-free products don't contain chlorine, period. Chlorine is not green. It is a severe irritant and corrosive to the skin, eyes, and lungs. It's dangerous to breathe and touch and is acutely toxic to aquatic life. Oxygen bleach and enzymatic ingredients offer the same disinfecting and whitening properties as chlorine without the human and ecological hazards.

Solvent free and nontoxic solvents. Chemical solvents are usually used in heavy-duty cleaning. They effectively cut grime, dirt, oil, and soil. But they are also harmful to lung tissue, skin, and human organs, and they are dangerous to touch or breathe. Petrochemical solvents (such as glycol ethers, 2-butoxyethanol, and ethano-lamines) aren't biodegradable, period. Nonbiodegradable chemical solvents contaminate distant rivers, lakes, and streams and build up in and contaminate our homes. There is a bevy of solvent-free, nontoxic HHCPs capable of heavy-duty action without the harmful hazards posed by chemical solvents. Look for solvent-free cleaners and those that call on the strength of plant-based solvents.

Phosphate free. Phosphates have long been used in laundry and dish detergents as water-softening agents (to keep detergents from leaving scum all over everything) and for deflocculating action (to keep dirt and grime from settling back during washing). Though phosphates are cheap ingredients that do make detergents work better, they're on the ecological no-no list because they wreak havoc in water ecosystems, causing algae blooms, suffocating fish and other aquatic life, and throwing everything wickedly out of whack on a large scale. The good news is that even major laundry detergent manufacturers are phasing out phosphates, thanks in part to governmental efforts to restrict and ban them altogether. The bad news is that some of those manufacturers are opting for petro-based synthetic phosphate substitutes, which cause a different set of eco-hazards. Phosphates are still prevalent in conventional automatic dishwasher detergents. Look for natural laundry and dish detergents that are phosphate free.

Natural fragrances. Who doesn't love a fresh-smelling room? The difference between a fresh, clean smell and a toxic chemical cloak is a very blurry line in the conventional HHCP world. Undisclosed (synthetic or artificial) fragrances are generally dodgy chemicals and can include just about anything. Look for HHCPs that tap into the good smelling and purifying power of natural fragrances derived from plants and essential oils.

Colorants. Bright colors can be a beautiful thing, especially in flowers, sunsets, and crayons. But the colorants used in conventional HHCPs don't make products work better. Synthetic colorants are generally derived from petrochemical ingredients, and you wouldn't want the residues hanging around on your dishes or clothing or in your home. Look for natural HHCPs that don't contain colorants or those that opt for harmless plant-based colorants.

HEAVY-DUTY CITRUS CONCENTRATES
Getting Tough on Grime

Citra Solv Natural Cleaner and Degreaser is a versatile, concentrated citrus solvent with mighty natural muscle to clean and degrease the toughest grime and stains inside and outside your home. Made from orange peel extract, essential oils, and biodegradable cleaning agents, it can be applied full strength for especially tough jobs—even to remove stuck-on gum, waxy lipstick stains, and crud burnt to barbecue grills. This concentrated cleaner is available in 2-, 8-, 16-, and 32-ounce screw-top bottles and can be diluted with water to tackle most general household cleaning tasks, including floors and walls. A version of this cleanser is available in a lavender bergamot scent. (www.citra-solv.com)

BioKleen Citrus Soy Solvent uses soybean oil extract in place of petrochemicals or high levels of citrus extract. This superconcentrated formula is a multipurpose cleaner for heavy-duty degreasing and dissolving of substances including gum, wax, paint, adhesives, tar, and more; dilute for light cleaning. It has low volatile organic compounds (VOCs) and is gentle to both your skin and the environment. (www.biokleenhome.com)

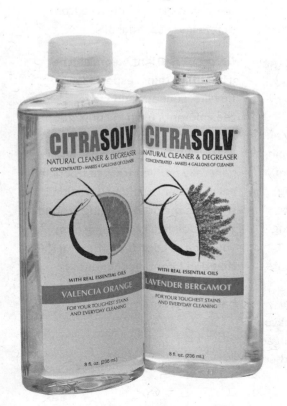

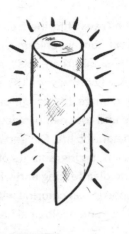

SCOURING SCRUBS
Shake and Shine

Bon Ami has been earth friendly since 1886, offering a tried-and-true, nonabrasive powdered surface scrub in a classic shake-top canister called Bon Ami Polishing Cleanser. This 100 percent biodegradable formula is made from natural calcite and feldspar mineral abrasives, biodegradable detergent, and sodium carbonate to condition hard water and remove hard water mineral deposits without the use of chlorine, dyes, phosphates, or perfumes. Bon Ami is recommended for sinks, counters, showers and tubs, plumbing fixtures, cookware, and appliances—and even grills, garage floors, and outdoor furniture. (www.bonami.com)

Mrs. Meyer's Surface Scrub is tough on grimy surfaces and does so in a delightful selection of scents derived from plants and essential oils. Made with naturally safe calcium carbonate, oxygen bleach, and plant-based surfactants to scour safely without scratching, this shake-canister surface scrub is excellent for porcelain, stainless steel, cookware, tile, and more. (www.mrsmeyers.com)

Or give your kitchen and bathroom surfaces a spa-treatment scrub with **Caldrea**'s Powdered Scrub, available in several delicious scents derived from essential oils and well-researched, biodegradable, human-safe synthetic sources. This nonabrasive shake-canister powder is made from all-natural plant and mineral ingredients with no phosphates or chlorine. Use it on virtually any surface in your kitchen or bathroom. (www.caldrea.com)

HARD FLOOR CARE PRODUCTS
Feet Friendly

★ **Bona** has been taking care of hardwood floors with nontoxic, waterborne cleaners since 1919. Bona became the first floor care product certified by the nonprofit GREENGUARD Environmental Institute—which means Bona's products pass stringent indoor air quality criteria. Bona Swedish Formula Hardwood Floor Cleaner, Concentrate, Polish, and Refresher are solvent-free, biodegradable formulas good for all finished hardwood floors. Bona Stone, Tile & Laminate Floor Cleaner is a go-to for easy, nontoxic cleaning of sealed hard surface floors, and Bona Stone, Tile & Laminate Floor Polish refreshes flooring's appearance without polluting indoor air. Look for Bona's Premium and Ultimate Floor Care Systems, which include everything you need to safely clean and care for your hardwood and sealed hard surface floors. (www.bonakemi.com)

★ **Method** debuts forward-thinking eco-cleaning care with the OMop collection, each packaged in a 100 percent recycled plastic bottle with an ergonomically designed shower-nozzle spray for easy, no-puddle coverage. Nontoxic and biodegradable, these floor cleaners won't leave hazardous residues behind. OMop All Floor Cleaner is a no-wax, no-nonsense formula in lemon ginger. OMop Wood for Good Floor Cleaner smells like delicious almond. For complete, eco-friendly floor care, OMop All Floor Care Kit and OMop Wood Floor Care Kit contain a bottle of cleaner, a washable microfiber pad, three compostable sweeper dusters made from corn-based plastic, and a magic mop that bends so your back doesn't have to—all in an übergreen box made of a blend of bamboo fiber and recycled paper that's compostable. (www.method home.com)

CARPET CLEANING PRODUCTS
Spiff Up Shag and Pamper Pile

★ **Begley's Best** Spot Remover and Household Cleaner is one of the ultimate all-purpose stain removers for carpets, laundry, and upholstery. Formulated by actor and eco-pioneer Ed Begley Jr., this plant-based, biodegradable, multipurpose whiz is concocted from pine, citrus fruits, maize, fermented sugarcane, and olive seeds with zero chemicals, chlorine, solvents, or phosphates. Try this revolutionary formula on dingy, coffee-stained car floor mats, and they will come out looking brand-new. (www.begleysbest.com)

★ **Earth Friendly Products** Everyday Stain & Odor Remover is specifically formulated with enzymes and plant ingredients that tackle organic stains and odors caused by food, dirt, urine, and other natural soils. It's excellent for stains and odors on carpets, fabric, and laundry. For deep carpet cleaning, Carpet Shampoo with Bergamot & Sage is a renewable, ecologically sound cleaner designed for use in hot- or cold-water extraction machines. Entirely free of harsh chemicals, this rug and carpet shampoo is formulated with pure, natural ingredients—no phosphates, chlorine, petrochemicals, or toxins. One 32-ounce bottle of this concentrated formula will clean three average-size rooms. (www.ecos.com)

★ **Mrs. Meyer's** Odor Removing Carpet Cleaner is designed for pet mishaps on wool, nylon, and stain-resistant carpet. Scented with the essential oils of chamomile and clary sage, this nontoxic, biodegradable stain and odor buster is formulated with natural solubilizing agents, minerals, and enzymes. (www.mrsmeyers.com)

★ **Seventh Generation** Carpet Spot & Stain Remover eliminates odors and leaves your carpet soft, fresh, and truly clean. Formulated with hydrogen peroxide for active stain removal and featuring a delightfully clean white flower and bergamot citrus scent derived from essential oils and plant extracts, this all-natural carpet-care product is nontoxic and biodegradable. (www. seventhgeneration.com)

The spectrum of household cleaning product (HHCP) formulas today is dizzying. We often demand multitasking action from our cleansers, which is why many HHCP formulas have become so complex. To help you understand the ingredients and how they work, here are the basic categories of almost all HHCP ingredients:

Abrasives. Found in powdered or liquid form, abrasives consist of small particles (usually minerals) that help scour stains and grime from hard surfaces, especially sinks, tubs, pots, and pans. Look for natural abrasive products (like Bon Ami powder) that don't contain chlorine, and be mindful, as some abrasives can scratch delicate surfaces. Baking soda is a cheap, excellent, gently abrasive alternative to store-bought abrasive formulas.

Bleaches. Bleaching agents are used to whiten, brighten, and lift stains as well as for disinfecting properties in laundry products, stain removers, scouring powders and liquids, automatic dishwasher detergents, and tub and tile cleaners. Chlorine is the commonly used bleaching agent in conventional HHCP, but it's toxic and hazardous to humans and the environment. Oxygen bleaching agents, on the other hand, are safe, effective, eco-friendly alternatives to chlorine bleach.

Enzymes. Enzymes are protein-based ingredients that actively break down dirt, oil, soil, and stains basically by eating them. They are natural and effective aids for laundry and dish detergents, stain removers, and drain-cleaning products.

Solvents. These are usually found in liquid form and act by dissolving such substances as greasy and oily soils. The solvents in conventional HHCPs (degreasing products, glass and all-purpose cleaners, spot cleaners, rug and upholstery cleaners, stain removers, and furniture polishes and waxes) are mostly made from petrochemicals (ironically called *organic solvents*) and are highly toxic. Chemical solvents may offer no-elbow-grease action for heavy-duty chores, but they are linked to some pretty dicey human and environmental concerns. Look for solvent-free products or those that contain plant-based solvents such as citrus solvents or grain alcohol.

Surfactants. A nifty abbreviation of *surface-active-agents*, surfactants are cleansing agents that reduce the surface tension of water so it can spread out (as opposed to bead) and get beneath dirt and grime to slough them off. Used in detergents, these agents also help suspend soil and grime so dirt isn't redeposited on clothes, dishes, or surfaces. Most conventional surfactants are derived from petroleum and are slow to break down. Look for HHCPs with plant-based surfactants, which cleanse and suds like champs and biodegrade with ease.

AIR FRESHENERS
Clear the Air

★ **Air Therapy** is a 100 percent natural purifying mist distilled from pure essential citrus oils and nothing else. This 2.2-ounce nonaerosol spray contains millions of ions (electrical charges) that attract, neutralize, and eliminate odors and airborne pollutants. Choose from five scents such as key lime, spruce, and vanilla. (www.miarose.com)

★ **Mrs. Meyer's** Room Freshener refreshes any stale space. Made with nontoxic, natural ingredients, essential oils, and well-researched, human-safe, biodegradable synthetic fragrances, the freshener comes in four scents (soothing lavender, bright lemon verbena, sunny geranium, and baby blossom) dispensed from 8-ounce pump-top sprayers. (www.mrsmeyers.com)

★ **Ecco Mist** brings a bit of paradise to freshen rooms. Made from pure essential oils, a natural emulsifier, and nothing else, Ecco Mist comes in three scents: citrus, lavender, and summer fruit. Each 8-ounce pump-top aluminum bottle offers 2,000 sprays of aromatherapy, and the bottle can be recycled when you are through. (www.eccobella.com)

★ **Air Scense** naturally refreshes and neutralizes air using nontoxic, plant-based ingredients dispensed from 7-ounce pump-spray bottles. Choose from four fresh scents: orange, lime, vanilla, and lavender, all derived from essential oils and plant extracts. (www.citra-solv.com)

★ **Orange Mate** Air Freshener Mists are 100 percent pure citrus air fresheners that use high-quality, biodegradable citrus ingredients in a nonaerosol spray to destroy odors instead of simply masking them. Choose from four citrus scents (grapefruit, lemon, lime, and orange) plus the newest fragrance, cinnamon, all sold in 3.5- and 7-ounce nonaerosol pump-top spray bottles. (www.orangemate.com)

★ **Earth Friendly Products** makes two natural air fresheners. Eco-Breeze Fabric Refresher is an all-natural, 22-ounce trigger-spray bottle of plant-based ingredients in fresh scents such as lavender mint, lemongrass, and citrus. Uni-Fresh Air Freshener is a 4.4-ounce pump-spray bottle of nontoxic, plant-based ingredients with clean smells such as cinnamon, citrus, lavender, vanilla, and parsley. (www.ecos.com)

★ **Smells Begone**'s proprietary blend of natural ingredients and plant-based fragrances eliminates odors safely and quickly. Dispensed from 12-ounce nonaerosol pump-top bottles, Smells Begone is nontoxic, non-staining, and safe for fabrics and pets. Available in three scents (calming rain, energizing citrus, and soothing breeze) as well as fragrance free. (www.punati.com; www.amazon.com; www.gaiam.com)

FYI

Worn-out T-shirts make the ultimate absorbent, lint-free rags. One tee will yield two to four towels: The front and the back will each yield one good-size rag, or they can be cut lengthwise to yield two longer rags each.

WAVE GERMS GOOD-BYE

Purelight UV Sterilizing Wand allows you to sterilize household surfaces with the simple wave of an ultraviolet-light-emitting wand. This germ-killing wand is designed to reduce and control bacteria and viruses, as well as dust mites and bedbugs, with 99.9 percent efficacy in minutes. No chemicals, no residues, no waiting period. The UV light waves generated by the wand act as a germicide at close range and deactivate the DNA of dust mites and pathogens like bacteria and viruses, preventing them from multiplying. It's cordless for easy use anywhere in your home. While this magic wand is not inexpensive, it's a good investment for those who have allergies or asthma. Use for mattresses and bedding, knives and cutting boards, carpets, toilet seats, baby bottles and toys, and even personal hygiene items such as razors, hairbrushes, and nail files. (www.gaiam.com; www.amazon.com; www.comforthouse.com)

SHOWER FILTERS
Get the Chlorine Out

Install a shower filter and you improve the quality of indoor air by reducing chlorine pollution—and you also protect your skin and hair from drying out. Most shower filters can be screwed on any kind of showerhead, including low-flow heads, without affecting water flow, and they don't cost much. Filters should typically be replaced every 6 months.

Aquasana offers basic, plastic-housed models such as the Shower Filtration System and an adjustable handheld Shower Filter with Handheld Massager for deluxe convenience. You can sign up for Aquasana's Water 4 Life auto-ship program to automatically receive a replacement filter cartridge every 6 months at a discount price. (www.aquasana.com)

Custom Pure uses nifty patented filtration media in their models: the High Output, in plastic housing; the Slim-Line All Brass, in chrome or polished brass; and the handheld Royale Filtered Shower Handle, in chrome or brass, with built-in filter. (www.custompure.com)

Gaiam's online store sells simple and fancy models from different brands. The white and polished chrome **Royale** All-in-One has five adjustable spray options. The **Wellness Shower Filter** (www.wellnessfilter.com) filters out impurities, increases dissolved oxygen for an antioxidant effect, and includes a backwashing system. Or take a look at the gorgeous rainfall-style **Sunflower Showerhead** in chrome. (www.gaiam,com)

The Shower Filter Store has good-looking models to fit your needs. The April Shower Deluxe Metallic Filter, available in polished chrome, gold tone, or satin nickel, includes a sleek, adjustable showerhead. The handheld, eight-spray April Shower Pure Mist comes in white, polished chrome, and satin nickel. (www.showerfilterstore.com)

SHOWER, TUB, AND TILE CLEANERS
Clean Green, Clean Often

★ **Earth Friendly Products** Shower Kleener eliminates and prevents hard-water stains and soap scum with plant-based surfactants, corn cleaners, and clean-smelling antiseptic essential oils of tea tree and lavender. The bonus: It's nontoxic and biodegradable. (www.ecos.com)

★ **Method** Tub 'n Tile Bathroom Cleaner busts soap scum, hard-water stains, and mildew, leaving a spalike eucalyptus mint scent in its wake. This biodegradable plant- and mineral-based cleaner contains no petrochemicals and is manufactured using renewable energy. Now that's green! Once your shower is clean, apply Method Daily Shower Spray; the nontoxic, biodegradable formula contains ingredients like lactic acid to dissolve soap scum. Just spray, no scrubbing or rinsing required (it works best if you start with a clean shower and use regularly as a preventive). It smells great and is packaged in a 100 percent recycled plastic bottle. (www.methodhome.com)

★ **Ecover** Limescale Remover eradicates soap scum and hard-water lime deposits; apply it to bath, shower, tiles, tubs, and basins. Made completely from plant-based ingredients—hence its fresh, clean fragrance—this cleaner quickly biodegrades with minimum impact on aquatic life. (www.ecover.com)

★ **Seventh Generation** Shower Cleaner–Green Mandarin and Leaf prevents mold, mildew, and soap scum buildup without generating harsh fumes. This nontoxic, biodegradable formula contains plant-based agents, the oxygen bleach power of hydrogen peroxide, and clean, bright-smelling essential oils and botanical extracts. Seventh Generation Tub and Tile Cleaner removes tough crud and prevents scummy buildup in your bath and shower and on tile surfaces. Nontoxic and biodegradable, this no-fume formula comes in a spa-scented emerald cypress and fir fragrance, derived from essential oils and botanical extracts. (www.seventhgeneration.com)

the bathroom

SOFT SCRUBS AND CREAMY CLEANSERS
Gentle Giants

Soft scrubs and creamy cleansers are gentle giants when it comes to tackling grime and gunk on porcelain, stainless steel, tile, and other hard surfaces in the bathroom (and kitchen, too).

Method helps you say "adieu" to grimy gunk and soap scum, hard-water deposits, and mildew and "bonjour" to sparkly clean results with Le Scrub Bathroom Cleaner. This biodegradable, finely milled marble formula has the whistling-fresh scent of eucalyptus. Packaged in a sleek, chic bottle made from recycled plastic and with a functional sponge holder, Le Scrub is even produced with renewable energy. Very snazzy. (www.methodhome.com)

A little squeeze of **Earth Friendly Products** Creamy Cleanser goes a long way in cleaning power. Formulated with crystalline silica, this lemon oil–based cleaner is tough on stains yet nonabrasive and gentle on the earth. (www.ecos.com)

Ecover Cream Scrub is a tub, tile, and basin soft scrub made with a mild abrasive that cleans up mildew and soap scum in a snap. It is nontoxic, biodegradable, plant based (including the fresh fragrance), and suitable for every surface in the bathroom; in the kitchen apply it to pots and pans, countertops, and stovetops. (www.ecover.com)

BioKleen Soy Cream Cleaner cleans, shines, and protects surfaces without scratching and without the need for toxic chemicals. Formulated with volcanic perlite and lime peel extracts, this creamy soft scrub is safe and effective for linoleum, porcelain, chrome, stovetops, sinks, countertops, tub and tile, grout, your hands, and the earth. (www.bio kleenhome.com)

TOILET CLEANERS
Spanking-Green Choices

Cleaning the can is not the most sought-after household chore. Fortunately, you don't need bleach, solvents, or harsh chemicals to deodorize your toilet and make it sparkle. Nontoxic, biodegradable toilet cleaners are a smart green way to think beyond the bowl—they're better for you, your family, and the planet.

Seventh Generation Emerald Cypress & Fir Toilet Bowl Cleaner with a handy squirt-top thoroughly deodorizes and cleans just as well as conventional toilet cleaners and without harsh fumes, harmful chemicals, or dyes. The clean-as-a-whistle scent of this plant-based, nontoxic, biodegradable toilet cleaning whiz is naturally derived from antiseptic essential oils and botanical extracts. (www.seventhgeneration.com)

Mrs. Meyer's Toilet Bowl Cleaner makes cleaning the loo like taking a trip to the spa. Well, almost. The divine aromatherapy scents of crisp basil, calming lavender, sprightly lemon verbena, and sunny geranium deodorize and linger long after the task is complete. Harnessing hard-working plant-derived surfactants and lactic acid to munch away grime, this biodegradable, squirt-top cleaner makes toilet chores more bearable. (www.mrsmeyers.com)

Method Lil' Bowl Blu detoxes, deodorizes, and decalcifies toilets and does it with a spanking-clean eucalyptus-mint scent. Method put brains behind this nontoxic, biodegradable formula to come up with just the right mix of lactic acid, natural thickening gum, and plant surfactants to clean the porcelain throne and bust ring-around-the-rim—all in a mod-looking, easy-to-squirt bottle. Recognized by Design for the Environment's Cradle to Cradle protocol, this toilet formula is manufactured using renewable energy so that the planet doesn't go down the drain with it. (www.methodhome.com)

Other nontoxic, tough toilet cleaners include **Earth Friendly Products** Toilet Kleener (www.ecos.com) and **Ecover** Toilet Bowl Cleaner (www.ecover.com), both formulated with plant-based surfactants; clean, natural scents; and no chlorine, fake fragrances, dyes, or caustic or chemical solvents.

A Whiter Shade of Green

Life without toilet paper and facial tissues would be inconvenient and messy to say the least. Unfortunately, there's no way around manufacturing the stuff with paper from trees. Yet even when it comes to one-time-use disposables like TP and tissue, we can still take steps to preserve precious forests and to stop the contamination of the planet with dioxins generated when paper goods are bleached with chlorine.

One simple step doesn't cost much money: Use naturally bleached, recycled tissue products that have a significant postconsumer waste (PCW) content. If the idea of recycled tissues and TP brings to mind sandpaper-grade burlap, relax—things have noticeably improved since the 1970s. You can save trees and have snowy white TP and tissues, thanks to eco-sensitive products whitened with oxygen and ozone instead of chlorine.

Some brands once relegated to health food stores are now available in mainstream markets, including 100 percent recycled Earth First toilet paper (80 percent PCW), Seventh Generation toilet paper (80 percent PCW), Green Forest toilet paper and tissues (40 percent PCW), Natural Value toilet paper (10 to 25 percent PCW), and Trader Joe's toilet paper (35 percent PCW), all bleached without chlorine, of course. And now many mainstream brands are hip to using 100 percent recycled content and nonchlorine bleaching processes, including April Soft and Fiesta toilet papers (80 percent PCW) and Cascades and Pert toilet paper (80 percent PCW). Marcal makes a slew of 100 percent recycled toilet paper and tissues with 40 percent PCW content under several brand names, including Marcal and Sofpac toilet paper, Fluff Out tissues, Hankies tissues, and Marcal tissues. Of all the toilet papers on the market, Whole Foods' 365 Everyday Value gets the highest green marks because it's made with 100 percent recycled and 80 to 95 percent PCW content, processed chlorine free.

GREEN CLEANING GOES MAINSTREAM

Clorox is renewing a good name with a platform of natural cleaning products called Green Works. Built from the ground up for natural efficacy and made from a profile of clean, green plant–based ingredients, all Green Works products are "at least 99 percent natural" with a goal of "100 percent natural." Green Works has teamed up with two very visible partners, the Sierra Club and the EPA's Design for the Environment, to raise the bar for natural cleaning products with stringent standards that are widely available, affordable, and effective. Look for Green Works All-Purpose Cleaner, Glass Cleaner, Dilutable Cleaner, Dishwashing Liquid, Cleaning Wipes, and Bathroom Cleaner. (www.greenworkscleaners.com)

FYI

Water-guzzling toilets account for about one-third of indoor water use at home. Look for ultra-low-flush toilets, which use about 50 percent less water than older ones, or retrofit any toilet for lower-flow efficiency without compromising performance by displacing water in the toilet's reservoir. Install a toilet dam (a water displacement device available in hardware and plumbing stores), or simply submerge a full plastic water bottle or two in the tank.

HAND SOAPS

Getting in a Lather

★ **Kiss My Face** is obsessively organic about its self-foaming hand soaps. Loaded with certified organic ingredients, the soaps have divine fragrances derived from plant extracts and essential oils. Kiss My Face was the first to bring to market a nifty nonaerosol pump that foams a small amount of soap into a sudsy puff of cleansing pleasure. This aerating dispenser makes a little soap go a long way: One bottle lasts for months. Larger refill bottles save on wasteful packaging. This is as good as it gets—no synthetics, chemicals, sodium lauryl sulfate (SLS), artificial preservatives—just clean, soft, good-smelling paws. (www.kissmyface.com)

★ **Avalon Organics** liquid glycerin hand soaps are enriched with vegetable glycerin for hydrating moisture even with frequent washing. Infused with organic essential oils and pure botanicals, they come in five scents—lavender, lemon, peppermint, rosemary, and chamomile (extragentle baby soap). Avalon also offers bar soaps created with organic vegetable and essential oils. (www.avalonorganics.com)

★ **Burt's Bees** liquid hand soaps help clean up the dirtiest hands with strong yet gentle plant-based cleansers. The soaps' coconut and sunflower oils form a richly foaming cleansing complex, and honey and glycerin lightly moisturize and soften hands. Choose from the Citrus & Ginger Root Hand Soap to sweetly wash away dirt, Green Tea & Lemongrass for a perfect combination, or hand-healing, cream-based Naturally Nourishing Milk & Shea Butter for hardworking hands. All of Burt's Bees hand soaps are free of petrochemicals, parabens, synthetic fragrances, and colors. (www.burtsbees.com)

BAR SOAPS

Raising the Bar

Some bar soaps have sophisticated skin-healing ingredients and natural moisturizing agents. **Aubrey Organics** bar soaps are made from pure plant ingredients, botanicals, and essential oils, and they lather up beautifully without drying out your skin. Choose from nine varieties. (www.aubrey-organics.com)

Dr. Bronner's has been the leader in pure, liquid castile soaps for more than 60 years and also offers bar soaps made only from pure organic plant oils, essential oils, and vitamin E. Choose from eight varieties, including eucalyptus, lavender, peppermint, and rose. (www.drbronner.com)

Druide uses exquisite cold-pressed vegetable oils in its handmade bar soaps, which are air-dried for 2 months to achieve perfect softness. The soaps are 100 percent pure, with no synthetic ingredients whatsoever; different selections are adaptable for several skin, body, and facial types. Choose from 13 eco-certified varieties, including Ginseng & Rose, Hibiscus Flower & Shea Butter, Chamomile & Calendula, and unscented Pur & Pure. (www.druide.ca)

Juniper Ridge offers moisturizing, pure olive oil and shea butter bar soaps scented with pure, wild-crafted, and sustainably harvested plant extracts that guys will especially enjoy. Choose from six varieties, including Coastal Sage Scrub, California Bay Laurel, and Western Juniper. (www.juniperridge.com)

Kiss My Face bar soaps are made with only pure palm oil, olive oil, herbal extracts, and natural fragrances. Choose from 15 varieties in three collections: Organic Big Kiss Soap (palm oil), Organic Sudz Bar, and Olive Bar Soap. (www.kissmyface.com)

Pangea Organics handcrafted bar soaps are made with the finest cold-pressed plant oils, pure essential oils, and herbal extracts to cleanse and moisturize with seductive aromas, all packaged in 100 percent recycled cardboard. Choose from nine varieties, including Indian Green Tea with Mint and Rose Petals; Italian White Sage, Geranium & Yarrow; and Pyrenees Lavender with Cardamom. (www.pangeaorganics.com)

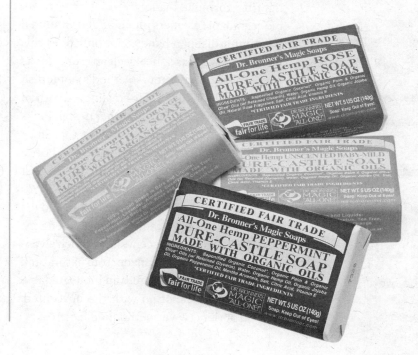

DISH SOAPS
Better Bubbles

If you'd like a little spa treatment with your dish duty, **Mrs. Meyer's** and **Caldrea** both offer seductively scented suds made from biodegradable, plant-derived surfactants and soap bark extract (one of nature's best degreasers), and only natural colorants and preservatives. Choose from Mrs. Meyer's signature scents like basil or lemon verbena or from Caldrea's collection (including ginger pomelo and lavender pine), with fragrances derived from essential oils and some well-researched, biodegradable, human-safe synthetic sources. (www.mrsmeyers.com; www.caldrea.com)

Seventh Generation natural dish liquid is my personal go-to for dishes. It suds up beautifully and biodegrades, and it's made from non-toxic, plant-based ingredients that are tough on grease but kind to your hands and the planet. One bottle goes a long way and is usually a good buy when compared to other products. Lavender floral mint is my favorite scent, derived from essential oils and plant extracts, and unscented is a good alternative for anyone with sensitivities or who just likes it that way. (www.seventh generation.com)

Method dish soap is a supersudsy, grease-fighting formula made from plant-derived, biodegradable cleaners plus aloe and vitamin E to counter dishpan hands. Not only does this product get dishes squeaky clean, but it looks very cool on the counter—Method's iconic dish soap bottle looks like a chic bowling pin with an easy-to-squeeze feature; another design looks like a bullet with a convenient twist-top. Since it's an ultraconcentrated formula, one bottle will do a heck of a lot of dishes. This was the first ever dish soap to be recognized by the EPA's Design for the Environment program, and it's even manufactured using renewable energy. Choose from enticing scents like French lavender and pink grapefruit, made from natural and well-researched, skin-safe, and biodegradable synthetic sources, or go with the unscented, undyed option. (www.methodhome.com)

FYI

White distilled vinegar is one of the most effective and inexpensive dishwasher rinse aids. Simply fill the rinse-aid compartment of your dishwasher with white vinegar. The machine will do the rest.

DISHWASHER RINSE AIDS: SQUEAKY-CLEAN SPARKLE

Rinse aids are made of specialized surfactants that reduce spots by lowering the surface tension of the water so that it can't form into droplets but instead drains off dishes, glasses, and flatware in thin sheets. That yields spotless results. Opt for natural rinse aids that use plant-based surfactants instead of synthetic ones, many of which are accompanied by chemical fragrances, neither of which will biodegrade and may leave residues on your dishes, glasses, and flatware. **Earth Friendly Products**' Wave Jet rinse aid and **Ecover** rinse aid are both formulated with biodegradable, plant-based surfactants and zero chemicals. Neither will leave residues or create fumes—you'll just see squeaky-clean sparkle. (www.ecos.com; www.ecover.com)

DISHWASHER POWDERS AND GELS

A Shiny, Green Clean

Earth Friendly Products' Wave automatic dishwasher powder, gel, and tablets are made with minerals and plant-based surfactants that will totally biodegrade and with pure fragrance from lavender oil. Wave tablets are also available unscented. These patent-pending formulas are some of the best performing on the market and are entirely free of caustic chemicals, chlorine, and phosphates. (www.ecos.com)

Ecover automatic dishwasher powder and tablets are also fantastically clean, green options for auto-dish duty. Chock-full of grub-busting, degreasing minerals, oxygen bleach compounds and enzymes, and a fresh, plant-based fragrance, both will clean and degrease dishes without leaving residues on your dishes or creating chlorine fumes, and they quickly and easily biodegrade with minimum impact on aquatic life. Powder and tablets both come in boxes that are made out of 95 percent recycled cardboard. (www.ecover.com)

Seventh Generation Free & Clear automatic dishwasher powder is as clean as it gets. Made from mineral-softening and china-protecting agents and plant-based surfactants that are especially designed to prevent water spots, this dish powder contains oxygen bleach in the form of sodium percarbonate and nonanimal-derived enzymes instead of chlorine. It is free of phosphates, fragrances, and dyes of any kind. Seventh Generation automatic dishwasher gel will make your dishes sparkle without the use of phosphates or chlorine. The fresh lemon and green apple scent is derived from essential oils and botanical extracts. (www.seventhgeneration.com)

If you are an auto-gel kind of dish master, **Biokleen** automatic dishwasher gel is a potent green pick because it's biodegradable, nontoxic, dye free, chlorine free, and phosphate free. The three-times concentrated formula cleans tough, baked-on food and grease by using plant-based surfactants and the power of grapefruit seed and orange peel extract. Biokleen's automatic dishwasher powder and Free & Clear powder with oxygen bleach are both excellent concentrated formulas; however, they are packaged in bulky plastic tubs, which the planet could do without. (www.biokleenhome.com)

Ditto on **Method** Smarty dishwasher tablets. Great product but excessive plastic packaging, which is, however, made from 25 percent recycled content. (www.methodhome.com)

OVEN AND GRILL CLEANERS

A Recipe for Success

Most modern ovens come with a high-temperature self-cleaning cycle that will burn off caked-on spills so that you don't need to use an oven-cleaning product. If your oven is not self-cleaning, nontoxic all-purpose cleaners such as scouring scrub powders, degreasing citrus concentrates, and/or a simple paste of baking soda and water will usually do the trick. Or you can select a product that clean grills and ovens.

SoyClean BBQ Grill Cleaner is a biodegradable, soy-based formula with 100 percent natural, nontoxic ingredients that are nonflammable. It will not create caustic fumes. It loosens and softens soiled surfaces and removes char, grease, and burnt residue from hard-to-clean surfaces such as barbecues, smokers, grills, and stoves. Pick up a 22-ounce spray bottle or an economical 1-gallon jug. (www.soyclean.biz)

SunBrite Grill and Oven Cleaner is a nontoxic, biodegradable, industrial-strength cleaner for grills, grease, carbon, ovens, ranges, barbecues, and more. This nonabrasive, water-soluble cleaner is available in a 22-ounce spray bottle or a 1-gallon jug. (www.sunbrite.biz)

Wipe It Right

Bamboo is a durable, highly renewable material valued for its quick-drying and antibacterial properties, so putting it to use in a cleaning cloth is a brilliant no-brainer. **Twist** Bamboo Cloth #35 is soft and lint-free; it can be used again and again to wipe, dust, and polish, and it's ultimately biodegradable. White towels with a mod-bubble print are sold in three-packs. (www.twistclean.com)

Pacific Dry Goods' EcoTowels are superabsorbent and reusable and made from 82 percent bamboo and 18 percent corn. These durable, machine-washable towels perform well wet or dry in the kitchen, on floors, andfor dusting and polishing. Two white towels with a green bamboo imprint come in each pack. (www.pacificdry goods.com)

Twist and Shout

Spongemaker **Twist** greens kitchen clean-up with sponges made from completely natural, biodegradable materials. Twist Loofah Sponge #50 features superabsorbent undyed cellulose on one side and a natural loofah scrubbing layer on the other—sturdy enough for when you need a little scrub-a-dub power to clean everything from spills to pots and pans. Twist Naked Sponge #55 is made from 100 percent cellulose, with no dyes, for absorbent clean-up capacity. Twist Euro Sponge #10 is an eco-twist on a classic European sponge design. Made from biodegradable materials, this chic, colorful, highly absorbent sponge has a thinner, larger dimension than most domestic sponges, and it offers durable mop-up and dishwashing capabilities.

If a sponge and a paper towel had a love-fest, Twist European Sponge Cloth #20 would be the offspring. This versatile, colorfully spongy cloth wipes up kitchen and bath surfaces like a paper towel and absorbs like a sponge. And it's biodegradable, of course. (www.twistclean.com)

For long-lasting dishwashing finesse and drip-free, superabsorbent wiping, give a shout for EcoSponge, purveyed by **Pacific Dry Goods**. Tough enough to scour and scrub yet soft enough to wash fine china, wineglasses, and crystal, these incredibly absorbent, drip-free sponges can absorb 15 times their weight in liquid. Available in regular size (4 x 3 inches) and large (6 x 4 inches), the EcoSponge will outperform and outlast ordinary sponges. (www.pacificdrygoods.com)

FYI

A well-stacked, fully packed dishwasher is more water-efficient than hand washing when you curb excessive pre-rinsing. Opt out of the "heated dry" cycle and open the door to air-dry dishes for loads of energy savings.

Something Old, Something New

Target has stepped up its green presence at stores nationwide. Look for four-packs of organic flour sack towels sold under Target's house brand, Home. These naturally soft and durable towels are made from 100 percent certified organic cotton and are packaged in a sleeve made from 80 percent postconsumer waste recycled cardstock. The towels are manufactured in a facility certified by the Institute for Marketecology. (The IMO certification is an emerging standard for international commodities like cotton that combines organic certification with fair-trade criteria to ensure a socially accountable, ecologically responsible, economically stable fair shake for small farmers. Visit www.imo.ch for details.)

Williams-Sonoma also proudly purveys organic flour sack towels made from unbleached organic cotton that is extrasoft, absorbent, and lint free. A fabulous favorite, sold in sets of three. (www.williams-sonoma.com)

Not Just for Glassware

Target offers four-packs of absorbent, textured organic bar towels under the in-house Home brand. They are far too handy to be relegated just to the bar. Made from 100 percent certified organic cotton fiber with IMO (Institute for Marketecology) certification, these reasonably priced towels are soft and durable and will withstand plenty of household abuse. (www.target.com)

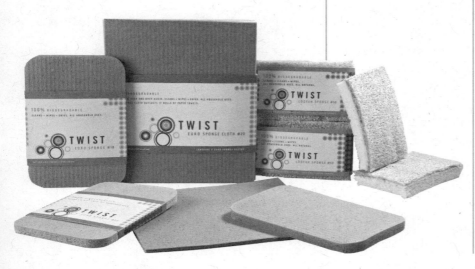

PAPER TOWELS
Recycled Content Is Key

Truth to tell, reaching for cloth towels over paper is the greenest choice of all. But when disposable paper towels are called for, opt for eco-friendly products made with recycled, chlorine-free content. Also, select paper towels with high postconsumer waste (PCW) content. PCW products are made from paper that was used in a finished product, then separated from the waste stream and repulped into new paper. Compare this to simple recycled paper, which could be leftovers from a virgin paper run.

There are plenty of PCW towel and napkin options. Check 'em out:

★ Marcal and Sunrise paper towels are made with 100 percent recycled paper, with more than 60 percent PCW content, and are processed without chlorine. Marcal also makes Bella dinner napkins (100 percent recycled, 40 percent PCW) and Marcal napkins (100 percent recycled, 60 percent PCW), both bleached without chlorine.

★ Atlantic and Fiesta paper towels are both processed chlorine free and made with 100 percent recycled paper and 80 percent PCW content.

★ Some mainstream markets and retail chains now carry brands that were once found only in natural markets, such as Planet Inc.'s 100 percent recycled Green Forest paper towels (40 percent PCW) and Planet paper towels (80 percent PCW), both whitened without chlorine. For eco-friendly paper napkins, look for Green Forest napkins, made with 100 percent recycled, chlorine-free paper and 40 percent PCW content.

★ Earth First paper towels and napkins are 100 percent recycled with 80 percent PCW content and processed without chlorine.

★ Trader Joe's paper towels are chlorine free and 100 percent recycled with 35 percent PCW content.

★ Whole Foods' 365 Everyday Value paper towels and napkins are made with 100 percent recycled paper and 80 to 95 percent PCW content, made bright white without chlorine.

★ If you prefer the back-to-the-land brown of unbleached paper towels, Seventh Generation paper towels are just for you, made from 100 percent recycled paper and 80 percent PCW content.

Helpful or Harmful?

Antibacterial soaps and hand sanitizers have become enormously popular accessories beside sinks everywhere and even within handy reach of supermarket shopping carts. It's not that there are more germs and bacteria at large than there were 20 years ago, but we've grown much more paranoid about them. Yet antibacterial soaps and hand sanitizers may not be the best answer for confronting them. Consider the following:

1. A lot of bacteria are benign and helpful—such as those in our digestive tracts, that are in large part responsible for healthy digestion and nutrient absorption and are essential to our immune system. Antibacterial products kill bacteria indiscriminately, wiping out the good with the bad.

2. Constant use of antibacterial cleansers may mess with our immune systems. While bacteria and germs are everywhere, they have a tough time infiltrating our bodies because our bodies are designed with many levels of defense. However, our immune systems get lazy when all of the low-grade, day-to-day defense work is done for us. This can become a big issue when the nasty stuff comes along. A strong immune system is one that's kept in fit, fighting form.

3. Casual, regular use of antibacterial products promotes the growth of resistant strains of bacteria and germs. This may spell trouble for antibiotic medicines in the long run. Over time, our most effective antibiotics will be rendered powerless. We need antibiotics for the really nasty bacteria and pathogens, such as Staphylococcus and E. coli, not for the common kinds that mill around in the bathroom and kitchen.

4. Research actually links excessive hygiene with an increase in allergies, asthma, and eczema in some individuals.

ENZYME DRAIN CLEANERS: DIGESTING DEBRIS

For an unstoppable drain aid, Bio-Clean's Granulated Powder is a concentrated blend of natural bacteria and enzymes (not genetically modified) that digest the waste that accumulates in pipes and drains in no time. (www.statewidesupply.com)

Citra Solv Citra-Drain is made with natural enzymes, bacterial cultures, and a biodegradable surfactant to keep drains and pipes flowing freely without damaging the plumbing. (www.citra-solv.com)

Earth Friendly Products Earth Enzymes Drain Opener is a granulated powder that effectively digests clogged debris with natural enzymatic action. (www.ecos.com)

Naturally Antibacterial Essential Oils

For eons, essential oils derived from plants and flowers have been valued for their medicinal and therapeutic properties. Modern science has verified the value of many traditional oils, especially their antiseptic, antibacterial, antimicrobial, and antiviral qualities. Most notable in this regard are cinnamon, clove, lavender, lemon, lemongrass, orange, oregano, rosemary, tea tree, and thyme.

Essential oils are effective additions to homemade cleaning formulas made from basics like vinegar and baking soda. They can be added to a liquid hand soap to improve the antibacterial action of soap and water. And they smell fantastic. Why not enjoy some aromatherapy with your cleaning and cleansing?

Pure essential oils are available at most natural markets and from online sources. They aren't cheap, but a little goes a long way, and one bottle can easily last a year. Aura Cacia (www.auracacia.com) offers one of the most complete selections, with close to 80 types of 100 percent pure essential oils and 28 types of 100 percent organic essential oils. Floracopia (www.floracopia.com) offers a large selection of well-known oils, as well as unusual, uncommon, and relatively unknown oils from unique botanical species.

RECYCLED-CONTENT TRASH BAGS

Talking Trash

Recycled-content plastic bags save energy and resources, requiring 40 percent less energy to produce.

Seventh Generation's tall kitchen drawstring bags hold 13 gallons of trash and are made of 16 percent PCW and 39 percent preconsumer content. Seventh Generation also makes 30- and 33-gallon large trash bags from 80 percent recycled plastic, 24 percent of that PCW and 56 percent preconsumer plastic. (www.seventhgeneration.com)

Webster Industries manufactures two lines of recycled trash bags: EarthSense liners made from 100 percent recycled plastic (but zero percent PCW) in 13-, 30-, 33-, and 39-gallon sizes; and ReClaim heavy-duty liners made from 80 percent recycled plastic (10 percent PCW) in sizes ranging from 7 gallons to 56 gallons. (www.greenlinepaper.com; www.amazon.com; www.buyonlinenow.com)

ZEOLITE REFRIGERATOR FRESHENERS

A Fridge's Best Friend

Keep the inside of refrigerators fresh and deodorized with odor-munching, mold-inhibiting zeolite, a naturally occurring, highly absorbent mineral found in lava rock. Available in granules or chunks, zeolite neutralizes migrating odors and is said to curb staleness and freezer burn. And pure zeolite is rechargeable! Once it has soaked up funky odors and moisture for about a year, it can be laid out in direct sunlight for a day to dry and be ready to work again. Before long, you'll find other homes for zeolite's deodorizing power, such as closets, cars, and garbage cans.

The **Caldrea** Refrigerator Freshener is the loveliest zeolite product I've seen on the market. The charming, antique French–looking ceramic pot (4½ inches tall) makes a pretty home for zeolite to absorb odors in the fridge and other small spaces such as kitchen cabinets or closets. (www.caldrea.com)

Omni-Zorb Odor, Moisture and Mold Eliminator from **Cycletrol Diversified Industries** is an effective freshener made from pure, high-grade, granulated zeolite plus amino acids for ultimate odor control. ZeoFresh Refrigerator Packets, also from Cycletrol, are handy packets of zeolite that will keep fridges and freezers fresh by controlling odor and preventing odor cross-contamination. (www.omni-zorb.com)

Nature's Odor and Germ Control Refrigerator and Freezer Packets can be conveniently stashed in the fridge or freezer to soak up odors for up to a year. (www.nogc.com)

STAINLESS STEEL CLEANERS
Look, Ma, No Streaks

★ **Method** Steel for Real Stainless Steel Polish is a nontoxic, biodegradable, nonabrasive formula that cleans and polishes stainless steel surfaces without streaking and leaves a protective layer for long-term shine. Enjoy the lovely, nontoxic orchard blossom scent. Packaged in a 100 percent recycled plastic trigger-spray bottle, this supergreen steel polish is manufactured with renewable energy and recognized by the EPA's Design for the Environment for its eco-savvy formulation. Method Steel for Real Wipes are made with 100 percent renewable and biodegradable bamboo fiber and contain no plastic binders—just nontoxic, biodegradable polishing agents and fragrances for spiffy results and delightful smells. (www.methodhome.com)

★ **Caldrea** Stainless Steel Spray offers a nontoxic spa treatment experience for stainless steel surfaces packaged in a sturdy, reusable brushed-metal trigger spray bottle. It takes advantage of an old-school remedy using olive oil for lustrous shine. Delectable fragrances such as basil blue sage, citrus mint ylang-ylang, and ginger pomelo are derived from essential oils and biodegradable sources. (www.caldrea.com)

★ **Mrs. Meyer's** Stainless Steel Spray is a creamy, nontoxic formula that uses old-fashioned olive oil and plant-derived surfactants to clean and shine stainless surfaces. Choose from three fragrances derived from essential oils and natural sources: lavender, lemon verbena, and geranium. (www.mrsmeyers.com)

DEGRADABLE TRASH BAGS: On the Fast Track

Degradable plastic contains additives that accelerate the breakdown and degradation of plastic. It looks, feels, and functions just like ordinary plastic, but it reduces waste because it disintegrates in 1 to 2 years, whereas regular plastic can take hundreds of years. **Natural Value EcoSafe** degradable tall kitchen bags (13 gallon) and EcoSafe degradable large trash bags (33 gallon) are made from plastic with an additive called TDPA that "will totally fragment and disintegrate in 12 to 24 months." These bags have undergone stringent testing to ensure that they will lose at least 90 percent of their molecular weight in just 10 months, safely returning to the natural biocycle as fragments of carbon that can be ingested and mineralized by microorganisms to reduce the volume of landfill disposal. (www.naturalvalue.com)

BIODEGRADABLE, COMPOSTABLE TRASH BAGS
From Potato to Plastic

Biodegradable plastic trash bags are made from plant-based (think corn and potatoes) polymers that will entirely decompose, leaving no toxic residues. The manufacturing of bioplastic uses about 68 percent less energy and creates 80 to 90 percent less greenhouse-gas pollution.

BioBag makes 100 percent biodegradable and compostable kitchen and yard-waste bags (and even dog-waste bags and kitty-litter pan liners). Look for 3-gallon food-waste bags; 13-gallon tall kitchen bags, and 33-gallon lawn and leaf bags. Check out BioBag's Garden Bio-Film, a biodegradable plastic wrap. It's sold for garden use but works brilliantly and safely to wrap food. (www.biobagusa.com)

Al-Pack Compostable Bags are made with 100 percent biodegradable and compostable plastic in 3-, 14-, 39-, and 63-gallon sizes. (www.mycompost.com)

Fortune Plastics' Comp-Lete 33 x 39-inch lawn and leaf bag will hold 33 gallons and is made with 100 percent biodegradable and compostable plastic. (www.fortuneplastics.com)

Heritage Bag BioTuf Compostable Bags, available for home and commercial use, are available in 30-, 32-, 48-, and 64-gallon sizes. They're 100 percent biodegradable and compostable. (www.heritage-bag.com)

Bio-Solo bags come in a huge selection of 100 percent biodegradable and compostable trash and waste bags for home and commercial use. Choose from the 4-gallon mini, 13-gallon jumbo, 33-gallon garbage, 39-gallon leaf and yard, 55-gallon heavy-duty industrial, and 64- or 94-gallon cart liner. (www.biosolo.com)

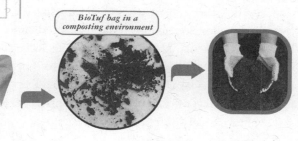

BioTuf bag in a composting environment

WOOD AND FURNITURE POLISHES AND CLEANERS
Go for the Glow

Plant-oil-based soaps and wood cleaners are gentle yet effective ways to keep wood furniture lustrous and polished. **Murphy Oil Soap** is one of the oldest and best products to care naturally for wood. It's biodegradable, water-based, phosphate free, and ideal for any wood surface, including furniture, cabinets, paneling, and floors. The original concentrated formula goes a long way—use just 2 ounces in a gallon of warm water—and is available in 32-ounce and 1-gallon screw-top bottles. Murphy Oil Soap Multi-Use Clean & Shine spray for wood offers a convenient way to clean dust, grease, grime, and wax buildup to reveal wood's natural beauty without leaving residue. (www.colgate.com)

Method Wood for Good will clean and buff wood surfaces in a snap. This naturally nontoxic formula contains glycerin and oleic acid (the omega-9 fatty acid found in olive oil); nontoxic, degradable surfactants; and polishing agents to keep wood fresh and clean and a natural almond scent for good measure. Wood for Good is packaged in a convenient trigger-spray bottle made with 100 percent recycled plastic. (www.methodhome.com)

Earth Friendly Products Furniture Polish contains only natural olive and orange oils and an emulsifier to clean, restore, and beautify wood surfaces with all types of finishes (even Formica, particleboard, and vinyl surfaces). It's 100 percent biodegradable and nontoxic and contains no phosphates or petroleum ingredients. (www.ecos.com)

Caldrea Lavender Pine Wood Furniture Cream blends lemon balm, carnauba wax and beeswax, jojoba oil, and vinegar to create a balanced wood cleanser and moisturizer for a rich luster for all finished wood surfaces. Thanks to the essential oils of lavender, pine needle, and cedar, the lingering aroma is divine. (www.caldrea.com)

Citra Solv CitraWood Natural Wood & Furniture Polish uses the gentle power of orange oil and soybean oil to polish, protect, preserve, and beautify your finest wood surfaces, leaving behind only a hint of pleasant Valencia orange fragrance. It contains no petroleum distillates, synthetic perfumes, or dyes—just pure, clean care for wood. (www.citra-solv.com)

EARTH FRIENDLY SILVER POLISH
Tarnish Trappers

Over time, the brilliant luster of sterling silver will tarnish to a dull, oxidized pallor. Sterling silver flatware, candleholders, and jewelry (the latter commonly plated with a thin coat of special silver to keep it shiny) will benefit from a good polish from time to time to return the lustrous shine. Conventional silver cleaners are generally chemical dips, but Earth Friendly Products offers a biodegradable plant-derived silver polish that is free of formaldehyde, phosphate, and chlorine. (www.ecos.com)

EVAPO-RUST REMOVER
Get the Red Out

Evapo-Rust is an eco-friendly, biodegradable, water-based rust remover that is safe on your skin. It also won't harm chrome, plastic, rubber, unrusted steel, vinyl, or wood, so you can safely treat mixed-material objects. Nontoxic, noncorrosive, and nonflammable, it won't create fumes, VOCs, or bad odors; and it removes heavy rust completely and safely. (www.evapo-rust.com)

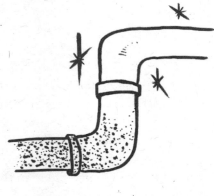

ROMANCING THE STONE

Method Daily Granite Polish cleans and buffs granite and marble surfaces to a shine using supereffective, nontoxic, biodegradable cleaners made from plants like corn and coconut. Packaged in a 100 percent recycled plastic trigger-spray bottle, this polish has a lovely orchid blossom scent. (www.methodhome.com)

LIQUID LAUNDRY DETERGENTS

Sensible Suds

★ **Method**'s liquid laundry detergents are superconcentrated, so less is more (use 1 ounce per full load). These mighty laundry liquids are made of nontoxic, biodegradable plant-based surfactants and natural brightening agents. They're compatible with high-efficiency (HE) washers and are available in four great-smelling natural scents. (www.methodhome.com)

★ **Mrs. Meyer's** liquid laundry detergent is a hardworking formula that's tough on dirt and grime yet gentle on clothes and safe for skin. Formulated with biodegradable anionic surfactants from plant-derived sources, cotton extract, borax, and dirt-fighting enzymes, this nontoxic liquid detergent gets its garden-fresh scents from essential oils. It smells fantastic! You'll get 32 loads per 64-ounce bottle. (www.mrsmeyers.com)

★ There's one problem with **Caldrea**'s laundry detergents: They smell so delectably good that you will want to wash your clothes more often than you probably need to. Mild yet highly effective and containing powerful plant-derived surfactants and borax to get your whites white and colors bright, these liquid detergents are biodegradable and contain no phosphorus. Choose from six special formulations of essential oils; their enticing fragrances gently linger in your clothes long after they are dried and folded. (www.caldrea.com)

★ **Seventh Generation**'s laundry detergents are among the best buys on the market. The Natural 2X Concentrate liquid is formulated with plant-based surfactants and enzymes to power out even the toughest stains. Anyone with sensitivities will appreciate the unscented, undyed Free & Clear. The Baby Laundry liquid is also free of dyes and fragrances and specially formulated to be tough on stains yet gentle on baby's clothes. All are free of phosphates and optical brighteners and effective in both HE and standard machines. (www.seventhgeneration.com)

THE POWER OF O

Oxygen bleach is the supreme way to whiten whites and keep colors bright while sidestepping the ecological and human hazards of chlorine. **OxiClean** Versatile Stain Remover contains 50 to 60 percent active oxygen ingredients from sodium percarbonate. It's sold in 3.5- and 6-pound tubs. For on-the-go spot treating, look for OxiClean Spray-A-Way Instant Stain Remover in a handy, 0.47-fluid-ounce tote-size spray bottle. Very nifty. (www.oxiclean.com)

Clorox Oxi Magic Multi-Purpose Stain Remover Powder and Spray opts out of chlorine in favor of a 50 to 60 percent active oxygen content from sodium percarbonate. Look for the powder form in two sizes of tubs or in liquid form in a convenient spray bottle. (www.oxymagic.com)

Why Oxygen Bleach?

Oxygen bleach releases oxygen to whiten whites and keep colors bright. Like chlorine bleach, it oxidizes, burning away stains and grime; unlike chlorine bleach, it won't harm fibers. But oxygen bleach is not hazardous to humans or the environment. When it's done working its magic, oxygen bleach breaks down into oxygen, water, and natural soda ash (sodium carbonate). It has antiseptic properties, is safe for colors, and boosts the power of laundry detergent for any type of load by naturally softening water. It's a winner in any form, powdered or liquid. Here are more benefits of oxygen bleach:

Prevents yellowing and graying of fabric. Oxygen bleach can be used continuously.

Safe for all washable fabric. It doesn't weaken fibers and fabrics.

Disinfects and deodorizes.

Safe with other products. Oxygen bleach can be mixed with other cleaning and laundry products without hazard.

Environmentally friendly. The release of oxygen is actually beneficial for agriculture and aquaculture.

FABRIC SOFTENERS
Fluff before Folding

Who doesn't like cushy, good-smelling clothes that resist static cling? There's no need to compromise your skin or the environment to get just that—simply find natural fabric softeners that are free from dangerous chemicals.

Method offers a nontoxic and biodegradable choice. Formulated with plant-based softeners and surfactants, its fabric softener is vegan—meaning it contains no animal tallow. The two scents are derived from both natural and well-researched, human-safe, biodegradable synthetic sources. (www.methodhome.com)

Mrs. Meyer's fabric softener smells delightful and keeps clothes fluffy and soft with nontoxic, biodegradable, plant-based softening ingredients and naturally derived fragrances, including basil, lavender, lemon verbena, and geranium. (www.mrsmeyers.com)

Seventh Generation's nontoxic, biodegradable fabric softener is manufactured with plant-based ingredients and without tallow derivatives. It's hypoallergenic and fetches a pretty lavender scent from various essential oils and botanical extracts. (www.seventh generation.com)

Caldrea fabric softener is made from plant-derived softening elements. It uses a special formulation of essential oils for deliciously lingering fragrances, including ginger pomelo, basil blue sage, and green tea patchouli. (www.caldrea.com)

FYI

Vinegar is a good fabric softener, especially for absorbent materials like towels and diapers, as well as heavy fabric like denim blue jeans. Add 1/2 cup white distilled vinegar to the rinse cycle.

STAIN REMOVERS
Spot Be Gone

Some of the best all-purpose stain removers are sold as carpet spot removers, including **Begley's Best** Household Cleaner and Stain Remover. As one of the ultimate all-purpose cleaners and stain removers on the market, this nontoxic, biodegradable formula of sophisticated plant-based ingredients works like magic on whites, lights, and colors. It contains zero solvents or chemicals. (www.begleysbest.com)

Biokleen Bac-Out Stain & Odor Eliminator uses live enzyme-producing cultures that attack stains and odors, digest them safely and naturally, and leave no residues. The nontoxic, biodegradable formula contains lime peel extract to boost cleaning power and to deodorize and destroy the toughest odors. It's excellent for removing mold, mildew, and pet stains from clothing, carpets, and upholstery. (www.biokleen home.com)

Citra Solv Citra-Spot Natural Enzymatics uses natural enzymes and bacterial cultures to break down organic stains and odors, including blood, pet stains, grass stains, and more. Nontoxic and biodegradable with no synthetic perfumes, dyes, or chemical solvents, this mighty spray leaves behind only a gentle hint of Valencia orange. (www.citra-solv.com)

Ecover Stain Remover includes a handy built-in brush to remove all types of obstinate oil and protein stains such as grass, mud, blood, sweat, food, and more. Formulated with plant-based, nontoxic ingredients that quickly and easily biodegrade, this stain remover is safe for use on both whites and colors. (www.ecover.com)

If you want a delightful scent to linger long after stains are removed, **Caldrea** Sweet Pea Stain Remover is just for you. Highly effective on all types of organic stains, especially for garments and linens of kids and babies, this stain remover gets its pleasant fragrance from an essential-oil blend of geranium, orange, jasmine, coriander, rose, and bergamot. (www.caldrea.com)

DRYER SHEETS: AIN'T MISBEHAVIN'

Tame static with dryer sheets that condition by means of plant-based agents and are scented with natural fragrances or are unscented. **Bounce** Free fabric softener sheets release biodegradable softening agents and contain no dyes or perfumes. (www.bouncesheets.com)

Method believes that "wet is the new dry" when it comes to its softener-infused dryer sheets. Moist to the touch, these dryer sheets are made with renewable plant oils, which reduce static and infuse plant-based softeners right into the fabric of clothes as they dry, instead of just leaving them on the surface. Choose from natural fragrances, such as sweet water, nectarine blossom, and lavender, or unscented for static-free softness. (www.methodhome.com)

Mrs. Meyer's dryer sheets are a perfect way to reduce static cling and add a lovely aroma to your clothes. They contain a vegetable-derived softening agent and essential oils on a biodegradable paper sheet. Choose from four fragrances: cool basil, soothing lavender, warm geranium, and fresh lemon verbena. (www.mrsmeyers.com)

Caldrea once again offers sumptuous-smelling solutions with its dryer sheets. These biodegradable sheets contain a vegetable-derived softening agent and are infused with delectably fresh smells that are beyond the beyond, such as basil blue sage, ginger pomelo, and lavender pine. (www.caldrea.com)

DRYER BALLS
Give Linens a Lift

Dryer balls are alternatives to disposable dryer sheets or expensive liquid softeners. Typically sold in sets of two, these rubbery balls are covered in soft, spiky nodules that lift, separate, and relax fabrics as they tumble in the dryer. Dryer balls produce softer clothing and fluffy, more absorbent towels with less lint and wrinkling. They even reduce drying time by up to 25 percent. Now that's the kind of green that will save you green (cash, that is).

Most dryer balls are made of nontoxic silicone, a sturdy, eco-friendly material that can handle high heat without degrading. They're an inexpensive, chemical-free solution to laundry softeners for those with sensitivities. A set of two will last several years, which equates to a small mountain of dryer sheets (read: save more money). Brands to look for include **Nellie's** All-Natural Dryerballs (www.nelliesallnatural.com), guaranteed to last up to 2 years, and **Dryer Max** (www.ontelproducts.com).

DETERGENTS FOR DELICATES
Gentle Yet Mighty

★ As a tried-and-true detergent for delicates, **Woolite** has been around a long time. It's designed to gently clean silk and wool without stripping the natural oils from the fiber or leaving residue. Woolite uses biodegradable surfactants and contains no phosphates. Who knew? (www.woolite.com)

★ **Dr. Bronner's** Baby Mild pure castile liquid soap is as pure as it gets, made from 100 percent vegetable oils, such as olive, hemp, and coconut oils. Among a multitude of uses, it's ideal for hand-washing cashmere, rayon, and silk. Dr. Bronner's saponified coconut oil allows for excellent lathering and less soap residue, even with extremely hard water. This thin liquid is superconcentrated, so a little goes a long way. It's 100 percent biodegradable and packaged in 100 percent postconsumer recycled plastic bottles, which are easy to recycle after use. Bravo! (www.drbronner.com)

★ **Earth Friendly Products** Baby liquid laundry soap is not just gentle enough for babies' clothes, it's also suitable for hand-washing silk, wool, cashmere, and other delicates. It's hypoallergenic and good for sensitive skin, and its pure fragrance comes from the essential oils of chamomile and lavender. (www.ecos.com)

★ **Ecover** Delicate Wash is made from biodegradable plant ingredients and ideally suited for washing fine fabrics like silk, cashmere, and wool. Its inviting fresh fragrance is derived from plant-based sources. (www.ecover.com)

★ **Seventh Generation** Delicate Care laundry liquid is formulated to gently and effectively clean without leaving residue on clothing, so it's especially good for those with sensitivities and for washing delicate clothing. This nontoxic, plant-based, biodegradable detergent contains no fragrances, dyes, optical brighteners, or enzymes. (www.seventhgeneration.com)

FYI

For clothes you care about, consider hand washing. You'll save money on your energy bills and prolong the life of your best-loved duds.

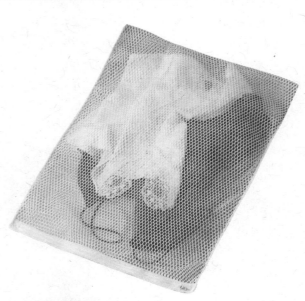

LINGERIE WASH BAG
Preserve and Protect

Extend the life of beloved delicates by washing them in lingerie wash bags. Just think—no more tangling with other garments, which can damage decorative features. Stockings and pantyhose will also benefit from this simple step. Lingerie wash bags are widely available. Look for **Bare Necessities** (www.barenecessities.com) lingerie wash bags (17 x 13 inches) and large lingerie wash bags (18 x 22 inches); **Laundry Essentials** mesh lingerie wash bags (12 x 15 inches); and **Whitney-Design** (www.whitney-design.com) mesh lingerie wash bags (14 x 18 inches).

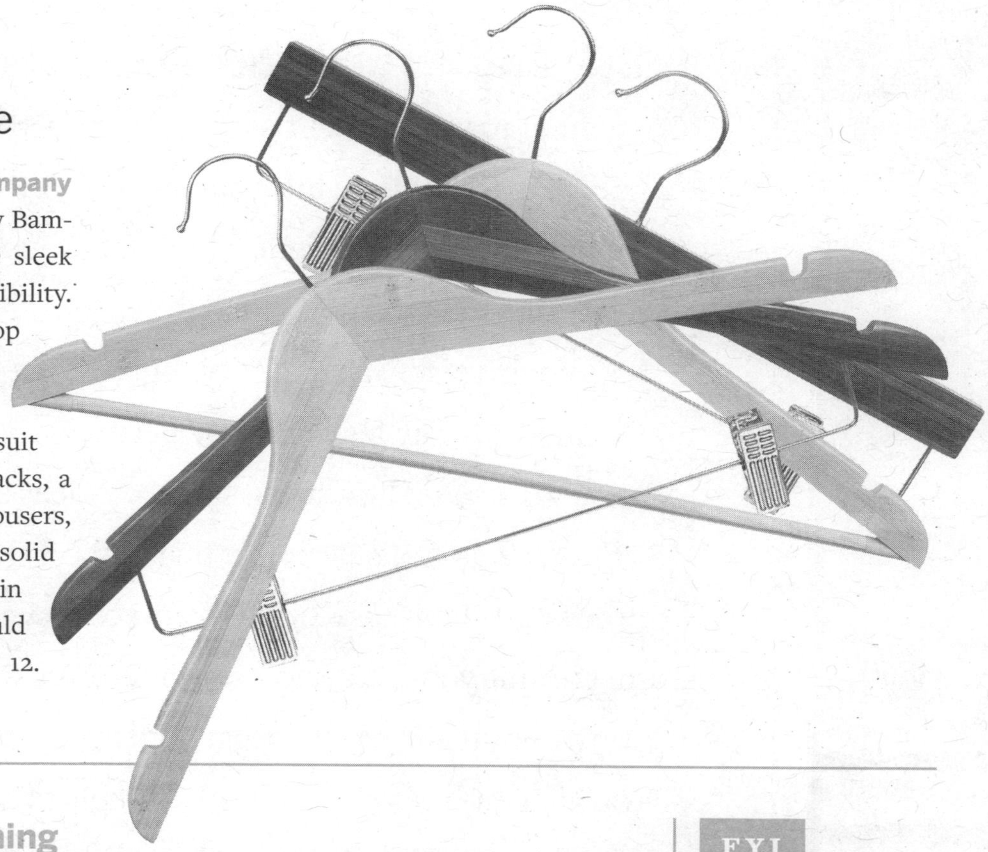

BAMBOO CLOTHING HANGERS

An Übergreen Alternative

The Great American Hanger Company offers beautiful, durable, earth-friendly Bamboo Collection hangers that combine sleek function with environmental responsibility. Choose from five styles, including a top hanger for shirts and tops, a bottom hanger with a horizontal top and two clips to hang trousers and pants, a suit hanger with a rod to accommodate slacks, a combination hanger with two clips for trousers, and an extrasturdy coat hanger. These solid accessories will keep your clothes hung in eco-style and are so well made they could last a lifetime. Available in sets of 12. (www.hangers.com)

Tips for Hang-Drying Clothing

Whenever possible, keep clothes out of the dryer and out on the line! You'll save energy (and money), and your laundry will smell clean and fresh courtesy of Mother Nature. Here are handy tips for easy and effective hang-drying of laundry:

★ Use a clothespin bag. This canvas bag has a lightweight internal metal frame that hooks over the clothesline to hold your clothespins within easy reach.

★ Hang clothing upside down to prevent stretching in visible places like the shoulders.

★ Turn colored garments inside out and ideally hang them out of direct sun to prevent fading. A few hours in the sun is unlikely to fade colors, but continuous, long-term exposure might.

★ Fold a large item like a sheet or tablecloth in half and place three or four clothespins at the hem edge, allowing the folded edge to billow in the breeze for the quickest drying.

★ Prevent towels from stiffening up by giving them a curt snap before hanging. Drape a few inches of the narrow end over the line and place clothespins at the corners (and one in the middle if it's an extralarge bath sheet). Towels may be taken from the line when they are still a touch damp and tossed in the dryer for 5 to 10 minutes to fluff up nicely.

★ If you are setting up a clothesline, aim for a length of 25 to 35 feet and hang the line half an arm's length above your head. This should be long enough to accommodate a full load of wash; any longer and the weight of wet clothes may cause the line to sag. If possible, scout a strategic place that will allow a breeze to pass through hanging laundry for the shortest drying time.

FYI

You can make your own wash bag for delicates using a clean, white pillowcase. Simply place your delicate items in the pillowcase, tie the pillowcase closed, wash in cold water on the delicate cycle, and hang-dry.

Buy Local. Buy Organic. Eat Seasonally. We face a whole menu of mantras to choose from, enough to produce a case of purchase paralysis: Should you buy your apples from the local farmers' market, even though they're not organic? Or should you go with the organic apples from Argentina?

Your grocery list can be a blueprint for a greener life if you simply strive to Eat Well. Buy less, but buy better. Start by learning where your food comes from and how it was grown, processed, packaged, and transported. The green goal is to "eat low on the food chain," to make fresh, minimally processed plant-based foods from your own region the cornerstone of your diet. Limit your intake of resource-intensive animal products, and when you do buy meat, poultry, eggs, or dairy, select the pasture-raised products. Navigate the seafood aisle with the help of a consumer guide to sustainably raised or harvested fish.

As an environmentally savvy shopper, you have the power to help curb climate change, prevent pollution, preserve farmland, save endangered rain forests and oceans, and support more humane conditions for farm-workers and animals. That's a lot of weight to put on your plate. But consider this: While Americans are now just 5 percent of the world's population, we burn through about 30 percent of the planet's resources—and generate one-quarter of the world's greenhouse gases. Adding insult to injury, we throw away nearly 40 percent of the food we produce, sending it to landfills where it rots and generates methane, a greenhouse gas that traps 20 times as much heat in the atmosphere as carbon dioxide does. We pay through the nose for this noxious practice, spending about $1 billion annually to pitch food waste into landfills.

Another waste-not strategy: Have some recipes in mind before you head to the market. You'll be less likely to make impulse buys that don't get eaten. If you're not inclined to plan your meals in advance, just keep your pantry and freezer stocked with staples. That way, you'll have the means to throw together a soup, salad, or stew on the fly.

When you build your meals around fresh fruits and vegetables, you reduce another source of waste—the excess packaging of processed convenience foods. That's another worthy reason to shop at the farmers' market. The buy-local movement is an effective way to support farmers whose values are in sync with your own. Bear in mind that buying local is often the most low-impact choice—but not always: An out-of-season local tomato grown in a fossil-fuel-heated greenhouse could consume more energy than one that's been field grown and shipped from Mexico.

Then there are those items that you simply can't get locally. A region rich in avocados and oranges will have no blueberries or maple syrup. So save your food miles to splurge on spices, oils, chocolate, tea, coffee, and other staples that you cannot get domestically.

The "buy organic" edict has a panoply of meanings.

Many people associate organic farming with the back-to-the-land movement of the '60s and '70s, but the methods we now label "organic" were simply the way the world fed itself for centuries before the advent of industrial agriculture. The "certified organic" label remains a useful tool for consumers seeking to avoid foods that have been produced with chemical fertilizers and pesticides. Many farmers who do grow their crops organically choose, for a variety of reasons, not to seek organic certification. Some of these farmers define themselves as "beyond organic," while others describe their growing practices as "sustainable." These nuances are another incentive to buy food directly from the folks who grew it.

Choose low-carbon foods produced through photosynthesis rather than petroleum-based chemicals, and place plant-based foods front and center on your plate. When you make fruits, vegetables, and whole grains your axis of Eat Well, you'll be well on your way to a healthier diet—and to curbing your carbon "foodprint."

—Kerry Trueman

Private Security for the Food Chain

In theory, the Food and Drug Administration ensures the safety of our food supply, and the United States Department of Agriculture supports rational agricultural policies that benefit both farmer and consumer. In practice? Not so much. The reality is that our chronically underfunded FDA barely manages to inspect 1 percent of the foods imported to this country, and it often stumbles when faced with a domestic outbreak of contaminated meat or produce.

The USDA is saddled with the schizophrenic agenda of promoting the interests of agribusiness while exhorting Americans to adopt healthier eating habits. Over the years, the USDA has proposed dietary guidelines advising us to, say, curb our sugar intake, or eat less meat—only to have the powers that be in the food industry start throwing up roadblocks. Consumers have consistently voiced concern over genetically modified organisms (GMOs), cloning, the widespread use of hormones and antibiotics, irradiation, and the long list of potential toxins that taint our food supply.

food&waterwatch

So who is looking out for the little guy? Several nonprofit organizations are dedicated to acting as watchdogs over our food supply, among them the **Center for Food Safety** (www.centerforfoodsafety.org), **Center for Science in the Public Interest** (www.cspinet.org), **Consumers Union** (www.consumersunion.org), **Food and Water Watch** (www.foodandwaterwatch.org), and **Organic Consumers Association** (www.organicconsumers.org).

Miso, a soybean-based paste, is best known as an essential ingredient for Asian soups. This versatile fermented seasoning can also enhance salad dressings, stews, sauces, and just about any other dish. A staple of Japanese cuisine for centuries, miso is high in probiotics—the "good" bacteria that aid digestion and boost immune systems.

The Closer to Home, the Better

There's no need to wait till the price of solar panels plunges to get your energy from the sun. Solar power's a great source of calories as well as kilowatts. When you fuel up on fresh, unprocessed fruits and veggies that haven't been grown with petrochemicals or transported from hither and yon, your diet shifts, in the words of Michael Pollan, "from a foundation of imported fossil fuel to local sunshine."

Farmers' markets are your best source for local, sustainably grown produce, and the odds of finding one near you get better all the time. In 1970, there were just 340 farmers' markets in the United States. As of 2008, there were 4,685, according to the USDA. You can find the farmers' markets in your region through online directories at www.eatwellguide.org and www.localharvest.org.

The **Eat Well Guide** and **Local Harvest** Web sites also feature listings of CSAs (community supported agriculture). When you become a member of a CSA, you're buying a share of the bounty from a farm in your neck of the woods. In return for an investment of several hundred dollars or so at the start of the growing season (the cost varies depending on a range of factors), you get a weekly assortment of produce that changes with the seasons, from spring through fall.

This arrangement ensures that your fridge and fruit bowl stay filled with fresh, local produce. The CSA model works best for those blessed with an adventurous and eclectic palate, since you'll get a grab bag of whatever's ready for harvest that week. Some CSAs offer eggs, dairy, and meat products, too—or even cut flowers. If you're ready to embrace a truly seasonal approach to eating, a share in a CSA is an investment that pays delicious dividends.

When a supermarket or natural food store is your only option, your most sustainable choices will generally be the produce that's grown closest to home and organic fruits and vegetables from North American farmers.

COFFEE

Equal Exchange Is Greenest

Do you get your get-up-and-go from a cuppa joe every morning? If so, you've got plenty of caffeinated company; coffee's the second most traded commodity in the world after oil, according to the Rainforest Alliance. And as with that other fuel, its production has a profound impact on the environment.

The gold standard in sustainable coffee is triple certified: shade grown, organic, and fair trade. Coffee trees thrive in the rich, moist soil and under the lush canopy of the rain forest. Migratory birds flock to this biodiverse habitat and keep the insect population in check.

But back in the 1970s, some coffee farmers began clearing forests to plant coffee trees in full sun, where they grow faster. Though this method yields more beans, their flavor is inferior, consistent with industrial agriculture's "quantity over quality" ethos. Lacking the rain forest's balanced ecosystem, these farmers must employ chemical fertilizers and pesticides to counter the monoculture that evicts wildlife and erodes the soil.

Most certified organic coffee is, therefore, shade grown. But in some deforested areas, organic coffee farmers are restoring habitat through a method of farming called agroforestry, in which trees, shrubs, and crops are interplanted to create a biodiverse, productive environment where coffee crops flourish.

Fair-trade certification, verified in the United States by the nonprofit **TransFair USA**, ensures that your coffee beans weren't harvested by child labor and that they come from a cooperatively owned farm where the growers are guaranteed a premium for their coffee beans. Fair-trade certified farmers also receive assistance in switching to organic farming methods. (www.transfairusa.org)

Fair-trade pioneer **Equal Exchange**, a worker-owned co-op based in Massachusetts, started importing fair-trade coffee from Nicaragua in 1986. Over the past two decades, Equal Exchange has grown to become one of our primary purveyors of fair-trade coffee, tea, cocoa, and chocolate in partnership with small farmer organizations in Africa, Asia, Latin America, and the United States. (www.equalexchange.coop)

EQUAL EXCHANGE: FAIRLY DARK CHOCOLATE

Dark chocolate is chock-full of the same flavonoids that make deep-colored fruits and vegetables so rich in antioxidants. It's still a high-fat indulgence, but those flavonoids have been shown to lower blood pressure and cholesterol and protect against heart disease.

Sadly, the way most cocoa beans are harvested is a human rights scandal more likely to make your heart sink and your blood pressure rise. Much of the world's cocoa comes from plantations in West Africa, particularly the Ivory Coast, where children, many under the age of 10, are forced to harvest the pesticide-laden crops. Conventional cocoa cultivation practices deplete the soil and contaminate the water.

So do your heart doubly good by choosing fair-trade, organic chocolate from **Equal Exchange**, which works with farmer cooperatives in the Caribbean and South America dedicated to sustainable, humane cocoa production. (www.equalexchange.coop)

FYI

You can prolong the life of your produce dramatically with Evert-Fresh Green Bags or the Healthy Harvest Freshness Extender, available on Amazon.com. Both products delay decay by reducing the ethylene gases that cause produce to ripen.

Front Yard Farmers

Look out, lawn lemmings! The grassroots revolt against grass is spreading like dandelions. Weirdly ironic, isn't it? The more fertilizers, weed killers, and water you pour on your lawn, the less green it gets.

You can have your lawn and green it, too, by replacing those thirsty, fussy, nonnative grasses with slow-growing, drought-tolerant native species such as buffalo grass or a blend of fescues.

But why settle for a low-impact lawn when you could have a high-yield yard? Enhance your landscape by adding edible plants that are lovely to look at *and* tasty to eat.

No land? No problem; plenty of fruits and vegetables thrive in containers on a rooftop or a terrace. A window box can become a "cut-and-come-again" salad bar. Find the sunniest spot you've got; add soil, seeds, or plants; and water. You'll be on your way to a homegrown harvest.

You can also get in touch with your inner farmer by joining a community garden. Check out the American Community Garden Association Web site at communitygarden.org to find—or start—a community garden in your neighborhood. For inspiration on the rewards of tearing out turf and building up gardens, read Heather C. Flore's permaculture manifesto *Food Not Lawns: How to Turn Your Yard into a Garden and Your Neighborhood into a Community* (Chelsea Green, 2006).

The kitchen garden revival is in full swing on the White House lawn and beyond. Seed sales have skyrocketed as millions of Americans follow First Lady Michelle Obama's lead and get growing. If you're a novice gardener, the best tool for digging may be the Internet, where savvy gardeners share their wisdom with the greenest of green thumbs at Kitchen Gardeners International (kitchengardeners.org).

Other sources of garden guidance: Architect Fritz Haeg's Edible Estates project has recruited a new army of amateur agrarians to launch the next generation of victory gardens. His book *Edible Estates: Attack on the Front Lawn* (Metropolis Books, 2008) documents four grass-to-garden conversions Haeg undertook in collaboration with home gardeners in different regions. *Edible Estates* features contributions from some of America's foremost proponents of edible landscaping, including Michael Pollan's seminal essay "Why Mow? The Case Against Lawns," and an entry from edible landscaping pioneer Rosalind Creasy, who literally wrote the book on this topic, *The Complete Book of Edible Landscaping* (Sierra Club Books, 1982). A new edition of this essential but long-out-of-print classic is due out in 2010.

Choose Pastured Over Factory Farmed

Livestock production generates nearly 20 percent of the world's greenhouse gases, so eating less meat is a surefire way to curb your carbon "foodprint." Follow Thomas Jefferson's example; our founding father/foodie regarded meat as merely "a condiment" to accompany the vegetables that dominated his dinner table.

But don't just move meat to the margins. Support farmers who raise pastured or grass-fed livestock humanely. The factory farms that churn out cheap chuck also breed misery, disease, and pollution. These CAFOs (concentrated animal feeding operations) cram animals into tight, filthy pens and pump them full of antibiotics to speed growth and combat disease—a practice that may be creating drug-resistant strains of bacteria in humans.

The grain grown for feedlots squanders resources, encourages deforestation, and uses petroleum-based fertilizers. And the CAFO manure lagoons contaminate soil, water, and air.

Pastured livestock is healthier all around—higher in "good" fats, antioxidants, and vitamins. As more farmers go grass-fed, pastured products are becoming easier to find. Eatwild.com offers a comprehensive directory of pasture-based farms and a list of farmers who will ship their products to you.

D'Artagnan (www.dartagnan.com) and **Organic Prairie** (www.organicprairie.coop) ship a wide range of organic and grass-fed meat and poultry products. If you're worried about racking up food miles, search your local market for products from Organic Prairie and **Applegate Farms** (www.applegatefarms.com).

MEAT ALTERNATIVES

Get Your Animal-Free Protein

Vegetarians have been tinkering with tofu and wheat gluten for centuries in search of satisfactory mock-meat concoctions. It all began with seitan, the wheat-gluten-based meat substitute reportedly invented by Buddhist monks in 7th-century China.

Many vegetarians—as well as carnivores seeking to eat less meat—find that seitan, along with its venerable vegan cousins tofu and tempeh, is a good source of animal-free protein. Look for locally made, organic versions at natural food stores; if they're not available, your second best bet is a brand that's made from non-GMO, organic ingredients.

Tofu dogs and veggie burgers are essentially a Western variation of these ancient Asian foods, but if your motivation for choosing these products stems from a love of animals or the environment, you need to vet your soy dogs carefully. Most of the nationally distributed brands are owned by corporations that make their fortunes from commodity-crop-based processed foods and factory farming. Read the labels, and if the soy is neither organic nor non-GMO, you can bet it's genetically modified, as is 92 percent of America's soy crop as of 2008, according to the USDA.

The happy exception is **Turtle Island Foods**, best known for its **Tofurky** products. This family-run, Oregon-based company makes a wide range of faux deli meats, burgers, sausages, soy dogs, tempeh, and its namesake Tofurky, using certified organic, non-GMO soybeans and tofu. (www.tofurky.com)

A relative newcomer to the alternative meat market, Seattle-based **Field Roast Grain Meat Company** offers an excellent line of what it calls "grain meats," featuring savory, well-seasoned sausages, deli slices, and its signature product, the field roast loaf. (www.fieldroast.com)

The Cheese Bible

Artisanal cheese making is enjoying a revival all over the country, so seek out a local cheesemonger for fresh and aged cheeses from small-scale, sustainable farms. Whether looking for mozzarella, ricotta, feta, goat cheese, cave-aged Cheddar, blue cheese, or raw milk varieties infused with that distinct regional flavor the French call *terroir*, you'll find America's finest sustainable cheese makers listed in Jeffrey Roberts's **Atlas of American Artisan Cheese**, published by Chelsea Green (2007).

EGGS

Choose Carefully

Egg producers slap so many claims on their cartons these days—cage free, free range, omega-3-enhanced, organic, certified humane—that it takes an egghead to figure out what these labels really mean. The one label you *won't* see is "battery caged," although the vast majority of eggs produced in this country fall into that category. Egg manufacturers who use battery cages presumably prefer not to advertise that their eggs come from industrial operations where hundreds of thousands of hens are so confined that they can't even flap their wings. This highly efficient method of production yields tons of eggs—and tons of toxic waste, which contaminates the surrounding air and water.

So consumers are increasingly seeking more environmentally friendly, ethically produced eggs, and producers are scrambling to meet the demand, to varying degrees. Cage free simply means that the hens aren't stuck in those miserable little cages; instead, they're packed into cavernous barns where they're crowded but unconfined. Free range goes a step further, generally permitting the hens not only to roam indoors but also to go outside on occasion (whether they actually avail themselves of this opportunity is another matter).

Certified organic eggs come from uncaged hens that are given outdoor access and fed an organic, all-vegetarian diet free of antibiotics and pesticides. Your best option, which may or may not be officially organic, is the pasture-raised eggs you can get, in season, from your local farmers' market. Small, biodiverse family farms often raise a few chickens to keep the bugs in check and help fertilize the soil. Pasture-raised eggs are not only kinder to the environment, they taste better and are more nutritious, too.

Low-Carbon Cooking

The most energy-efficient way to prepare food is, of course, to not cook it at all. Simply eat it raw. Raw food may be the preferred diet of hemp-happy hipsters and weed-eating survivalists, but it's really not so exotic. Every time you eat a salad with fresh fruits or vegetables, you're eating raw.

If the idea of giving up hot food leaves you cold, consider quick-cooking methods that generate the fewest greenhouse gases: steaming, sautéing, blanching, and (my favorite) pressure-cooking. You can conserve by doing your roasting and braising in a slow cooker and your baking in a toaster oven instead of a conventional gas or electric oven.

Is there a place for the microwave in the low-carbon kitchen? It is, after all, a fast and energy-efficient way to heat food. But, as the title of Sandor Katz's marvelous manifesto—*The Revolution Will Not Be Microwaved* (Chelsea Green, 2006)—about America's underground food movements declares, food is your friend—cook it, don't nuke it! Save the microwave for reheating leftovers and defrosting frozen foods. And please don't microwave plastic. Researchers have found that even so-called microwave-safe plastics may release the toxic chemical bisphenol A when heated.

It's easy to make tasty, low-carbon meals when you focus on fruits, vegetables, grains, and legumes. You don't need to go whole hog and become a "vegangelical"; try skipping animal products one day a week—say, Monday (see meatless-monday.com). Here are five fabulous cookbooks to inspire you: *Short-Cut Vegan* by Lorna Sass (William Morrow, 2009); *The Real Food Daily Cookbook* by Ann Gentry (Ten Speed Press, 2005); *The Balanced Plate* by Renée Loux (Rodale, 2006); *Veganomicon* by Isa Chandra Moskowitz and Terry Hope Romero (Da Capo Press, 2007); and *Get It Ripe* by Jae Steele (Arsenal Pulp Press, 2008).

SEAFOOD

Troll the Internet for Fresh Information

Should you skip the skipjack tuna? Chill on the Chilean sea bass? You need a scorecard to keep track of which fish you can eat with a clear conscience. Thankfully, there are several organizations that offer just such a list on their Web sites: the **Blue Ocean Institute** (www.blueocean.org), the **Environmental Defense Fund** (www.edf.org), and the **Monterey Bay Aquarium** (www.montereybayaquarium.org) all provide rankings of seafood to help you choose wisely; each site also lets you download a pocket-size guide to consult when you're at the supermarket or the sushi bar. You can even dial up a cell-phone-friendly version of the guides from the Blue Ocean Institute (www.fishphone.org) and the Environmental Defense Fund (www.m.edf.org/seafood).

The **Marine Stewardship Council**'s ecolabel program gives you another way to select sustainable seafood. When you see the blue MSC ecolabel on a package of fish at the market—or next to a menu selection at a restaurant—it's an assurance that you're purchasing a product from a sustainable fishery. Currently there are more than 1,600 MSC-labeled products available around the world, including canned and frozen fish as well as fresh. (www.msc.org)

TEECCINO

Cuppa Faux Joe

Faux-coffee fans mourned the passing of Postum when Kraft pulled the plug on that century-old caffeine-free coffee substitute in 2007. Happily, there's a great post-Postum alternative called Teeccino. This is a line of grain-based "herbal coffees" that you brew just as you would a cup of coffee. Organic Teeccino Maya Herbal Coffee gets its rich roasted flavor from the ramon nut, an ancient Mayan crop whose cultivation supports the preservation of the Mayan rain forest. (www.teeccino.com)

TEA

A Rainbow of Green Choices

Teatime used to be a late-afternoon ritual; now, with an ever-expanding array of teas available—from black, green, oolong, and white to new-kids-in-the-pot rooibos and yerba maté—there's a tea for every time of day. But whether you wake up with the classic English breakfast brew, grab an iced chai on the fly, or calm down with a cup of chamomile, there's a fair-trade, organic version of your favorite blend that lets you steep easy, knowing your tea was harvested sustainably and ethically.

Choice Organic Teas, founded in Seattle in 1989, started out with just four varieties of organic Japanese tea. In 2000, Choice Organic Teas became the first American tea company to offer fair-trade certified tea. Today, it offers more than 70 kinds of tea grown by organic farmers all over the world, from Sri Lanka to the United States.

The company strives to minimize its carbon footprint from crop to cup; beyond supporting sustainable agriculture, it minimizes its packaging, uses unbleached tea bags, purchases 100 percent wind-generated energy for its facilities, and recycles more than two-thirds of its waste. Choice Organic Teas even provides incentives for its employees to walk, bike, or take the bus to work. The company's "tea shirts"—made of unbleached organic cotton, of course—are printed with an eco-friendly ink and produced by a women's sewing cooperative in Nicaragua. Could your green tea possibly get any greener? (www.choiceorganicteas.com)

Guayakí's yerba maté, a tea made from the dried stems and leaves of the South American yerba maté tree, sets the bar for sustainable sipping even higher. Guayakí's organically shade-grown yerba maté boasts a negative carbon footprint; the cultivation of this evergreen shrub in sub-tropical rain forests captures so much carbon dioxide that these products *subtract* carbon from the environment. (www.guayaki.com)

Other widely available brands of tea that feature organic and fair-trade varieties include Alter Eco, Art of Tea, Eco Teas, Equal Exchange, and Rishi Tea.

WINES

Think Inside the Box

Choosing wines made from organically grown grapes is a great start, but don't overlook how the wine is produced, packaged, and transported. If you live in New England, a bottle of wine trucked from the Napa Valley burns more fossil fuel than one shipped from France—good reason to seek out local vineyards. There are now winemakers in every state.

How a wine is packaged counts even more. Now's the time to think *inside* the box: Boxed wines require far less energy to ship than bottled wines, and well-respected European vintners have now enhanced the quality of boxed wines. French Rabbit, one of the first companies to box wine, offers a line of wines made from grapes grown sustainably in the South of France. Its pinot noir, cabernet sauvignon, chardonnay, and merlot are sold nationwide. (www.frenchrabbit.com)

But if you're nearer the Pacific than the Atlantic, your best bet is a West Coast wine. Fetzer Vineyards in Mendocino County, a "zero waste" winemaker, relies entirely on alternative energy to produce its wines, and then it bottles them in lightweight glass. Founded in 1968, Fetzer has been a leader in environmentally friendly wine production for decades. Its wines aren't technically organic, as Fetzer, like many vintners, believes that a small amount of added sulfites is necessary to preserve and stabilize its wines, thus disqualifying it from organic certification.

Many winemakers, though farming sustainably, prefer not to pursue organic certification. Others go beyond organic to be "biodynamic," a holistic approach to agriculture that creates a self-sufficient closed loop. All these vintners help you to raise a toast without toasting the planet. (www.fetzer.com)

Suds Are Going Organic

The resurgence of microbreweries all over the United States gives thirsty locavores plenty of brews to choose from. But "locally brewed" doesn't necessarily mean "locally sourced." Looking for a beer that's local *and* organic? That's a tall order—and a sticky one, too.

You might think that a beer labeled "certified organic" would be brewed exclusively from organic ingredients, but under current (and controversial) USDA standards, organic beers may contain up to 5 percent nonorganic ingredients. That may sound insignificant, but it only takes a small quantity of hops to make a batch of beer. Brewers can easily meet the organic standard using hops that have been grown using all sorts of chemicals. Unfortunately, hop vines are prone to mildew, so farmers rely on fungicides and chemical fertilizers to ensure good yields.

Most organic hops currently come from New Zealand and Europe, but the worldwide demand for sustainable stout has created a chronic shortage in recent years. This poses a challenge to microbrewers who'd like to go beyond the letter of the law and be 100 percent organic.

One of America's first certified organic brewers, Vermont-based Wolaver's Certified Organic Ales, is working with small organic farmers to increase domestic production of organic hops. This collaboration has enabled Wolaver's to market its 100 percent certified organic All American Ale in limited editions. Wolaver's is best known for its more widely available year-round brews and seasonal ales, but the company's efforts to expand the domestic organic hops crop hold the promise of more locally sourced ales that are truly, entirely organic. (www.wolavers.com)

Your local microbrewer could be a model of sustainability, too. Some small brewers find the process of becoming certified too expensive or onerous to pursue, even though they rely predominantly—or even exclusively—on organic ingredients. One way to ensure that your beer is wholly organic (not to mention ultralocally brewed) is to make it yourself. Seven Bridges Cooperative offers certified organic brewing kits at www.breworganic.com.

FYI

Puzzled by the plethora of labels popping up on food products these days? *Consumer Reports'* eco-label center at www.greenerchoices.org will fill you in on whether "free range" is really free or if "natural" is an artificial appellation.

Take It from the Tap

The production and distribution of bottled water squanders resources and leaves behind depleted aquifers and heaps of discarded bottles.

You could argue that bottled water is a safer, purer product than tap water—but you'd be wrong. The EPA holds tap water to a higher standard than bottled water, which is more loosely regulated by the FDA. In fact, nearly half the bottled water on the market is just municipal tap water that's been needlessly filtered or otherwise "enhanced" to justify the extra expense. Tap water, on the other hand, is freely available, though not as widely as before private vending machines displaced public water fountains as the primary source to quench one's thirst.

But in some places tap water still has problems, including contamination from agriculture, industry, antiquated plumbing, and chemicals of unknown origin whose impact is also largely unknown—and unregulated. Our municipal water sources need greater protection.

You can see how your community's tap water stacks up by consulting the Environmental Working Group's national tap water quality database at www.ewg.org/tapwater/yourwater. Better still, have your water tested; if the results are unsatisfactory, invest in a filtration system. Find a state-certified lab to test your water at the EPA's Safe Drinking Water Hotline (800-426-4791; epa.gov/safewater/labs/index.html). For information on water filtration systems, consult Food and Water Watch's *How to Choose a Water Filter* at www.foodandwaterwatch.org.

There's no denying that bottled water comes in handy at times, and it's a good idea to keep a few gallons on hand for an emergency. If you can find a brand that's been bottled nearby, so much the better. But for everyday on-the-go hydration, adopt the habit of carrying a refillable bottle and go with the flow from the tap.

PASTA AND NOODLES
Whole Grain Is the Way to Go

Noodles are the quintessential comfort food. From ramen to rigatoni, nearly every culture seems to have its particular pasta. But most of the popular brands you'll find at the supermarket are made of refined flour from industrially grown wheat—not good for you *or* the environment.

Whole grain pastas with the taste and texture of cardboard haven't helped the cause of sustainable spaghetti, but, thankfully, the quality of whole grain pastas has improved dramatically in recent years. There's a much wider selection to choose from, including gluten-free alternatives such as quinoa- or rice-based pastas. Eden Foods relies on certified organic family farmers to grow the Kamut, spelt, buckwheat, quinoa, whole wheat, and rye in its whole grain pastas and its Japanese-style udon and soba noodles. Eden also offers organic crushed, diced, or whole canned tomatoes to complement its pastas, as well as pizza and spaghetti sauces. (www.edenfoods.com)

If mac 'n' cheese is your preferred pasta, look for the bunny on the box that says Annie's Homegrown. Annie's is the anti-Kraft, the all-natural alternative to that all-American icon of unnatural neon orange cheesiness. Founded in 1989 by Annie Withey, a Connecticut organic farmer, Annie's caught on with folks looking for a more wholesome take on their favorite comfort food, and the company now offers crackers and breakfast cereals along with an expanded line of pastas. Annie's demonstrates its commitment to sustainable food production by sponsoring school and community gardening programs as well as providing scholarships to college students studying sustainable agriculture. (www.annies.com)

Planet to Food.   Food to People.   People to Planet.

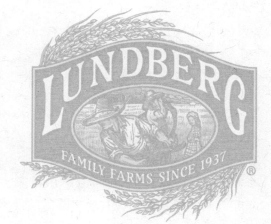

HOMEGROWN AND DELICIOUS

Thanks to the Dust Bowl, you can fill your rice bowl with Lundberg Family Farms' sustainably grown grains. In 1937, that Depression-era ecological disaster inspired Albert Lundberg to move his family to Northern California from Nebraska, where he had witnessed the catastrophic soil erosion caused by shoddy farming practices and drought. On Sacramento Valley's rich farmland, Lundberg became a pioneer in sustainable rice production; three generations later, Lundberg Family Farms continues to lead the way, developing innovative, organic methods of pest and weed control and relying on alternative energy to process its grains. You'll find Lundberg Family Farms rice—including aromatic, nutty Wehani and delicious blends such as basmati and wild rice—on grocers' shelves throughout the nation. (www.lundberg.com)

PRESERVING FOOD
Yes, We Can!

Basing your meals on what's in season in your neck of the woods is another way to conserve in the kitchen. Eating seasonally doesn't have to mean living on parsnips and pumpkins all winter (not that there's anything wrong with that); learn how to prolong the bounty of summer and fall right through till next spring with an Excalibur dehydrator, a Harsch fermentation crock, the Food Saver vacuum sealer, or an All-American Pressure Canner, all available on Amazon.com. In the words of President Obama, "Yes, we can!" Recommended reading: *Preserving Summer's Bounty: A Quick and Easy Guide to Freezing, Canning, Preserving, and Drying What You Grow*, edited by Susan McClure (Rodale, 1998).

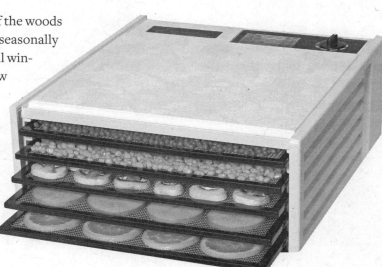

In my book *The Art of Simple Food*, I outlined my eight basic principles for cooking and living well:

★ **Eat locally and sustainably.** Learn where your food comes from and how it is produced. Seek out a diverse variety of vegetables and fruits from small, local producers who take care of the land. Buy eggs, meat, and fish from producers whose practices are organic, humane, and environmentally sound.

★ **Eat seasonally, and shop at farmers' markets.** Farmers' markets create communities that value diversity, honesty, locality, sustainability, and beauty.

★ **Plant a garden.** It's deeply satisfying to eat food you have grown—even a pot of herbs on your windowsill can transform your cooking and connect you to the changing seasons!

★ **Conserve, compost, and recycle.** Take your own basket to the market; reuse packaging whenever you can. The more you conserve, the less you waste, the better you feel.

★ **Cook simply, engaging all your senses.** Plan uncomplicated meals. Let things taste of what they are.

★ **Cook together.** Include your family and friends, especially children. When children grow, cook, and serve food, they want to eat it. The hands-on experience of cooking teaches children the value and pleasure of good food almost effortlessly.

★ **Eat together.** No matter how modest the meal, create a special place to sit down together and set the table with care and respect. Savor the ritual of the table. Mealtime is a time for empathy and generosity, a time to nourish and communicate.

★ **Remember food is precious.** Good food can only come from good ingredients. Its proper price includes the cost of preserving the environment and paying fairly for the labor of the people who produce it. Food should never be taken for granted.

EASY-TO-GROW GREENS

Stand Back and Enjoy

Why settle for garden-variety greens when you could be growing exotic Asian varieties? Bold brassicas like mizuna, tatsoi, and mustard greens add spice and texture to mesclun mixes, and they can liven up your salad patch, too—especially dramatic varieties like 'Ruby Streak' mizuna and 'Osaka Purple' mustard greens. Nasturtium flowers make a piquant, gorgeous garnish for your salads, but don't overlook their less showy but equally spicy leaves. And they're all easily grown from seed.

For seeds, try **Johnny's Selected Seeds** (www.johnnyseeds.com) or **Fedco Seeds** (www.fedcoseeds.com).

BEANS

Your Protein Partner

Beans are a versatile, affordable, delicious source of protein. Lentils, chickpeas, cannellini beans, black-eyed peas, pintos, and kidney beans are perennial favorites, but there are dozens of lesser-known varieties with wildly varying tastes and textures, guaranteeing that you'll never be bored by beans.

You can find organic brands of canned beans such as **Eden** and **Westbrae** in markets nationwide. But dried beans offer better texture and greater variety, including heirlooms from speckled beauties like appaloosas and cranberry beans to meaty black soybeans—and best of all, the sweet, nutty tepary bean.

Teparies, a North American staple for centuries before they lapsed into obscurity, are due for a revival, thanks to climate change. One of the most drought-tolerant legumes in the world, teparies have superb flavor and are exceptionally high in protein and fiber. Order sustainably grown teparies and other choice heirloom beans online from **Rancho Gordo** at www.rancho gordo.com. Steve Sando, Rancho Gordo's founder, has made it his mission to rescue rare beans from oblivion; he also founded The Family Farm League, a Napa Valley, California–based nonprofit dedicated to promoting local food production.

Cayuga Pure Organics is another great source for small batch-produced beans, featuring such staples as pinto, kidney, and black beans along with a growing selection of heirlooms. Cayuga's founders, who have been farming organically in upstate New York for decades, offer sustainably grown grains as well as beans. (www.cporganics.com)

Intrigued by all this beany goodness but not sure how to cook them? Check out bean revivalist *Elizabeth Berry's Great Bean Book* (Ten Speed Press) and Steve Sando and Vanessa Barrington's *Heirloom Beans* (Chronicle Books).

BREAD
Think Flour, Water, Salt, Yeast

Those presliced, preservative-laden, plastic-wrapped loaves sold in supermarkets bear no resemblance to the freshly baked breads that once filled America's breadbaskets. Much of the stuff on the supermarket shelves contains industrially grown ingredients like partially hydrogenated soybean oil, high-fructose corn syrup, and a bewildering array of additives intended to improve texture and prolong shelf life.

Real bread requires only four ingredients: flour, water, salt, and yeast. What we now call "artisanal bread"—the fresh, fragrant loaves our local bakers make with pure, simple ingredients—was the norm before the commercial baking industry emerged at the turn of the 19th century.

Happily, the real bread revolution's got a growing army of artisanal bread bakers led by pioneers like **Acme Bread** in Berkeley, **Amy's Bread** in New York, and **Zingerman's** in Ann Arbor. It's easier than it's been in decades to find fresh handmade breads, but if you can't find a source near you (and you're willing to splurge on the food miles), you can order online from both Amy's (www.amysbread.com) and Zingerman's (www.zingermans.com). If you can't finish a whole loaf before it goes stale, keep in mind that bread freezes well and can be easily defrosted later. Enjoy your bread with preserves, not preservatives!

FYI

Want to be more green, but unsure of how to begin? It's simple: Stop eating meat. Agriculture causes more greenhouse gas emissions than transport. The only source of greenhouse gas emissions that is larger than agriculture is electricity generation. And cutting out meat is a lot easier than getting off the grid.

—Peter Singer,
Princeton University

SIMPLY ORGANICS
Kinda Spicylike!

When recipes call for fresh herbs, nothing beats dashing to your own kitchen garden and snatching a handful of thyme. But even if you grow your own herbs, you'll still need an assortment of dried herbs—not to mention spices. **Frontier Natural Products** is a cooperatively owned manufacturer of organic herbs and spices whose Well Earth sourcing program supports organic, sustainable production, funds community projects, and provides small farmers with fair market prices.

Founded in 1976 in Iowa, Frontier now offers an extensive line of seasonings under the name Simply Organics in addition to its namesake spices. (www.frontiercoop.com)

BIGGEST AND BEST OF THE ORGANICS

Nature's Path, North America's biggest manufacturer of organic breakfast cereals, has been making whole grain cereals for more than two decades. This family-owned Canadian company has helped grow the market for overlooked grains such as Kamut, millet, quinoa, amaranth, and spelt, in keeping with the mission to "increase organic cropland and maintain sustainable family farms."

Nature's Path, equally committed to reducing waste and conserving resources, offers its "heritage grain" cereals in bulk 32-ounce "eco-pacs," which use 66 percent less packaging than traditional cereal boxes. (www.naturespath.com)

Books to Savor

How we wound up saddled with SAD—the fatty, sugary, chemical-laden Standard American Diet—is the focus of historian Anne Vileisis's *Kitchen Literacy: How We Lost Knowledge of Where Food Comes from and Why We Need to Get It Back* (Island Press, 2007). *Kitchen Literacy* traces the triumph of ready-to-eat over made-from-scratch.

Hungry Planet: What the World Eats by Peter Menzel and Faith D'Aluisio (Ten Speed Press, 2005) depicts how a week's worth of groceries in a typical American household compares to other countries' cuisines.

Joan Dye Gussow's memoir, *This Organic Life: Confessions of a Suburban Homesteader* (Chelsea Green, 2001), celebrates the bounty of her suburban backyard and launched the "locavore lit" genre exemplified by Barbara Kingsolver's bestseller *Animal, Vegetable, Miracle: A Year of Food Life* (HarperCollins, 2007). Kingsolver's account of her family's yearlong exercise in eating only local foods makes a compelling case for the reregionalization of our food chain.

Sam Fromartz's *Organic, Inc.: Natural Foods and How They Grew* (Harcourt, 2006) documents how the skyrocketing demand for pesticide- and chemical-free foods led to the paradox of "industrial organic."

Nutrition professor Marion Nestle's indispensable aisle-by-aisle guide *What to Eat* (North Point Press, 2006) will help you dodge military-industrial-strength snack attacks. Her strategy is simple: Shun prepackaged ersatz foods loaded with dubious ingredients. Stick with minimally processed produce and unrefined whole grains.

Let Nestle, Gussow, and their colleagues lead you out of our culinary wilderness; be well read and you'll be well fed.

EATING OUT
Helpful Internet Tools

The restaurant industry wastes vast quantities of energy and water and generates tons of garbage. Food waste goes to the landfill, where it rots and produces methane instead of being composted. And don't forget the menus featuring factory-farmed fillets served with jet-lagged vegetables, washed down with a bottle of foreign water.

But restaurateurs across the country are discovering that what's good for the planet is also good for business. The Green Restaurant Association (www.dinegreen.com), Chefs Collaborative (chefscollaborative.org), and Eat Well Guide (www.eatwellguide.org) all feature directories that let you search for sustainably minded dining in your region.

Finding fresh, local food when you're on the road is easier than ever, too, thanks to the Eat Well Guide's Eat Well Everywhere interactive mapping tool, which helps you plan a customized "eat-inerary" of restaurants, markets, farms, and even B&Bs where you can get off the beaten—or, rather, battered and deep-fried—path.

BROTH AND MISO
Save Time, Stay Organic

In an ideal world, we'd all make our own stock from scratch. It's simple to do, and it's a great way to use up vegetable scraps and animal bones—after all, if you *do* eat meat, isn't it more ethical to adopt Fergus Henderson's "nose-to-tail" philosophy of eating? As the famed British chef says, "If you're going to kill the animal, it seems only polite to use the whole thing."

But most of us are more inclined to reach for a quart of store-bought broth. It's an essential shortcut that lets you throw together an otherwise home-cooked soup or stew in minutes.

There are several decent brands of organic broths and stocks. If you're on a budget, you can't beat Whole Foods and Trader Joe's own store brands, which run about $2 a quart. For a dollar or two more (depending on your retailer), Pacific Natural Foods, a locally owned natural food company founded in Oregon in 1987, offers a line of broths bearing their Certified to the Source trademark, Pacific's promise that they use only the finest, predominantly US-sourced organic and natural ingredients.

Look for low-sodium misos made from certified organic, non–genetically modified soybeans, such as California's Cold Mountain Miso, which offers a range of misos from sweet to savory in 14-ounce tubs that sell for around $4. Miso Master Miso, a North Carolina–based company, makes organic, non-GMO misos from barley, brown rice, and chickpeas as well as the traditional soy-based varieties, all in 1-pound tubs for about $7.

MILK ALTERNATIVES
Soy Milk and Beyond

Folks who are lactose intolerant or who don't wish to consume animal products for ethical or health reasons have a choice of a wide range of alternative milks. Soy milk is the most common, but there are nut milks made from hazelnuts or almonds as well as rice milk, oat milk, and hemp milk.

You can ensure that your soy milk comes from non–genetically modified soybeans by sticking with an organic brand such as **Silk**, **Edensoy**, **Vitasoy**, or **Pacific**. Pacific also makes organic hazelnut, almond, rice, and oat milks.

Two Canadian companies, **Manitoba Harvest** and **Living Harvest**, offer organic milk made from the highly nutritious hemp seed—a crop that's illegal to grow in the States because our government lumps it in with its psychoactive sibling even though hemp lacks marijuana's ability to alter one's state of mind. Hemp is an easy-to-grow crop that needs no herbicides and is a great source of both food and fiber, so perhaps this plant, which was widely grown in the USA prior to the war on drugs, will be legal again someday.

FYI

Look for independent natural-food manufacturers who haven't sold out to multinational corporations. Consult Michigan State University professor Phil Howards's chart tracking consolidation in the organic food industry at www.msu.edu/~howardp/organicindustry.html.

SWEETENERS: BEWARE OF HIGH-FRUCTOSE CORN SYRUP

Nutritionists will tell you that your body doesn't distinguish between refined white sugar and less-processed sweeteners such as raw cane sugar, honey, or maple syrup. As Dr. Andrew Weil has noted, "They are all sugar to be converted to glucose for metabolic fuel."

However, there is evidence that high-fructose corn syrup (HFCS)—the preferred sweetener of the processed food industry—may be wreaking havoc with our metabolisms. If you've seen the documentary *King Corn* or read Michael Pollan's *The Omnivore's Dilemma*, you know about the downside of our corn-crazed food chain. So steer clear of products with HFCS.

Conventional sugarcane production is hard on the environment; that's another incentive to opt for more low-impact sweeteners. Some other forms of sugar are manufactured in a more eco-friendly way. **Wholesome Sweeteners** offers an extensive line of organic, fair-trade-certified sugars as well as molasses, honey, agave, and an organic light corn syrup. (www.wholesomesweeteners.com)

OILS, VINEGARS, CONDIMENTS
Spectrum and Eden Organics Fit the Bill

Adventurous chefs often keep a veritable arsenal of exotic culinary oils and vinegars on hand. But even if you don't consider toasted sesame oil and balsamic vinegar essential to a well-stocked pantry, you need at the very minimum a few bottles of high-quality oils for cooking and salad dressings, as well as several vinegars.

Olive and canola are two of the most commonly used oils for cooking and salad dressings because they're high in heart-healthy monounsaturated fats. But how healthy they are for you—and the environment—also depends on the method of extraction. Many cheaper brands of vegetable oils are made by a chemical process that uses hexane, a toxic solvent. You can avoid them by choosing oils labeled "mechanically pressed" or "expeller pressed."

And unless you're eager to be a guinea pig for the biotech industry, steer clear of oils derived from genetically modified crops. **Spectrum** offers a nationally distributed line of organic, expeller-pressed oils guaranteed to be free of any genetically engineered ingredients, as are their organic vinegars, salad dressings, and mayonnaises. (www.spectrumorganics.com)

Eden Organic also offers a line of organic oils, vinegars, and other condiments, plus Asian culinary essentials such as soy sauce, wasabi powder, and sea vegetables. (www.edenfoods.com)

DAIRY
Good National and Regional Choices

Glass-bottled milk from grass-fed cows was once a fixture on everyone's front step. Now, it's a pricey, nostalgic novelty found only in specialty shops and some farmers' markets. The milkman's gone the way of the dodo bird, and most dairy products come from intensive industrial operations much like their meat-producing cousins.

So it's a good idea to dial back on your dairy consumption and switch to organic—and, ideally, pasture-based—dairy products. Such products are becoming more widely available, thanks, ironically, to the factory farms' reliance on rBGH, the synthetic bovine growth hormone that lets farmers wring more milk out of their cows. The writing's on the stall: A grassroots consumer revolt against dairy products from rBGH-treated cows has fed a growing market for products that are organic and rBGH free.

You'll find grass-fed milk, cheese, and yogurt—from sheep and goats as well as cows—at most farmers' markets. Many supermarkets offer plenty of organic dairy products, too. Choose those from the dairies nearest you, and from pasture-raised livestock whenever possible. Several nationally distributed brands provide an alternative to factory-farm dairy products. One of the biggest is **Organic Valley**, a dairy cooperative owned by family farmers. Founded by seven farmers dedicated to humane, sustainable dairy production back in 1988, the cooperative now includes 1,322 family farmers committed to community building and sustainable agriculture. Organic Valley's products include milk, cream, butter, sour cream, cottage cheese, and cream cheese. (www.organicvalley.coop)

Natural By Nature is another cooperative that offers a similar range of dairy products that are 100 percent grass-fed as well as organic. (www.natural-by-nature.com)

On the West Coast, the **Straus Family Creamery** offers all of the above plus yogurt and ice cream (www.strausfamilycreamery.com). The **Springfield Creamery** in Eugene, Oregon, has been making Nancy's organic dairy and soy-based yogurts for decades, using locally grown fruits as much as possible and sweetening their yogurts with honey, agave, and grape juice (www.nancysyogurt.com). In the Northeast, look for yogurt from **Butterworks Farm** in Vermont, a small family-owned organic dairy that's been farming sustainably for 25 years (www.butterworksfarm.com).

ENERGY FROM START TO FINISH

For sustainably produced on-the-go sustenance, try a **Clif Bar**. These wholesome, nutrient-dense energy bars are made from mostly organic ingredients and wrapped in foil rather than plastic. But the Berkeley-based, independently owned company doesn't stop there. With a full-time "sustainability manager," the folks at Clif Bar curb their carbon footprint at every step: building wind turbines; running the company fleet on biofuels; using recycled materials to reduce waste; providing their staff with incentives to make their commutes—and even their homes!—more energy efficient, with cash rewards for employees who walk, bike, or carpool to work or who buy a hybrid or biodiesel-fueled car.

When it comes to carbon-lowering carb loading, Clif Bar's the best—bar none. (www.clifbar.com)

FYI

Know what kinds of produce are most likely to be contaminated with pesticides: Download the Environmental Working Group's pocket-size shopper's guide to the "dirty dozen" fruits and vegetables at www.foodnews.org. The guide provides a list of the "Cleanest 12" fruits and veggies, too.

SNACKS
Thank You, Paul Newman

How our ancestors survived on a mere three meals a day separated by hours of fasting is a mystery. Today, we nibble nonstop on sweet, salty, fatty, crunchy snacks in plastic packets. This double whammy of excess calories and excess packaging widens our waistlines and heightens our landfills.

For a healthier, more carbon-neutral nosh, try raw veggies dipped in hummus. Not ready to ditch the cookies or chips? Make those (mostly) empty calories count for something with snacks from **Newman's Own Organics** and **Guiltless Gourmet**. With these brands, you're driving demand for organic products, and, in the case of Newman's Own, the profits go to Newman's Own Foundation, which donates dollars to organizations that promote sustainable agriculture. (www.newmansown.organics.com; www.guiltlessgourmet.com)

KUHN RIKON PRESSURE COOKER
What's Old Is New

There is no single appliance that makes it easier—and faster—to prepare veggies, grains, and beans than the 21st-century pressure cooker. Forget about the old-school, "jiggle-top" pressure cooker that spattered your grandma's ceiling with spaghetti sauce; the next generation of pressure cookers lets you make 5-minute risottos, 10-minute stews, whole grains in half an hour—and all without blowing your lid. The Kuhn Rikon Duromatic, known as "the Mercedes-Benz of pressure cookers," is available at better housewares shops or may be ordered online at www.pressurecookerworld.com. And there's no better book to bring you up to speed on cooking under pressure than Lorna Sass's *Great Vegetarian Cooking under Pressure* (William Morrow, 1994).

A Greener Way to Slow-Cook

The slow cooker may not seem like a low-carbon appliance, given that you generally leave it on for anywhere from 4 to 8 hours. But for roasting or braising, it's far more energy efficient than a standard gas or electric oven. Best of all, if you take a few minutes in the morning to prep the ingredients for a soup or stew and toss them into your slow cooker, you'll be rewarded at the end of the day with a meal that's ready when you are.

There are fancy high-end slow cookers with elaborate settings, but this is one appliance that you really don't need to splurge on; a fairly basic Crock-Pot from **Rival**, the folks who made the first slow cookers back in 1970, will serve you well. Choose a 5-quart or larger crock for maximum utility. For ease of use, you'll want one with a timer that shifts to a "keep warm" setting when your dish is done. (www.crock-pot.com)

FYI

Fertilize your kitchen garden with TerraCycle's ultra eco-friendly organic liquid fertilizer, made from worm poop and packaged in repurposed soda bottles. TerraCycle is widely available in stores and online. (www.terracycle.net)

VITA-MIX
Stirring Things Up

The Vita-Mix is an überblender favored by chefs and smoothie bars, but its allure for the eco-conscious home cook lies in its ability to quickly (if noisily) transform wholesome raw ingredients into delicious, ready-to-eat treats. It's more of a pulverizer, to be precise, with a motor so powerful that it can puree the most fibrous vegetables into microscopic particles.

It's the ultimate smoothie maker, but the Vita-Mix also enables you to grind your own flour from whole grains, knead bread dough, make nut butters and baby foods, and create nearly instant hot soups and frozen desserts. That high horsepower comes with an equally high price tag ($350 and up), but this versatile appliance will give you your money's worth. It's built to last, too, so you can shop around for a vintage Vita-Mix on eBay or Craigslist—or invest in a new model. (www.vitamix.com)

KITCHEN COMPOST BUCKET
Kitchen-to-Compost

Your kitchen scraps can be a boon or a bane to the environment, depending on how you dispose of them. Those coffee grounds, eggshells, and onion peels you toss in the trash end up in the landfill, where they decompose and emit methane, a potent greenhouse gas. Composting your scraps, on the other hand, yields a rich fertilizer that gardeners call "black gold."

So try to treat those scraps like garbage only as a last resort. There's a compost bin for nearly every budget and household.

Whether you opt to compost at home or participate in a neighborhood program, it helps to have a kitchen compost bucket in which you store your scraps for emptying later at your convenience. **Gardener's Supply Company** offers kitchen compost buckets from plastic to ceramic to stainless steel. (www.gardeners.com)

SPORT SOLAR OVEN
Green in So Many Ways

The ultimate carbon-neutral way to cook is the solar-powered oven. This "negawatt" novelty uses only the sun's rays to bake your food, like an unplugged slow cooker.

The Sport Solar Oven, manufactured by the nonprofit Solar Oven Society (SOS), is a light-weight, easy-to-use solar oven that can cook just about anything, weather permitting: meats, fish, chicken, vegetables, breads, grains, pastas, rice—you can even bake cakes and cookies. It's made partly from recycled plastic soda bottles, and the Solar Oven's profits fund its mission to fight deforestation by distributing sun ovens in developing nations where forests are routinely cut down to provide firewood for cooking. (www.solarovens.org)

Plants for the Edible Landscape

Any of a number of plants and shrubs that you can plant in your yard will not only look great but also make for fine eating. Here are a few examples that may thrive in your climate:

★ **Blueberries.** If you've got rhododendrons, azaleas, or other acid-loving shrubs standing sentry at your entry, why not replace them with blueberries, another acid lover? Blueberries bear delicate white blossoms in spring that become delicious berries in summer, followed by gorgeous fall foliage. With the right soil conditions, they're remarkably low-maintenance shrubs, requiring little or no care. Plant a mix of early-, mid-, and late-season varieties and you'll have baskets of berries all summer long.

★ **Hazelnut.** Dwarf hazelnuts are another choice ornamental edible; they make a terrific hedge or can be grown individually as a specimen shrub reaching 4 to 12 feet in height. The nuts grow in clusters, encased in a frilly green cover. In fall, the leaves turn varying shades of gold, orange, and scarlet, followed by charming catkins that cling to the branches through winter. The one labor-intensive thing about hazelnuts is shelling them—and that's only a problem if the squirrels decide to leave you any.

★ **Hardy kiwi.** If you have a trellis or an arbor in need of a vine, plant a pair of hardy kiwis and you'll reap a rare and tasty fruit. The hardy kiwi is a smaller, sweeter cousin to the familiar fuzzy kiwi, with a smooth, edible skin that lets you just pop it in your mouth as you would a grape. Sadly, few American farmers grow this marvelous fruit because it takes about 5 to 7 years to begin bearing. Luckily, the vines feature deep green, leathery leaves that are decorative in their own right, so you'll have something to admire while you're waiting.

★ **Pawpaw.** Organic gardeners like the pawpaw because it has few pests and, unlike most fruit trees, grows well in light shade. The fruit is said to taste like banana custard, but most folks have never tasted a pawpaw—even though it's native to North America—because the fruit is too delicate to ship. A graceful tree with large, tropical leaves, the pawpaw grows up to 25 or 30 feet eventually but can be pruned to stay more compact. You'll need to plant two for pollination. Choose your varieties carefully—some are reportedly much tastier than others.

★ **Alpine strawberries.** Alpine strawberries make a great groundcover or edging plant and produce small, intensely sweet berries. They do well in hanging baskets, too. Unlike their larger siblings, which spread by sending out runners, most alpines remain compact and devote all their energy to fruiting from spring through fall. Plant one of the white or yellow varieties if you want to baffle the birds—they mistake these kinds for unripe red berries and so don't bother to steal them.

GREEN STAR TWIN GEAR JUICE EXTRACTOR

The Wonder of Triturating

Juicing's an excellent way to incorporate more fruits and vegetables into your diet. Two types of juicers dominate the market: the centrifugal juicer and the masticating juicer. Each has strengths and drawbacks. Some models are efficient at extracting the juice but may be harder to clean; others excel at juicing carrots and apples but not leafy greens.

The Green Star Twin Gear Juice Extractor eliminates these dilemmas by utilizing a more efficient method of extraction called *triturating*, which works well for nearly every kind of fruit and vegetable. The twin gear's kinder, gentler extraction process preserves a higher percentage of the enzymes and nutrients that can be oxidized by high-speed, high-heat methods of juicing. Like the Vita-Mix, the Green Star also makes nut butters, baby food, sauces, pastas, and frozen desserts. And, as with the Vita-Mix, efficiency and versatility command top dollar—the Green Star starts at around $400. (www.greenstar.com)

FYI

Get religious about curbing your consumption with the Church of Life After Shopping, led by Reverend Billy. This mock man of the cloth has a true message: that consuming less is "the single most effective and immediate response" you can take to avert the climate crisis.(www.revbilly.com)

GROCERY STORES/SPECIALTY MARKETS

Large and Small Going Organic

Demand for more wholesome, environmentally friendly foods has compelled even the most conventional supermarkets to stock their shelves with organic products. Safeway and Stop & Shop are among the giant chains that have launched their own lines of organic foods in recent years.

Wal-Mart—America's number-one food retailer—offers a growing array of organic foods, too, which is either a plus or a minus, depending on how you feel about this big-box behemoth with the Sasquatch-size carbon footprint. I'd rather shop at a small regional chain like Oregon's New Season Market or Wegmans, a family-owned business with 71 stores in the Northeast. In 2007, the Wegmans founded the Wegmans Organic Research Farm in upstate New York, with two goals: to grow produce for their stores and to educate both farmers and consumers about sustainable agriculture.

If you're lucky, you might live near a one-of-a-kind enterprise that supports small-scale food producers, like San Francisco's Bi-Rite or Zingerman's in Ann Arbor. The Eat Well Guide (www.eatwellguide.org) and Local Harvest (www.localharvest.org) can help you find nearby green-minded grocers plus food co-ops for folks who'd like to get connected to a truly alternative food chain.

Those who live in the upscale, urban Arugula Belt likely have a Whole Foods nearby. This mecca of ethical edibles offers foods preselected to meet the conscientious consumer's criteria, so you don't have to separate sustainable wheat from industrial chaff.

Folks accustomed to cheap conventional foods grumble about Whole Foods' prices, while hardcore locavores lament the produce aisles piled high with "industrial organic" vegetables and out-of-season foreign fruits. But Whole Foods' higher prices are due in part to the true cost of producing real, wholesome foods sustainably, without relying on the subsidized commodity crops and environmental shortcuts that shortchange us all in the long run.

Whole Foods has stepped up its efforts to sell more local products and remains America's premier market for natural and organic foods, giving shelf space to modest mom-and-pop operations as well as megabrands. Trader Joe's has upped its organic offerings in recent years, too, and provides a fair number of affordable pantry staples and convenience foods notable for their relatively unadulterated, wholesome ingredients.

If you haven't got access to any of these outlets, try an online alternative such as Gold Mine Natural Foods (www.goldminenaturalfood.com) or Diamond Organics (www.diamondorganics.com).

Diamond Organics

Wegmans

LocalHarvest

Green Power

Energy issues have been on people's minds lately. There is great uncertainty and anxiety about fossil fuel supplies, especially with rising worldwide demand from developing countries like China and India.

Many green enthusiasts now believe that the fossil fuel era may sunset within our lifetimes, making way for what could be a cleaner, more sustainable future. That change is spurred by the specter of global warming, which threatens inundation of coastlines, intense storms, and planetwide disruptions of weather patterns and ocean currents that will affect wildlife, food supplies, and ordinary peoples' lives in ways we can hardly begin to predict.

The next few years could see a tipping point to radical change. In the 1970s, then-president Jimmy Carter responded to the Arab oil embargo by creating the federal Department of Energy and kicking off a national energy policy that promoted innovation and deployment of clean sources of energy. Carter famously installed solar panels on the White House roof, turned the thermostat down to 68°F to save energy, and donned a now-iconic sweater. He opened the floodgates of federal funding to renewable energy and promoted energy conservation.

Many of Carter's changes failed to survive the booming, instant-gratification '80s. But we can learn a great deal from the past even as we realize that today's challenges require a renewed commitment. There are now many more Americans on the planet and many, many more people in other countries. There is less oil in the ground; there are more greenhouse gases in the atmosphere. An estimated 65,000 Americans die prematurely every year due to illnesses aggravated by air pollution, mostly rising from the coal-fired power plants that still supply half our energy.

At the same time, prices of gasoline, heating oil, natural gas, and electricity have risen dramatically, and for a while some parts of the United States experienced double-digit increases. Economists, policy analysts, and recent trends all suggest that in the long run, it's only going to get worse.

Here's the good news: The clean, renewable energy sector is experiencing rapid growth, also in the double digits. More families and businesses than ever are taking a serious look at energy conservation, and a maturing industry is helping them take advantage of green renovations, tax credits, and innovative financing plans. One of the lessons from the California energy crisis of 2000 and 2001 was that conservation works, that an educated, empowered public can drastically slash energy use if given incentives to do so. Many Californians, for example, signed up for a program in which regulators could remotely turn down their air-conditioning during peak loads.

The typical family or business can save big money on energy by taking many small steps. The average American can boost home efficiency up to 65 percent, according to the Department of Energy, using technologies that are readily available. One good step is to purchase Energy Star–rated products. Another is to do a home energy audit to find trouble spots.

For many folks, the most exciting parts of the clean-energy revolution are the emerging sources of renewable energy, from iconic solar and wind power to wave and tidal power, piezoelectric motion generators, fuel cells, and more. Research funding is increasing, breakthroughs are being made, and new tax incentives are coming online at the state and federal levels.

Solar energy use has been growing 40 percent a year for the past 20 years. It offers great potential in terms of direct electricity generation (photovoltaics) and solar thermal systems. Federal incentives were extended as part of the Emergency Economic Stabilization Act of 2008, and several states have initiated their own stimulus programs, from sunny California to New Jersey, Connecticut, Massachusetts, Ohio, Colorado, and others.

On a global scale, wind power is enjoying spectacular growth, particularly in offshore and other large deployments. As turbines get bigger, the amount of power they can generate increases exponentially. Large-scale wind power is approaching the cost of (scrubbed) coal-generated energy in many markets.

The energy revolution is upon us.

—Brian Clark Howard

Slaying Energy Vampires

Many electrical and electronic devices draw power even when they're not in use. Americans throw away 8 percent of their annual electric bills this way, wasting billions of dollars. Defang this phantom-load problem by plugging electronics into a surge protector—then turn off the strip when you're done using the devices. Make it even easier by investing in "smart strips" that automatically cut the power when you switch off select devices.

One great example: the Smart Strip Power Strip from **Bits Ltd.**, which can pay for itself in reduced utility costs in as few as 6 weeks. Several sizes are available, with or without fax/modem or coaxial cable protection. Smart Strips also include regular plugs that are always "on." (from $30.95; www.smarthomeusa.com)

THE ENERGY DETECTIVE

Get the Facts on Your Energy Use

The quickest way for homeowners to see energy savings is to install a widget that displays how much energy is used to dry clothes, run an electric toothbrush, or heat breakfast. It's called The Energy Detective (TED).

TED's compact display shows household electrical usage in real time, and it predicts your monthly bill. Once consumers see their spending in progress, they get motivated to make changes. It may never have occurred to you how much it costs in hair-dryer power to whip up that Flock of Seagulls wave, but one look at the numbers on TED and you may decide to tone down your grooming. Or you may be shocked by how much power it takes to dry clothes, when a line in the backyard will do the job for nothing.

According to the manufacturer, typical TED users save 15 to 20 percent on utility bills, which amounts to hundreds of dollars a year. TED can pay for itself in just a few months. To go further, hire an electrician to wire TED into your house's main power line. TED can also interface with your computer, opening up advanced tracking and graphing options. (from $139; www.theenergydetective.com)

KILL A WATT MONITOR: THE LOWDOWN ON POWER

It's a cinch to measure the energy use of your appliances and electronic devices—and it won't require any math. All it takes is a small, handheld, $20 device called the Kill a Watt electric usage monitor, from **P3 International**. Just plug the Kill a Watt into a wall socket, then insert the plug for the device you wish to monitor. The large LCD display will give a breakdown of the device's energy use. A "money button" shows how much the appliance or device costs to operate by the day, week, month, or year.

If some appliances show a high operating cost, it may be time to upgrade to high-efficiency models. Or it may be time to use the less important appliances more sparingly. (www.p3international.com)

FYI

Some 90 percent of desktop computer users fail to optimize software settings for energy efficiency. According to Intel, using built-in settings can save 400 kilowatt-hours annually, or $40 to $80. Just find your operating system's energy options, and set to shut off components after idling.

SUPERBRIGHTLEDS AND EARTHLEDS

The Future of Lighting

Just a few years ago, lighting experts cautioned that LEDs weren't ready for daily domestic use. The technology works fine for specialized applications like clock displays, they said, but LEDs couldn't be made very bright. That's no longer the case; a number of companies are bringing out super-energy-efficient LED lightbulbs for regular fixtures.

For instance, the model E27-W8 bulb from **Superbrightleds.com** has a light output comparable to a 40-watt incandescent, yet it consumes just 8 watts of power and lasts 20,000 hours. It has a normal "Edison base," so it will fit in typical fixtures. It's available in cool white, natural white, or warm white. Buy it for $49.95.

This LED bulb cannot be used with a dimmer, and operating it at temperatures above 73°F can shorten its life. But Superbrightleds.com offers a 1-year warranty on all bulbs. (www.super brightleds.com/edison_spot.html)

Another source for advanced home LEDs is Advanced Lumonics' **EarthLED.com**, which warranties its products for 2 years. The company says its bulbs are up to 10 times more efficient than conventional lightbulbs, with life spans that can exceed 10 years. EarthLED's dazzling, revolutionary EvoLux line matches the light output of a 100-watt incandescent at only 13 watts. They are available in two color temperatures, warm white and cool white. The bulbs cost a hefty $79.99 to $99.99, but they last an estimated 50,000 hours and cost only about $6 a year to operate.

EarthLED.com's dimmable bulb, called EvoDim, cannot be used with traditional dimmer switches; the company will soon replace it with newer technology compatible with dimmers. Another new line from EarthLED.com is ZetaLux, which packs the power of a 50- or 60-watt incandescent in a mere 7-watt bulb.

Energy Audit: The First Step to Saving

It's easier to boost energy efficiency if you know how much power you are currently using and can assess your biggest problem areas. Simple air leaks can sap your home's energy efficiency by 5 to 30 percent a year, says the US Department of Energy. It pays to do a thorough accounting of your home energy budget. Hire a professional to do a full energy audit, or conduct your own walk-through.

To perform your own audit, first look for leaks in your home's envelope. The tighter a house is sealed against the elements, the more efficiently it can be heated or cooled. Take a close look at places where two different building materials meet, such as at corners, around chimneys, where pipes or wires exit, and along the foundation. Make sure good seals form around all doors and windows. Find gaps or holes? Carefully plug them up with caulk (choose low-VOC brands!).

Then try the famous "candle test"—or better yet, use the incense test: Light a stick of incense, then blow it out and carefully move it along walls. Where the smoke wavers, air is sneaking in or out.

Next, examine insulation. In the right climate, you could do the sublimely simple "snow test": If snow melts from your roof faster than your neighbors', they have better insulation. Make sure the floor of your attic, including the hatch, is well insulated and that the material isn't compacted or crumbling. Basement ceiling and walls should be insulated, as should all exterior walls. You can get some idea of the wall insulation of an older home by removing the cover from a power plug or by drilling a small inspection hole in the back of a closet. If there's little or no insulation, your house may be a candidate for blow-in insulation. Don't forget that hot-water pipes, ducts, and water heaters can be insulated. Be sure to examine heating and cooling equipment, including filters.

When you finish your energy audit, make as many improvements as time and budget allow. Then do a repeat audit a month or two later so you can compare your energy bills. You should see savings. A Web-based energy audit tool, such as the one developed by the Environmental Energy Technologies Division at Lawrence Berkeley National Laboratory (http://hes.lbl.gov), can inform the whole process.

To get even more detailed information, hire an energy audit professional. The service typically costs around $300, but many utilities and local governments offer deep discounts. An audit professional will spend a few hours carefully inspecting every room of your dwelling, poring over your utility bills, and asking questions about energy usage patterns. The audit rep is likely to measure the tightness of your home with a device called a blower door and look for leaks with a thermographic (or infrared) scan. Find qualified energy auditors in your area by calling your utility or state department of energy.

SYLVANIA CFLs
Efficient Bulbs of All Stripes

One barrier to more widespread adoption of energy-efficient compact fluorescent lightbulbs (CFLs) has been that people don't like the bulbs' now-iconic swirl shape. And many people use lamps with shades that clip directly onto the old rounded-top lightbulbs.

That's no longer an excuse not to get a CFL. Several manufacturers now make CFLs with standard bulb shapes. One is Osram Sylvania, the North American division of German lighting giant Osram. Sylvania's CF14EL/A19 14-watt CFL (in traditional A-shape) is rated for a lifetime of 8,000 hours and produces the amount of light equivalent to a 40-watt incandescent bulb. Pick it up for $5.

Got pendants, chandeliers, or wall sconces? No problem! Sylvania offers a CFL with a converter enabling it to fit both candelabra and medium screw-base decorative fixtures. This CFL type cannot be used with dimmers.

Can efficient lightbulbs also be cute? Sylvania's Mini-Twists are just that, and they are among the smallest CFLs available. They screw into regular bases but can fit small sconces, decorative lamps, and other spaces where you don't want to see the bulb. They sip energy at 13 or 7 watts. (www.sylvania.com)

EARTHMATE BULBS
New Dimmable CFLs

Hosting a dinner party? Want to set a reflective or romantic mood? Now CFLs are available that work with many dimmer switches—something that was unheard of a few years ago.

Dimmable CFLs work differently from their incandescent cousins. Earlier models in particular aren't compatible with all switches, so it's a good idea to test a bulb before investing in a large supply. The first dimmable CFLs on the market could dim only 20 to 50 percent of their output, in contrast with dimmable incandescents, which function from 0 to 100 percent. However, new dimmable CFLs from Earthmate are designed to dim down to 15 percent of their output or more—and they work fine with traditional dimmer circuits.

Earthmate's reflector-style dimmable CFL (for recessed fixtures) can reduce output to 5 percent and uses only 8 watts. A 5-watt candle-style bulb also dims down to 5 percent and comes with a candelabra or standard-size adapter.

For the commercial market, Earthmate bulbs are sold under the Litetronics brand and offer CFLs in color temperatures from restaurant yellow to warm white and halogen white. (www.earthmatelighting.com)

SATCO LED NIGHT-LIGHT
Can You Believe 100,000 Hours?

LED (light-emitting diode) night-lights are cheap, extremely inexpensive to power, and last for a long time. Sound like a bright idea? An added advantage of the LED multidirectional night-light from Satco is the rotatable head, so light can be directed where you want it. It is designed to last a whopping 100,000 hours, and the built-in photocell turns the light on or off automatically depending on the surrounding darkness.

Based on 10 hours of use per day, the annual operating cost will be less than a dollar per year. Now that's low cost. The night-light always remains cool to the touch, so there's little fire hazard. (www.lightbulbsdirect.com)

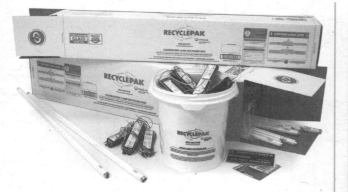

SYLVANIA'S RECYCLEPAK

Recycling Made Simple

Because CFLs contain a small amount of toxic mercury, they should not be tossed in the trash after use. But most consumers have no idea what to do with broken bulbs. Bulb maker Sylvania offers an easy solution with its Recyclepak program. First, order a consumer pack on Sylvania's Web site for $15, including shipping. When you receive it, fill it with about 12 burned-out bulbs, attach the prepaid shipping label, and (carefully) drop in the mail. Your retired CFLs will then be responsibly recycled. Larger sizes and community packs are also available. (www.sylvania.com)

Feeling burned about having to pay for recycling? Perhaps one day America will have the kind of product take-back laws found in Germany. But until that time, take heart in knowing that the recycling cost amounts to just about 1 percent of the total you'll spend on a bulb in its lifetime, since energy use makes up the vast majority of the expense.

FYI

Power down TVs, unused appliances, and computers at night. In 1 year, if you shut off your machine before bed each night, you'll save an average of $90 in electricity.

Compact Fluorescents: Bulbs for Any Fixture

The lightbulb has turned on over the heads of many Americans, who find that they can save energy easily by switching to compact fluorescent lightbulbs (CFLs). CFLs accounted for nearly 20 percent of the lighting market in 2007, up from 5 percent earlier in the decade.

CFLs already meet the new US standards being phased in for lightbulb efficiency, since they use a quarter of the energy of incandescents. CFLs also last six to 15 times longer (some discount brands have been known to last less than that). CFLs give off little heat, so they don't add much to cooling loads. A single 20-watt compact fluorescent lamp replacing a 75-watt incandescent will save about 550 kilowatt-hours over its lifetime yet produce the same light. That saves nearly 500 pounds of coal and prevents 1,300 pounds of carbon dioxide and 20 pounds of sulfur dioxide from entering the atmosphere. If every US household replaced just one regular bulb with a CFL, the energy saved could light 2.5 million homes for a year.

CFLs now come in sizes and shapes to fit nearly any fixture, from candelabra to flood. The color of the light emitted by CFLs is improving, so the best "soft white" models now approach incandescents. Other colors are available.

Begin by switching out the bulbs you use the most, especially those left on for extended periods. CFLs won't last as long if they are frequently flipped on and off. It's also smart to try one or two bulbs and see how you like them before buying a whole-house set.

What about their mercury content? CFLs do contain up to 5 milligrams of mercury, which is a small amount compared to that in older home thermostats and mercury fever thermometers. Even if all the mercury from a broken bulb vaporizes into the air, the concentration would still likely be lower than OSHA safe standards. And since 40 percent of the mercury being released into our environment comes from coal-fired power plants, 13.6 milligrams of mercury are released in generating the power needed to light one incandescent bulb, whereas only 3.3 milligrams are released running a CFL.

If a CFL does break, ventilate the room. The EPA recommends picking up all the fragments with paper towels. Wipe the affected area clean, then place the fragments, towels, and gloves in a sealed plastic bag. It's against the law to toss CFLs in the regular trash. Take them to your local hazardous waste collection site.

PHILIPS LED HOLIDAY LIGHTS

No Lumps of Coal Needed

Make like the Rockefellers and switch to LED-strand holiday lights. Holiday displays at New York's iconic Rockefeller Center, at Cincinnati's Fountain Square, and in other cities cost less money because new LEDs use so little energy.

Although they've been around for more than a decade, LED holiday lights are more affordable than ever. They cost only a few pennies to run for a whole jolly season, and since they don't get hot, they carry much lower risk of fire. LEDs also have a lower failure rate, giving you more even lighting and less worry about bald spots on your tree.

A traditional 26-light string of incandescents burns at 125 watts and lasts for about 1,000 hours. The same size string in LEDs burns at 2.3 watts and lasts 20,000 hours. Discount LED strands retail for under $10, and fancier designs—from icicles to snowflakes—typically go for $20 to $30. The colorful Philips 25-light C9 LED display costs about $12 and includes replacement bulbs; it's suitable for indoor or outdoor use. (www.philips.com)

WESTINGHOUSE AND ECO OPTIONS BULBS

Lights for Bugs and Beasts

George Westinghouse was one of Thomas Edison's bitterest rivals, and today his namesake company makes advanced bulbs that threaten to unseat Edison's traditional incandescent design. Fans of back porches, patio barbecues, and summer cabins will be glad to know that Westinghouse Lighting Corporation now offers an antibug CFL for outdoor use. Its yellow coating emits an eye-pleasing hue that, unlike incandescent bulbs, does not attract insects.

Need to see what's rummaging through the compost or trash bins at night? Get CFL floodlights from Home Depot's Eco Options line. Weatherproof and durable, these 23-watt bulbs disperse intense light over a wide area. So you can watch the raccoons at work.

RAB OCCUPANCY SENSORS

Ignore Those Switches

Many businesses discovered years ago that they could save money by installing occupancy sensors in restrooms, stairwells, and hallways. The technology works well, saves energy, and ensures that no one need remember to turn off the lights when leaving a room.

This energy-saving convenience can work well in your own home. The RAB LOS800 wall-mount unit costs a mere $29 and pays for itself in a short time. It fits into a standard light switch space and takes about 5 minutes to install, and the sensor has a range of 1,000 square feet. For 360-degree sensitivity, consider the RAB LOS2500 ceiling occupancy sensor. Easy to install, the $53.85 unit offers delay times of 10 seconds to 8 minutes. (www.elights.com)

FYI

Take advantage of the movement of the sun through the day to warm your house in winter or cool it in summer. Close blinds on the sunny side when it's hot; open them and welcome the sun when it's cold.

Freely Down the Garden Path

Solar-powered accent lights, which come in many styles, are easier to install than conventional path lighting. Better yet, their operating cost is zero. Activated by a built-in photocell, most solar lights turn on automatically at night. A four-pack of **Sunforce** Solar Accent Glow Lights costs $29. Designed for gardens or paths, the molded plastic bubble lights have white LEDs and come with ground stakes, solar cells, rechargeable batteries, and mounting hardware. (www.target.com/gp)

COOPER LIGHTING MOTION SOLAR FLOODLIGHT

Sunlight and Surprise

Some homeowners leave their exterior lights on all night for security or for convenient access. That is, of course, a huge energy expenditure. Additionally, bright outdoor lights can severely disrupt wildlife. What are the energy-saving solutions? Use timers or occupancy and motion sensors.

Studies are inconclusive on whether outdoor lighting actually deters crime, but most security experts say the startling effect of a motion-sensor-activated light probably helps. Cooper Lighting MSL180W ($65 from Amazon) includes a solar panel that recharges the battery during the day, ensuring that the unit's 13-watt halogen bulb comes on when motion is detected. (www.amazon.com)

CONSERVING GREEN INSULATION JACKET

A Jacket for Your Tank

Heating water is one of the biggest uses of energy in the home, yet it provides an opportunity for savings. If your hot-water tank is in a cold space, or if you can feel heat radiating from its sides, it's time for an insulation jacket. Kits can be picked up from many building and hardware stores or ordered online.

Look for insulation jackets with the highest R-value you can find. Follow the directions carefully; you don't want to impede the heater's function or block critical air vents on gas or oil-fired units.

The water heater jacket from Conserving Green provides an R-value of 6. The kit fits electric and gas water heaters up to 80 gallons in size and includes aluminum tape. The company says the jackets typically pay for themselves in a short time. (www.conservinggreen.com)

For formal, traditional, and upscale outdoor lighting, check out the sleek pewter Gatsby light from GreenCulture Lighting, which works on a riser, shepherd's hook, or table-top. Order one for $161, or pay $292 for a set of eight. Or go with the elegant copper post light for $185; $340 for a set of eight. (www.eco-lights.com/solar-lighting.php)

REAL GOODS LED SOLAR LIGHTS

Sun-Run Holiday Brilliance

Real Goods LED solar holiday lights require no fossil fuels, so you can feel good about lighting up the winter night. During the day, the sun charges a battery via the included small solar cell. When darkness falls, a sensor automatically turns on your lights. The lights are sure to be a conversation piece for any of your holiday guests. They are available in red, white, and multicolor, and they come in 34-bulb ($89) or 68-bulb ($109) strands. For $89, Real Goods also offers a festive wreath, with faux evergreen boughs made of recycled plastic, and red or white LED lights powered with a solar cell. (www.realgoods.com)

As semiconductor and solar technologies continue to drop in price, such products will become even more affordable. Santa's way will eventually be lighted entirely without fossil fuels. No coal on Christmas.

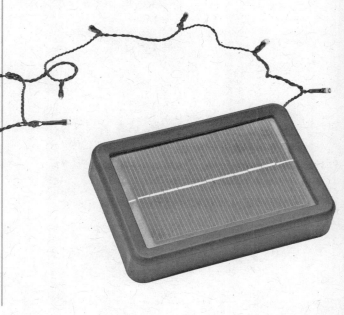

RINNAI TANKLESS WATER HEATERS

Antitank Strategy

If it's time to replace a water heater, consider upgrading to a tankless model, also called an on-demand or instantaneous water heater. It heats up water only as needed. And with a properly installed tankless system, no one in the family will run out of hot water in the middle of a shower.

Tankless water heaters cost more up front than conventional water heaters, but the savings over time may come as a pleasant surprise. Note that gas-fired tankless models tend to be much more energy efficient than the electric models.

Rinnai tankless heaters are up to 30 percent more energy efficient than a traditional natural gas water heater and up to 50 percent more efficient than an electric water heater. Unlike tank heaters, which take up an average of 16 square feet of floor space, Rinnai tankless units are compact and wall mounted. The appliances are expected to last 20 years, twice as long as typical tank heaters.

Rinnai tankless heaters can provide hot water at a constant temperature for up to three outlets simultaneously. They can accommodate a flow rate up to 9.8 gallons per minute. Or choose a different model with a different flow rate and Btu output. (www.rinnai.us)

REAL GOODS SOLAR UMBRELLA

Under the Rainlight

Entertain alfresco with a solar patio umbrella. By day this one-of-a-kind item from Real Goods stores energy; at night it gives off light from LEDs embedded in the inner ribs. A full day's charge yields 6 to 8 hours of light from AA NiMH batteries. There's an on/off switch for convenience.

The umbrella's webbing is made of UV-protected, water-resistant polyester fabric. At $229, it's priced competitively with other patio furniture. (www.realgoods.com)

It's Clearly Green

It may not sound classy, but installing a sheet of clear plastic film over the interior side of windows in winter can save energy and a nice chunk of change. If the idea of putting up plastic shrivels your design sensibilities, fear not. Installed carefully, the plastic coverings are surprisingly inconspicuous. The Shrink & Seal window kit from **M-D Building Products** makes it easy. The clear plastic film is applied to a window frame with the kit's double-faced tape. A once-over with a hair dryer shrinks the film taut, making it virtually invisible. Once in place, the film blocks cold drafts, making rooms more comfortable, and by trapping still air the film boosts the insulating value of windows (as measured by R-value) up to 90 percent. In drafty old houses, especially those with original double-hung windows, the plastic can make a big difference. It's a lot cheaper than putting in new double- or triple-glazed Energy Star windows. (www.mdteam.com)

ELECTROSTATIC AIR FILTERS

Clearing the Air

Disposable fiberglass filters were originally designed to protect HVAC equipment, not improve indoor air quality. That's why fiberglass filters trap only 10 to 40 percent of the debris passing through them. In contrast, newer electronic filters trap 88 to 97 percent and are much better at controlling bacteria, mold, viruses, and pollen. Electronic air filters, also called "electrostatic filters" since they rely on static electricity, range in price from $1,000-plus for high-end models to as little as $50.

LifeTime electrostatic air filters have been designed to remove 97 percent of all allergens and airborne dust particulates, from pet dander to dust mites—making a big difference in indoor air quality (www.lifetimeelectrostaticfilter.com). HVAC leader Carrier offers high-quality electrostatic filters as well. (www.residential.carrier.com)

Heating and Cooling Systems Can Be Efficient

Most households shell out 50 to 70 percent of their energy budgets on heating and cooling. Fossil fuels still dominate for these tasks, but natural gas burns cleaner than oil, which burns cleaner than coal. Electric heat is inefficient for most applications, and burning wood produces polluting smoke that contributes to smog and can endanger those with asthma and allergies.

Heating and cooling equipment is important as well as expensive to run, so it pays to take good care of it: Perform visual inspections and regular maintenance on your systems. Change filters as needed, up to once a month during peak seasons. Save time, cut down on waste, and breathe cleaner air by using an electronic furnace filter instead of the common throwaway fiberglass screens. The filters in electronic (electrostatic) models are permanent, washable, and easy to install and clean. To improve indoor air quality, add a high-efficiency particulate air (HEPA) filter to your HVAC system (but first make sure your blower is strong enough to service the house). HEPA filters block 99.97 percent of the particles that cause breathing problems. Beware of imitators, often advertised as "HEPA-like filters," which are much less effective.

Air ducts aren't just handy escape passages for spies or criminals. According to the US Department of Energy, 10 to 30 percent of conditioned air in an average system escapes from ducts. Sealing ducts can save the average home up to $140 annually—and reduce problems with mold and dust. So examine your ductwork for dirt streaks, which indicate leaks. Small problems can be patched with duct tape or a bit of insulation. If your ducts look very dirty or worn, contain mold growth, are infested with rodents or insects, or are actually clogged, call in professional help for thorough cleaning or replacement. Some utilities may offer incentive programs to help with the costs of repairs.

Cautions: Most HVAC systems don't need commercial duct cleaning services as a matter of routine. Cursory cleanings often don't improve performance or indoor air quality and can make problems worse. Also, the Environmental Protection Agency (EPA) does not certify cleaners, contrary to some advertising claims. The National Air Duct Cleaners Association can provide advice and assistance in locating a reputable provider.

Central air-conditioning is technically more efficient than window units at cooling, but judicious use of room units can result in lower energy expenditures overall. If your house has central air-conditioning, check the coils both inside (usually in the basement) and outside. If they show dirt, carefully vacuum it off. Schedule an annual HVAC system inspection by qualified pros. Many utilities offer this service free or at a low rate. Some HVAC manufacturers may provide inspections, depending on your sale agreement.

Finally, consider professional installation of an advanced home energy monitoring and control system that integrates lighting, audio, home theater, security, and HVAC systems. That can provide maximum control over total energy use.

HONEYWELL AND LUX PROGRAMMABLE THERMOSTATS

Controlling Climate and Family

Many homeowners argue over thermostat settings. Someone forgets to turn the heat down or the air-conditioning up, and not everyone shares the same concern about environmental impact or the size of the utility bills.

A programmable thermostat can make life simpler, at least where climate control is concerned. It can save approximately $150 a year, according to the EPA. Since they generally cost $35 to $75, this unit will pay for itself in just a few months. Most HVAC installers now sell them as the default choice on new systems.

A word of warning: Some programming is essential. To make it easier, many models come with built-in energy-saving programs designed to cut heating and cooling costs by up to 20 percent—simply set the time and date. Better yet, customize your thermostat based on the daily patterns of your life. (Many models allow for separate weekend schedules.) For example, many people set their programmable thermostats to turn down the heat at bedtime and then to raise room temperature 10 minutes before they rise in the morning.

Programmable thermostats are easy to install, or you can hire a pro to do it for you for a small fee. Look for a model with a battery backup for times when the power goes out.

The EPA's Energy Star program certifies efficient programmable thermostats—and the Energy Star Web site (www.energystar.gov) now lists 11 pages of them. One leading brand with all its models certified by Energy Star is **Honeywell** (http://yourhome.honeywell.com/Consumer). Another brand that has won acclaim for its ease of use, precision, and large, highly visible display is **Lux** (www.luxproducts.com). Check their Web sites for rebates you might qualify for.

PORTABLE EVAPORATIVE COOLER

For only $169, you can have efficient, small-scale cooling right where you need it for your office, bedroom, garage workshop, or other small space. The portable, sleek **Whynter** 4-in-1 swamp cooler lowers air temperature 15°F more than a regular fan. It's called "4 in 1" because the compact unit can function as a cooler, fan, air purifier, and humidifier. It even comes with a remote control! (www.comfortchannel.com/prod.itml/icOid/6323)

FYI

To save energy, unplug appliances you aren't using, most of which draw down power even when they aren't on. This is particularly true of electronics with standby modes, but it applies to TVs (especially new models), computer peripherals, and many other devices.

LEHMAN'S SOLAR-POWERED ATTIC FAN

Cut Those Cooling Loads

Notice how hot attics get in the summer? All that collected heat makes it harder to cool the living spaces below. If it's 90°F to 110°F outside, attics can reach a sweltering 140°F to 150°F.

One solution is to install an attic fan, which typically removes hot air through vents (often on the gables) and pulls in cooler outside air through soffit vents. According to the utility Austin Energy, reducing the attic temperature by 10°F or more saves up to 10 percent on A/C costs. Of course, some electricity is needed to run the fans—that is, unless you select a solar-powered attic fan like the one from **Lehman's** ($479). This American-made fan is mounted through the roof and powered by its own built-in solar panel. The fan can reduce attic temperatures by 50°F to 60°F and help prevent floors from warping and shingles from deteriorating. Further, when it's cold outside, the attic fan will help keep moisture from condensing. (Condensation can damage rafters and floors and soak insulation.) The silent fan runs only during the day, when needed most.

Installation is relatively easy: Cut a hole on the south side of your roof, mount the fan, caulk the flashing with the included 50-year silicone, and orient the solar panel toward the sun. (www.lehmans.com/shopping)

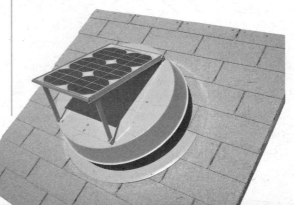

energy

AIRSCAPE WHOLE HOUSE FANS
Bringing Breezes Home

Whole-house fan systems use roughly one-tenth the energy of central air-conditioning. Mounted in the ceiling, a high-capacity whole-house fan is designed to draw a stream of cooler outdoor air inside through open windows and then discharge the air out through a vent in the roof. Such systems can work well in mild and dry desert climates, or elsewhere in spring or fall when cooling loads are low. However, whole-house fans are only effective when the humidity isn't too high and when outdoor air is cooler than indoor air. Another downside is that they can pull in pollen, dust, and pollution.

Installing a whole-house fan can cost between $300 and $1,500—significantly less than central air. AirScape is known for ultraquiet and high-efficiency fans. AirScape uses industrial-grade damper systems that automatically seal tight when the unit is off. They're designed for easy drop-in/plug-in installation and wireless remote control. (www.airscapefans.com)

SOLARROOFS.COM WATER HEATING SYSTEMS
Gateway to Renewable Energy

For people interested in renewable energy, solar water heating is a good entry point. The relatively simple technology has a long track record, great reliability, and an affordable buy-in. Solar water heaters have been mandated in Israel for some time, they are the de facto standard in much of the Caribbean, and they will soon be required for new construction in fossil-fuel-strapped Hawaii. Solar hot-water systems produce three or more times the energy of solar electric photovoltaic (PV) per dollar installed.

For example, Sacramento, California–based SolarRoofs.com can install a rooftop solar water heater for $6,000 to $8,000. Considering that the federal tax credit covers 30 percent of a system and that heating water typically accounts for 17 percent of a home's energy bill, the economics quickly make sense. If you're handy, you can acquire your own solar collectors and other components from SolarRoofs.com and save a chunk of change with a self-install.

HUNTER CEILING FANS
Comfort from Above

The easiest and most efficient way to cool off in the summer heat is to use portable floor fans or to install ceiling fans, both of which use 90 percent less energy than air-conditioning. Fans can cool a room by a perceived 4°F to 10°F simply by moving air, which leads to greater evaporation of perspiration. Most fans have multiple speeds, and many ceiling units have a setting to run the blades in reverse (clockwise), which will push warm air down when it's cold and reduce heating costs by 10 percent.

To facilitate maximum airflow, ceiling fan blades should be at least 10 inches from the ceiling and 18 inches from the walls. Installing a fan isn't difficult if a ceiling light mount already exists. Otherwise you'll probably need an electrician or skilled handyman. Just make sure there is enough clearance for tall folks!

What is the proper size ceiling fan for your room? First determine the square footage of your room (length times width), then check the manufacturer's guidelines. In general, 52-inch blades (the most commonly used) are good for rooms of 225 to 400 square feet. Seek out Energy Star–certified fans, which promise quality and energy efficiency. Energy Star ceiling fan/light combination units are about 50 percent more efficient than conventional fan/light combos, and they will save $15 to $20 per year on utility bills. Energy Star fan-only models are typically 14 to 20 percent more efficient than competitors and are currently available from some 30 manufacturers.

Many of the stylish, finely crafted models offered by **Hunter Fan Company** are certified by Energy Star. Hunter's modern Palermo model comes with a brushed nickel base, CFL lightbulb in a large dome housing, and blades in cherry or maple. The Sonora line features bleached oak blades and an elegant housing for a CFL, and the Jackson Square is finished with antique pewter and a red veneer on the blades. (www.hunterfan.com)

If a ceiling fan is not an option, you can use tabletop or floor fans to get the air moving. To create a "wind tunnel" that pulls outdoor air—when it's cooler than indoor air—through the house, position one fan in a window to face inward and position another fan at an opposite window to blow warm air out.

55

SWIFT ROOFTOP WIND ENERGY SYSTEM

Up on the Housetop…

Developed by **Renewable Devices** in Scotland, the unique Swift turbine has been providing nearly silent, vibration-free power to homeowners, community groups, and businesses for more than 4 years. The Swift does not require the towers or poles that neighbors dislike and that may not be permitted by local laws. Instead, the Swift turbine is mounted on a short aluminum mast, with a minimum blade-roof clearance of about 2 feet.

The Swift is usually mounted at the highest point of a roof, in a position that benefits from maximum prevailing wind. The unit's unique dual tail keeps it optimally positioned in the wind. The five-blade design, with an outer ring diffuser, minimizes turbine noise. The Swift's mounting brackets include a damping system to minimize vibrations.

The Swift turbine has a diameter of 7 feet and a rated power of 1.5 kW (at 31 mph wind speed). The estimated annual power supplied is up to 2000 kWh, roughly a fifth of the average home's energy budget. The Swift is designed to be grid integrated, so your home will use wind-power electricity first, then make up any energy shortage from the electric utility. If net metering is available from your state and utility, you could see your meter run backward during high winds.

Swift turbines cost an estimated $10,000 to $12,000, including installation. For the US market they are manufactured and assembled by Cascade Engineering of Grand Rapids, Michigan. (www.swiftwindturbine.com)

**SUNPOWER SOLAR PANELS:
HIGH EFFICIENCY, COOL DESIGN**

Today's solar panels aren't the ones installed by your forward-thinking parents in the 1970s. New designs are much thinner and can be installed nearly flush to roofs, so they blend better with the lines of your home. Leading this trend is **SunPower**, an American company that makes attractive all-black solar panels that are the most efficient models currently on the market.

SunPower recently completed the high-profile installation of a 205-kilowatt system atop the US Department of Energy's Washington, DC, headquarters. Or consider the experience of the Bunka family of Sunnyvale, California. After they installed their 5 kW SunPower system on the roof of their house, they saved more than $2,000 per year on energy costs. SunPower estimates the Bunkas will reduce their carbon emissions by 143,349 tons over the 30-year life span of the system—equivalent to planting 30 acres of trees or not driving 179,187 miles.

SunPower panels are up to 50 percent more efficient than typical panels on the market and up to 100 percent more efficient than thin-film solar panels. They're backed with a 25-year warranty. (www.sunpowercorp.com)

FYI

Take advantage of natural light! Open shutters, blinds, and shades to let that free sunshine in! When it's nice outside, take your reading into the garden or on the porch. (Yes, go ahead and encourage your boss to hold that meeting outside.)

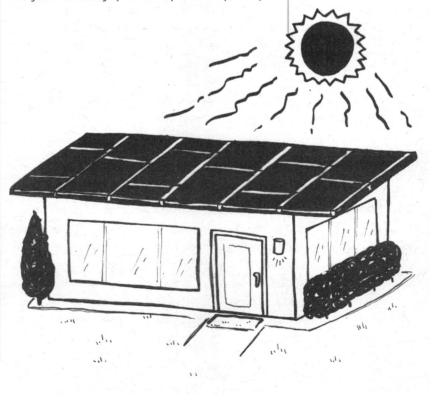

CHOOSING THE BEST AIR CONDITIONER
Chill Out, Save Money

When buying an electric air conditioner, look for an Energy Star–rated model, which for a room air conditioner means it must use at least 10 percent less energy than a conventional model; ideally look for an energy-efficiency ratio (EER) above 10. It's important to get the right unit for the space and to get one that can deal with local humidity levels.

The following models are top performers: Friedrich's $870 SS10L10 (with an EER of 12; www.friedrich.com), GE's AGM06LH and AGM08LH ($180 and $240, with EERs of 10.7 and 10.8; www.ge.com), and Frigidaire's FAA067P7 and FAA087P7 ($150 and $180, with EERs of 10.7 and 10.8; www.frigidaire.com).

While central air-conditioning may be a sign of status in Dallas or a de facto requirement in Florida retirement communities, it is an energy hog. Energy Star–registered models, with higher seasonal energy-efficiency ratings (SEERs), are not that much more efficient (about 8 percent on average) than standard models.

According to the American Council for an Energy-Efficient Economy, top-rated central units include the Lennox HSXA19 Series (with a SEER range of 14.6 to 17.5; www.lennox.com), American Standard Allegiance 18 (SEER 16.5 to 18.3; www.americanstandardair.com), and Trane XL19i (SEER 15.5 to 17; www.trane.com).

FYI

Wash clothes in cold water and line-dry. Your garments will last longer, and sun and wind help disinfect and break up stains.

SHARP SOLAR ELECTRIC SYSTEMS
Solar Shingles = Invisible Power

The world's largest seller of photovoltaic products is Japan-based Sharp; the company developed the first solar-powered calculator. Sharp produces outstanding solar panel arrays for rooftops and ground-mounted applications, but it also excels in what's called building-integrated systems—the most famous example being "solar shingles."

Solar shingles are small photoelectric arrays built directly into sturdy roof tiles. They blend seamlessly with properly planned architecture. The technology was developed largely to get around opposition to unsightly solar panels; neighbors can scarcely object to something they don't notice. An added benefit is that solar shingles serve double duty as electricity generators and true structural elements. On the downside, building-integrated solar cells are less efficient than dedicated hardware, and they are more expensive up front. Solar shingles are also more difficult and time-consuming to install than flat panels, as they require more wiring and piecing together. Building-integrated products generally make sense only for new construction and for major renovation projects. (www.sharp usa.com/solar)

Energy Labels You Should Watch For

Energy Star: Trying to figure out the actual operating costs of an appliance or electronic device can be a knotty task for the average consumer. Luckily, one handy label makes it easier. The blue-and-white Energy Star label instantly conveys that an appliance is 10 to 50 percent more efficient than standard models, depending on the class of device. The label was developed by the Environmental Protection Agency (EPA) and the Department of Energy (DOE). More than 18,000 products in 35 different categories qualify for this label by meeting efficiency standards and providing solid performance at a reasonable price.

A home fully equipped with Energy Star products will use about 30 percent less energy than standard houses, saving an average of $600 a year. Actually, entire homes can be Energy Star certified. (www.energystar.gov)

Green Seal: Green Seal maintains a system of rigorous, independent certification that takes into account many variables. Heating and cooling units can qualify, as can paper, paints, adhesives, household and industrial cleaners, windows, and more. (202-872-6400; www.greenseal.org)

HELIXWIND S322 WIND TURBINE
Mighty Winds, Vertical City

Vertical-axis wind turbines are thought to be better suited for urban locations than traditional propeller styles, since city winds are more swirling and less directional. When the rotor spins around an upright axis, wind coming from any direction can turn the blades and provide power. However, a vertical turbine is less efficient, because during part of its rotation it will have to move against wind. Vertical-axis turbines tend to be extremely quiet, and they pose a reduced risk to bats and birds.

One innovative, eye-catching vertical turbine is the HelixWind with solid, scooplike rotors arranged in a helix pattern. They are designed to provide smooth power across a broad range of wind speeds. The units require no furling or shutting down, are simple to install, and are intended for urban environments and low-draw, off-grid applications.

HelixWind's S322 turbine is rated at 2.5 kW and is 4 feet by 8.66 feet. Helix also offers the S594, which is double the size and capacity of the S322. Both can produce energy with winds as low as 10 mph, although the company recommends use on sites that routinely get winds above 14 mph.

Interconnect HelixWind's turbines with the grid or use them with optional storage batteries for off-grid applications. The turbines are mounted on the company's modular monopoles. Total mounting heights of 15 or 20 feet are common, with a maximum of 35 feet. The Helix doesn't have to be as high as propeller designs to generate reliable power, which lowers installation costs and makes it easier to meet zoning guidelines.

Helix turbines are estimated to cost from $6,500 to roughly $16,500 installed. Made of aluminum alloy and steel, they should last for 30 years. (www.helixwind.com/en).

ENVISION GEOTHERMAL SYSTEM
Heat from Underground

Want to heat and cool your home without greenhouse-gas emissions or the limitations of solar and wind energy?

Consider geothermal power. An Envision system from Indiana-based WaterFurnace International harvests latent energy stored in the ground through something called an *earth loop*, which is an underground piping system. Envision provides 5 units of energy for every 1 unit of electricity used. Even the most efficient gas furnaces, approaching 94 percent efficiency, provide less than 1 unit of energy per unit used.

Envision can save your family up to 70 percent on cooling, heating, and water heating costs over the course of a year. That means units can pay for themselves in a few years, need less maintenance than conventional systems, and enjoy better reliability. (800-GEO-SAVE; www.waterfurnace.com)

ESSENTIAL SOURCES AND REFERENCES

Solar Living Sourcebook, by John Schaeffer (Gaiam, 2007). Thirty years ago John Schaeffer compiled the *Solar Living Sourcebook*, which became one of the most useful guides for those aspiring to go off the grid. This new edition is packed with 600+ pages of practical, easy-to-understand information on energy sources and efficiencies.

Green Home Improvement: 65 Projects That Will Cut Utility Bills, Protect Your Health, and Help the Environment, by Dan Chiras (Robert S Means Co, 2008). A former professor of sustainable development, Chiras spent the past 30 years studying sustainability and applying and communicating what he learned.

The Homeowner's Handbook to Energy Efficiency, by John Krigger and Chris Dorsi (Saturn Resource Management, 2008). From simple fixes to large-scale renovations, ways to save energy that will fit every budget, ability, or time.

Home Power Magazine A great resource on all types of renewable energy, from solar panels to wind turbines. www.homepower.com

Mother Earth News Living lighter on the earth, via home renewable energy, gardening, natural health, transportation, and more. www.motherearthnews.com

OK SOLAR PORTABLE POWERPACK

OkXPower Powerpack 1600 provides a clean backup for temporary service off the grid. The portable system can deliver up to 1,600 watts of electricity—enough to run almost any electronic product or appliance at home. The rugged, wheeled OkXPower Powerpack consists of a battery pack, electronics that convert 12 volts from the battery to household power, and AC or DC outlets. No moving parts to break down or fuels to add. (www.oksolar.com/portable)

SKYSTREAM 3.7 BY SOUTHWEST WINDPOWER
One Answer Is Blowing in the Wind

Unveiled in 2006, the Skystream 3.7 is the first fully integrated wind generator designed specifically for the grid-connected residential market. Arizona-based Southwest Windpower is the world's largest producer of small wind turbines, having produced some 130,000 for distribution in 88 countries.

Depending on the wind at your location, the 2.4 kW–rated Skystream generates between 30 and 80 percent of the power required by a typical home. Some users have reported a savings of more than 50 percent on their energy bills. The unit produces approximately 400 kilowatt-hours per month in a 12 mph wind, and it can produce some energy starting at 8 miles per hour. Skystream 3.7 costs approximately $12,000 to $18,000 to purchase and install and could pay for itself in as few as 5 years. The Emergency Economic Stabilization Act of 2008 included a new federal-level investment tax credit for small wind turbines, up to $4,000, for units installed through 2016.

The Skystream's three blades have a diameter of 12 feet and a swept shape for efficiency and decreased noise. Skystream can power your home directly and can sell electricity back to the grid.

Is your property a candidate? According to the company, you need more than a half acre, unobstructed (the top of the tower should be a minimum of 20 feet above surrounding objects within 300 feet). Your average wind speed should be at least 10 miles per hour; greater than 12 mph is better. Local zoning laws must allow a structure that is at least 42 feet tall, and your electric utility must have an interconnection agreement. Your local Skystream dealer will help you navigate the process. Wind maps can be checked online before you make the call. (www.skystreamenergy.com)

HARMAN XXV PELLET STOVE
Burning Down the Waste

Pellet stoves are vastly more efficient than traditional fireplaces or woodstoves, yet they produce cozy warmth by slowly and cleanly burning wood pellets. They produce very little smoke and ash, are easy to install, and don't require a masonry chimney. They do, however, use a little electricity for their fans and controls.

Pellets are made out of compressed sawdust, wood scraps, and other wood waste material. Therefore, they are an environmentally friendly fuel. Pellets are widely available, typically sold in 40-pound bags.

In their 25th anniversary model, the XXV, Pennsylvania's Harman Stove Company created a high-efficiency pellet stove loaded with advanced technology but sporting a classic look. The cast iron XXV Pellet Stove is rated at 50,000 Btu. It can heat an impressive 1,700 square feet and features fully automatic ignition and temperature controls. All you have to do is fill the hopper with pellets and set the desired temperature.

You have to remove the ash, but a large, easy-to-reach pan makes that simple. The stove has different venting options, from taking advantage of an existing vertical pipe (so you can seamlessly replace a regular woodstove in your home) to using only outdoor air. The XXV comes in colors from classic black to charcoal, forest green, brown, red, and blue. Harman stoves are made in the USA. (www.harmanstoves.com)

Check out the fuel cost calculator from the Pellet Fuels Institute for comparisons to heating with other fuels, from hardwood to coal, natural gas, oil, electricity, and more. (www.pelletheat.org/2/index/index.html)

A house is like the human body. Studs, rafters, and beams are the bones. The structural parts are covered by a protective exterior skin that's several layers thick, containing siding, sheathing, roof shingles, and insulation. Like humans, houses need to breathe and maintain a comfortable temperature; that's the job of the heat, ventilation, and air-conditioning (HVAC) systems. And like humans, houses depend on attentive care and quality materials to stay in good shape.

What makes a house green? There's no short or easy answer to this question. For starters, a green house probably won't be extravagant in size. And no matter what its size, a green house must have features that conserve energy: high levels of insulation, a superefficient HVAC system, appliances and lighting that consume minimum amounts of electricity, and even solar panels that generate electricity or heat water. Water conservation is also an important factor; this goes beyond the use of efficient bathroom fixtures to include such practices as rainwater collection.

Green design is about how a house performs. It's also about how a house is built. Green home design involves materials and products with eco-friendly qualities. A building product may be considered green if it's made at least partially from recycled material, such as countertops that contain recycled glass. If recycled content isn't present, then the product should be made from sustainably managed resources in a manufacturing facility that utilizes green technologies. Other factors being equal, locally produced products are greener than those from afar because less fuel is required to transport them from manufacturing site to building site.

Here are some basic principles of sustainable home design:

★ Small to moderate size: under 3,000 square feet for a family of four; under 2,000 square feet for a couple

★ Minimal waste during the construction process

★ High levels of insulation in a tightly built "envelope," or shell

★ Energy-efficient appliances and lighting

- ★ Water-conserving fixtures, appliances, and design features
- ★ Building materials with green value
- ★ Healthful interior environment
- ★ Renewable energy use—solar, wind, wood heat, geothermal

Many manufacturers now promote the green or sustainable value of their products. But since "green" may be broadly and creatively defined, it's a good idea to double-check manufacturers' claims. These questions are a good starting point:

- ★ Is the product locally made from renewable resources?
- ★ Does the product contain significant recycled content?
- ★ How much energy is required to manufacture the product?
- ★ Does the manufacturing process itself have harmful environmental effects?
- ★ How far does the product travel from manufacturing site to end user?
- ★ Can the product be readily recycled?
- ★ How long will the product last, and how much maintenance will it require?
- ★ Does the product emit harmful gases after installation or if it burns?

Here are some of the most important products and services that will help in achieving and maintaining a truly green home.

—Tim Snyder

MANUFACTURED HOMES

Greener Dwellings from the Factory

When many people hear the term *manufactured housing*, they think of trailer parks. But a growing number of architects are teaming up with manufacturers to produce high-quality houses with worthy green details. Fossil fuel is required to transport the house from factory to home site, but there are plenty of features to offset the fuel use.

Some companies pioneering this new segment of the manufactured home industry are:

★ **Ideabox** (www.ideabox.us). Based in Oregon, Ideabox specializes in sleek, energy-efficient houses assembled from 215-square-foot cube-shaped modules. House packages up to 1,250 square feet are available, and Ideabox will even help you find a building lot.

★ **Michelle Kaufman Designs** (www.mkdarc.com). Architect Michelle Kaufman has pioneered the field of factory-made houses that are green and well designed. Her team offers six standard house packages and a custom-design service.

★ **FlatPak House** (www.flatpakhouse.com). For modern, edgy design, FlatPak is worth checking out. Their houses are boxy but beautiful, with lots of glass and open-plan interiors. Their Web site says a lot about their innovative approach to manufactured housing.

★ **Envision Prefab** (www.envisionprefab.com). This company takes steel cargo containers and makes houses ranging from 740 to 1,280 square feet by cutting holes for windows and doors, covering the shell with siding, and stacking or joining containers together. Envision houses feature foam insulation, gray-water recycling systems, and optional solar panels.

Advantages of Manufactured House Construction

★ **Precision.** Studs, joists, sheathing, and other parts are readily cut to exact dimensions. Flat, uniform work surfaces ensure flat, straight, and square walls and floors.

★ **No bad weather.** Indoor work conditions eliminate slowdowns due to bad weather and protect materials during assembly.

★ **Skilled workers.** Factory workers use special equipment and assembly-line techniques to maintain high quality.

★ **Better insulation.** Insulation is typically installed into wall and ceiling assemblies under good lighting conditions, eliminating energy-robbing empty spaces or voids.

★ **Minimal waste.** Well-planned manufacturing minimizes scrap wood and other unused materials.

★ **Predictable and affordable cost.** The factory can maintain reliable assembly times and costs, and buying materials in bulk enables manufacturers to pass savings on to buyers.

INSULATED CONCRETE FORMS

Going Green with Foam

Insulated concrete forms (ICFs) are foundation and wall forms made from lightweight rigid foam. Like giant Lego blocks, ICFs are engineered to stack and interlock. The cores of the blocks are hollow and are designed to be filled with poured concrete and steel reinforcement rods (rebar). Although size and interlocking details vary from one manufacturer to the next, all ICFs share qualities that make them popular in green houses.

For one thing, they create an insulated masonry wall, something you don't get with conventional poured concrete walls or walls built from concrete blocks. ICFs minimize the amount of concrete required to create a masonry wall, which is a good thing from a green point of view, because the manufacture of concrete contributes to air pollution and requires significant energy.

Most ICFs are made from expanded polystyrene (EPS), the same lightweight white foam used to make disposable coffee cups. Though this type of foam is derived from petroleum products, it's more environmentally friendly than other types of foam. ICF construction saves time, because the forms don't need to be stripped and moved; they stay in place, providing an insulated wall that can be finished in a number of ways. On the exterior side of an ICF wall, a waterproof coating and drainage mat material should be applied to keep the interior dry. For more information and a list of manufacturers, visit the Insulated Concrete Form Association (www.forms.org).

ENGINEERED LUMBER
A Green Builder's Dream

For green building, there's plenty to like about engineered lumber (EL) products. Unlike solid wood joists and rafters (traditional "two-by" framing lumber) that need to be cut from mature stands of timber, most EL components are made from waste wood and faster-growing, lower-value trees. Engineers who develop these products evidently excel at figuring out how small pieces of wood shaped like chips, flakes, or longer strands can be bonded together with glue and resin to create panels, joists, boards, and beams that are dimensionally stable and uniform in size and strength.

I-joists are named for their I-shaped profile. A pair of plywood chords are connected by a thin web made from oriented strand board (OSB), a green panel product that's now often used instead of plywood. Available in different sizes, I-joists are lighter, easier to handle, and more uniform than the traditional 2 x 8, 2 x 10, and other dimension lumber they replace. Other EL products that replace solid wood components in house construction include OSB panels, rim board (installed around the perimeter of a floor), laminated veneer lumber (LVL), and laminated strand lumber (LSL). These last two EL products are frequently used as beams that support floor joists.

Find out more from the primary EL trade association at www.apawood.org. Weyerhauser has developed a house construction package called iLevel that integrates numerous EL components. (www.ilevel.com)

TOOLBASE SERVICES
Zero-Energy Houses

A zero-energy house (ZEH) will, over the long term, produce enough energy to offset energy purchased from utility companies, resulting in a net-zero energy bill. A ZEH uses many of the same products found in ordinary green houses but in larger quantities: There will be photovoltaic panels that generate electricity, a solar hot-water system that helps heat water, and many other energy-conserving elements. Although a ZEH can operate off the utility grid, there are advantages to staying connected: Excess electricity generated by the house's photovoltaic panels may be sold back to the electric utility.

Of course, it costs a bundle to achieve zero-energy performance, but every ZEH that gets built is a laboratory for testing the technologies that may become mainstream in the future. For a clear summary of ZEH technology, go to www.toolbase.org. ToolBase Services is the result of a collaboration between the National Association of Homebuilders (NAHB), the Department of Housing and Urban Development (HUD), and the Partnership for Advancing Technology in Housing (PATH).

FYI

An energy-efficient house should be "tight"—with a minimum of air leaks—so that wintertime drafts can't come into the house through holes and cracks in the building shell or "envelope."

WHAT'S A CARBON FOOTPRINT?

Carbon footprint is one measure of environmental impact, in units of carbon dioxide—a greenhouse gas that contributes to global warming. Products have carbon footprints, and so do activities and even people. A building material that requires a lot of energy to make and transport from factory to job site will probably have too big a carbon footprint to be considered green. A personal carbon footprint depends on numerous factors, including the type of car you drive, how much air travel you do, and even how much locally produced food you eat. To calculate your approximate carbon footprint—and learn ways to reduce it—try the formula at one of these Web sites:

★ www.climatecrisis.net

★ www.carboncounter.org

★ www.carbonfootprint.com

★ www.whatsmycarbonfootprint.com

STRUCTURAL INSULATED PANELS

Tight Houses Made Easy

Ever marveled at how long a cup of coffee can stay hot in a foam cup? Well, that's part of the magic of structural insulated panels, also known as SIPs or stress-skin panels. With these factory-made components, a house can now be built that's extremely tight and well insulated, minimizing energy requirements for heating and cooling.

An SIP is made by sandwiching a thick panel or "blank" of rigid foam insulation between two sheets of exterior sheathing. By themselves, the sheathing and foam aren't very strong. But when bonded together to form panels that are at least 4½ inches thick, 4 feet wide, and 8 feet long, SIPs can be joined at their edges to build structural walls and ceilings, creating a complete building shell—with insulation already installed.

SIPs were introduced to residential construction by timberframe builders in the 1980s, as a means of enclosing and insulating a structure's post-and-beam frame. But SIP manufacturers soon discovered that properly made panels could provide interior and exterior sheathing, insulation, and structural support without the need for a supporting framework. The labor and lumber required to frame exterior walls and roof assemblies is eliminated.

What makes SIPs green? Let's start with the minimal amount of wood that's required for a house with an SIP shell: Eliminating the need for a large number of studs and rafters means that fewer trees need to be cut down. What's more, the oriented strand board sheathing used to face SIPs can be made from waste wood and fast-growing, lower-value trees.

Today, a builder can buy a complete building shell package from numerous SIP companies in the United States. Advanced manufacturing processes make it possible to cut window and door openings at the factory, which saves time and helps to minimize job-site waste. Once completed, a house with an SIP shell is not only well insulated, it's also very tight. These two characteristics mean that the house may be heated and cooled efficiently.

For more technical information and a list of SIP manufacturers, go to www.sips.org.

More Is Better

The *R* in **R-value** stands for resistance to heat flow, and it's the standard measure for insulation value. There is quite a variation in R-value per inch for different types of insulation. Higher R-value per inch doesn't make one insulation better than another; it just means that you don't need as much insulation to achieve a target R-value.

Here are some R-values (per inch) for different types of insulation:

* ★ Standard fiberglass batt (roll) 3.2
* ★ High-performance fiberglass batt 3.8
* ★ Loose-fill fiberglass 2.5
* ★ Loose-fill rock wool 2.8
* ★ Loose-fill cellulose 3.5
* ★ Expanded polystyrene foam board 3.8
* ★ Extruded polystyrene foam board 4.8
* ★ Polyisocyanurate foam board 5.8
* ★ Polyisocyanurate board, foil-faced 7.0
* ★ Spray polyurethane foam (low density) 3.6

ULTRATOUCH INSULATION

New Use for Old Jeans

Waste material from making blue jeans and other fabric-based products supplies the raw material for manufacturing insulation that installs like traditional fiberglass batts—but poses no handling or inhalation hazards. UltraTouch insulation is made from 100 percent postindustrial denim and cotton. The batts are sized to fit standard stud, rafter, and joist spacing (16 inches and 24 inches on-center). They cut and install just like fiberglass batts. Insulation value is about the same as fiberglass (R13 for 3½-inch thickness; R19 for 5½ inch). (www.bondedlogic.com)

BIO-BASED INSULATION

Spray Foam to Seal and Insulate

Many of us have used spray foam insulation that's sold in pressurized cans at home centers and hardware stores. The stuff is supersticky, and its expansive qualities make it great for filling gaps and stopping drafts in numerous places. This same technology can work on a whole-house scale. Today you can call in a foam insulation installer who will arrive in a truck that contains separate tanks of polymer and foaming agent. The two liquids are mixed right at the nozzle, and the mixture starts to foam and expand as soon as it hits the surface.

Insulating a house with spray foam costs more than using fiberglass batts (rolls) or cellulose. Despite the extra cost, many homeowners, architects, and builders are choosing this insulation method over others because it seals air leaks in addition to insulating effectively. Once in place, spray foam insulation won't settle, shrink, degrade, or support mold growth.

Is spray foam a green material? In terms of its energy performance, the answer is yes. But at least some of the chemicals commonly used in spray foam are derived from petroleum products. BioBased Insulation (www.biobased.net), however, uses air as a blowing agent, which doesn't contribute to ozone damage. Also, BioBased Insulation uses soybean-derived polymers as a partial substitute for petroleum-derived ingredients.

There are two basic types of foam. Closed-cell foam (like BioBased foam) has the greater R-value (around R6 per inch) and can serve as a vapor barrier in certain applications. Low-density and open-cell foam such as Icynene (www.icynene.com) provides R3.6 to R4 per inch. This type of spray foam insulation is often used between rafters because it may be applied in a thicker layer for greater overall insulation value. Its vapor permeability allows roof and wall assemblies to "breathe," or absorb and release moisture—essential to any healthy house.

VINYL SIDING: IS IT GREEN?

How about a siding product that's inexpensive, easy to install, completely immune to mold and moisture damage, resistant to splits and cracks, and able to look good for 20 years or more without painting or major maintenance? That's vinyl siding. But is it green? Of course, vinyl siding manufacturers say yes, and the NAHB Model Green Home Building Guidelines consider vinyl siding a green product because it requires no applications of paint, stain, or caulk during or after installation. But other green rating organizations aren't as positive, because polyvinyl chloride (PVC, the main ingredient in vinyl siding) is a petroleum product, and it releases toxic gases when it burns. The verdict? You decide. But consider this: The savings you score by using this less-expensive siding option might enable you to make more green choices elsewhere in your house.

CELLULOSE INSULATION

Old News Can Still Be Useful

Could anything be greener than insulation made from old newspapers? It's not just the trash-into-treasure factor that makes cellulose appealing; the manufacturing process uses less energy than other types of insulation. Another green point: Cellulose insulation doesn't come from a centralized source; instead, it's produced by many companies, so there's probably a manufacturing plant near you. This type of insulation can be bought at building supply outlets and home centers.

But what is more flame friendly than shredded newspaper? Cellulose insulation must be treated with a flame retardant, and it is effective.

There are two basic types of cellulose insulation: dry and wet. Dry, or loose-fill, cellulose may be poured into an attic space right from the bag. Alternatively, you can rent a blower unit and blow loose-fill cellulose into place. Wet cellulose contains a liquid adhesive or binder; it's formulated to be sprayed between studs. The binder helps the cellulose stick together and to the surrounding wood surfaces, but if the mix isn't formulated correctly, the insulation can settle. This is one reason why loose-fill cellulose tends to be a more popular option. (www.cellulose.org)

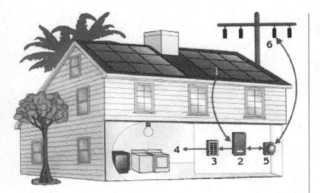

PHOTOVOLTAIC SYSTEMS

Get to Know the Parts

To install a PV system, the best bet for most homeowners is to contact a qualified local solar installer. In most cases, a grid-tied system makes the most sense—though a PV system that includes a bank of batteries and a generator will enable you to act as your own electric utility. For a good overview of PV systems and all the components that make them work, check major suppliers like Solar Direct (www.solardirect.com), Ready Solar (www.readysolar.com), Silicon Solar (www.siliconsolar.com), and Affordable Solar (www.affordable-solar.com).

Solar Electricity

Believe it or not, the first experiments with harnessing the sun's energy to generate electricity took place in the late 1800s. But practical photovoltaic (PV) panels only arrived with the space age, when NASA needed a reliable source of electrical power for orbiting satellites. Today, photovoltaic technology has spread around the world. Working in combination with home-based electric generators, photovoltaics enable people to live off the grid—independent of electric companies. But the greatest growth area for photovoltaics is in grid-connected communities where more and more people are interested in saving money on electric bills while helping to reverse global warming. Sunlight is free, and with every watt generated by a photovoltaic cell, less coal, natural gas, or oil is required to power electric generators.

UNI-SOLAR

Solar That Can't Be Seen

When thinking about solar power, visions of large, roof-mounted panels come to mind. Despite their green appeal, these devices are unsightly to many people. But some manufacturers are now incorporating photovoltaic cells in standard roofing materials like shingles and roof tiles. These building-integrated photovoltaics (BIPV) promise to make photovoltaic systems less conspicuous and more appealing. The solar roll roofing membranes available from Uni-Solar (United Solar Ovonic; www.uni-solar.com), for instance, are made using thin-film PV technology. The PV material is flexible, waterproof, and designed to be easily integrated with standard asphalt-fiberglass roofing shingles. Other companies making strides in BIPV include BP (www.bp.com) and Kyocera (www.kyocera solar.com).

DSIREUSA.ORG

Get Paid to Upgrade!

That's right: There is money available to help offset the cost of adding solar panels, upgrading to a more efficient HVAC system, improving insulation levels, and completing other work that will improve home energy efficiency. Some of these financial incentives are rebates; others are tax exemptions. Depending on locale, there may also be grants and low-interest loans available. It can literally pay to check these options out.

To get an overview of the most current programs, visit the Database of State Incentives for Renewables and Efficiency (DSIRE; www.dsireusa.org). There's also good information at the Energy Efficiency and Renewable Energy division of the U.S. Department of Energy (www.eere.energy.gov/states/maps.cfm#spp).

ECOROCK
Let's Rock the Walls!

Gypsum-based wallboard, commonly known as Sheetrock (a popular brand) or just "rock," is by far the most commonly used finish material for interior walls and ceilings; the United States and Canada produce around 35 billion square feet of drywall paneling every year. The trouble is that the gypsum-based core of a standard drywall panel is a very energy-intensive material. Just one 4 x 8-foot sheet can require over 100,000 Btu of energy to manufacture—and it'll put 16 pounds of greenhouse gases into the atmosphere.

Here's some good news for builders and remodelers: The folks at Serious Materials have come up with an interior wallboard called Eco-Rock that's much more environmentally friendly than standard drywall. The core material in EcoRock is made from 85 percent postindustrial recycled content. EcoRock is greener to manufacture because it doesn't require the energy-intensive heating and drying processes necessary for standard drywall. Considering all the interior wall and ceiling surfaces there are in a house, any alternative to standard drywall is worth considering, and EcoRock doesn't cost much more than regular rock. (www.seriousmaterials.com)

Certification Programs

It is not surprising that many architects, designers, and builders claim to be experts in green home design. How can you make sure you're really getting a green design, not one that's been "greenwashed" with clever marketing? One way is to insist that a house be certified green by a recognized certification program. There are several nationally recognized green certification agencies and many more regional certification programs. Check these Web sites:

National Programs

★ Leadership in Energy and Environmental Design (LEED): www.usgbc.org

★ Energy Star: www.energystar.gov

★ National Association of Home Builders National Green Building Program: www.nahb.org

Regional Programs

For a state-by-state list of Web sites, go to the PATH Web site (Partnership to Advance Technology in Housing): www.pathnet.org

---

SMARTSIDE
Like Solid Wood Siding, But Better

From red cedar clapboards and white cedar shingles to pine board-and-batten siding, solid wood sidings have long been considered premium-choice materials. And they're green, too, provided that they're milled from sustainably harvested trees. One alternative to expensive solid wood siding is composite wood siding that cuts, installs, and holds up like solid wood but has less tendency to warp, crack, or split. Louisiana Pacific's SmartSide siding has the same composition as oriented strand board (OSB); it's made from wood strands and flakes that are mixed with resin and formed under pressure into panels, trim boards, and clapboard and other lap siding. SmartSide comes with a factory-applied primer coat, so finish coats can be applied as soon as the siding is installed. In addition to being strong, durable, and dimensionally stable, SmartSide is green because it's made from wood waste and low-grade trees. (www.lpcorp.com)

FYI

Healthy indoor air quality can be achieved with a ventilation system designed to exhaust stale interior air while drawing in a balanced supply of fresh exterior air without compromising the insulation or tightness factors.

FATMAX XTREME FUBAR TOOL
Demolition Done Right

If you're interested in recycled lumber and other reclaimed building materials, you probably won't need to look beyond your own neighborhood for salvage opportunities. A little networking with local contractors who specialize in remodeling and small additions can yield big opportunities to stockpile building materials that might otherwise end up in the landfill. To liberate used lumber and other stuff, make sure you have Stanley's FatMax Xtreme Fubar Demolition Tool (model 55-099; around $40). The Fubar is one lean, mean hand tool that excels at prying things loose, pounding in protruding nails, and pulling loose nails. Good online sources include Amazon (www.amazon.com) and Northern Tool (www.northerntoolcom).

LINOLEUM
Making a Green Comeback

Linoleum is an old material that's making a comeback because of its green value. This flooring was invented in the mid-1800s by an Englishman who discovered that a mixture of linseed oil, fine sawdust, and pigment could be pressed into canvas backing and cured to create flooring material that's resilient, waterproof, durable, and attractive. Linoleum's popularity grew (especially for use in wet zones like kitchens and bathrooms) until vinyl flooring began to take over in the 1960s. Vinyl flooring offered all linoleum's advantages plus brighter colors, slightly easier installation, and a streamlined manufacturing process. But vinyl's troublesome environmental rap—it's made with petroleum products and produces toxic gases

when burned—has led homeowners and builders to reconsider the sustainable, all-natural appeal of linoleum. Today, the big flooring companies like Armstrong (www.armstrong.com), Forbo (www.forbolinoleumna.com), and Johnsonite (www.johnsonite.com) once again offer a wide range of linoleum patterns and colors. If you're building or remodeling a kitchen, bath, or mudroom, try it—you'll like it. Linoleum is sold in sheet and tile form, and it's among the easiest types of flooring to install.

RECLAIMED WOOD COUNCIL
Wood Flooring Sourced Wisely

Trees are a renewable resource as long as they're sustainably harvested. And if you want to go from good to great, consider flooring made from salvaged (aka reclaimed) wood. It might be reclaimed from an old barn or even from the bottom of a swamp.

Regardless of the source, reclaimed wood earns points in any green building certification program and offers other advantages. Salvaged wood flooring is likely to be denser, stronger, more stable, and more beautiful than the same species of wood that's freshly harvested and milled. Some wood species—chestnut, heart pine, and redwood—are rarely harvested today because they're too rare or too protected by environmental regulations. But you can find these species in stock at a number of reclaimed lumber dealers. Builders and preservationists involved in historic restoration or reproduction rely on reclaimed wood flooring to make their projects authentic.

A number of companies specialize in flooring made from reclaimed lumber. Most will also sell salvaged wood for cabinetry and other uses. You can get basic information from the recently formed Reclaimed Wood Council (www.reclaimedwoodcouncil.org), and you'll find much more detail at the Web addresses of individual companies. There's excellent information at the Goodwin Heart Pine Company (www.heartpine.com), Duluth Timber (www.duluthtimber.com), Mountain Lumber (www.mountainlumber.com), Pioneer Millworks (www.pioneermillworks.com), the Woods Company (www.thewoodscompany.com), and Vintage Lumber (www.vintagelumber.com).

PROGRAMMABLE THERMOSTATS
Saving Energy Automatically

If you haven't upgraded your heating and cooling system with this electronic device, stop right now, do not pass GO, and put off any other energy-saving strategies until you've made this key upgrade. Though there are many brands of programmable thermostats available, they all work the same way: You program the time periods when less heating or cooling

is required. When you're warm and cozy in bed during winter nights, for example, you program the thermostat to allow for cooler interior temperatures until about 20 minutes before you have to get up in the morning. If the house is vacant during weekdays while everyone is at work or at school, program the thermostat to minimize HVAC action until just before you get home. Good information on selecting a programmable thermostat is available on the Energy Star Web site. (www.energystar.gov).

Where Does It Come From?

Sometimes referred to as reclaimed wood, **salvaged wood** comes from some sources that you might expect and from others that will surprise you. A substantial amount of old wood is reclaimed from old buildings—factories and industrial sites in urban zones and barns in rural areas. Old wine vats, abandoned wood bridges, and water towers contribute a limited supply of reclaimed redwood, oak, and other species. Still other salvaged wood comes from the bottoms of lakes and rivers where "sinkers" (logs harvested for lumber that were too dense or waterlogged to float) have rested for generations. There are even some companies reclaiming trees left standing at the bottoms of reservoirs.

CORDLESS CIPS: CUTTING IT DOWN TO SIZE

The cordless "cip" saw—that's contractor lingo for "reciprocating saw"—will more than earn its keep by cutting big lengths of lumber to manageable size, sawing through layers of plaster or plywood, and slicing off finishing nails that hold valuable vintage molding in place so that the face of the board isn't damaged. Cordless saws are available from every manufacturer of portable power tools (**Bosch**, **Porter-Cable**, **Makita**, **DeWalt**, **Ryobi**, etc.), with prices starting under $200. **Milwaukee**, whose famous Sawzall reciprocating saw set the industry standard many years ago, has a great 18-volt saw (model 6515-27) available for around $220 (try Amazon or the Tool Barn; www.toolbarn.com).

FYI

Look for a local source of salvaged exterior siding. Many types of siding (including vinyl, fiber cement, and lap siding) can be removed without sustaining much damage when older houses are remodeled. Shop around for some. You may be surprised!

PAPERSTONE COUNTERTOPS
Recycled Beauty and Strength

Judging by heft and hardness, you'd never guess that this brand of countertop relies on paper as its primary ingredient. But Paper-Stone is definitely more like stone than paper. This Washington-based company uses postconsumer recycled cardboard and office paper in combination with petroleum-free resins and organic pigments to produce panels in different thicknesses. Though PaperStone products have other uses, they're most popular as countertops. Currently more than a dozen standard colors are available. PaperStone may be cut and shaped with the carbide-tipped blades and router bits used in portable power tools. (www.paperstoneproducts.com)

BAMBOO FLOORING
A Great Floor from Grass

Though it may not look like the green stuff that's growing on your lawn, bamboo is a species of grass with impressive and unusual qualities. It grows very quickly, so it's an exceptionally renewable material. And though the manufacture of bamboo flooring (and other bamboo building products) requires many small pieces of the material to be glued together, the end result is harder than oak flooring. Most of the bamboo flooring currently available comes in strip (2¼ inches wide) or wider plank form, with tongue-and-groove edges. The material typically comes with a factory-applied finish, and two tones are available: natural and a darker caramelized finish.

Bamboo flooring installs just like other solid wood flooring. It looks beautiful and can stand up to heavy use. The only glitch in its green appeal is where it's made and how far it has to travel in order to get here: Most bamboo flooring, paneling, and countertop material is made in China and then shipped to distant markets. Order bamboo flooring online from a number of national suppliers, including **iFLOOR** (www.ifloor.com) and **simpleFLOORS** (www.simplefloors.com). For other bamboo products (plywood, paneling, blinds, fencing, etc.), including flooring, check out **Cali Bamboo** (www.calibamboo.com).

FYI

Every year, 50 to 70 percent of home energy expenses are attributable to heating, ventilation, and air-conditioning (HVAC) equipment. It's time to take advantage of new, state-of-the-art HVAC systems that will save you money while helping heal the planet.

ICESTONE COUNTERTOPS
Broken Glass + Concrete = Beauty

A great way to recycle old glass bottles is to put them into concrete countertops. That's what Icestone (www.icestone.biz) and several other companies are doing. The glass is crushed into small fragments before being added to the concrete; the mix then gets poured into forms, where it hardens. Grinding the cured material with progressively finer abrasives yields a smooth-surfaced countertop that's durable, beautiful, and green. The countertop may be tailored to taste by tinting the concrete and specifying different glass colors, so color combinations abound.

Another company that manufactures glass and concrete countertops is **Enviroglas** (www.enviroglasproducts.com). Worth noting: You can probably find a local concrete countertop specialist who can create this type of countertop. If you go the local route, you may even be able to add your own glass, if you've got something special in mind. To find a local fabricator, go to the Concrete Network (www.theconcretenetwork.com).

BAMBOO BUTCHER BLOCK

Bamboo is tough enough to use on the floor, so it's a sure bet for countertops. Although bamboo countertops typically are fabricated overseas (mostly in China), they're made from an exceptionally renewable resource. **Teragren** (www.teragren.com) sells a variety of bamboo products, including butcher-block-style countertop panels. For bamboo with a different look, check out **Totally Bamboo**'s countertop material in both butcher block and edge-grain styles (www.totallybamboo.com).

WOOD COUNTERTOPS
Looking Good

With the variety of countertop materials available today, it's easy to overlook the original green countertop: *wood*. A wood countertop provides a beautiful, one-of-a-kind work surface that wears well in any location except around a sink. You can treat the surface with a simple oil finish or go with a more durable clear polyurethane varnish.

There are companies that specialize in fabricating wood countertops in just about any size and style, and with a variety of wood species. Pennsylvania-based **Grothouse Lumber**, for one, will build a custom countertop in any size and style and ship it anywhere. A greener option is to have the fabrication done close to home at a local cabinet shop or perhaps in your own workshop. If possible, use wood species native to your area or reclaimed wood. While end-grain-type countertops demand more in the way of tools and time to fabricate, you can make great countertops by gluing boards edge to edge—though that's a project involving more tools and techniques than you might want to take on. (www.glumber.com)

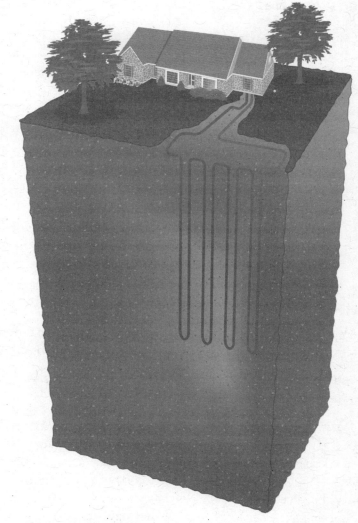

GROUND-SOURCE HEAT PUMPS
Dig Deep for Supergreen HVAC

Is a ground-source heat pump (GHP) the greenest HVAC system you can buy? Some experts think so. That's because this type of heating and air-conditioning system (also known as a geothermal heat pump) saves energy by taking advantage of a very renewable resource: the fairly stable temperature that prevails about 6 feet below the earth's surface.

A GHP provides heat during winter months, air-conditioning during hot summer days, and (with some models) hot water for washing in all seasons. A GHP operates on the same principles that make air conditioners and refrigerators work: By circulating a refrigerant through expansion and compression cycles, heat can be moved from one place to another. In a GHP, a refrigerant or an antifreeze solution is pumped through long coils of tubing that are buried underground. Though a year-round underground temperature of around 55°F may not seem hot to us, it's warm enough for the refrigerant to change from a liquid to a vapor, undergoing the phase change that makes heat transfer possible.

Largely because of the underground piping that's required, a GHP can cost about twice as much as other HVAC systems (around $8,000 for an average-size house). But if you're interested in green value and reliable long-term energy savings, this is a great system to go with. For more background, check out the US Department of Energy's Energy Efficiency and Renewable Energy Web site (www.eere.energy.gov).

Woodstove Heat

The oil shortages that hit in the mid-1970s brought about a woodstove revival that abated when oil prices dropped. Today, wood heat is back in style, and there are many brands of stoves to choose from. But it's important to use caution when buying, installing, and using a woodstove. Clean-burning woodstoves (like those certified by the Environmental Protection Agency) can be 50 percent more efficient than lower-quality stoves. You'll find good general information at www.woodheat.org and at the EPA's Web site (www.epa.gov/woodstoves).

Why heat with wood?

★ You can stay warm during power outages.

★ Wood is a sustainable resource.

★ Firewood is (in many parts of the country) a locally harvested product.

★ Many woodstoves are manufactured in the United States, reducing transport costs.

★ Heating with wood is greener and more economical than heating with oil, gas, or electricity (as long as you're using a clean-burning woodstove).

★ A woodstove is easy to understand and operate. Unlike more complicated heating systems, it won't break down or require expensive, expert maintenance.

★ Don't forget that famous French saying: *Qui coupe son bois se chauffe deux fois*. Cut your own firewood and you're twice warmed.

If you start looking for a woodstove, you'll find that most manufacturers offer both catalytic and noncatalytic models. In a catalytic woodstove, a special honeycomb-shaped insert is incorporated in the design to bring about a secondary combustion process. This burns off pollutants that remain after the primary combustion and helps the stove to burn more completely and, thus, more cleanly. Noncatalytic woodstoves provide for secondary combustion without a catalytic converter, so they tend to be simpler and easier to operate. Also, there's no need to clean or replace the catalytic converter.

Some US-based woodstove manufacturers include:

★ **Lopi Stoves** (www.lopistoves.com). Lopi sells gas, pellet, and wood-burning models. Most models are made from steel plate instead of cast iron, and you can dress up their plain, boxy design with optional legs and doors that have gold or porcelain finishes.

★ **Buck Stove** (www.buckstove.com). All but one of the woodstoves from Buck Stove are made from thick steel plate rather than cast iron. These stoves share a rugged, basic design, and they all have large glass doors for viewing the fire. Inserts and pellet stoves are also available.

★ **Hampton** (www.hampton-fire.com). If you like traditional-looking cast-iron woodstoves, Hampton's models are worth checking out. Several porcelain colors are available if you want something other than flat black.

★ **Harman Home Heating** (www.harmanstoves.com). Harman's Exception model incorporates a large ash pan in the pedestal support, a practical design feature that simplifies the basic maintenance task of removing ashes. Stoves that burn pellets, coal, and gas are also available.

★ **Vermont Castings** (www.vermontcastings.com). This company started out with just a few cast-iron woodstoves, but after acquiring several companies, they now have a broad selection of products, including downsized models suitable for heating small spaces. Gas, pellet, and coal-burning stoves and inserts are available.

RADIANT FLOOR HEATING

Warm Feet Can't Be Beat

Most of us know that if your feet are warm, so is the rest of your body. With radiant floor heat, a room's air temperature doesn't need to be as high as with a forced-air heating system. Warm feet and cool air is healthier than hot air and cold feet. Radiant floor heating has another health benefit that is especially important to people with allergies: It doesn't blow air through a network of ducts, which is how forced-air heat operates. Forced-air systems are inexpensive, but they can fill interior air with dust and even irritating mold spores that sometimes grow in air ducts. Radiant floor heat works without ducts. There is also an interior-design benefit: With no heat registers or baseboard radiators, interior spaces are more attractive and easier to furnish.

There are two types of radiant floor heat: electric and hydronic. Electric radiant floor heat is like having an electric blanket beneath your flooring. Heating cables in the floor are connected to a wall-mounted thermostat that controls in-floor heating. This type of radiant floor heating isn't necessarily green, since it relies on electrical power, and it's best used in small areas like bathrooms.

For higher green value and greater energy savings, hydronic radiant floor heating is the way to go. The floor is heated by warm water or a water and antifreeze solution that circulates beneath the finished floor surface in specially designed polyethylene tubing called PEX. The entire floor surface acts as a giant radiator, which contributes to economy and comfort. Like other hot-water heating systems, hydronic radiant floors can get heating assistance from solar panels. Solar-heated water can help to heat the house, making a green heating system even greener.

Most of the technology behind modern radiant floors has come from northern European countries, where high fuel costs and comfort in cold weather have been concerns for many years. The key word here is *system*: A radiant floor heating system consists of PEX tubing that is allocated to different heating zones, special programmable thermostats, and a high-efficiency boiler that usually supplies hot water for washing as well as for heating. It's best to contact companies that supply systems of fully integrated components: **Uponor** (www.uponor-usa.com), the **Radiant Floor Company** (www.radiantcompany.com), and **Hannel Radiant Direct** (www.radiantdirect.com) are good examples.

Volunteering Is Very Green!

Want to lend a hand in building affordable housing that's also green? There are many opportunities to volunteer for organizations devoted to housing folks in need. Here are a few suggestions.

Habitat for Humanity. Based in Atlanta but with affiliate offices across the country and around the world, this well-known organization gives volunteers the opportunity to build and rehab houses for families who otherwise would go without adequate shelter. (www.habitat.org)

Builders without Borders. In existence since 1999, BWB is an international network of builders who promote and demonstrate the use of straw, earth, and other local, affordable materials in construction. BWB organizes hands-on workshops and partners with other organizations to build affordable sustainable housing. Past projects have taken place in the United States as well as in Mexico, Israel, South Africa, and Siberia. (www.builderswithout borders.org)

Common Ground. Founded in response to the devastation of Hurricane Katrina, this organization's mission is to provide short-term relief for victims of natural disasters in the Gulf Coast region and long-term support in rebuilding affected communities in and around New Orleans. (www.commongroundrelief.org)

COMBINED HEAT AND POWER (CHP)

An All-in-One Solution

Would you be interested in a single appliance that could provide your home with electricity, heat, air-conditioning, and hot water for washing? Such systems exist, but until recently, combined heat and power (CHP) technology (aka cogeneration) has developed more in Japan and Europe than in the United States. CHP is sure to become more popular stateside as fuel prices rise and power outages due to storm damage increase in frequency.

The easiest way to understand how CHP works is to think about a system you've probably been using for years—the engine in your car. An auto engine not only provides power to move your car down the road; it also generates electricity and utilizes the heat of combustion to keep the car interior warm in winter weather. The heart of a home-size CHP system (sometimes referred to as "micro CHP") is a small engine that runs on natural gas or diesel fuel. The CHP engine drives an electrical generator and also (as needed) the air-conditioning compressor. The engine's heat is transferred to a storage tank that can supply hot water to the household.

Depending on house size, a residential CHP system can cost between $10,000 and $20,000, which is more than twice the price of other HVAC systems. But remember: Conventional systems don't supply you with electricity and hot water for washing. Although it's easier to design and install a CHP system in a new house, retrofit applications are possible. The key is to go with HVAC companies with experience in residential CHP. **Climate Energy** (www.free watt.com) and **Aegis Energy Services** (www.aegisenergyservices.com) are examples.

FYI

A green house will have more insulation than local building codes require. In fact, it should have enough extra insulation to be at least 15 to 20 percent more energy efficient than a standard code-compliant house, according to Energy Star guidelines (www.energy star.gov).

TURNED ON BY TINY LIGHTBULBS

We've been exploiting the bright illumination and tiny size of light-emitting diodes (LEDs) for years. LEDs, also known as solid-state lighting, are used extensively in digital clocks, auto directional signals, and display screens for appliances. But LEDs are now being adapted for general household lighting. The screw-in LED bulbs that are currently available from suppliers like **SuperBrightLEDs** (www.superbrightleds.com) are comparable to compact fluorescent lights (CFLs) in energy efficiency, but they contain no mercury (CFLs contain trace amounts of mercury) and burn even cooler than CFLs. Because of their tiny size, LEDs have great potential for the low-profile lighting that goes under cabinets, inside display shelving, and in other  tight spots. Keep your eye on this technology and the companies that drive it (such as **Philips Electronics**; www.consumer. philips.com), because LED lighting development is moving ahead at near light speed.

RAIN HARVEST SYSTEMS

Let It Rain!

In greenspeak, it's called rainwater harvesting. In plainer language, it's simply a strategy for collecting rainwater so that it may be used for watering plants and other purposes. The components in a small-scale rainwater harvesting system are pretty basic. Your building needs gutters and downspouts to collect rainwater, rain barrels to store it, and some sort of screen or bypass valve to filter out leaves, twigs, and other debris. Companies like Rain Harvest Systems sell all these components. But depending on your budget and the scale of your project, you might be fine just buying a barrel or two. **Rain Harvest Systems** sells plastic rain barrels equipped with tops and spigots (for connecting a garden hose) for around $160. (www.rain harvest.com)

Make Your Water Work Harder

It's a shame to let the water from taking showers, rinsing dishes, and washing clothes just drain off uselessly into your septic tank or municipal sewage system. Instead, this "gray water" can be put to work in your lawn or garden or used for flushing toilets if you install a gray-water system. The simplest gray-water system might consist of a polyethylene tank that serves as a collection point for gray water, a filter to capture lint and other impurities, and a pump that delivers gray water to a garden hose. For a great overview of gray-water systems, check out a book called *The New Create an Oasis with Greywater* (around $20 from **Oikos Green Building Source**; www.oikos.com). If you want a plug-and-play gray-water system that recycles water from the bathroom sink for use in flushing the toilet, check out the AQUS system from **WaterSaver Technologies** (www.watersaver tech.com). This small-scale system is simple enough for any plumber (or an experienced DIYer) to install.

Here are some of the benefits of a gray-water system:

- ★ Reduced demand is placed on wells and municipal water supplies.
- ★ Less strain on septic systems means they last longer and don't require pumping (saving you money).
- ★ Gray water is purified naturally when used to water gardens and lawns, since phosphates and other chemical compounds leach into soil and can actually nourish plants.
- ★ Groundwater supplies are recharged when gray water is used to water plants and lawns.

Check with your local building department before ordering or installing gray-water components to ensure you're in compliance with local ordinances.

Save water by changing your landscaping to plants or other objects that don't need regular (or any) watering.

Heat Water Naturally

Instead of paying the electric utility or your fuel company to heat water for bathing and washing clothes or dishes, let the sun do the work. Depending on available sunshine in your area, a solar water heating (SWH) system can cut your hot-water heating expenses by 50 to 80 percent. The most basic SWH system can cost as little as $1,000, but most people choose a more expensive (in the $4,000 range) closed-loop system that uses an antifreeze solution to transfer solar heat. This eliminates freezing problems during cold weather.

Although solar collectors may be mounted on the ground, most are installed on the roof. **Velux**, a relatively new entry into the SWH market, has developed a collector that looks exactly like a skylight. All piping and structural supports are housed in the skylight well; they don't show on the roof. (www.veluxusa.com)

Clothing and fashion have substantial environmental impacts in every stage of production and consumption. Our choice of clothing may ostensibly mirror our mood, preference, and residential climate, but what they're made of and how they're made echo who we are and what we believe in. Consciously or not, we are models of our choices.

If you want to look chic while doing your part to save the earth, rest assured that there are more eco-friendly choices than ever before. Ecology and economics are intersecting in a new sector of the garment industry: eco-fashion. As supply expands to meet demand, some of the fashion-forward eco-designs are about as granola as a pair of Christian Louboutin stilettos. Savvy consumers are now privy to an unprecedented selection of styles.

Eco-fashion has come a long way, baby. Just a few years ago, when I was filming the pilot of my first TV show, I scrounged to find just eight wardrobe changes of sophisticated threads. While I knew the camera couldn't read the fiber-content labels, I could. Today, there are far more designers and brands proffering eco-collections than could be covered in this book. And we're not just talking back-to-the-land burlap styles or even workout wear. Sure, it's nice to bum around in drawstring pants and a hoodie at home, but what about eco-threads you can wear to a critical interview, to your cousin's wedding, or for a night on the town? Innovations in natural and recycled fiber technologies translate to organic and eco-friendly fabrics that perform as well as—and sometimes better than—conventional counterparts. In short, eco-fashion is not a compromise.

Today's green fibers include organic cotton, bamboo, soybean fiber, hemp, SeaCell, and sasawashi; eco-friendly hybrid fibers such as Tencel and Modal; repurposed vintage fabrics such as cashmere, leather, silk, and wool; and recycled fibers made from soda pop bottles, mill-end surplus fabrics, cotton, wool, and leather. Designers are using exceptional, luxurious fibers to forge sustainable styles that leave nothing to be desired.

The thing to remember is that the true cost of fashion is not printed on the hangtag. What about the cost paid by the planet and the people who produce the garments? Fashion is ephemeral, but its environmental impact is not. Cotton saturated with pesticides and fabric dyes laden with heavy metals; oil extracted from the land and processed to make synthetic fabrics; chemicals used to scour, bleach, and finish fabrics; garment manufacturing practices that violate human rights—these less-visible costs of fashion may take a heavy toll on the ecosystem and the communities who live in it.

Buying sustainable clothing made from eco-friendly fabrics, colored with low-impact dyes, and constructed by means of fair-trade labor is one step toward conscientious consumerism. But buying smart and better are also part of true eco-fashion. Those skinny jeans that were shunned in favor of boot cuts and bell-bottoms a few years ago are back in fashion. And if this book is in print long enough, the inverse will soon be true. Buy smart—that is, select classic pieces that won't go out of style. Buy better—purchase less stuff of better quality that will last longer. Buy eco—next time you need a new piece of clothing, stop, drop, and roll: Scout for an eco-version that will make you feel good long after the transaction high is over.

—Renée Loux

Important Facts about Eco-Clothing Materials

As the wave of sustainable supply meets the crest of green demand, understanding the basics about the leading green fabrics will help you make the best choices for function and fashion.

BAMBOO

Why it's green: Bamboo regenerates and grows prolifically without the use of pesticides or extensive agricultural tending. Some varieties grow several inches to several feet a day. After the stalks are cut, many bamboo root systems send up new shoots to replenish growth without being replanted. Bamboo cultivation gets high eco-friendly marks: It improves soil quality, shores up erosion, and sequesters carbon out of the atmosphere at an impressive rate.

Fabric benefits: Bamboo fabric is lusciously soft and supple yet strong. It drapes beautifully. It feels softer than the softest cotton and has a natural luster similar to that of cashmere. It is highly breathable, is as absorbent as cotton, dries quickly, and is a thermal regulator, keeping you cool in hot weather and warmer in cold weather. It's easy to care for in a washing machine and dryer. Proponents say that it has natural antibacterial, hypoallergenic, and deodorizing properties due to a naturally occurring bacteriostatic agent that helps bamboo fiber resist odors and bacteria.

The trade-off: Making stiff bamboo stalks into silky fiber can require a lot of harsh chemical solvents. Newer processing technologies, such as the lyocell process, dissolve pulp using less toxic and nontoxic chemicals in a closed-loop system that captures and recycles the chemicals to be efficiently used again and again.

HEMP

Why it's green: Hemp grows like a weed. It's sustainable and highly renewable, and it grows more easily than cotton in less-than-ideal conditions without the use of pesticides. Hemp can produce two to three times more fiber per acre than cotton.

Fabric benefits: Hemp is absorbent, extremely durable, and versatile—it blends beautifully with other natural fibers and can be as soft as soft cotton, as sturdy as denim, and as flowing as linen. Thanks to the hollow core of the fiber, hemp is a thermal regulator, keeping you cooler in warm weather and warmer in cool.

The trade-off: The stigma of hemp, due to its drug-related cousin marijuana and the early burlap-sack eco-designs, have made it an often-overlooked fiber for fine clothing, though that's changing. Like linen, hemp needs to be ironed for a smooth appearance, and it does wrinkle.

INGEO (CORN FIBER)

Why it's green: Made from corn, Ingeo is one of the few truly renewable synthetic materials. It's 100 percent biodegradable.

Fabric benefits: Ingeo combines the comfort and feel of a natural fiber with the specialty performance of synthetics: It's extremely strong, resilient, and dimensionally stable. It's more absorbent, is resistant to UV light, and has a lower density than synthetics like PET polyester. Plus, it doesn't cause environmental contamination in disposal. Ingeo can be beautifully blended with natural fibers such as cotton and wool.

The trade-off: Since Ingeo is made from corn, it may contain genetically modified organisms (GMOs), because most corn does.

MODAL

Why it's green: This bio-based synthetic is made from reconstituted beech trees via a renewable process and is 100 percent biodegradable.

Fabric benefits: Modal blends the best qualities of a natural and synthetic fiber—it's luxuriously soft, is 50 percent more absorbent than cotton but dyes just as well, doesn't pill or shrink, and is colorfast and resistant to fading. It dries quickly and can be blended with cotton for a silky smooth finish and structure that holds even after repeated washing.

The trade-off: Like pure cotton, Modal needs to be ironed after washing for a smooth appearance.

ORGANIC COTTON

Why it's green: Certified organic cotton is grown without chemical pesticides, insecticides, or fertilizers. It supports a healthy ecosystem, improves soil quality, often uses less water than conventional cotton, and won't contaminate water with toxic chemicals.

Fabric benefits: Organic cotton is often very high quality. Cotton is extremely versatile, breathable, durable, and delectably soft. It can be blended with almost any other fiber, natural or synthetic, is easy to care for, and takes dye beautifully.

The trade-off: Organic cotton can have a longer growth cycle, require more skill to grow, and cost more to produce than conventional cotton. Therefore it's often more expensive. Be aware that some companies use organic cotton only in part or uncertified cotton and still make the claim to green fame. Not all organic cotton is dyed or bleached naturally, so look for companies with transparent practices whenever possible.

LOOMSTATE JEANS
Stylish *and* Green

Loomstate started making foxy and laid-back certified organic jeans when most other eco-fashion looked like it was cut for Gilligan. The collection has grown from just jeans and tees to a fine spread of classic American casual wear that looks great without trying too hard. Based in New York City, Loomstate takes a design approach based on timeless style rooted in environmental and social responsibility. Loomstate's modern fits and uncompromised attention to construction are rendered in high-quality, comfy, 100 percent certified organic materials that have been ecologically washed and softened. The company directly manages every stage of manufacturing—from the fabric mills, to the cut-and-sew facilities, to the laundries—all to ensure responsible manufacturing up and down the chain of production.

Loomstate's blue jean cuts are "classic modern" and won't go out of style. The core collection is supplemented with seasonal collections for year-round sustainable wear. (www.loomstate.org)

DEL FORTE
Organic Through and Through

Del Forte is a premium denim brand with chic design and eco-ethical production. Made in the USA from 100 percent organic cotton denim with just the right blend of figure-flattering fabric weight and stretch, Del Forte's savvy, sexy collection ranges in style from classic to fashion-forward. Medium and dark denim washes complement mid-rise and high-rise cuts, leg styles, and top-stitch details. Choose from classic boot cuts, hip wide-leg cuts, in-vogue slim-leg skinny jeans, and versatile trouser cuts.

Del Forte takes its sustainable commitment to heart and has linked up with the Sustainable Cotton Project to build mutually beneficial bridges between farmers, manufacturers, and consumers to promote sustainable farm-to-finished-fiber practices. The results are gorgeous, top-quality denim designs with classy versatility that can be dressed up or down.

Del Forte has launched an in-house program called Project Re*jean*eration, designed to recycle your jeans and refresh your wardrobe. When you've had enough of your Del Fortes, send them back to the company, where they will be recrafted by hand into a second generation of denim.

Each season brings a new piece of Rejeaneration Denim, such as the Janelle Skirt, trimmed with kimono fabric, hand-stitched embroidery, and a spray of hand-made rosettes. As a reward for recycling, Del Forte will give you 10 percent off your next purchase, or will donate your 10 percent to the Sustainable Cotton Project. It's the ultimate rebirth of denim in style that sustains its resources. (www.delforte.com)

JEANS WITH ECO-ATTITUDE
Good Society presents an affordably priced, forward-thinking collection of blue jeans that are fully sustainable—both ecologically and socially. Constructed from fairly traded, 100 percent organic denim, Good Society jeans join form and function with clean styling and a fit that ensures you look good and feel great. From hangtags to dyes, everything is eco-friendly and follows fair-labor practices. Good Society was founded by the genius team at Sling & Stones as a less-expensive denim line that doesn't sacrifice quality, style, or socio-eco-responsibility. Good Society jeans are available in low-rise boot cut and slim cut and mid-rise straight-leg cut. (www.goodsociety.org)

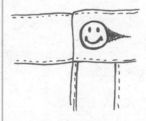

A Giant Goes Green

Arguably the original and authentic leader in blue jeans for more than 150 years, **Levi's** is a brand icon. Now Levi's takes its long-term position of responsible manufacturing and business practices to a new, sustainable level with Levi's Eco and Levi's Capital E, certified organic denim versions of its most popular and classic styles.

Levi's Eco offers popular fits and finishes at affordable prices, including the men's Vintage Straight 539, Low Boot 527, and forward Skinny 511. Women's jeans include classic mid-rise Straight 552, Boot 553, and fitted trouser; forward fit low Skinny 531; and a few Eco shorts. Levi's superpremium line, Levi's Capital E, comes at a more precious price, but the price reflects quality and attention to detail, including the use of recycled buttons, rivets, and zippers and natural indigo dyes that have minimal impacts on the earth. Find  much-loved, classic styles in men's boot, loose, and straight cuts, and in women's classic-cut Ruler, boot-cut Swank, and skinny Skimmer. (http://us.levi.com)

LINDA LOUDERMILK
Eco-Luxury to the Nines

Linda Loudermilk is the nexus of eco-fashion. In her words, it "is all about saving the planet one sexy little number at a time." Combining beautiful design with luxurious eco-fabrics, Linda Loudermilk's collections flatter women's shapes and give back to the earth. Spearheading the luxury eco-fashion marketplace, Linda Loudermilk Designs is dedicated to well-made, high-quality designs that will withstand seasonal fashion trends. Seasonal collections feature tops, pants, dresses, and jackets that are off the charts in style and sustainability. From casual to couture, the sophisticated cuts and styles range from classic to edgy and feminine to fashion forward. If you like the look of a tailored blazer or suit, Linda Loudermilk is as good as it gets. Luxurious eco-fabrics include organic cotton, buttery-soft bamboo, jersey-draping wood fiber, sasawashi (a Japanese allergen-free lint), SeaCell seaweed, organic wool, Ingeo (corn fabric), recycled denim, and soy. Loudermilk garments are manufactured by meticulously researched, sustainable business practices and under fair-labor standards. (www.linda loudermilk.com)

DENIM THERAPY
First Aid for Jeans

If you've worn your all-time favorite jeans to shreds but are reluctant to part with them, get some therapy—for your jeans, of course. **Denim Therapy**'s unique reconstructive technique weaves new cotton fibers into existing denim fabric to repair holes and worn sections. Color-matched to the current color of the worn and torn jeans, the inserted fabric impressively mimics the grain, hue, and feel of the original denim. It's not a patch, it's a veritable resurrection of your old jeans! Denim Therapy accepts all types of denim jeans, not just high-end brands, plus denim jackets, skirts, or any other denim article you want to restore. All you have to do is wash  your garment to ensure color accuracy, fill out and submit a simple form, and await a confirmation number for shipping and tracking the process. When Denim Therapy receives your beloveds, they will inspect them and e-mail an estimated cost of repair, which is charged by the inch ($7 an inch). Once you OK the estimate and submit payment, they'll return your revamped jeans in a matter of weeks (quicker if you upgrade for rush processing). These guys are geniuses. And you keep it green by rendering a second life to your much-loved threads. (www.denimtherapy.com)

EDUN
Fair-Trade Fashion

EDUN makes it cool to care. This company was founded to create trade, not aid, and to foster sustainable communities and long-term economic growth in developing areas around the world. Launched in 2005 by activist Ali Hewson and her husband, U2 rocker Bono, with a mission to fashion beautiful, ethical clothing for a thinking consumer, the EDUN collection is produced with respect for the communities in which the garments are made, for the earth and the materials produced, and for the consumer who wears the threads. As Bono says, "We carry the stories of the people who make our clothes around with us."

EDUN's T-shirts are all made from organic cotton, as is about half of the rest of the collection. Denim, knits, woven tops and shirts, blouses, dresses, sweaters, graphic tees, hoodies, and casual jackets are made from organic cotton, silk, alpaca, and wool. The EDUN collection infuses beauty with backbone, weaving fashion and form in modern, edgy classic looks for men and women in a genre somewhere between rock 'n' roll and punk rock. All cool, all fair trade, all the time. (www.edunonline.com)

HURRAH FOR VINTAGE MATERIALS!

Recycling something that already exists is greener and more sustainable than making anything new. Reuse saves energy and reduces pollution and waste, even when compared with producing new, natural organic fibers.

It seems that almost anything can be recycled into something usable. Clothing designers are getting fantastically creative with recycling materials, whether it's using polyester made from recycled soda pop bottles and discarded garments or deconstructing vintage pieces to fashion new ones.

Dream a sustainable dream: a rain jacket or swimsuit made from recycled polyester; a cashmere sweater perfectly pieced together from hand-selected pieces; a chic trench coat made from recycled wool; a smart button-down from reclaimed cotton; a sophisticated blouse made from a combination of vintage scarves; a handbag made from discarded candy wrappers, pop tabs, or vintage auto upholstery. If our imagination knows no bounds, neither does sustainable style.

LOYALE
Loyale Is Loyal

Loyale embodies alluring, understated sophistication with built-to-last styles made from the ground up in New York City with Texas-grown certified organic cotton. Loyale founder (and winner of the Eileen Fisher Grant for socially responsible women-owned companies) Jenny Hwa is FIT-trained and one of the most authentic and committed designers around. Her keen eye for wearable, simple styles evokes the vibe and silhouettes of 1950s and '60s Americana, suggestive of an era of optimism. Scoop backs, fluttery sleeves, ruffle bottoms, pencil skirts, smocked blouses, playful frocks, and feminine details characterize Loyale's retro, ready-to-wear collection.

Loyale *is* loyal. In an effort to keep the garment industry thriving in America, the entire collection is grown and sewn in the USA. Loyale utilizes only low-impact dyes, and it continues to expand its color-grown organic cotton collection, in which garments are made with strains of cotton that naturally bloom in tones of green, blue, and brown and thus don't require dyes. It's clear that Loyale is walking the eco-talk—even its hangtags and marketing materials are printed on postconsumer recycled and tree-free paper using nontoxic inks by a printer that offsets its energy with wind power. (www.loyaleclothing.com)

H&M

Green Garb Goes Main Street

H&M carries men, and women's fashions—from tailored classics to modern basics and accessories—at affordable prices. So what's new? H&M has introduced organic and recycled fibers throughout its concepts for men, women, teenagers, and kids. H&M started blending organically grown cotton into garments in 2004, and its long-term commitment to organic cotton continues to grow: Garments made from 100 percent organic cotton are now found in all departments, and H&M aims to increase the use of organic cotton by 50 percent a year for the next 5 years.

H&M is using new green fabrics made from recycled materials, too—polyester recycled from PET plastic bottles and textile remnants, reclaimed wool from worn-out garments and fabric remnants, and recycled cotton from fabric remnants. The main objective is to create garments that are both fashionable and environmentally compatible. This objective is reinforced by policies up and down the supply chain that champion overall environmental awareness and sustainable use of resources. All clothing in H&M's organic range must pass rigorous quality and safety tests from supply through manufacturing to the final products.

Given that H&M is an international company, the impact of transportation is on its radar. In partnership with eco-aware transport companies, the company continues to work toward efficient transport by optimizing freight handling to reduce fuel consumption and by increasing the use of renewable fuels. It's certainly not claiming to be perfect, but H&M is making some good green waves and bringing eco-fashion into just about everyone's reach. (www.hm.com)

FYI

When greening your wardrobe, start with the basics. Opt for organics and sustainable fibers for clothing staples like jeans, T-shirts, socks, and underwear.

STEWART + BROWN

Socially Conscious Cashmere

Stewart + Brown believes in sustainable clothing design that attains the highest standards of quality and functional style while extracting a bare minimum from the earth's precious capital. The company's seasonal collections are fashioned of organic plant fibers such as organic cotton pima, jersey, terry, and crepe; green fabrics such as renewable Tencel, hemp, silk, and linen; and sustainable, eco-friendly, premium knitwear such as merino wool, yak down, and Mongolian cashmere. The cashmere is produced exclusively with fibers hand-combed from the downy undercoat of cashmere goats from the remote, rugged steppes of Outer Mongolia. Stewart + Brown mindfully harvests, spins, and knits the garments in Mongolia to help sustain the centuries-old nomadic way of life of Mongolian herders. And the designs are beautiful, with classic and modern flair. (www.stewart brown.com)

COVET
Green Avant-Garde

Covet is a fusion and balance of contemporary, vanguard style. And this company is as green as can be. Based in Montreal and New York, until recently Covet was under the radar about being green, quietly working sustainable fibers into its aesthetic-forward, avant-garde seasonal collections. But now, uninhibited, Covet has gone completely eco. Translating organic cotton, organic French terry, bamboo, hemp, Modal, Tencel, soybean fiber, recycled cotton, and poly-wool blends into collections that both men and women will "covet," the line is infused with edgy Japanese style and handcrafted detail that is eco-conscious to the core.

Touted as "handcrafted redemption," the collection doesn't skimp on original style. Urbane streetwear, cropped trench jackets, cargo skirts, body-conscious textured sweaters and cardigans, whimsical long coats, high-waist tailored pants, mod dresses and skirts, skin-baring halter tops, and spiffy collared shirts fuse fashion and sustainability. (www.covetthis.com)

lara miller

LARA MILLER FLIP
Play with Your Fashion

Lara Miller puts a signature spin on eco-fashion with her FLIP design—convertible clothes that can be worn multiple ways for different looks. Made from sustainable materials including organic cotton, soy, hemp, silk, bamboo, SeaCell, and recycled cotton, these sassy styles offer classy defense against fast fashion and keep your wardrobe fresh with choices. The easy-to-wear pieces are designed to unleash your creativity: Depending upon how you tie, twist, and gather it, a dress can be transformed into a cowl-neck top or cardigan. Sleek silhouettes can be turned upside down to reveal a whole new garment; long ties can be twisted to suit your mood. Lara Miller's designs are grounded in geometry and architecture and conceptually animated—the pieces within each collection are designed to be played with, flipped, and re-created for each individual wearer. All this chic, feminine tailoring and distinctly detailed style is made in the USA and dyed with only low-impact dyes. (www.laramiller.net)

VINTAGE VERVE

For the fashion forward and style savvy, Deborah Lindquist creates exquisite apparel with fun and funky character out of a mix of reincarnated vintage garments. Her vintage cashmere collection is made from recycled cashmere that has been refashioned into "new" pieces with spunky character and sustainable style. Each piece, by nature, is one of a kind. The core cashmere collection includes buttoned cardigans and ruffle-sleeve shrugs, perfect for layering, and every season offers new styles like sleeveless sweater vests. (www.deborah lindquist.com)

FYI

Take pride in "Made in the USA." Purchases that are manufactured domestically not only bolster our national economy, they also conserve resources and fuel required to ship goods from overseas.

83

BURNING TORCH CASHMERE
Second Life

If you covet cashmere, Burning Torch's collection is absolutely to live for, and live in! Made from 100 percent recycled vintage cashmere that has been deconstructed and reconstructed into new garments for women, men, and children, each piece is tailored with character and quality to last a lifetime. Whether a simple woven knit or a pattern of beautiful cables, each new garment takes an average of six vintage sweaters to create.

The cashmere coat by Burning Torch is a modern and classic "lifetime" piece. Sporting a flattering, tailored cut and adorned with an asymmetrical, oversize collar, the coat is constructed of 100 percent recycled vintage cashmere in a rich, elegant charcoal gray. It's gorgeously versatile and can be dressed up or down thanks to quality and character that won't go out of style.

Karyn Craven, founder of Burning Torch and senior designer, does not forget about clothing for the guys. The Recycled Cash V-neck sweater is a classic in light gray and blue stripes. Talk about sexy and snuggly (and über-eco-friendly to boot). Here's a little tip for you men: Wear cashmere. Ladies will want to touch you. Wear stylish, vintage recycled cashmere. Game, set, match: No woman can resist a smart, sensitive, stylish man.

About half of the Burning Torch collection is constructed of vintage fabrics and materials like cashmere, silk scarves, and army fatigues and snow camouflage; the other half uses virgin organic fibers like cotton. (www.burningtorchinc.com)

BURNING TORCH BLOUSES
Vintage Silk Is the Secret

Burning Torch rescues vintage silk scarves and gives them new life as flattering, feminine blouses in stunning colors and patterns. Carefully hand-selected scarves are cut and perfectly pieced together in chic, one-of-a-kind combinations. One top has some retro scarf pieces that you might swear you saw swathing Pan Am stewardesses. The blouses are effortlessly classic and sophisticated yet freshly exciting and unique. They're versatile enough to layer under a dressy blazer with slacks or over a summery skirt or jeans. If these catch your fancy, be sure to browse Burning Torch's collection of recycled scarf halter tops and dresses: Just add oversize sunglasses and perennial summer spirits. Fabulous, darling, just fabulous. (www.burningtorchinc.com)

FYI

Support ethical, fair-trade, and fair-labor practices. Use your dollars to vote for ethical codes of manufacturing and socially conscious protocols that offer a fair shake for people who farm fibers and make garments. Look for companies with transparent labor and trade practices.

VIRIDIS LUXE
Divine Design

Viridis Luxe is on a mission to create sustainable, ethical clothing for those who want to tread lightly on our planet and still revel in an aesthetic of effortless chic. Working with signature fabric blends of bamboo, cashmere, hemp, silk, and organic cotton in an indulgent array of decadent textures, Viridis Luxe's style is influenced by a casual yet classic vintage era that goes against the grain of throw-away fashion. The bamboo–organic cotton blend yields a soft jersey fabric with gorgeous drape, and the sumptuous bamboo-cashmere blend is a fine, lightweight knit with simple elegance and buttery-soft comfort.

If the idea of hemp clothes brings to mind coarse burlap, welcome to the future of luxury fashion. Viridis Luxe takes hemp to a stratosphere of splendor using a proprietary blend of hemp and cashmere that brings out the best of both fibers: The supremely soft knits have a structure not found in cashmere on its own. The collection also features hemp jersey and hemp-silk jersey blends that will make even the softest cotton jealous. Viridis Luxe sources the finest long-fiber Mongolian cashmere tended by traditional methods on high-altitude family farms.

Considering the fabrics, it's no surprise that Viridis Luxe collections are beautiful. The looks are elegant yet modern, and feminine silhouettes are flattering and versatile enough to dress up or down. And the feel of the fabrics? Simply divine. (www.viridisluxe.com)

Fair Trade in Fashion

The concept of fair-trade clothing has been emerging in the fashion trade to indicate an ethical, socially responsible code of manufacturing. In the market of specialty foods like coffee and chocolate, the term "fair-trade certified" refers to an established, verifiable standard with clear criteria. When it comes to clothing, the term "fair trade" is used more casually, with a looser definition, less monitoring, and less authenticated documentation. This is not to say that fair-trade clothing doesn't exist; it's just that it's up to individual companies to define their own ethical and fair-trade practices and to monitor and enforce them.

For the most part, companies that tout fair-trade clothing follow a manufacturing code of conduct that includes fair wages and working conditions, bars child labor and sweatshop practices, adheres to civil labor and safety laws, supports environmental sustainability, and advocates equitable partnerships between overseas producers and North American marketers. To get a more solid picture of what fair trade means to a given company, dig into the company's code of conduct or mission statement description (often found on the company Web site) and look for details. Most companies that are genuinely adhering to fair-trade protocol will not be shy to post their measures of standard.

Demand for ethical, fair-trade garments has come of age, partly in response to media exposure of global corporations that moved manufacturing out of the United States to developing countries where few ethical labor standards may exist and even fewer may be enforced. But terrible labor conditions exist in the States also. Some of the biggest brand-name corporate bullies, however, are changing their ways, thanks in large part to consumer demands. It's becoming cool to care. "Activism is the new chic," writes *Newsweek*'s Jessica Bennett, "and we, the consumers, have become the new activists—saving the world one credit-card transaction at a time."

The EDUN collection, created by U2 singer Bono and his wife, Ali Hewson, raises the bar. EDUN makes ethical clothing as cool as it gets by working through the premise of "trade, not aid" to foster sustainable communities and long-term economy in Africa, South America, and India. Environmental sustainability is woven into the socially conscious protocol of companies like EDUN. Other fashion brands are following suit.

While a gap still exists between the need for standards and their realization, it's important to note that ethical fashion is now on the radar. In time, through the vote of consumer dollars, a certified fair-trade standard for the garment industry can be established, as it has been in the food industry, with meaningful criteria, enforceable standards, and a bona fide stamp of approval.

WOMEN'S ORGANIC BLAZERS AND JACKETS
From Sporty to Chic

★ **Burning Torch** organic canvas blazer sports a casual yet tailored look that can be dressed up with slacks for the office or dressed down over jeans for clean style. Made from soft, organic cotton, this natural-paper-colored blazer is fashioned with pin-tuck details for figure-flattering shape, long-cut sleeves, four buttons, and two pockets at the hip. (www.burningtorchinc.com)

★ **Grace & Cello** Twill Metropolis blazer is smart and eco-savvy, made from 100 percent organic cotton twill in cool gray. With a short, tailored, feminine fit, three-quarter-length sleeves, flap pockets at the hips, and notch collar, this blazer is sporty and chic. (www.gracecello.com)

★ **Stewart + Brown** French Terry tailored blazer offers put-together style and natural design. The midweight fabric is made of an organic cotton blend and features a mid-rise mandarin collar, front pockets, antiqued buttons down the front and on the cuffs, a yoke across the chest, and a tailored back. Choose from gray heather and rich brown sable. (www.stewartbrown.com)

★ **Hessnatur** designs beautiful apparel, as pure in its creation as it is a pleasure to wear. The velvet jacket, made from 100 percent certified organic cotton from Turkey, has a tailored fit that hits the hips with shaped seams and two buttoning flap pockets. In a caramel taupe color that begs to be touched, this blazer is lined with a high-quality piped finish. (www.hessnatur.com)

★ **Eileen Fisher** Convertible Collar shaped jacket in hemp twill is a natural classic. Woven with bone-white eco-friendly hemp and cotton, this smart blazer is designed with a collar that you can wear up or folded down, princess seams finished with welt pockets, thread-covered buttons, and slits in the back and at the cuff. (www.eileenfisher.com)

THE LITTLE (GREEN) DRESS

Beau Soleil designs simple, chic, and casual dresses fashioned from delectably drapey blends of organic and sustainable fibers that make the mission to "reduce, recycle, renew" a pleasure. The collection calls on sustainable fabrics (such as vegetable-dyed organic cottons, renewable bamboo, and eco-friendly Tencel) that are trimmed and studded with recycled, surplus materials.

Beau Soleil also stands for eco-friendly manufacturing—all of its mill and manufacturing partners are certified fair trade and fair labor and meet strict, eco-friendly European standards. The seasonal collections bring regular renewal with versatile dresses in a pretty palette of colors. (www.shopbeausoleil.com)

> ### FYI
>
> Resist the fashion roller coaster and the fetish of trendy styles. Buy classic pieces that will survive the revolving door of seasonal fads.

ORGANIC WOMEN'S SUITS
Style from Overseas

Yes, purchasing clothing that is made far away takes a greater toll in fuel to ship than those produced domestically, but some imported designs are top shelf in quality and style and thus can live in your wardrobe for decades. Buying fewer things of superhigh quality is a sound green approach.

Amana, based in London, makes clothes that marry beautiful design with ethical production practices. *Amana* means "delivered in trust" in Moroccan Arabic, and these garments are made from certified organic fibers by women artisans working on a fair-trade basis in a mountain village in Morocco. Amana Rima suit jacket and trousers, made from 100 percent organic cotton, have chic style. If you like a more feminine fit, the flattering open neck and collar of Amana Naila suit jacket is right up your alley. Pair this gorgeous cut with Naila suit trousers for the whole 9 yards. Both are dyed black with azo-free dyes. (www.amana-collection.com)

Hessnatur infuses comfort with eco-chic style in its classic charcoal gray jacket and pant set with a subtle check pattern. It's made from a blend of 78 percent organic cotton and 22 percent new wool and is lined with 100 percent organic cotton. The low-cut pants sport a wide, stylish tab waistband. (www.hessnatur.com)

Noir has a signature tailored sexiness and is one of the most stylish and high-end ethical fashion lines. Made from certified organic fabrics, the seasonal collections feature crisp blazers and feminine silhouettes. Noir Cyril cropped blazer in white looks perfect with Noir Demetrius trousers in black. Both are made from Oeko-Tex–certified organic cotton. Noir Cato silver gray jacket is a sharply tailored yet feminine piece that goes perfectly with skinny jeans, wide trousers, or the matching Noir Dan silver gray slim pants. (www.noir-illuminati2.com)

MEN'S ORGANIC BLAZERS: WEAR 'EM WITH PRIDE

Sameunderneath is taking steps toward sustaining our earth with eco-friendly textile and business practices and dashing style. The men's knit blazer is classic, fitted with a casual but sophisticated look. Made from a blend of organic cotton and a little polyester for just the right structure and hang, this blazer sports smart, trimmed lapels, two front flap pockets, three-button cuffs, and a full lining in a contrasting print. (www.sameunderneath.com)

H&M renews its organic collection in seasonal styles, including men's smart-looking blazers in affordable eco-style. Get it on with matching organic cotton slacks and a button-down for put-together sophistication without spending a fortune. (www.hm.com)

RAWGANIQUE THREE-PIECE SUIT
For Men, Hemp Is Hip

Rawganique's Eco-Couture three-piece hemp business suit is simple, elegant, understated, classy, polished, extremely well made, and—most important of all—pure and sustainable. It's made in Europe from organically grown European hemp and produced under sweatshop-free fair-labor practices. Each piece—jacket, vest, and slacks—is available individually in natural, black, and earth brown. The classic three-button styling of the dress jacket is tailored and timeless: Check out the silky organic cotton sateen lining and the subtle padding that creates the perfect, classic shape and look. Choose from straight-leg flat-front hemp slacks with a visible button; or low-rise flat-front hemp slacks, which feature a hidden inside button to keep the zipper up and the front true and flat; or even the low-rise for a modern look. The dapper five-button vest complements this debonair ensemble for a formal style. (www.rawganique.com)

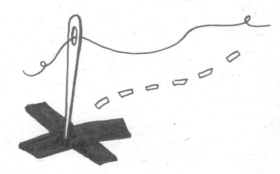

Fibers of the Future

Bagir is quietly leading the garment industry with innovative ecological integrity. As one of the preeminent global manufacturers of suits, Bagir private labels appear in an impressive number of clothing brands, guiding industry needs and trends from fiber and fabric to design and display. Bagir has spearheaded a new generation of two fibers, ECOGIR Recycled and ECOGIR Organic, that are being used throughout their private label brands and in accordance with the corporate mission "to strive to business success while committing to social and environmental values."

ECOGIR Recycled is made from 100 percent recycled postconsumer content, fashioned into cool, trendy men's suit designs, such as in the Covington brand, that you'd never suspect were created from erstwhile discarded PET plastic bottles. It's estimated that about 27 plastic water bottles are reincarnated into each ECOGIR Recycled suit, the development of which is aimed at producing a product that maximizes quality while reducing carbon footprint. ECOGIR Recycled garments reduce the impact on the environment, including significant reduction of CO_2 emissions compared to manufacturing virgin fiber and diverting tons of waste from landfills.

Truly brilliant in form and function, ECOGIR Recycled suits and garments have great structure and wear well long term. Plus they're machine washable, an attribute intentionally designed by Bagir to reduce the environmental impact of dry-cleaning and personal expense typically associated with caring for nice clothes. Bagir's ECOGIR Organic is showing up in brands like Dockers, a Levi Strauss imprint manufactured by Bagir.

ECOGIR Organic products are produced with strict standards for the details and trimmings, including all of the numerous components that go into making an article of clothing, such as the trim and inner linings. Bagir's manufacturing process recycles most of the leftover scraps from cutting to use in the trimmings, which makes good business and ecological sense.

Bagir includes a carbon footprint measure on garment hangtags to identify the amount of energy used to create the garment. Bagir practices transparency in sustainable fiber ventures, which are 100 percent certified by third-party assessment in every step of design and manufacture.

Visit www.bagir.com to learn more about ECOGIR and the numerous brands produced by Bagir. Look on the label for "ECOGIR by Bagir" to know you are in good green hands.

THEY'VE GONE ORGANIC!

Bamford & Sons is a London-based menswear institution selling timeless elegance, refined details in artisan quality, and the perfect combination of form and function. And now they've gone organic! **Bamford & Sons Organic Collection**, made with 100 percent organic cotton, embodies subtle distinction through a portfolio of classic, sophisticated, and relaxed styles. Created with care and responsibility, this intelligent organic collection features fine muslin shirts, raw-edge cotton T-shirts, chalky denim jeans and jackets, canvas trousers, and chinos. (www.bamfordandsons.com)

JOHN PATRICK ORGANIC

Dress It Up

John Patrick Organic evokes the style of the past century with effortlessly chic poise. The sensible yet modish collections are individual and irreverent. Laundered finishes, classic shapes, and muted colors with cohesive style are quietly infused with deeply rooted ethics of agrarian sustainability. The men's clean, classic, soft yet crisp collection is renewed seasonally with a hint of earthy panache. Button-down shirts and vests, jackets and blazers, trousers and slacks, sweaters, and ties are all made with the highest caliber organic and recycled cotton and wool. The women's collection is equally well put together. (www.johnpatrickorganic.com)

NAU MEN'S SHIRTS
Form and Function

Nau is raising the bar for functional, elegant design, offering sporty men's button-downs made from organic cotton, some 100 percent pure and some blended with a bit of spandex for just the right stretch and structure. The Deviant Polo takes a twist on the classic polo. Stay fast and light without sacrificing comfort or style in Nau Triptych Is Shirt. This lightweight piece is made from 99 percent organic cotton and 1 percent spandex for just enough freedom of movement and greater durability. (www.nau.com)

SEACELL MEN'S DRESS SHIRTS: FEED YOUR SKIN
Can you imagine a stylish and sophisticated button-down shirt made from a soft, natural fiber that actually nourishes your skin? The fabric is called **SeaCell**, and it is a luxurious natural fiber woven from nutrient-rich seaweed and combined with eco-friendly lyocell manufacturing technology to yield gorgeous, soft, breathable fabric that actively nourishes your skin: Nutrients such as calcium, magnesium, and vitamin E are released by natural body moisture when the fiber is worn. Numerous international studies confirm the beneficial effects of this fiber, which remains unchanged even after regular washing cycles.

FYI

Vintage and secondhand clothing are often high quality, chic, and inexpensive, and garment reuse gives existing clothing a second life. Plus it's a fabulous way to create a personal style that can't be duplicated.

CASUAL COTTON BUTTON-DOWNS
Easy Does It

Dockers, an easygoing imprint of Levi Strauss, is now featuring a collection of 100 percent cotton organic menswear button-down shirts with casual classic style. The organic oxford shirt is cut for a slightly tailored fit and eco-friendly enzyme washed for softness and a worn-in look—available in stucco white and several plaid patterns. The Peabody organic long-sleeve shirt offers versatile sportswear style with a slightly tailored fit, spread collar, set-on placket of buttons, and buttoned single spade pocket on the chest. The Pikes organic overshirt provides substantial, heavy-weight warmth with soft, broken-in style and an oversize fit for layering. Available in yarn-dyed plaid colors with faux tortoiseshell buttons. (www.dockers.com)

Of the Earth makes casual, short-sleeve button-downs made from 100 percent organic cotton that will keep you cool in comfort and style. The cowboy-style Mod shirt in six solid colors sports snap buttons down the front and on the chest pockets and Asian-inspired embroidery across the back shoulder line. The Western Plaid shirt has snap buttons along the placket and cuffs and western-style tailored chest pockets. Ultracomfy and perfect for backyard barbecues. (www.oftheearth.com)

TOPO RANCH SHIRTS: WEAR 'EM, COWBOY

Topo Ranch believes that greener pastures lead to a brighter future. That's why their western-style of men's button-down shirts are made from 100 percent certified organic cotton. In a well-versed collection of plaids, stripes, and solids in short and long sleeves, Topo Ranch button-down shirts will up your cool factor in eco-friendly cowboy style. Their extremely well-made construction means they're built to last. If spiffy, western-style plaid prints are your speed, choose from long-sleeve classics like Hombre and Truckee. Or keep your cool in lightweight short-sleeve plaids like Baja, Padre Rick, and classic Gingham, most of which come in several colors. (www.toporanch.com)

LADIES' HOODIES

Snuggly and Stylish

★ **Prairie Underground** hoodies are divinely comfy and cut to flatter the female figure. All are made from luscious 100 percent organic cotton fleece, each with standout details and character. Seasonal collections spotlight new pieces alongside tried-and-true styles that stay in demand for good reason. The Prairie hoodie is one of the bestsellers, combining a knee-length sporty style with feminine touches. The Long Cloak hoodie is another favorite—it features a long cut, a nipped-in waist, and gathered front pockets. (www.prairieunderground.com)

★ **Stewart + Brown** Tailored Hoodie is casually stylish, made from 90 percent supersoft organic cotton and 10 percent polyester for just the right fit and hang. Gathered through the chest and sleeves with the feminine yoke, this hoodie features eyelet fastenings and flat metal buttons from waist to just under the chin. (www.stewartbrown.com)

FYI

Donate whatever clothing you can. When you edit your closet, donate the goods you no longer want rather than send them to the landfill. Be considerate and launder garments before donating.

GUYS' AND GALS' HOODIES

Down to Earth, Layered Up

★ **Loomstate** has ongoing seasonal collections of hoodies for men and women, made from the best quality 100 percent organic cotton. Each sports different designs, such as the women's two-tone Rising Sun zip-up hoodie with a stitched outline graphic of the sun, and the men's Act Natural Zip hoodie with a graphic on the back. Both feature front pockets and well-tailored seams. (www.loomstate.org)

★ **Of the Earth** offers relaxed to refined apparel with a reputation for innovative fabrics, superior design, and performance. You'll want to live in their hoodie sweatshirts, made from 100 percent soft organic fleece. The men's Mega hoodie has a zip front and thumb holes inside the cuffs to keep your hands protected. The Cypress jacket is a zip-up terry with clean, crisp style. (www.oftheearth.com)

★ **Threads for Thought** is a casual eco-fashion brand focused on a lifestyle of movement, sustainability, and awareness for the planet. All Threads for Thought garments are produced from organic and recycled materials in certified fair-trade environments, and they offer hoodies for men and women made from 100 percent organic cotton in a nice range of colors and graphic prints. These guys even donate 2 percent of *sales*, not just profits, to two charitable concerns. (www.threadsforthought.com)

WOMEN'S OUTERWEAR JACKETS

Wrap Up Green

★ **Loomstate** Thorn peacoat is a classic, midweight, double-breasted peacoat made from 82 percent organic cotton and 18 percent recycled polyester for versatile seasonal comfort. It's fashioned with two hand pockets and cinchable sleeves with buckle straps. (www.loomstate.org)

★ **Grace & Cello** Isabella jacket is chic and versatile; it will never go out of style. Made from black recycled wool in a traditional double-breasted peacoat cut, it stands at three-quarter length with a dashing motorcycle-style collar for extra warmth. Grace & Cello Awnee jacket makes a sharp, snappy statement with a contrast of color—upper half in cream and lower half in black—made from recycled wool. (www.gracecello.com)

★ **Stewart + Brown** long-sleeve mini-trench is a fleecy, cropped revamp of a classic trench made from organic cotton. It has button folding pockets, an extrawide collar, and a ruched seam just under the bust that creates a sweet, feminine fit that hits at the hip. Or dash around town in the organic cotton swing jacket, a simple cut with a foldover collar lined with hemp silk. (www.stewartbrown.com)

★ The **Emily Katz** Portland swing coat, made from 100 percent organic water-resistant cotton fleece, is a catch. The beautiful blend of vintage and modern style is versatile enough to dress up or down. (www.emilykatz.com)

★ If edgy style is your thing, the **FIN** jet-black biker jacket, made from 100 percent fair-trade certified organic cotton, is a foxy find. The two-way front zipper zips on the bias, and zipper cuffs convey chic, sophisticated attitude. FIN is a carbon-neutral company headquartered in Oslo, Norway. (www.finoslo.com/en)

FYI

Be a conscious consumer. Less is more—buy fewer things of higher quality to get the most for your money and to conserve the planet's resources.

MEN'S JACKETS AND COATS

Sustainably Macho

★ **Loomstate**'s classic American style and respect for the planet are evident and in accord in the Hawkeye jacket, a zip-and-snap, anorak-style, hooded piece of versatile comfort. It's made from 82 percent organic cotton and 18 percent recycled polyester for water resistance and windproof action. Loomstate Roman Surplus Winter Army jacket sports a midweight distressed style with an organic cotton canvas exterior. The warm recycled poly fill is lined with a diamond-quilted sateen interior and a plush trim neck for warmth and comfort. Loomstate's seasonal collections are continuously supplemented with new styles. (www.loomstate.org)

★ **Nau** is an eco-savvy company that is something like a cross between Patagonia and Prada. Performance, style, and sustainability are the name of Nau's game. The riding jacket is tailored and clean, an eco-friendly update that honors its roots in English riding jackets with moto style and minimalism. This dialed-in fit made from recycled poly fabric is highly breathable yet wind and water resistant, making it the ultimate all-in-one piece for work, travel, and play. The double-weave, postconsumer recycled polyester soft shell has four-way stretch and matte finish to shed wind, water, dirt, lint, and even pet hair. The brushed interior disperses moisture to help keep your cool, even under duress. And it's machine washable. (www.nau.com)

NO SNOW REQUIRED

Burning Torch Snow Camo coat is one of the most ingeniously stylish pieces around. Made from 100 percent recycled snow camouflage, this one-of-a-kind, lightweight coat is printed with Burning Torch designs, specially washed and hand-detailed. It's the perfect windbreaker or daily-wear coat, fashioned with a figure-flattering belt. (www.burningtorchinc.com)

FAUX, FAIR-LABOR FUR

Indulge your inner need for furry luxury without harming animals. **Loyale**'s Costilla jacket flaunts gorgeous vegan faux fur in bone white, made from 100 percent organic cotton. Lined with 100 percent organic twill, this jacket features a generous collar, front pockets, and faux tortoiseshell buttons. It falls to high thigh. Designed by the one and only Jenny Hwa, founder and senior designer of Loyale, and crafted in New York City with fair-labor practices. (www.loyaleclothing.com)

FYI

Cut up old cotton clothing to use as household rags. One hundred percent cotton T-shirts, sweatshirts, sweatpants, flannel garments, and socks are the best candidates.

LADIES RAINCOATS AND JACKETS

Greenin' in the Rain

★ **Emily Katz** Wow rain jacket could have been the muse for Leonard Cohen's song "Famous Blue Raincoat." The signature style and elegance that this all-weather coat brings to your wardrobe is sound reason to sing. Emily Katz is a native of Portland, Oregon, and she clearly knows about rain and how to stay stylish under gray skies. Water resistant, wind resistant, and made from recycled polyester with a white, soft organic cotton fleecy lining—no wonder it's called Wow. (www.emilykatz.com)

★ **Nau** Urbane jacket is the quintessence of form and function, elegance enveloped in a recycled polyester shell with chic style. This waterproof, windproof, breathable beauty is woven from two layers of stretch fabric made from postconsumer and postindustrial sources with a matte finish in a sophisticated dobby-weave texture. It's even machine washable, and tumble-drying on low heat will rejuvenate water repellency. (www.nau.com)

★ **Eileen Fisher** Eco-Poly hooded anorak reflects the simplicity, creativity, and delight through design that Eileen Fisher is known and loved for. Made from 100 percent recycled polyester, which reflects the designer's mission to guide Eileen Fisher products and practices toward sustaining the environment with responsible business, this classic water- and wind-resistant anorak is simple and stylish in an earthy mussel color. (www.eileenfisher.com)

WOMEN'S LONG AND LUXE COATS
Bundle Up, Eco-Style

★ **Grace & Cello** proffers eco-gorgeous, elegant, and sharp designs ethically produced in Canada. Drawing from a portfolio of materials that have a minimal impact on the environment, Grace & Cello's chic and classy collections are updated seasonally with fashionable designs that won't go out of style. Grace & Cello wool coats are classic and elegant; made from 80 percent recycled wool to keep you warm and in eco-vogue. (www.gracecello.com)

★ **Kelly B** Taylor trench coat is a classic, heavy-weight, double-breasted trench made from 100 percent organic cotton fleece. Proudly made in the USA. (www.kellybcouture.com)

★ **Rebe** coats are classic, modern, and eco-chic, made from recycled fibers, including repurposed cotton and polyester, with fantastic and flattering cuts. The Maryanne coat is their bestseller. The Hazel coat is feminine and practical. Both are available in six rich colors. (www.myrebe.com)

★ **FIN** is exquisite, made with elegance and style, expertly fusing design and awareness in fashion. FIN pleated trench coat is elegantly classic yet modern and sophisticated. It's also beautifully feminine and feels luxuriously soft. Made from 100 percent organic cotton in black. FIN is a carbon-neutral company headquartered in Oslo, Norway. (www.finoslo.com/en)

★ **Stewart + Brown** make bundling up eco-chic and stylish. The Shine Trim duffle coat is versatile and cozy, made from organic cotton fleece lined with silky smooth hemp silk. (www.stewartbrown.com)

FYI

Store your threads carefully. Taking care of clothing and storing it properly will grant it the longest life possible, especially as the seasons change and your wardrobe changes, too.

Put a Green Foot Forward

Fashionistas with a shoe fetish are not the only ones who will bask in the beauty of **Form & Fauna**'s gorgeously chic shoes made from sustainable and renewable materials. They're comfy and designed for living, working, walking, and standing in sustainable style. Handcrafted in the USA, the fashion-forward collection is designed with a "less is more" philosophy: Let's all buy fewer things that are built to last longer. Working with materials that are ethically produced and sustainably derived and constantly upgrading components with better alternatives, Form & Fauna taps into many fabulous mediums: the best quality Italian synthetics with the highest environmental ethic of any coagulate producer ("no noxious substances in final products, biodegradable, and in cases of combustion, do not spread toxic gases"); organic hemp fabric; heels made from bamboo and regenerative wood; outsoles made from rubber latex or compressed fermented oak; insole boards made from recycled fiber; plush yet breathable eco-liners; and water-based glues. Each season brings fresh styles and pragmatic designs. (www.formandfauna.com)

Look for low-impact-dyed garments and those that have been whitened without chlorine:

LADIES, BAMBOO UNDERWEAR

Ultimate Eco-Undies

Bamboo fabric is sumptuously soft, comfortable, and breathable—ideal qualities for intimate undergarments. Bamboo fiber wicks moisture brilliantly (four times more than cotton) and is a thermal regulator, which means it will keep you cool in warm weather. Bamboo even prevents odors due to its mineral content, its ability to absorb moisture, and its natural antibacterial properties.

Cosabella, a leading designer of intimate apparel manufactured in Italy, presents its Bamboo and Eden collections designed in an ecologically innovative bamboo fiber and micro-Modal blend. Cosabella has sourced a bamboo fiber that has been rigorously tested to meet international environmental standards and can be considered a fully natural fabric. Cosabella's Bamboo collection features three cuts for the bottoms (bikinis, thongs, and hot pants) and two styles of camisoles. The Eden collection presents low-rider thongs as well as some cute tops. (www.cosabella.com)

Spun Bamboo offers simple and sensuously soft Panty Boo undergarments made from a perfect blend of organic, panda-safe bamboo and organic cotton. These high-quality undergarments are available in three styles: low-rise bikini, high-leg brief, and thong. Athletically oriented women should also note the spun bamboo women's sports bra, made of 70 percent organic bamboo, 25 percent organic cotton, and 5 percent spandex. (www.bambooclothes.com)

MEN'S ORGANIC UNDERWEAR

Eco-Savvy Undergear

★ **American Apparel**'s Sustainable Edition organic baby-rib men's briefs are an organic version of their best-selling nonorganic original. Made from 100 percent organic cotton with an elastic waistband and trim, these babies come at a wallet-friendly price. (http://store.americanapparel.net)

★ **Calvin Klein** has gotten hip to the organic trick with a collection of dapper natural hip briefs and boxer briefs made from organic cotton and fitted with an organic waistband and a functional fly pouch contour. (www.calvinklein.com)

★ **Red Dog** Eco Sportswear introduces Eco-Sport boxer briefs, trunks, and sports briefs. Made with SKAL certified organic cotton (exclusive of trim), these supersoft skivvies offer comfortable and supportive cuts for active men. Red Dog uses low-impact, eco-friendly dyes to print the waistband. (www.reddogsportswear.com)

★ **Patagonia** champions a flock of eco-u-trou made from 100 percent recycled polyester for moisture-wicking performance and quick drying. Choose from briefs, boxers, and boxer briefs in a bunch of different colors. All can be recycled through Patagonia's Common Threads Program. (www.patagonia.com)

★ **Osaj** men's boxers and briefs are made in the USA from 100 percent unbleached organic cotton. The boxers are available in classic sateen and flannel, and the briefs offer supportive form. (www.osaj.com)

★ **Rawganique** organic cotton boxers are made entirely in the United States and Europe under fair-labor conditions and are available in flannel and sateen. Rawganique hemp boxers are made in Europe with fair labor and processed without chemicals of any kind. They're available in two styles: eco-classic and Euro-style original with a narrow waistband. (www.rawganique.com)

★ **Spun Bamboo** makes two of the most comfortable boxers you'll ever find. They're made from a blend of 70 percent organic, panda-safe bamboo and 30 percent organic cotton jersey. Choose from spun bamboo men's boxers in a classic, straight cut or men's two-button-fly boxer briefs, which offer freedom of movement along with the support necessary for an active lifestyle. (www.bambooclothes.com)

LINGERIE
Sustainably Sexy

Sustainable has never looked so sexy when lingerie is made from sensuous, eco-friendly materials. Perfectly Imperfect offers hot and cool lingerie made from organic cotton with lace details. Their Lace Wrap panty and thong and Sweetie Lace cami and chemise come in jewel tones like berry and teal. Ivory and chocolate Sporty Boy shorts are trimmed in black and blue. Nighties and the flirty, ruffle-bottomed Sunday cami dress are perfect for covering up just enough. And they're made in the USA. (www.piorganic.com)

Cosabella presents the Devon collection, a bevy of organic lingerie with gorgeous lace and soft-as-a-petal feel, made from 100 percent organic cotton. The simply elegant bra offers sumptuous support and matches your choice of a low-cut thong or string bikini, all detailed with lovely lace in just the right places. (www.cosabella.com)

Enamore infuses eco-under-there with irresistible va-va-voom. The Anabel Ruched Shorty set is a flirty camisole and short set made from a crisp, white organic stretch silk, and the Sophia Ruffled Shorty set is a black set made from stretch soybean and organic cotton jersey. Release your inner animal in the Bedrock Betty bra and knicker set (soft bra and knickers) or sleep short set (camisole and shorties) in a racy leopard print made from soft, bamboo jersey. Made in the United Kingdom. (www.enamore.co.uk)

Ever heard of pine fiber lingerie? G=9.8 is a French lingerie company producing beautiful undergarments out of recycled pine fiber, which is enzymatically processed into a sustainable, soft material. The company's name represents the constant acceleration of the earth's attraction, or in other words, gravity. The G=9.8 Triangle bra is made from 94 percent recycled pine fiber and 6 percent spandex. It's comfy and adorable with elastic crossover straps in the back and pairs perfectly with the boy shorts fashioned with lace detailing. And the thigh-high tights leave just enough to be desired. (www.organiclingerie.fr)

WOMEN'S ORGANIC COTTON UNDERWEAR
Simple Styles

Soft, comfy, and kind to the earth, certified organic cotton underwear is a simple, sustainable, and sexy secret worth sharing. Blue Canoe has been perfecting organic cotton underthings for over a decade and offers styles for sensible, sustainable comfort while pampering your feminine side. Choose from a low-cut lace panty or boy shorts, both made from a lightweight blend of 90 percent organic cotton and 10 percent spandex. For ultrasoft, ultralight, barely there comfort with just enough spandex for gentle support, Sheer Body is just what you're looking for. Choose from sheer low-cut panty, thong, high-cut panty, and boy shorts, also made from a blend of 90 percent organic cotton and 10 percent spandex. If you are a purist who prefers 100 percent organic cotton without the spandex stretch, Blue Canoe's Just Cotton collection is naturally soft, cool, and comfortable. (www.bluecanoe.com)

American Apparel Sustainable Edition presents 100 percent organic cotton underwear that is friendly to the earth and your wallet. Choose from two styles: organic baby-rib flat bottom panty, with a low-rise 1970s appeal and elastic trim, and organic baby-rib thong that looks and feels sensational. (http://store.americanapparel.net)

Louella Bloom Organic Dainties specializes in cute and comfy organic hipsters, boy shorts, and thongs made from a blend of organic cotton and soy and a bit of spandex for the perfect fit. For supreme comfort, no elastic is used. Made locally by a cooperative of women in need. (www.louellabloom.etsy.com)

Osaj Intimates integrate the finest organic cotton with simple, sensual design. Choose from four styles (low-cut, hi-cut, briefs, and thong) created domestically from 100 percent unbleached organic cotton. (www.osaj.com)

In 1900 the automobile was brand-new, and all the latest models were on display in New York City at the very first National Automobile Show. Even though there were fewer than 500 cars in New York State at the time, some 60,000 people turned out to see the invention that would replace the horse.

The cosmopolitan visitors to that show were polled, and they overwhelmingly chose electric as their first choice for automobile travel, followed closely by steam. Gasoline ran a distant third, getting only 5 percent of the vote. There were 1,681 steam, 1,575 electric, and only 936 gasoline cars made that year.

Now we're at a similar crossroads. At today's auto shows, electric battery cars sit alongside hybrids, plug-ins, and fuel-cell vehicles. And again, no one technology has a clear lead, reflecting considerable uncertainty as the world's energy picture goes through rapid and profound changes. Under the twin specters of climate change and peak-price oil, the 21st century will of necessity be a time of big decisions—by governments and by us as global citizens.

Energy experts agree that we cannot continue to burn fossil fuels—coal, oil, and natural gas—at our current accelerating pace. World consumption of oil grows 1 percent each year. In 2007 the world used 85.7 million barrels of oil per day, and that number is expected to jump to 118 million barrels per day by 2030 under current projections. As demand grows faster than supply, oil prices will rise once again—and then are expected to stay high.

To understand why we're using more oil every year, take a look at China, whose auto industry is growing at the fastest rate in the world. There were fewer than 2 million private cars in China in 1996; in 2007 there were 35 million.

The Chinese obviously have the same right to drive alone to work as the rest of the world, but if they do, the environmental consequences will be devastating, especially in terms of the greenhouse-warming gases those cars will emit. But when it comes to auto dependence, the United States leads the way.

A 1982 children's book called *The Kids' Whole Future Catalog* imagined that by 2000, surely, we'd have replaced our gas guzzlers with the full range of low- and zero-pollution transportation, from battery electrics to fuel cells. What's holding us back is a national commitment like the one that built the hugely effective national rail link that peaked in 1920, when there were 300,000 miles of federally regulated track. There's only half that now. The automobile has divided and conquered like no invention before it.

In 2008, public transit ridership was the highest it had been in 52 years, reports the American Public Transportation Association (APTA). Cities are expanding bus lines, putting in light-rail, and building bike paths. But all the activity masks how far we have to go to curtail our dependency on cars. A recent US Department of Transportation survey showed that of the billion trips a day Americans make, 900 million were by car and just 19 million by public transit (though the latter number is rising).

Automobile showrooms are featuring green options, including newly viable battery-powered electric cars. Hydrogen fuel cells and other future technologies are said to be just around the corner (but don't hold your breath). The *Wall Street Journal*'s Joseph B. White notes rather pessimistically, "An automobile revolution is coming—but it's traveling in the slow lane. . . . This revolution will take years to pull off." By summer of 2009, however, electric cars were headed to the showrooms.

In the meantime, consider the alternatives. Americans lead the world in bike ownership but are somewhere near the bottom in actual bike use. Is your bike in the back of the garage on flat tires? Time to get it out again. Riding your bike benefits the environment because the only emissions are your exhalation of carbon dioxide. You will increase heart and lung function, get the same aerobic workout you would from jogging, and build stronger leg muscles.

Walking reduces your risk of heart attack and type 2 diabetes, helps lower your blood pressure, and can, of course, get you back in touch with your waistline. There are walking trails right-around the corner, and city pavement yields a good walkabout, too.

The Onion, a satiric publication that delights in revealing hard truths through parody, ran a story entitled "98 Percent of U.S. Commuters Favor Public Transportation for Others." Citing a fictitious APTA report, it noted that four out of five Americans recognize the need for "everyone else" to take the train or the bus.

A lot of cities now have light-rail systems, which are ideal for commuting, and light-rail is on the agendas of many planning agencies. Americans are also developing a new appreciation for what Amtrak offers, and new routes may help make up for what was lost during the decline of rail travel.

Don't forget the bus, the redheaded stepchild of American transit. APTA figures reveal that more than 60 percent of public transportation trips are made on buses, despite the fact that transit agencies routinely shortchange bus service in favor of rail and other services. Bus routes are mature in most American communities, and chances are you can walk to a stop.

Car sharing offers an opportunity to have the convenience of a car without actually owning one. Carpooling and van pooling are coming back as great ways to get to work, and telecommuting is more viable than ever as work-at-home technology improves. The greener options are there if you look!

—Jim Motavalli

TOYOTA PRIUS

High Standards

Back in 1999, the editor of a prominent American car magazine declared that the Toyota Prius, already a moderate hit in Japan then, would fail in America. It was too complicated, not big enough, and clueless when it came to towing large recreational vehicles and big boats. Further, nobody cared about fuel economy.

Instead, the Prius, especially in its second-generation, 2004-to-2009 version, caught on big-time. Toyota has sold more than 600,000 Priuses in the US since 2000. The redesigned 2010 Prius is crucial to Toyota's fortunes. It's much improved, says the company, which really piled on the innovative features, many of them standard. The car got more power (134 horsepower) from an engine that grew from 1.4 to 1.8 liters, but despite that, it achieves an overall 50 miles per gallon. Prices start at $21,000, though that is for a stripped-down fleet car—consumer models are more like $23,000.

The third-generation Prius is not a big departure from the second. It's the same basic shape but with a nose more in line with current company designs—it's almost Yaris-like. The key to getting that improved gas mileage is a really slippery shape, with a .25 coefficient of drag. That means a steeply raked windshield, which creates an ideal space for Toyota's new Touch Tracer system, which puts vital information at eye level to prevent distraction. The optional sunroof solar panel, which supplies power to the ventilation system, keeps your car's interior cool while it's parked on a hot day. The key fob can also start up the air conditioner a few minutes before you get in the car.

Push the "EV" button, and the 2010 Prius has a 1-mile battery-only cruising range. It's a preview of what drivers will be able to do with the forthcoming Toyota plug-in hybrid. The "LKA" button is for Lane Keep Assist. Drift out of your lane, and the Prius uses a bit of torque steer to get you back in line (while also sounding an alarm in case you're falling asleep).

Standard safety features include vehicle stability control, traction control, brake assist, ABS, and electronic brake force distribution. There are seven airbags, and in the event of a collision, the active headrests come up to cushion your head while the seat belts tighten. Get in that fender bender and an OnStar-like Safety Connect system triggers a phone call from Toyota headquarters to make sure you're okay.

All this comes in a car with a very low carbon footprint. Toyota guarantees that its nickel-metal-hydride battery pack will get recycled, too. (www.toyota.com/prius-hybrid)

Fuel Economy in Real Time

Fuel economy starts with awareness. If your car gives you no way to track your mileage in real time, consider a plug-in device like the fuel economy computer known as **ScanGauge II**, which tracks that information, along with other useful data such as engine speed. It can turn off that pesky "check engine" light, too. The compact three-in-one (trip computer, digital gauge set, scan tool) computer costs $169 including shipping and is easily moved from one car to another. It works with all 1996 and newer vehicles, including hybrids. (www.scangauge.com)

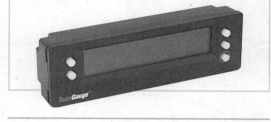

ULTRA MOTOR A2B

The Electrifying Bicycle

Electric bicycles have had trouble finding a niche in the American market, but they're getting a second look as urban commuting vehicles and auto alternatives. The new lithium-ion-battery-powered Ultra Motor A2B ($2,500) weighs 73 pounds and has a 40-mile range (if you buy the optional secondary battery pack). The range is extended if you provide some pedal assist to get the bike up to cruising range. And, of course, you can always pedal it home if it runs out of juice. The 500-watt motor offers surprisingly peppy performance at speeds of up to 20 mph. (http://ultramotor.com)

ELECTRIC SCOOTERS: CHARGING AROUND

Love the idea of a wind-in-the-face motorcycle that will save you gobs of money on commuting costs, but hate all the noise and tailpipe fumes? Have we got a choice for you!

Electric scooters are coming of age, and there are a dozen on the market, from Vectrix, ZAP, eGo, eMoto, and Skeuter. One popular choice is the EVT America Z-20b ($2,499, including charger), which can reach speeds of 45 mph, with a range of 30 to 45 miles on a charge to its 12-volt batteries. It can carry two riders (though range and speed will suffer), with storage room under the seat. The upgraded Z-30 ($2,750), with a larger motor for better torque and climbing ability, is also available. (www.evtamerica.com)

BMW 128I COUPE

Back to the Basics

If cars are cold, hard, steel juggernauts of power and potential destruction, why do we have such emotional reactions to them? Why do we like them so much? Well, the best cars do have personalities and even a certain quality of soul. Just ask any Italian Ferrari or Alfa fan, who gets as worked up about these vehicles as they do about a primo red wine.

BMW has made some brilliant cars, especially the legendary 2002 model. It was popular precisely because it was basic and quick. It was better than every sedan on the market in the late 1960s because North American cars of that era handled so badly. But then BMW went bigger, heavier, and more expensive, even offering big SUVs and the opulence of 12-cylinder models like the 760Li. It's safe to say the company lost the thread. But the newest BMW incarnation, the $26,000 128i coupe, is moving back in the right direction. It's cheerful, unpretentious, and fun to drive, gets 28 mpg on the highway, and is stirred by a great six-speed transmission (auto or manual) that makes it a really relaxed highway cruiser. The 24-valve six-banger generates some 230 hp at 6,500 rpm. The rear-wheel-drive 128i has some sophisticated standard features to keep it on the road, including dynamic stability control, traction control, and more. You'll have as much fun with 6 cylinders as the 760Li has with 12. (www.bmwusa.com)

CHEVROLET VOLT

Will It Jump-Start GM?

Will the Chevrolet Volt save General Motors? Probably not. It will be a niche vehicle, initially selling no more than 50,000 a year (and that only if prices can be kept down). But what a concept, and what a shift for one of the industry's most conservative (and beleaguered) automakers!

The 2010 Volt is the first series hybrid on the market. What's a series hybrid? Well, think of a battery electric car with a range extender that in this case is a small gasoline engine. The motor isn't connected to the wheels; instead, it drives a generator to keep the batteries charged for as much as 350 miles. With the latest generation of lithium-ion batteries, the car is designed to travel 40 miles on battery power alone. Since the average American commute is 33 miles round-trip, that could mean a lot of electric travel.

"For someone who drives less than 40 miles a day, Chevy Volt will use zero gasoline and produce zero emissions," says GM. The car could also be called a plug-in hybrid, since the batteries can be recharged by plugging into house current overnight.

The Volt was first shown in 2007, and it became the talk of the industry. The finished car was unveiled in the fall of 2008. According to Michael Simcoe, GM's exterior design chief, "The design is different from the show car mostly because of the need for greater aerodynamics to get the 40-mile battery range."

The Volt is definitely a "halo" product for a company that could use some good publicity. The four-door Volt is expected to run close to $40,000, but high costs could push that estimate higher. (www.chevrolet.com/electriccar)

FOLDING BIKES
Ride It 'n' Hide It

It's a rather ridiculous catch-22. Some rush-hour trains and buses refuse to let their passengers bring bicycles aboard, thus thwarting this environmentally friendly form of commuting at the point where it would become intermodal and very practical.

Cities such as Portland, Oregon, have addressed this problem by putting bike racks on buses and offering space for bikers on the light-rail systems. There's another approach: Folding bicycles have been around for decades, but they're getting much better both as bikes and as objects you have to lug around. A few brands to consider:

Brompton bikes ($1,000 and up) are a bit pricey, but they are high quality and, despite being equipped with a rack and fenders, fold into an easily carried package 22 inches by 23 inches by 11 inches. Weight is between 20 and 28 pounds. The company has been making them for more than 15 years.

Dahon bikes are the industry leader, capturing more than two-thirds of the market in the United States. The company produces very light 20- to 26-inch folding bikes (made in Taiwan and China) that start at $350 (the budget Boardwalk) and climb to $3,000.

Montague Corporation makes the Swiss-Bike TX ($629), which is full-sized and rides like a normal bike but folds to fit in the trunk of a small car. The concept is to drive part way to work then bike the rest of the way.

There are many other folding bikes on the market. Find them online at www.optimalride.com/folding-bicycles.

Bike Tune-Up Time

Bicycle fanatic Jim Langley, author of *Your Home Bicycle Workshop* (Bicycle Aficionado Press), maintains a helpful Web site at www.jimlangley.net. His online Basic Bike Care guide makes these important recommendations:

★ **PUMP IT UP.** Bike tires lose air: It's a fact of life. Road bike tires will soften in a week; mountain bikes in a month. If you ride with soft tires, you can damage rims, tubes, or tires on potholes or rocks. It's a good idea, then, to check road bike tires before every ride and mountain bike tires weekly.

★ **LUBE IT OR LOSE IT.** Your chain and pivot points on brakes and derailleurs need to be regularly lubricated with a light oil such as Triflow. Chains that are shiny and squeaking need to receive a light coat of oil. Spinning parts with bearings (including wheels and pedals) should be dismantled and repacked with grease about once a year. Unless you're adept, leave this to your bike shop mechanic.

★ **KEEP IT CLEAN.** Mountain bikes, especially, get filthy and need to be sprayed down. To avoid getting water into vital bearings, spray from above, not from the side. Then fill a bucket with water, add some environmentally friendly cleaner, and scrub down with a sponge.

★ **STORE IT.** Bicycles should be stored inside, if possible. Although a covered porch might seem fine, moisture in the air will corrode the bike's metal parts. If space is a problem, consider mounting the bike on an interior wall with a vinyl-covered bike hook. "These provide convenient storage while displaying the bike like a work of art," Langley writes.

★ **INSPECT IT.** If you ride infrequently, a monthly checkup is probably OK. Heavier riders should schedule weekly inspections. Take a look at the brake pads—if the grooves have disappeared, it's time for new pads. Operate the brakes and shift lever and closely inspect all four cables on both ends for signs of fraying, cracks, or rusting. Check key bolts (seat, seatpost, wheel quick release, stem and handlebars, brakes and shift lever) to make sure they're still tight. Tighten clipless pedal screws and bolts that attach accessories.

FORD ESCAPE
America's First Hybrid

The **Ford Motor Company** lost $2.7 billion in 2007, which is an improvement from 2006 (when it lost $12.6 billion). The financial problems have probably killed Ford's goal of producing 250,000 hybrid vehicles a year by 2010.

Ford has talked about hybrid versions of vehicles including the Ford Edge, Mercury Montego, and Lincoln MKX. The Ford Fusion and Mercury Milan hybrids were new for 2009.

Ford was, however, the first American carmaker with a hybrid, the small Escape SUV (34 mpg city/30 mpg highway for the two-wheel-drive version in 2008). The car has been a bright spot in recent dismal sales results but was down in 2009 along with the rest of the market.

The Escape (the Mercury Mariner is similar) was given rounder styling in 2008, which includes a new front spoiler that reduces aerodynamic drag and increases fuel economy. In the hybrid version, a 2.3-liter, four-cylinder engine is coupled with two electric motors and an electronically controlled continuously variable transmission (CVT) to produce 155 hp.

Improvements to the Escape's battery pack mean it can now reach 40 mph in electric mode (it was 30 mph). Like the Prius, the Escape shuts off automatically at stoplights, and this process has been smoothed out, so that there is less shudder than in previous models.

The Escape uses some technology from the Toyota Prius, and it's better for it, being generally more sophisticated and fuel friendly than its main domestic competitor, the Saturn Vue Green Line. Prices start at $27,445. (www.fordvehicles.com/suvs/escapehybrid)

FYI

That cargo pod on the roof of your minivan is shaving up to 5 percent off your fuel economy. Do your car a favor and store the darned thing in your garage.

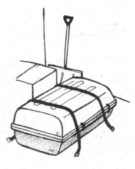

HONDA FIT
Great Mileage, Fun Ride

The **Honda** Fit was already one of the most versatile and fuel-efficient cars on the market, but redesigned for 2009 it got a little bit bigger and even better. The subcompact starts at $14,550 for the base model and $16,060 for the Sport, which adds jazzy-looking trim and a paddle-shifting option.

The key to understanding the four-door Fit is usable space. It's only 13 feet long, but it has 90.8 cubic feet of passenger volume and 20.6 cubic feet of rear cargo area. The rear seats accommodate three passengers easily enough, but they also fold down in multiple ways, and on the new car they can dive down flat to the floor without the need to remove the headrests. You can and will move large, bulky things that would challenge a station wagon.

The Fit compares well against its main competitor, the Toyota Yaris. It's far more versatile and considerably more fun to drive. The steering is particularly sharp, and the Fit benefits from a sporty suspension featuring MacPherson struts in the front, torsion beams in the rear. And the optional electronic stability control will keep everything well balanced. It also boasts better-than-average brakes.

The Fit's 117 hp, 1.5-liter, four-cylinder engine is slightly more powerful than the earlier car's, but fuel economy is actually improved at 28 mpg city/35 mpg highway for manual models. Adding an automatic doesn't carry too much of a penalty, as the mileage figures are still 27/33. Also impressive is the fact that the Fit was rated an ultra-low emission vehicle (ULEV-2) by the California regulators. (http://automobiles.honda.com/fit)

BMW HYDROGEN 7
Luxury + H2

Yes, there is a production car running on hydrogen in the United States, but only the very lucky are able to park one in the garage. There are just 40 Hydrogen 7 BMWs on the road here. These vehicles can switch back and forth between burning hydrogen and gasoline with a flick of the "H2" button, and the only difference is a slight increase in noise from the fuel injection.

These cars carry trunk-mounted, superinsulated, reinforced tanks of liquid hydrogen. And brrr, this gas liquefies at −423°F. To run smoothly on hydrogen, the big V-12 is detuned to 260 hp. Despite this, it still tops out at a speed-limited 143 mph, and it reaches 60 mph in just under 10 seconds. There is an exhaust pipe, but emissions from it are almost negligible—the Hydrogen 7 is almost as clean as a fuel-cell car.

There are no sacrifices for hydrogen power. This is a 7-Series BMW, with such functions as soft-close doors, a rear-seat TV monitor with six-DVD changer, a car telephone, and (only Europeans would do this) a "smoker package." And, oh yes, if there's even a tiny hydrogen leak, the door locks glow red and the car sends a GPS-backed text message to BMW headquarters. (www.bmwusa.com)

NOVICA CHESS BOARD: TURNING GEARS INTO GAMES

Let's face it, the car is among our more recyclable products; even so, human ingenuity is doing a bit more for the cause. Armando Ramirez, for instance, pondered the issue and decided to recycle auto parts into a rather fantastic (and heavy at 20 pounds) chess set, available from www.novica.com. The $224.95 chess set turns spark plugs into bishops and gears into castles. Horses' manes are made from galvanized wire; bases from ignition parts. The queen has legs that began life in the electrical system, and the king's cross is made of nails. The artist notes, "Smudges and scratches may be present."

THE HONDA INSIGHT
Look Out, Prius!

There are winners and losers in the hybrid race. The first two generations of the Toyota Prius reached an incredible 757,000 cars (630,000 of them 2004 and beyond) on the road by fall 2008. Honda sold only 277,000 hybrids total in the period, despite being first out of the gate in the United States (1999) with the two-seater Insight. Although the Insight was a dedicated hybrid like the Prius (and achieved fuel economy of better than 70 mpg on the highway), its limited seating and bare-bones accommodations turned off buyers.

But now the Honda Insight is back as an approximately $18,000 five-passenger hatch-back Prius fighter, and it's much better looking this time (sharing styling with the company's sleek FCX Clarity hydrogen fuel-cell car). The platform is all new, with the battery pack and controller safely tucked away below the cargo area. As with the earlier Insight and Civic Hybrid, the new generation of the Integrated Motor Assist system runs mainly on the gas engine and uses the electric motor as a booster.

Honda has huge ambitions for new Insight sales, anticipating a not-impossible 100,000 a year in North America (half of the worldwide sales). Honda spokesman Chris Naughton says the original Insight, beloved of "hypermilers" working on "can you top this?" fuel economy, "made a few people very happy." The new model could make a lot of people very happy and get the company a long way to its goal of 500,000 hybrid sales a year. The United States, Japan, and Europe are targeted. (http://automobiles.honda.com/insight-hybrid)

Smart Tips for Fuel Savers

Bizarrely, tire pressure became an issue in the 2008 presidential election. But go to the Department of Energy's site Fuel economy.gov, and it proclaims: "You can improve your gas mileage by around 3.3 percent by keeping your tires inflated to the proper pressure. Underinflated tires can lower gas mileage by 0.4 percent for every one psi [pound per square inch] drop in pressure of all four tires."

Underinflated tires have more rolling resistance, and their tread life goes down something like 25 percent because of uneven wear. Steering and cornering are also negatively affected.

To check your tires, you need a handheld gauge, because few stations with an air pump have any way of measuring pressure. Add some air, check pressure, add some more. Refer to the vehicle owner's manual for correct tire pressures. Overinflation is bad, too, because the tire has less contact with the road surface. Overinflated tires ride harsher, transmit more noise, and can get damaged more easily.

You can take further steps to save gas:

★ AVOID JACKRABBIT STARTS. Smoking your tires, putting the pedal to the metal, and then jamming on the brakes wastes fuel by as much as 33 percent at highway speeds and 5 percent around town.

★ DON'T BE A LEAD FOOT. Observing the speed limit pays off at the pump. Every 5 mph you drive over 60 is like adding 30 cents a gallon to your gas bill.

★ DEJUNK THE TRUNK. Beware, cargo has a fuel bill attached. If you're carrying around an extra 100 pounds, mileage will go down by 2 percent. Get rid of that box of old books you're saving for your next trip to Goodwill.

★ AVOID EXCESSIVE IDLING. This is a particular fuel waster if you have a big vehicle.

A couple of other things that are good for the planet: Use your cruise control, because it maintains a constant speed. Don't warm up your car in the winter—can't you just be cold for a few minutes? Warming the engine is not necessary for your car's health. (www.edmunds.com/reviews/list/top10)

NISSAN CUBE

Electric Commuting

Electric cars have been thin on the ground until recently. But as fuel prices climb and battery technology improves, that's slated to change. Nissan will have its first mainstream electric car available for fleet customers by 2010 and to the general public by 2012. With the notable exception of GM's EV1, no major manufacturer has sold a battery-powered car in the United States since the 1920s. The fact that Nissan believes it can do this profitably now shows how far we've come.

According to the online Motor Authority, the car will have a conventional electric motor in the front, but the company is also working with small 20 hp motors in each of the four wheels (a version that could be on the market by 2015). In concept vehicles such as the Mixim and Cube, Nissan has worked with lithium-ion batteries, so those are a virtual certainty, too. The boxy Cube has both gasoline and battery versions.

Auto Week says the electric car will have a range of 100 miles and will reach 75 mph, charging fully in 8 hours. According to Carlos Tavares, a Nissan executive vice president, more than 90 percent of drivers travel less than 62 miles a day, so there is "a huge, huge potential there for EVs."

On the surface, the Nissan's numbers are not overwhelming. GM's EV1 could probably meet them and was certainly faster than the Nissan will be. The company intends the cars for commuters who have no need to set speed records. (www.nissanusa.com)

WHEEGO WHIP

Affordable (and Local)

The concept of a vehicle that can't exceed 25 mph isn't likely to get anyone's heart racing, especially with that speed demon the Tesla Roadster around. But they may be onto something with the Wheego Whip.

The car is an LSV, which is short for low-speed vehicle. Through federal regulations, they're permitted on roads with speed limits of 35 mph or less but can't exceed 25 mph. Also known as neighborhood electric vehicles, some are more like glorified golf carts. But the GEM PeaPod and the Wheego Whip are different: real enclosed cars, similar in shape and concept to the Smart. For $18,995, Wheego will sell you a two-seater with air-conditioning, power windows, power locks, four-wheel disc brakes, and an MP3- and iPod-ready stereo. A federal income tax credit covers 10 percent of the purchase price.

Cars like this work for gated communities, college campuses, sprawling tech centers, and resorts. According to the *Christian Science Monitor*, there are 40,000 already rolling on American roads.

There's an interesting history here. As President Jeff Boyd explains it, the company was founded as Ruff and Tuff Products several years ago in South Carolina, primarily to make golf carts.

Ruff and Tuff, after an expansion, will now sell you anything from a golf cart to a camouflage-painted four-wheel-drive hunting vehicle. For $24,000, Wheego is also selling a highway-capable small car, based on the Whip, with lithium-ion batteries and a 100-mile range.

The Wheego Whip costs three cents a mile to operate, and the highway car not much more. (www.wheego.net)

SMALL IS BEAUTIFUL

Space is indeed the final frontier. Ford has announced that it is going the fuel-efficiency route and will refashion three of its truck plants to produce six smaller cars currently aimed solely at the European market. GM and Chrysler are frantically retooling for small cars as well. The Big Three got lazy. The huge vehicles they turned out for record profits didn't need to make efficient use of space. There was always room for three kids, the family dog, and luggage, too. But now the challenge is to get everything to fit in vehicles half the size.

Make no mistake, that's where we're going. The Smart car hit the beach first, but there will be many more like it coming along. Hatchbacks will be big again, because they're great for getting humongous things into small packages. The luxury car of 2012 will be a tricked-out, Civic-size vehicle with leather seats and a high-end stereo.

TESLA MODEL S

A Glamorous Electric Sedan

Tesla has proven many people wrong with its $109,000, 248-horsepower battery-powered Roadster, which can hit 60 mph from a standing start in under 4 seconds. Although the company went through financial problems, it shook them off and got the car on the market despite a daunting economy in 2009. The Roadster is not a family car, but Tesla's strategy is to make an early splash and then develop other models.

The Model S, which goes into production in 2011, is the next step. It has the potential of 300-mile range from lithium-ion batteries, zero to 60 in 5.6 seconds, seating for seven if you put in the two rear-facing child seats, and ample storage. Tesla claims its battery cars are twice as efficient as hybrids.

The Model S looks handsome from every angle in a vaguely Maserati way. It is also very fast and fairly quiet and exhibits good build quality with few rattles or squeaks. The interior, which is snug but not cramped for both front and rear passengers, is dominated by a huge 17-inch touch screen offering Internet access, streaming audio, and other features. The seats (vegetable-tanned Italian leather) offer good support.

A few things deserve clarification. The quoted price of $49,900 is actually $57,400 minus a $7,500 federal tax credit. That buys the base car, which has 160-mile range and a 42-kilowatt-hour battery pack. The company plans to offer two battery upgrades, with 230 and 300 miles on a charge. (www.teslamotors.com)

SMART CAR
Small Is Beautiful

It started out as a side project by a Swiss watch company. Producing what was originally known as the "Swatchmobile," the Smart ("Swatch Mercedes ART") team partnered with Daimler-Benz after negotiations with Volkswagen fell through. The goal was to create a car so small that two of them would fit in one parking space. The Smart was launched in 9 European countries in 1998, and soon it was available in 25 (but not the United States).

Smart sold more than 750,000 cars before finally coming to the States in 2008. Before that, it had been available only as a gray-market import, with a few brought in by California-based retailer ZAP. Now they're sold here officially through the Penske Automotive Group.

The Smart is certainly fuel efficient at 33 mpg in the city and 41 on the highway, but it dims that luster somewhat by requiring premium gas. People love the Smart's distinctive styling, which—like the Prius—says, "I'm an environmentalist." The problem is that the Smart isn't an especially good car. Acceleration is achingly slow; the car is noisy and rough riding. And like the original Honda Insight, its utility is limited by having only two seats. Interior materials do not meet the standard normally associated with a car that passed through Daimler-Benz. It's very easy to park, however.

The Smart models are the basic pure ($11,590), the upgraded-for-two passion coupe ($13,590), and the passion cabriolet ($16,590). The latter is rather whimsical: Putting the top down requires removing side roof rails and stowing them in the tailgate. Perhaps the best model will be the all-electric version, with a range of 120 miles. (www.smartusa.com)

TESLA ROADSTER
Electric Wizardry

For the ultimate green car experience, there is the long-awaited Tesla Roadster, which finally began reaching excited customers in 2008. Based on the British Lotus Elise, the Tesla Roadster is a battery-powered sports car produced by California-based Tesla Motors.

The Tesla is not for everyone. It costs $98,000, for one thing, and it is a tiny two-seater with limited luggage space. Few people would own one as their only car. But for a "green" car, the Tesla Roadster is astonishingly fast, able to accelerate from zero to 60 mph in just 3.9 seconds. Top speed is an electronically governed 125 mph.

It does this while enjoying the equivalent of 105 mpg from its lithium-ion battery pack, which (thanks to the very light weight of its carbon-fiber body) can move it 244 miles on a single charge.

Tesla's "Signature One Hundred" cars were sold out by August 2006, and the entire 2008 production run of 650 was reserved by the beginning of that year. But Tesla was slow to fulfill the orders. Production for 2009 is projected to more than double to 1,500 cars.

Some environmentalists see more utility in Tesla's forthcoming Model S, a $60,000 sport sedan. Set to go on sale at the end of 2010, the made-in-California Model S will travel at least 160 miles on a charge. (www.teslamotors.com)

AN INCREDIBLE VOLKSWAGEN

There's an absolutely amazing fuel-efficient Volkswagen on the European market, but VW won't let us have it over here. It's the Polo BlueMotion, and it achieves a combined fuel economy rating of 61 mpg in the European driving cycle. On one tank of fuel, it can travel 700 miles.

The Polo BlueMotion is a state-of-the-art green car, featuring reduced weight (just 2,389 pounds), improved aerodynamics, direct fuel injection, low-rolling-resistance tires, and a five-speed manual with very tall gears. But it also has a 79 hp, three-cylinder turbodiesel engine, and diesels just never have done well on the American market. High diesel fuel prices are one reason. In addition, greens don't like them much, although today's diesels are much cleaner and better performing than the slow, smoky vehicles of the 1960s and '70s.

It's possible the Polo BlueMotion will come here after Volkswagen's new plant in Chattanooga, Tennessee, opens in 2010. The BlueMotion garners only 5 percent of worldwide Polo sales, but as fuel prices rise, its cachet is growing. (www.autobloggreen.com/tag/polo+bluetec)

VESPA SCOOTERS

Two Wheels, 70 mpg

When it comes to fuel-efficient transportation, the Italian-made Vespa motor scooter can claim a long history. The company has been around since 1946, and its low-cost scooters made life easier for many a Roman boulevardier in the 1960s.

Vespas are well made, with excellent dealer and parts support. They began a sales renaissance once gas prices soared to $4 a gallon. "Demand has doubled or tripled in the last year," says Rich Watson of Connecticut-based Valley Motorsports. "And it's totally because of high gas costs."

At the top end of the Vespa line are 200 cc, low-emission models with four-stroke, liquid-cooled engines that can travel on the highway. But for really stellar fuel economy, there are the 50 cc models, which have to stay on local roads (but do not have to be licensed or insured in some states).

The Vespa LX, for instance, costs $3,299 in 50 cc form, averaging 70 to 80 mpg and running on regular unleaded fuel. Of course, you won't be able to go above 39 mph. Interestingly enough, you don't lose that much economy with the 150 cc upgrade (72 mpg). That one costs $4,399 and can reach 59 mph. Vespa builds a wide range of models, including a hybrid with 140 mpg.

The prices may seem steep, but beware of inexpensive ($500 to $1,500) alternatives, many built in Korea, which lack the build quality and dealer support. (www.vespausa.com)

FYI

Carpools and ride-share programs can cut weekly fuel costs by 50 percent and save wear and tear on your car. In many places, you'll also be able to take advantage of the high-occupancy vehicle (HOV) lanes for car-poolers.

FORD FUSION/MERCURY MARINER HYBRID

Competitive US-Made Hybrids

There's a lot to like about the new midsize Ford Fusion Hybrid, which will offer 41 mpg in the city and 36 on the highway. Those numbers make it actually more fuel-efficient than the very good Toyota Camry Hybrid.

The new sedan and its cousin, the Mercury Mariner Hybrid, reach 47 mph in pure electric mode—more impressive than the Prius (which switches on its gas engine around 35 mph). It has a range of 700 miles between fill-ups, too.

Advanced features of the new Ford, which should give it many advantages over the current Escape Hybrid, include a 2.5-liter, 155-horsepower, four-cylinder engine coupled to a fuel-saving continuously variable transmission, smaller and lighter nickel-metal-hydride batteries, a very efficient regenerative braking system, and an electric air-conditioning compressor that allows the air to work without the gas engine running. Enhanced electronic throttle control improves fuel economy on restarts. Drivers can monitor fuel economy different ways through a built-in SmartGauge with EcoGuide.

If there's a drawback to the Fusion, it's that Ford may not sell many of them. For one thing, mass production of hybrid battery packs is a challenge. Ford America's president Mark Fields said that Fusion production could be "constrained by the amount of components, including batteries, that the supply base can provide us." American carmakers are precariously dependent on outside suppliers for their batteries, and nobody is yet producing in volume the lithium-ion packs needed for plug-in hybrids. Toyota has the right idea by partnering with Panasonic in building and co-owning two battery factories.

Despite this caveat, the Fusion and Mariner hybrids are smart products and well-timed, too. (www.ford.com)

Auto Emissions: It Pays to Check

Let's face it: Cars are dirty beasts. Every one produces an average of 5 tons per year of carbon dioxide (CO_2), the main global-warming aggravator. But air pollution would look much worse if we hadn't begun equipping all US-market cars in the late 1960s with catalytic converters and other smog-reducing equipment. At the time, the auto industry said "cats" would bankrupt them, but now they swear by the technology. The next step may be finding a way to warm up converters before you start your car, since they're ineffective when the car is cold.

The other big breakthrough was removing lead from gasoline, the health benefit of which is estimated at 10 to 13 times the cost, or at least $17 billion per year. It's been illegal to sell leaded gasoline here since 1996.

Some cars are much dirtier than others: As few as 10 percent of the automobiles on the road, usually older ones, contribute as much as 50 percent of the pollution. Is your car one of them? If it's 10 or more years old and hasn't had an emission inspection in several years, it may well be.

The Environmental Protection Agency (EPA) estimates that smog maintenance can improve fuel economy by 15 percent. Don't assume your car is fine just because it's running well. Up to a third of the cars

tested at emission stations fail due to excessive carbon monoxide, hydrocarbons, or oxides of nitrogen. And don't remove or modify emission controls to get the car to breathe easier. The EPA says it is not only illegal "but is likely to have a negative effect on vehicle performance and durability."

All the clean-air benefits we've achieved through emission controls in recent years could be lost with increases in US population and vehicle miles traveled (VMT). One saving grace of expensive gas is that VMT actually declined for the first time, and people are driving smaller, more fuel-efficient cars. In April 2008, for instance, cumulative miles traveled dipped 2 percent from 2007. The same month saw a precipitous drop in midsize SUV sales. (www.epa.gov/OMS/consumer/05-autos.pdf)

ZIPCAR

Sharing Is Cool

What's not to like about America's premier car-sharing service, Zipcar? As many as 300,000 people in 50 cities are Zipcar customers, which means instead of owning a car, they pay a monthly fee and, depending on their need, "share" one of the company's strategically located hybrids, subcompacts, or pickup trucks.

Car sharing originated in Europe, but it has found an enthusiastic base in the United States. There are nonprofit and government-owned car-sharing operations around the country, and new entrepreneurial start-ups, too. Zipcar, founded in Cambridge, Massachusetts, in 1999, has grown rapidly. In 2008, for instance, membership jumped 80 percent over 2007, and the service is constantly expanding to new locations. The green benefits are obvious, because Zipcar users drive much less than car owners. Each new car in Zipcar's 5,500-vehicle fleet replaces as many as 15 privately owned vehicles. As many as 40 percent of users decide against buying a car, or they sell the one they have. Zipcar also points out that:

★ Older private cars are replaced with newer Zipcars.
★ Green space is preserved because fewer parking spaces are needed.
★ Reduced fuel consumption spares the planet from greenhouse gas emissions.

Zipcar rates include a $25 one-time application fee plus usage charges that range from $9.35 an hour up to $65 a day. A variety of plans are available. Gas and insurance are included, which is one reason Zipcar has found it hard to make a profit as fuel prices have risen. But for consumers, it's one excellent deal. (www.zipcar.com)

PZEV CARS: ASK FOR ONE

There are hundreds of thousands of them on the road, and some people are even unknowingly driving them. They look just like any normal Chevy, Ford, Honda, or Volvo, but they're up to 90 percent cleaner out of the tailpipe. What are they? Why, PZEVs, of course!

PZEV stands for "partial zero emission vehicle," and they're ultralow-emission versions of many popular cars, sold only in the dozen states that have embraced the stringent California tailpipe and greenhouse-gas regulations (mostly on the East and West Coasts).

Although PZEVs are several hundred dollars more expensive to produce, the public often gets their clean-air benefits at no extra cost. But let's face it, no matter what clean-air benefits these cars bring with them, the acronym PZEV (pronounced "pee-zev") has simply not caught on. The PZEV joins the LEV, the ULEV, and the SULEV (all California emission standards, and increasingly clean iterations of "low-emission vehicle") in confounding the public. SULEV, for instance, stands for "super-ultra-low-emission vehicle," a designation that could only have emerged from some bureaucratic basement.

Also part of the PZEV package is elimination of evaporative emissions—solving a problem few motorists ever worried about. Evaporative emissions are gasoline fumes that escape during refueling or, especially on hot days, from fuel tanks and lines. The car doesn't have to be running to emit evaporative emissions, and this invisible pollution can be significant. According to the California Air Resources Board (CARB), which sets state tailpipe standards, PZEVs "have fewer emissions while being driven than a typical gasoline car has while just sitting."

Ask your dealer if a PZEV version is available or can be ordered. Chances are you'll be met with a blank stare, but the information is available. And if you can find a PZEV, you'll be rewarded with a car whose exhaust is, in some parts of the United States, cleaner than the ambient air. (http://alternativefuels.about.com)

If you have a car with a manual transmission, drive in the highest gear possible when cruising at a steady speed. It's not the sportiest way to go, but it will save gas.

HONDA CIVIC GX

As Clean as They Come

Although most environmentalists would walk right past one to get to a Toyota Prius, the Honda Civic GX is actually the cleanest-burning car on the market. It looks like any other Civic, but the GX runs on natural gas. And according to Honda, the GX produces "near zero" smog-forming emissions and is "the cleanest internal-combustion vehicle in the world."

The GX is also the only natural gas car in regular production currently on the US market—most of the 150,000 natural gas vehicles (NGVs) on our roads today are conversions from standard gasoline cars. Natural gas is 40 percent less expensive than gasoline at the pump right now, but there aren't nearly enough of those pumps (just 1,600, compared to 180,000 gasoline stations). And most of our current natural gas stations are used for fleets, with no retail sales to the public. Lower energy density than gasoline is also an issue; the Civic GX tops out at 250 miles of cruising range.

Actor and environmentalist Ed Begley Jr. drove across the country in a natural gas car in 2000 and noted that he had a rough time back then: "I've got 10 different natural-gas fueling cards and it's still not enough! It's like the late 1970s, when you had to have a different ATM card for each bank."

The only other drawback to natural gas power is a much smaller trunk. The 113 hp, 1.8-liter VTEC engine has plenty of pep, and it's mated to a five-speed automatic. Both side and side-curtain airbags are standard. The manufacturer's suggested retail price (MSRP) is $25,090, but that can be offset by a $4,000 federal tax credit, and there are some state and local incentives as well.

You can order a GX at any Honda dealer, and it can be augmented with a $3,400 home-based fueling station called the Phill, produced by Fuelmaker. The cost is less than at a public station, but the gas is under lower pressure, so refueling takes overnight. (http://automobiles.honda.com/civic-gx; www.myphill.com)

EARLY HYBRIDS: PORSCHE WAS FIRST

Do you think hybrid cars are a brand-new development? Not exactly. In 1898, Ferdinand Porsche (yes, *the* Porsche) hooked up with the Austria-based Lohner and Company to develop an electric car (with motors in the wheel hubs). Porsche's Elektromobil could travel 38 miles on a charge. But he wasn't finished. By 1901, Porsche had added a 2.5 hp Daimler gas engine to his design, creating the Mixt hybrid system. It was revolutionary, but not a success.

Another early hybrid, the Woods Dual Power coupe, was a resounding flop when it was produced in Chicago from 1917 to 1918. The Woods Dual Power had a four-cylinder gasoline engine under the hood and an electric motor/generator behind it.

Woods had been producing electric cars since 1899, and the market was slowly dying as gasoline cars rapidly improved. The hybrid was Woods's attempt to have it both ways, but the car was relatively expensive, and its advantage in fuel economy meant little in an era when gasoline was cheap. The Dual Power worked well, but, alas, few were sold. Hybrids were off the US market until the Honda Insight made it here in 1999. (www.hybrid-vehicle.org/hybrid-vehicle-porsche.html)

GREASECAR

Biofuel Made Easy

Super Duper Weenie in Fairfield, Connecticut, has received national attention (from *Gourmet* magazine, *Cigar Aficionado*, and the *David Letterman Show*) for its gourmet hot dogs, all-beef burgers, made-from-scratch coleslaw, and melt-in-your-mouth homemade fries. But few of the people lining up at lunchtime are aware that Super Duper is also a transportation pioneer.

Until recently, co-owner Gary Zemola had a costly disposal problem at the end of the week: 35-gallon jugs of depleted and contaminated soy oil. But that old oil is now an asset. Instead of piling up in the storage shed, it goes (after filtration) straight into the tank of Zemola's 1978 Mercedes 300D, which has been converted from diesel fuel to 100 percent fryer-based biofuel. The car's license plate? SOYBNZ.

"They laughed when I said what I was going to do," says Zemola. "But with $4-a-gallon gasoline, who's nuts? My veggie car is good for the environment and good for business."

The Mercedes was converted with a kit from Greasecar that includes a special biofuel tank, filters, heat exchangers, and plumbing to deliver the fuel to the engine. Conversion kits cost $995 to $2,900, depending on the make of car; having Greasecar install it for you is another $1,100 to $1,400.

Standard diesel vehicles can run, without any modification, on a processed blend of 20 percent vegetable oil and 80 percent standard diesel fuel. This "B20 biodiesel" can be made at home, provided you have the right equipment and don't mind working with such toxic chemicals as lye and methanol.

Zemola's converted car burns straight vegetable oil. Since vegetable oils congeal in cold weather, biofuel vehicles start up using standard diesel in the winter months, then switch to veggie oil after it has been heated by the warming engine.

When compared to conventional diesel, burning B100 reduces particulate matter by 47 percent, unburned hydrocarbons by 67 percent, and carbon monoxide by 48 percent, according to the EPA. It is dirtier only in nitrogen oxide emissions (a 10 percent penalty). Biodiesel also has a very high energy balance, generating 3.2 units of energy for every single unit of fossil energy expended to produce it.

Biofuels are versatile and will burn in home furnaces as effectively as in car engines. Oil companies are beginning to blend them in with standard fuel oil in 5 percent concentrations. As oil prices soar across the board, interest in biodiesel is soaring, too. (www.greasecar.com)

FYI

Think small for your everyday vehicle, and think creatively for those special occasions: Rent a truck, borrow an SUV, or investigate car-sharing options.

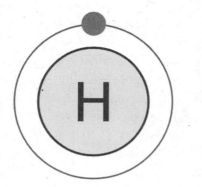

HYDROGEN CARS

Making Progress

Sir William Robert Grove (1811–1896) was the first scientist to describe and build a filament light, and he also invented the fuel cell, although nobody could find a practical use for his invention until long after he was dead.

Fuel-cell technology can be compared to that of a car battery, in that hydrogen and oxygen are combined in a chemical process to produce electricity. The fuel cell's major by-products are water and waste heat. The process is "zero emission," however, only if the hydrogen was generated through clean sources such as solar or wind power. Right now, most hydrogen is a by-product of natural gas.

The conversion of hydrogen to electricity is much more efficient than burning gasoline in an internal-combustion engine, but it has still taken several decades of research to get fuel-cell vehicles to rival the cruising distance of average cars and trucks today. This is because hydrogen gas has much less energy per volume than gasoline, so it has to be compressed (at up to 10,000 pounds per square inch) in an onboard tank.

Honda's FCX Clarity and General Motors's Sequel are state-of-the-art hydrogen fuel-cell cars (with 300 miles of range, an extremely quiet ride, and all the creature comforts), but both are being produced only in minute numbers for test fleets.

No auto company has a date for putting fuel-cell cars in showrooms, but the technology is progressing rapidly, with smaller cell stacks producing higher power output. The trick in the next decade will be to dramatically lower costs both for hydrogen and for the fuel-cell cars that run on it. (http://automobiles.honda.com/fcx-clarity; www.chevrolet.com/fuelcell/)

Ethanol: A Homegrown Alternative

Ethanol wins points as the homegrown biofuel alternative to expensive imported oil from the volatile Middle East. In the United States, ethanol is distilled mostly from fermented corn, which makes it not only an alternative to fossil fuel but a boon to midwestern farmers. If the ethanol process sounds a bit like making corn liquor in a still, that's because ethanol is an alcohol fuel.

In 2008, the United States had 139 ethanol plants in operation, with the capacity of producing 7.8 billion gallons of the biofuel annually. Production of ethanol nearly tripled between 1998 and 2005. Tom Slunecka, executive director of the Ethanol Promotion and Information Council, believes that the US production number could rise to 40 billion gallons by 2025.

The Alternative Motor Fuels Act, passed in 1998, enabled automakers to get federal Corporate Average Fuel Economy (CAFE) credits for producing ethanol-ready "bifuel" vehicles that could also run on gasoline. The catch is that our embryonic ethanol infrastructure dooms most of these environmentally friendly vehicles to run on gasoline most of the time.

General Motors's Live Green, Go Yellow campaign boasts that it has produced more than two million ethanol-compliant vehicles. There were an incredible six million ethanol-capable vehicles on American roads in 2007. But there are only 1,200 pumps dispensing E85 ethanol (which contains 15 percent gasoline) in a country with approximately 180,000 gas stations.

Most of us burn ethanol even without bifuel vehicles because it is blended into our gasoline (in 10 percent concentrations) as an oxygenating replacement for MTBE, which has water-pollution issues. Although the United States produces ethanol almost exclusively from the corn it grows in abundance, other countries are achieving higher energy yields from "cellulosic" ethanol made from such sources as sugarcane (Brazil), forestry waste (Sweden), sugar beets (France), and sweet sorghum (India). Switchgrass also shows promise.

Ethanol could lead the way to a modest green-energy revolution, but the cellulosic form will probably have to be in the lead. The US Department of Energy recently set a goal of replacing 30 percent of current gasoline and diesel for transportation use with biofuels by 2025.

A study by the Natural Resources Defense Council concluded that by 2050, biofuels could be cheaper than gasoline or diesel, saving us $20 billion in annual fuel costs and reducing greenhouse gas emissions by 1.7 billion tons a year. (http://epicinfo.org)

THE SOLAR BUS
A Solar Energy Classroom

Gary Beckwith, a sometime technical writer and former Deadhead, is the Solar Bus's creator, instigator, and chief propagandist. The Vermonter runs a dedicated Web site at www.solarbus.org, and he takes his vehicle (a 1982 Crown Supercoach that looks much older than it is) all over the country to spread the word about affordable solar panels.

"It was a school bus in California until 2003," says Beckwith. "We yanked out the seats, put some solar panels on the roof, gave it a paint job, and started driving around showing

and teaching people about the real uses of renewable energy."

Now let's get this straight. The Solar Bus, green though it may be, is not solar powered. "Everybody asks, 'Does the bus really run on sunlight?' But there's just not enough surface area for the panels. With a solar-connected electric motor, we simply wouldn't be able to keep up with the power demand."

The bus has undergone a biodiesel conversion and runs for the most part on used veggie oil. In that it is not unique, since people are doing such conversions on everything from Mercedes station wagons to VW convertibles. According to Beckwith, "Vegetable oil is a form of solar power anyway."

Beckwith's mission is about solar power, not biodiesel. His bus can and does provide electricity for rock concerts and the amplified speeches at solar festivals (though it helps if it's a sunny day). The onboard "solar DJ" can entertain at weddings and parties. Its solar oven bakes solar cookies at more than 300°F. The bus also holds a portable store with solar gadgets and a solar library.

It's clear that Beckwith and his dedicated group of followers would love to proselytize full-time about the advantages of solar power, but economic reality limits their outreach right now. "Renewable energy is not a future technology," reads a flyer. "It's here, it's now, and its time has come!" (www.solarbus.org)

WINTER DRIVING WITHOUT AN SUV

Consumers have been abandoning gas-guzzling SUVs in droves because of high gas prices, but some people cling to the behemoths because of their perceived safety advantage. Guess what. The "king of the road" image doesn't square with reality, particularly in winter driving.

Cheryl Campbell is a police officer in Buffalo, where they're certainly used to driving in snow, but that didn't prevent her from spinning her GM Jimmy sport utility vehicle on ice. "I came around a curve too fast, hit a patch of black ice, and did three 360-degree spins without the four-wheel drive helping one bit," she said. "Having an SUV definitely makes winter drivers overconfident. We see it all the time."

Stan Barney of Wreckerman Towing in Anchorage agrees. He has pulled many hotshots out of the local ditches. "Drivers of top-heavy SUVs are the worst," he said. "I see a lot of Blazers and Broncos upside down."

In Toronto, Brent Mikstas, the local commander of the Ontario Provincial Police, sees his share of snow, too, and he concurs that macho four-wheel-drive vehicles are often the first to get in trouble. "The logical inference is that big SUVs with big tires will stop quicker, but ice is ice," he said. "Did overconfidence lead those drivers to go too fast for the conditions? I believe it did."

Because SUVs handle off-road or deep-snow conditions better than cars and will get away faster from a stoplight during bad conditions, drivers tend to assume they will perform better than cars in all situations. In fact, SUVs may require even more careful driving on slippery winter roads than cars do, not only because of their propensity to roll over when a driver swerves but because they require longer distances to stop.

Liz Neblett, a spokeswoman for the National Highway Traffic Safety Administration, says an SUV's longer stopping distance is a matter of simple physics. "Bigger vehicles are harder to

stop, particularly in the winter," she said. "If you hit ice and put your foot on the brake, four-wheel drive isn't going to help you—you're going to skid for a long time."

According to Jerry Donaldson, the senior research director at Advocates for Highway and Auto Safety in Washington, "For 99 percent of winter driving, with highways regularly plowed, there's little advantage to four-wheel drive and no reason to buy an SUV." (http://redmonk.com/sogrady/2006/12/28/winter-driving-101)

AUTOMOBILE RECYCLING
We Could Do Better

Ever looked at the vehicles stacked on top of each other in a junkyard and thought, "Wow, that's a whole lot of cars"? Now think about the end-of-life vehicles (ELV) from sea to shining sea—about 15 million every year—and you understand the scope of our disposal problem.

Fortunately, the scrap metal from American cars and trucks is a valuable commodity, so 75 percent or more of the materials from the average vehicle get recycled. Ninety-five percent of all cars go through the recycling process, and that produces an average of more than 14 million tons of scrap steel annually. It sounds pretty good, doesn't it?

Well, it could be better. The European Union is phasing in a law that mandates a much higher recycled percentage by 2015, up to 85 percent. To attain that goal, they'll have to get creative with the usually landfilled automotive shredder residue (ASR), also known as "fluff," which constitutes 25 percent of the vehicle by weight. We produce 2 billion pounds of ASR annually.

Japan passed a recycling law that required reuse of ASR beginning in 2005. Higher recycling rates are not mandated by US supply-and-demand rules, which are buffeted by market forces. But a coalition called the Vehicle Recycling Partnership (including the Big Three automakers) is working with the Department of Energy and the American Plastics Council to increase ASR recycling.

Research is taking place at a plastics-sorting pilot plant on the grounds of Argonne National Laboratory, near Chicago. Project manager Sam Jody shows off large containers filled with unprocessed ASR scrap (nasty stuff with visible tire treads and crumbly bits of foam) and its increasingly more refined (and usable) final product. The process is not all that complex: Water baths separate the various plastic types. What remains is 95 percent pure polyethylene and polypropylene plastic that can be pelletized and sold. Automotive products that are made from it include knee bolsters and headlight liners.

Overall, 15 to 20 percent of ASR plastic is currently recoverable, plus 10 to 15 percent of the rubber. But to get close to European-level recycling rates, we'll have to ramp up that small-scale pilot plant many times over. (www.ecarcenter.org)

Greener Car Choices

The American Council for an Energy-Efficient Economy (ACEEE) publishes an annual list of greener choices for new car buyers, based on factors that include fuel efficiency and emissions. There's a separate list of the very greenest cars at www.greenercars.org. It features the best picks across the spectrum, from subcompacts to large trucks. Here are the rankings for 2008:

1. Toyota Prius (48 mpg city/45 mpg highway; green score 53)

2. Honda Civic Hybrid (40/45 mpg; green score 51)

3. Smart for two convertible/coupe (33/41 mpg; green score 49)

4. Honda Fit (33/41 mpg; green score 43)

5. Ford Escape Hybrid (34/30 mpg; green score 42)

6. Hyundai Sonata (21/30 mpg; green score 39)

7. Subaru Outback Wagon (20/26 mpg; green score 37)

8. Nissan Rogue (22/27 mpg; green score 37)

9. Toyota Tacoma (19/25 mpg; green score 34)

10. Toyota Sienna (17/23 mpg; green score 33)

11. Chevrolet Tahoe Hybrid C1500 (21/22 mpg; green score 28)

12. Nissan Frontier (14/19 mpg; green score 27)

greenercars.org
ACEEE'S GREEN BOOK®

It's Catching On

Tighter municipal budgets have meant cuts for one in five of the nation's transit agencies, reports the American Public Transportation Association. Despite those cutbacks, public transportation ridership is up sharply: Americans took 2.6 billion trips in the first 3 months of 2008—88 million more than in 2007. One of the fastest-growing forms of transit is the local urban service known as light-rail, which is enjoying huge public support and, in many cases, adding new lines.

Light-rail systems showing double-digit ridership increases in the first quarter of 2008 included Buffalo (45.9 percent); Philadelphia (34.9 percent); Kenosha, Wisconsin (26.9 percent); Sacramento (26.3 percent); Salt Lake City (19.4 percent); Minneapolis (16 percent); Baltimore (13.7 percent); San Francisco (12.2 percent); and Pittsburgh (12 percent). US cities with light-rail systems, streetcar, or vintage trolley lines include:

Baltimore
Boston
   (number 1 in ridership nationally)
Buffalo
Charlotte, North Carolina
Cleveland
Dallas
Denver
Detroit
Fort Worth, Texas
Houston
Jersey City, New Jersey
Kenosha
Little Rock, Arkansas
Los Angeles
   (number 3 in ridership nationally)
Memphis
Minneapolis/St. Paul

New Orleans
Newark, New Jersey
Philadelphia
   (number 4 in ridership nationally)
Pittsburgh
Portland, Oregon
   (number 5 in ridership nationally)
Sacramento
St. Louis
Salt Lake City
San Diego
San Francisco
   (number 2 in ridership nationally)
San Jose, California
Seattle
Tampa
Tucson
Washington, DC

Systems have been proposed or are under construction in these locations, among others: Atlanta; El Paso, Texas; Fort Lauderdale; Fort Worth; Hawaii (Kauai and Maui); Kansas City; Las Vegas; Louisville; Madison, Wisconsin; Miami; Norfolk, Virginia; Orlando; Raleigh, North Carolina; San Antonio; Spokane, Washington; Phoenix, Arizona; and Tampa.

FUELECONOMY.GOV:
YOUR ONLINE MILEAGE AND CLIMATE GUIDE

If you're researching the purchase of a new car online, your surfing should include a stop at fueleconomy.gov, a joint project of the Department of Energy and the Environmental Protection Agency that offers the green skinny on every new car and truck on the market.

Check out the 2009 Dodge Ram 1500 pickup with four-wheel drive, for instance, and you'll discover that it gets 13 mpg in the city, and just 18 mpg on the highway. In a year, it will use 22.8 barrels of oil and emit 12.2 tons of carbon dioxide—not too great on a scale of 3.5 to 16.2 tons. By contrast, the Smart Car for two (33 mpg city/41 highway) uses only 9.5 barrels of oil annually and emits 5.1 tons of CO_2. You can also use the site for used cars, since it goes back to 1985 models.

There's plenty of other useful information on the site, including tips for driving more efficiently. "Observe the speed limit" is one of them. Every 5 mph you drive over 60 mph is like paying an additional 24 cents a gallon for gas. The site has recently been upgraded with considerable environmental information, including the fact that cars and trucks account for 26 percent of US climate emissions and the fact that the average vehicle emits 6 to 9 tons of CO_2 every year.

ZELECTRIC BOATS

Run Silent

Imagine traveling across a still lake with your boat's wake barely breaking the surface. Instead of an outboard's roar, there is absolute silence from your electric motor, which allows you to watch passing wildlife undisturbed. Also imagine no blue exhaust haze on the water.

Such a scenario is not that far-fetched. Electric boats currently on (and under) the water include military submarines (which are diesel-electric hybrids) and the *Queen Elizabeth II*. But you're probably going to want something smaller in your own battery-powered boat.

One great option with an electric boat is a clean-energy loop. Some users report mounting photovoltaic panels on their docks and getting about 40 percent of the electricity they need that way. There is a complete list of electric boat companies at www.econogics.com/ev/evboats.htm. Many look interesting, but for starters check out the range offered by Canada's Tamarack Electric Boat Company. The Loon, for instance, is a great party platform. It's a 20-foot-long, 8-foot-wide pontoon boat powered by a 3 hp electric motor connected to lead-acid batteries. The Loon can cruise at 6 knots and travel 30 miles on a 6-hour charge.

The Heron is much more intimate, a four-passenger rigid inflatable with a similar 3 hp electric motor. It's capable of 7 knots and can travel 20 miles, with 4-hour grid recharging. (www.tamarackelectricboats.com)

AMTRAK

Fun and Relaxing

Have you ridden Amtrak recently? It's a whole lot of fun, as well as the most relaxed way to travel. To make your trip more comfortable, check out the range of tips online at http://on-track-on-line.com/amthints-on-train.shtml. Here are a few hints you might find useful:

★ **TRAVEL LIGHT. Amtrak** limits you to two carry-ons per person, and individual bags cannot weigh more than 50 pounds. Due to post–9/11 security regulations, you won't always be able to check bags in advance. If you're in a sleeping compartment, it's best to carry on only one overnight bag, because there isn't much storage space. For detailed information about bringing your bicycle, call Amtrak at (800) USA-RAIL.

★ **RELAX.** Bring binoculars, because you'll definitely find a use for them. Earbuds are a must for your iPod or portable DVD and CD players. Some Amtrak snack bars stock decks of cards if you're caught short. Amtrak no longer shows movies in lounge cars, although films are still offered on the Auto Train and the Cascade Service. To listen, you'll need to buy the headphones or use your own.

★ **WHERE AM I?** The *SPV Railroad Atlas of North America* offers the best route maps (www.spv.co.uk/atlases.shtml). Another good choice, though without the rail maps, is the *Rand McNally Road Atlas*. Basic route information is available at www.amtrak.com. Read about using a GPS device onboard at http://on-track-on-line.com/gps-train-tracking.shtml.

★ **TAKE A WALK.** It's OK to leave most of your belongings (though not electronics and cameras) at your seat when you take a stroll onboard; you don't have to stand guard. Schmoozing and making new friends are required parts of the Amtrak experience.

★ *BON APPÉTIT.* Long-distance trains always have a snack bar and usually a dining car. Prices are not higher in the dining car, in case you were wondering. Unless you've brought a party of four, you'll be seated with other people. View a sample menu at www.amtrak.com. Special meals, including vegetarian and kosher, may be accommodated with 72 hours' advance notice. Soft drinks are probably cheaper in depot vending machines than they are on the train, but you'll find tap water on the train—and even ice on request. It's okay to bring your own corkscrew and bottle of wine! (www.amtrak.com)

Growing Greens

What is organic gardening? The simplistic answer is gardening without using synthetic fertilizers or toxic pesticides on plants. But gardening organically is much more than what you *don't* do. When you garden organically, you think of your plants as part of a whole system within nature that starts in the soil and includes the water supply, people, wildlife, and even insects. An organic gardener strives to work in harmony with nature and to continually replenish resources the garden consumes.

You could say that building soil is the defining act of organic gardening. The best way to ensure soil success is to regularly add organic matter, using locally available resources wherever possible. Everyone has access to the raw ingredients of organic matter, because our lawns, gardens, and kitchens produce them every day. Grass clippings, fallen leaves, vegetable scraps from your kitchen, and other such decaying plant waste are the building blocks of compost, the ideal organic matter for your garden soil. The microbes in soil (specifically bacteria and fungi) feed on organic matter, breaking it down into nutrients that can be taken up by plants' roots. By regularly mixing organic matter into the soil, you collaborate in the natural cycle of birth, growth, decay, and regeneration.

The plant nutrients in synthetic fertilizers, on the other hand, offer no benefits to the helpful organisms in the soil. During heavy rains, synthetic fertilizers wash away and into streams, rivers, and lakes, where they cause rampant algae growth that chokes out other aquatic life. Synthetic fertilizers affect plants in much the same way that steroids act on our bodies. That is, they may stimulate remarkable growth in the short term, but over time they weaken plants' natural defenses and make them vulnerable to pests and diseases. What's more, many synthetic fertilizers are petroleum based, so they exact a toll on the environment even before they're used in your garden.

If you concentrate on building your soil, you'll grow healthy, robust plants, and you'll have countless insects in and around your organic garden. That's a good thing, because the majority of insects in your garden are either beneficial or at least not destructive. Many gardeners become anxious and want to react decisively when they see "bugs" on their plants. Before you consider using chemical pesticides, bear in mind that many of them have been linked to increased rates of cancer and other diseases among people and pets. They also harm songbirds, freshwater fish, and other wildlife.

Does that mean organic gardeners must allow their plots to be decimated by pests? No. Remember the central principle of organic gardening: growing plants in harmony with nature. Insects are a crucial part of that system. When you see insects eating your plants, take some time to watch what they're really doing. Are they actually destroying the plant or just nibbling it a bit? Many plants can outgrow minor damage. Also, insects typically attack stressed-out plants. Do you have enough healthy plants to spare the sickly ones? Can you restore sickly plants to robust health so they can resist insect attack?

The best defenses against most garden problems are preventive measures. Grow plants suited to the site and they'll be less stressed. Design a diverse garden so that pests of a particular plant won't wipe out an entire section of the garden. Most important, encourage the natural predators of pest insects to hunt in your garden: Beneficial insects (such as the familiar ladybug), birds, frogs, and lizards control pests by eating them. Make your garden hospitable for these natural allies by keeping a water source nearby and by not wiping out the entire pest population with a pesticide.

When a pest or weed infestation demands direct intervention, organic gardeners can rely on a wide variety of products and techniques to help control the problem. Options include physical barriers, tools, traps, and nontoxic sprays that affect only the target pest. These are effective without causing collateral damage to the environment. You'll learn more about them in this chapter.

The organic method, however, is more than a safer set of products or just a way to garden successfully. Tending an organic garden is an act of environmental stewardship. Grow some vegetables, fruits, and herbs and you diminish the considerable ecological impact of producing and transporting your food. Fill your yard with trees, shrubs, and flowers—especially species native to your region—and you help to maintain wildlife corridors that birds, reptiles, and mammals increasingly depend on for food and shelter as open space is developed into housing developments and shopping centers.

When you grow even a fraction of your own vegetables and fruit, you understand how fresh, healthful food is produced and what it tastes like. That's sure to lead you to seek out local, organic producers for your food. When you garden the organic way, you don't rely on the labels on packages of fertilizers and pesticides to tell you what to do. You tune in to the weather and the seasons. You notice the butterflies and bees. You act according to how your plants are performing. Through this focused attention, an organic gardener builds a deep and real bond with the earth. That bond makes preserving our planet and all of its resources a personal matter.

—Scott Meyer

*Pam Ruch, Therese Ciesinski,
and Willi Evans Galloway also
contributed to this chapter.*

SOIL TEST: THE FIRST STEP

Before you decide what to plant, before you add an ounce of lime or other amendment to your garden beds or lawn, take the time to have your soil lab-tested. The results will tell you the soil's pH, the levels of essential nutrients like phosphorus and potassium, and the percentage of organic matter (more than 5 percent is ideal). That information, in turn, tells you which plants are suited to your conditions and what you need to add to your garden soil. You'll find private soil testing labs in many regions, but the cooperative extension service in nearly every state offers soil testing. Click on "Soil" at www.organicgardening.com for a state-by-state listing of soil test services.

SOIL-BUILDING PLANTS

aka Green Manure

What's the most valuable thing you can do for your garden soil? Grow a cover crop. Think of it as compost-in-training. And ask yourself: Which is easier—shoveling a cubic yard (that's about 1,400 pounds) of compost around the garden, or spreading 3 pounds of seed?

After you pull out your cucumbers and tomatoes, rough up the soil and sprinkle a cool-weather seed mix over the plot. Multiple benefits ensue: The crop will scavenge nutrients and minerals from the soil; it will prevent erosion; it will nourish beneficial soil organisms; it will increase organic matter and available nitrogen. Best of all, it will crowd out weeds. Come

spring, whack the crop down and turn it root side up. After 2 or 3 weeks, you'll be able to work the residue in. By the end of the season you'll see dramatic improvements in your garden's soil from growing cover crops.

There's a cover crop for every garden situation. Buckwheat will scavenge nutrients from the soil while preventing weeds in the heat of summer. Crimson clover acts like a living mulch under tomatoes and corn. Hairy vetch injects your soil with a supernitrogen fix. Cereal rye can be planted even after frost. And there's more. Check out the **Peaceful Valley Farm & Garden Supply** catalog (you can download it from the groworganic.com Web site) for a host of options, a handy chart that explains individual benefits of each, appropriate inoculants (for kick-starting certain seeds' nitrogen-fixing action), and even a cover crop glossary. (www.groworganic.com)

SUNFLOWERS

Bird Magnets

A fun and fail-safe way to make your garden a stopping station for seed-eating birds is to plant sunflowers. Planting sunflowers is, literally, child's play. The seeds are big enough for little hands to maneuver into the ground, and when the plants bloom approximately 60 days later . . . wow! Plant them in straight formation, as a summer screen, or in a circle to create a private fort for children. Use them as climbing props for flowering vines, or space them 3 or 4 inches apart in a row so they stretch for light and give you armloads of long-stemmed flowers. However you use them, try hard to resist the urge to "neaten up" the garden in late summer. You'll get another season of interest as the birds do acrobatics to dislodge the tightly packed, nutritious seeds.

Check out the hundreds of varieties available. You'll find dwarfs and giants, branching reds and single-stemmed oranges, multiple small flowers and humongous heads. You'll also find pollenless sunflowers. Choose whatever turns you on—some say the pollenless types make better cut flowers, and even they will make seeds if other sunflowers with pollen grow nearby. One word of advice: For bird-feeding purposes, the wilder, branching types are more generous and last longer in the garden than the once-and-done single-stemmed varieties.

Other seed-producing flowers that birds like to pick at (if you let the flower stalks stand through the winter, that is) include black-eyed Susan, purple coneflower, cosmos, aster, and 'Purple Majesty' millet. A limited selection of seeds is generally available from retail seed racks. Some mail-order sources, such as **Johnny's Selected Seeds**, have sunflowers in dozens of colors and sizes, as well as a good selection of other bird favorites. (www.johnnyseeds.com)

Seeds versus Starts

You've decided to grow a vegetable garden. (Great decision!) So you sit down with a cup of tea and a pile of seed catalogs and begin marking pictures of purple peppers, heirloom tomatoes, and "bolt-proof" lettuces. You draw a sketch of your garden with all of your vegetables in neat rows, surrounded by a gorgeous flower border. You make a list. You place your order. You complain (brag) to your friends, "I can't believe I spent $130 on seeds!"

Soon, too soon, the seeds arrive. You read the backs of the seed packages. Uh-oh. They make unreasonable demands like "Sow 3 to 4 seeds per inch in sterile seeding mix 3 weeks prior to planting outside" or, worse yet, "Start seeds indoors 8 weeks before transplanting. Transplant when nighttime temperatures are above 50°F." You realize, with a sinking feeling, that you will be a slave to your baby plants from March until May. What to do?

Take heart, you're not alone—every novice gardener gets carried away on the February garden fantasy ride. Here are your choices:

1. Buy some plant lights and form a playgroup with other seedling moms and dads. (This is actually a very good choice.)

2. Sort through your seeds and put those that can be sown directly in the garden in one pile, those that need 6 to 8 (or more) weeks in another pile, and those that need a month or less in the third pile. Then count up piles 2 and 3 and decide which you really, really want to grow, favoring pile 3.

3. Donate your seeds to someone with a greenhouse and hope that he or she will have a reciprocal attack of generosity when the seedlings are ready to plant out.

Experience will soon teach you which plants you'll want to grow from seed and which you might be better off buying from a garden center, or, better yet, from your local farmers' market. But here are a few hints:

Start from seed

★ Unusual plants are often unavailable as transplants, so pick out a couple of packs of fascinating flower and vegetable seeds just for fun. Discover something new every year.

★ If you plan to plant big masses of one or two flower types, seed growing is an economical way to go.

★ Zinnias are easy from seed—they reach transplant size in just 4 weeks. In fact, they grow so big so fast

that garden center employees have trouble keeping them watered, so you often find only stressed-out plants to buy.

★ Lettuces and other salad greens, beans, cucumbers, squash, root vegetables, and sunflowers can all be sown right in the garden. Buy seeds.

★ If you plan to grow things like spinach, broccoli, or lettuce in fall, buy seed in spring to start in mid- to late summer. Stores sell out.

Buy plants

★ Tomatoes, peppers, eggplants, or any plants you don't need in huge quantities can often be bought singly. Buy as many different varieties of tomato plants as you can fit into your garden, and discover which grows best for you.

★ Some flowers, like pentas and wax begonias, really take their time getting to transplant size. If a seed pack tells you to start the seed 12 weeks or more before planting out, well, that's just too much windowsill time.

★ Some flowers, like marigolds and petunias, are easy to find and inexpensive. Buy them as plants and save your precious window light for more exotic choices.

★ Perennial flowers and herbs can take years to size up when started from seed. And purchased plants can often be divided the second year. This usually makes plants the better choice.

Aside from all that, you may find there are a few plants that you'll start from seed year after year—the ones you must have. Maybe the garden center will have your favorite varieties, but if they don't, well, the consequences are just too dire to contemplate! Ask experienced gardeners you know and they'll confirm what I'm telling you. In this writer's case, the must-haves are 'Genovese' basil (for pesto) and triple-curled parsley (for edging). Oh, and 'Benary's Giant' zinnias, for butterflies.

ACHIEVE THE PERFECT BALANCE

A garden's success depends in large part, if not completely, on the quality of its soil. So before you plant a new bed and about every 3 years thereafter, get a soil test.

When your soil test indicates a nutrient deficiency, you can remedy it with purchased ingredients that target the specific problem. These soil amendments include ingredients that are animal, mineral, or vegetable. For instance, if your garden soil needs phosphorus (a major nutrient essential for healthy root growth), you might use bonemeal, which is made from (you guessed it) pulverized animal bones. Treat a bed that is in need of calcium with gypsum, a mineral also known as calcium sulfate. Alfalfa meal, a popular food for pet rabbits and hamsters, is a rich source of nitrogen.

The old saying "If a little is good, a lot is better" is not true when it comes to soil amendments. Your goal is to get the soil balanced, and an excess of one nutrient can inhibit plants from taking up others. That's why you need the soil test before you apply amendments.

COMPOSTUMBLER
High-Speed Composting

You can make compost two ways: fast or slow. Lazy man's compost is a no-brainer: Mix your organic materials once, then walk away and let time take over the decomposition process. But if you need finished compost and don't want to wait, turn to the CompostTumbler. Put everything in, add water, and spin the barrel five revolutions a day for a few weeks. Round and round and round it goes, and when it stops, you have black gold. The constant mixing ensures that everything inside heats up, then breaks down. Clean, easy, and yes, fun to use. (www. compostumbler.com)

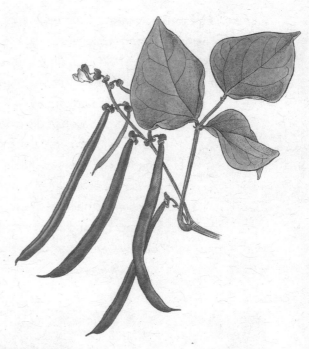

BUSH BEANS
Symbiotic and Snappy

Green beans, or snap beans as some gardeners call them to distinguish them from dried beans, deserve a spot in every organic vegetable garden for a simple reason: They add nitrogen to the soil. Beans have a symbiotic relationship with Rhizobium bacteria. The bacteria act like little nitrogen factories for the beans. They form nodes on the plants' roots and convert nitrogen from the air into a form that the beans can use. In return, the beans provide the bacteria with carbohydrates and minerals. How cool is that?

Green bean pods come in green, yellow, and purple varieties, and you can choose from two different growth habits: pole or bush. Pole beans grow, flower, and produce beans all season and need a sturdy trellis to climb. Bush beans grow to a certain height and concentrate their flowering and pod set within a set period. Both bean types have their advantages, but bush beans are a better choice for gardeners interested in canning or freezing beans for the winter.

Adding bush beans into a succession planting plan helps ensure that even the smallest vegetable garden yields big results. Try planting a bush bean variety such as 'Jade Green' in early summer following a spring crop of lettuce. Once the beans are harvested, pull the plants and sow beets, radishes, or garlic in their place. John Scheepers Kitchen Garden Seeds offers many varieties. (www.kitchengardenseeds.com)

SEED SAVERS EXCHANGE: PROTECTING DIVERSITY

For centuries, farmers and gardeners saved the seed from their best plants and grew them the next year. And they handed seeds down from one generation to the next. The advent of commercial plant breeding in the 20th century brought growers new varieties, and many of the heirlooms began to disappear from common use.

In 1975, Iowa farmers Kent and Diane Whealy launched Seed Savers Exchange, a crusade to preserve the old-fashioned varieties and protect the diversity of the seed pool. Members share varieties of everything from asparagus to zucchini, including treasures such as 'Brandywine' tomato and 'Country Gentleman' corn. Nonmembers can buy seeds of classic varieties. (www.seedsavers.org)

RAISED BED KIT
Build Up

Gardeners set up raised beds to give plant roots fluffy, rich soil in which to spread out. The soil stays loose, because raised beds make it clear where to walk and not walk. They warm up and dry out early in spring, giving you the opportunity to plant sooner. Many gardeners believe that raised beds give their plots a neat appearance.

To make a raised bed, simply mound up the soil 4 to 6 inches above the ground. Give the soil a nutrient boost and add bulk by mixing as much compost as soil into the mound. You can round off the sides and pick up a little extra growing space that you can plant with low growers like lettuce.

Or you can give your beds the finishing touch by framing them. Stones or bricks are simple to install. Naturally rot-resistant cedar planks or lengths of recycled plastic lumber take a little more know-how, but they're stable and last for years. Easiest of all is to buy a kit with the pieces cut to size, the holes predrilled, and the necessary hardware included. At Raised-Garden-Beds.com, you'll find nicely designed kits that let you configure your garden in many shapes, not just the traditional rectangle.

'BRANDYWINE' TOMATO
Big and Bold

Of the more than 1,500 varieties of tomatoes available to home gardeners, the one most celebrated for its flavor is 'Brandywine'. It has sweetness and acidity in perfect balance, and a melony softness in its texture, but it tastes like nothing so much as long days of summer sunshine. The tomatoes are big—up to 1 pound each—and ripen to their finest about 100 days after you transplant them to your garden. They are deep pink, almost purple, when fully ripe. Inside, they are meaty. The only drawback: As with many heirloom varieties, Brandywine's yields are modest, often just a few fruits per plant.

Brandywine's history dates from at least the 1860s, when it was offered in the earliest American seed catalogs. It later fell from favor, as newer hybrid varieties replaced the old open-pollinated types. Brandywine survived outside the commercial seed industry because gardeners and farmers saved the seeds each season and passed them along to the next generation. In 1982, it surfaced at the Seed Savers Exchange and was soon after winning taste tests and the hearts of organic gardeners again.

The renewed popularity of Brandywine means you can find started plants in many garden centers and at online vendors. But think how much more rewarding it will be if you join the chain of gardeners who have been growing, preserving, and replanting the seeds of this heirloom variety for so many seasons. In spring, look for transplants and seeds at Burpee. (www.burpee.com)

BABY GREENS

Grow 'Em Yourself

Baby greens fetch a high price at the super-market, but these little vegetables are inexpensive and easy to grow at home. All you need is a small patch of bare soil, or a container filled with potting mix, and a packet of seeds.

From April through September, simply sow the seeds thinly in 3-inch-wide, 2-foot-long bands spaced 18 inches apart. Cover the tiny seeds with a dusting of soil and water them gently. Keep the soil consistently moist.

Baby greens grow up fast—within a month the leaves are 4 to 5 inches tall and ready to cut. To harvest your homegrown salad, use scissors to shear the leaves down to 2 inches. New leaves regrow soon, as long as you keep the plants well watered and fertilize them after each harvest with a liquid organic fertilizer.

You can create a custom blend of these "cut and come again" greens by sowing lettuces, mustards, spinach, arugula, and endive together. Or buy a preblended mix, such as the Paris Market Mix by **Renee's Garden**, which features lettuces, arugula, chervil, curled endive, escarole, and chicory. (www.reneesgarden.com)

Local Smarts

The **Cooperative Extension Service** is the go-to organization for gardening questions in your community. Extension offices and their agents exist to teach the community how to garden: They give advice, identify insect and disease damage, and host fairs, clinics, and seminars. Most, but not all, of their advice is organic. It doesn't usually cost you anything; it comes courtesy of your tax dollars. Get online and go to www.csrees.usda.gov/Extension to find the extension office in your area.

KNOW YOUR ENEMIES

Why should we care about invasive species? Kudzu's on the march, and bark beetles are boring into the elms, so why shouldn't we just get on with it? Here are three reasons:

★ Invasives cost us money by damaging farmland and waterways.

★ They crowd out other plants and animals and destroy habitats.

★ Most of all, look at it this way: We've made a mess of things by thoughtlessly putting our wants ahead of the planet's health, so let's proceed mindfully from here and now—because it's the right thing to do.

The USDA has teamed up with the University of Georgia to create a comprehensive set of invasive plant images. Click on any one of the pernicious weeds at **www.invasive.org** and you'll learn why you should steer clear of it. Also at your service are photos of diseased plants, as well as pesky critters from flathead catfish to large red slugs—in living color, you'll be happy to know. A complementary Web site is **www.invasive speciesinfo.gov**, managed by the National Invasive Species Information Center. This will tell you everything you want to know and more about what *invasive* means, what impact invasive species have on our environment, and what various agencies are doing about them.

FYI

Trees add value to your property, keep your house cool, and provide food and shelter for songbirds. A traditional proverb says the best time to plant a tree is 20 years ago; the next best time is today.

HAWS WATERING CANS

The Sustainable Choice

Vegetable and flower plants growing in containers need frequent watering; in some climates, as often as twice a day. That makes a well-designed watering can an essential tool. The best models are balanced so that you can carry them easily and tip them without dumping all the water out at once. They have a rosette (the sprinkler part) that can be replaced separately from the rest of the watering can. And they're made of galvanized steel, brass, or copper.

Most experienced gardeners agree that **Haws** makes the best watering cans. The company offers lots of models for specific uses, and while they tend to cost more than those you'll find at the discount store, they are the sustainable choice because they last for years, maybe even for generations. (www.hawswatering cans.com)

MASON BEES
The Buzz on Pollination

In recent years, scientists, farmers, and bee-keepers have reported an alarming decline in the population of honeybees, with many hives suffering from colony collapse disorder. The causes of this epidemic are still being sorted out, but all agree that it poses a significant threat to our food supply—and our gardens—because of the critical job of pollination that honeybees do.

But they are hardly the only pollinator to visit your garden. Along with the moths, beetles, and flies that also carry pollen from plant to plant, many bee species beyond honeybees abound in cultivated landscapes. Among the most appealing is the gentle orchard mason bee (*Osmia lignaria*).

Named for their habit of making compartments of mud in their nests, mason bees are native to North America (honeybees are an import from Europe). Mason bees tend to be slightly smaller than honeybees and a shiny dark blue. They are not social in the way that honeybees are. Every mason bee female is fertile and makes her own nest, and there are no worker bees. As solitary bees, they do not produce honey or beeswax.

With no honey to defend, mason bees sting only if squeezed or stepped on. Because they both pollinate plants and rarely sting, they are popular with organic gardeners. They nest in holes other creatures make. You can attract them to your yard by putting up a mason bee house, made by drilling short holes (use a 5⁄16-inch bit) in a block of wood. Be sure not to use treated wood, which contains compounds that may be toxic to bees. You can buy a mason bee house, too—Gardeners Supply Company (www.gardeners.com) is one source.

FYI

When building frames for garden beds, don't use treated wood, including used railroad ties and utility poles. They contain toxic substances that leach into the soil. Pass on planting in tires for the same reason.

BASIL
Easy and Flavorful

If you have space for only one herb, make it basil. Its leaves are a must for pesto, pizza, tomato sauce, and myriad other dishes. Grow it in your vegetable or herb garden, tuck it in among your flowers as an accent, or keep it in containers on your patio or windowsill.

Basil is easy to grow. Start it indoors from seed or buy plants—but since basil cannot tolerate the cold, don't put it in the ground until soil and air temperatures are above 70°F. Plants need to be kept moderately moist and receive at least 6 hours of full sun a day. If you start harvesting leaves *before* the plant sends up flower spikes, you'll have leaves all summer long. With basil, flowers equals seeds equals time-to-die, so cutting the stems keeps the leaves coming and the plant from making flowers. Basil dies at first frost, but by then your freezer will be stocked with pesto. Its white or blue flowers attract bees and beneficial insects.

Lemon, lime, cinnamon, 'Purple Ruffles', 'African Blue', 'Aussie Sweet', Thai, 'Red Rubin', 'Holy' basil—there are dozens of types. All are edible, but most people prefer the taste of green for eating and the look of the red and purple types for ornamental use. Sweet basil is the best known; 'Genovese' is one of its most flavorful cultivars. Johnny's Selected Seeds offers more than 25 kinds of basil seed. (www.johnnyseeds.com)

VEGGIES' BEST FRIEND

If you grow cabbage, broccoli, or kale, you'll want some Bt on hand. No, Bt does not stand for "Bug toxin," but maybe it should. *Bacillus thuringiensis* is a naturally occurring soil bacterium that kills the destructive caterpillar larvae chewing holes in your cabbages, yet Bt will not harm bees, lady beetles, or other desirable insects. Fungus gnats, mosquito larvae, and potato beetle larvae are other prime Bt targets. Different strains are effective against various pests, so read the label carefully to be sure you buy the product you need. Since the bug-slaying bacteria degrade rapidly in sunlight, you'll need to reapply Bt frequently. You'll find Bt at Arbico Organics. (www.arbico-organics.com)

Starting a New Garden

Whether you want a new vegetable garden or flowerbed, the first steps are the same. The best time of year to start a new garden is in fall, though you can begin in spring, too.

Step 1: Look around your yard at different times of day, taking note of which areas get full sun, which are shaded all day, and which are sunlit for part of the day. Also notice which spots tend to be constantly damp and which dry out very fast. Use that information to choose the site for your new garden. The popular garden vegetables—including tomatoes, peppers, cucumbers, and peas—are most productive when they get full sun (that is, 8 to 10 hours of sunlight a day during the peak of summer). Many flowers, including favorites such as zinnias, cosmos, and roses, grow best in full sun, too. Leafy vegetables, such as lettuce and spinach, and many herbs thrive in partial sun, as do many flowers, including impatiens and geraniums.

Step 2: Mark the perimeter of your new garden with stakes and string. A practical size for a garden bed is 4 feet wide—so you can reach into it from either side—and 8 to 10 feet long. In most climates, vegetables and herbs grow best in raised beds, which are built up 4 to 6 inches above the surrounding ground.

Step 3: If the area where your new garden will go is covered with grass, you have a couple of options. The fast but hard approach is to use a sharp spade to slice through the sod and lift it right off the soil like a carpet. The slower but less labor-intensive way is to smother the grass with a layer of newspaper (about six to eight sheets thick), topped by compost, grass clippings, shredded leaves, straw, and other organic matter. Do this in fall, and the following spring you will be able to dig a hole and plant right through those top layers.

Step 4: If you have removed the sod, prepare the soil in your new garden beds before you buy plants. Loosen the soil with a shovel, garden fork, and/or tiller 6 to 8 inches deep, then add several inches of compost.

Step 5: Choose plants that will fare well in your garden's conditions. When you select plants that thrive in your conditions, you don't have to lavish them with attention to keep them healthy. Also, many novices make the mistake of overplanting because the seedlings look so small and the empty garden seems so big. But as the plants grow, they compete with each other for water, nutrients, and sunlight. Go with fewer plants and leave plenty of room between them when you plant.

Step 6: Bare soil is an invitation to weeds. Cover every inch not planted with a layer of mulch—straw, grass clippings, shredded leaves, or bark chips—and you'll prevent weeds from sprouting, conserve moisture in the soil, protect against erosion, and nourish the soil with organic matter as it decomposes. Replenish the mulch layer each season, and your new garden will flourish for years to come.

WINTER SQUASH
Garden Bounty in Cold Months

Eating fresh food from your garden need not come to an end when the growing season finishes. Plant winter squash and you will harvest a load of supernutritious vegetables that keep through the cold months. You can choose from varieties including acorn, butternut, delicata, buttercup, banana, kabocha, Hubbard, and spaghetti. (Pumpkins, by the way, are simply orange winter squash.) They differ from summer squash, such as zucchini, because they develop a thick skin that protects them through months of winter storage.

If you have a short growing season, start squash seeds indoors about 3 weeks before your last frost and set out transplants a week or two after all danger of frost has passed. In warmer regions, simply sow squash seeds directly in your garden a couple weeks after the danger of frost has passed. Generally, your goal is to have winter squash maturing in late summer and early fall. Squash vines need a lot of space, so plant "hills" of two or three plants about 4 feet apart in rows 6 feet apart.

When your squash is ready to harvest, look for the telltale ripeness clues that each type reveals. Where an acorn or delicata touches the ground, it develops an orange spot that darkens as the fruit ripens. Buttercups, bananas, kabochas, and Hubbards have large, spongy stems that turn corky as they ripen. Butternuts are ready when they turn from a greenish hue to a peanut color. Mature spaghettis, acorns, and butternuts should resist the light pressure of your thumbnail on the skin.

Set ripe squash in a warm, dry place to cure for a week or so after harvest to seal the skins and dry out the stems. Then move them to a cool, dry place for long-term storage. Unheated rooms or cool cellars work well. Wait about 3 weeks after storing before you sample them, to give the sugars time to develop.

CROSS-COUNTRY NURSERIES' PEPPERS
Add Heat to Your Garden

Hot pepper lovers are a breed apart from other gardeners. They eat the pungent fruit partly as a sacrament and partly as a test of machismo. And they seek out the rarest of varieties, often swapping the seeds with other chile-heads.

The rest of us may simply enjoy adding a bit of fiery flavor to salsa or chili, or we may want a few hot peppers to use in a homemade pest control spray. No matter what level of heat is best for your needs, you will find many suitable choices at **Cross-Country Nurseries** in Rosemont, New Jersey. There you can pick from hundreds of varieties, from 'Aji Benito' (from the Andes) to 'Zimbabwe Bird' (from Africa).

Order an assortment early in spring and you'll get healthy, robust, organically raised pepper plants ready to transplant to your garden when the time is right. No seed starting necessary. (www.chileplants.com)

FYI

In spring, summer, and fall, turn your compost pile weekly to keep it cooking steadily. But in winter, turning the pile slows the decomposition process by exposing the microbes in the warm center of the pile to frigid temperatures. Turn it only during long warm spells or wait until spring.

GARLIC
Grow Your Own!

You don't have to look hard to find credible science about garlic's health benefits, particularly as a natural immune system booster. This pungent herb isn't medicine, though—it's a popular culinary ingredient around the world because of the zing it brings to many cuisines.

Growing garlic is nearly effortless. Plant it in the fall, then harvest the following summer. Planting your own lets you enjoy varieties of many colors (including ones with purplish pink, red, pearly white, or silvery skins) as well as flavors.

You must first choose between softneck and hardneck varieties. Softnecks keep longer in storage, tend to mature faster, and are the best choice for the South, the West Coast, and wherever winters are moderate. Hardnecks are more colorful and offer more flavor variety. Go with them where winters are cold, spring is damp and cool, and summer is dry and warm—that is, in the Northeast, Midwest, northern-tier states, and Canada.

Plant garlic by breaking a bulb apart into individual cloves, being careful to keep the papery skins covering each clove intact. (Each clove will produce a new bulb.) Fill a quart jar with water and mix in 1 tablespoon of baking soda and 1 tablespoon of liquid seaweed (available in garden centers). Soak the cloves in this mixture for 2 hours prior to planting to prevent fungal disease and encourage vigorous growth.

Dig a 3-inch-deep furrow in rich, well-drained, weed-free garden soil. Plant the presoaked cloves 6 to 8 inches apart in the furrow, with the flat root end down and the pointy end up. Cover the cloves with 2 inches of soil mixed with compost. Water the bed, then spread a 6- to 8-inch layer of straw mulch. You should see shoots poking through the mulch in 4 to 6 weeks. Garlic stops growing in the winter months and resumes in spring.

When half to three-quarters of the garlic's leaves turn yellow brown, typically in late June or early July, harvest the garlic by carefully digging up each bulb. Do not pull, or you may break the stalk from the bulb, which can cause it to rot. Once it's harvested, get it out of the sun as soon as possible.

Tie garlic together in bundles of 6 to 10 bulbs and hang them to cure for about 4 to 5 weeks in a shaded, dry, and preferably drafty area. When the garlic is thoroughly dry, trim the roots, taking care not to knock off the outer skin. Cut off the stalks about 1½ inches above the bulb if you plan to keep the garlic in bags. Recycled mesh onion bags are perfect for storage.

Farmers' markets and the many garlic festivals held throughout North America each year are excellent places to find varieties suited to your conditions. **Filaree Farm** offers more than 100 varieties. (www.filareefarm.com)

COMPOST TEA
Beneficial Brew

Compost is an essential ingredient in successful organic gardening. Microbes in the soil turn compost into nutrients plants thrive on, and compost helps manage moisture in the soil and prevent plant diseases. A liquid version called compost tea offers a quick, effective way to deliver many of compost's benefits.

You make basic compost tea just the way you'd imagine: Fill a burlap sack or an old pillowcase with compost and soak it in a bucket of water for a few days or even weeks. (Toss the used compost back into the pile.) The longer it steeps, the stronger the tea. You can sprinkle it on your plants with a watering can. Just be sure to dilute really strong tea before using it on seedlings or other tender plants.

Recent research has found that actively aerating compost tea during the brewing process dramatically increases the number of beneficial microbes in it. Many gardeners are now so enthusiastic about the benefits of aerated compost tea that they are setting up home brewing systems. You can assemble one with parts purchased where aquarium supplies are sold, or you can order a complete starter kit, in sizes ranging from 1 to 1,000 gallons, from **Keep It Simple, Inc.** (www.simplici-tea.com)

The Organic Scoop

The complete name of this research-based manual is *Resource Guide for Organic Insect and Disease Management.* But we'll just call it *The Place to Go for Organic Garden Solutions.* It tells you the best ways to grow lettuce, tomatoes, broccoli, and other crops if you want to prevent or manage problems organically (and who doesn't?). It sorts through approved organic products and explains which to apply when, for example, the dreaded black scurf is scarring your potatoes. Turn to the appendices for the scoop on preventive techniques such as trap cropping (look it up) or creating habitats for beneficial insects. (www.nysaes.cornell.edu/pp/resourceguide)

FYI

Gardeners are often advised to place rocks, bricks, Styrofoam peanuts, or broken pottery in the bottom of plant containers to help water drain through the soil. Don't you believe it. Research has shown that reducing the volume of soil in a pot inhibits root growth and hinders plants' development.

LACEWINGS
A Must for Your Garden

Aphids, spider mites, thrips, whiteflies, leafminer eggs, and beetle larvae are all considered "dinner" by lacewing larvae, which inject prey with venom and suck out their body fluids. That's why you want hungry lacewings in your garden or greenhouse. They're a better choice for outdoor jobs than lady beetles because they stick around and work, whereas lady beetles will fly off to your neighbors' buggier gardens once they finish supping on aphids at yours. You can buy lacewing eggs and larvae, ladybugs, miniwasps, and other helpful predators from a number of sources, including **GreenMethods.com** (http://greenmethods.com). Before you buy, however, keep a couple of things in mind:

1. Buy beneficial insects from a reputable source and request fast delivery. Freshness is ultraimportant. Insect eggs and larvae are perishable and delicate, so give them shade when they arrive.

2. If you're in a hurry, buy lacewing larvae rather than eggs. You'll pay more, but they'll arrive hungrier than grizzlies just out of hibernation.

3. Don't expect to witness the injecting and sucking part; lacewings work the night shift. You should see clean new plant growth and some sucked-dry aphids, however.

Another thing: Purchasing good bugs is one way to get them into your garden. The other way is to plant a flower border. Beneficial insects love dill, cilantro, sweet alyssum, calendula, and cosmos. In fact, most anything that blooms attracts allies to your cause. Try leaving your kale in the garden over winter—it will break out in pretty yellow flowers in spring, a handy source of early-season nectar for your beneficial friends.

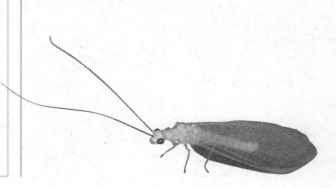

ROW COVERS
Shelter from the Storm

Floating row covers act like a safety blanket for vegetable crops. When placed over plants, the lightweight, spun-polyester fabric lets light, air, and water in while keeping pests out. The covers are especially useful for protecting eggplants from flea beetles, cauliflower and broccoli from cabbage moths, and squash from squash bugs. Row covers also help you to extend the gardening season in fall and start earlier in spring by insulating the plants and keeping them safe from freezing temperatures, wind, and harsh rain. Different weights provide varying levels of frost protection and light transmission. Reemay row cover from **Territorial Seed Company** offers a nice balance, allowing 75 percent of sunlight in and protecting plants down to 30°F. (www.territorialseed.com)

SLUG TRAP
They Love Their Brew

In damp, shady gardens, the shell-less gastropods known as slugs munch their way through rows of salad greens and beds of irises and other perennials. And they are sneaky about it—feeding at night and hiding during the day. Birds, snakes, and toads are helpful slug predators to have around your garden, but when they can't keep up with the job, you can set out baited traps for the slimy pests. They flock to beer like European soccer fans. The slugs fall into the traps, get loaded, and then can't get out. You can make your own traps by reusing plastic food containers or order Slug-X from **Gardener's Supply Company**. (www.gardeners.com)

FENCES
Wildlife-Gardener Harmony

Organic gardeners have a love-hate relationship with wildlife. The sight of wild animals in our yards is evidence that we have created a safe haven for them and are contributing to their survival. But the sight of garden plants denuded of leaves or chewed to the ground, and tomatoes gone or damaged before you've had a chance to pick them, is disappointing and frustrating enough to tempt you to take arms against the varmints what done the dirty deed.

All manner of gadgets and potions are touted as capable of keeping deer, woodchucks, rabbits, and other critters from turning your garden into their private buffet. Those products may be effective in some conditions, but the only deterrent that's sure to work without harming the animals is a fence. For deer, the fence needs to be no fewer than 8 feet high, ideally set at an angle away from the garden. For rabbits, woodchucks, and other ground-dwelling invaders, install the bottom of the fence 2 to 3 feet belowground. If you want to make sure the animals still frequent your yard and get enough to eat, plant a few of their favorite plants outside the fence where you can watch and appreciate them. **McGregor Fence Company** offers fencing ideas at www.invisible-deer-fence.com.

INSECTICIDAL SOAP
Spray Your Plants Clean, Naturally

If aphids or other pests attack your garden, wait and observe the situation for a few days before you reach for a spray. Ladybugs and lacewings often take care of an aphid problem quickly and efficiently if you give them a chance. But if the infestation doesn't subside (or if it's taking place inside your house), you can use an insecticidal soap spray, such as Safer soap. This organic insecticide contains fatty acids and salts that degrade the protective coating on soft-bodied insects like aphids, thrips, mealybugs, and whiteflies, causing them to die. The spray is safe to use around most beneficial insects. Find Safer soap at many garden centers, including the online **Planet Natural**. (www.planetnatural.com)

BUILD IT AND THEY WILL COME

Urban legends aside, bats aren't interested in flying into your hair. Mosquitoes and some other airborne morsels that plague your garden are what they're after. And boy, do they eat: One bat can catch up to 2,000 bugs a night. Normally bats nest in caves and mines, but they'll take up residence in your attic if it's near a body of water. Provide them with a safe, convenient bat house instead. One house holds up to 50 bats (that's potentially 100,000 bugs a night!). Not only does Bat Conservation International sell bat houses and kits, it's also the place to learn about this amazing flying mammal. (www.batcon.org)

MILKWEED
A Butterfly's Best Friend

They don't call milkweed "butterfly weed" for nothing. Plant it and you'll provide for two stages of butterfly growth. Monarch butterflies lay their eggs on plants in this genus (*Asclepias*) so their larvae can eat the leaves. In addition, varied and sundry butterflies sip nectar from milkweed's flowers.

Feeding butterflies is always a two-course affair. The first course is for the caterpillars: You need to plant milkweed or parsley or another larva meal and then just stand by and watch it get eaten up. Your reward will come when the striped larva that's been stripping your parsley morphs into a beautiful swallowtail butterfly that daintily sips nectar from your garden phlox. Plants that feed the larvae are known as host plants and include (in addition to milkweed and parsley) cherry trees, spicebush shrubs, and violets. The list of nectar plants reads like a who's who of garden favorites: verbena, zinnia, coneflower, aster, goldenrod, blazing star, joe-pye weed, and many others. It's important to provide butterflies with water, too, even if it's just a shallow birdbath.

Prairie Nursery (www.prairienursery.com) offers flowers favored by butterflies and sells complete butterfly garden kits that include plants and plans for gardeners short on time or knowledge. Armed with a good plant list, you can create a stunner of a butterfly garden by shopping at a local well-stocked nursery. It's best to check with your local cooperative extension office first to learn about the butterflies that frequent your area and their favorite snack foods.

NATURAL HERBICIDES
Safer Alternatives

Weeds can drive a gardener to distraction. Pull one and it seems two more pop up. Gardeners tired of hoeing, digging, and pulling often turn to herbicides—chemical weed killers. But synthetic herbicides can be toxic to people, pets, and wildlife, plus they kill organisms in the soil that contribute to plant growth and health. Natural herbicides, derived from natural sources, are effective, safer alternatives.

Corn gluten meal is the only true preemergent weed killer available that's also organic. It works by inhibiting the germination of seeds. For treatment of weeds after germination, turn to natural herbicide sprays. They are simply stronger concentrations of products you'd find in your kitchen. Your choices include horticultural vinegar (not supermarket vinegar, which is too weak); oils such as citrus, clove, and cinnamon; and sprays made from fatty or citric acids. Some work by clogging airholes on the plants' leaves, some by burning the foliage with their acidity. Most natural herbicides kill off the top growth but not the root system. You will need to periodically reapply to new growth (and after it rains) to ultimately see results.

Remember: Just because a spray is organic doesn't mean it's harmless. Full-strength vinegar and some oils and soaps can burn if you get them on your skin or in your eyes, so when applying, always wear gloves and eye protection. Follow the directions on the label, and avoid spraying bees and other insects.

Natural herbicides are also nonselective; they will kill or burn any desirable plants they come in contact with. Dipping a paintbrush into the solution and painting the leaves with it is the safest way to use most natural herbicides. A spray bottle or backpack sprayer works for larger areas. A wide selection of natural herbicides can be found at Planet Natural. (www.planetnatural.com)

BAMBOO: Wanted—Dead, Not Alive

Bamboo stakes are about the most useful and versatile props you can have in the vegetable garden. After all, bamboo is renewable, strong, lightweight, and inexpensive. You can fashion it into bean trellises and tomato tepees. Or create fancy grids that will keep your zinnias from napping by using twine (or, easier yet, zip ties) to connect the joints. At the end of the season, just disassemble the structures and store until the next year. But here's the thing: To make good, strong structures, you'll need to buy 7- to 8-foot stakes that are at least ½ inch in diameter. Generally these are available only in bales of 50, which means you should gather a cadre of gardening friends and order a few bales. Soon.

Beware of trying to grow your own bamboo. It tends to spread rapidly and uncontrollably, so that soon after planting you wish it dead and gone. Look for bamboo stakes in bulk at **www.amleo.com**.

EARTHBOX SELF-WATERING POTS
Lighten Your Gardening Workload

Living in an apartment or urban setting is no excuse for not growing tomatoes, when pots are available that water themselves. Mind you, you still need to water—just not as often. There are lots of different models, some utilitarian, some elegant, but they all contain a water reservoir that will help keep your plants continuously, but not overly, hydrated. Often it's a false bottom, but sometimes it takes the form of a pot inside a pot. The clunky EarthBox (www.earthbox.com) is a time-tested model that gets overwhelmingly favorable performance reviews. Here's why:

★ It's big enough to grow tomatoes!
★ The reservoir is sized right for the large, boxy container, allowing water to be wicked to the roots as needed to keep plants healthy when they're growing like wild in late summer.
★ It has an overflow hole, so you can't overwater.
★ It's on casters, so you can wheel your plants around to catch more rays.

Get several and put them in full view so that the idea of growing food will spread through the land—and with it the notion that we can control our destinies (or at least our diets). If you're a DIY sort of person, google around for plans to build your own self-watering planter. Many are available.

CONTAINER MIXES
An Eye on Ingredients

Potting mix choices, it often seems, are severely limited. Our advice: Search for natural and sustainable ingredients. Instead of purchasing the standard peat moss and encapsulated chemical fertilizers, go for coir, compost, bark, rice hulls, and worm castings.

Let's take a look at some ingredients, good and bad. The nutrient-free material that makes up the base in many commercial container mixes is either peat moss or coir, or a combination of the two. Most peat is harvested, on a massive scale, from Canadian bogs. Yes, it will regenerate, but probably not in your lifetime. Coir, on the other hand, is a waste product. It's the fiber from the husks of coconuts. Likewise for rice hulls, which are the indigestible protective coverings on rice grains, often used as cheap filler in pet food. As for fertilizers, odor-free organic worm castings are, no exaggeration, nature's most complete plant food as well as the perfect soil conditioner. Skip the mixes with the blue crystals of synthetic fertilizers blended in.

If you're fortunate, you may find a local producer of compost-based potting media, such as the Organic Mechanics Soil Company in West Chester, Pennsylvania, which sells a premium product using good ingredients to a limited market, in this case to the Mid-Atlantic states. TerraCycle (www.terracycle.net) produces a peat-free potting mix, packages it in used gallon milk jugs, and is working to get it on the shelves of retailers, both mega and mini. Now that's sustainable thinking!

FYI

The best time to harvest vegetables and herbs from your garden is in the morning, after the dew dries. Later in the day, the plants lose moisture and freshness. When the plants are still wet from dew, however, you risk spreading fungal diseases as you touch each of them.

SPADE
Dig, Cut, Pry, and Edge

Don't confuse a spade with a shovel; they're not used for the same jobs. A shovel, with its scooped-out head and rounded edge, is for lifting and throwing loose material, such as sand, soil, or gravel. A spade has a squared-off blade and is meant for cutting, digging, and more. Its primary purpose is to open a hole in the ground for a plant, but a spade's sharp edge also makes it perfect for edging beds and slicing through roots or under turf. And those are just its recognized uses. You'll discover more on those days when you're too tired to go back to the shed for the proper tool. You'll use your trusty spade to smash clods of dirt, hammer in stakes, lever up rocks, and carry plants from one place to another.

A high-quality spade has a carbon or stainless steel head. The shaft and handle are made from hardwood—usually ash—and the handle is shaped in what's called a "YD" shape. (Take a look at the **Spear & Jackson** digging spade at www.gardentalk.com.) Most important is how the steel and the wood join—either by a socket design or with straps that are riveted to the shaft. This lessens the possibility of the spade breaking when you use it as it wasn't intended.

Buy the best you can afford, then keep the blade sharp and rust free, and the wood oiled. You'll never need another.

HO-MI KOREAN HAND PLOW
A Hands-Down Favorite

Just as every cook has a favorite knife, every gardener has a pet hand tool. For many, the ho-mi is it. Strong yet lightweight, it multitasks furiously: digging planting holes, creating tidy seed furrows, banishing dandelions, and cultivating tight little rows of onions. Use it with whole-arm action to dig or to extract weeds by using the strong, curved blade for leverage, and you'll avoid the wrist problems that can result from trowel digging. Some retailers call this tool the EZ Digger—for good reason. It's available from **Garden Hardware Company**. (www.gardenhardware.com)

SEEDS OF CHANGE CUT FLOWERS
Mix It Up

You can fill your home with bouquets of fresh organic flowers all summer long for less than $25. How? Plant a cutting garden. Many of the best cut flowers grow quickly and easily when planted from seed in late spring. These cheerful plants demand nothing more than sun, a patch of well-drained soil, and deep watering once a week. And they bloom exuberantly from midsummer until frost. You get bouquets for your home (and to share with family and friends) that have not been doused with chemicals, unlike those imported posies you find in most florist shops.

The Cut Flower Collection from **Seeds of Change** contains an especially nice mix of long-lasting, attractive flowers, including old-fashioned favorites like sunflowers, marigolds, cosmos, and zinnias, plus larkspur, Mexican sunflower, nigella, safflower, and coreopsis. Each type of flower comes packaged individually, rather than premixed, so you can design your cutting garden however you like. (www.seedsofchange.com)

FORK
Spear a Good One

The garden fork is a spade's slightly more refined sibling. While the four-tined fork digs and loosens soil like a spade, it also turns compost, untangles roots, and coaxes potatoes and carrots from their earthly beds. And does it with less chance of slicing into things better left unsliced, like worms or tree roots.

A good fork is made of the same materials, and by the same manner, as a spade. The head and shaft should be forged from one piece of carbon or stainless steel. This way, if a tine bends against a boulder, you can bend it back without the tool losing strength. Forks made from stamped steel are cheaper, but once bent, the fork is never again as strong. It should have a YD handle for comfort and leverage.

A good fork is heavy and solid in your hand. This is a tool where quality construction counts. Look for steel garden forks made in England; they're built to be heirlooms. **Lee Valley Tools** has a selection of steel garden forks and spades in different sizes so that small and tall gardeners alike sacrifice neither comfort nor efficiency. (www.leevalley.com)

FYI Until the late 20th century, clover was included in many lawn seed mixes, but now many homeowners try to eliminate it. That's misguided, because clover pulls the vital nutrient nitrogen out of the air and holds it in the soil for other plants (like grass) to feed on. And when clover blooms, it attracts and nourishes the bees that pollinate your garden.

RAIN BARRELS
Channeling Raindrops

Did you know that every time lightning strikes, nitrogen combines with hydrogen and gets washed out of the sky? In other words, *there's fertilizer in them thar drops*. If you think of that next time you watch the rain gushing down the driveway, along the curb, and into the storm drain, you may be more inclined to say, "Stop! Enough!" Add to that the soil erosion caused by major storms, the depletion of our precious groundwater, and the flooding caused by rampant development, and you'll be convinced that each small step you can take toward water conservation is important.

That's where rain barrels come in. They allow you to collect your roof water for use in your garden. Check **Clean Air Gardening** (www.cleanairgardening.com) for a diverse selection of ready-mades. Some companies, such as **RainWater Solutions** (www.rainwater solutions.com), offer discounts to encourage group purchases by municipalities and civic groups. Think how much runaway rain you could halt by turning your town on to this idea! For DIY types, consult YouTube (www.youtube.com) for tutorials that show how to adapt a barrel to function as a rain collector.

Here are useful rain barrel facts and tips:

★ More than 15 percent of the average household water usage is for lawns and gardens.

★ An inch of rain on a 100-square-foot roof will fill a 60-gallon rain barrel.

★ Water pressure increases about a half pound for each foot your barrel is raised off the ground. A barrel raised 2 feet flows at about 2 gallons per minute.

★ Rain barrels must be well secured—a full barrel weighs more than 400 pounds.

★ Every rain barrel should be outfitted with an overflow pipe directed away from the house's foundation.

★ Add a screen to the top of your rain barrel to keep out insects and debris.

VIBURNUM
Multitalented Performers

Most shrubs are one-trick ponies, drop-dead spectacular for 2 weeks, invisible (if not downright gawky) the other 50. Not viburnums. This huge plant family multitasks its way through the year. Viburnums flower in large clusters of white, cream, or pink-tinged blooms. Not all are fragrant—some stink, actually—but the ones that are will have you swooning with their spicy scent. After the flowers come colorful berries that birds love. Most viburnums obligingly end their growing season by turning vivid colors in fall. When you add in the shelter they provide wildlife, and the fact that there's a viburnum right for every area of the country, you have the perfect plant for organic landscapes. Forestfarm (www.forestfarm.com) has dozens of viburnums to choose from. Bet you can't stop at just one.

WHERE IT ALL STARTED

In 1942, J. I. Rodale coined the term *organic* in its current context, meaning growing food without toxic chemicals and living in harmony with nature. Rodale launched *Organic Farming and Gardening* magazine as the practical guide to producing the most healthful food, using resources efficiently, and protecting the ecosystem around your home. The magazine that is now known as *Organic Gardening* and its Web site, OrganicGardening.com, are still delivering the latest research and the real-world insights of experienced gardeners to readers tending their first plot as well as to longtime earth-turners. (www.organicgardening.com)

FYI

When feeding plants with liquid fertilizer, add ¼ teaspoon of dish soap to a quart of water. Then mix in the fertilizer, per the package's instructions. The soap helps the fertilizer coat the leaf surface.

DRIP IRRIGATION
A Little Drop'll Do You

Rainfall is the best source of water for your garden, but when conditions demand that you supplement, a drip irrigation system is the most efficient—and therefore eco-conscious—way to give your plants a drink.

Drip irrigation systems typically come in a kit with plastic tubing, emitters from which the water drips, and some connectors and end pieces. You lay out the tubing in your garden with the emitters near your plants. The water goes straight where it needs to—the plants' roots—and isn't wasted where it's of no use.

You can find drip irrigation systems designed for vegetable beds, landscape plantings, even plants in containers. For a greener, more efficient system, go for the timer option. This allows you to water plants early in the day—the ideal time for the roots to soak up moisture before it evaporates—and when you are away from your garden. (www.dripworksusa.com)

STIRRUP HOE
A Weed's Worst Enemy

Weeds grow in gardens. It's a fact of life. But you absolutely do not need to blast them with toxic chemicals or spend hours on your knees to create a neat and tidy landscape. Instead, invest in a stirrup hoe—a tool developed specifically to remove small weeds quickly and easily, no stooping required. Going after weeds while they are young has two main advantages: Weed seedlings are easier to remove than plants with mature root systems, and you eliminate the pesky plants before they have a chance to set or spread seed.

You can reduce your weed problem to almost zero if you spend just a few minutes each week removing small weeds with a stirrup hoe. The tool's oscillating stirrup-shaped blade cuts about ¼ inch deep in the soil, slicing off the roots of young weeds without disturbing the soil enough to bring new weed seeds to the surface. The 3¾-inch stirrup hoe from Johnny's Selected Seeds features a sturdy ash handle and a replaceable, tempered steel blade that maneuvers easily between established perennials and rows of vegetables. (www.johnnyseeds.com)

GREENER LAWN MOWERS
Power of the People

Repeat after me: "I do not need a noisy, fume-spewing, gas-powered mower to cut my quarter-acre lawn." Did you know that as 54 million Americans mow their lawns every weekend, they contribute as much as 5 percent of the nation's air pollution?

The **Brill** Razorcut reel mower is not your grandfather's push mower. It's sleek in design and weighs only 17 pounds. You won't get quite the workout your grandfather achieved with his hefty version—but we'll count that as a plus. Here's a tip: Don't let your lawn get too shaggy. The blades slice through your grass much more easily if you mow often. One drawback with the Brill is that it shaves the lawn to 2 inches or shorter—and many lawn grasses crowd out weeds better if shorn at 2½ to 3 inches tall.

There are other options: **Sunlawn** reel mowers are not quite as lightweight, but they adjust for higher cuts. Next in rank of eco-correctness is a corded electric mower. Just think, no more yanking on a starter cord, no more running out of gas. The average small-lawn owner will find the cutting and mulching performance of an electric machine perfectly adequate. Battery-powered, cordless electric mowers are also an ecological step up from gas-powered mowers and a good option for midsize lawns. Something to be aware of: Lead emissions occur during the manufacture of the batteries.

Start your investigations at Clean Air Gardening. Their Web site has several reel, electric, and cordless mowers to choose from. (www.cleanairgardening.com)

CORN GLUTEN MEAL
Crabgrass Buster

A 100 percent weed-free lawn not only is wholly unnatural but demands regular applications of harsh chemicals that threaten the health of your family, your pets, and the environment. A perfect lawn isn't worth it. Deal with a few weeds.

That said, you can defend your lawn from a weed invasion without turning to the toxins. Raise your lawn mower blade to its highest setting (typically about 3 inches). Taller grass shades out weeds, has deeper roots, and looks more lush.

If crabgrass is a problem, apply corn gluten meal in spring. A by-product of corn processing that's often used to feed livestock, it has been found to inhibit seed germination. Bear in mind that once the weeds have gone beyond the sprout stage, corn gluten will not affect them. Also, corn gluten doesn't discriminate between seeds you want to sprout and those you don't, so avoid using it where you've recently sown seeds. It has terrific long-term effects. Studies have found that 3 years after application, it suppressed weeds more thoroughly than it did in the first year.

Corn gluten meal comes in a pellet form, so you can use it in an ordinary spreader. Apply it early in the season, before the soil reaches 55°F, at a rate of 20 pounds per 1,000 square feet. Bonus: Corn gluten meal is a rich source of nitrogen for your grass, so it works just like the popular "weed-and-feed" products—only without risking harm to any living thing.

You can find corn gluten meal in bulk at many feed stores, or look for bags of **Espoma** Natural Weed Preventer Plus Lawn Food. (www.espoma.com)

'CAREFREE BEAUTY' ROSE
No Prima Donna

Roses demand constant pampering and regular dousing with chemicals to look beautiful, right? Wrong! Choose the right roses for your conditions, plant them where they get morning sun and steady airflow, and they'll thrive with minimal attention. Roses' most common problems—fungal diseases such as blackspot—are easily (and safely) treated with 1 tablespoon of baking soda mixed in 1½ quarts of water, with a few drops of vegetable oil. Spray this mix directly on affected leaves.

You can choose from hundreds of rose varieties, but stay away from hybrid tea roses, because they tend to be the most susceptible to problems. Go with shrub roses instead. They don't bear tight buds atop long stems like you get in florist's bouquets, but they are enchanting plants for your yard. If you are new to organic rose growing or have struggled to successfully grow roses in the past, plant 'Carefree Beauty'. It comes with natural resistance to pests and diseases. It blooms repeatedly in spring and fall, opening countless clusters of 4-inch, lightly fragrant pink flowers all over the 3- to 5-foot shrub. When 'Carefree Beauty' is finished blooming for the season, it sports large orange hips that nourish birds through the winter.

You can find it in garden centers or from online rose retailers, such as the Antique Rose Emporium. (www.antiqueroseemporium.com)

ESSENTIAL BOOKS FOR GARDENERS

The Garden Primer by Barbara Damrosch (Workman, 2008). Encyclopedic, down-to-earth, fun to read, she has all the answers.

How to Grow More Vegetables Than You Ever Thought Possible on Less Land Than You Can Imagine by John Jeavons (Ten Speed, 1991). The biodynamic, French intensive system shows how to get maximum yield from any size space.

The Organic Gardener's Handbook of Natural Insect and Disease Control edited by Fern Marshall Bradley, Barbara Ellis, and Deborah L. Martin (Rodale, 2009). Search by crop or pest to identify problems and find the best organic solutions.

Four-Season Harvest: Organic Vegetables from Your Home Garden All Year Long by Eliot Coleman (Chelsea Green, 1999). Organic guru shares his passion and techniques for growing food 12 months of the year in any climate.

Armitage's Native Plants for North American Gardens by Allan M. Armitage (Timber Press, 2006). A renowned scientist names the best species and varieties for backyard ecosystems.

CHICKENS
Best Breeds for Small Flocks

Take an early-morning stroll through a residential neighborhood in Portland, Oregon; Austin, Texas; or Brooklyn, New York, and you might hear an unexpected sound: clucking chickens. Cities and towns across the country are lifting bans on backyard chickens, and organic gardeners are discovering that raising a small flock of hens offers plenty of rewards—fresh eggs, a constant supply of natural fertilizer, great compost, and hours of entertainment.

Chickens come in both large and miniature—or bantam—sizes. Large-breed birds work well for backyard flocks because they produce bigger eggs than bantams and are too heavy to fly very high or far. Chickens are decidedly social creatures, so you'll need at least three birds. Poultry hatcheries such as **Murray McMurray** (www.mcmurrayhatchery.com) offer dozens of breeds to choose from. Since most backyard chickens double as pets, consider choosing a breed like the Black Australorp.

Bred in Australia, Black Australorps have gorgeous, shiny black plumage and bright red combs; they reliably produce brown eggs in winter, when other breeds' egg production tapers off. They are gentle, curious, and fond of human company, but they don't mind being secured in a coop—as long as they have plenty of room to stretch their legs. Black Australorps get along well with other breeds, so consider building a flock with a mix of breeds, including Buff Orpingtons and Silver Laced Wyandottes.

CHICKEN COOPS
Backyard Poultry Palaces

Keeping a few hens in the backyard makes a lot of sense for organic gardeners. Chickens produce nutrient-rich manure; they devour slugs, snails, and weed seeds; and they lay dozens and dozens of eggs each year. All they ask for in return is food, fresh water, plenty of room to exercise, and a safe place to live.

Coops such as the **Henspa** and **Eglu** are available online (www.henspa.com), but these premade henhouses cost upward of $1,000, are made from plastic or new wood, and must be shipped across the country. A more sustainable option is to purchase chicken coop plans and build your own coop with locally sourced or recycled materials. Chickens can survive in cramped quarters, but you'll have happier, healthier birds if the coop has at least 4 square feet per bird, plus a large enclosed outdoor run. Plan to include a roost for the hens to rest on off the ground, a nest box for laying eggs, and a waterer and feeder.

The chicken supply company **My Pet Chicken** sells plans for an attractive, barn-style coop that comfortably and safely houses up to five chickens. It features a large sheltered outdoor run and an elevated henhouse that keeps the birds safe from predators at night. Materials for the 4 × 8-foot chicken coop run between $300 and $500 new, but you can reduce the cost to your pocketbook and the planet by using salvaged wood. (www.mypetchicken.com)

Your home is where you can fully express your desire for a greener, more socially responsible planet. And thanks to the growing number of green products on the market, it's increasingly easy to incorporate eco-friendly appliances and home furnishings into your everyday life. This chapter highlights some of the greenest options out there—and maybe saves you a little green, too—including products that span the spectrum from innovative machinery to traditional crafted goods.

More efficient appliances will become more important as energy prices rise and concerns over climate change grow. The improved appliances now on the market show that manufacturers are willing to meet those needs. Whether making a first-time purchase or replacing an older model, paying more up front often saves money in the long run. We spend about 20 percent of our household energy bills to power appliances, so it makes sense to find appliances that reduce energy and water demands—and utility bills.

Greener appliances can perform well, too. There's no sense in buying any product, green or not, that doesn't work effectively. Because it's also true that small is beautiful when it comes to saving energy, some appliances are considered green simply because they save energy based on size alone.

Since most manufacturers don't advertise what their products are made from or who makes them, it can be difficult to identify appliances made from environmentally friendlier materials or made in socially responsible ways. Many large appliances are made with a minimum of 25 percent recycled steel, for instance, but you're not likely to see that fact displayed. It's worth noting that some of an appliance's most significant impacts occur once you get it home. Knowing how to use appliances efficiently can go a long way toward conserving energy or water.

Many home furnishings are chosen on looks and function alone. But what appears lovely on the outside may not be so worthy on the inside. As manufacturers have sought to bring furnishing products to market more quickly and at lower price points, concerns about renewable materials, safety, and labor practices have often gone by the wayside.

Here's the good news: You can select products that do not sacrifice style or function for sustainability. The purchase of many home goods, from kitchen accessories to bedding, can have a positive impact on the environment and people who produce them.

Textiles are a case in point: While many are made from synthetic fabrics like polyester or nylon that are derived from nonrenewable petroleum resources, there is a growing number of sustainably produced natural textiles. Certified organic, fair-trade fibers, for example, are produced without the application of most synthetic fertilizers and pesticides and are grown by farmers who make a living wage.

Some natural fibers, such as hemp and linen, can grow quickly and easily without chemical inputs. Choosing organic is especially important when it comes to cotton. Conventionally grown (nonorganic) cotton accounts for about 11 percent of all pesticide use in the world.

Choosing greener home furnishings, then, means selecting natural, organic fabrics; opting for products that are low in volatile organic compounds (VOCs); and avoiding products that receive chemical treatments for things like stain resistance during the manufacturing process. Textiles, for instance, can contain and emit formaldehyde, a known carcinogen. In your home, products can off-gas that chemical and other VOCs, posing a health hazard to anyone who breathes them. According to the Environmental Protection Agency, our indoor air can be up to 10 times as polluted as outdoor air, in part due to home furnishings.

In light of ethical issues surrounding forestry, wood furniture is another area where it's important to seek sustainable sources. Many small producers now craft their wares from sustainable sources, as do a few larger manufacturers. For the best assurance that furniture supports environmentally sound practices, opt for wood that is certified as sustainable by a credible source, such as the Forest Stewardship Council. It's just one of many ways that your choices can lead to a greener, healthier home—and a better planet.

—Kristi Wiedemann

appliances

CLOTHES DRYERS

Dryers with Eco-Sensibility

First, the bad news: Dryers are one of the few large household appliances that haven't gained much in efficiency over the years. Try to find an Energy Star model, and you won't—that program doesn't exist for dryers, since they don't vary much in efficiency. The good news: many newer dryers have a built-in moisture sensor that knows when the load is dry and shuts off the machine. Compared with timed drying, that one feature can cut energy use by about 15 percent. And since dryers are typically the second-largest electricity consumer in your home, the long-term savings can go a long way. What's more, shorter drying times mean less wear and tear on your clothing and linens.

Two well-rated options with moisture sensors come from **LG** (www.lgusa.com) and **Frigidaire** (www.frigidaire.com). The 7.3-cubic-foot LG SteamDryer is part of the company's chic and colorful TrueSteam series. One feature is the machine's capability to steam your clothes, minimizing the need for ironing. For something more basic but still versatile, consider Frigidaire's 5.8-cubic-foot dryer. It includes seven automatic cycles and four temperature options. Both dryers offer a natural gas option for $50 to $150 more. Gas is typically cheaper than electric, and it emits fewer greenhouse gases.

DISHWASHERS

Dishes Dried for Free

Quick quiz: What's more efficient—washing dishes by hand or washing them in a dishwasher? If you guessed the latter, you're spot on. Thanks to dramatic improvements in efficiency over the past decade or so, dishwashers can use as little as half the energy and one-sixth of the water required to wash by hand.

Although most dishwasher energy goes toward heating the water, a chunk of it goes toward drying, too. That's why most energy-saving advice suggests forgoing the heated drying option. But now some dishwashers offer heated drying cycles without using additional energy. These machines recycle heat snagged from the hot water used in cleaning and put that heat to work in the drying cycle.

Eco-conscious European manufacturer **Bosch** offers this "recycled heat" feature in many of its dishwashers. One well-rated option is the full-featured 800 Series Integra dishwasher. A pared-down version, the 300 Series Integra dishwasher, sells for about half as much.

In addition to energy-free drying, both models come with the EcoSense feature, which cuts back on unnecessary water use if soil levels don't demand a full wash. They also have built-in booster heaters, allowing you to turn down the temperature on your home's water heater to save even more energy. (www.boschappliances.com)

> **FYI**
>
> As tempting as it may be to peek, keep the oven door closed when cooking. Every time the door opens, the oven can lose 25°F of heat. Instead, watch a clock or use a timer.

COOKTOPS

Greenest Cooktop You've Never Heard Of

When it comes to choosing a greener cooktop, you might think your choice is between gas and electric. But the most energy-efficient technology is one you may not have heard of—induction. Induction cooking elements have been widely used in Europe and Asia for years, but the technology has only recently begun expanding into home kitchens in the United States.

The energy savings of an induction cooktop can be significant, because each time you cook on an electric burner, you can lose nearly 25 percent of the heat. With a gas burner, you can lose 60 percent. Induction burners deliver as much as 90 percent of their energy directly to the pan.

Induction cooktops work by heating up the pan itself through magnetic energy. They require cookware that's magnetic—iron or stainless steel. To check whether your cookware is compatible, see if a magnet sticks to your pans. If it does, you're ready to cook induction-style.

The stainless steel and black 30-inch **Electrolux** Icon induction drop-in cooktop includes four induction elements that range in size and power. It boasts 15 digital preset heat settings for precise cooking. (www.electro luxicon.com)

The **Kenmore** Elite electric induction cooktop is another well-rated option at a slightly lower price. This cooktop is also stainless steel and black with four heating elements, but it provides less power. (www.kenmore.com; www.sears.com)

And don't forget that *how* you cook can be just as important as what you cook on. For a list of energy-saving cooking tips, check out the American Council for an Energy Efficient Economy's Web site: www.aceee.org.

FYI

Use any oven's self-cleaning feature sparingly. Experts say using the self-cleaning feature more than once a month can counteract any savings from purchasing an energy-efficient model.

JUICERS

Drink Those Nutrients

You've heard it all before: Eating lots of fruits and veggies every day—an average of nine servings, to be exact—can help ensure you live a long and healthy life. But how many of us actually follow that sound but admittedly daunting advice? One way to help ensure that you get your daily recommended servings of fruits and vegetables is to extract them in liquid form from fresh organic produce using a juicer. Or better yet, use a dual stage "masticating" Nutrition Center. Omega Products offers such a countertop device that can meet all your juicing and extracting needs. It can whir up everything from pulpy fruits like peaches to leafy greens and a whole lot more.

This is a hardy unit, so strongly constructed that it is UL approved for both home and commercial uses, and Omega is so confident of the Model 8003's durability that they guarantee it for 10 years. The fresh-squeezed tastes alone will likely keep you coming back for years.

The **Omega Nutrition Center** is available in a clinical white as well as a snappy chrome-and-black model. (www.omegajuicers.com)

COFFEE PRESS: GREENING YOUR COFFEE HABIT

If you're already drinking sustainable coffee, you're well on your way to minimizing the impacts your daily java fix had from the field to your cup. Ready to take the next step? Consider brewing your joe in a French press that will not only eliminate the need for disposable filters but also keep your coffee warm, so that you spend less energy reheating it. The elegantly designed Columbia thermal press from **Bodum** does both in stainless style. The press comes in 3-, 8-, and 12-cup capacities. (www.bodumusa.com)

OVEN/RANGES
Cooking That's a Breeze

After all that measuring and mixing, wouldn't it be nice if your oven could help ensure your results reflect your efforts? A convection oven might be just the helping hand you're looking for.

Most ovens heat food from the bottom up, but the built-in fan in a convection oven sends that heat swirling around your cookies and casseroles, creating a breezy environment. Those air currents not only contribute to more even cooking, they allow you to lower the oven temperature and enjoy the fruits of your labor more quickly. Convection ovens cut down on energy use by about one-third compared with their non-fan-equipped counterparts. And they can be gas or electric powered.

Whether you're looking for a wall oven or a range, Maytag offers well-rated models in both categories with its EvenAir convection technology. The 30-inch Maytag freestanding gas range delivers uniform browning and top-notch baking. Its five-burner cooktop includes a center simmer burner. The freestanding range comes in black, white, or stainless steel and is available in an electric model.

The 30-inch electric Maytag single built-in oven delivers equivalent results using the same convection technology. It also comes in black, white, or stainless steel. The built-in oven does not have a comparable gas model.

Both models are self-cleaning, which means—aside from the obvious—they're well insulated, so heat is less prone to escape during use. (www.maytag.com)

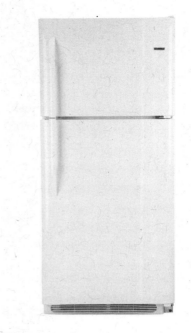

REFRIGERATORS
Size and Style Matter

Refrigerators are the single-biggest energy-consuming kitchen appliance in most households, but they are significantly more efficient than they were just 8 years ago, so there is good reason to consider buying a new one.

The larger the fridge, the more energy it consumes. Choosing a size that's just big enough to meet your family's needs is the first step toward energy savings. Less obvious is the fact that energy efficiency varies by style and feature. Top-mounted models are the most energy shrewd of the bunch. Side-by-sides take the cake for being the most consumptive. Ice makers and through-the-door ice dispensers draw more energy.

Some of the most energy-efficient top-mounted refrigerators available are made by Sun Frost. The 14.3-cubic-foot Sun Frost RF16 model boasts energy savings of 36 percent compared to refrigerators that meet required federal efficiency standards. With its relatively small capacity, the RF16 provides good incentive to buy and store your food judiciously. At about $3,000, it's a real investment in energy efficiency. (707-822-9095; www.sunfrost.com)

If you're looking for something less costly, consider an Energy Star top-mount refrigerator made by Kenmore. Like most Energy Star–qualified refrigerators, the 20.6-cubic-foot Kenmore 78254 top-freezer model uses about 20 percent less energy than others in its class, even with an ice maker. (www.kenmore.com; www.sears.com)

FAN: LOWER-TECH CLIMATE CONTROL

Among the simplest, most energy-efficient ways to keep cool is with a tried-and-true fan. By creating a windchill effect, a fan helps you feel cooler without actually lowering the temperature—and with much less energy than an air conditioner uses. Ceiling fans are most effective for cooling a whole room, but if you're looking for a quick, subtle burst of cool, a portable or window fan can be a good compromise.

Honeywell makes two fans known for their cooling powers: the Honeywell Dual window fan and the Super Turbo High Performance oscillating table fan. (www.kaz.com)

Seeing the Forest for the Trees

In theory, wood is one of the most eco-friendly products we use. Its seeds are readily available, and its main energy sources are sunlight, soil nutrients, and water. On top of that, wood is completely recyclable and biodegradable. All sounds good, right? But things get more complicated when we look at the practices of growing and processing this resource.

Thankfully, there are now ways to reward the best practices of forest management: certification.

One example is the Rainforest Alliance's forestry certification program, SmartWood, founded in 1989 in response to the crisis of tropical rain-forest destruction. The goal was and still is to provide economic incentives to businesses that practice responsible forestry management. The work of this group spurred the 1993 formation of the Forest Stewardship Council (FSC), an international, independent, not-for-profit organization that promotes the responsible management of the world's forests. FSC's representatives include environmental and social advocates, timber traders and foresters, indigenous peoples, corporations, and community forestry advocates.

How does third-party certification for forests work, and what does it mean when you see an FSC label? First, standards are developed for responsible forestry that reflect social, economic, and ecological needs. FSC relies on a set of 10 principles and other criteria, which include compliance with local laws; protection of the rights of indigenous peoples and forest workers; management of environmental impact; and monitoring and assessment of the forest and the impacts of the process from forest to store.

The use of independent, third-party auditors allows the practices of timber companies and forest landowners to be evaluated and certified to ensure they're meeting FSC's standards. The end products carry the FSC label in the consumer marketplace.

To guarantee that products on the market are those that were certified in the forest, FSC uses a "chain of custody" system: The wood product is tracked at every stage of production, from harvest to processing, and finally to the marketplace. Environmental groups like the Natural Resources Defense Council consider FSC the most credible of certification programs.

Another forest certification is the Sustainable Forestry Initiative (SFI). Established by the American Forest & Paper Association, SFI is now a wholly independent nonprofit organization that certifies North American forests. SFI certification involves compliance with standards and has a chain-of-custody tracking system. But some environmentalists argue that SFI's standards aren't rigorous enough.

In the end, forest certification programs may differ in the stringency of their requirements and certification, but they offer a structured system that ensures that some sustainable forest-management practices are followed.

WASHING MACHINES
A New Spin on Efficiency

Despite all that agitation and spinning, most of the energy used for washing your clothes in a traditional washing machine goes into heating the water. So it makes sense that the most efficient machines use less water to get the job done.

Front-loaders, also known as horizontal-axis models, are designed to do just that, cutting water use nearly 40 percent and energy use by about 50 percent. While a typical washer uses about 40 gallons of water per load, a full-size front-loader uses only 20 to 25 gallons. These machines also spin more water out of your clothes, resulting in shorter drying times, and are gentler on clothes, reducing wear and tear.

In LG's TrueSteam series is the top-rated 4.2-cubic-foot LG SteamWasher that has Allergiene. This Energy Star–qualified model uses steam to achieve better performance and efficiency, saving an estimated 7,600 gallons of water per year compared with a traditional washer. (www.lgusa.com)

For a less costly front-loader that still performs well, consider the slightly smaller, Energy Star–qualified, 3.5-cubic-foot Frigidaire front-load washer. (www.frigidaire.com)

Still drawn to loading your clothes from the top? All is not lost. Despite trouble with quality in earlier models, some high-efficiency top-loaders now perform well. One of the best is the 3.7-cubic-foot Fisher & Paykel Intuitive Eco. This Energy Star–qualified machine senses just the right amount of water required. (www.fisherpaykel.com)

FYI

When possible, install your dishwasher away from your refrigerator. With the heat and moisture given off by a dishwasher, a nearby refrigerator will have to work extra-hard to keep things cool, thus consuming more energy. If the two must be neighbors, separate them with a sheet of foam insulation.

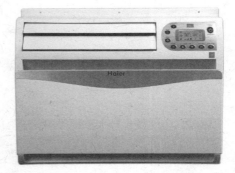

AIR CONDITIONERS
Ozone-Friendly Cooling

If you've ever questioned whether your everyday product choices *really* make a difference in the big picture, consider this: What was once a gaping hole in the earth-protective ozone layer is now on its way to closing up. That's in part because the refrigerants used in consumer products today are more ozone friendly.

Among the friendliest air conditioners to the ozone layer is the Haier Paragon Eco-Conditioner (ESAD4066). It's Energy Star–qualified, which means it uses at least 10 percent less energy than conventional models. As it cools, it also aims to reduce airborne odors, allergens, and pollutants. With 6,000 Btu of power, this model is built to cool a room that's between 150 and 200 square feet. (www.haieramerica.com).

If the space you wish to cool is outside the range of the Eco-Conditioner, consider an Energy Star–rated A/C from Frigidaire. Frigidaire window-mounted air conditioners are consistently well rated and come in various power capacities. Not quite sure what size A/C to buy? No worries—Frigidaire's Web site offers a sizing guide. (www.frigidaire.com)

SMALL FOOTPRINT SAVES ENERGY

Whether you want to bake a side dish or a miniature meal, a toaster oven can be an ideal way to cut down on cooking kilowatts—in fact, about half as many kilowatts compared to a full-size oven. Not sure whether a toaster oven offers enough versatility to cook what you want? Check out the Black & Decker Toast-R-Oven Classic Countertop. It comes with plenty of settings (including bake, broil, toast, and warm) and accommodates six slices of toast or a 12-inch pizza. (www.blackanddeckerappliances.com)

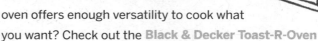

AIR PURIFIERS
Clear the Air

Despite smokestacks and tailpipes puffing pollutants into the atmosphere 24/7, it's the air indoors that tends to be the dirtiest—as much as 10 times as polluted, according to the federal Environmental Protection Agency. While your grandmother might tell you there are some simple steps you can take to clear the air—and she'd have a point (think opening windows)—if you're concerned about indoor air pollutants, you might want to spring for an air cleaner.

That's where Blueair comes in. With a combination of mechanical and electrostatic filtration, Blueair purifiers claim to capture 99.97 percent of particles as small as 0.1 micron—tiny airborne impurities like dust mites, pollen, pet dander, and other microirritants best kept out of our lungs.

Blueair aims to produce its products with minimal environmental impact. Each purifier is designed for recycling—meaning it can be broken down at the end of its useful life into its component parts, namely polypropylene (#5 plastic) and galvanized steel—and used again. All Blueair purifiers have earned Energy Star approval.

The latest, and greenest, Blueair purifier is the ECO10. It uses a mere 10 watts of power to run at high speed and can clean a room up to 300 square feet. This top-of-the-line model sells at about $930, but Blueair offers seven less-expensive options in various sizes to meet your needs and budget. The company also sells refurbished purifiers at a discount with a 10-year limited warranty. (www.blueair.com)

And for a budget purifier, check out the Honeywell Enviracaire Permanent True HEPA air purifier. It has three air cleaning levels and can purify the air of a room up to 374 square feet. (www.kaz.com)

EVAPORATIVE COOLERS
Nature's Way to Be Cool

If you live in an arid climate, such as the southwestern United States, an evaporative cooler can be a smart replacement for a traditional air conditioner. Taking a hint from nature, the aptly nicknamed "swamp cooler" pulls outside air over water and cools it by as much as 30°F. This chilled air is created with about 75 percent less energy than an equivalent air conditioner would use and for about half the price.

Humidity can cause evaporative coolers to lose effectiveness. So, despite their nickname, they work best where the air is hot and dry—ironically, in unswamplike conditions.

Like a room air conditioner, a swamp cooler should be chosen according to the size of the space you wish to cool for the most effective results. But unlike an air conditioner, whose cooling capacity is measured in Btu, a swamp cooler's output is measured in terms of the amount of air the cooler can blow into the room, otherwise known as cubic feet per minute, or cfm.

Air & Water, Inc., offers swamp coolers in different sizes, and their Web site includes a chart and buying guide to help you find the best fit. One model that's received rave reviews is the portable NewAir AF-330 evaporative swamp cooler with HEPA (high-efficiency particulate air), which is built to cool up to 150 square feet. It's the first cooler of its kind to do double duty by having a built-in HEPA filter that claims to remove 99.7 percent of particulates while it cools. It retails for $189. (www.air-n-water.com)

MICROWAVES

High-Tech Convenience

It's no secret that microwaves tend to be better for reheating than for cooking. That's because the typical microwave technology cycles the waves on and off, which all too often can result in under- and overcooked areas.

Now, with the use of inverter technology, microwave ovens can cook more like the real thing. One well-rated product with this feature is the **Panasonic** inverter microwave oven. The inverter allows for more consistent, faster heating, so food is cooked at the desired level without cycling. (www2.panasonic.com)

Microwaves use a lot of energy, but because they cook quickly, they can cut energy use by up to 80 percent compared to a conventional oven. And because they generate less heat in the kitchen, they avoid the need for additional cooling from an A/C during warm months.

But are microwaves safe? A federal safety standard limits the amount of waves that can leak from an oven throughout its lifetime to a level considered far below that known to harm people. If you're concerned, just take a few steps back. Microwave energy decreases dramatically as you move away from the oven. The government standard also requires all ovens to have two interlock systems that stop the production of microwaves the moment the latch is released or the door opened.

YOUR MOTHER WAS RIGHT

Just like bell-bottoms, the popularity of pressure cookers has risen and fallen over the years. But with newfound focus on saving energy, pressure cookers are one of several green throwbacks coming back in style. And for good reason—they are now made to be safer and can cut cooking time by as much as 70 percent.

A regular cooking pot allows heat to escape, especially when the lid's not on. In contrast, pressure cookers create and trap steam from a minimal amount of water and put it to use. The steam reaches 257˚F (45 degrees higher than boiling) and is infused through your food, resulting in quicker, more even cooking. Less cooking time means more flavor and nutrients are retained instead of cooked away.

Back in the day, pressure cookers were known to "lose their lids," so to speak, but manufacturers have since added features that ensure safety along with quality results. Stainless-steel pressure cookers made by **Fagor America** are among the best rated in the category.

The Fagor Duo pressure cooker line includes different-sized models. Each features a visual pressure indicator and an automatic pressure release position for ease of use. They'll work on any kind of cooktop. All models contain three safety features that permit steam to escape when overpressurizing occurs. So unlike older models, the lids will not open until all the steam has dissipated and pressure has been completely released. (www.fagoramerica.com)

PORTABLE SPACE HEATERS

Just Enough Warmth

When you need just a little added warmth, save energy by turning on a portable space heater instead of cranking up the heat in the entire house. Or if a room is not connected to your existing heating system, using a space heater is less expensive than installing a new system.

The Italian-designed **De'Longhi** mica panel radiator is praised by users for being quiet, lightweight, and capable of producing heat quickly. Unlike traditional oil heaters, the De'Longhi heater uses a relatively recent innovation: the mineral mica. The heat from this convection heater rides the waves of air currents in the room—a good choice if you wish to heat a whole room consistently.

The mica panel radiator has a built-in room thermostat; you set a desired room temperature and the radiator maintains it. You can easily tote the heater from room to room . Or mount it on the wall—a wise choice if you have small children or pets running around. Additionally, the heater comes with automatic shutoff features that kick in if it becomes too warm or accidentally tips over. (www.delonghiusa.com)

WATER FILTERS

Improving Tap Water

The flood of bottled water onto the beverage scene in recent years caused many of us to question the safety and cleanliness of tap water. In truth, the United States has some of the cleanest tap water in the world. So is it worth fretting over water quality?

Unfortunately, some unpalatable contaminants do exist in our nation's water supply, things such as chlorine and, in some locations, traces of heavy metals. But bottled water isn't necessarily safer, and those bottles take a collective toll on the planet: It's estimated that more than eight in 10 of the astonishing 28 *billion* single-serve plastic water bottles purchased each year end up in a landfill or incinerator, according to the Container Recycling Institute. Hundreds of millions more end up as litter. What's an eco-conscious consumer to do?

In your home, one of the most convenient bottled-water-free ways to remove potential contaminants, as well as foul tastes, is with a stand-alone water filter. A water filter can be used over and over to help trap contaminants before they reach your glass; just drop a replaceable cartridge into the filter, put the filter in the fridge, and fill it up as needed. How often you replace the cartridge will depend on the product.

The **Pur** 2 Stage water filter is a well-rated option that provides up to 40 gallons (1 to 2 months) of clean water. It claims to reduce chlorine and heavy metals, like lead and cadmium, as well as 99 percent of microbial bugs, such as cryptosporidium and giardia, which are linked to digestive ailments. (www.purwater.com)

How Clean?

Left wondering how clean your own tap water is? Check out your city's drinking water scorecard and see how it compares to those of other US cities on Pur's Web site. You'll also find Pur's online guide to built-in filtration systems. But if you're looking for a simple solution, a stand-alone water filter's the way to go.

VACUUM CLEANERS

Dirt in Its Place

The last thing you want after you've worked so diligently to remove dirt from your floors and upholstery is to discover that very same dirt scattered about again. Unfortunately, that can happen if your vacuum doesn't have a good built-in filtration system; dirt can merely pass through the machine and right into the air before settling back down. What's worse, some of that airborne dirt can be inhaled and get trapped in your lungs, where it can lead to respiratory problems. But have no fear, advanced filtration's here.

At **Miele**, each German-engineered vacuum is built with the company's unique Sealed System and includes a Super Air Clean filter with triple-layer filtration bag, ensuring that up to 99.95 percent of particles down to 0.5 micron, plus other indoor air pollutants, stay put. The Antares canister model is touted for its ability to clean bare floors as well as carpeting, a feature that uprights tend to be better known for. The Antares offers two other filters, including a HEPA filter, in case you want additional filtration. (www.miele.com)

If you prefer a vacuum that sucks a little less green from your wallet, check out the new upright **Eureka** Envirovac. It comes standard with a washable HEPA filter, which you can reuse multiple times. The Envirovac claims to be 33 percent more energy efficient than comparable upright vacuums. It's sold exclusively at Wal-Mart. (www.walmart.com)

SOLAR OVEN
Sun-Powered Cooking

Via solar chargers and solar panels, the sun is being harnessed to power everyday gadgets and equipment. Putting the sun to work is really nothing new, especially in parts of the world where wood and other fuels can be scarce and costly.

That's where the Global Sun Oven comes in. It's a durable, high-performance solar oven that captures sunlight to cook food. Invented in the mid-1980s as a solution to deforestation in developing countries, today it's an alternative for anybody who wants to use the most reliable and powerful energy source we have. And to have a little fun while you're at it.

Don't let the name "oven" fool you: This appliance can boil, steam, roast, or bake food. Cooking temperatures are expected to reach 360°F to 400°F, which you can monitor on a built-in thermometer. Cooking times and methods will be similar to that of a conventional oven. For meals that require more than 30 minutes, you make a simple adjustment to one of several preset positions to capture the optimum angle of the sun as it travels overhead. Or you can use the oven for slow cooking, much like a slow cooker, without any readjusting. The most important factor in using a Global Sun Oven is the brightness of the day, rather than the outside air temperature.

The best cookware for a solar oven are dark, thin-walled pots with lids that hold steam. Glass casserole dishes with lids also work. The price of a Sun Oven includes one black, round, covered enamelware pot.

With every oven purchase, you help fund the introduction of solar ovens around the world, wherever Sun Ovens International is involved in solar cooking projects. To date, thousands of portable models have been shipped to more than 126 countries around the globe. (www.sunoven.com)

HAMMOCK
Reasons to Relax

What better reminder to slow down and unwind than the sight of an empty hammock swaying in the breeze? We all know that relaxation can bring real benefits to our hearts and minds, and now experts are finding that just being in green surroundings can boost our spirits, too. So the next time you need a good excuse to take a siesta, consider the Envirope Hammock. Twisted into soft, weather-resistant Eco-Spun fiber from 100 percent postconsumer plastics (e.g., soda bottles), the hammock is recycled, recyclable, and repairable. Even the wooden bars are made from locally grown white oak and processed in a worker-owned mill in rural central Virginia. (www.twinoakstore.com)

SOLAR LIGHTS

Now you can brighten your landscape with two of the cleanest, greenest lighting technologies out there: solar  power and light-emitting diodes (LEDs). While the familiar draw of solar lies in its ability to create energy from the sun, the fact that LEDs can create light with little energy and continue to illuminate for about 35,000 to 50,000 hours over their lifetime makes them a perfect solar partner. For beautifully designed outdoor solar lights, check out Soho Décor. (www.sohodecor.com)

BAMBOO FURNITURE
Great Grass Things

Not too long ago, many of us were most familiar with bamboo as a material for chopsticks and a favorite food of the giant panda. Today bamboo has become one of the most coveted materials for green furniture and accessories, thanks to its numerous eco-friendly attributes.

Actually a grass and not a tree, bamboo is lauded for its ability to grow, well, like grass. In short, very rapidly. Some types grow more than 2 feet per day! Bamboo can be harvested in as few as 3 years in a managed forest and yield twice the amount of fiber as a fast-growing pine forest would in the same amount of time. It even regenerates itself from its own roots, so it doesn't require replanting. Strengthwise, some bamboo can be compared with red oak, which is widely considered one of the most durable hardwoods.

Just as quickly as we're learning about the green benefits of bamboo, companies are selling it. But not all bamboo products are created equal, so it's good to know what to look for. One of the main differences can be traced to the glues used to bind pieces of bamboo together to create final products. Some glues are more toxic than others and can emit harmful chemicals, such as formaldehyde, a known carcinogen.

A company that's using safer glues while producing beautiful furniture is **EcoDesignz**. The American-Chinese company offers high-quality tables, chairs, and other products produced entirely from bamboo. They only use glues that meet stringent European E-1 standards for off-gassing chemical content.

FYI

Make the most of natural sunlight. Place furniture like reading chairs and desks in locations that let you put the sunlight to work for you. Then turn the lights off.

OUTDOOR FURNITURE
Sitting Well with Nature

For those bright sunny days and warm starry evenings, what better way to get in touch with your home's natural surroundings than to take it all in on environmentally friendly outdoor furniture? With sustainably produced wood and recycled-plastic options just a click away, it's never been easier to find outdoor furnishings that fit right into their environment.

The **Crate & Barrel** Graceful Arbor line includes elegantly styled tables and chairs made from plantation-grown eucalyptus, a fast-growing hardwood. All of the wood is certified by the Forest Stewardship Council, a nonprofit organization that promotes sustainable forestry. Although the deep reddish brown pieces come treated with mineral oil, the company recommends further sealing to prevent discoloration. (Use a product marked low in volatile organic compounds, or VOCs, to minimize off-gassing of potentially harmful solvents.) The nine-piece Graceful Arbor ensemble includes a 94-inch-long rectangular table and eight chairs, and it retails for $1,699. (www.crateandbarrel.com)

If you prefer weatherproof recycled plastic, then **Polywood** is your source. The company takes recycled milk jugs and transforms them into furniture for the patio or yard, including several classically styled Adirondack lounge chairs, tables, and ottomans. The nature of the sturdy materials means you never have to treat them. And they're all made right in Syracuse, Indiana. (www.polywood.com)

How to Spot Sustainable Textiles

Whether grown from seed or derived from petroleum, conventionally produced textiles are associated with major environmental and social impacts. The textile industry relies heavily on chemical inputs on the farm and in the factory and is infamous for employing a low-wage workforce. By seeking out the labels below, you can help to support a more sustainable textile industry.

★ **Certified organic:** You probably have a good idea of what the US Department of Agriculture organic label means on fruits, vegetables, and grains. "Organic" essentially means the same thing on textiles, with one main caveat—how the fiber is processed. On the farm itself, plants are grown without toxic and persistent pesticides or fertilizers. Farmers employ natural, biological methods to control pests. Keeping soils productive by managing compost and rotating crops is also key to organic production. Genetically modified organisms and ionizing irradiation are prohibited in organic production. Once organic fibers leave the farm and are processed into textiles, however, there are no further restrictions. To avoid harsh processing chemicals, ask the manufacturer what processing chemicals, if any, it uses.

★ **Transitional fiber:** This label is a general claim that fibers are grown using organic practices, but grown on land used for conventional (nonorganic) production fewer than 3 years ago. The US Department of Agriculture says any land that's being converted from conventional to organic production must undergo a 3-year transition period. But neither the department nor any other entity officially certifies this label. Any type of finishing chemical can be used in processing transitional cotton fibers.

★ **Green cotton:** Labeling cotton "green" implies that the cotton was grown conventionally but wasn't treated with bleach, dyes, or formaldehyde. Since no independent agency certifies this claim, it's only the manufacturer's word.

★ **Recycled fiber:** More textiles are being labeled "recycled," which means the same thing as it does on paper or plastic products. Today you can find textiles in home furnishings and apparel that are made from recycled plastic and recycled cotton. The more recycled content, the better. The claim is a voluntary one that's not independently certified.

★ **Fair-trade certified:** This is an antisweatshop label for textiles. It means that farmers and workers in developing countries are guaranteed a minimum price for their products. Crops are grown using conservation measures that restrict the use of agrochemicals. While the term "fair trade" is commonly used in the textile world, it carries the most credibility when it's certified by the Fairtrade Labelling Organization or one of its member groups. (www.fairtrade.net)

Recycled and Underfoot

No longer are plastic bottles and containers destined only to become new versions of their old counterparts. Plastics are now being "upcycled" into brand-new products with entirely new uses. Great examples include **Mad Mats**, colorful mats handwoven from 98 percent recycled plastic bottles and packing materials. By their nature, Mad Mats are weatherproof and washable and ideal for outdoor porches and patios. You can choose from more than two dozen patterns—including florals with names like Oriental and Wildflower and geometrics like Zipper and Scotch—in three rectangular sizes. (www.outdoorrugsonly.com)

BUDGET GREEN FURNITURE

Whether you're looking to go green on a budget or would just like to add a little green flair to your home's decor, check out the eco-friendlier home furnishings offered by **IKEA**. The Swedish retailer blends Scandinavian style with an element of sustainability that you won't find in most big-box retailers. The company is working toward sourcing wood only from forests certified as responsibly managed. They also have an active commitment to use safer chemicals throughout their product lines. (www.ikea.com)

CERTIFIED WOOD
Woods of a Lifetime

Wood furniture is among the greenest materials on earth, with a caveat: While wood is natural and renewable, not to mention beautiful, it doesn't always originate from sustainable sources. Knowing what to look for and where to find it can help ensure your purchase has both environmental and social benefits.

Some of the finest-quality sustainable furniture is made by **The Joinery**, an Oregon-based company that understands why forest stewardship is critical to the long-term health of their craft and the planet. The company offers an exquisite line of hardwood furniture that blends old-world construction techniques and tools with modern machinery. Styles range from traditional to contemporary to custom. Any piece can be ordered in your choice of wood types from responsibly managed forests. Each piece is finished with natural oils and guaranteed for life. (800-259-6762; www.thejoinery.com)

On the opposite side of the country sits **Vermont Woods Studios**. This nature-inspired company offers somewhat more affordable heirloom-quality sustainable hardwood furniture, all carrying a lifetime guarantee on craftsmanship and materials. Go online to view a full line of traditional and contemporary styles, as well as custom pieces, all with natural finishes. Most of the wood originates from well-managed forests in Vermont's Green Mountains or in neighboring northeastern states. If you prefer rain-forest woods, like mahogany or teak, the company ensures that its wood is certified by the Forest Stewardship Council. (www.vermontwoodsstudios.com)

FYI

That compact fluorescent lightbulb *finally* burned out, so now what do you do? Because the bulbs contain small amounts of mercury, they should *not* go in the trash. Instead, log on to www.earth 911.org and enter your ZIP code into the locator for a listing of nearby drop-off locations.

CERTIFIED, SUSTAINABLE FABRIC FURNITURE
Pure *and* Elegant

Looking at the surface, it's hard to imagine everything that goes into upholstered furniture. But on and beneath those cushions are typically a host of potentially hazardous chemicals, including glues and stain-resistant fabric treatments that can off-gas into your home and contribute to poor air quality. Luckily, several furniture products are now produced in various shades of green.

Some of the greenest furniture is made by **Furnature**, a company committed to making high quality, environmentally sound products that don't sacrifice the health or prosperity of future generations. The company's quest to create a natural and nontoxic line began in the early 1990s with a chemically sensitive customer's request for a chemical-free sofa. A few years later, Furnature was born. An inspiring example of what can happen when you ask a company to change its practices, eh?

Today Furnature offers an extensive line of furnishings (including chairs, sofas, loveseats, ottomans, and more) made from nontoxic, organic, and natural materials. In striving to be as green as can be, they use natural rubber and wool (not synthetic petroleum-based foam) in their cushions and apply only water-based glues. No synthetic dyes or finishing sprays are used at any stage of production. You can choose from organic and chemical-free fabric coverings. All wood frames are sustainable and carry the Forest Stewardship Council's certification.

Prices vary by fabric type and style. Upholstered chairs are $2,000 and up, and sofas start at $4,000. The furniture comes with a 25-year frame warranty and a 10-year natural rubber cushion filler warranty. (800-326-4895; www.furnature.com)

MODERN GREEN FURNITURE
Online Decorating

Mix an innovative furniture design company with a Web site and what do you get? An online tool you can use to create your very own green furniture. The Los Angeles–based furniture company **Viesso** lets you select the furniture layout, filling, fabric, and legs. Once your design has been submitted, you'll be lounging on your sofa in about 3 weeks. And with a spectrum of choices of materials, you can decide just how green you want your seating to be. All furniture is made in L.A. with water-based, low-emissions glues, stains, and finishes. Prices vary; the Blumen sofa, for example, starts at $1,547. (www.viesso.com)

SUSTAINABLE WOOD FURNITURE
The Past Is Pro-Log

Experts estimate almost half of the earth's original forest cover has been converted to other land uses. While the total amount of forest area continues to decline worldwide, the rate of deforestation appears to be slowing. As the largest consumer of wood products in the world, we in the States can lessen our impact by buying wood that's already been harvested.

The fittingly named **Urban Woods** furniture company, based in Los Angeles, has made it their mission not to harm any trees to produce their wood products. Instead, they source all of their wood from local, vintage buildings that have been slated for teardown. Their reclaimed collection features richly hued, tightly grained pieces for the dining room, living room, and bedroom. All pieces are made by hand in L.A. from solid wood with nontoxic water-soluble glues, stains, and finishes. The Sunset Collection, a popular bedroom set, comes in your choice of hardwood that can be upholstered or tufted. (www.2modern.com)

A similar philosophy operates at **2-Day Designs**, where they use recycled antique lumber whenever possible. The company got its start 15 years ago by creating furniture from reclaimed lumber from abandoned Sears catalog warehouses. When that supply ran out, 2-Day Designs turned to other reclaimed sources, including solid white oak wine barrels, of which hundreds of thousands are produced each year and discarded only a few years later. From those barrels, they produce expertly crafted, often imaginative pieces with "vintage" character only an aged wine barrel could produce. (www.2-day designs.com; www.daxstores.com)

FLATWARE
Plantation-Grown Flatware

Much like food, trees can be grown on farms, otherwise known as plantations. When sustainably managed, these land areas can be a useful way to cultivate trees that are endangered in the wild and otherwise restricted from commercial use. One coveted tree is teak, a tropical hardwood indigenous to South and Southeast Asia. Teak's extreme durability led to its being commercially logged for centuries, which sharply reduced its habitat, and as a result some types were listed as endangered. But now, plantation-grown teak is being used in all kinds of products, including Vivaterra's Teak Flatware. Delicate as they may look, the utensils are dishwasher safe. (www.vivaterra.com)

TABLE LINENS
Raw Beauty for Your Table

Adorn your table in sustainable plant fiber fabrics with 100 percent certified organic linens from Rawganique. The line reflects the spirit of the intimate French bistro it was inspired by, and the table linens work for everyday use as well as for special occasions. Each piece is handwoven in Europe from organic hemp or linen. No chemicals of any kind are used in manufacturing. To emphasize their raw and natural beauty, tablecloths are finished simply. Choose from round, square, or rectangular shapes in an array of tablecloths, napkins, and accessories in different colors. (www.rawganique.com)

NEXT WAVE LIGHTING

Lighting creates ambience and sets a scene like little else in a home. Because it's also responsible for about 10 percent of your utility bills, it's a good idea to take advantage of the energy-efficient technologies out there. Following closely on the heels of compact fluorescents (CFLs) are light-emitting diodes (LEDs), which save even more energy and last longer than those penny-pinching CFLs. Thanks to IKEA, LEDs are affordable, too. Check out the Jansjo series of LED lamps in floor, table, wall, and clamp versions, each with an adjustable neck for easy focusing. (www.ikea.com)

KITCHEN ACCESSORIES
Recycled, Recyclable Tools

Today a yogurt cup, tomorrow a colander. That's a recycling coup brought to life every day at Recycline, where since 1996 they've been creating a growing line of colorful, 100 percent recycled products called Preserve. The company got its start when the founder decided plastics were best kept out of the waste stream and recycled into new products that didn't sacrifice style or quality.

The sole type of plastic used in Preserve products from the get-go has been polypropylene, otherwise known as #5 plastic. Since most communities don't accept #5 plastic for recycling, Preserve products provide an important eco-destination for those plastics. Number 5 plastic is considered safer than some others, because it is free of bisphenol A and phthalates, chemicals linked to hormone disruption.

The Preserve kitchen line includes vividly colored colanders, cutting boards, and food storage containers, all designed by food lovers. The dishwasher-safe line takes its designs and colors from the real thing: Colanders were modeled after strawberries; food storage containers after Granny Smith apples.

All of Recycline's plastic products are recyclable through the company's postage-paid mailers or at the curb in those communities that recycle #5 plastic. To find out which types of plastics are accepted in your community and where you can recycle all kinds of products, visit http://Earth911.org.

In the end, by helping to reduce our dependence on the nonrenewable petroleum resources that virgin plastics are made with, Preserve products are accomplishing what they set out to—helping to preserve the earth one home at a time. Buy them online or find them at a local Whole Foods Market. (www.recycline.com)

COMPOST KEEPER
Kitchen-Born Fertilizer

Hard as we might try, it seems just about impossible to avoid having to toss food left on our plates. Food leftovers make up the single largest component of the waste stream by weight in the United States. On a household level, it's estimated we toss 12 percent of the food we buy, or about 1.3 pounds every day. Some of that waste could help you grow a healthy, sustainable garden and lawn, so it makes sense to compost it.

Good compost can reduce or eliminate the need for chemical fertilizers, suppress plant diseases and pests, and promote higher yields. It can even help sandy soils retain water.

The **Ceramic Compost Keeper** is an ideal place to store your kitchen scraps until you are ready to transfer them to your outdoor composter. Acceptable items are vegetables and fruits, bread, grains, spoiled food, coffee filters and tea bags, eggshells, and some paper products. Do not add meat, fish, poultry, or dairy products, which will attract pests to your compost pile. To minimize odors, the compost keeper has a carbon filter, which will last about 6 months, and comes with two filters. (www.earth easy.com)

BAMBOO EVERYWHERE

Here's a new entry to the list of certified organic products: bamboo kitchen utensils. **Bambu** offers a full set of handcrafted utensils, from salad tongs to spatulas, each formed from a single piece of certified organically grown bamboo. Unlike other bamboo products, which are often made by gluing individual pieces of plant fiber together, Bambu utensils are free of adhesives and are hand-finished with a top-grade natural, food-safe oil. No need to worry about nasty glues being that "secret ingredient" in your meals. With their natural strength and durability, Bambu utensils stand up to heat and resist stains. (www.greenfeet.com, www.bambuhome.com)

POTTERY MUGS
From Their Hands to Yours

Most mugs are a dime a dozen, mass-produced by machines in factories around the world. But wouldn't it be nice to take in your favorite brew or infusion from a mug made by a true artisan? Well, you don't have to wait for the next craft fair, because there's a Web-accessible company whose pottery has been handmade and hand-painted in Virginia since 1977.

From the Blue Ridge Mountains of Virginia, **Emerson Creek Pottery**'s master potters and artisans bring colonial-era pottery-making methods to the contemporary world. Some ceramic-making practices used today have led to questions about pottery product safety. But take heart: Emerson Creek Pottery's commitment to toxin-free glazes, paints, and clays will give you the peace of mind to sip with serenity.

Emerson Creek Pottery's Go Green Earthware Mug (2680-054) is just one piece of the company's Go Green Handcrafted ceramic dinnerware line. The 16-ounce, handcrafted mug's deeply colored earth tones and classic, smooth design are sure to soothe. Emerson Creek offers 13 other pottery lines. All products come shipped in recycled boxes with cornstarch peanuts. (www.emersoncreekpottery.com)

SUSTAINABLE DISHES, SUSTAINABLE MEALS

Beach glass lovers, rejoice. The frosted textures and wavy shapes in the colorful Seaglass dishware line from **Riverside Design Group** are reminiscent of the real thing. Each time you reach for a dish, you can capture a bit of that feeling you get when you discover a colorful sea-weathered gem in the sand. The Seaglass line is crafted from recycled postindustrial glass at the company's Pennsylvania studio. It comes in 12 shapes and 14 colors, like citron, grass green, and pearl. Riverside's dishes can be washed in the dishwasher or used to heat food in the microwave. A set of four 7-inch plates can be ordered from www.vivaterra.com.

For your altruistic side, you can choose from an array of

recycled glass plates, each linked to a different nonprofit organization in the Pittsburgh area, where Riverside is housed in a certified green building. For every dish that's purchased in their Plates With Purpose line, the company donates 15 percent of the proceeds to the cause illustrated on that plate. Choose a heart and support Habitat for Humanity, or pick a forget-me-not and help the Alzheimer's Association. All plates come in pearl white with a custom design. (www.plateswithpurpose.com)

GREEN GLASS

Trash into Treasure

Ever wonder where old wine and beer bottles end up once they're tossed in the recycling bin? While most are crushed to produce the raw materials for tomorrow's bottles and containers, some make their way into the hands of the **Green Glass Company**, now the largest maker of reclaimed glassware in the world. By infusing new life into old glass bottles, the company brings new meaning to the old adage "turning trash into treasure."

Launched in South Africa in the early 1990s, the Green Glass Company is now headquartered in the north woods of Wisconsin, where all of its glassware is made. The company collects used bottles from West Coast wineries and purchases rejected bottles from bottle-making companies. Their golden Topaz glass tumblers, goblets, and vases began as California Chardonnay bottles, and their emerald-green Forest collection can be traced back to yesterday's Bordeaux.

The product line includes both clear and frosted glassware in a variety of colors and etched designs, including galloping horses and Hawaiian flowers. Unlike most frosted products manufactured today, which are etched with acid, Green Glass products are frosted by sandblasting.

But Green Glass doesn't stop at glass. The company also creates vases that are supported by the inner springs of unusable mattresses donated by Goodwill. How's that for resourceful recycling!

Prices start at $32.50 for a set of four tumblers. (www.greenglass.com)

COOKWARE

The Case for Basic Metals

Designed to fix the problem of hard-to-clean cookware in the kitchen, nonstick surfaces may have introduced another risk—potentially harmful chemicals. Some studies show that heating nonstick coatings (to 572°F, to be exact) can create a suspected cancer-causing fume from tetrafluoroethylene (TFE) and other toxic chemicals. The Environmental Protection Agency says there's no reason to avoid nonstick cookware if you use it properly, but there are good quality non–nonstick cookware products.

One line comes from **Lodge Cast Iron**, a company that's been producing cast-iron cookware since 1896. Four generations later, the family-owned company expanded their legendary iron cookware line to include a collection of enamel-coated cast-iron cookware. Lodge's Logic Skillet with Assist Handle comes in a variety of sizes. The company is working to minimize their environmental footprint at the Tennessee foundry where the cookware is produced. They've upped their recycling, decreased their waste, and improved the water quality of a stream that runs through their foundry so that water lilies, cattails, and fish now thrive. (www.lodgemfg.com)

Stainless steel is another option that'll help you steer clear of undesirable chemicals. You'll find practical, quality pots and pans in the Revereware cookware line. The **Revereware** Copper Advantage line couples stainless steel with a protected copper base for quick and even heat distribution and comes with a limited 25-year warranty. (www.revereware.com)

BLANKETS
Cotton Blankets Over Again

If you've ever shopped at a thrift or consignment store, you know there's no shortage of old cotton duds out there. But did you know that in the United States alone, an estimated 1 million tons of fabric per year end up on the cutting-room floor without ever becoming garments? The founders of **in2green** do, and they've formed a whole company around creating blankets and other textiles from scraps and materials that might otherwise head for a landfill or incinerator.

In2green uses environmentally responsible, regenerated fibers and yarns that are spun into what's called Eco2cotton. After collection of preconsumer fibers and clippings that result from the cutting and sewing process in garment factories, the fragments are sorted by color and blended and spun into "new" yarn that's used to make the company's recycled cotton blankets and other products. All products are made in the USA or Central America in sweatshop-free environments. In2green's recycled cotton blankets feature colorful, nature-inspired and monogram designs. Each blanket sells for $125.

When second-generation products are used, many of the impacts typically associated with textile manufacturing are avoided. Less new cotton means less land needed for growing, less water used for irrigation, and fewer fertilizers or pesticides applied to crops. And since the regenerated fibers retain the color of the original recycled T-shirt or garment, the recycled fabrics don't even have to be dyed, which is another kindness to the environment. (www. in2green.com)

MATTRESSES
Sleep Naturally

Ah, sleep. What could be more refreshing than a good night's rest? How about one that's free from potentially harmful chemicals? An appealing notion, especially when you consider that some mattresses can off-gas substances linked to health hazards and that we spend about a third of our lives in bed. But the good news is, potentially safer alternatives abound.

Many mattresses made from natural and organic materials don't contain potentially harmful chemicals found in the conventional counterparts, including hormone-disrupting flame-retardant chemicals, otherwise known as PBDEs. While newer mattresses are less likely to contain PBDEs today, polyurethane foam mattresses are made from petroleum, which can emit potentially harmful volatile organic compounds (VOCs). Who wants to cozy up to those chemicals?

The family-owned **Lifekind** company offers a collection of natural and organic mattresses, including some for cribs. All are made by hand from combinations of 100 percent certified organic cotton, pure wool from Northern California sheep, and sustainably harvested rubber tapped right from the tree. Mattresses are made in the company's eco-factory in Southern California and have been certified to meet Green Guard's strict indoor air quality guidelines for off-gassing chemicals. (800-284-4983; www.lifekind.com)

PILLOW DREAMS
Purposeful Pillows

Isn't it nice to know you can buy something beautiful and affordable while investing in a more socially responsible world? That's the idea behind the Pillow Dreams Project. The project provides a direct channel for women in Vietnam, Thailand, and South Africa to sell their intricately designed pillows. A full 50 percent of the profits from each pillow sold is donated to support a specific project where the pillow was made. For instance, buying a Vietnamese pillow benefits homeless teens, while an African pillow supports an orphanage in Malawi. Among the most eco-friendly options are the Thai Hmong pillows, made from hemp. Prices start at $20. (www.pillowdreamsproject.com)

BEDDING
Organic Nights

You might think that soft, fluffy white cotton is one of the purest fabrics you could use in bedding. The truth be told, cotton's actually one of the most chemically intensive crops to grow, using about 11 percent of the world's pesticides. Luckily, there's eco-friendlier organic cotton.

Some of the finest 100 percent organic cotton bedding is made by Coyuchi, a California-based company that offers a fine line of white and ivory-colored bed linens and a line for baby that features little embroidered animal and nature scenes. The cotton comes from India, where it's grown rotationally with lentils and chickpeas. Insects are controlled with practices that mimic nature in lieu of chemical fertilizers and pesticides. The farmers, who grow and harvest the cotton by hand, are paid a fair wage for their work. (www.coyuchi.com)

Another organic cotton bedding collection comes from Amenity. Their plant- and flower-printed duvet covers and shams are especially fitting for nature lovers, and the nursery line features blankets and pillowcases with charming animal scenes printed on plush organic fabrics. They also offer organic cotton crib sheets and accessories in natural colors to serve as a neutral backdrop. All of Amenity's fabrics are sewn locally from minimally processed natural fibers and printed with nontoxic, water-based eco-friendly dyes. (www.amenityhome.com)

WHITE LOTUS PILLOWS
Comforting You and the Planet

When you finally climb into bed at the end of a long day, you want to feel good about where you lay your head. But like so many other textile products that can be treated with potentially harmful chemicals (like formaldehyde, a known carcinogen), pillow covers are no exception. The insides of a pillow typically aren't much better. Most are filled with petroleum-derived polyurethane foam or polyester or with down feathers linked to inhumane practices.

For safer, greener options, check out the pillows from White Lotus Home: hand-stuffed and hand-sewn pillows made from natural organic cotton, buckwheat, wool, and kapok. White Lotus also offers a "green cotton" pillow, which means the cotton wasn't treated with bleach, dyes, or formaldehyde. With so many options, how can you choose?

★ Want the feeling of down without the guilt? Try kapok-filled pillows. They're filled with soft, silky fibers sustainably harvested from the seeds of the tropical kapok, or ceiba, tree.

★ Organic cotton pillows provide an alternative for people with allergies to wool, buckwheat, or latex but may not resist dust mites.

★ Buckwheat pillows are like beanbags, so they contour to your neck as you sleep. Each is filled with 100 percent organic buckwheat hulls grown in the United States. They are inherently pest resistant.

★ Wool is a good choice if you prefer a softer, more resilient pillow. Wool can keep you cool in the summer and warm in the winter and is naturally resistant to fire, mold, mildew, and dust mites.

White Lotus pillows come in different shapes, sizes, and materials, and you can request the softness you want. (http://whitelotus.net)

CARPETING
Eco-Friendly Flooring

When it comes to choosing greener flooring, carpeting is often shunned. That's because carpets are typically made from nonrenewable petroleum-based fibers that can offgas volatile organic compounds, creating indoor air pollution. But before you dismiss carpeting altogether, check out **FLOR**.

FLOR carpet tiles are some of the greenest, most stylish options you can find. Because the tiles come in squares that measure fewer than 2 feet on each side, you can use as many or few as you like. The most natural options in the collection include coconut fibers, wool, and hemp. You can also choose among colors and patterns featured in their nylon collection without much green guilt. All of their carpet tiles meet strict VOC standards. They are recyclable, too.

Through FLOR's trade-in and recycling program, you can return any tile at any time and they'll cover the full charge of shipping back the products. This is one company that walks the talk not only through its recycling program but also by manufacturing the tiles in the first place with renewable energy sources and energy-efficient technologies in their Georgia facilities. FLOR's parent company, Interface, is a leader in the sustainability movement and has set a bold goal to minimize any negative impact the family of companies has on the environment by the year 2020.

You can install FLOR carpet tiles in just about any room that has a clean, hard, dry surface. You can also choose among thicknesses, depending on where you want to install them. (www.flor.com)

Carpeting not only reduces noise, it also provides an extra layer of warmth and insulation to help conserve energy in those colder months. Just be sure to choose natural or recycled carpeting that can be recycled itself.

AREA RUGS
Rugs au Naturel

If you want to grace your floors in truly natural fibers, you'll unroll many beautiful options from New Hampshire–based **EcoRug**, a small company devoted exclusively to natural fiber rugs. Their earth-friendly floor mats come in nearly 50 weaves made from durable natural fibers. Among them are natural grasses, like East African and Brazilian sisal, coir, and jute; wool blends; and a stunning, must-see woven paper mat. You can select or custom design your weave, border, and size online. Prices start around $140 a square foot. (www.ecorug.com).

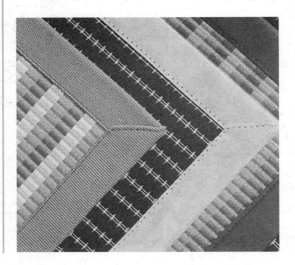

BREATHE EASIER IN YOUR SHOWER

If you've ever been overwhelmed by the smell of a new plastic shower curtain, chances are it was made from polyvinyl chloride, or PVC. That's what most plastic shower curtains are made from. Unfortunately, PVC can off-gas potentially hormone-disrupting phthalates and contain heavy metals like lead, so it's a good idea to shop for alternatives. **Real Goods** offers a 100 percent linen shower curtain made from flax that's grown without harmful pesticides and resists mold and mildew. It comes with stainless steel grommets. (www.realgoods.com)

WINDOW SHADES

Natural Light Control

Some windows provide better insulation than others, but all happen to be responsible for a portion of energy loss in your home. Short of installing the most energy-efficient windows available, a simpler, cheaper step is to hang old-fashioned shades. Although most shades on the market today originate in China and Southeast Asia, where labor and environmental practices can be questionable, now you can buy them from a socially responsible mom-and-pop company whose commitment to the cause runs deep.

The couple's window treatment business, fittingly named Earthshade, offers a natural, aesthetic solution to help you block out unwanted summer heat and keep in desirable winter warmth. The product line features nearly two dozen natural shades made from renewable, wild-crafted grasses and reeds like bamboo and sisal. They also carry an undyed hemp-and-cotton blend.

Raw materials are gathered primarily in Central and South America before being sun-dried and deftly twisted or braided into final products in Mexico and Texas by workers who earn a fair wage. You can choose from a range of colors, patterns, and styles such as Sanctuary, Tibetan Twine, and Malaysian Moss and have the shades cut to fit your windows exactly.

It's worth a mention that the company scored a listing in GreenSpec, the green building industry's bible of the most reliably green products. (800-528-5443; www.earthshade.com)

FYI

One way to avoid both daily and nightly encounters with synthetic chemicals is to surround yourself with bedding and bath linens that have been dyed naturally with veggie or mineral dyes. Or, for a more pure and simple approach, consider purchasing fibers in their unbleached, natural color.

THE GREENEST DRYER MONEY CAN BUY

Long before there were dryers, there were drying racks and clotheslines. Then technology and convenience stepped in, and most folks never looked back. While a dryer is certainly nice to have as a backup, if you really want to green up your laundry practices (and save a little green), consider incorporating fresh air and sunlight into your laundry routine. For a selection of drying racks made from sustainably grown New England eastern white pine often left over from wood mills, check out www.abundantearth.com. For clotheslines, visit www.clotheslineshop.com.

ORGANIC BATH LINENS

Soft and Colorful Organic Cotton Towels

If wrapping yourself in soft, chemical-free cotton sounds like a good way to start the day, you've come to the right place. Each LOOP organic cotton towel is woven from high-quality organic cotton fibers into plush, absorbent terry cloth. The company uses hydrogen peroxide for whitening in lieu of chlorine bleach, and it achieves its earthy colors of sandstone, seaglass, and clove with low-impact dyes. All production is carried out in responsible, sweatshop-free environments. (www.looporganic.com)

closing the Circle

Did you know that dinosaurs unwittingly served as the first recyclers? According to the California EPA's *Illustrated History of Recycling*, their decaying bodies combined with desiccated sea animals and plants on the sea bottom 65 million years ago to recycle gradually, through heat and pressure, into the petroleum that powers our modern economy.

Eons later, human beings took up the mantle. The first municipal dumps date to 500 BC in Athens. The first recorded instance of recycling of paper by the Japanese was way back in 1031. Seven hundred years later, American colonists declaring independence from Britain conducted scrap drives because raw materials from the mother country weren't available. By 1865, the Salvation Army was founded to recycle unwanted household goods, and curbside recycling began in Baltimore in 1874. Plants to recycle aluminum cans opened in Chicago and Cleveland in 1904.

Given all this activity and the rapid growth of America (and its waste materials), it's surprising that Congress didn't significantly regulate trash until the Solid Waste Disposal Act of 1965—5 years before the first Earth Day in 1970. And the first bottle bill (in Oregon) didn't become law until 1972.

By 1995, however, Americans were getting into the swing of recycling. That year, 47.5 *billion* soft drink containers were recycled. Some 63 percent of all aluminum cans were being processed. There were then 10,000 recycling centers in the United States and 4,000 curbside programs up and running.

Unfortunately, we've stagnated in many ways since the high-water mark. We recycle a smaller percentage of glass today than we did in 1996. We've gone backward on aluminum cans, too, recycling just 50 percent of them.

The regression on plastic polyethylene terephthalate (PET) bottles illustrates that one of the big problems with current recycling is *volume*. Back in 1995, we recycled almost 40 percent of those bottles, but by 2005 that rate had dropped to only 23 percent. Why? Two words: *bottled water*. According to Salon.com, the total poundage of PET recycling, at 775 million pounds in 1995, stayed relatively steady, but the number of bottles sold had more than doubled by 2005. "Those of us who do recycle aren't necessarily recycling less as the years go by, we just haven't been able to keep up with the deluge," Salon claims.

Sadly, another issue is apathy. Have people gotten bored with recycling? "Orphaned garbage barges no longer make headlines," reports *USA Today*. "Politicians don't pose with recycling trucks for glitzy photo-ops. Recyclers don't get restaurant coupons or cash prizes anymore. . . . Today, although more Americans recycle than vote, the sense of urgency has faded."

But the 2008 election of President Barack Obama, who has made volunteerism and the environment cornerstones of his presidency, may signal a recycling rebirth. During the campaign, Obama set an example by creating ObamaCycle (www.obamacycle.com) to press for the recycling of his own get-out-the-vote materials.

So although the effort has plateaued in recent years, there is great hope that Americans will once again recognize the urgent and ongoing need for recycling and get us back on the road to the ultimate goal: zero waste.

—Jim Motavalli

FREECYCLE NETWORK
Global Recycling

In 2003, Deron Beal started the Freecycle Network, working with a dream and a loose network of willing friends in the Tucson, Arizona, area. Beal saw a lot of perfectly good stuff being thrown away, so he and his associates started offering the unwanted goods to local nonprofit groups for free. After expending a lot of shoe leather, they took the concept online with an e-mail network to match free goods with willing recipients.

Soon Freecycle was national, then international. It has grown to more than 85 countries, involving (at last count) 4,619 groups and almost six million members. The group says it keeps 500 tons of material a day out of landfills, annually equivalent to a stack of garbage trucks five times the height of Mount Everest.

Taking part is simple enough. Enter your state in the finder on the Web site home page, and local groups pop up. You do have to join the local group, but it's free. And of course you can post your own free stuff, providing a short description and an approximate location. (www.freecycle.org)

THE ULTIMATE RECYCLING REFERENCE

Choose to Reuse (Ceres Press) by Nikki and David Goldbeck is an incredibly thorough reference work, with more than 2,000 resources grouped into 200 topics, with information, as the authors put it, "on how to reduce, reuse, recycle, repair, restore, reclaim, refill, recharge, and resell everything from air filters to zippers." Printed on recycled paper with soy inks, the book is packed with good advice on finding repair sources and keeping the things you already own in good condition. It also provides copious listings for charitable and volunteer organizations that take in unwanted goods.

Remember, there are three Rs, and recycle is only one of them. We've neglected the reuse part of the equation, but this book does its best to address that unfortunate turn of events.

Recycling is all well and good, but how about practicing "precycling"? That means shopping smart, buying in bulk, and most important, looking for minimally packaged or loose produce that was never entombed in plastic wrap.

MOTOR OIL
Give It a Second Life

Here's a sobering statistic: You can contaminate a million gallons of fresh water—a year's supply for 50 people—simply by dumping your used motor oil in the wrong place. Since it's usually cheaper to change your own oil than have someone else do it, home mechanics routinely face the question of what to do with 4 or 5 quarts of contaminated motor oil.

Luckily, there are 30,000 US locations that take back used motor oil, including auto parts stores, service stations, and government agencies. An easy-to-use locator box at Earth911.org brings up locations when you enter your ZIP code.

According to the American Petroleum Institute, "Motor oil has value even after it has been drained from an engine. The oil you take to a collection center . . . can be reprocessed and used in furnaces for heat or in power plants to generate electricity for homes, schools, and businesses. It can also be sent to a refinery that specializes in processing used oil and rerefined into lubricating base oils."

If you do change your own oil, the *New Car Buying Guide* from **Consumer Reports** (www.newcarbuyingguide.com) offers some sensible advice: "Drain your oil into a clean container with a tight-fitting cap. A one-gallon, plastic milk jug or water container works well. Do not mix the recovered oil with any other liquids such as antifreeze or automatic transmission fluid. Make sure the oil is free from dirt, leaves, and other debris. Then take it to an oil collection location." (877-EARTH911; www.earth911.org/recycling)

RECYCLED STEEL

It's Number One!

Who knew that steel would become such a performance leader? Believe it or not, it's our number-one recycled material, and we recycle more of it than aluminum, paper, and glass combined!

The environmental numbers are impressive. The steel industry reduces its energy consumption 75 percent with recycling, enough to power 18 million homes for a year. Every ton of steel recycled (and 76 million tons were recycled in 2005) saves 2,420 pounds of iron ore, 1,386 pounds of coal, and 121 pounds of limestone.

Steelmaking furnaces are designed to melt down scrap, and they have a voracious appetite for the stuff. Chances are that the car you're driving has recycled steel in it. At least half of the steel produced in the United States has been recycled through the network of more than 2,000 ferrous scrap processors, says the Steel Recycling Institute.

Some 63.4 percent of our steel cans (also known as containers) were recycled in 2006, up from just 15 percent in 1988. Just 20.4 percent of steel appliances were recaptured in 1988; in 2006 it was 90 percent. The overall rate for steel recycling has slipped a bit, though: from 75.7 percent in 2005 to 68.7 percent in 2006. (www.recycle-steel.org)

FYI

Want to get off junk mail and catalog lists? Visit www.donotmail.org.

What's with the Numbers in Triangles?

Since the system was created by the Society of the Plastics Industry in 1988, plastic containers intended for consumer use (from 8 ounces to 5 gallons) are embossed (on the bottom, as close to the center as possible) with the chasing triangle recycling symbol. The number inside the triangle tells you whether that container should be thrown in the recycling bin or the garbage can. **Number 1** (PETE) is the most common, used for soda and water bottles, vinegar bottles, and medicine containers, among many other things. It's recyclable everywhere.

Number 2 (HDPE) is used for laundry and dish detergent, fabric softeners, bleach, milk, shampoo, conditioner, motor oil, and some toys. It's generally recyclable, too. You're also fine with **number 4** (LDPE)—filmy polyethylene plastics such as wrap and plastic grocery and sandwich bags.

Some commonly used plastics are not generally recyclable, including **number 3** (V, for polyvinyl chloride) used for pipes, shower curtains, cooking oil bottles, clear medical tubing, coffee containers, and seat covers. **Number 5** (PP, for polypropylene) is another one for the garbage can, and it's found in Tupperware, yogurt tubs, diapers, outdoor carpet, and syrup bottles. It's unfortunate that **number 6** (polystyrene) isn't recyclable, because billions

of coffee cups are made from it, as well as both clear and colored disposable cups and cutlery, plus Styrofoam insulation and packing peanuts. **Number 7** ("other") is a grab bag of uncommon plastics, some made from a combination of numbers 1 through 6.

If there's no symbol on the container, you should probably assume it's made of multiple plastics and not recyclable. Grocery bags aren't always recyclable in the bin, but many supermarkets take them back. If you're in doubt about a potential recyclable, you can always call your local recycling center for clarification. (www.pslc.ws/mactest/work/recycle.htm)

THE WAY FORWARD FOR RECYCLING

We've come a long way, according to the Natural Resources Defense Council (NRDC). We are recycling 28.5 percent of our municipal solid waste, compared with just 5 percent in 1970. Our recycling efforts have the same climate effects as taking 39.6 million passenger cars off the road.

There was no curbside recycling in the United States before 1973, but now there are 8,660 programs. That's progress, but we still recycle less than a third of plastic soft drink bottles, less than a quarter of water bottles, about half of all aluminum cans, and less than half of postconsumer paper. Airports and airlines generate 425,000 tons of passenger-related waste each year, and less than 20 percent of it is recycled.

One way forward is extended producer responsibility (EPR), launched in Germany in 1991 with a packaging ordinance prompted by limited landfill space. The Germans saw that packaging waste accounted for 30 percent by weight and 50 percent by volume of all municipal waste.

The law set up the waste management organization **Duales System Deutschland** (DSD) and required every producer to either join it or set up an independent system to take their packaging back. Packaging from DSD members carries a green dot, which alerts consumers that they can put it in their DSD-collected yellow bin (for plastic, metals, and composites), with separate bins for glass and paper. Germany's commitment to recycling packaging has been successful, but it's also expensive. Germans pay roughly $28 per person per year to operate the system. Nevertheless, the German law has been widely imitated in Europe.

Packaging laws have a cousin in ordinances aimed at electronic devices, such as TVs and computers. A Japanese law, enacted in 2001, requires takeback of refrigerators, air conditioners, TVs, and washing machines. In Sweden, EPR is applied to automobiles, tires, and magazines. Other countries that are embracing EPR include Brazil, Japan, Taiwan, and Korea.

EPR has a few lonely proponents in the States, but powerful lobbies would make it difficult for the concept to get a fair hearing in the country that undoubtedly produces the most packaging per capita. (www.informinc.org)

HOUSEHOLD BATTERIES
Check the Specs

The good news is that after 1997, household batteries (including the commonly used AA, AAA, C, D, and 9-volt types) were reengineered to remove mercury and other dangerous toxins. Thank the Mercury Containing and Rechargeable Battery Management Act of 1996 for that change, which means you can throw your used batteries in the garbage with a relatively clear conscience. Keep in mind, however, that if you're throwing out a dozen or more AA batteries annually, it will more than pay to switch to rechargeables.

The rules are not so simple for other battery types. Tiny button batteries can contain silver, zinc, or other nasty substances and should be recycled rather than discarded. A handy locator for recycling these batteries is at www.earth911.org/recycling.

For nickel-cadmium (Nicad), lithium-ion (Li-ion), or nickel-metal hydride (NiMH) rechargeable batteries, the rules are complicated. Nicads definitely should be recycled, because they contain toxic cadmium. Li-ion and NiMH are less toxic but should be recycled anyway.

The 1996 law that got mercury out of batteries also set up the Rechargeable Battery Recycling Corporation (RBRC), which accepts Nicads, NiMHs, and Li-ions. It would make things easier if RBRC also took alkaline and button batteries, but unfortunately they don't. Take a close look at your worn-out rechargeables, which should have RBRC symbols on them. The next step is using the locator tool on the nonprofit group's Web site to find drop-off locations.

If these options sound like too much trouble, there's the alternative of the **Big Green Box**, an international program offered to businesses, municipalities, and individuals. The box (actually white and green) gets gradually filled up with batteries and dead portable electronics at your location, then it's loaded into a container and shipped to a recycling facility. The only obstacle is the $58 up-front cost. (www.rbrc.org/consumer; www.biggreenbox.com)

FYI

Many chain stores that ship packages, including UPS, Mail Boxes Etc., Postal Annex, FedEx, and Kinko's, will reuse your unwanted packing peanuts. Call ahead and check.

RECYCLED GLASS
We Need to Do Better!

Glass is dense and heavy, which means it's a big part (by weight) of our household and industrial waste stream. That stream includes bottles and broken glassware, lightbulbs, and miscellaneous products. Recycling glass uses much less energy than making it new from sand, soda, and lime. And every ton of waste glass, crushed and ready to be recycled, will save 693 tons of global warming gas.

The state of glass recycling is not the prettiest picture, with recapture rates in the United States declining from a none-too-impressive 30 percent in 1996 to just 20 percent in 2006. The good news, according to Earth911.org, is that a typical glass container contains 70 percent recycled material, and that 80 percent of recycled glass will end up as new containers. If bottles go into a landfill, they will take a million years to break down. The many uses for recycled glass include using it to make sports turf, kitchen tiles, and even sand for depleted beaches.

The Container Recycling Institute says that one reason for the low recycling rate is that curbside recyclers commingle different colors, which means fewer tons of color-sorted glass are available. An even bigger reason is that only 11 states have bottle bills, meaning they offer cash incentives for reclaimable bottles. Those states are California, Connecticut, Delaware, Hawaii, Iowa, Maine, Massachusetts, Michigan, New York, Oregon, and Vermont.

We need to do a whole lot better than this! A major step forward would be industry support for bottle bills, but the bottlers have instead thrown their weight behind antilittering campaigns, which put the onus of waste collection on the consumer. (www.earth911.org)

FYI

Cork is a delightfully sustainable product that is gradually being replaced (even in high-end wine bottles) by plastic stoppers. Old wine and champagne corks, however, can be recycled into other cork products by sending them to Wine Cork Recycling, Yemm & Hart Ltd, 610 South Chamber Drive, Fredericktown, MO 63645; www.yemmhart.com.

CAR BATTERIES
Getting the Lead Out

Some 97 percent of our automobile batteries are recycled rather than dumped in landfills. That's great news. The lead in these lead-acid batteries (21 pounds per battery) is highly toxic, and keeping it out of landfills is essential. The five million batteries that do get landfilled annually contaminate the earth with millions of pounds of lead and millions of gallons of sulfuric acid. Luckily, the lead is nearly 100 percent recyclable, has value, and can be resold, so the auto parts store that sells you a new battery should happily take the old one.

Another option is the **AAA Great Battery Roundup**, handled by your local Automobile Association of America office, usually around Earth Day. Dead batteries are collected and your current auto battery checked. Many towns hold hazardous waste collection days that take in car batteries. (www.batteryroundup.com)

But the story does not end there. Industrialized countries, such as the United States and Great Britain, have strict laws governing lead smelting, forcing the industry to install emission controls. As Greenpeace reports, third-world smelters can take batteries for recycling without installing such controls, and that has propelled much of the secondary lead industry out of North America entirely. So your battery may travel halfway around the world before its lead is imperfectly recovered.

Given all this, it's a good deal for the earth to keep your car battery working as long as possible. That means keeping fluid levels topped off and disconnecting the battery from the car if it's going to be stored for weeks or months. (www.roadandtravel.com/carcare/2005/battery recyclingtips.htm)

NEWSPAPERS
Many Ways to Reuse 'Em

Some 139 million Americans have access to curbside recycling programs, and more of us recycle than vote. Newspapers are overwhelmingly welcome in the blue bins. But if you're unlucky enough to be without that essential service, Tip Diva (www.tipdiva.com) has useful alternatives to throwing your old papers into the garbage:

★ **Line the bird cage.** Newspapers make great cage liners and are easy to dispose of when soiled.

★ **Control weeds.** Lay newspapers about 10 sheets thick around your plants, wet them thoroughly, and top with mulch. It's cheaper than the black plastic sheets of weed blockers, and it decomposes after a year.

★ **Wrap presents.** The comics page makes particularly good and unique wrapping paper and can still go in the recycle bin after its useful second life.

★ **Wash windows.** Use newspapers instead of paper towels, and the result will be sparkling glass with no streaks.

★ **Fireplace kindling.** Rolled-up sheets of newspaper make a great fire starter.

★ **Compost.** Assuming that the newspapers were printed with nontoxic ink, you can shred them and add them in with your food scraps.

★ **Help with packing.** Cushion your breakables with multiple newspaper sheets.

State Champion Recyclers

As Americans, we produce an average of 1.3 tons per person per year of municipal solid waste. According to the 2006 "State of Garbage in America Report," conducted by Columbia University and *Bio-Cycle* magazine, we're not doing all that well at recycling that staggering load. We reclaim overall only 28.5 percent of our municipal trash (equal to 110.4 million tons).

The Columbia/*Bio-Cycle* report says the state with the highest rate is Oregon, which recycles 45.8 percent of its trash. Close behind are Minnesota (43.2 percent), New York (43 percent), Tennessee (42.2 percent), and Washington (40.5 percent). An earlier *Bio-Cycle* report also praised California (40.2 percent), Iowa (41.7 percent), Missouri (38.9 percent), and New Jersey (37.9 percent).

Exceptionally poor performance was recorded circa 2004 by Colorado (2.8 percent), Georgia (8.3 percent), Idaho (8.4 percent), Louisiana (8.1 percent), New Mexico (6.5 percent), North Dakota (9.4 percent), Oklahoma (1 percent), South Dakota (3 percent), Utah (4.8 percent), West Virginia (6.9 percent), and Wyoming (1.7 percent).

The EPA says the most commonly recycled material in the waste stream (as of 2003) was paper and paperboard (40 million tons), followed by yard trimmings (16.1 million tons).

A New Hampshire environmental report points out that states calculate their recycling rates differently. Some states put limits on what municipalities can count in achieving their rate, "while others allow them to include everything from automobile hulks to chicken droppings." And some jurisdictions count "biosolids," or industrial waste, as municipal solid waste. (www.jgpress.com/biocycle.htm)

PAINT

Donate It or Dry It (Unless It's Oil)

Your first priority should be to not create paint waste in the first place—a gallon of house paint covers 250 to 350 square feet, so plan accordingly. (There are online calculators to help with this task.) If you have small amounts of various colors left over from a job, you can combine them and reuse the mixed paint as a primer coat that will eventually be covered by a final finish.

Sooner or later, however, everyone accumulates unwanted paint. But not all of it is hazardous waste. Leftover water-based latex paint, for instance, can be safely discarded in household trash, provided you dry it out beforehand. Remove the lid and let the paint harden. If there's more than a quarter can left, kitty litter (or a proprietary paint hardener) can be used to aid in the drying process. Then put both can and lid into a plastic trash bag and discard it with the weekly trash.

Two cautions with old latex: If it was made before 1992, it may contain mercury. And if it was made before 1977, it may contain lead. Check the dates of manufacture on the cans.

Oil-based paint is definitely toxic and cannot be landfilled safely. The solvents in oil-based paint are flammable, and resins, solvents, pigments, and additives can be toxic when breathed or touched. If you have unwanted oil-based paint in still-usable amounts, consider donating it to a school, community, or theater group so that it may be safely used and not landfilled. Unopened cans can probably be returned. If none of these options are available, oil paint should go to your local hazardous waste collection site or dropped off on a special waste collection day. (www.dec.ny.gov/docs/materials_minerals_pdf/paint.pdf)

PLASTIC BAGS

From Grocery to Environment

Paper versus plastic? Most people have already voted for plastic grocery bags, which the American Plastics Council says have grabbed 80 percent of the market. That switch has had a heavy environmental impact.

Reusablebags.com points out that our global society consumes 500 billion to one trillion plastic bags annually, or a million per minute. (The US number alone is 380 billion, according to the EPA.) And billions of those end up as litter.

Plastic bags don't biodegrade—they "photodegrade," meaning they break down into small pieces that contaminate soil and bodies of water. The Center for Marine Conservation says that plastic bags are among the 12 types of debris most often found in coastal cleanups. The bags are mistaken for food by sea turtles, whales, and other marine mammals, and hundreds of thousands die each year after accidentally ingesting them.

The solution is as old as shopping itself: reusable cloth bags. When Ireland (which consumed 1.2 billion plastic bags in 2001, 316 per person) introduced PlasTax, a consumption tax on plastic bags, it reduced consumption of plastic bags by 90 percent. "Each high-quality, reusable shopping bag you use has the potential to eliminate hundreds, if not thousands, of plastic bags over its lifetime," says Reusablebags.com. Many municipalities in the United States are now considering or have enacted plastic bag bans. San Francisco was the first, in 2007.

Most grocery chains sell reusable bags for $1 or less, and some, such as Trader Joe's, offer perks for people who bring their own bags. Whole Foods gives a 5-cent discount. A Web site known as One Bag at a Time has sold more than

3.5 million reusable bags, which it says has saved the use of 624 million plastic bags (and enough petroleum to drive a car 112 million miles). Bags on the Run is similar. (www.reusablebags.com; www.onebagatatime.com; www.bagsontherun.com)

DECONSTRUCTION
The Reuse Alternative

When Vermont's Middlebury College decided to replace its six-story science center with a new library in 2001, it hired a New Hampshire company to take the old building apart instead of demolishing it. More than 1,350 tons of material (97.4 percent of the total) was recovered, including concrete, copper, rebar, stainless steel, limestone, and scientific equipment. The science equipment was donated to 14 Vermont high schools. It wasn't exactly "zero waste"—36 tons went to landfills—but it was impressive.

The reuse idea is gaining in popularity, particularly because the recovered materials are valuable and can be resold. The Port of Oakland is using deconstruction to take down large military buildings. Rick Denhart of Mercy Corps, which dismantled many New Orleans buildings in the wake of Hurricane Katrina, defines deconstruction as "the dismantling of buildings by hand for maximum reuse of materials." He also likes the description he heard from a local resident as "removing the house with dignity: board by board, brick by brick."

Habitat for Humanity ReStores are retail outlets offering affordable prices on used and surplus building materials. The proceeds help fund Habitat home reconstruction projects. Some of the stores raise enough money to build 10 additional homes per year. The materials are typically donated by demolition crews, building supply stores, and contractors. (www.habitat.org/env/restores.aspx)

The Building Materials Reuse Association has a wealth of information to help explore the environmentally friendly deconstruction approach. (www.buildingreuse.org)

CLOTHING
Creative Reuse

Recycling used clothing is hardly a new process: It's called a thrift store. Take a look in the yellow pages under "secondhand stores," "thrift shops," or similar listings. Thrift shops are run by charities such as the Salvation Army, Goodwill Industries, St. Vincent de Paul, and the American Cancer Society (Discovery Shops). You can stock up on some great stuff—including new duds for yourself—at unbelievable prices. Most offer tax deductions for your donations.

Tap into the national directory of thrift stores, searchable by ZIP code, at TheThriftShopper.com. Homeless shelters would probably be grateful for your clothing donations. Another great idea is selling your unwanted outfits at a home sale, which have regionally specific names depending on where you live, such as "tag," "yard," "garage," "lawn," or "rummage" sale. Advertise your sale in the local paper (or with flyers on lampposts and community bulletin boards), and you'll be amazed at the turnout. The online Craigslist ("clothing and accessories") and Freecycle.com are other options. (www.thethriftshopper.com; www.craigslist.com; www.freecycle.com)

CARPETS
A Small Cost for Caring

You're renovating, and that means the old, worn carpet has to go. But is there an alternative to throwing it in the Dumpster? Yes, if you're prepared to commit your wallet to the cause.

Five billion pounds of carpet go to landfills every year, and to date only 500 million pounds have been recovered—but it's a start. There's no national resource for carpet recycling, but there are great local resources, including LA Fiber in California (323-589-5637), CarpetCycle in the New York/New Jersey area (908-353-5900), ERCS in the Boston area (978-664-5050), and NYCORE in Minnesota (770-980-0000).

Carpet America Recovery Effort (CARE) says, "Please keep in mind, recycling costs money; it's not free. Costs vary with location and available systems." On average, that means 5 to 25 cents per pound (and carpet usually weighs 4 to 5 pounds per square yard).

According to CARE, old carpet can be made into composite lumber, roofing shingles, railroad ties, auto parts, stepping-stones, and more. (www.carpetrecovery.org)

CFL LIGHTBULBS
Don't Just Throw 'Em Out

There's no question that compact fluorescent (CFL) bulbs are a huge help to the environment, lasting much longer and using a fraction of the energy of incandescent bulbs. What was once a trickle of CFLs on the marketplace has become a flood, and they've overcome initial light quality issues and become affordable and widely available. But there's an end-of-life disposal issue, because all fluorescents contain very small amounts of the toxic metal mercury. And the mercury from just one bulb can make up to 6,000 gallons of water dangerous to drink.

The bad news is that people throw out 600 million fluorescent lamps containing 30,000 pounds of mercury annually. And some 187 incinerators nationwide emit 70,000 pounds of the stuff every year.

It's actually illegal to dispose of fluorescents as normal waste in California, Minnesota, Ohio, Illinois, Indiana, Michigan, and Wisconsin. Fluorescent bulbs should not go into recycling bins, *ever*. That said, there are no easy disposal options. You need to be motivated.

Services such as LightBulbRecycling.com will take your used CFLs and conventional fluorescents, but at a price. You fill up one of their safety bags with used bulbs, seal them in a shipping container, and address the shipping label, then FedEx delivers the lot to an EPA-approved recycling station. You get a certificate with the date your bulbs were recycled. To recycle 30 bulbs in a big green bucket costs $120.

To address the problem locally, check with the local transfer station to see if it has a hazardous waste recycling program. State environmental departments offer guides to hazardous waste collection dates and locations. Home Depot also has a recycling program for CFLs.

You can store your CFLs while waiting to safely deliver them, perhaps in a large plastic bucket with a tight-fitting lid. It's more work than using third-party services, but it should be more affordable. (www.lightbulbrecycling.com)

It's Open Season on Copper and Brass

By the time copper hit a new record of $4 a pound on the New York Mercantile Exchange's Comex Division, it had become a runaway target of theft, joining aluminum, bronze, lead, and any other metal that can be pried loose.

Welcome to the wonderful world of scrap metal theft. Let's look at the record in just one state, Connecticut. One of the lowlights of this creative crime was the theft in 2008 of 32 bronze nozzles from a fountain on the New Haven Green, a stone's throw away from Yale University. It caused $20,000 worth of damage but probably netted the thieves less than $100. The replacement nozzles are made of plastic.

Scrap dealers and police say they cooperate to prevent the sale of stolen goods, and laws have recently been toughened, but it hasn't ended the epidemic. The list of metals recently purloined around Connecticut includes:

★ Four bronze plaques on a historic statue of P. T. Barnum in Bridgeport's Seaside Park.

★ The copper onion domes on a venerable and significant brownstone building in the same city.

★ Spools of copper wire from a Connecticut Light and Power substation in New Canaan.

★ Metal Little League benches from a field in Bristol. In the same town, a plaque commemorating actor and native son Ted Knight also disappeared, though it was later recovered.

Because the increased demand for scrap metal is worldwide, the theft problem is also global—and apparently no site is off-limits to metal thieves: In Edmondthorpe, England, the 800-year-old St. Michael and All Angels Church lost much of its lead roof in long strips, leaving a 100-square-foot hole. The thieves' motive was simple economics. The price of lead had increased by 700 percent in the past 6 years.

In 2001, scrap metal sold for an average of $77 a ton, but the price had climbed to $500 a ton in 2008. The bull market is inspired by demand increases in China, India, and South Korea. Metal theft has become the crime of choice for drug addicts, police say, because the metal can be quickly turned into cash from dealers who often don't ask many questions.

Separation Anxiety: How We Recycle

What's the best way to collect recyclables, anyway? The debate continues, with pluses and minuses on both sides.

According to the Container Recycling Institute, the predominant recycling method until the late 1980s was "source separation," which required consumers to separate just about every material into its own bin. Trucks had compartments for everything from glass bottles to aluminum cans.

In the simpler **"commingled"** system, there are two basic waste streams. One is food and beverage containers, including cans and bottles; the other is newspapers and mixed paper, which is placed in either another bin or a paper grocery bag.

The **"single stream"** recycling method was introduced in the late 1990s because it costs a whole lot less on the front end. All the recyclables can be jumbled together, easily picked up and hauled. The problem, critics say, is that the waste streams contaminate each other and reduce their value. For instance, glass from broken bottles and plastic from PET bottles can get mingled with paper waste and cause problems at the recycling mill. But municipalities benefit from lower overall recycling costs.

With commingled systems, the two major waste streams stay separate. The paper is delivered unsorted, but the cans and bottles are separated, either by automatic equipment or by hand. In either case, it adds postpickup costs.

As if this weren't complicated enough, there are also hybrid commingled systems that only separate glass from the other waste types. All these systems have their benefits, and unfortunately none is ideal. (www.container-recycling.org)

FYI

Old Christmas cards can be recycled as Christmas tags simply by cutting out the design and writing on the other side. And the front panels by themselves make great postcards. Old cards can also be donated to St. Jude's Ranch for Children Card Recycling Program, 100 St. Jude's Street, Boulder City, NV 89005.

TREX
Deck Your Halls

Trex decking, railing, and fencing is made from 50 percent recycled polyethylene plastic (including used grocery bags) and 50 percent reclaimed wood scraps. The plastic protects the wood from damage due to moisture and insects, and the wood shields the plastic from UV light damage.

The company claims its operations keep 300,000 tons of plastic and wood scrap out of landfills every year. The wood is sourced from woodworking operations, used shipping pallets, and sawdust—some 300 million pounds annually.

Here's an amazing statistic: Seven out of 10 recycled grocery bags in the United States go into Trex products. That's 1.5 billion bags every year.

Trex costs more, but its products don't need to be painted and are unlikely to splinter or rot. Trex can be bent or curved, and it won't warp. There are no harmful chemicals, and at the end of life, Trex can go safely into landfills. (www.trex.com)

ZERO WASTE

A Long Time Coming

It's a beautiful idea but a long way from realization. It's "zero waste," and its time has come, at least in New Zealand, where it's a national policy goal.

There are several basic tenets that govern zero waste programs. The first is to embrace extended producer responsibility concepts and redesign both products and packaging to reduce waste—"designing products for the environment, not for the dump."

Zero waste advocates (ZWAs) think 90 percent of waste can be diverted from the landfill with a combination of reuse facilities (such as the free shops that have sprouted in New Zealand), social policies, and market signals. ZWAs like the idea of leasing or renting products from their manufacturers rather than buying them outright. They also think that taxpayers should not be asked to subsidize polluting industries by making it cheaper for them to use raw materials instead of recycled or recovered ones. And, of course, consuming less per capita is one of their basic tenets.

Zero waste creates jobs out there, too. The Institute for Local Self Reliance says, "On a per-ton basis, sorting and processing recyclables alone sustains 10 times more jobs than landfilling or incineration." And paper mills that produce recycled paper and plastic employ 60 times more workers (on a per-ton basis) than do landfills.

According to Boulder, Colorado-based Eco-Cycle, US companies committed to zero waste include:

Fetzer wine, which has already cut its garbage 93 percent and uses solar energy to fill and cap 1.2 million bottles of wine. All Fetzer packaging is recycled.

Interface, a carpet company whose goal is "to take nothing from the earth that is not renewable and do no harm to the biosphere." Interface carpets are offered through an "evergreen lease" that minimizes waste, recovers worn carpeting for recycling, and replaces carpet in sections rather than the entire rug.

Lexmark, which uses a recyclable egg-carton-shaped paperboard packaging for its printers instead of Styrofoam. The packaging itself is made from recycled paper.

Eric Lombardi, executive director of Eco-Cycle, asks, "Is there really anything to like about landfills or incinerators? As Jean-Paul Sartre said after a lifetime of seeking the meaning of life, 'The root of all significance lies in comparison.' So which do you choose?" (www.ecocycle.org)

The Frugal Shopper suggests that egg cartons make great seed starter trays. When you take the seedlings out to plant, the cardboard can be buried next to the plants to decompose. You can make ice cubes in egg cartons, too.

RUBBER TUBS

Made from Recycled Tires

There are hundreds of millions of junk tires clogging up America's landfills, so it's always refreshing to hear how they can be reused. How about a flexible 8-gallon bucket made from 100 percent recycled tire rubber?

This all-purpose bucket has two sturdy handles and is ideal for such tasks as collecting garden rubbish and weeds, carting picnic supplies to the beach, feeding animals, spreading mulch, mixing compost, or displaying items at yard sales. We imagine you can think of a few more uses. The surface of the bucket is nonreactive, so it shouldn't stain or stick to anything you leave in it. (www.cleanairgardening.com/flexible-tub)

Biodegradable Alternatives to Plastic

Remember when Dustin Hoffman's character in *The Graduate* was told that his future lay in plastics? Well, he'd probably get different advice these days. "The image of plastics among consumers is deteriorating at an alarmingly fast pace," Larry Thomas of the Society of Plastics Industries has said. "At this rate, we will soon reach a point from which it will be impossible to recover our credibility."

More than 20 million tons of plastic made it into US landfills in 1995, and by 2010 that number is expected to be 20 percent higher.

Now imagine an additive that can be blended into standard plastic resins that makes them biodegradable. Ohio-based ECM BioFilms says it can do exactly that with its pellet technology, which is not dependent on the presence of light or moisture to degrade.

Biodegradable plastics have been introduced to the market, usually with a corn (starch) base combined with resins. ECM's pellet technology is different, consisting of organic and inorganic chemicals (the formula is proprietary) that can then be combined with any standard polyethylene or polypropylene resin to produce a plastic that is fully biodegradable. It can be used to make bags, agricultural films, diaper liners, and many other products.

Lab tests show that ECM-treated plastics are nontoxic, and they do break down in landfills under anaerobic (meaning cut off from a supply of oxygen) conditions. (www.ecmbiofilms.com)

CANDLES: MAKE YOUR OWN!

Recycling your burned-down stubs into new candles is not a hard job, and it's a fun project to do with your kids. According to the Web site Kaboose, what you'll need from a crafts shop are wicks, craft glue, and wax boil bags. You supply the old candles and some glass jars (preferably with lids).

Fill the boil bags with your old candle fragments, then heat them to melting on the stove. Cut the wicks to size and position them in the center of the jars. If the wicks are not straight, the candle will not burn well. You can use twist ties to position the wicks, crossing two of them over the middle of the jar in an "X" shape. Pour the melted wax into the jars, let cool, and there are your new candles. The craft glue (and ribbon, if you'd like) is for decorating the outside of the jars.

Safety is important here. Melted wax is very hot and can cause skin burns. Never heat wax in a microwave oven, and make sure that children have adult supervision during the whole process. (www.kaboose.com)

RECYCLED ALUMINUM

Big Energy Costs Can Be Saved

Where does aluminum come from? We start with an ore, in this case the red clay-like ore known as bauxite, which contains many aluminum compounds. Bauxite mining itself is environmentally destructive. Then smelters (such as those that dot the landscape in Iceland) separate the aluminum using abundant amounts of electricity.

That electricity use (7.5 kilowatt-hours for a pound of aluminum, enough for 34 cans) is avoided when aluminum is recycled. For instance, aluminum can recycling saves 11.5 billion kilowatt-hours annually, enough to light the city of Pittsburgh for 6 years. With the recycling of just four aluminum cans, the energy in a cup of gasoline is saved. Recycling aluminum produces only about 5 percent of the carbon dioxide generated by raw aluminum.

Today, 50 percent of aluminum cans are recycled, making it the most recycled product in the United States. But only 31 percent of scrap aluminum is currently recycled, largely because (assuming you don't worry about the environmental consequences) producing it new is cheaper. Aluminum scrap for recycling has to be collected, identified, separated, and cleaned. If paint is present, that's a complicating factor because the paint releases toxic fumes when heated. (www.aluminum.org)

FYI

Large, bulky items, such as plastic jugs and cardboard boxes, should be crushed or folded to conserve space in your recycling bin and, later, in the truck that picks them up.

SPORTS BOTTLES
Choose Recycled

Everybody's drinking a lot of water these days, and when that H2O comes from a single-use plastic bottle, a huge amount of waste is created that clogs landfills and litters the landscape. But the PETE (#1 recycled) plastic that goes into water bottles is eminently recyclable. Too bad only 11 states have bottle bills.

Fight back with the affordable, reusable, recycled, and recyclable 20-ounce sports bottles from Maple Leaf Promotions, which can be imprinted with your group or company's logo for promotional use. The bottles (but not the lids) are molded from 100 percent recycled plastic, and they become biodegradable, high-density polyethylene plastic (#2 recycled). They're available in eight colors. (www.mapleleafpromotions.com)

FLAGS
Respect and Recycle Old Glory

Do you have to burn an American flag that touches the ground? Not according to the Flag Code. If it's an outdoor flag, you can simply hand-wash it with laundry detergent. Some dry cleaners will process your flag free of charge (especially in July). To keep your flag in good condition, bring it inside during bad weather, and make sure it's fully dry before storing it to avoid mold or mildew.

If your flag is beyond saving, the Flag Code says it should be retired, and a preferred method is burning (although this seems counterintuitive in an age of anti-flag-burning ordinances). You can also seal the flag in a box or bag and bury it, or deliver your flag to the American Legion or the local Boy Scout or Girl Scout Council, for a flag retirement ceremony.

Burning nylon flags releases toxic fumes. According to DuPont, "Hazardous gases/vapors produced in fire are formaldehydes, ammonia, carbon monoxide, cyclopentanone, oxides of nitrogen, traces of hydrogen cyanide, [and] incompletely burned hydrocarbons." A green alternative is to write the word "recycle" on the header before handing it over. Then the nylon can be used to make new flags, and the Stars and Stripes will wave again.

Wisconsin-based American Flag Recycling will take your worn-out banner for a fee: $4 for flags 3 x 5 feet to 8 x 12 feet and $5 for flags 10 x 15 feet and larger. (www.americanflagdisposal.com)

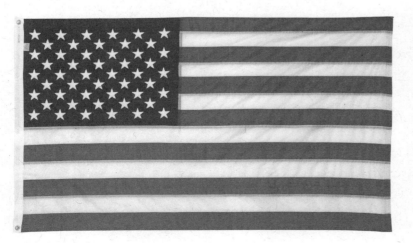

ANTIQUES
Furniture to Last a Lifetime

As devout fans of *Antiques Roadshow* are well aware, antiques can be big business. Some thought that dealer (and *Roadshow* regular) Leigh Keno was crazy for paying $731,000 for the Biddle-Drinker family's 18th-century American highboy—sight unseen. But when the piece was auctioned at Christie's in late 2008, it fetched more than $1 million.

Let's face it: Every old piece you buy at a tag sale or inherit won't make you rich (although the show makes it seem that way sometimes). But old furniture and furnishings can be beautiful, are usually well made, and will probably appreciate in value.

According to Ken Melchert, a furniture restorer and co-owner of the Harp Gallery antique store in Wisconsin, "Living with antique and vintage furniture has a very positive effect on the environment. Recycling treasures from the past not only saves landfill space but also has many other positive 'green' effects on our planet.

"Recycling vintage furniture saves trees and breathes new life into beautiful old wood. Much of the finest old-growth hardwood has already been cut down and made into furniture years ago. Refurbishing these irreplaceable pieces substitutes for further decimating of more prime mature hardwood trees in endangered forests."

Oscar Wilde said: "Nothing is so dangerous as being too modern. One is apt to grow old-fashioned quite suddenly." But some modern techniques are good, particularly the safer and gentler processes to strip old varnish, and the new water-based finishes that are vastly less injurious to the earth than petroleum-based lacquers and solvents. (www.antiquesroadshow.com)

RECYCLED PAPER
We're Halfway There

Americans are amazing paper gluttons, using an average of 700 pounds per person annually, seven times the usage of the average global citizen. Despite the promise of the "paperless office," 95 percent of all business information is still stored on paper.

We've been making paper for 2,000 years and recycling it one way or another ever since. It's heartening that approximately half of our paper production (360 pounds per capita) is currently recycled, and 36 percent of new paper comes from recycled sources. But there's certainly room for improvement—the industry's goal is 60 percent by 2012—and big incentives. We save 6.7 cubic yards of landfill space with every ton of paper recycled. Eighty-seven percent of us have access to paper recycling of one form or another, so there's really no excuse.

According to Carnegie Mellon Green Practices:

★ Making new paper from old paper uses 30 percent to 55 percent less energy than making paper from trees and reduces related air pollution by 95 percent.

★ Typical offices generate 1.5 pounds of waste paper per employee per day, and 77 percent of paper waste in offices is recyclable.

★ Commercial and residential paper waste accounts for more than 40 percent of waste going to the landfill. Eliminating paper waste would nearly double the lives of current landfills.

★ Newspaper is recycled into newspaper, game boards, egg cartons, gift boxes, animal bedding, insulation, and packaging material.

★ Office paper is recycled into office paper, tissue paper, paper towels, and toilet paper.

★ Corrugated cardboard is recycled into new cardboard and cereal boxes. (www.cmu.edu/greenpractices/)

FYI

Do you have a drawerful of unmatched socks? Here are six uses: Give them to your kids for sock puppets; take them camping to use as pot holders; make a pad to dust around the house; tie one into a knot to use as a dog toy; turn them into rags when refinishing furniture; and use them to clean up after painting or arts and crafts projects.

RETREAD TIRES
Recapping Means Nil Goes to Landfill

Junk tires are not only a huge waste-disposal issue but also a potential health problem. Sitting around in landfills half full of water, they are breeding grounds for mosquitoes. So why not give them a second life?

If you thought the retread tire market had vanished, guess again. In 2006, 18.6 million retreads were sold in North America. It's a more than $3 billion business. If you're not familiar with the industry, it's because the major customer of the 900 retread plants in North America is the medium-size truck market.

According to the **Tire Retread and Repair Information Bureau** (yes, there is such a thing), retreaded tires (which cost 30 to 50 percent less than new ones) are used on school buses, race cars, taxis, trucks, and US government and military vehicles. Almost all airlines use retreads.

Harvey Brodsky, managing director of the bureau, thinks that retreads get a bad rap for "rubber on the road" syndrome. "Rubber on the road, also known as road alligators or tire debris, is a menace and can cause fatal accidents if not cleaned up promptly," he says. "Unfortunately, far too many people believe the cause of rubber on the road is retreaded tires, but the fact is that much of the rubber on the road comes from tires that have never been inside a retread plant." He says improper tire maintenance causes first-time-around tires to shred.

The bureau's unusually ambitious Web site has everything you could possibly want to know about retreads, including buyers' guides, searchable databases of recap tires near you, and detailed accounts of the recapping process. (www.retread.org)

RECYCLED PLASTIC
Ban the Bottles!

The big culprit in plastic is bottled water, a category that barely existed 30 years ago. Average consumption in 1976 was only 1.6 gallons annually; by 2006, it was 28.3 gallons. Some 29.8 billion plastic water bottles were sold in 2005. And we drink and toss: In 2006, Americans guzzled an average of 167 bottles of water, but only 23 percent were recycled. And so 38 billion plastic water bottles (8 out of 10) went into landfills, and others were left clogging storm drains or turned into unsightly and non-biodegradable roadside waste.

Overall, plastic PET (polyethylene terephthalate) recycling has been in decline since the mid-1990s high of about 30 percent. Today, the rate is not much more than 20 percent.

Sales of 10- to 12-ounce plastic water bottles increased 900 percent between 2002 and 2005, from 1.9 billion to 18.9 billion. One thing that indicated was a move from larger sizes to "on the go" single serves—a switch that dramatically increased plastic waste.

Bottled water is a big energy consumer: A year's US supply uses up 1.5 million barrels of oil, enough to keep 100,000 cars on the road. We're leaving a problem for future generations. When they go into landfills, these robust containers will stay intact for an estimated 700 years.

There is a gratifying backlash against bottled water that could, over time, return us to the tap-water-dependent 1970s. And it's amazing how quickly the savings will accummulate. According to Earth911.org, if everyone in New York City gave up water bottles for 1 week, they would save 24 million bottles from being landfilled; 1 month would save 112 million bottles, and 1 year would save 1.328 billion bottles from going into the landfill. (www.container-recycling.org)

BAGS FROM BILLBOARDS
Tote with Pride

Did you know that today's billboards aren't painted on paper but are printed on vinyl plastic? When they are taken down, that's a lot of potentially toxic plastic waste headed for landfills. A green alternative is reusing the colorful material for no-two-alike purses, totes, and sports bags. Green with Envy Gifts has a wide selection of billboard bags. They will even work with a specific billboard of your choosing when possible. (www.greenwithenvygifts.com)

Robin Janson and Nicola Freegard of Vy and Elle say their company has recycled about 100 tons of billboards into 50,000 bags. "Vinyl billboards are usually discarded into landfills, where they create toxic pollution," says Vy and Elle. "Instead, the strength of PVC vinyl makes it an ideal material for reuse. And because of the different images printed on the vinyl, it's even more interesting as a fabric. It offers colorful graphics that take urban art into everyday living." (www.vyandelle.com)

The Story behind the Recycling Logo

Gary Anderson was a 23-year-old college student in 1970 when he came up with the logo that is now universally recognized as the symbol of recycling. Chicago-based Container Corporation of America (CCA) sponsored a design contest for high school and college art students, who were asked to create a logo that represented recycling—with college tuition as the prize.

More than 500 students responded, and a team of designers chose Anderson as the winner at the 1970 International Design Conference in Aspen, Colorado. His design was three arrows chasing each other in a Möbius loop. That same year, the logo was adopted by the three principal paper industry groups. CCA initially tried to trademark the symbol, but it eventually dropped its application and the icon went into the public domain.

Anderson, who received a master's degree in urban design from the University of Southern California, served as a research fellow at Johns Hopkins University and is now a senior planner at a Baltimore firm. Still environmentally involved, he is a board member of 1,000 Friends of Maryland.

"One thing is certain," Anderson said. "It seems to belong to everybody—and that is fine with me."

Working Green

Green is the new black—that's the word in the workplace. What that means is that going green in the office is both chic and a powerful marketing statement for all who share a concern for the environment. This is a transformational change for all workplaces, including home offices. There are five reasons for this shift in thinking.

Reason one: Going green won't necessarily cost more money, because recently there has been a flood of high-quality, attractively priced, and green-hued office furniture, equipment, and tools. So why not go green?

Reason two: The quality of green goods is way up. A generation ago, recycled paper, for instance, often was mottled, absorbed ink erratically, and did not feed smoothly into printers and copiers. For many people 20 years ago, their first ream of recycled paper was their last. Now it is time to revisit the matter. There is no discernible quality difference between 100 percent postconsumer recycled paper and virgin. So a simple starting point for going green at work is to buy a ream of recycled copy paper. Since most offices still use a lot of paper, this switch has an immediate positive impact.

Another easy green jumping-off point: Use remanufactured inkjet cartridges and save money while aiding the environment. Remanufactured cartridges perform as well as brand-new but cost 10 to 20 percent less. Again, performance is key: Green now performs at the same high level as conventional office supplies.

Reason three: Green office products are plentiful. Big-box stores from Office Depot to Wal-Mart sell them, as do online retailers that ship products directly to your door. Time was, a plausible excuse was "I can't find anything green when I need it." That no longer applies.

Reason four: We are where we work. Big companies recognize that employee attitudes about themselves and their jobs are influenced by the office environment. That is all the more true when the office is at home. What we surround ourselves with says volumes about who we are and how we see ourselves in relation to the planet. The good news is that home offices often are comparatively small spaces, which means they can be greened up on the cheap. Going green in a 10 x 8-foot space might mean buying just a few smart products and following a handful of ecologically aware practices.

Reason five: There are plenty of very low-cost—even no-cost— ways to make a big green statement. Think recycling: Think about old doors, for instance, which are easy to find, often at no cost at all (check www.freecycle.org), and have many uses. Place one on a pair of two-drawer filing cabinets and that is not just a workstation, it's a statement. It says: "I am running my business with minimal environmental impact."

Another smart no-cost strategy: Reduce waste. The less we throw out, the greener we are. Most waste still lands in landfills, for which we have less and less room. Yet we still aren't good at recycling: New Jersey, for instance, calculates that only 54.7 percent of what should be recycled actually gets recycled, which means 45.3 percent of potential recyclables still go to the dump. Yes, ours has long been a disposable culture, but when we commit to recycling everything that can be recycled, that puts us farther along the green path.

Daylighting is one of the simplest of no-cost green tactics: Simply open the blinds, pull the curtains away, and let the sun in. Too often, when we think about going green, our mental cash register rings as we picture buying everything from solar arrays to geothermal heat for the office. Yet when we focus on the basics, something as simple as letting the sun in helps us to be greener.

More broadly, conservation of energy often is the biggest and easiest step to take. Turn off the computer at day's end. Open a window and use a fan instead of an air conditioner. In winter, pull on a sweater and turn down the fossil-fuel heat. Little steps add up to a big green statement—and anybody can take them. Want still more green suggestions and products to mull over? Check the pages that follow for some of the coolest, most innovative green gear out there.

—Robert McGarvey

RECYCLED PAPER
Getting Better All the Time

Just a few years ago, recycled paper was funky and expensive and did little to project a professional image. Today it's every bit as good as virgin paper when it comes to printing and photocopying, and prices are competitive. The midweight (24-pound) paper from Xerox, for example, has a minimum of 30 percent post-consumer recycled content—which means fewer trees get chopped down. What's particularly cool is that it comes in vivid colors such as lime green or orange. (www1.officedepot.com/)

There's more: Paper made from 100 percent postconsumer recycled content is becoming affordable. Office Depot (www.office depot.com), for instance, sells **Wausau** Exact Eco 100 (20 pound, white) for $8.39 per ream. A bonus: This is acid-free paper that won't yellow over time. (www.wausaupapers.com/products)

Earthchoice paper is another option. It's not recycled, but it is Forest Stewardship Council (FSC) certified and endorsed by the Rainforest Alliance. By most estimates, around half the paper we buy winds up recycled, but that volume is not enough to meet the demand for new paper. So some will perforce be virgin, but the FSC badge is a promise that the source forests are well managed and environmental impacts are minimal. (www.domtar.com)

RECYCLED NOTEBOOK
Notes on Green

Here is the green notebook you've been looking for: The cover is 100 percent recycled cardboard, and inside there are 100 sheets of unlined recycled paper. This journal can be personalized with your logo. Whenever you take it out to record meeting notes, you'll also make a statement about the importance of going green. Price, in quantity, is just $3.60. (www.onsale promos.com/products)

YOLO COLORHOUSE PAINTS
Cutting VOCs

Freshening up an office with new paint has long been a drag on the environment, because conventional paints throw off quantities of volatile organic compounds (VOCs) that may contribute to global warming and can smell terrible. Early-generation low- and no-VOC paint provoked howls of discontent, mostly for poor coverage. But that is changing fast as new environmentally sensitive paints win good reviews for quality. Speeding up adoption are state and federal laws that take old-fashioned VOC-laden paints off the market.

Low-VOC paints are becoming commonplace as big-box retailers such as Lowe's and Home Depot stock them, but a little hunting can turn up no-VOC paints that, as the name suggests, contain none of those damaging organic compounds. No-VOC paint costs more ($39 to $50 a gallon is typical), while conventional paints usually run $10 to $20 a gallon cheaper. But no-VOC paint is free of odors and the greenhouse gases that contribute to global warming. The no-VOC paints from **Yolo Colorhouse**, at about $39 per gallon, have won favorable notice in publications such as the *New York Times* and are now beginning to garner praise from pro painters for quality and ease of use. Yolo paints are not yet widely available at retail, but check the company's Web site for local distributors— and yes, the company does ship paint nationally. (http://yolocolorhouse.com)

Just the Green Fax

How many pages of paper are you routinely wasting on junk faxes? The worst of conventional faxing is that every incoming page gets printed automatically, consuming paper and inks. Good news: Paperless faxing is yours with eFax, a computer-based service that delivers incoming faxes as e-mail attachments. Review them on screen, then print only the ones you really need on paper. A big plus: When documents are digital, they are easy to search for. It's much easier to find that one important fax on your computer than in a filing cabinet.

eFax comes in a free version with limits on incoming fax pages (currently 20 pages per month are permitted free). As faxing continues to decline in volume, the free version just may be enough for many home offices. Power users will want to sign up for fee-based editions that offer users the opportunity to get many more faxes; for instance, eFaxPlus is $16.95 per month, which includes an area code of choice, 130 pages of incoming faxes per month, and 30 pages of outgoing faxes per month. (www.efax.com)

Biodegradable Writing Stalk?

Throw it away and just 12 months later, this pen is no more—because the world's first pen made from corn naturally decomposes in a compost pile or landfill. The feel in hand is similar to that of a conventional plastic pen. But those ordinary pens never break down, while the Grass Roots corn pen decomposes after it runs out of ink (only blue ink is available). Price: just $1.99. Also available: imprinting with your company name. Hand out these pens to customers and colleagues and make a surprising statement about your commitment to going green. (www.grass rootsstore.com)

When Good Machines Die

Don't throw out that dead printer with the trash. And hold that old fax machine and PC, too. This equipment fills up the landfill, and most high-tech gear comes with unwanted toxins and chemicals that simply don't belong in the soil. European consumers have been adamant that manufacturers offer end-of-life take-away policies, and such programs are growing in the United States. Hewlett Packard, for one, will take away most equipment it sells. Check out the terms at (http://www.hp.com/recycle). Although it charges a fee, it offers coupons that cover the full charge. A PC and monitor, for instance, cost $46 for HP to recycle, but the company provides a $50 coupon redeemable at its online store.

Dell offers free end-of-life recycling. In fact, all major manufacturers offer some form of end-of-life recycling, and these policies can be an important part of purchasing decisions. Small businesses, including sole-proprietor home offices, ought to follow suit. You don't want to get stuck with equipment that cannot practically be disposed of in an environmentally responsible way. Let professionals who know how to handle this equipment do so. That often means turning it back over to the manufacturers.

What does a manufacturer do with the gear it collects? HP says it recycles and reuses what it can and promises to dispose of anything left over in an environmentally sensitive way. Other major manufacturers make similar promises. HP also suggests that where possible, unwanted gear be donated to organizations that want it. Unfortunately, many nonprofits have become picky about which electronics they will accept. The Cristina Foundation, dedicated to the support of training with donated technology, currently accepts PCs, peripherals, printers, and more. It's supported by Dell, HP, and many other manufacturers. It does set some age limits; for instance, it won't accept very old Pentium I and II computers anymore, but Cristina will accept most working devices. A tax deduction may even result for the giver. (www.cristina.org)

In many communities, schools and charities may accept direct contributions of high-tech equipment. They will likely decline very old stuff, but that 3-year-old laptop that no longer is needed in your office may be just the machine a seventh grader in a low-income school district could use. Lately, the US Environmental Protection Agency has jump-started broad recycling electronics with its Plug In to eCycling campaign. (www.epa.gov)

What about the personal content left on your hard drive? Don't worry; just go to Download.com, search for "erase hard drive," and pick the program best suited to your needs. Most such software is based on the same idea: It literally overwrites the hard drive with nonsense, often two or three times. Thus all data get destroyed.

Before buying any new gear, get the answer to this question: When this machine comes to the end of its useful life, how will the manufacturer help me dispose of it in an environmentally and socially responsible way?

Go Used

Want to know the lowest-impact way to furnish an office? Go used. Whatever environmental impacts were involved in the manufacture occurred years ago, and if volatile organic compounds (VOCs) figured into the furniture, the emissions have probably dissipated with age. You cannot get much greener than using a 50-year-old, indestructible, government-issue metal desk and matching file cabinet. Lots of used furniture is free, too. A recent search on **Craig's List** (www.craigslist.org) turned up a free wooden teacher's desk ("It won't fit in my new apartment"), a free desk with extra bookcase shelving, a free IKEA bookcase, and a free desk chair. Why do people list their items for giveaway? Often, people wish to reduce their personal impact on the landfill. Also, it feels good to give unwanted belongings to people who have a use for them.

Another time-honored way to find free furniture is to scout the streets for discards, especially near the end of the month, when renters move out. Many urbanites brag that they have furnished their entire dwellings with castoffs, which may include paintings, exercise equipment, and lots of office equipment and furniture.

All this goes into overdrive at the **Freecycle Network** (www.freecycle.org), a nationwide network that facilitates giving away the unwanted. And what finds! A recent search turned up a gorgeous mahogany filing cabinet—current home is a pricey Upper West Side Manhattan apartment. One company put out an alert that it was closing and giving away all kinds of furniture (printer stands, desk chairs, desks). Put in a few minutes a day on the Freecycle site and odds are good that you'll be able to furnish a home office at no cost.

Tip: The mother lode of free furniture may often be a college campus area at the end of the spring semester. Come mid-May, as the students race to get home for summer, all manner of furniture is deposited on the curb. Savvy New Yorkers, for instance, mark their calendars to track the end of the New York University spring semester, so when they patrol the Greenwich Village and East Village neighborhoods where NYU students live, they can pick up everything from telephones to IKEA workstations.

Don't forget the **Salvation Army**. Furniture there isn't free, but prices usually are nominal, and delivery is available in many locations (a lot of office furniture is just too big to fit into a car). A fresh coat of paint can make used wooden furniture look great. Buy some low- or no-VOC paint and have at it.

The best part of furnishing a home office with used furniture is that it means having a positive impact on the environment by keeping more stuff out of landfills.

GREENPRINT
Print Less, Save More

In printing, there is waste. Just about every time we print anything from the Internet, we get more than we want or need. Print a brief op-ed piece and you're liable to get 37 pages of reader comments in which you have no interest. GreenPrint can highlight the pages we don't need and, when those are deselected, print only the truncated essentials. It even keeps a running tally of pages not printed and money saved. The company says the average user will save $90 in paper and ink in the first year. The free World Edition probably suffices for most users, but souped-up versions with more robust features are for sale. The Home-Premium edition, appropriate for commercial users, costs $29. (www.printgreener.com)

greenprint

FYI

So many office buildings are stuck with permanently sealed windows (though newer office buildings tend to have windows that open). In a home office, you can open the window to provide the fresh air and cooling you need.

TEAK DESKS

The Old-Wood Way

You *can* have a teak desk and not contribute to rain-forest destruction. How? Buy a desk made of recycled and reclaimed woods. More furniture designers are using recycled wood content, and the resulting desks—typically with a weathered, well-used look—are outstanding.

One such product is the Lini Desk, made in Thailand from reclaimed teak, that takes the form of a fanned-out barrel. Once, such wood would just have been burned, but now innovative designers are putting it to new uses in distinctive furniture.

The form of this desk is determined by the half-circle steel top, fashioned from steel that's been salvaged from junkyards. The steel writing surface sits above a drawer, supported by strips of reclaimed teak. $3,500 will buy a beautiful unique desk that will stand as a functional centerpiece of your green office and will endure for years. Designed by Singh Intrachooto and built in Thailand, it's available from Natural Territory. (www.naturalterritory.com)

PETSMART INKJET CARTRIDGE RECYCLING: GREEN *AND* PET-FRIENDLY

Discarded inkjet cartridges clutter our landfills, but there is now an environmentally savvy alternative that's also-kind to animals. Stop at any PetSmart store, pick up a supply of postage-paid envelopes, and mail in empty cartridges. PetSmart Charities, which is dedicated to saving the lives of homeless pets, receives $2 and up for the cartridges, which get refilled and returned to the consumer marketplace—reducing the landfill burden. And with the money, PetSmart Charities funds adoption programs, emergency relief for pets in natural disasters, and other good works. For our part, all that's required is to pick up the envelope and mail in an empty that otherwise would have been tossed in the trash. Over 150 types of cartridges are acceptable; check the PetSmart Web site for specifics. PetSmart claims its charity has saved the lives of at least 3.5 million dogs and cats. (www.petsmartcharities.org/donate)

STOREX AND RUBBERMAID DESKTOP GEAR

Green Tools of the Trade

Little plastic holders litter most desktops today. There's a pen holder, something for paperclips, probably an in-box . . . on and on. A generation ago, those items were usually made of metal and occasionally glass, but in the 21st century, plastic has won the battle of the desktop, and that is not good for the environment; plastic comes from oil or natural gas. Now we can reduce the impacts of plastic by choosing *recycled* plastic desktop gear. Check the Storex line of plastic desk accessories, all made from 50 percent postconsumer recycled content, and, like the old Model T Fords, all in your choice of color, as long as you like black:

- ★ Paper clip holder: $3.79
- ★ Pencil cup: $2.29
- ★ Mini desk organizer (holds scissors, pens, reading glasses): $3.99
- ★ Business card holder: $1.99
- ★ Stacking letter trays: $5.99
- ★ Magazine file: $9.99
- ★ Three-compartment incline sorter (for holding phone messages, to-do lists, etc.): $4.29
- ★ Rotary organizer (for scissors, pens—a bigger version of the mini organizer): $5.99

Another choice? Rubbermaid offers a similar array of desktop accessories at about the same prices and with the same color choice. The Rubbermaid collection is 25 percent postconsumer content, half that of the Storex line.

What's terrific about these products is their affordability. Spending forty dollars creates a well-equipped desktop and could even bring some order into your life. (www.staples.com/office/supplies)

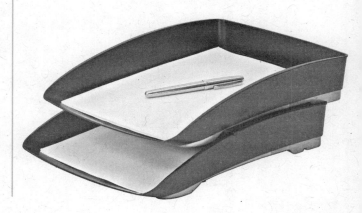

THE WOODY PEN
Earth-Friendly Writing Tool

Y ou want a pen that feels solid in the hand? Woody just may be your solution. Made from sustainably harvested white birch, the substantial Woody Pen writes in your choice of blue or black ink. Even cooler, the Woody Pen looks more handsome with use. If you must discard it, eventually it will biodegrade. Price: $6.99. (Other wood models come with more frills and are priced up to $15.50.) (www.grass rootsstore.com)

BRETFORD STEEL BOOKSHELF
Like a Rolling Shelf

I t's on wheels and the content is 30 percent postconsumer recycled. This rolling shelf handily holds reams of printer paper, notepads, a postage scale, magazines, and other sundry office stuff. With the strength of steel, the bookshelf is nearly indestructible and lasts for years. The maker is Bretford (www.bret ford.com), a distinguished creator of handsome office pieces. The only color is putty. Dimensions: 28 inches wide, 24½ inches high, 13 inches deep. Price: $257.09, from the Green Office. (www.greenoffice.com)

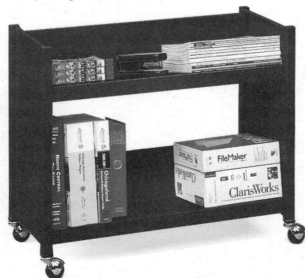

FYI

Do you really need to print that document? Many of us print out of habit. For an "extra," security copy, e-mail it to yourself at a free address set up for this purpose at www.gmail.com. Make that digital storage your virtual filing cabinet, with zero ecological impact.

BITS AND WATTSTOPPER
Power Strips Wise Up

I t is a monumental waste of energy to leave home office gear running 24/7. Forget that myth that turning printers, faxes, and home computers on and off is somehow bad for them. There's no proof of that, but there is ample evidence of widespread laziness when it comes to switching off and/or unplugging all the equipment that hums in our offices. Ironically, emerging technology just may have the antidote for slack behavior.

Case in point: BITS Ltd. LCGv3 power strip, a new generation of very smart power bar. It's a bit pricey at $47.95, but it may well pay for itself in a matter of months. Here's how: Plug a computer into a designated slot, then plug the peripherals—printer, camera, digital voice recorder, speakers—into their designated slots. Next comes the magic. Turn off the computer and, whoosh, the peripherals also turn off because this is one smart power strip. Of course, it also provides standard surge protection. (http://catalog.bitsltd.us)

WattStopper is another supersmart power strip that ups the ante. It features a built-in motion detector that turns off whatever is plugged in when nobody is in the office. Walk into the office and WattStopper turns on all the equipment. You can leave some things plugged in and running 24/7, because two outlets are uncontrolled. Price: $90. It is a sure way to lower energy bills. (www.wattstopper.com/products)

ECO-HEATER: CHEAP HEATS

The Eco-Heater is a compact and very efficient electric panel wall heater designed to stay on for long periods of time—while using a minimum of energy so it can keep your home office toasty all day. It operates at a relatively low surface temperature of 165°F, so it is less hazardous to children and pets than other heating sources. Because of that low temperature, the Eco-Heater can be painted any color to match your office. No harmful pollutants are emitted from the Eco-Heater, a claim that can't be made by gas-fired central-heating systems or fuel-oil boilers. Installation is DIY and usually takes under 10 minutes (the company promises no skills are required). With its low power consumption and high efficiency, the Eco-Heater costs under 4 cents per hour or 96 cents per day to run in most parts of the country. (www.eco-heater.com)

FYI

Invoice electronically: Ask your clients if they'll accept invoices as e-mail attachments. That eliminates a lot of printing and postage. And ask if clients can pay electronically with direct deposit into your checking. It's convenient, fast, and reliable.

BLUE MAX DIMMABLE DESK LAMP

When You Can't Have Sunlight

The Blue Max Dimmable Desk Lamp has a flicker-free bright light that is a perfect substitute for sunlight. It provides illumination at any hour but is especially helpful for late work nights. Using the Blue Max dramatically cuts down on greenhouse gas emissions. By the reckoning of the manufacturer, a user of a 300-watt halogen bulb would have to plant over 1,000 trees to achieve the net environmental impact of the Blue Max over its lifetime.

It can be dimmed down to 20 percent illumination. Bulbs (replacement cost: $29.50) have a life of 10,000 hours (over a year of nonstop use; a couple of years in more ordinary settings). Just as cool: This lamp comes with a 100 percent lifetime warranty. Blue Max Lamp price: $169. (www.bluemaxlighting.com)

Certified Green

Want proof that your office is green—or maybe you want still more pointers on taking your green commitment to the next level? Take Greenline Paper's certified green test; if you pass, you get a certificate for framing. Just answer basic questions:

★ Is your equipment Energy Star certified?

★ Is it turned off at night?

★ Is your lighting energy efficient?

★ Do you have double-pane windows? Do they open?

★ Are you using recycled office paper? Toilet paper? Paper towels?

★ Are your cleaning supplies earth friendly?

★ Do you recycle?

★ What happens to your old office equipment?

Some questions in the survey don't pertain to home offices ("Is there bike parking for employees?"), but just working through this test is a strong reminder of the key areas for going green in your workspace. And if your score is high enough, there is that certificate to hang on the wall. Good luck! (www.greenlinepaper.com)

Cloud Computing

Do you really need that new computer? A technology revolution is occurring that may enable us to squeeze years' more use out of the tools we have. It's called "cloud computing," where the heavy lifting happens not in the machine in front of you but in remote areas on the Internet. It means is that any computer capable of running a reasonably late-model browser (such as Google Chrome or Opera or Mozilla Firefox) and with high-speed Internet access can stay on equal footing with a brand-new ultraspeedy computer.

If you use Gmail, the e-mail application from Google, you probably are aware of cloud computing. Cloud computing via Google offers much of the functionality of applications such as Microsoft Outlook or Mozilla Thunderbird. But all the computing takes place online on Google-owned and -maintained computers. Google Apps, for example, is a suite of business applications that offers most of the functionality of Microsoft Office, including presentation software that rivals PowerPoint. The price is unbeatable—it's free.

Is cloud computing slower than computing on the desktop? Not usually. Broadband Internet access, via cable modem or DSL, ought to allow super-speedy computing in the cloud. Cloud providers increasingly offer tools that let users do work while offline; Google lets users read, respond to, and write new Gmail while offline. So even when the power is out or the Internet is inaccessible, some work can be done with cloud tools.

The cloud may even put superpowerful software at your disposal. Sun Microsystems, for one, makes available very powerful tools on an à la carte basis via its Network.com. Want to create 3D tools? You could buy software for that, or you can pay nominal fees to use Sun's Blender application, which lets you tap into much more robust computing power than you are likely to have in your office.

One way to get started in cloud computing is to stop backing up files on the desktop; instead, back everything up to the cloud. That service was pricey just a few years ago, but now there are many low-cost options such as Mozy.com for just $4.95 a month; it's owned by EMC, a powerhouse in business-to-business computer gear. Amazon's JungleDisk (www.jungledisk.com) charges by the gigabyte, and the cost should work out to just a few dollars monthly. Backing up in the cloud means you don't need to buy that extra drive for the desktop, plus you gain the safety and security of offsite, redundant backup. If your computer is destroyed in a fire or other disaster, your files are safe because they are kept on remote servers.

Bottom line: Cloud computing just may be the step that allows you to go another year or three without a hardware upgrade.

WEIGHING PAPER

Using 10 pounds of conventional paper a year throws off 28 pounds of greenhouse gases, creates 95 gallons of wastewater, and results in 11 pounds of solid waste. With numbers like that, it is time to hop on the recycled-paper bandwagon—which is the whole point of the Environmental Defense Fund's **Paper Calculator**, an easy tool for understanding the consequences of your paper choices. Switch to 100 percent recycled content paper and annual greenhouse gases go down to 16 pounds, solid waste dips to 3 pounds, and wastewater is cut to 10 gallons. All aboard! (http://edf.org/Paper Calculator)

CHECK GALLERY
Checks in Balance

Electronic paperless online banking is the greenest way to go. It's faster and easier than old-fashioned paper checking. But there are times when you still need those paper checks: It's tough to give a holiday gift to a nephew electronically, and some small merchants still aren't set up for electronic banking. Try checks made of recycled paper. Check Gallery's checks are printed with soy-based ink on recycled 24-pound bond paper for minimal environmental impact. Checks even can be designed to reflect support for green causes such as Zen gardens or African wildlife. Just $10.95 buys a first box of imprinted checks. (www.checkgallery.com)

PRESENTATION FOLDERS
Show 'Em the Green

How better to flaunt your green stance than to use eco-marketing presentation folders? Made of 100 percent recycled fibers (56 percent postconsumer) and handsome as well, these folders are a natural for press kits. Constructed of sturdy unbleached chipboard and available in natural tan color, a box of 75 goes for $50. It's a sweet way to build an earth-friendly commitment into every business presentation. (www.greenhome.com/products)

MULTITASKING MACHINES
Scan, Man—And Fax and Print

Scanning is the secret to the green office of the future. Don't mail that signed contract back to the client—scan it instead and attach the electronic file to an e-mail. That cuts lots of energy use by you and the US Postal Service. And the truth is that files are much easier to organize and find in an office using digital documents rather than paper ones. Programs like Google Desktop can find pretty much anything on your hard drive, but even the Google geniuses have no strategy for figuring out what's squirreled away in paper filing cabinets. More good news: Multifunction machines (typically combining printer, fax, and scanner) just keep getting cheaper. As little as $60 now buys an Energy Star–certified multifunction machine. Ink for printing in a multifunction machine can get pricey—but that's all the more reason to make heavy use of its scanning feature, which does not use ink.

How to choose the right multitasking machine for your office? On the Web site of your favorite online retailer, search for multifunction printers and start reading descriptions. If a product is not labeled Energy Star, go to the next printer. (Energy Star devices pay for themselves in reduced electricity use.) Beyond that, we won't take sides in the HP versus Canon versus Lexmark versus Epson wars. All make durable workhorses that will churn out scans, faxes, and printed copies.

FYI

Never throw away a cell phone. There always are people and charities that want your discards. Remove the SIM card (the identifier linked to you), then donate the phone.

EPIC FURNITURE POLISH
Back to Nature

All right, just what's in conventional furniture polish? That lovely sheen comes with an environmental price tag: Petroleum, emulsifiers, fragrances, and worse make up conventional furniture polishes. Think about this: People polished furniture for hundreds of years before modern polishes were developed. Age-old polishes are in most respects as effective as the contemporary goo, and the old classics are much less damaging to the environment. One long-standing favorite is beeswax; for $11.95 you can buy 5 ounces of beeswax and lavender essential oil that is absolutely free of chemical additives. Epic is another polish that combines orange with soy oils and uses no dyes, no petroleum products, and no chemicals. It's $4.99 for an 8-ounce bottle. (www.bravisa.com/myb store/greenmart)

GREENLINE'S RECYCLED ENVELOPES
Chlorine-Free Mailing

E-mail is the green way, but every week we still need to send out five or 10 envelopes of hard copy, like invoices to clients who won't accept them via e-mail or checks to vendors that aren't set up for e-payment. So an office must-have is recycled envelopes. Greenline Paper's contain 100 percent recycled content, with no chlorine used in the manufacturing, which means minimal environmental impacts. The standard 6.75 size ($3\frac{5}{8}$ x $6\frac{1}{2}$ inches) will run you $17.95 for a box of 500. Recycled index cards are also available from Greenline; it's another good idea for your green office space. (www.greenlinepaper.com)

FYI
Use a laptop, not a desktop computer. Most experts say laptops use one-third less energy than their bulkier brethren—one reason that laptop sales have eclipsed desktop sales.

DESKTOP CALENDAR
Reminders in Green

Recycled paper (100 percent recycled, minimum 30 percent postconsumer, with soy ink) can work atop the desk to keep track of appointments and deadlines. This desk pad, $18\frac{1}{2}$ x 13 inches, features holiday notations and leaves plenty of room for scribbling reminders and honey-do's. (www.greenlinepaper.com)

GREAT GREEN STYLE

Who would have thought that the world's best desk chair is also one of the greenest? That's Herman Miller's Aeron, long touted as *the* must-have chair, with its sleek design, cool features such as lumbar support, and ability to adjust to fit most bodies. Much of the chair is made from recycled material— vivid proof that recycled goods can stand with the best. The Aeron isn't cheap—around $1,000 and up—but it comes with a 12-year warranty, and users report no-hassle repairs and customer service. (www.hermanmiller.com)

RECYCLED FILE STORAGE BOX: FOR THE PAPER-FULL OFFICE

Seventy percent recycled content (50 percent post-consumer) distinguishes the Snap-N-Store filing box—and boy, do we need filing boxes. Even in the supposed era of the paperless office, we all still produce many reams of paper that need storing, often for years. File storage boxes are an office must, and these, with their comparatively high recycled content, are a sound choice. They'll accommodate both legal- and letter-size storage. Color: stylish black. Price: $6.80. (www.amazon.com)

BUSINESS CARDS
Green Greetings

It is obvious that products from **U.S. Business Card** are made of 100 percent postconsumer recycled content: They are printed on cereal boxes (no kidding), and segments of the original boxes are visible on the back side of the card. Prices aren't cheap—$115 buys 200 cards—but this is a card that emphatically endorses recycling. (www.usbcards.net)

Looking for something less flamboyant and more affordable? Try 250 business cards for $45 from **Natural Printing**. These cards are made from 100 percent recycled paper and soy ink. (www.naturalprinting.com)

BARNWOOD DESK
Slabs of Americana

Tens of thousands of aged barns dot America's rural landscape, and for every one saved by an agrarian preservationist, way more get torn down, with the wood trucked off to landfills or just bonfired. But wait, this is a building material with the unmatched character that comes from aging for 50 years, 100 years, or longer. A growing number of aware artisans are repurposing this highly useful barnwood. Refinished, it can become a gorgeous desk. For example, check out the barnwood desk from **Cottage Home** that sells for $1,275, or the barnwood pub table that can double as a distinctive desk for $1,475. Using used wood naturally saves a tree or two. (www.cottagehomemaine.com)

EARTHDRIVE
Corn Fed

EarthDrive is what the manufacturer calls this USB drive, and the name fits: It's the world's first recyclable USB drive with a housing made from polyactic acid (PLA) materials such as corn. Plastic from petroleum is the main ingredient in conventional housings, and USB drives (aka thumb drives) are replacing other portable storage media such as CDs and floppy disks. As storage memories grow exponentially, what is likely to be done with yesteryear's tiny 256 MB thumb drive? It probably gets tossed. Consequently, discarded traditional USB drives end up in landfills, where they will languish for many years.

The EarthDrive is designed knowing that the day will come when it will be obsolete and expendable. Until then, EarthDrives are waterproof, shockproof, and dustproof. **ATP** offers models ranging from 1 GB to 8 GB. About $26 currently buys a 2 GB drive, which is plenty to hold PowerPoint presentations, photo albums, and many hours of music. (www.atpinc.com/newweb)

Free Lighting, No Impacts

Turn off the lights in your office and open the shades. Taking that simple step places you squarely in the vanguard of a design trend called daylighting, which is revolutionizing illumination inside offices. A typical application sees ceiling fixtures eliminated in favor of light through a window paired with a small task lamp on the desk for pinpointed illumination as needed. Try lights-out when on a telephone call or surfing the Internet—a monitor usually throws off plenty of light.

It's easier, of course, to incorporate daylighting in new construction, but any home office with a window can cut down on some lighting by positioning work spaces to increase the use of natural daylight. Get more information about daylighting from the Energy Center of Wisconsin's informative Web site www.daylighting.org.

BULLETIN BOARD: PIN UP

Now coming to an office wall near you: a 12 x 12-inch bulletin board made of recycled paper for just $22. Just the thing for pinning up to-do lists, big ideas, revolutionary changes, irresistible cartoons, essential numbers, and more. (www.elements chicago.com)

SOLAR CALCULATORS
No-Cost Math

The first solar calculators hit the market in 1978 and went mainstream in 1981, when Texas Instruments introduced its first solar-powered model. So by now there is no excuse for using battery-operated models. Functionality in solar-powered calculators equals that of the battery powered, and most are so sensitive that they can get the juice they need sitting indoors on your desk. Twenty dollars buys a terrific TI solar-powered calculator—and other brands are available. (www.officemax.com)

DIGITAL VOICE RECORDERS
Look, Ma, No Tape!

Technology marches forward. For decades, recording interviews, spoken notes, and telephone calls involved using lots of often-fragile cassettes made from lots of plastic. Digital voice recorders now have swept the market, offering high recording quality and zero operating costs. No need to buy tapes. High-end models allow for easy interface with a computer, so files can be transferred to the hard drive. Cheaper models do not have that capability, so it is probably worth spending the few extra dollars to buy an interfacing unit. The recording capacity of digital recorders is staggering. The simplest units typically can record 50 hours, sometimes even 100 hours! In the cassette era, that would have meant buying dozens of tapes. About $50 will buy a recorder with interface capability. (www.olympusamerica.com)

FYI

Set your computers to go into standby mode when they are inactive for 30 minutes. That puts every computer on an energy diet. The US Department of Energy says sleep mode cuts computer energy use by 90 percent.

REMANUFACTURED INK CARTRIDGES AND TONER
The Ink Goes Round and Round

Complete the recycling circle by buying remanufactured ink cartridges. Then you'll learn what happens to those cartridges you donated to support good causes. Most of them come back on the market again, refurbished and refilled with ink. That saves a few bucks compared to prices of new cartridges, and by every measure, the remanufactured cartridges work every bit as well. Anytime something is reused and doesn't have to be made from scratch, it's a plus for the environment. Remanufactured toner drums for laser printers also are easy to come by. The same principles apply. Users save money and the environment benefits. (www.officedepot.com)

CELL PHONE RECYCLING
Win-Win-Win

How many cell phones languish in your desk drawers? Nationwide, some 500 million unwanted, deactivated cell phones lie dormant, and the ones that eventually go to landfills throw off lead, mercury, cadmium, and arsenic. Put obsolete phones to a better uses by giving them away—smartly. Start by visiting www.collectivegood.com. Then select a worthy charity. Choices range from the Humane Society to EarthWorks and CORA (a group focused on domestic violence). It gets sweeter. Collective Good helps you calculate the tax deduction your gift warrants (for donations under $250, no receipt is required by the IRS). What happens to the unwanted phones? They get sold into developing nations such as India, where there are millions of potential users who want that phone you no longer use. And that keeps your old cell phone out of a landfill, so this truly is a win-win-win.

RECHARGEABLE BATTERIES
Beats the Energizer Bunny

Inventory the batteries in your office: digital camera, wireless mouse, digital voice recorder, maybe more. That's on top of the specialty batteries that power cell phones, laptops, calculators, and other equipment. Batteries wear out and get thrown out in phenomenal numbers. By some estimates, we toss 84,000 *tons* of batteries every year. The overwhelming majority is not properly disposed of. On the trip from your garbage receptacle to the landfill, batteries typically are crushed, they leak, and out seep mercury and other toxins.

The simple green solution? It's a no-brainer. Buy and use rechargeable batteries. Yes, the start-up cost is higher, but over the long term, rechargeables will return dividends both economically and ecologically. They can be reliably recharged perhaps a thousand times, and that subtracts lots of regular batteries from the landfill. It also eliminates the packaging waste involved in every battery purchase. What does it cost to get started? About $25 buys a set of four Sony AA batteries plus recharger. Similar investments will set you up with AAA and D batteries. (www.amazon.com)

When a rechargeable battery dies, the Rechargeable Battery Recycling Corporation will help you find a nearby retailer that will accept it free of charge and dispose of it properly. Radio Shack, Best Buy, and plenty more participate. (www.rbrc.org)

Free Time

Under $10 will buy you a wind-up alarm clock—no electricity, no batteries, just green time. They worked a century ago, and they'll keep time today. They keep on ticking if there's a power outage and your clock radio goes dead. Put those old-fashioned mainsprings to work and cut the fossil-fueled electric bill. (www.amazon.com/Advance-Clock-2060-Keywind-Almond)

FYI

Buy stationery in smaller quantities. Do you really need 1,000 business cards? Ditto for letterhead. Save money, cut down on waste—it's win-win.

MOBIVOX

MOBIVOX

MOBIVOX
Send Your Voice, Not Yourself

Exactly what is the carbon impact of flying to Dublin, Ireland? Tons, not pennies. But you can call Ireland for pennies (1.9 cents per minute, to be exact) with Mobivox, a clever service that lets any phone tap into the inexpensive voice routing of VOIP (voice over Internet protocol). Need to call India? A conventional phone service might charge several dollars per minute, but Mobivox does it for 7.9 cents per minute. Sweet, too, is that Mobivox works on cell phones. (That call to India might cost $4 per minute on a cell phone.) Dial a local number, then input the distant foreign destination for your call. Audio quality is good, usually indistinguishable from quality over traditional phone lines. (www.mobivox.com)

GUIDES, GOALS, AND RESOURCES

Greening Your Office, from Cupboard to Corporation by Jon Clift and Amanda Cuthbert (Chelsea Green Publishing, 2008). An A-to-Z guide with a stress on practical tips that let a business go green and often save money, too.

True Green at Work by Kim McKay, Jenny Bonin, and Tim Wallace (National Geographic, 2008). Written for everybody who works, this book's aim is to give practical advice about reducing your carbon footprint on the job.

101 Ways to Turn Your Business Green, by Rich Mintzer (Entrepreneur Press, 2008). Still more practical tips.

Innovations in Office Design: The Critical Influence Approach to Effective Work Environments by Diane Stegmeier (Wiley, 2008). New thinking about the design of effective work spaces.

DESKSLIDER BIN
Recycling Made Easier

Face it, good intentions alone don't guarantee recycling. To make it easier—and more likely—put a clearly dedicated recycling bin within reach. Pop one of these blue bins, made of postconsumer recycled content, into the desk well so it's always there to catch discarded papers. Busy offices that generate lots of different kinds of waste will want to buy several bins, some for glass and some for plastics. Price: $7.85 each. (www.recyclingsupply.com)

JIMNIE PEN
Trash Talk

Take auto headlights, discarded CDs, and junked cell phones, then mash them up, and you could end up with the Jimnie Pen. It's concocted of 75 percent recycled content and priced affordably for the office ($14.77 per dozen). Ink colors include black, blue, and red, and the color of the rubber grip matches the ink. The pen is a great conversation starter: "Would you believe my pen used to be car headlights?" This trash-to-treasure device is another sign of where our society, with diminishing places to bury trash, is heading. And if glass can beget pens, what else can trash be transformed into? (http://recycledproducts.org)

RESOURCE REVIVAL OFFICE PRODUCTS
Bike Chain Magic

Bike chains break, and then what good are they? The folks at **Resource Revival** are transforming bike chains into cool products such as a picture frame—$37.95 for a 4 x 6-inch frame made from chains. A bottle opener is $14. A business card holder is $19.95, with space for about 30 cards and a pen. An 8-inch wall clock, of chains and recycled rubber, is $68. (www.resourcerevival.com)

FYI

Turn the lights off when you leave the workplace. The federal government says lighting represents 29 percent of the energy use in an office.

VOLTAIC SYSTEMS
Solar Charging en Route

Voltaic's handy messenger bag, made from recycled soda bottles, is the consummate multifunction device. It's well-designed, with ample room for a laptop and business documents. Slick solar panels built into the bag suck in the sun's energy and can recharge your cell phone, digital camera, iPod, and GPS unit. The bag comes with a wide array of standardized plug-ins to accommodate just about any electronic device. Color choices: black, silver, orange, and green. Price: $229. (www.voltaic systems.com)

⊖C⊕ Voltaic

RECLAIMED WOOD BOOKCASE
Pricey But Impressive

Talk about stylish: A bookcase made of reclaimed wood has a patina that newly milled wood could never provide. A tall model (72 inches tall, 60 inches wide) is priced at $990 and will be a visual centerpiece in any home office. (www.naturalterritory.com)

BROOKSTONE BAMBOO OFFICE CHAIR MAT
Grass Underfoot

Chances are your office chair currently rolls around on a large, petroleum-based plastic mat floor protector. There is a greener way: a bamboo mat. One-quarter-inch thick and made of the sturdiest part of the bamboo stalk, Brookstone's mat is a handsome way to add green character to the office. Felt backing with nonskid dots holds the mat firmly in place. Available in dark cherry or natural, the 55 x 57-inch version costs $199.95; the 48 x 72-inch is $249.95. (www.brookstone.com)

FYI

When buying new equipment, insist on products bearing the Energy Star label. Everything that wears that merit badge uses less energy and saves money.

GREEN THROWBACK

It doesn't get greener than Earth-write. These pencils are 100 percent biodegradable and are composed of 60 percent postconsumer recycled content (newspapers, to be specific). And the price is really right at 99 cents for one dozen. Half a century ago, most writing was done with a pencil—an old tool that was easy on the earth and on the pocketbook. Still is. (www.greenearth officesupply.com)

HASSOCK FANS
Winds of Change

Turn off the air conditioner, but keep your cool with an ottoman (aka hassock) fan, which puts out 360 degrees of cooling. A staple of the 1950s, these units still provide a comfy place to rest one's feet. Sadly, hassock fans are no longer readily found new. They are plentiful in used markets, where they are emerging as chic period pieces—still functional and adding a note of character to any home office. A search on the Antique and Artisan Center (www.antiqueand artisancenter.com) recently turned up a gorgeous green hassock fan priced at $340. A search on eBay (http://search.ebay.com) found a dozen for sale, some with a "buy now" price as low as $29 (admittedly for a down-market unit). By some estimates, a fan uses only 1/30th of the electricity a window-unit air conditioner consumes, so when a fan will suffice, give it a try.

NEW TOOL FOR OLD SKILLS

Steno pads are a terrific size, perfect for jotting notes—whether or not you know the ancient art of stenography. Ampad's Green Cycle 6 x 9-inch steno pads feature 50 percent recycled content. Eighty sheets per book, $1.97 apiece. (http://recycledproducts.org)

Natural Beauty

Most of us groom ourselves without giving much consideration to the ingredients in the products that we apply to our skin and the most intimate nooks and crannies. It's not only beautifying agents but also basic daily maintenance materials like shampoo, toothpaste, deodorant, shaving cream, and soap that are now worth a good, green look. Whether personal upkeep is a pleasure or a daily chore, selecting products created with natural ingredients is a clean, wise way to green your regime. True beauty may come from within, but eco-friendly products and savvy health aids on the outside certainly help.

The pursuit of beauty and health is as old as the hills, whether undertaken for vanity, social vogue, or a deep-seated biological drive for self-preservation. In the search for good hygiene, lovely skin, clean teeth, and good smells, humans have been developing prized formulas and special solutions for eons.

From Roman and Egyptian times well through the Victorian era, people used lead oxide dusting powders for porcelain-smooth skin, lead and antimony eye makeup for drama, and mercury-based rouge for cheeks and lips, with negative health consequences that now are well understood. The potions and lotions we now use for grooming and beauty have improved since those times. But while modern science has gotten hip to some of the worst of what's around, and the product market has begun to reflect changes for the better, there are still plenty of questionable products crowding the shelves.

Reading labels is the most effective tool for discovering what's in the products we slather, lather, and anoint our bodies with and for learning just how green they may be—for us and the environment. While words like "natural" and allusions to "botanicals" frequently occupy real estate on many product labels, the ingredient list is the text to pay attention to. Companies that formulate clean, green products will generally tell it like it is, defining and disclosing ingredients clearly without shrouding them in vague, often mysterious terms. The bottom line: If you can't identify ingredients, either because of their chemical terminology or because they are ambiguous, you might want to reconsider using the product on your body.

The skin is our largest organ, and it's also a key player in our immune systems. Our teeth not only make smiling with confidence a pleasure, but maintaining them in good form also is vital to our long-term health. Keeping armpits naturally fresh not only makes close encounters more pleasant, but it also supports healthy lymph nodes and breast tissue that are nestled in close proximity. Shaving may look sexy, according to modern marketing, but in reality it's a chore, and the chemicals used in most conventional shaving products are anything but sensual.

Choosing clean, green beauty products and health aids is simply sensible. Opting for plant-based products that harness the beautifying benefits of botanical ingredients over synthetic, petroleum-laden ingredients, preservatives, and perfumes is not a radical choice, especially when plant-based products work terrifically and smell fantastic. Greening your personal regime no longer calls for compromises; now it's an absolute must, for both your own health and the well-being of the world around you.

—Renée Loux

FACE WASHES AND CLEANSERS
Clean 'n' Green

★ **Kiss My Face** has long been known for natural, clean products at reasonable prices. Their face washes are no exception. Kiss My Face Start Up Exfoliating Face Wash is made with 82 percent certified organic ingredients and nothing artificial. Formulated with natural fruit acids to gently exfoliate and with antioxidant, anti-inflammatory, and antimicrobial lemongrass to stimulate cellular growth, this face wash will clarify, cleanse, and revitalize skin. For creamy, soap-free, nondrying facial cleansing, Kiss My Face Clean for a Day Creamy Face Cleanser is rich with certified organic ingredients to cleanse and hydrate and even contains highly absorbable Ester-C to combat free radicals. Its natural vanilla and tangerine scent soothes and brightens your senses. (www.kissmyface.com)

★ **Jurlique** has earned an eco-savvy reputation for sophisticated skin care products born from biodynamic botanical blends and defined by sustainable connections to humans, farms, and the earth. Biodynamic farming methods go beyond organic with careful, conscious, constant hands-on cultivation to plant and harvest with the natural rhythm of the earth and seasons. Instead of simply treating symptoms of dryness, oiliness, and sensitivity, Jurlique's Facial Foaming cleansers and cleansing lotions tap botanical intelligence to lift and remove surface impurities and leave skin clean, balanced, and hydrated. Take your pick: For overall balance and hydration, try Jurlique's Balancing Foaming Cleanser, rich with calendula and daisy. Rebalance dry skin with Replenishing Foaming Cleanser and Replenishing Cleansing Lotion, both laden with viola and rose. Skin with excess oil can be refreshed with Purifying Foaming Cleanser and Cleansing Lotion. Sensitive skin will rejoice with Soothing Foaming Cleanser and Soothing Cleansing Lotion. They aren't cheap, but in this case you get what you pay for. This stuff is divine. (www.jurlique.com)

302 FACIAL SERUMS
Green Medicine for the Skin

The serum 302 Drops is a naturally derived, chemical-free, self-preserved, oil-free topical product formulated to restore skin elasticity and correct visible natural aging flaws. With some serious scientific backbone, this simple, clear lipid formula moisturizes and normalizes troubled and aging skin. Results? Smooth, resilient skin surface and pretty plumpness. Wrinkles, scars, and weak or thin skin? Consider them on the road to recovery. For best results, use a few drops once every other day, applying them to clean, slightly damp skin.

For those who prefer a traditional emulsion, 302 Serum is a light lotion. It will yield the same age-defying feats as the drops—both contain the same concentration of Avogen (avocatin 302). If you desire a little something extra, 302 Plus Serum is the most potent regeneration formula in the 302 line. It's a bit like a topical face-lift. Loaded with Avogen, 302 Plus Serum is laced with rice peptides (the silver bullet of antiaging these days), the amino acid fibronectin (for moisture retention and silky smoothness), and other naturally derived ingredients for instant plumping and soft-as-a-baby's-butt results. Begin with a single application every other day and increase to daily applications after 1 week.

Elegant, simple 302 regimens of exceptional value reflect the cutting edge of regenerative skin aesthetics and science. 302 has brought together the best of what nature and science have to offer. (www.302skincare.com)

Start small, start anywhere. Greening your grooming regime doesn't mean chucking everything you have and spending a fortune. Start reading the ingredient list of each product you currently use to evaluate if it's something you want to keep in your medicine chest.

JUICE BEAUTY
It's All About the Juice

Juice Beauty has raised the bar of organic standards for the beauty industry worldwide with an innovative collection of juice-based skin care products that contain a total certified organic content of an unparalleled 98 percent. It's all about the age-defying juice, which infuses powerful antioxidants, fortifying vitamins, vital phytonutrients, and essential fatty acids with potent action. Every drop of the 40-plus skin and body care formulas deeply feeds skin, thanks to the patent-pending, antioxidant-packed 100 percent organic juice base of over 25 different organic fruit juices and over 60 active organic ingredients. Backed by science, Juice Beauty is clinically validated by age-defying results that show an 85 percent reduction in free radical skin cell damage and an impressive increase in skin moisture and hydration.

Juice Beauty has raised the bar of internal company practices, too. With more than 100 ingredients locally produced by family farms and over 80 percent of products manufactured using solar power, Juice Beauty even uses recycled and recyclable content packaging and VOC-free veggie ink. Look for Juice Beauty cleansers, toners, exfoliants and peels, moisturizers, products for men, and SPF protection for pure organic pleasure. (www.juice beauty.com)

Regulations, Anyone?

There is alarmingly little regulation of the landslide of personal care and cosmetic products on the market. Loopholes in federal law allow for virtually any kind of chemical in any amount to be used in personal care products. Absolutely *no* federal law requires companies to test personal care and cosmetic products for safety *before* they hit the shelves. No joke. A major part of the problem is that no one is responsible. The FDA sort-of-kind-of looks out, but then again not really. The FDA officially states that "neither cosmetic products nor cosmetic ingredients, other than color additives, need to be approved by the FDA before they are sold to the public." Apparently, the "FDA cannot require companies to do safety testing of their cosmetics before marketing." This is none too reassuring, and there's absolutely no mention of environmental impact. The reality is that it is up to us as consumers to make clean, green purchasing choices—choices that are good for our bodies and the planet. Taking care of our skin, hair, and teeth means knowing what we apply to them—what goes *on* our bodies ultimately gets *in* our bodies, and the rest washes down the drain, and that has a huge impact. By gathering knowledge and by reading labels, we can pick personal care and cosmetic products that can do their job gracefully, without human hazard or eco-harm.

GRN
Grow, Restore, Nurture

GRN Blue Chamomile Cleanser is a gentle foaming cleanser derived from plant surfactants for skin-kind yet deep cleansing action that can even remove makeup. Infused with certified organic extracts of chamomile, rosemary, and green tea and free of harsh chemicals and sodium lauryl sulfate (SLS) or sodium lauryl ether sulfate (SLES), this blend is suitable for all skin types and won't dry or irritate skin. It can be used daily.

GRN Hydrating Face Serum is incredibly addictive. All skin types (including sensitive and oily) will benefit from and glow with the synergistic blend of certified organic aloe, corn silk, and plant extracts such as konjac mannan—the latter derived from an Asiatic tuber renowned for its healing properties. This formula is clean, green, non-greasy, highly absorbable, and skin-drinking good: effective to firm and moisturize facial skin. Packaged in a frosted glass bottle that is easy to recycle, it is reasonably priced and the right size to tote along on an airplane ride. (www.exhalespa.com)

JURLIQUE FACE MOISTURIZERS
Organic and Biodynamic Face Care

Jurlique formulates a sumptuous line of face moisturizers with nourishing, clean, organic, and biodynamic ingredients. The result is sophisticated, natural, efficacious products that do the skin and the planet a world of good.

Jurlique Day Care lotions are light-textured moisturizers that are absorbed easily and are rich with organic botanical and flower extracts to hydrate and balance the skin. Jurlique Clarifying Day Care Lotion moisturizes oily skin and helps minimize visible signs of aging. Soothing Day Care Lotion is infused with organic botanicals to restore delicate skin. The lightweight texture of both these organic face lotions is perfect for daily use and ideal to apply over a serum.

It doesn't get better than Jurlique's top-of-the-line Biodynamic Beauty skin care line, featuring proprietary blends of organic and biodynamic ingredients. Biodynamic Beauty Night Lotion is a light, restorative lotion to support skin renewal while you sleep. Rich with biodynamic herbs and flowers, this treatment will help fade discolorations and brighten skin. Heighten the lotion's hydration and skin-smoothing properties by using it in conjunction with Jurlique Biodynamic Beauty Serum, which goes on smooth and absorbs quickly to strengthen skin, diminish fine lines and wrinkles, and restore youthful radiance. Biodynamic Beauty Eye Cream is formulated for delicate skin around the eye area. Active ingredients such as euphrasia and arnica renew and brighten tired skin and reduce puffiness. Jurlique products are supremely good and superclean. Though not inexpensive, they go a long way. (www.jurlique.com)

DR. HAUSCHKA SKIN CARE
Biodynamic Pioneer

Dr. Hauschka has pioneered a holistic approach to skin care using plant-based healing remedies for skin since 1967. Offering a complete line of skin care based on a thorough understanding of the therapeutic properties and healing power of plants, Dr. Hauschka utilizes some of the most vital, effective, and mindful botanical preparations on the market. Each and every ingredient is carefully selected for its effect to work in harmony with your skin's natural function. No synthetics are used, and all products meet the most selective European criteria for "Certified Natural" standards.

Dr. Hauschka's holistic philosophy is rooted in biodynamics, a self-sustaining form of agriculture that dates back to the 1920s and takes into account the natural rhythms, cycles, and interrelationships of the soil, seasons, plants, and people. Biodynamic practices yield plants with paramount quality, potency, and vitality. Dr. Hauschka draws on these botanical benefits for formulas that restore and maintain healthy skin and foster the well-being of the earth, beautifully and naturally. Look for a complete range of Dr. Hauschka face care products, including advanced options for mature, acne-prone, and hypersensitive skin, as well as a wide selection of cosmetic makeup and body care products like moisturizers, deodorants, body oils, body powders, and hair care at prices that are quite reasonable considering the caliber of the goods. (www.drhauschka.com)

FYI

Plenty of green beauty products use kitchen staples like oatmeal and honey. Try concocting your own mask with 1/4 cup oatmeal, 1/2 cup water, and 1 teaspoon honey. You'll save money, and your skin will thank you.

SPA TECHNOLOGIES
Green Magic from the Sea

Seaweed is sensational! Seaweed is said to have the wealthiest portfolio on the planet of essential minerals and vitamins critical to skin cell function and regeneration. The nourishing good stuff in seaweed reflects what is found in seawater, which is similar to the fluid of our body tissue. In short, seaweed is akin to our skin and provides deep nourishment and conditioning.

Spa Technologies harnesses the healing power of the sea in its active seaweed complex moisturizers and serums, all of which contain a 70 percent concentrated seaweed base gel. The seaweed base is blended with natural active ingredients that have been clinically shown to reduce fine lines and wrinkles by 50 percent over a 90-day period. Spa Technologies uses the highest-quality food-grade algae available, harvested from pure waters off the coasts of Brittany and Iceland. The products in its Age-Defying Skincare Program are formulated to fight environmental stress, scavenge surface free-radicals, improve skin tone, replenish lost minerals, and diminish fine lines. (www.spatechnologies.com)

Mermaid Beauty is an ambrosial collection of skin care products divinely formulated with skin-renewing Hawaiian seaweeds, potent antioxidants, vitamins, premium botanical ingredients, hydrating organic hydrosols, and pure essential oils locally distilled on Maui. Exquisitely crafted in small batches by an unpretentiously wonderful company with decades of experience and a dossier of efficacy, Mermaid Beauty is a superlative secret to rejuvenate, nourish, and revitalize skin (especially sun-exposed skin) with remarkable results. (www.mermaidbeautyskincare.com)

REN ANTIAGING CREAMS AND SERUMS
Green Peter Pan in a Bottle

REN is all about clean, bioactive skin care. Each of their face moisturizers is formulated to treat individual skin types via savvy skin care technology tailored for optimum moisture, nutrients, and prime conditioning. All face moisturizers contain REN's powerful proprietary antioxidant complex to combat premature aging, sun damage, and environmental stress; none contains anything synthetic. REN Vita-Mineral Radiant Day Cream is chock-full of bioactive trace minerals and plant-based vitamins (like vitamin F from Arctic cranberry seed oil) designed to boost collagen production and tone, firm, and energize normal skin types. Dry and dehydrated skin can drink deeply with Osmotic Infusion Ultra-Moisture Day Cream. Expressly designed to infuse dry skin with long-lasting moisture, this cream is formulated to release hydration deep into the skin as needed.

REN Revivo-Lift H11 Intensive Night Serum is formulated to restore skin's elasticity and vitality. Laden with peptides (some patented for the way they are delivered to the skin) to plump skin and smooth fine lines, this serum is concentrated with bioactive ingredients, vitamins, trace elements, and ginsenoside to increase the supply of oxygen, nutrients, and bioactive compounds to the skin. Revivo-Lift Radiant Day Serum is a lighter serum with a similar profile designed to lift, smooth, and brighten the complexion with daily use.

Skin undergoing hormonal changes will find a friend in REN Sirtuin Phytohormone Replenishing Cream. Formulated to treat the needs of pre- and postmenopausal skin, this advanced moisturizer is loaded with cell-life-prolonging and anti-skin-sagging bioactives and replenishing phytohormones derived from wild yam. REN products range from pretty expensive to quite expensive, but their purity and quality and their effective bioactives return the expense with replenishing renewal. (www.renskincare.com)

BLEMISH TREATMENTS
The au Naturel Approach

★ Burt's Bees has long been loved for simple, all-natural products; a friendly persona; and unfussy packaging. Even though Burt's Bees has grown exponentially since its craft-fair peddling roots and has been acquired by a giant company, the core values have remained true—natural, earth-friendly personal-care products that contribute to the greater good at prices that are affordable. Burt's Bees Herbal Blemish Stick banishes blemishes botanically. This powerful roll-on glass stick harnesses 10 no-nonsense herbal ingredients, including willow bark (nature's version of synthetic salicylic acid) to clarify and exfoliate skin for clear pores, tea tree and juniper oils for their antiseptic and astringent qualities, and calendula to calm inflammation. (www.burtsbees.com)

★ Desert Essence is all about clear skin with a clear conscience. As the first company to introduce tea tree oil products to the United States in the early 1980s, Desert Essence is in large part responsible for the now-ubiquitous embrace of tea tree oil as a multitasking miracle worker with naturally antiseptic, antimicrobial, antibacterial, clarifying, and astringent qualities. Desert Essence Blemish Touch Stick taps the efficacy of tea tree oil to bust blemishes in combination with nine natural extracts and essential oils such as rosemary, lavender, thyme, birch, petitgrain, chamomile, and calendula. It even works healing, soothing wonders on insect bites. This roll-on blemish stick contains Desert Essence's Eco-Harvest Tea Tree Oil, which is grown by a federation of farmers using strict, sustainable agricultural methods and guaranteed to be free of chemical pesticides, herbicides, and fungicides. FYI: All Desert Essence products are manufactured using wind-energy offsets. Now that's clear skin with a conscience. (www.desertessence.com)

★ For bigger blemish concerns like acne, 302 Acne Drops are clinically proven to deliver visible, fast results. The proprietary combination of potent, pure, natural, and organic ingredients in the clear lipid drops helps stabilize and normalize troubled skin and cystic acne. 302 Acne Drops are formulated to dissolve excess sebum and treat skin aggravated by sebaceous gland imbalance. Use this simple formula once every other day, and follow with daily applications after 1 week. (www.302skincare.com)

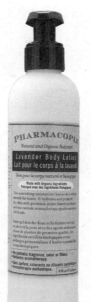

PHARMACOPIA
Smells Great, Works Wonders

Pharmacopia believes that what you put on your skin is just as important as what you eat. And they certainly make it smell good. Behind the clean, apothecary-style packaging of Pharmacopia is a crop of lotions, balms, soaps, salts, and oils formulated with premium ingredients that are sustainably sourced and organically produced. Infused with herbs and emulsified oils, distinctive blends of antioxidants, vitamins, and exceptionally high-quality essential oils that elicit aroma-therapeutic delights for all of the senses, Pharmacopia body care products are designed with the utmost integrity to keep skin healthy and supple. No synthetic ingredients are used—just pure, plant-based good stuff that smells like heaven. The delicate, organic scent blends used through each category of the line are complex without being overpowering and carefully crafted to comfort and soothe the body, mind, and spirit. Look for organic body lotion, hand cream, body and massage oil, soap, body wash, lip elixir, and bath salts imbibed with four signature bouquets of divinely balanced aroma: lavender, their all-time bestseller, combined with Roman chamomile to calm, quench, and heal skin; citrus, an uplifting balance of neroli, tangerine, grapefruit, and a whisper of lavender; rosemary, a revitalizing fusion with hints of peppermint and eucalyptus; and ginger, a warming, sensual blend with notes of lemongrass, tangerine, and a touch of cinnamon. (www.pharmacopia.net)

RED FLOWER
Sumptuous-Smelling Green Body Moisturizers

Red Flower purveys pure pleasure and sensuous scent through their line of more than a hundred 100 percent botanically based, essential-oil-derived products that are sustainably sourced. Rich with unusual regional ingredients—including certified organic, biodynamic, and wild-crafted botanicals, extracts, and flowers—Red Flower products perform with the utmost integrity and environmental consciousness. All of them are free of dyes, parabens, SLS, petrochemicals, and synthetic preservatives.

Red Flower moisturizing body lotions are formulated in eight opulent scents, with a mirrored selection of cleansing body washes. Choose from magic-carpet-ride aromas such as Moroccan Rose, made with evening primrose to repair damaged cells, olive leaf to increase elasticity, and highly absorbent silk extract for penetrating moisture; or Indian Jasmine, infused with centuries-old ingredients such as honey from gardenia flowers, vitamin-rich almond oil, and deeply healing and purifying neem extract.

Unisex scents include Icelandic Moonflower, an evocative blend of Arctic river flower, sea rocket, and antioxidant-rich cassiope; and Ocean, a dreamscape scent that includes laurel to open the lungs and cool the skin on contact. Red Flower's two treatment collections, Red Flower Japan and Red Flower Hammam, are highly recommended luxuriant celebrations of Eastern bathhouse customs. (www.redflower.com)

A Bodaciously Green Experience

If you like to lather with liquid body wash in the shower, but you prefer to steer clear of synthetic surfactants and fake fragrances, you'll find plenty of eco-friendly shower products. The pores of our skin open in a steamy shower, which may increase absorption of materials, so choosing plant-based products with clean, green ingredients will do your body and the planet good.

REN body washes are eco-luxurious picks for soft, clean skin. Formulated with mild, plant-based cleansing agents derived from oats, corn, and sugarcane, REN products avoid synthetic sulfates like SLS and chemical preservatives, which can be harsh to the skin and the ecosystem. REN uses 100 percent natural fragrances with tantalizing aromatherapeutic benefits. Savor the refreshing, mood-enhancing neroli oil distilled from Tunisian orange blossoms and the cold-pressed grapefruit oil, renowned for its skin toning properties, in REN Neroli and Grapefruit Zest Body Wash. Rose petals, harvested at dawn and steam-distilled, exquisitely scent the Moroccan Rose Otto Body Wash to relieve stress and soothe dry and sensitive skin. (www.renskincare.com)

If you like the gliding texture of shower gels, Pangea Organics offers a great-smelling collection of plant-based formulas made with pure, cold-pressed oils, which are naturally saponified to retain the vegetable glycerin for good clean suds that won't dry and strip your skin. Made entirely without synthetics, Pangea Organics shower gels are fortified with skin-nourishing organic herbal extracts and infused with pure, organic essential oils. The unusual and enticing scents suit different skin types. The Pangea Organics Pyrenees Lavender with Cardamom gel is designed for thirsty to balanced skin; its organic essential oils clarify the mind and smooth the body. Egyptian Basil & Mint is formulated for demanding skin and to stimulate the mind and awaken the body. Indian Lemongrass with Rosemary is the choice for balanced to oil-rich skin and to rejuvenate the mind and refresh the body. (www.pangeaorganics.com)

FYI

The jury is out on the long-term health effects of many of the chemicals commonly used in skin care products. Always read the ingredient list before buying. Better safe than sorry!

The Ins and Outs of Skin Absorption

Skin is the largest organ of our bodies. It is in the frontline of immunological defense, and it performs an essential role in respiration in the form of perspiration. Skin is adept at absorbing substances that are applied to it—dermal absorption is one of the most efficient delivery systems to the bloodstream, so what you apply to your skin really does matter. Factors that affect skin absorption include the concentration, surface area, and duration of contact; the physiological condition of the skin; and the part of the body exposed (some skin is more delicate and permeable).

Skin is a two-way street, expunging sweat and waste and absorbing what it comes in contact with. It needs to "breathe" and be nourished. Some synthetic and petrochemical ingredients may offer superficial moisture but occlude the exit of sweat and waste, thus clogging pores. All the chemicals, additives, fragrances, dyes, and preservatives found in conventional personal care products wouldn't be much of an issue if our skin weren't so darn good at absorbing stuff. But since it is, choosing clean, plant-based products is a must to keep skin functioning optimally. Opt out of products that contain synthetic and petrochemical ingredients in favor of those that harness nature's healing cornucopia of nourishing plants, minerals, and botanicals to keep skin young, clean, and balanced and to protect the planet, too.

NATURE'S GATE AND TOM'S OF MAINE DEODORANTS
Bust BO sans Aluminum

★ **Nature's Gate Organics** deodorant sticks are made from an effective formula of certified organic botanical, fruit, and flower extracts for natural protection. These odor-absorbing deodorants bully bacteria with baking soda, witch hazel, echinacea, and rosemary. None contains propylene glycol (otherwise known as antifreeze) or paraben preservatives. The fresh fragrances are unisex and derived from plant extracts and essential oils, which do double duty with antiseptic, antibacterial antifunk action. (www.natures-gate.com)

★ **Tom's of Maine** natural, aluminum-free deodorants call on the powers of plant extracts, like the antimicrobial action of hops, to inhibit the growth of odor-causing bacteria, and on natural botanicals to neutralize any odors that do arise. The deodorants contain only natural fragrances derived from essential oils and plant extracts; none contains paraben preservatives. Tom's of Maine Natural Long-Lasting Care Deodorant Stick and Roll-on formulas use the odor-binding properties of zinc ricinoleate, sourced from castor beans, and silica-encapsulated natural fragrances for long-lasting good smells. Sensitive underarms have a fine-tuned friend in Tom's of Maine Natural Sensitive Care Deodorant Stick, a dermatologically tested, aluminum-free formula with chamomile extract and organic aloe vera to sooth skin. (www.tomsofmaine.com)

ASTARA BIO GENIC SKINCARE: LOW-TEMP PROCESSING = PURE SKIN FOOD

Get your natural glow on with Astara's formidable formulas to feed your skin with the finest botanical ingredients in the plant kingdom. Astara Bio Genic Skincare was born from the philosophy that our skin, like our bodies, can repair and rejuvenate itself when properly nourished. Sourcing supreme-quality, raw ingredients is a fundamental element, but what makes Astara truly exceptional is the careful, low-temperature processing to harness, preserve, and enhance the best of nature's endowment. Utilizing low-temperature processing techniques that never exceed 105°F (36°C) may be more costly, but it retains and preserves the active efficacy of enzymes, antioxidants, and vital proteins when compared to common manufacturing procedures that employ heat and processes that deplete and denature the vital and delicate constituents of natural ingredients. The results are beautifully evident. Astara Activated Antioxidant Infusion is a definite star in the line. This

rich yet lightweight emulsion is formulated with antioxidant-rich borage seed oil, green and white tea, and vitamins A, C, and E, designed for timed-release delivery over 5 hours to deeply penetrate, hydrate, and promote cellular repair for all skin types. (www.astaraskincare.com)

CRYSTAL MINERAL DEODORANTS
Relief from the Rock

Once upon a time, crystal deodorants were available only as small hunks of clear mineral rock that you moistened and then rubbed on your armpits. Strange but effective. Now these deodorants are available as convenient roll-ons, pump sprays, and sticks. Crystal deodorants don't stop you from sweating, but when applied to freshly cleaned pits, these mineralized crystal salts (collectively called alum) form a layer on the skin that prevents odor-causing bacteria from growing.

The products from **Crystal Body Deodorant** are as clean and straightforward as they get. Available in your choice of stick, roll-on, rock, or spray, they're made from 100 percent natural mineral salts and nothing else. Unlike some other crystal bacteria-busters, this line of underarm products doesn't contain fragrances or paraben preservatives. Crystal Body Deodorant Stick, a handy, patented twist-up stick, is a modern evolution of the "original rock," Crystal Body Deodorant Rock. Both need to be moistened before applying to clean skin, and both are good for 6 to 12 months of use. Crystal Body Deodorant Roll-on and Crystal Body Deodorant Spray are both liquid versions of the rock and convenient for folks who don't want to prewet the rock or the stick. (www.thecrystal.com)

Naturally Fresh Deodorant Crystal is another superclean pick for fresh pits. Available in stick, wide stick, roll-on, spray, travel size, and stone forms, Naturally Fresh Deodorant Crystal products are purely without paraben preservatives, artificial fragrances, or colorants. Super-long-lasting and highly economical, this brand is a clean, green way to go. (www.tccd.com)

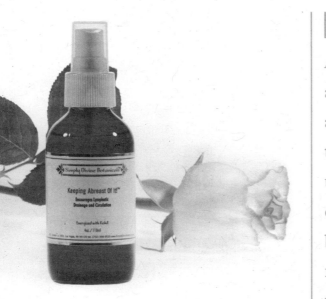

KEEPING ABREAST OF IT!
Deodorant with a Purpose

A little-known company called **Simply Divine Botanicals** has created a uniquely effective natural deodorant with multitasking components that encourage healthy lymphatic drainage and circulation. Keeping Abreast of It! is a proprietary deodorant spray formulated with angstrom zinc and silver, which efficaciously snuff odor-causing bacteria, and a potent and balanced blend of herbs and essential oils specifically crafted to aid lymphatic flow, circulation and drainage, and healthy breast tissue (lymph nodes are clustered in the underarm and breast). Keeping Abreast of It! contains 24 karat gold, which has been scientifically shown to promote penetration of oxygen molecules, and coenzyme Q10, a potent antioxidant and a key player in cellular respiration. Packaged in a 4-ounce, cobalt-blue glass pump-top bottle, this mighty formula has a gentle, unisex-friendly scent. Although it feels as if you are spraying water on your underarms, it is quite effective.

Simply Divine Botanicals makes another fabulous deodorant spray called Crystal Ally Deodorant Tangerine, formulated with crystallized mineral salt, angstrom zinc and silver to kill off stink-inducing bacteria, 24 karat gold, and pure essential oils of tangerine for antibacterial properties and a bright, clean scent. (www.simplydivinebotanicals.com)

FYI

Apply deodorant *immediately* after bathing to get an upper hand on odor-causing bacteria. It's not our sweat that smells; body odor is caused by the bacteria that naturally grow on our skin.

COLORESCIENCE SPF TREATMENTS
The Magic of Minerals

Colorescience has stepped forward with a top-shelf collection of SPF mineral powders made from micronized titanium dioxide and micronized zinc and designed to color, protect, and correct skin. Housed in a nifty, convenient tube with a retractable brush, each loose mineral formula is available in a sophisticated palette of naturally pigmented, light-reflective colors that give your skin a natural-looking, flawless finish. Colorescience SPF Minerals protect skin from sun damage and aging by offering broad-spectrum, physical sun protection that will not dry skin or clog pores. Formulated with naturally occurring antioxidants, Colorescience SPF Minerals are designed to correct imbalanced skin tone, rosacea, and hyperpigmentation. They're even rated as "very water resistant."

Colorescience Suncanny Foundation Brush SPF 20 is available in 11 shades for weightless-feeling, full-coverage protection with the ease of a brushstroke. Corrector Brush SPF 20 offers a little extra help to balance skin tone, correct color, and camouflage imperfections. It is available in two problem-solving colors. Create contour and a safe, healthy, sun-kissed glow with the stroke of a brush using Bronzer Brush SPF 20, available in four shades.

For a soft, smooth, matte finish, Finishing Brush will balance skin tone through three barely there colors. Formulated with skin-beneficial pearl powders, rice peptides and starch to balance skin and oil, and oat beta-glucan and oat protein to absorb oil and nourish skin, this soft-focus finishing powder offers full-coverage SPF protection and a naturally radiant look. Bring a little sparkle and glow to cheeks, shoulders, legs, or décolletage using Afterglow Brush, formulated with light-reflective pigments for a touch of shimmer and contoured highlights and available in three colors. Colorescience Brush Blush creates a look of healthy color from the inside out in a flattering palette of 10 colors for a spectrum of skin tones and a blushing glow. (www.colorescience.com)

SKINCEUTICALS
Encapsulated Sunscreen

If you love the sun but don't care for chemicals, you probably favor hats and cover-ups over sunscreen. But here is a sunscreen that offers enduring, full-spectrum protection that won't make your skin freak out, feel suffocated, or absorb questionable chemicals. Skinceuticals UV Defense SPF sunscreens work two ways: First, they are formulated with a patented transparent titanium dioxide and zinc oxide called Z-Cote, which offers broad-spectrum UVA/UVB protections while minimizing the pasty-white, frosted-lifeguard look of most sunscreens. Second, these cosmetically elegant sunscreens contain encapsulated sunscreen ingredients, which means they can do their job on the *surface* of the skin but do not get absorbed through the skin, reducing the chances of irritation. Skinceuticals Ultimate UV Defense SPF 30 contains 7 percent transparent zinc oxide. It is designed for broad-spectrum daily protection and is perfect for high-altitude climates. Physical UV Defense SPF 30 is optimal for sensitive or traumatized skin and safe for children—containing 5 percent transparent zinc oxide, 10 percent titanium dioxide, and two nonirritating encapsulated active ingredients for broad-spectrum daily protection. If you have an active lifestyle, Sport UV Defense SPF 45 offers waterproof and sweat-proof maximum protection for high-energy activities by way of transparent zinc oxide and encapsulated active sunscreens and UV blocks. (www.skinceuticals.com)

HYDRATING SUN SHIELD

Dry, dehydrated skin is more susceptible to sun damage than well-hydrated skin. For hydrating sun protection, MyChelle Dermaceuticals has created Sun Shield SPF 28, an extraordinary antiaging, non-eye-irritating, full-spectrum sunblock. Formulated with the physical protection of a proprietary clear zinc oxide called ZinClear and titanium dioxide, Sun Shield SPF 28 contains anti-inflammatory organic aloe vera to preserve skin's moisture.

MyChelle's Del Sol is a safe sunless tanner made with natural tanning agents such as erythrulose and dihydroxyacetone (both derived from sugar) for an even, long-lasting tanning effect. (www.mychelleusa.com)

HAIR WAXES
Think Milk and Honey (and Alcohol!)

Waxing is a popular method of hair removal that plucks the hair at the root, on almost any area of the body. Most conventional waxes contain petroleum-based paraffin, which is none too eco-friendly, and a slew of questionable chemicals that may be unhealthy for your skin, but there are greener natural options, whether you choose to DIY or splurge for salon services.

GiGi Organic Milk & Honee Wax is an all-natural wax blend formulated with honey and milk extract. It contains no mineral oil, artificial fragrances, or harsh chemicals. (http://gigi.aiibeauty.info)

Sally Hansen offers Naturally Bare Honey Wax Hair Remover formulated with all natural honey, sugar, chamomile, and lemon that can be rinsed away with water. This fragrance-free formula has no added colors, doesn't need to be heated, and comes in a kit with clear, biodegradable removal strips made from corn. (www.sallyhansen.com)

L'Orbette Liquid Organic Wax is a fragrance-free wax made from natural resins and purified alcohol. This naturally light and thin wax is skin-friendly for all types, especially sensitive skin.

SHAVING CREAMS
For a Clean, Green Shave

Conventional shaving creams and gels are loaded with petroleum-derived ingredients, chemical fragrances, and artificial colorants. If you're concerned about the synthetic surfactants used in the name of a foamy glide that can enhance penetration of chemicals into your bloodstream, you should be. Those ozone-munching aerosol cans? Forget 'em. There's good news when it comes to cleaner, greener options for sharp shaving and smooth skin.

Burt's Bees has introduced Natural Skin Care for Men to inspire even you strong, silent types. The shaving cream promises a close, smooth shave with all-natural plant-based ingredients and botanical extracts like soothing calendula, calming linden, and hydrating chamomile. Pacify, shield, and protect dry and sensitive skin with Burt's Bees Natural Skin Care Aftershave, chock-full of moisturizing sunflower and coconut oils and appeasing aloe and vitamin E. Burt's Bees prefers plants over petroleum and flowers over fake fragrances in all their products, and the company has innovated a naturally effective preservative system using sugar enzymes. (www.burtsbees.com)

REN Tamanu High Glide Shaving Oil is designed to guide a clean, close shave and curb postshaving dryness and irritation with 100 percent pure plant oils, including tamanu, which lubricates, moisturizes, and nourishes skin. Using shaving oil feels different from shaving with conventional creams and gels but offers silken-soft results. Couple the oil with Multi-Tasking After Shave Balm formulated to calm and condition the skin. REN products are making green waves thanks to progressive, natural ingredients—such as biosaccharide to ease inflammation from a razor's edge, ward off bacteria, and kindle endorphins for happy brains and blood; polyphenols from peppermint leaf juice to cool, tone, and protect the skin from oxidative stress and pollution; and pumpkin enzymes to foil ingrown hair. (www.renskincare.com)

ORAL HYGIENE PAR EXCELLENCE

The Dental Herb Company has a handful of professional oral hygiene products that are unequivocally in a league of their own. Only the purest high-grade ingredients are used, including certified organic and ecologically wild-crafted herbs, extracts, botanicals, and essential oils. Brilliantly developed by a dentist, these proprietary formulas are powerfully potent and chock-full of botanical antimicrobials. They contain no chemicals or artificial flavorings, colors, preservatives, sweeteners, SLS, or fluoride.

It doesn't get better or more pure than the Dental Herb Company's Tooth & Gums Tonic for a seriously no-nonsense mouthwash. This epic oral rinse is concocted with herbs, essential oils, and botanical agents in stimulating and invigorating proportions to maintain superhealthy teeth and gums. It's not cheap, but a little goes a long way. One bottle will last about 2 months when used once daily. Unfortunately, Dental Herb Company products are sold only through dental professionals. If you can't find one in your area who carries them, the company will sell to you directly with a note from your dentist. It's worth the effort—this stuff is superpure and powerfully good. (www.dentalherbcompany.com)

RAZORS THE RIGHT WAY

If the idea of the estimated 38 million disposable razors purchased every week ending up in the landfill makes you want to forgo shaving altogether, have no fear—there's no need to let stubble rear.

Recycline presents Preserve eco-friendly shaving products that don't compromise on performance or the planet. Try Preserve Double Razor and Triple Razor with easy-to-grip ergonomic handles made from 100 percent recycled plastic (65 percent of that from Stonyfield Farm yogurt cups). Take your pick from four vivid colors and stay sharp with Preserve Razor Double or Triple Razor Replacement Blades, both made with titanium-coated blades and vitamin E and aloe-lubricated strips for a soothing, smooth shave. The handles can be used with other major brand blades, including Gillette Sensor Blades and Personna Acti-Flexx, and are fully recyclable wherever #5 plastics are accepted. Old handles (as well as Preserve toothbrushes and tongue scrapers) can be returned to Preserve for another re(cycled) incarnation; just download and print the free postage-paid mailer from their Web site. (www.recycline.com)

Whole Green Catalog

202

RADIUS DENTAL PRODUCTS
Bio-Based Toothbrushes and Floss

Dentists recommend replacing a toothbrush every 3 months. That might keep brushing up to snuff, but it amounts to a mountain of waste—an estimated 1.2 billion toothbrushes discarded annually in the United States.

Radius offers snazzy oral solutions for greener brushing. Known for innovative design, Radius created a new generation of toothbrushes in the early 1980s using a wide oval head with thinner bristles in a high tuft count that distributes brushing pressure and protectively massages sensitive gum tissue. The wide handle of the Radius Original Toothbrush is made from renewable bioplastic cellulose with an ergonomic thumbprint impression for right- and left-hand orientation. Available in six nifty colors, it is approved by the American Dental Association. The Radius Source Toothbrush, made from 93 percent recycled material and 47 percent renewable resources, is the next era of eco-friendly oral care. The standard-size wooden handle, molded from recycled wood and bioplastic, will last for years. It can be fitted with replacement heads available in soft and medium bristles, which reduces environmental impacts because only 7 percent of the toothbrush is discarded as compared to 100 percent of ordinary toothbrushes.

Eco-friendly flossing just got better with the good-for-you glide of Natural Silk Floss, also by Radius. Unlike the traditional petroleum-based, paraffin-coated nylon dental floss, this floss is made from pure silk spun in natural beeswax to remove plaque softly and effectively.

Radius products are made in the USA with dedication to durability, design, and environmental responsibility. (www.radiustoothbrush.com)

TRUE-BLUE TOOTHPASTE

If you have a passion for a naturally clean kisser and pristine pearly whites as well as the planet, Jason Natural has a dozen clean, green oral options to choose from. Jason Natural toothpastes and gels blend the art and science of natural oral care with the highest-quality ingredients in pure formulas that contain no SLS, fluoride, synthetic ingredients, or artificial preservatives, colors, or sweeteners. Blast away bad breath and plaque-causing bacteria the eco-friendly way with Jason Sea Fresh Toothpaste. It's an all-around champ for choppers with innovative, naturally effective ingredients including perilla seed extract (to neutralize bacteria and sugar acids), biologically active blue-green algae, sea salts and minerals (to help heal, detoxify, and strengthen gums and teeth), bamboo powder, vitamins and nutrients, grapefruit seed extract (a natural preservative and antiseptic), and natural herbal sweeteners like stevia. (www.jason-natural.com)

RECYCLINE DENTAL PRODUCTS
Recycled Content and Natural Flavors

Recycline, founder of the eco-friendly Preserve Razors, also offers the Preserve Toothbrush, made from 100 percent recycled plastic, including Stonyfield Farm yogurt cups. Medium, soft, and ultrasoft bristled brushes are available in seven snappy colors and can be returned to Preserve for recycling by using the postage-paid label provided on their Web site.

Make oral patrol for kids eco-friendly with Preserve Jr.; the 100 percent recycled plastic pea-pod-shaped handle makes gripping easy for 2- to 8-year-olds. As a proud sponsor of the National Wildlife Federation, Recycline has designed each toothbrush color to highlight a different endangered species: Galapagos Turtle Green, St. Lucia Parrot Pink, and Tiger Orange.

For on-the-go oral grooming, Preserve Flavored Toothpicks offer a pocket-size punch made from sustainably harvested wood and are all natural flavors. Choose from spicy Cinnamint or superfresh Mint with Tea Tree, both packed in a handy 100 percent recycled canister. Don't leave home without them. (www.recycline.com)

Nail Polish with a Cause

Rated as some of the safest paint-based nail polishes on the market, PeaceKeeper Nail Paints are made with mineral pigments and are completely free of FD&C coloring, formaldehyde, toluene, phthalates, acetone, and parabens. They aren't tested on animals, either. The creamy, long-lasting enamel polishes are made with amino-acid-rich argan oil  to nurture the nails and for fabulous shine. Most of the nine inspiring shades are vegan. With a range of colors from rich berry shades and shimmering naturals to sheer pinks, each polish is given an endearing name such as Paint Me Patient or Paint Me Tender. (www.iamapeacekeeper.com)

For Strong, Healthy Nails

The neem tree, native to India, has been valued for centuries as a multipurpose medicine, including healing and beautifying hair and nails. With potent antimicrobial, antifungal, and anti-inflammatory properties, neem leaf is known to stimulate circulation and strengthen keratin protein, making it an ideal healer for nails in need. Dr. Hauschka Skin Care calls on the botanical brilliance of neem leaf extract with the Neem Nail Oil Pen, a daily treatment to fortify strong nail growth, discourage nail fungi, and create softer, healthier cuticles. Made with the purest ingredients, healing oils, and botanical and flower extracts, this formula is suitable for all skin conditions and benefits both soft and brittle nails. The handy pen comes with a felt-tip applicator and several replacement tips for long-lasting use. (www.drhauschka.com)

Natural Nail Polish Remover

The active ingredient in conventional nail polish remover is acetone, which, though effective, is pretty toxic stuff to inhale or touch and far from eco-friendly. When painted nails have started to chip, use nontoxic nail polish removers that are safe for your paws, toes, and the planet.

★ **SpaRitual** Fluent Gentle Conditioning Lacquer Remover is a nonacetone blend of nondrying, sugar-derived solvents and Italian red mandarin essential oil to safely and effectively remove polish and condition the nails in one swipe. (www.sparitual.com)

★ **No-Miss** Almost Natural Polish Remover is made from fruit acid solvents, amber acid from lichens, vitamin A to moisturize nails, and a natural vanilla fragrance. This cruelty-free, nonacetone remover takes a little rubbing to work, but it doesn't have a harsh odor and is packaged in a nifty spill- and leak-proof "Menda" pump for easy dispensing. (www.nomiss.com)

Choosing natural nail products is somewhat of a challenge. The materials used to achieve a chip-proof, high-gloss polish and to remove polish are typically anything but natural. However, there's no need to sport naked nails unless you want to. SpaRitual embraces a commitment to creating eco-friendly, human-safe nail products crafted from vegan ingredients free of formaldehyde, toluene, and DBP. SpaRitual's palette of more than 80 nail lacquers is formulated for sensational shine, quick dry time, and even coverage.

Fine fingers aren't just for the ladies. SpaRitual Amigo Matte Topcoat for Men provides a protective, subtle matte finish for well-groomed guys.

If you want to treat your nails to spa-quality, eco-friendly service at home, SpaRitual Nail Elixirs collection includes basecoats, topcoats, and cuticle care products, all completely free of formaldehyde, toluene, and phthalates. SpaRitual Lacquers and Nail Elixirs are packaged in glass bottles with up to 50 percent recycled materials. (www.sparitual.com)

ORGANIC COTTON TAMPONS
The Eco-Friendly Approach

★ In the late 1980s, Susie Hewson founded Natracare in a direct response to the human and environmental hazards associated with dioxins and synthetic rayon used in conventional tampons. Natracare developed the first 100 percent certified organic cotton tampon on the planet. They are certified not only to US standards but also to strict European Soil Association standards, ensuring organic certification from the growing of the cotton through the processing and manufacturing of the tampons. This means there is no risk of women's vaginal tissue being directly exposed to residues of toxic chemicals used to grow and process conventional cotton, and no risk of even low-level exposure to dioxins (a carcinogenic by-product of chlorine bleaching and known to accumulate in the fatty tissue of humans and animals).

Natracare snowy-white tampons are bleached with safe, dioxin-free, oxygen-based hydrogen peroxide. They contain no synthetics such as rayon, no chemical additives such as binders, surfactants, resins, or fragrances, and none of the risks associated with these materials. (www.natracare.com)

★ Seventh Generation's chlorine-free organic cotton tampons are made of 100 percent certified organic cotton and are certified by Quality Assurance International to meet rigorous international standards that protect soil, water, air, and the health of cotton farmers. Whitened without chlorine, Seventh Generation tampons are

guaranteed free of residues from chlorinated hydrocarbons, such as dioxins, as well as irritating dyes, fragrances, and rayon, so they're safe for the environment and safer for sensitive skin. The compact style of Seventh Generation tampons means less wasteful material, and the boxes are made from 100 percent recycled content. (www.seventhgeneration.com)

SEVENTH GENERATION AND NATRACARE PADS
Planet- and Pant-Protecting

Seventh Generation engineers highly absorbent, eco-friendly, chlorine-free pads and pantyliners for discreet and comfy protection. You need, they've got: soft, cottony pads for light flow, and several sizes of contoured pads and heavy-duty maxi pads with securable wings and highly absorbent cores made from nonchlorine-bleached wood pulp and a polymer gel derived from wheat. Although the maxi pads are covered with thin layers of nonwoven polyolefin plastic, they are overall a much greener option for superabsorbent reliability than conventional pads. (www.seventh generation.com)

With styles to suit every cyclic flow, Natracare liners and pads are made from natural plant cellulose pulp made of wood pulp from strictly sustainable managed forests. Natracare stands strong against the use of plant cellulose from ancient, endangered forests, an issue that has become the focus of a worldwide Greenpeace Awareness Campaign. Natracare abstains from the use of energy-intensive CTMP (chemo-thermal mechanical processing) for their cellulose pulp materials, a process that not only creates eco- and fish-toxic sulfur compounds and resin acids but also causes finished pulp materials to be slow to biodegrade. All of Natracare's liners and pads are nonchlorine bleached, perfume free, plastic free, and 100 percent biodegradable. (www.natracare.com)

FYI

True beauty comes from within in more ways than one—putting pure, clean stuff inside shows up on the outside like sunshine follows rain. Eating a rainbow of foods is key. Color is an indicator of beautifying agents such as antioxidants, flavonoids, and carotenoids, all of which help to neutralize damaging free radicals. Beautifying foods include organic berries, pomegranates, tomatoes, grapes, green veggies, dark chocolate, avocados, green tea, red wine, and good fats such as extra-virgin olive oil.

MENSTRUAL CUPS
Zero Waste and Reusable

Menstrual cups have been around in one form or another since the 1930s and have fairly recently returned to the market as the übereco par for the monthly course. Molded from either natural latex rubber or high-grade silicone, these minicups are designed to catch and collect the menstrual flow—kind of like a structured, inverted diaphragm. The DivaCup is made out of pure, medical-grade silicone. This latex-free, plastic-free, hypoallergenic menstrual cup is perfect for those with sensitivities to latex. The DivaCup has a little nipple on the bottom for easy insertion and removal and can be worn for up to 12 hours for light or moderate flows before emptying, washing, and inserting for another 12 hours (heavier flows may call for emptying more often). It's clean, comfortable, convenient, and reliable. Perfect for all activities including traveling, exercise, and swimming, this cup can also be worn overnight. (www.divacup.com)

REUSABLE CLOTH PADS
The Ultimate Eco-Friendly Solution

For ladies who wish to reduce their generation of feminine pad waste, reusable cloth pads are an advanced eco-option. They're very green although a little messy, and they may be more appropriate for use at home or for overnight protection.

GladRags makes washable and reusable soft cotton pads that offer a healthy, eco-friendly alternative to disposable feminine goods. All GladRags have one soft flannel holder (cover) with wings that snap for secure comfort and two inserts made from layered terry flannel. GladRags last 5-plus years, so in the long run, they're easy on your pocketbook. Available in regular cotton and organic cotton, they can be purchased individually or in packs of three. (www.gladrags.com)

NATRACARE FEMININE WIPES: ORGANIC COTTON'S THE KEY

Keep yourself fresh with Natracare Organic Cotton Intimate Wipes, formulated with gently cleansing calendula and chamomile. Unlike the vast majority of feminine and baby wipes on the market made of petroleum-derived polypropylene and polyolefin and a slew of chemical synthetic ingredients, Natracare's intimate wipes are made from 100 percent certified organic cotton and pure, plant-derived ingredients. They're soft, strong, clinically tested (but not on animals), and biodegradable. These personal wipes don't contain paraben preservatives, chlorine, SLS, harsh alcohols, skin-irritating propylene glycol, phenoxyethanol, or formaldehyde-releasing imidazolidinyl urea (a commonly used cosmetic preservative identified as the second leading cause of contact dermatitis). (www.natracare.com)

Sleep is the body's time to restore itself and reenergize the organs and skin, especially when a regular sleeping pattern is maintained.

THE BODY SHOP NAIL AND FOOT FILES
Eco-Friendly Shaping and Reduction

The Body Shop's Big Nail Filer is made from FSC-certified wood pulp, meaning it comes from sustainably managed forests that protect biodiversity. This durable, double-sided file has coarse emery grains on one side and fine grains on the other. For eco-nail filing emergencies, the Body Shop's Nail File Matchbook is the perfect solution: This handy, matchbook-style pouch contains 12 mini nail files made from recycled cardboard with rough emery grains on one side and fine on the other.

Treat tough foot calluses to a healthy filing the eco-friendly way. The Body Shop's Wooden Foot File is made from FSC-certified beechwood, sourced in partnership to provide steady employment, fair wages, and a social action fund to support children in Western Siberia, Russia, where the sustainably managed wood is grown. This foot file performs double duty—the coarse side smooths away stiff, stubborn, callused skin; the smooth side exfoliates the rest. (www.thebodyshop-usa.com)

JOHN MASTERS ORGANICS
Masterful Organic Hair Care

Part basement alchemist, part organic innovator, John Masters is truly a master of natural hair care. His John Masters Organics hair care products are brilliantly formulated using the purest, highest-grade ingredients and botanicals (with an emphasis on organic and sustainable wild-crafted plants), cold-pressed plant oils, and steam-distilled essential oils. These are among the purest and finest products on the market. Absolutely no synthetic or chemical ingredients of any kind are used—no SLS, SLES, paraben preservatives, petrochemicals, artificial fragrances or colors, or genetically modified organisms (GMOs).

John Masters Organics Evening Primrose Shampoo for dry hair is made from pure and gentle coconut and corn cleansers and infused with conditioning plant extracts and essential oils. It will gently wash away dirt without overstripping dry, delicate, or colored hair. Honey & Hibiscus Hair Reconstructing Shampoo is formulated with honey and hibiscus extracts for penetrating nour-

ishment and a delightfully clean scent. It will fortify and strengthen hair with linoleic and hyaluronic acids, which are found in young, healthy hair. Citrus & Neroli Detangler will condition and detangle hair without weighing it down and has an uplifting aroma. Hair will benefit from lipid replenishment via natural vegetable oils, such as borage seed oil, and its strength and shine will be restored by this protein- and vitamin-packed formula. Lavender & Avocado Intensive Conditioner is just what the master orders as an intensive way to bring moisture and vitality to dry hair. It is chock-full of avocado oils, vitamin B5, and more than a dozen plant extracts and essential oils to moisturize and strengthen the hair shaft naturally. (www.johnmasters.com)

TELA BEAUTY ORGANICS
Sophisticated, Sustainable Hair Care

Tela Beauty Organics combines the best of nature's sustainable ingredients with the most advanced science for sophisticated hair care products designed for performance and beauty. Each product is formulated with Tela Organic Core Blend, a proprietary base, which consists of 35 certified organic ingredients chosen to penetrate and enhance hair of all types. All are paraben free.

Tela's Measure Shampoo and Conditioner are both formulated to smooth and strengthen mature or weaker hair for improved texture and shine. Measure contains a certified organic "regenerating blend" of potent botanical ingredients such as structure-enhancing horsetail, antioxidant-rich organic red sage and Reishi mushroom, and protective burdock for stronger, longer, healthier hair. Color Atura Shampoo and Conditioner is designed to protect, restore, and enhance color- and chemically treated hair. The certified organic "enhancing blend" includes antioxidant-protective Chinese foxglove and milk thistle as well as replenishing wolfberry to keep hair color and chemical enhancements intact. (http://telahaircare.com)

FYI

Diluted apple cider vinegar is an excellent clarifying rinse to revive hair that is dull from product buildup, restore a smooth cuticle and add shine to your hair, and restore healthy pH levels to the scalp.

HAIRBRUSHES
Earth-Friendly Grooming Tools

Eco-glamorous hair styling is at hand with the Aveda Ceramic Round Brush, made with 100 percent postconsumer recycled content and manufactured without glue. This eco-friendly innovation is made with heat-resistant, PCW-recycled-content bristles to create lift and volume without tangling, and a ceramic-coated barrel that heats quickly and evenly to smooth and straighten hair with less blow-drying time (so you save on energy use, too). All Aveda products are manufactured with wind energy so you can get your glamour on and still be green. (www.aveda.com)

Widu offers an exquisite line of Italian hairbrushes made from Forest Stewardship Council (FSC) certified wood. Designed by a hair stylist in Milan, these brushes are handmade by artisans with impeccable old-world craftsmanship for long-lasting performance and durability. The wood bases of the Widu brushes are sustainably harvested from managed forests and finished naturally with purified linseed oil and beeswax. No toxic lacquers or finishes of any sort are used. A wide variety of ingeniously designed shapes, styles, and sizes is available with both wooden bristles and natural boar bristles. Wood bristles are made from the smooth, white wood of the hornbeam tree (from sustainable, managed forests, of course), chosen for its break-resistant grain. Wooden bristles can be replaced with individual replacement bristles, available in packs of 10, without impacting the overall brush. Ethically obtained wild boar bristles are hand-set into the boar bristle brushes. The supreme quality of all Widu handmade brushes is evident in the clever design and consummate character—they are clearly meant to last a lifetime. (www.widu.com)

INTELLIGENT NUTRIENTS
Organic, Multitasking Hair Intelligence

Intelligent Nutrients is the certified organic baby of natural-beauty mogul Horst Rechelbacher, founder of Aveda. This man is a genius when it comes to natural hair care, and he has taken it to a new level of purity and performance with Intelligent Nutrients (IN). All IN formulas utilize nontoxic plant-based surfactants, preservatives, fixatives, and fragrances. Every IN product contains a proprietary superantioxidant complex called Intellimune—a blend of seed oils designed to harness the antiaging properties of black cumin, pumpkin, red grape, red raspberry, and cranberry seed oils.

Intelligent Nutrients 70 percent Organic Hair Cleanser is an ultramild, pure, and healthy cleanser for all hair types, including color-treated hair. It can even multitask as a shave foam or to wash your produce (it's that pure). IN Certified Organic Hair Conditioner protects and detangles hair with multitasking function—rinse out, leave in, or use as a styling cream to reduce frizz and enhance control. IN Certified Organic Leave-In Conditioner is designed to hydrate and protect the scalp and doubles as a foundation for styling and skin moisturizer for the body. To detangle and soften uncooperative hair, IN Certified Organic Spray-On Detangler can be used on damp hair to condition and protect hair from damage, or sprayed on dry hair for antistatic conditioning or to activate curls. (www.intelligentnutrients.com)

CONDITIONING TREATMENTS

Eco-Hair Repair

Hair that has been abused or neglected by too much processing or too little TLC will see buoyant results from fortifying conditioning treatments that call on botanical renewing agents for deep repair.

Creative Airs makes Salon Choice Rinse-off Conditioner, Volume-Plus Deep Conditioner Hair Mask with certified organic herbal extracts, vital nutrients and moisturizers, provitamins, and phytoproteins to penetrate hair for healing manageability. The ingredients are as clean as it gets, and the results are magnificent. (www.creativeairs.com)

Intelligent Nutrients is a natural winner for multitasking function with the intensively hair-repairing 70 Percent Organic Hair Treatment. Thoroughly and brilliantly natural, this hair conditioner is made with pure plant emollients and the certified organic superantioxidant Intellimune Seed Oil Complex to protect and restore damaged hair. Leave in, rinse out, or use as a foamless cleanser for moisture restoration and curl control. It even doubles as a frizz-reducing styling cream. (www.intelligent nutrients.com)

Skin Deep—Find Out What's in Your Products

Given the elusive credentials, lack of government safety regulations, and vague labeling terminology, it's tricky to find out how safe and eco-friendly personal care and cosmetic products are. For the skinny, turn to the Environmental Working Group (EWG) database, Skin Deep. It's the ultimate safety guide for personal care products and cosmetics. With research into more than 25,000 products, which are cross-referenced against 50 toxicity and regulatory databases, Skin Deep is the largest integrated data resource anywhere. Products are rated on an overall scale of 0 to 10 (with 0 being harmless and 10 being extremely hazardous) and flagged for specific possible health hazards. Further, each ingredient of a reviewed product receives an individual 0-to-10 rating. The Skin Deep database is interactive, easy to navigate, and user friendly.

Who are the people behind this savvy database? EWG is a Washington, DC–based public interest watchdog. The EWG's team of scientists, engineers, policy experts, lawyers, and computer programmers scour federal data, legal documents, and peer-reviewed scientific studies for threats to human health and the environment and then test products in their own labs to expose hazards. Most important, they help find solutions.

When using this site, look closely at the ingredients responsible for a product's rating. Take advantage of EWG's Skin Deep database at www.cosmeticdatabase.com.

GIOVANNI HAIR CARE

Eco-Savvy Hair Styling

Being green does not mean succumbing to flat, lifeless locks. If you are seeking savvy style, va-va-voom volume, or a solution to bedhead, frame your mane and glamorize your tresses with clean, green styling products that are human-safe and eco-friendly. Giovanni Hair Care combines certified organic botanicals and incredible style. To boost bodacious body, Giovanni Natural Mousse Air-Turbo Charged builds hair to hefty heights with staying power and adds texture and shine. Formulated with infused herbal extracts such as rosemary, St. John's wort, yarrow, and red clover, this light styling mousse will boost hair body without bumming out the earth. Fickle, floppy locks can get a healthy root boost and directional control with Giovanni Root 66, chock-full of herbal extracts such as nettle, wild bergamot, and California poppy. The directional nozzle makes spritzing this root-boosting formula a cinch. Giovanni Straight Fast! offers sleek, chic style to smooth, soothe, and straighten hair temporarily until your next shampoo. Certified organic botanicals and soy protein protect hair from heat styling such as blow-drying and flat ironing. If you want to spike, smooth, or control hair with authority and without crazy chemicals, Giovanni L.A. Natural Styling Gel is your ally to secure shape with extreme hold. Loaded with herbs, botanical extracts, and trace minerals, this styling gel is hair healthy, planet safe, and preserved naturally with grapefruit seed extract. L.A. Hold Hair Spray secures hair safely, retaining firm hold and style all day long. It washes out easily, leaving a conditioned feel from all of the organic botanical ingredients. (www.giovanni cosmetics.com)

SUPERCLEAN WITH SPF

Kiss My Face 3-Way Color provides sheer coverage for cheeks, lips, and eyes for naturally blended color with everyday SPF 8 protection. Made with a base of pure, creamy antioxidant-emollient olive butter and moisturizing mango butter, this colored cream contains natural mineral pigments that add richness and depth to skin tone and titanium dioxide for natural sun protection against UVA and UVB rays. Mix and match the four lovely shades for a natural look to protect, even, and smooth skin tone. (www.kissmyface.com)

MINERAL FUSION

Clean, Natural Beauty

Mineral Fusion is dedicated to creating eco-friendly, human-safe cosmetic products from naturally processed mineral pigments, using sustainable technologies that won't deplete our planet of precious resources. Made from micronized minerals, which sit on the surface of the skin to do their job without being absorbed and clogging pores or getting cakey, Mineral Fusion cosmetics are entirely free of paraben preservatives, talc, chemical dyes, and synthetic fragrances. Since Mineral Fusion cosmetics don't contain talc, less product on the brush yields more coverage on the skin.

Put your best face forward with Mineral Fusion base basics in a range of complexion colors. There's concealer (three hues) for the eye area, loose base (seven hues) for flawless coverage, pressed base (15 hues) for a perfect matte finish, setting powder for touch-ups, and sheer tint base (three hues) for a natural wash of liquid coverage. Line and define eyes with eye pencils made from mineral pigments in a vegetable oil base, and complement eye shape and color with a rainbow of eye shadows in singles or trios. Accentuate your smile with confidence using Mineral Fusion lip pencil, plant-based lipstick, lip gloss, and richly pigmented Liquid Glass for high-gloss shine and an ultramoist look. (www.mineral fusioncosmetics.com)

LIPSTICKS

Plant-Based Lip Love

Perfect Organics introduces organic, vegan Lip and Cheek Shimmers made from pure, certified organic ingredients for supersmooth, glossy color and glow. Available in seven lovely colors derived from natural mineral sources, the ingredients are so clean you could practically eat them—which, in effect, is what slowly happens while you wear lipstick anyway. With a base of healthy, lip-healing certified organic plant oils and plant wax, this moisturizing shimmer has a seductive and bright scent from pure organic essential oils of peppermint and organic vanilla. Perfect Organics takes green integrity through all stages of manufacturing, including using stainless steel filling tubes to fill lipsticks instead of the disposable plastic filling tubes that are used once and then landfilled. Housed in an elegant, high-quality, twist-up stainless steel tube, Perfect Organics Lip and Cheek Shimmer isn't inexpensive, but the quality and performance are worth every penny. (www.perfectorganics.com).

Sustainable style and innovative integrity meet in **Cargo PlantLove Botanical Lipstick**. The plastic tube is made from corn—a renewable resource and 100 percent biodegradable—and the carton is made out of flower paper embedded with viable wildflower seeds that will grow if moistened and planted! How very. The PlantLove collection features sheer, glossy lipstick that is formulated with flower extracts, meadowfoam seed, nourishing jojoba oil, and protective shea butter. (www.cargo cosmetics.com)

cosmetics

NVEY ECO ORGANIC MAKEUP

Where Nature and Luxury Meet

Bred by years of stringent research, testing, and access to the expertise of nearly a half-century legacy in the beauty industry, **NVEY ECO** was born as the green child of the Australian cosmetic house NVEY Le Maquillage. NVEY (pronounced EN-vee) ECO organic makeup is masterfully formulated with a prudent blend of select plant and mineral ingredients, botanical extracts, antioxidants, and nutrient-rich restorative components. Meeting strict organic certifying criteria for all stages of production from ingredient sourcing, research, and development through processing and manufacture, all NVEY ECO products are free of synthetic preservatives (including parabens), SLS and derivatives, propylene glycol, GMOs, talc, and petroleum-based ingredients.

Achieve flawless foundational coverage with NVEY ECO Organic Moisturizing Liquid Foundation, made with chamomile, cucumber, calendula, and a touch of pure rose absolute to soothe dry and sensitive skin. The foundation is tinted with natural earth elements in six colors to suit a spectrum of skin tones and undertones. Five Organic Compact Powder colors and eight Organic Powder Blush colors enhance and define skin with a fresh, soft, seamless finish—both pressed powder compact products are formulated with corn silk; jojoba oil; vitamins A, C, and E; chamomile; and pure mineral earth colors. NVEY ECO Organic Eye Shadows are dreamy and sold in single compacts, but their Organic Creative Eye Color System is packaged in a sleek, mirrored compact and provides just the right variety of complementary colors to create looks from subtle and natural to deep and dramatic. (www.econveybeauty.com)

JOSIE MARAN COSMETICS

Eco-Makeup from One Who Knows

Josie Maran Cosmetics is the brainchild of earth-conscious moxie-model Josie Maran. With a decades-long résumé of gracing glossy magazine pages and an inside scoop about makeup from the best in the business, she's created a cosmetic line that doesn't sacrifice luxury or performance in the name of being skin-safe and kind to the environment. Made from everything you want and nothing you don't for a fresh, naturally flawless face and clean, green planet, each product is clearly labeled to illustrate the eco- and skin-friendly features and ingredients. Ingredient lists are identified with symbols to indicate paraben free, fragrance free, toxin free, petrochemical free, and organic formulas. Product packaging and components are made from glass, aluminum, biodegradable plastic, and paper, and each touts the mark of recycled content (percentage of recycled content is indicated) and whether it's recyclable or biodegradable. Even the display units at retail counters are constructed from sustainable materials. (www.josiemarancosmetics.com)

JANE IREDALE MINERAL COSMETICS

Mineral Makeup Maven

Jane Iredale was well ahead of the curve. She introduced her unique skin care makeup line based on minerals in 1994, the very first of its kind on the market and one that offered not just color enhancement but also clear benefits to the skin. What makes Jane Iredale Mineral Cosmetics different from all the others on the market is their proprietary processing technology. Earth minerals are pulverized into micronized flat crystals that overlap each other to form a filter that protects the skin from pollutants and allows it to breathe. The minerals used by Jane Iredale are inert and cannot support bacteria, therefore, no preservatives are required to keep these makeups fresh. They last indefinitely. Jane Iredale Mineral Cosmetics offers many cosmetic categories: bases, blushes, lips, eyes, kits, shimmers, concealers, and facial sprays. (www.janeiredale.com)

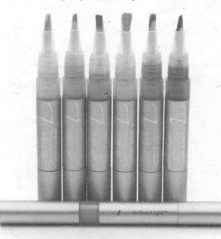

SUKICOLOR
Fresh Finish Mineral Cream Makeup

After years of studying with cosmetic chemists and tinkering with traditional medicinal blends in her own kitchen, Suki Kramer set out to formulate a truly natural skin care and cosmetic line that was not only effective and thoroughly green but also sensual, sophisticated, and stylish. SukiColor offers fresh-finish mineral cream cosmetics made from finely crushed, completely natural minerals and pure, targeted skin care ingredients. The resulting clean colors blend beautifully—not too glittery, not too flat—for a radiant, flawless complexion that looks like you, only better. SukiColor is clear of any synthetics, dyes, GMOs, petrochemicals, and FD&C and lake colors. SukiColor mineral cream makeup comes in five versatile cosmetic categories in a subtle range of hues.

SukiColor Tinted Active Moisturizer SPF is a light, creamy, tinted moisturizing foundation that offers sheer coverage to even skin tone and minimize pores. Made from organic and pure plant oils, anti-inflammatory white willow, antioxidant-rich vitamin C liposomes, natural sunscreens for full protection, and fresh-smelling steam-distilled essential oils, this tinted moisturizer is available in two colors. To banish blemishes and brighten under-eye circles, SukiColor Liquid Formula Concealer will correct and conceal, healing as it hides. Made with 100 percent organic, pharmaceutical-grade active ingredients, including anti-inflammatory white willow and nourishing borage, jojoba, and hazelnut oils, the pink and peach undertones of this concealer can cover up target areas and also be used as a tinted moisturizer for even the fairest of skin tones to provide protective coverage.

Triple Cream Eye Definer is a creamy cosmetic balm that works as a shadow, liner, and brow definer. Made with active vitamin and mineral-rich color, pure botanicals, and floral waxes, this ultrasilky formula will support delicate skin around the eyes with antioxidant moisture. Quench and color cheeks and lips with Pure Cream Stain for a silky, hydrated glow. This cream tint is made with natural crushed mineral pigments and protective, skin-nourishing rose wax, jojoba oil, and vitamin E. (www.sukicolor.com)

FYI

Hydrate skin from within: Drink eight glasses

of water a day to keep skin moist, supple, clear, and

fresh—and help prevent wrinkles and blemishes.

EYE MAKEUP REMOVERS
An au Naturel Solution

A clean, green, gentle formula designed specifically to remove eye makeup and impurities is a kind way to treat and protect eyelashes and the delicate skin around the eyes. Jurlique Eye Makeup Remover is a moisture-based cream that contains pure, biodynamically grown calendula, organic sunflower and jojoba seed oils, and botanical and flower extracts to safely and effectively remove eye makeup and leave skin feeling soothed and refreshed without oily residue. (www.jurlique.com)

Eminence Organic Skin Care offers a pH balanced liquid Herbal Eye Make-up Remover made with cucumber, lavender, calendula, and chamomile to decongest sensitive skin and with comfrey extract to protect and heal delicate skin around the eyes. (www.eminenceorganics.com)

Rotating Products

Every body is unique. Every body's skin and hair have different qualities and needs, so different products work well for different people. Certain products work brilliantly for a while and then lose their luster, so rotate your personal care product regime depending on the season and daily environment.

Is there any empirical backbone to product rotation? Yes. Some scientists and skin biology experts affirm that there are indeed scientific reasons for rotating products. In a nutshell, our skin and hair reach a level of saturation of even the best clean, natural ingredients.

JANE IREDALE LIQUID MINERALS

A Revolutionary Foundation

For light-diffusing, breathable liquid foundation, Jane Iredale Liquid Minerals supply nourishing coverage with timed-release antioxidants and phytosomes. This liquid foundation looks pretty wild. Suspended in a clear gel of pure aloe vera, lavender flower water, and vegetable glycerin, visible beads of mineral liposomes are encapsulated in seaweed lipids with active ingredients such as olive squalene, coenzyme Q10, vitamins C and K, willow bark extract, chamomile, and calendula. When these liquid minerals are applied and buffed onto the skin, the body's temperature naturally breaks down the liposomes for prolonged timed-release nourishment and protection. With a pH of 6, this formula is perfectly balanced. Jane Iredale Liquid Minerals is available in 18 colors. The suspended mineral colors can look different in the bottle than when applied to the skin, so try a combination of two to get the right flawless match. This liquid goes a very long way, so one bottle (though not inexpensive) will last a good long time. (www.janeiredale.com)

FYI

Protect yourself from excessively dry air in heated rooms and on airplanes by coating the inside of your nostrils with lip balm to keep your mucus membranes moist and less susceptible to airborne pathogens.

ECOTOOLS

Earth-Friendly Brushes and More

Gratify greener personal preening with eco-conscious hardware such as brushes, applicators, and grooming accessories. Eco-Tools offers a bevy of naturally chic green beauty gear at economically inviting prices. Featuring innovative earth-friendly materials to help make beauty routines a little greener, every aspect of this premiere mass collection has been meticulously planned and considered for its environmental impact. From the use of über-sustainable bamboo and recycled materials to cruelty-free bristles and reusable natural fiber pouches printed with plant-based ink, EcoTools is as green as it gets.

Choose from a bouquet of cosmetic brushes (available individually and as versatile five- and six-piece sets), engineered with durable bamboo handles and recycled aluminum ferrules that are made and professionally designed to maximize beauty and minimize effort. For perfectly tailored brows, the Recycled Brow grooming kit is a one-stop shop, including a bamboo-rimmed 5X lead-free mirror, recycled stainless steel scissors and tweezers, and two brushes. Don't miss other accessories to enhance beautifying bliss, such as reusable cleansing sponges made from soybean and cotton instead of petroleum, bamboo nail files, and even a recycled foot-smoothing stone made from ground recycled glass. (www.parispresents.com)

CLAIRSONIC SKIN CARE SYSTEM

Clairsonic has revolutionized skin cleansing with sonic technology. Micromassaging skin with 300+ minimotions per minute will not only clean skin and pores with unparalleled efficacy, but it also reduces your beauty footprint because less product is required to achieve stellar results again and again. It offers medi-spa results at home without harsh abrasion or chemicals. Gentle enough to use daily, Clairsonic leaves skin soft, smooth, toned, and at the ready to absorb serums and moisturizers ultra-effectively, meaning you'll need less of your favorite formulas for enhanced results, naturally. (www.clairsonic.com)

The green movement sweeping the nation has affected whole categories of products. Electronics is a fine example. Computers, printers, monitors, cell phones, and other electronic gadgetry might, by their nature, seem anything but green. After all, they're made from nonbiodegradable materials such as plastics and metals, and they tend to contain hazardous materials such as lead, mercury, and chromium. They consume electricity, which results in carbon emissions and other greenhouse gases (GHGs). Printers, fax machines, and copiers also consume resources such as paper and ink, which can have negative environmental consequences.

Enter green technology. Electronic devices are now being manufactured, operated, and retired with efficiency and a minimum of environmental impact. The underlying idea is to wring as much value as possible out of every resource—whether watts of electricity, sheets of paper, gallons of ink, or pounds of metals and plastics.

Green technology is good for the environment, but it's also good for your pocketbook, because greener, more efficient gear can save money on utility bills, paper, and ink and postpone the need to upgrade to even more new machines.

Why are these green improvements essential? First of all, the GHGs associated with powering computers, monitors, and other electronic hardware have increased around the globe as usage has ramped up. And CO_2 isn't the only harmful GHG linked with energy production. Look at coal, which is used to generate half of the electricity used in the United States. Burning coal produces dangerous sulfur dioxide, nitrogen dioxide, carbon monoxide, hydrocarbons, ash, and toxic sludge.

A second pollution issue is e-waste—electronic equipment that has reached the end of its useful life. One troubling trend is how much hardware ends up in landfills instead of being recycled. In 2007, only about 18 percent (414,000 tons) of discarded TVs and computer products were collected for recycling. Cell phones were recycled at a rate of just around 10 percent.

That e-waste is a source of hazardous substances, including lead, mercury, cadmium, chromium, and polybrominated biphenyls. By some accounts, e-waste represents 2 percent of America's trash in landfills, but it equals 70 percent of overall toxic waste.

Even machines that are sent off for recycling can cause harm to the environment and to people. Despite legitimate, major recycling efforts by several electronics manufacturers, some recycling programs send electronics waste to developing nations in Asia and Africa, where the very idea of "recycling" is mocked by the crudity and destructiveness of the methods: Devices are "dismantled" with hammers, and plastics are often burned to separate out the metal components.

So what makes technology greener?

Better power supply units. Manufacturers are using more-efficient power supplies as standard components in computers, monitors, and other electronic gear. The power supply components convert the AC power that flows into the machine from the wall into the DC power on which the system runs. In years past, as much as 40 percent of the energy that went through the power supply ended up wasted; vendors are now designing power supplies that are 90 percent efficient or higher.

More efficient cooling. Like a car engine, processors produce heat as they work and thus require cooling. The more powerful the processor, the more heat it produces and the more cooling it requires. Cooling isn't free; it is another burden on the electric bill. Vendors are developing processors and other components that don't run as hot. They're also rolling out machines with superior internal cooling systems.

Operational efficiencies. PCs, monitors, printers, and other electronics often sit idle for long periods of time yet remain powered and continue to draw electricity. Vendors have devised hardware and software that put machines into low-power modes when they're not being used, then automatically power those systems back on when they're needed. Further, we're seeing software that gets a better handle on waste associated with printing, copying, and faxing—such as software that eliminates superfluous pages.

Longer-lasting hardware. Companies are working to extend the life of electronic devices. The benefits of this are clear: You save time and money by not having to replace your computer or phone as often, and in turn fewer resources go toward retiring and recycling machines.

Easier disassembly. Vendors are making electronic devices simpler to disassemble. This means you can easily repair or upgrade a machine by pulling out one part and popping in another, rather than having to ship the machine out for factory repair or, worse yet, replace it entirely. Moreover, when a machine is easy to disassemble, its parts are more readily salvaged for reuse once the system is recycled.

Alternative power supplies. More products are emerging that draw on alternative energy sources—particularly the sun, manual power, and wind—thus reducing dependence on conventional pollution-prone sources of electricity.

Safer machines. Vendors now are building machines using fewer hazardous materials (such as lead and mercury)—with obvious environmental benefits.

Consumers—that's us—have a major role to play in terms of being responsible owners and operators of green technology. Do we turn our electronics off when they are not in use, or do we leave them powered up all the time? Do we use alternative means of charging devices, or do we rely solely on drawing power from the socket? Do we just throw our e-toys in the garbage when we're done with them, or do we recycle them responsibly?

The electronics industry has made strides toward offering greener products, and for that, manufacturers deserve credit. But there's plenty more progress to be made. Green-minded consumers can use the power of the pocketbook to urge companies toward even greener pastures.

The products noted here are by no means a definitive list, especially considering the speed with which new PCs, cell phones, and other electronic devices are produced. But these products can serve as benchmarks for what is currently available and what to look for in a green machine.

—Ted Samson

BELKIN CONSERVE

Stops Power-Wasting Electronics

You may not realize it, but your TV, DVD player, computer, printer, and other electronics are likely wasting electricity when you're not using them, just because you keep them plugged in. It's called standby power, or phantom power, and the California Energy Commission says it represents 15 percent of a household's electricity use.

Unfortunately, reaching below desks or behind television equipment to unplug your electronics isn't always practical. But there's a solution: the Belkin Conserve surge protector.

Equipped with eight outlets, the Belkin Conserve works much like any other surge protector, except that this protector comes with a handy remote control. Use the remote to completely and easily shut off the power to devices that would otherwise consume standby power. The Conserve has two "always on" outlets that allow you to operate devices that typically need to stay on. The remote can be mounted on a wall and works within a 60-foot range. (from $49.99; www.belkin.com/conserve)

HYMINI AND MINISOLAR PANEL

Free Energy for Your Handheld Device

Why pay for electricity when you can get it for free, compliments of Mother Nature, in the form of wind or sunlight? That mind-set is the inspiration behind the HYmini wind and solar power chargers for handheld devices.

The small, portable device is a simple lithium-ion battery pack that absorbs and stores 1,200 milliamp-hours (mAh) of electricity, rechargeable by wind or solar power. At the core of the system is the wind minigenerator, which houses the battery and a simple fanlike windmill. To charge the battery pack, expose it to a breeze of at least 9 mph by setting it outside, opening your car window as you drive, or even strapping it to your handlebars when you go for a bike ride. According to the company, 20 minutes of charging with a 19 mph wind delivers 30 minutes of charge to an iPod and 4 minutes of talk time to a cell phone.

The optional miniSolar Panel, available separately, connects to the charger and draws on the sun's power to generate juice for the battery.

The system is not limited to wind and solar power: Attachments let you power it up as you would a traditional charger by plugging it into a wall socket or a USB port. You can even purchase the mini-Handcrank to manually generate power for the battery. (from $49.99; www.hymini.com)

FYI

The average life of a cell phone in the United States is 18 months. Extending the service life of a phone from 1 to 4 years would decrease the environmental impacts by about 40 percent.

GAIAM SIDEWINDER CELL PHONE CHARGER

Battery-Free Charging

You're on the road. Your cell phone dies and you have an important call to make. And there's no place to plug in your charger. Feeling cranky? Well, crank away on the GAIAM SideWinder Cell Phone Charger, and soon your phone will have juice to make your calls.

This minute, 2.5-ounce device doesn't contain a battery. Rather, you generate power by manually turning the small handle on the side. Two minutes of turning gives you 6 minutes of cell phone time. This charger offers a nice off-the-grid alternative, even without an emergency. It also has a bright built-in LED emergency light that runs for over 5 minutes with only 30 seconds of charging. And it supports most models of phones. ($29; www.gaiam.com).

DELL STUDIO HYBRID DESKTOP

High Energy Efficiency in a Small Package

Like other good things, green computers come in small packages. In fact, a minute form is one of the eco-friendly selling points of Dell's Studio Hybrid desktop computer. The sleekly designed system is 80 percent smaller than standard desktops, so it contains less plastic and other nonbiodegradable materials than its rivals. The system also boasts 75 percent less printed documentation by weight compared to its competitors.

Adding to the Studio Hybrid's green appeal is its high level of energy efficiency: Consuming 70 percent less power than a typical desktop, it surpasses the requirements laid out by Energy Star for desktops. Even the system's packaging is earth friendly; it's made from 95 percent recyclable materials. These traits help earn the machine a gold rating from Electronic Product Environmental Assessment Tool (EPEAT).

Despite its green pedigree and minute size, this is a highly capable computing machine, muscular enough to run Microsoft's weighty Vista Home Premium operating system. It includes up to a 4 GB 667 MHz Intel Pentium dual-core processor, up to 320 GB of storage space, a CD/DVD writer, built-in wireless networking capabilities, optional Blu-ray functionality—and a TV tuner.

A rainbow of colorful, interchangeable sleeves are available for the Dell Studio Hybrid; to be extra eco-friendly, opt for one made from bamboo. (from $499; www.dell.com/hybrid)

Extend Cartridge Life and Save Cash

Printer ink can cost as much as $8,000 per gallon! And the process of having empty ink cartridges packed up and shipped for recycling is wasteful. Reuse is more efficient, and that's where your local participating Walgreens comes in. The drugstore chain with more than 6,700 locations throughout the United States now offers local printer cartridge ink refills at participating stores. Take your empties to the photo counter, and within minutes they'll be refilled with high-quality ink.

Black-ink refills cost $10; color-ink refills run $15 a pop. If you're skeptical of the results, the store offers a 100 percent satisfaction guarantee. However, Walgreens refills cartridges only for printers from Dell, HP, Lexmark, Okidata, Primera, Sharp, and Xerox. Epson, Brother, and Samsung users will have to go elsewhere. (www.walgreens.com/dmi/inkrefill/default.html)

APPLE MACBOOK AIR

A Laptop with Big Green Benefits

If your OS of choice is Mac instead of Windows, here's a tasty green Apple for you to sink your teeth into: the slick, slim MacBook Air.

The slender machine weighs in at a mere 3 pounds and measures 0.16 inch at its thinnest point: It can easily be slid into a manila envelope. That reduced size means it contains fewer plastics and other nonrenewable resources than other laptops.

Among its many green bragging points, the MacBook Air has a recyclable aluminum enclosure and a mercury-free LCD display with arsenic-free glass. Inside, the system contains no brominated flame retardant, and the cables are PVC free. The system complies with the European Union's Restriction on Hazardous Substances (RoHS). The lean, green machine consumes the least power among all Macs: It can run for 5 hours without recharging. These green criteria and others have earned the system a gold rating from EPEAT, which grades computing products based on their greenness.

The MacBook Air is powered by a 1.86 gigahertz (GHz) or 2.13 GHz Intel Core 2 Duo processor with 6 MB on-chip shared L2 cache and includes as standard features 2 GB of memory and a 120 GB hard drive. It also contains the NVIDIA GeForce 9400M chipset, which delivers a five-fold performance improvement over the previous Intel integrated graphics.

The system comes equipped with a 13.3-inch LED-backlit widescreen display, full-size backlit keyboard, built-in video camera, and ample-size trackpad. It brings to the table AirPort Extreme 802.11n WiFi networking, which Apple says delivers up to five times the performance and twice the range of 802.11g. It's Bluetooth 2.1 capable. (from $1,499; www.apple.com/macbookair)

FYI

Even when your cell phone isn't plugged into a charger, the charger is likely drawing electricity and raising your power bill. Many AC adapters (also known as "wall warts") continue to pull current even when not working. Be green: Pull the plug on all chargers when they're not actually charging something.

Buying a Greener PC

Computer and monitor manufacturers are working hard to develop greener and more efficient technology. That said, finding desktops, laptops, and monitors that meet your work (and play) needs as well as your environmental standards does take some work. Here are some tips to assist your research:

Shop within your needs. You may well dream of equipping yourself with the least energy-thirsty PC on the market. However, be realistic about your computing and viewing needs. The more you want from your system, the more powerful it needs to be, and that means it will require more power. It's counterproductive to wind up with a machine that lacks the capabilities you need for, say, art production or playing games. But it's wasteful to buy a device loaded with energy-draining bells and whistles that you don't require.

Know your operating system. Not all operating systems are created equal. Microsoft Vista's bare minimum (not recommended) system requirements are an 800 MHz processor, 512 MB of RAM, a 20 GB hard drive with at least 15 GB of available space, and support for Super VGA graphics. Ubuntu, a Linux desktop OS, has much lower power demands: Its minimum requirements are a 300 MHz processor, 64 MB of RAM, 4 GB of disk space (for full installation and swap space), and a low-end VGA graphics card with 640 x 480 resolution.

Consider the software you plan to run. Some applications require more processing power than others. Consider, for example, the array of office-productivity applications that are available for word processing, spreadsheets, and e-mail. Some have hefty system requirements. The same goes for graphic-intensive software such as games. Alternatively, you may find that you can make do with the lightweight Web-based applications, such as Google Apps for e-mail, word processing, and other tasks, which can be accessed and run through Web browsers.

Determine whether a laptop meets your needs. From a purely green perspective, a laptop is a superior choice to a desktop PC/monitor combo. It requires fewer parts to build; it's smaller and lighter and thus requires fewer resources to package and ship; and it uses less power and costs less to operate. The built-in keyboard and mouse give it a green advantage over buying those accessories separately.

Choose an appropriate monitor. Larger monitors with higher resolutions cost more and generally require more power. But some tasks are difficult to do without a large screen, such as working with large spreadsheets or editing images and video. Buy the size you need.

An LCD monitor is a greener choice than a CRT: LCDs require fewer parts than their bulky CRT counterparts and are more energy efficient in operation.

Look for the Energy Star label. Energy Star–branded PCs use at least 80 percent energy-efficient power supplies and operate efficiently in standby/off, sleep, and idle modes. They include power-management features. There are also Energy Star criteria for monitors.

Buy an EPEAT-rated computer. EPEAT (Electronic Product Environmental Assessment Tool) is an invaluable online resource for finding your perfect green desktop machines. Maintained by the Green Electronics Council, the registry contains a searchable listing of desktop computers, notebooks, and monitors that meet standards set by Energy Star as well as by RoHS, the European Union's Restriction on Hazardous Substances directive.

Know how to shop. Take advantage of information sources for the green computer of your dreams—among them, the Energy Star Web site, the EPEAT Web site, independent reviews from sources such as PCMag.com, and even your preferred vendor's Web site. Some vendors provide online resources to guide the purchase of eco-friendly machines.

EPAT

Searchable Registry of Green Computers

When shopping for a green computer or monitor, be sure to include a stop at the **Electronic Product Environmental Assessment Tool** (EPEAT) Web site. This searchable registry rates computers and monitors in bronze, silver, and gold categories and compares the electronics' greenness.

Bronze-rated products meet the minimum 23 required green criteria spelled out by the Green Electronics Council, the independent organization that manages EPEAT. Those criteria include compliance with Energy Star as well as with RoHS, the European Union's Restriction on Hazardous Substances directive. EPEAT-rated products must be built from a minimum of 65 percent reusable or recyclable materials, and the vendors must offer additional 3-year warranties for the products—which means the machines must be built to last.

EPEAT silver- and gold-rated products meet additional earth-friendly criteria, including the use of fewer hazardous materials than required by RoHS, easier-to-recycle packaging, and the availability of an alternative-energy power charger.

Be forewarned: You won't find much in the way of computer or monitor specs on the EPEAT site, so it's not well suited for comparing hardware features. But it's a great tool for creating a short list of computers or monitors to research further. (www.epeat.net)

MOIXA USBCELL BATTERIES

Cool, Flip-Top AA Batteries

Every year, 15 billion batteries get thrown away. Using rechargeable batteries spares the environment and, in the long run, your wallet. If you've got a computer with a spare USB port, along with an AA-powered device or two—camera, wireless mouse, laser pointer, or electric toothbrush—you might find uses for USBCell batteries from **Moixa**.

The Moixa USBCell batteries look like regular AAs, but you can flip their tops to reveal a USB plug. When they run out of juice, you simply plug them into a nearby USB outlet for a refill. Thus, if you happen to travel with your laptop and other electronics, you can simply leave your charger at home. Or bring the charger along, as these USB-Cells can be replenished with approved nickel-metal hydride (NiMH) chargers.

Convenience aside, the fact that they are NiMH batteries means they're more environmentally friendly than NiCAD models that contain cadmium, a hazardous substance. And they are recyclable.($17.50; www.usbcell.com)

SOLIO UNIVERSAL HYBRID CHARGERS

Sun Power to Juice Up an iPod

Nothing warms the heart quite like solar energy. Although solar panels might not be a viable option for your roof, on a smaller scale the sleek-looking **Solio** Classic Universal Hybrid charger works wonders for mobile devices, including most cell phones, iPods, PDAs, and other portable devices. Just let it bask in Mr. Sunshine's warming glow, and 1 hour of tanning time will generate 15 minutes of talk time on a cell phone or 40 minutes of music on an MP3 player. Fully charged, the Solio will recharge the average phone up to two times or deliver up to 15 hours of MP3 music. Weighing in at a mere 5.6 ounces, it's a pretty slim gadget, too, which makes for convenient portability. It even comes with a handy suction cup so you can affix it to a window for charging.

List price for the Solio Classic Universal Hybrid charger is $99.95; it comes in three colors: white, black, and silver. A lower-end model, the Solio Hybrid 1000, lists for $79.95. (www.solio.com/charger)

FYI

It is widely believed that turning a computer off between uses can cause the system harm. That's not true: Turning a computer on and off has no detrimental effects over the lifetime of the equipment. And of course, it saves energy when you turn off your computer.

HP TOUCHSMART SERIES

The Best of Both Computing Worlds

Looking for the large-display advantages of a desktop computer while reaping the environmental goodness of a laptop? Consider the HP TouchSmart series. Requiring only one cord to power it, the HP TouchSmart PCs combine a high-definition widescreen display with a powerful, energy-efficient Intel Core 2 Duo processor.

"TouchSmart" refers to the HP software designed specifically for *touch*: A finger tapped on or swept across the high-resolution screen delivers quick access to information, entertainment, and social networks. Without using a keyboard or mouse, you can play music and create playlists, zoom in or out of photos, and quickly check the weather or even watch TV.

The green advantages are many: TouchSmart uses 55 percent less metal and 37 percent less plastic than standard PCs and monitors. HP's power management technology provides up to 45 percent energy savings compared to PCs without it. Overall, the systems comply with the RoHS directive and have earned a silver rating from EPEAT.

The TouchSmart machines are available with two display sizes: 22 inches and 25.5 inches. The machines have a minimum 4 GB of memory; a large-capacity, high-speed hard drive; a wireless keyboard and integrated wireless local area network(WLAN); and HP Ambient Light to set a mood and illuminate the keyboard. (from $1,299; www.hp.com)

Consider purchasing an all-in-one system, also known as a multifunction printer or MFP. Many models are capable of scanning photos, copying documents, and faxing. Instead of having three or four bulky machines with separate power supplies, you will have a single machine that does it all—better for your power bills.

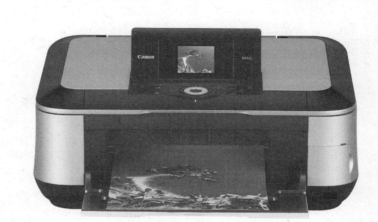

CANON MP620 ALL-IN-ONE PHOTO PRINTER

Saves Power, Cuts Waste

In the world of green electronics, all-in-one systems outshine their one-use brethren. The reason? Each additional machine draws that much more electricity. At the end of their life spans, that many more pieces of e-waste must be disposed of. The Canon MP620 all-in-one photo printer is one splendid solution: It does the work of a printer, a scanner, and a copier with a lone power cord.

Canon has made its MP620 a relatively green machine: It is Energy Star compliant and uses 91 percent less power than its predecessor, the MP760. It offers a paper-saving option: Four-in-one and two-in-one printing features allow users to print multiple pages on a single sheet. Moreover, the MP620 complies with the European Union's RoHS directive, meaning it restricts the use of cadmium, mercury, lead, hexavalent chromium, and other hazardous materials. And the machines are shipped with reduced packaging.

The MP620's five-color ink system is designed to ensure vivid colors and bold, black text. It produces long-lasting 4- by 6-inch photos with impressive 9600 x 2400 color dpi resolution in about 41 seconds. Scans yield 2400 x 4800 color dpi results.

Its wireless functionality means you can print to it from anywhere in the house—or even print without a computer: Photos can be printed directly from memory cards, previewing and enhancing images on the 2.5-inch TFT (thin-film transistor) display. Or print from a compatible digital camera—even from a camera phone. (list price $149.99; www.usa .canon.com)

ETON AMERICAN RED CROSS RADIOS

Tough Radios for Camping and Emergencies

Whether roughing it on a camping trip, upgrading your home's emergency preparedness plan, or just seeking a cool green radio, consider tuning in to the American Red Cross (ARC) **Etón** FR150 Microlink or FR500 Solarlink portable radios.

The ARC FR150 Microlink sports a built-in solar panel, making it a snap to charge up with sunshine. It also includes a hand crank for manually powering up the system's NiMH battery. The device can be charged via a separate USB cord as well.

In terms of features, the radio provides access to the FM, AM, and weather bands. You can also tune in FCC and EAS public alert systems. The device can easily be held in one hand to double as a flashlight and a cell phone charger. A useful bonus: Each radio includes American Red Cross disaster preparedness tips.

For a heftier, feature-rich alternative to the Microlink, check out the ARC FR500 Solarlink. It functions as an AM, FM, and shortwave radio with NOAA weatherband. It has a cell phone charger, a flashlight, an emergency beacon, even an emergency siren. Power source choices? Sunlight, hand cranking, an AC adapter, or AA batteries. (ARC FR150 Microlink $29.99, ARC FR500 Solarlink $79.99; www.eton corp.com)

VERDIEM EDISON

Manage Your PC's Power Consumption

The best things in life are free, and some things can even save you money while reducing your carbon footprint. Verdiem Edison is a prime example: This freely downloadable software is designed to power down your computer and monitor automatically when it's not in use. That can save you as much as $75 per year.

Installing the software is easy, as is setting up Edison to power down your equipment when it hasn't been used for a predetermined amount of time. Choose either preset guidelines suggested by Edison or enter time periods yourself. For example, choose to turn off your monitor and power down your hard drive after 5 minutes, 10 minutes, or a half hour, then put your PC into suspend mode after 30 minutes, 45 minutes, 2 hours—or never. It takes longer to resume your computer from suspend mode than it does to wake up powered-down hard drives. But suspend mode saves more energy.

You can also tell Edison your work and nonwork hours and have it power down according to your schedule. An added bonus: Edison estimates how much money, energy, and CO_2 you save by putting your monitor and PC to rest, so you can actually watch your green savings add up. (www.verdiem.com/edison)

ANYCOM SOLAR CAR-KIT

Bluetooth Device for Greener Driving

Holding a cell phone in your hand and talking while driving is downright dangerous (and illegal in some states!), which makes hands-free Bluetooth-powered alternatives a smart idea. Even smarter: a hands-free Bluetooth product that runs on solar energy. The ANYCOM Solar Car-Kit fits that bill splendidly.

The ANYCOM Solar Car-Kit easily affixes to a windshield with suction cups, enabling hands-free cell phone conversations. Its rechargeable lithium-polymer battery provides up to 15 hours of talk time. And it boasts a high-performance solar panel on the back to sunpower your calls. Three hours of charging can provide 30 minutes of talk time.

The device comes equipped with call-management features such as voice dial, last number redial, hold, mute, and three-way calling. Its digital signal processor filters the surrounding noise and can reduce the echo of your own voice. A powerful 95-decibel speaker delivers a loud and clear signal—a boon when dealing with loud driving noises. (from $56.99; www.anycom.com)

IQUA 603 SUN BLUETOOTH HEADSET

An Off-the-Grid Headset

Whether driving, cooking, or juggling, being able to talk on a cell phone using a hands-free headset is the way to go. And what better way to add to that convenience than by using an off-the-grid headset?

The Iqua 603 Sun Bluetooth headset is the first solar-powered Bluetooth headset in the world. This wireless device has a photovoltaic cell that uses any available light—outdoors and indoors—to charge itself and extend its operation times. The 603 Sun offers about 12 hours of phone time with a standard charge, but using sunshine or artificial light extends that time.

The headset offers all the usual features for answering or ending calls, including redial and voice dial, as well as the ability to switch a call between your phone and headset with the push of a button. There's also a volume rocker to adjust the loudness. Optional accessories for the 603 Sun include an ear hook, which some users find more comfortable than the standard earbud. (headset $99.99; www.iqua.com)

LENOVO THINKVISION L2440X WIDE

High Efficiency, Reduced Hazmats

Monitors can be power hogs, and many aren't built in environmentally responsible ways. One exception is the Lenovo ThinkVision L2440x Wide 24-inch LCD monitor.

With a gold rating on EPEAT, it is Energy Star compliant and meets the RoHS directive. It has also passed GreenGuard testing for more than 2,000 chemical emissions, such as carcinogens, allergens, and irritants. The ThinkVision draws just 29 watts of electricity—about 60 percent less power than conventional models. As Lenovo's first low-halogen product, it is also mercury free and arsenic free. The L2440x contains 28 percent postconsumer recycled content in its plastic parts. And the company uses 65 percent recycled packaging materials for it.

In terms of specs, the system supports 1920 x 1200p resolution, contrast ratios of up to 1000:1, and 5-millisecond response time. It features a USB 2.0 hub as well as a DisplayPort input, which offers superior digital display.

Also in the eco-friendly ThinkVision family are models ranging from 17 inches to 24 inches, including the L1700p, L1940 Wide, L1940p Wide, and L2240p Wide. According to ThinkVision, the entire line now consumes 30 to 60 percent less energy than older ThinkVision models. (Lenovo ThinkVision L2440x Wide from $469.99; shop.lenovo.com/us/accessories/monitors)

WATTS UP? PRO

Tracking the Energy Hogs

Curious to know how much juice that PC, monitor, refrigerator, or coffeemaker is consuming? Plug it into Watts Up? Pro, and this handy meter will log the energy-usage data at intervals from 1 second to 1 day. You can easily see how many watts of energy an electrical device uses, how much its operation costs in dollars and cents, plus more than a dozen other data points. Watts Up? Pro can store up to 8,000 records and transfer those data to your PC, where you can track trends using the included management software.

The uses for this meter are many, from tracking down power hogs such as old fridges or CRT monitors to measuring the savings from new Energy Star appliances.

The Watts Up? Pro is listed at $130.95. The Watts Up?, which doesn't include management software, costs $95.95. (www.wattsupmeters.com)

FYI

In the market for a new electronic device? Make sure the product bears the Energy Star emblem. It indicates that the product is primed for energy efficiency, meaning you will reduce greenhouse gases while you save some cash.

Recycling Electronics

Electronic waste is a fast-growing problem in the United States. In 2007, discarded televisions, computers, peripherals (including printers, scanners, and faxes), mice, keyboards, and cell phones totaled about 2.5 million tons. That's almost 2 percent of the entire municipal solid-waste stream, according to the Environmental Protection Agency. That number is steadily increasing as technological innovation makes products obsolete more quickly.

Fortunately, recycling electronics needn't be difficult. Here are straightforward steps to follow and organizations that help ensure that unwanted devices are disposed of in a safe and eco-friendly manner.

First, consider reusing the device. Are you sure that computer or television has reached the end of its life? Can it be economically repaired or upgraded? Perhaps your computer is operating more slowly than it used to, or it crashes a lot. The problem might not lie with the hardware; it could be the software. The life expectancy of a computer is around 7 years, but the life span of software is generally only 3 years. So before you replace your computer, try using software-optimizing utilities to clean up your system.

If you can no longer use an electronic device, consider finding it a new home instead of discarding it. This approach reduces the amount of new materials in the waste stream. Plenty of organizations are willing to take a functional machine off your hands. The most appropriate end organization for your equipment might be a charity, a local school, or a materials exchange. Businesses might be able to reap a tax incentive for donating computer equipment, thanks to the 21st Century Classrooms Act.

Before donating electronics, make sure the equipment is still usable, and check the donation organization's minimum requirements. Some might not accept a system with an old processor or one that runs only Windows 95 or 98. The same might be true for outdated equipment like a dot-matrix printer.

If reusing, repairing, or donating your electronics isn't a realistic option, then it's time to turn to recycling. Many municipalities offer computer and electronics collections as part of household hazardous-waste collections. Alternatively, many electronics manufacturers now accept used household electronics for recycling. In some cases, these services are free, though you might have to pay for postage.

Other disposal options may include a county recycling drop-off center, a TV repair shop, an electronics recycling company, or even a local electronics retailer that collects used products and sends them to a recycler. Staples, Office Depot, and Radio Shack are among companies providing these services.

One useful resource for finding recyclers is www.mygreenelectronics.org, a Web site run by the Consumer Electronics Association. It identifies local recyclers based on ZIP codes. For recycling cell phones or batteries, check out the Rechargeable Battery Recycling Corporation Web site at www.rbrc.org. It has a searchable database of drop-off locations for organizations that provide recycling services.

FYI

Still using a bulky CRT (cathode-ray tube) monitor? Consider investing in a flat-panel LCD (liquid crystal display). LCDs are 66 percent more energy efficient than CRTs and are as much as 80 percent smaller in size and weight, thus requiring less fuel and packaging to ship. LCDs are lower intensity and have steadier light patterns, making them easier on the eyes.

PHILIPS ECO TV

Draws Less Energy Than a 100-Watt Bulb

Eco-minded TV fans rejoice. Philips offers the Eco TV, a beautiful 42-inch television that will appeal to green sensibilities. The Energy Star–compliant set's major green claim to fame is its amazingly low energy consumption: A dimmable backlight and power-saver mode can drive the power consumption of this TV down to 75 watts, comparable to a standard incandescent lightbulb. Moreover, it has a standby mode power consumption of just 0.15 watt.

Eco TV contains no lead and just trace amounts of mercury, and it complies with the EU RoHS directive. The packaging is made from a combination of recycled material and materials from sustainably managed forests.

The set boasts a full high-definition (HD), widescreen 1920 x 1080p display; a Pixel Plus 3 HD engine for sharp pictures; and a powerful, invisible sound system that blends with the design of the cabinet. It's also got four HDMI inputs for full digital HD connection with one cable.

The full product name for the Eco TV is the Philips 42PFL5603D/27 42-inch 1080p LCD HDTV, which you might need to use to find the item online. ($1,249.99; www.usa.philips.com)

VERS 2X IPOD SOUND SYSTEM

Crafted from Sustainable Wood

The Vers Audio 2X is a compact iPod docking sound system with two 3-inch speakers, yet it produces a rich, natural, full-range sound. Its 14-function remote gives a high degree of control over iPod menu and playlist navigation functions as well as standard audio functions.

There's a big difference between the Vers 2X and its rivals: Its wood casing is one of the most renewable of all resources. The eucalyptus and pine used for the system come from locally sourced and managed plantations; all harvested trees are replaced by new plantings. And the entire tree—trunk, roots, bark, branches, and even twigs—is utilized.

The Vers 2X is a power-sipper: Its class D amplifier runs at 50 to 90 percent energy efficiency, and its power adapters draw 30 percent less power than traditional designs. Adding to the system's green résumé is the fact that it complies with the European Union's Reduction of Hazardous Substances (RoHS) directive, meaning it contains no lead, mercury, cadmium, hexavalent chromium, or other toxic materials. And the Vers 2X system is designed for easy disassembly to simplify recycling.

Each system takes more than a week to build by hand. The Vers 2X is available in natural cherry, natural walnut, dark walnut, and bamboo. ($179.99; www.versaudio.com)

PLX KIWI

Aids in Fuel-Efficient Driving

Are you a green driver yet? Plenty of techniques can improve mileage, but if you're not schooled in them, worry not: The PLX Kiwi can train you to be the greenest driver you can be, improving your fuel efficiency by as much as 33 percent.

The PLX Kiwi is a small device with an OLED (organic light-emitting diode) screen that connects to your automobile's onboard diagnostic port, which is found in all modern cars. Kiwi measures vehicle speed, rpm, engine load, and other data to determine the vehicle's optimum driving efficiency. It then uses those data to provide you with ongoing feedback—in the form of a score—to show how economically you're driving at a given time. The higher your score (the highest being 100), the better you're doing. The Kiwi also monitors average and real-time fuel economy with its mpg meter.

The device offers a Drive Green mode that includes a series of lesson plans designed to teach better driving behavior, letting you work on skills to improve smoothness, drag, acceleration, and deceleration. An added bonus: Kiwi has an engine check scan tool, enabling it to identify the cause of engine trouble. ($299; www.plxkiwi.com)

A SNOOZE BUTTON FOR YOUR COMPUTER

Alarm clocks have snooze buttons. Why not computers? Even the most well-intentioned computer user can forget to power down a system between uses. The makers of ecobutton offer a clever solution in the form of a visual reminder: a large, illuminated button that plugs into your Windows-based machine's USB port.

When taking a short or long break from computing duties, simply press the button, and the ecobutton software puts the system into an energy-saving deep-sleep "ecomode." The company says that ecomode saves more watts than standard standby. Press the button again and the system blinks back to life instantly, ready to resume work or play wherever it stopped. The ecobutton software also automatically tracks how much carbon, power, and cash it saved. (from $28; www.eco-button.com)

SAMSUNG E200 ECO, W510, AND F268

Raising the Bar for Green Cell Phones

There's demand out there for green cellular phones, and Samsung is one vendor who's all ears. The company offers a trio of green phones, two of which are made from bioplastic, a substance containing natural materials extracted from such plants as corn.

E200 Eco has an external case made of bioplastic. According to Samsung, using 1 ton of bioplastic instead of petroleum-based polycarbonate reduces CO_2 production by 2.16 tons. The phone contains no lead, mercury, cadmium, hexavalent chromium, polybrominated biphenyl (PBB), or polybrominated diphenylethers (PBDEs).

The 9.9mm slim phone comes equipped with a rechargeable lithium-ion battery. It boasts a 1.3-megapixel camera, an MP3 player, video-messaging capabilities, texting, e-mail, and speakerphone functionality.

The bioplastic-cased W510, which also contains no heavy metals, includes a 3-megapixel camera; supports video telephony and sharing; and offers Web browsing, e-mail, texting, and instant messaging.

Samsung's F268 contains no BFRs (brominated flame retardants) or PVC; the same can be said for all its accessories, including charger and headset. An alarm function reminds users to unplug it when it's fully charged. It features a 2-megapixel camera, a video recorder and player, an MP3 player, e-mail, texting, and Web browsing. All Samsung phone adapters comply with Energy Star standards.

There's a drawback to all three phones: None is available in the United States—at least for now. The E200 Eco is marketed only in Europe, the W510 in Korea, and the F268 in China.

ENERGY STAR

Find the Most Energy-Efficient Products

Power efficiency is one of the trademarks of truly green electronic devices. The less energy a device consumes, the fewer greenhouse-gas emissions released. Reduced utility bills are nice additional benefits. But how to find which products are energy efficient? Check them out on the Energy Star Web site.

Energy Star offers searchable databases of electronic devices and appliances that comply with the Energy Star standards. Washers and dryers, refrigerators, battery chargers, televisions, DVD players, computers, monitors, dishwashers, air conditioners, all types of office equipment—the list goes on and on.

Beyond providing names and models of energy-efficient wares, the site offers shopping tips to help you decide which products can best meet your needs. Not sure whether you want progressive scan on your DVD player? An analog or a digital cordless phone? A plasma flat-screen or an LCD TV? The Energy Star site will break down your features and choices. It also offers tips for saving money on the appliances and electronics you already own. Don't miss the section for searching for rebates; vendors or local utility providers often offer cash back for purchasing Energy Star products.

Fittingly, the Energy Star Web site doesn't cost a penny to use. (www.energystar.gov)

FYI

Instead of throwing batteries in the trash, take them to a toxic waste disposal area or a local recycler. Discarded batteries produce most of the heavy metals—lead, arsenic, zinc, cadmium, copper, and mercury—found in household trash. In landfills, those hazardous metals can contaminate groundwater and eventually make their way into the food chain.

POWER CONSERVATION

"Mr. Electricity" to the Rescue

How much electricity does the average laptop use? What kind of lightbulb is best? How can you reduce your heating or cooling costs? These are the kinds of questions that get answered for free at Saving Electricity, a site maintained by "Mr. Electricity," Michael Bluejay.

Bluejay tackles a wide range of power-saving topics in a refreshingly straightforward manner, guiding viewers through subjects such as lighting a home more efficiently, investing in energy-saving water heaters, even cooking in more energy-efficient ways.

On the site's home page, Bluejay outlines 10 simple investments that can shave upward of $2,300 per year off utility bills. Here's a sampling: Use space heaters to heat rooms instead of turning on the central heating system (saves $1,152 per year) or invest in ceiling fans instead of cranking on the air-conditioning (saves more than $600 per year). A handy calculator helps estimate how much it costs each year to power various appliances around the house. The Saving Electricity site is completely free—and free of those annoying pop-up ads! (http://michaelbluejay.com/electricity)

PCMAG.COM: UNBIASED REVIEWS OF GREEN MACHINES

Given the speed of advancements in technology, it's tough to keep track of the newest machines on the market. Finding the latest green machines can be even more difficult, because most computer magazines and Web sites don't give eco-friendliness much weight. Fortunately, there is one solid, unbiased source of information about the newest green machines on the market: the *PC Magazine* Web site.

PCMag.com provides in-depth reviews of and ratings for a wealth of desktop and laptop systems that take green criteria into account. Reviewers consider energy efficiency, recyclability, certifications, and all-important performance. Machines that hit a high green mark earn PCMag.com's GreenTech–approved seal. PCMag.com also looks at green gadgets and eco-friendly machines for the business world, with plenty of tips, facts, and advice to help you be greener in your work. Jump directly to the GreenTech coverage at http://go.pcmag.com/greentech.

Local Electronic Recyclers Database

Earth 911 has a noble goal: to deliver actionable local information on recycling and product stewardship, empowering consumers to live responsibly, act locally, and support sustainability.

The organization's Web site offers a rich, easily searchable database of recyclers throughout the country. Simply type in what sorts of items you want to recycle—from car batteries and used motor oil to toys and mobile phones—then enter your ZIP code or city and state. Click Go and you'll get a list of local recyclers who can properly dispose of your selected waste, with the address and phone number of each provider, as well as links to more details about the recycling services each offers. The site includes the recycler's hours of operation, a Web site address (when applicable), and a location map.

The Earth 911 site provides information about other earth-friendly topics, including shopping green, handling household hazardous waste, taking care of your car in an environmentally responsible manner, and composting. (http://earth911.com)

STAPLES ECOEASY

One-Stop Drop-Off for E-Waste Recycling

Old, unwanted computing gear—laptops, computers, monitors, printers, or fax machines—has a knack for piling up in the back of closets. If this sounds familiar, and if you're looking for a way to dispose of your e-waste responsibly, consider hauling it to your local **Staples** to take advantage of their EcoEasy technology recycling program. No matter what brand it is or where you bought it, Staples will pack and ship off unwanted electronics for proper recycling. The cost is 10 bucks per machine. They'll accept related peripherals such as mice, speakers, keyboards, and modems for free.

All gear is delivered to Staples's recycling provider, Eco International. The company uses industry-leading standards for data destruction to ensure your systems are purged of any personal information. The company then disassembles the equipment into its component parts—within the United States—for environmentally responsible recycling.

Staples will also take cell phones or PDAs for free recycling/refurbishing. The company has partnered with a nonprofit called Collective Good, which makes low-cost, refurbished phones available in developing nations. Moreover, Staples will give you $3 in Staples rewards for future ink purchases each time you recycle ink cartridges from Lexmark, HP, or Dell. (www.staples.com/ecoeasy)

GAZELLE

Recycle—And Get Paid!

Recycling unwanted electronic devices is rewarding in and of itself because it's good for our environment, right? But wait, there's more. When it comes time to discard an old cell phone, PDA, or video-game console, you can get some money back. If that sounds appealing, head on over to the **Gazelle** Web site, where you can arrange to ship electronics to them and in exchange be rewarded with monetary compensation via PayPal or check. Or have that payment donated to charity.

Here's how this free service works: Enter the name and model number of the item you want to unload. The company accepts cell phones, MP3 players, digital cameras, laptops, GPS devices, gaming consoles, camcorders, satellite radios, and portable hard drives. Fill out a simple form describing the condition of the electronic device and noting whether you still have the packaging, manual, and accessories. Based on that information, Gazelle will make you an offer for your item and display a graph showing the market value of the device you're looking to sell.

If you choose to accept Gazelle's offer, you log in to their site, and Gazelle will mail you a postage-paid shipping box so you can package your device and ship it to them. At their end, Gazelle will check that the item is in the condition you described. If so, you'll receive your payment in short order. If not, the company will alert you to their reduced offer. You can choose to proceed with the sale or to have the item sent back.

What does Gazelle do with your unwanted electronics? If they are in working condition, the company extends their life by removing all personal data and selling them through retail and wholesale outlets. Items without market value are recycled responsibly. (www.gazelle.com)

REDUCE UNWANTED SNAIL MAIL

If your daily mail pile includes unwanted catalogs, there's an easy, online way to reduce your daily delivery of paper waste: a free Web site called Catalog Choice.

A project of the Ecology Center, Catalog Choice is a one-stop location for unsubscribing from hundreds of retailers' mailing lists. Simply set up an account, then browse the searchable list of merchants whose mail you no longer wish to receive. Select the merchants, fill out your name and address, and you're done.

The site lists some merchants that do not honor requests submitted via Catalog Choice. In those cases, Catalog Choice will attempt to unsubscribe you but will also provide a phone number to call so you can unsubscribe directly. All personal information remains private, as Catalog Choice does not sell, rent, or otherwise share your contact details. As a nice added feature, Catalog Choice lists online catalogs so you can browse for goods without harming any trees. (www.catalog choice.org)

CARBON FOOTPRINT CALCULATORS

Get a Handle on Your Carbon Shoe Size

As the old adage goes, "You can't manage what you can't measure." So, if you don't know how much carbon dioxide you're responsible for emitting, how can you intelligently go about shrinking your carbon footprint? Fortunately, there are plenty of free carbon calculators available on the Internet, and one of the best is the Berkeley Institute of the Environment's Lifecycle Climate Footprint Calculator.

The calculator is pretty straightforward: You input data via drop-down menus and free-text fields, such as what state and region you live in, how many people are in your household, how much you drive and fly each year, how much you spend on various utilities per month, and what you spend per month on various household items, services, and food.

Based on all of those data, the calculator delivers colorful graphs and charts with such information as how many tons of CO_2 you release per year and how your rate compares with others throughout the world. (http://bie.berkeley .edu/calculator)

If you live outside the United States or you want to try out a different calculator, consider Carbon Footprint Ltd.'s Web site. While it doesn't take into account factors such as your income or your region, it supports users of any country, and in some ways, it's easier to use. For example, rather than asking how much you spend on particular goods or services, it asks about your lifestyle, such as what sort of diet you maintain (vegetarian, only fish, omnivorous), what you recycle, and other more general questions. (http://www.carbonfootprint.com/calculator.aspx)

FYI

Consumer electronics and computers account for approximately 15 percent of household energy consumption—a percentage that's expected to increase in coming years.

AISO.NET

Solar-Powered Web Hosting

Looking for a green place to park your personal or business Web site? Consider the services of AISO. In business since 1997, the company has a 100 percent solar-powered datacenter facility located in the inland desert of Southern California. Its solar panels soak up the sun year-round. By day, the company's Web servers feed directly off the site's 120 solar panels. By night, the servers are powered by batteries that store the excess solar energy. Even AISO's Web servers are energy efficient, using 60 percent less energy and generating 50 percent less heat than the average server.

Reliability of solar power is not an issue. If there's not enough sun for an extended period, AISO has a backup: a generator that runs on propane. Adding to their green credentials, AISO recently added a green roof—essentially a layer of soil and vegetation atop the building—that reduces cooling and heating requirements by up to 50 percent.

This award-winning company offers many competitively priced services, including personal and business Web hosting, colocation (where they'll host your personal Web server for you), e-mail, and mailing-list management. (www.aiso.net)

We live off the land, but it's hard for us to see how we do it. The chains of supply are long and convoluted, and the land and water on which we depend are over the horizon, out of sight, invisible. Most of our food, conveniently processed, is from grocery stores, so distant from the plants and animals that provide it that we need government-approved package labels to tell us about it. We live and work in buildings made of lumber and concrete and glass, not trees and stone and sand. The fuel that lights and heats our homes is from underground pipes and overhead wires, so far removed from its source that we don't know, except in the most abstract way, where it comes from or how it gets here.

Those long supply chains have great benefits but also great costs, and we pay. We pay in money and energy, in damage to our environment, and in the loss of a conscious connection to the things that make our lives possible. This chapter is about some ways to reestablish that connection with wildlife, woods, and water and to limit some of the costs.

Our relationship with wildlife, however remote and tenuous, has matured in the past century as we have slowly grown away from the notion that wild things need to be dominated or suppressed. Bird-watching is one of the most popular outdoor activities in North America, and it has been both a harbinger and a pioneer in the environmental movement. No other pastime has had such a dramatic effect on the way in which we see and preserve the natural environment. Our recognition that wildlife conservation requires international cooperation grew out of concern for migratory birds, and the enactment of treaties to protect them. Our understanding of how harmful chemicals accumulate and persist in the environment was forged in the fight to preserve birds by banning DDT. Even our grasp of the astonishing diversity of life has intellectual roots in the field guides used by bird-watchers. Birds and bird-watching have earned their place in this chapter, which recommends birding supplies as well as citizen-science projects that are fun and critically important to our knowledge of wildlife.

For more than a century, forestry in North America has been the nearly exclusive province of professional foresters and forestry companies. For the rest of us, however, there is one aspect of forestry work that remains in our hands: firewood. And with the increasing environmental, financial, and political cost of fossil fuels, firewood burned in modern, low-emission woodstoves is an affordable, renewable, carbon-neutral source of energy for our homes. In this chapter, you'll find recommendations for sources of firewood and for the tools you'll need to harvest and process this wood for home use, as well as for products that make working in the woods safer and easier.

Boats connect us to the outdoors in a remarkable way, almost but not quite immersing us in the stuff that covers most of the planet and makes life possible. They're useful and fun, but they're also tough on the environment. Wastes dumped from boats foul the water, the by-products of boat propulsion foul the water, the hulls and hull coatings that make boats float foul the water. Boaters know it, and the industry that supports them has made great progress in the past 30 years to put boats more gently on our waterways. You'll find some recommendations here for boating products that advance the cause.

The field sports—hunting and fishing—have in recent decades developed an uneasy relationship with environmentalism, but it shouldn't be so. Through their tax dollars and advocacy organizations, hunters and anglers are the source of most of the money and human energy spent on wildlife and habitat conservation. Without wildlands and clean water, there would be no hunting or fishing, and sportsmen and sportswomen are key players and natural allies in the struggle to preserve wilderness and wildlife. Anglers and hunters today have many new products to help make their sports cleaner for the environment, and this chapter highlights a few of them. It also looks briefly at a few ways in which anglers and hunters can help the environment through habitat improvement and the control of invasive species.

Let's get outdoors.

—Jeff Serena

WILD WINGS ORGANIC WILD BIRD FOODS

Birdseed That's Really for the Birds

Birdseed is a big industry, accounting annually for more than $2.5 billion in sales in the United States alone. Most of that seed is produced by industrial agriculture methods and carries some environmental baggage. Predictably, pesticides and other agricultural chemicals are part of that baggage. And this fact runs straight into a predicament. Since the publication of Rachel Carson's *Silent Spring* nearly 50 years ago, we've known that pesticides damage bird populations. A widely cited study of the environmental and economic costs of pesticide use, published in *BioScience* in 1992, estimated that agricultural pesticides alone kill 67 million birds each year in the United States. Poisoned bird bait, chemical bird repellents, and herbicides (to reduce bird breeding habitat) are commonly used to reduce bird damage to sunflower fields. The irony here is awfully thick: We're killing wild birds to help improve the yield of seed crops, some of which are then harvested and sold to feed to wild birds. It doesn't help that the birdseed industry has shown so little interest in changing the situation.

Wild Wings Organic Wild Bird Foods helps us out of this predicament by offering USDA-certified-organic birdseed products. Founded by veterinarian and avian health specialist Dr. Gary Harrison, Wild Wings is an offshoot of his Harrison's Bird Foods business, which specializes in high-quality, organic foods for pet birds. Wild Wings products include black oil sunflower, safflower, hemp seed, gray millet, nyjer seed, and peanuts, as well as seed mixes with whimsical names like Feeder Frenzy and No-Filler Bird-Thriller. They're not inexpensive, and they will likely cost more than the nonorganic (and generally much poorer quality) birdseed sold at your local grocery store, but they're an environmentally responsible solution to the problems posed by big-agriculture birdseed. (www.wildwingsorganic.com)

RUBICON INTERNATIONAL BIRDFEEDERS

Better for Birds

Heavy-duty plastic birdfeeders and birdhouses have distinct advantages over old-fashioned wooden ones: They don't split or rot, they're stain resistant, they require no repainting, and they're easy to clean. In short, they're more sanitary for the wild birds that feed on them. Rubicon International, a company in Tyler, Texas, has made the plastic feeder even greener. Their plastic birdfeeders and birdhouses are constructed almost entirely of polylumber, a building material made from postconsumer plastic bottles.

Founded in 1996, Rubicon offers a wide range of products, including 22 different styles of birdfeeders, five birdhouses, and a bat house, available in subtle greens and earth colors. The construction is top quality, with exterior-grade screws employed, wherever possible, in place of nails, and heat bonding used for added strength. All of the company's products are covered by an unconditional lifetime guarantee. The wren house and the small seed feeder are available as kits, and Rubicon company president Bill Farrar recommends them as great nature projects for kids. (www.rubiconinternationaltx.com)

Building Shelter for Birds

Providing housing for wild birds has its roots in colonial times. More than 80 species of birds that reside in the United States and Canada—from various ducks and owls to some species of wrens and all woodpeckers—nest in holes that occur naturally or are excavated in trees. Habitat loss is a significant threat to many of these species. Fortunately, most of them will happily take up residence in artificial nesting boxes. In fact, the purple martin of eastern North America depends almost entirely on nesting boxes, and the wood duck and eastern bluebird have both been brought back from the threat of extinction in substantial part by volunteer efforts to provide nesting boxes in appropriate habitats. Nesting boxes, also called birdhouses, are widely available from general and specialty stores and online retailers. You can also build excellent birdhouses with untreated lumber and a very modest set of hand tools. There are free birdhouse plans available on the Internet at www.craftybirds.com and www.freebirdhouseplans.net. **Ducks Unlimited** has plans for a specialized wood duck nesting box at www.ducks.org/Conservation/WaterfowlBiology/2716/WoodDuckBoxes.html.

10 Tips on Feeding the Birds

About 50 million Americans feed wild birds. It's a great hobby, bringing birds into our yards and our lives and getting us a little bit closer to nature. And there's little doubt that feeding has broadened the range of some songbirds, like the northern cardinal and Carolina wren, and that feeding helps birds through cold winters, when their need for food is high and availability is low. But there are some possible downsides. Poorly maintained feeders may help to spread avian diseases such as house finch disease (mycoplasmal conjunctivitis), which afflicts eastern house finch populations and some other songbirds. Moldy or rancid birdseed, suet, or hummingbird nectar can sicken birds that feed on it. Feeders attract house cats and other predators that kill birds. And putting feeders around our homes increases the likelihood that birds will be killed by flying into windows and glass doors.

Here are 10 things you can do to make feeding less dangerous for the birds that come to your feeder.

1. Store your birdseed in a cool, dry place indoors. Keeping your seed in a clean container with a tight-fitting lid will also keep house mice at bay.

2. Store suet in your freezer to prevent spoilage.

3. Store hummingbird nectar in your refrigerator, and don't make up more than you will use in a week.

4. Build or purchase feeders made of plastic or metal, which are easier to clean than wooden feeders.

5. Thoroughly wash your seed feeder twice a month and your hummingbird feeder every time you fill it. Many small, plastic feeders can be efficiently washed and sanitized in your dishwasher.

6. To reduce window collisions, locate feeders either very close to your house (within 3 feet) or well away from your house (30 feet or more).

7. Place yard feeders in the open (about 10 feet from the nearest heavy cover) so the birds can see approaching house cats, or use garden border fencing around your feeder to deter felines.

8. If you see sick or dead birds near your feeder, disinfect your feeders and stop feeding for a few weeks to allow healthy birds to disperse.

9. Don't use insecticides, such as wasp and ant sprays, near hummingbird feeders.

10. Relocate seed feeders when the ground beneath them becomes covered with seed hulls and bird droppings.

NIKON MONARCH ATB 8 X 42 BINOCULAR

Best Value in Birding Optics

Sports optics have made great strides since the 1990s, and the absolute proof is the Monarch ATB 8 x 42 binocular from Japanese optics giant Nikon. Its combination of superb optics; top-quality lens coatings; lightweight, ergonomic design; rugged construction; and affordability may make it the best binocular *ever* for birders looking for excellent value and top performance. The Monarch ATB 8 x 42 (that's 8× magnification with 42 mm objective lenses) sports a lightweight, roof-prism design and weighs in at just over 21 ounces. Its field of view is 330 feet at 1,000 yards. It's good for eyeglass wearers, with eye relief of almost 20 mm. The "ATB" in the name stands for "all-terrain binocular," and the Monarch lives up to the name: It's waterproof and fogproof and has hard rubber armor to absorb shocks. The warranty is outstanding: 25 years, no-fault, repair or replacement, against defects or accidents of any kind, for a flat $10 fee. This is a perfect binocular for general bird-watching and wildlife viewing.

Nikon is a world leader in corporate social and environmental responsibility. It established its first antipollution corporate office in 1970 and in 1992 implemented a cutting-edge corporate environmental management policy. Nikon is an active participant in the UN's Global Compact, which supports 10 basic principles of ethical behavior in human rights, labor, the environment, and anticorruption. And it has been an industry leader in the use of lead-free solders, hexavalent-chrome-free surface treatments, and Eco-Glass, the lead-free and arsenic-free optical glass that is used in the Monarch's top-quality optical lenses. (www.nikon.com)

SIBLEY FIELD GUIDES
The Portable Authority

In 1934, Roger Tory Peterson published *A Field Guide to the Birds*, and it changed the way we see nature. That little book, in its various and steadily improved editions, and the battery of Peterson field guides that it spawned, created a window through which the interested layperson could see the diversity of the natural world.

Three-quarters of a century later, bird-watchers in the United States and Canada are blessed with dozens of fine and useful guidebooks to birds. Of these, the best portable field guides available today are David Sibley's twin volumes, *The Sibley Field Guide to Birds of Eastern North America* and *The Sibley Field Guide to Birds of Western North America*, the first covering the continent east of the Rocky Mountains, and the latter covering the West. The books weigh in at just over a pound each, and they're published in a small trim size that fits conveniently into a shoulder bag or an empty binocular case. A tough, sewn, turtleback binding and high-quality paper make each book durable even with hard use in the field.

Good illustrations are at the heart of any field guide, and in this regard Sibley's field guides excel. Artfully rendered and with just the right amount of detail, his paintings strike a nice balance between simplicity and lifelike quality. Multiple illustrations are used to show birds in various plumages and to depict birds both when perched and in flight. Short, informative species write-ups describe each bird's typical habitat, highlight key physical and behavioral attributes, and describe typical vocalizations, including flight calls. Small range maps show the distribution of each species through the seasons.

The Sibley field guides are indispensable tools for amateur birders and professional ornithologists alike. (www.sibleyguides.com)

EBIRD
Birding on the Computer

Launched in 2002 as a cooperative project of the Cornell Lab of Ornithology and the National Audubon Society, with support from the National Science Foundation, eBird provides a way to record your observations of birds in a computer database that is used by professional ornithologists and amateur bird-watchers to monitor bird populations and movements across the Americas.

eBird replaces the dog-eared birder's checklist with a sophisticated program that allows you to create weekly, monthly, and yearly summaries of your own observations. You can create maps and tabular reports of all bird observations from the database, searching by date, range, and location (a county, state, user-created birding "hotspot," or American Birding Association Bird Conservation Region). You can also generate maps showing the distribution and frequency of bird species.

eBird is citizen science at its best, linking professionals and amateurs in a real-time, information-sharing network, and giving everyone immediate access to the data with a variety of summary and statistical tools. Since its inception, some 35,000 bird-watchers have submitted 1.6 million birding checklists to eBird, covering over a half million locations. Available in English, Spanish, and French, eBird is remarkably easy to use—and it's free. Sign up online to participate in eBird at http://ebird.org/content/ebird.

Volunteers for Wildlife

Citizen science is the participation of volunteers, most with little or no scientific training, in scientific research. It allows researchers to harness the observations and labor of the general public, while helping the public to understand the work of the scientific community. Most citizen science today supports research about wildlife and the environment—and is easy and fun.

The **Christmas Bird Count** (CBC) is the granddaddy of citizen science projects, and its founding provides a lesson in the evolution of environmental responsibility in North America. The "side hunt" was once a Christmas tradition in many parts of the United States and Canada. In a side hunt, participants formed teams, or sides, that would go afield with sporting arms on Christmas Day to shoot as many wild animals as they could. The side that killed the most animals, feathered and furred, was the winner. In 1900, Frank Chapman, an ornithologist at the American Museum of Natural History and an activist in the nascent Audubon Society movement, proposed an alternative to the side hunt. Teams would go afield on Christmas Day, but instead of shooting animals, they would count wild birds. And so the annual CBC was born.

That first CBC had 27 participants in the United States and Canada who counted birds in 25 locations. Today, participants number in the tens of thousands and count birds in more than 2,100 locations from Alaska to Argentina. Here's how it works: Teams of at least 10 individuals, including a compiler who keeps the team's count, select locations in which to count birds. Each team's location is circumscribed by a 15-mile-diameter circle on the map. Each team counts birds in its circle on 1 day during the period from December 14 to January 5. The compiler for each team reports the numbers and species of birds to the Audubon Society's CBC headquarters, where the counts are compiled. Results are summarized in the annual *American Birds* (a copy is sent to each participant), and the data are made available for study. Professional ornithologists use CBC information to assess changes in the range and populations of North American birds.

You don't have to be an expert birder to participate. Novices are teamed up with experienced birders. A $5 entry fee helps defray the cost of compiling and publishing the CBC results.

To learn more about participating in the CBC, go to www.audubon.org/bird/cbc/getinvolved.html in November or early December to find links to local compilers. Or get in touch with your local Audubon Society chapter, which you can find using the search tool at www.audubon.org/states/index.php.

FOR PROS AND AMATEURS ALIKE

Project FeederWatch is an annual winter survey of birds that visit some of the more than 50 million birdfeeders in the United States and Canada. A joint project of the Cornell Lab of Ornithology and Bird Studies Canada, the project asks volunteers to count the number and species of birds at their feeders on a few days each month from November to April. Anyone with an interest in birds, regardless of birding experience, can participate, and it's a fun activity for families and schools.

Ornithologists use the observations submitted by FeederWatch participants to track winter bird movements and populations. The cost is $15 per year in the USA, $35 in Canada. Participants receive a kit that contains instructions, a bird-identification poster, a calendar, a guide to feeding wild birds, a quarterly newsletter, and the project's annual report. You can join Project FeederWatch by signing up at the Web site, www.feederwatch.org.

FYI

Regular cleaning of birdfeeders is a real chore, and the chlorine bleach solutions often recommended for the task are definitely not green. Many feeders made from metal and plastic can be quickly brushed to remove seeds and droppings, then cleaned in your dishwasher.

Firewood Permits

You don't have to own a big woodlot or clear-cut your backyard to get your own firewood. National and state forests and parks, forests managed by the Bureau of Land Management, and many public utility companies issue firewood-cutting permits, usually at a very low cost—as little as 10 bucks a year in some western forests. In woodlands that are managed for high-value saw timber for the lumber industry, you will typically be assigned a woodlot in which damaged, diseased, and other low-value trees are marked by the agency's forester for firewood cutting. In other places, you may receive a permit to cut in a particular area of the forest, with relatively few restrictions on which trees you can take. You'll usually have a limit on the amount of wood you can cut with a single permit (5 cords is pretty typical), and permits can often be renewed from year to year. A quick phone call to the office of the nearest public land agency may be all that's needed to get you on the road to firewood self-sufficiency.

A recent trend in the management of public forestlands is to encourage firewood cutting or collecting as a way to help solve specific management problems, such as limiting the spread of tree pests or reducing the threat of catastrophic wildfires. Agencies will sometimes offer free permits to the public to remove unwanted trees. As an added bonus, these free permits are often issued for trees that have already been felled and sometimes limbed and cut into rounds. Free permits are usually available for only a short time (often in the early fall) and on a first-come, first-served basis, so call your local public land agency in the summer to see if they are planning to offer free firewood. Also, check online for press releases announcing free-firewood programs.

FYI

For a quick course on chain-saw operation, maintenance, and safety, Stihl has a terrific five-part video that can be viewed online at http://stihldealer.net/video library. It's also available in DVD format in English or Spanish for just $4.99 by calling 800-732-0054.

HOMEOWNER CHAIN SAWS
Choose Carefully

If you're a current or prospective woodstove owner who enjoys burning sustainable, energy-efficient wood fuel, a good chain saw is a must-have piece of equipment. Stihl, Echo, and Husqvarna make chain saws with fine reputations for quality, durability, and safety features, and they all support their products through networks of local dealers. In addition, all three companies are making continual progress in improving their saws' efficiency and reducing hydrocarbon emissions. For home woodcutting, here are a few models you might want to consider:

The Stihl MS 250 is a real workhorse—a reliable, high-performance chain saw with an excellent power-to-weight ratio. The saw comes with either a 16- or 18-inch bar, puts out 3.0 horsepower from a 45.5 cc engine displacement, and weighs just 10.1 pounds. The MS 250 retails for about $320. The MS 250 C-BE, a version with an easy-start system, is available for about $40 more. Stihl has a network of more than 8,000 US and 1,000 Canadian authorized dealers providing parts and service. (www.stihlusa.com)

Echo makes fine chain saws that are generally well regarded by their owners. A recent addition to the line, the Echo CS-400 weighs 10.1 pounds with a 40.2 cc engine and comes standard with an 18-inch bar. The saw offers some state-of-the-art technology. First, air is precleaned before entering the air filter by means of a mechanical feature that spins dust and dirt away from the filter. The air filter itself is a pleated, automotive-type filter that promises much better filtering than the single-layer fabric filters that are found on most competitors' saws. The CS-400 also comes standard with an easy-start system. It retails for about $300 and is available from authorized Echo dealers. (www.echo-usa.com)

A popular, high-quality chain saw from a top manufacturer, the Husqvarna 445 has an engine that displaces 45.7 cc and has a power output of 2.8 horsepower. You can use it with chain-saw bars ranging in length from 13 to 20 inches. It weighs 10.7 pounds and retails for about $320. The 445 is sold through Husqvarna's network of authorized dealers and through Lowe's home improvement stores. (www.usa.husqvarna.com)

YOUNGSTOWN CUT-RESISTANT GLOVES

Protecting Your Hands in Forestry Work

Youngstown Equipment Company of Agoura Hills, California, manufactures cut-resistant gloves that are fully lined with Kevlar to help minimize cuts. These gloves feature breathable cuffs for comfort and wrist support and terry cloth brow wipes on the backs of the thumbs. They're double-stitched for durability and are well designed to provide good dexterity. Youngstown's cut-resistant gloves are also useful for clearing brush, pulling thistle, and a thousand other chores in the woods and around the house. (www.ytgloves.com)

LABONVILLE 850KP CHAPS

Protecting Your Legs

Chain-saw chaps provide significant protection against deep leg cuts. When put into contact with a moving chain, fibers woven into the multilayered fabric of the chaps clog the chain or sprocket to minimize the potential injury to the wearer. **Labonville Inc.** of Gorham, New Hampshire, manufactures top-quality chain-saw chaps. Their model 850KP chaps are constructed from a six-ply Kevlar/polyester blend. The outermost layer of fabric is 1,000-denier Cordura Plus for durability and snag resistance and for repelling oil and water. Thick (1,440-denier) Kevlar strands do most of the hard work of slowing down a fast-moving cutting chain. Labonville's chaps are UL Class A classified and meet all relevant OSHA standards. When deciding on the size to buy, get chaps that are just a little long, so that they cover the top 2 inches or so of your boots. Don't get them so long, however, that they drag on the ground. (www.labonville.com)

Sharp = Green

The single most important thing you can do to reduce pollution from your chain saw is to keep your cutting chain sharp. Even a moderately dull chain can double or triple your saw's cutting time and its consumption of fuel and chain lubricant. In addition, dull chains are more prone to kickback than sharp chains are, and longer cutting times lead to fatigue and frustration—both factors in chain-saw accidents.

OREGON makes the tools you need to sharpen your cutting chains like new. The company manufactures kits complete with a round file, a file guide, a flat file, and two wooden handles. Replacement files are available in convenient two-packs. It's a good idea to touch up the edges of your chain saw's cutting teeth before every cutting session—it only takes a few minutes, and in the end it will save you time and will make your chain saw a safer and much more environmentally friendly tool. (www.oregonchain.com)

TASCO WOODSMAN FORESTRY SYSTEM 6000

Head Protection for the Home Woodcutter

Chain saws throw off a small blizzard of wood chips and sawdust, and you simply have to protect your face when you're running a saw. You also need to protect your hearing from the 100-plus-decibel scream of a chain saw at high revs. A good hard hat provides protection from a potentially disastrous kickback, and it also shields your head from falling branches when you're felling trees. You can cobble together an outfit with safety glasses, a hard hat, and earmuffs or ear plugs, but there's a better alternative: an integrated system that protects your face, your hearing, and your noggin, all in one piece.

The **Tasco** Woodsman Forestry System 6000 is professional-quality equipment at an affordable price. It includes a Class A, nylon hard hat featuring a six-point ratchet system for easy adjustment and a comfortable fit. The steel mesh facemask, coated to resist rust, can be rotated back over the top of the hard hat when you're not sawing, and it isn't subject to the fogging that is the curse of plastic masks. The low-profile earmuffs provide 22-decibel hearing protection and, like the facemask, rotate up over the hard hat when they're not in use. Tasco is an industry leader, and the Woodsman 6000 is a great value. (www.tascocorp.com)

STIHL BIOPLUS
Vegetable-Oil Chain Saw Lubricant

Chain saws provide lubrication to the bar and chain automatically by use of a "total loss lubrication system"—the lubricant delivered from your saw's oil tank briefly lubricates the bar and chain and is then thrown off the spinning chain as a fine mist. It goes directly into the environment: the ground nearby, the log you're cutting, the surrounding air, your clothes, your lungs. Not a pretty picture when you're using traditional, petroleum-based lubricants. These oils foul the soil, run off into nearby lakes and streams, and can irritate your skin and respiratory system.

There's an alternative: vegetable-oil-based lubricants. They're far more environmentally friendly than petroleum-based lubricants, typically around 90 percent biodegradable within 21 days. Stihl BioPlus is a chain lubricant based on canola oil. It has received excellent reviews from users, as well as Germany's coveted Blue Angel award for environmentally friendly products. (www.stihlusa.com)

Another alternative to petroleum-based chain lubricants is pure vegetable oil. Users of power-equipment chat boards on the Internet are increasingly advocating the use of grocery store cooking oil as chain lubricant, and it's hard to find anyone who has tried it and doesn't like the results. Some say that it works as well as the lubricants specifically designed for chain saws, keeps the saw cleaner, and won't shorten the life of the bar and chain. And, of course, if you buy too much, you can always use the extra in your cooking!

POCKET CHAIN SAW
Quiet, Quick, and Green

If you drive on forest back roads or just have a long driveway through the woods, you will sooner or later need to clear fallen trees and tree limbs out of your way, sometimes on a moment's notice. If you're like most people, you won't have a saw—and certainly not a chain saw—handy. The Pocket Chain Saw from Supreme Products Inc. solves the problem.

This clever little tool weighs less than 5 ounces and stores in a box small enough to fit in your hip pocket. It superficially resembles a chain saw's cutting chain, but it's not a loop. It's a single strand of cutting chain with a simple handle on each end and triangular teeth that cut bidirectionally (on both the forward and back strokes). It's designed to be used by one person but can be used by two.

The Pocket Chain Saw will cut firewood for campfires and saplings for shelters and will help clean up fallen limbs around the yard. (www.pocketchainsaw.com)

PLANTSKYDD DEER REPELLENT
Sure, We Love Bambi, But . . .

Plantskydd Deer Repellent was developed in Sweden in 1991 to protect tree plantings while meeting strict environmental protection standards. It proved so successful that it was brought to North America in 1993, and today it is manufactured in the United States and used by households and commercial forestry operations.

Plantskydd is formulated from bovine or porcine blood and vegetable oil. There are no synthetic ingredients, and it's completely nontoxic and biodegradable. It repels animals by releasing the blood odor that animals associate with predator activity, and the vegetable-oil binder makes it adhere to plants for long-lasting plant protection—typically 6 months in the winter and 3 to 4 months during the growing season.

Plantskydd has other benefits. It has been shown in tests conducted at Pennsylvania State University to be an effective foliar fertilizer. It is safe to apply around children and pets. It is safe and effective in protecting ornamental plantings and orchard trees. And it has been shown to be effective in repelling not only deer and elk but also rabbits, voles, squirrels, and other small animals.

Plantskydd is available as a premixed liquid, as a powdered concentrate that you mix, and in a granular form for scattering around plantings for protection from small animals. (www.plantskydd.com)

CORONA CLIPPER MCLEOD

The Most Useful Forestry Tool You've Never Heard Of

Invented around 1905, the McLeod (rhymes with *cloud*) was the brainchild of Malcolm McLeod, a ranger in California's Sierra National Forest. It was originally designed for use by wildland firefighters to build firebreaks in the flammable forests of the American West. It's a rugged multitool, featuring a steel head with a heavy-duty rake on one side and a broad, sharp hoe blade on the other. Affixed to a long wooden handle, it is used to remove brush, fallen branches, and other organic matter from a firebreak, effectively fuel-starving an approaching wildfire into submission.

You don't have to be a firefighter or live in the West to put a McLeod to good use. It's a terrific tool for cleaning up brush around your home, repairing potholes, spreading and tamping gravel on an unpaved driveway, shaping trails, raking and tilling garden soil, edge trimming, and planting bareroot tree seedlings.

Corona Clipper Inc. of Corona, California, makes a dandy McLeod. Sold as the McLeod Hoe, Corona's version of this venerable tool features a tempered head; a long, 48-inch ash handle; a rake with six broad tines crimped for added strength; a hoe blade nearly a foot wide; and a removable head for easy transport and storage. Corona's McLeod is one of the most affordable on the market, and it's covered by the company's lifetime guarantee against manufacturing defects. (www.coronaclipper.com)

OUTDOORS SOURCES AND REFERENCES

Boater 101: A Full Reference Guide to Boating Basics by Marine University (Rainbow Books, 2007) is a complete boating course in a paperback of just 132 pages, priced at $12.95. Emphasizing safety and environmental stewardship, **Boater 101** has been approved by the National Association of State Boating Law Administrators for boating safety courses.

The Harrowsmith Country Life Guide to Wood Heat by Dirk Thomas (Camden House, 1992) is a superb guide to wood-cutting, firewood preparation, and home wood burning that includes an excellent section on responsible woodlot management and good forestry practices for the home wood burner. Thomas's book is now out of print, but so entertainingly written that it's worth tracking down a used copy through Bookfinder.com or Amazon.com.

AMES TRUE TEMPER WOOD-SPLITTING MAULS

Splitting Firewood by Hand

Most professional firewood operations split wood with gas-powered, hydraulic log splitters, but those machines are expensive, polluting beasts. The greener alternative is to split your wood by hand, and the best and most popular tool for the job is a splitting maul.

Ames True Temper makes a pair of fine splitting mauls in 6-pound and 8-pound sizes. The Model 1189600 has a 6-pound head, a FiberPro handle of fiberglass and polypropylene, a handle guard, and a sledge head opposite the blade. It has an overall length of 36 inches. The Model 1189700 offers the same features with an 8-pound head. Both retail for about $35 and come with a lifetime warranty against manufacturing defects. Both are excellent tools at an affordable price. (www.ames.com)

ENVIRON-METAL HEVI-SHOT

Get the Lead Out (of Your Shotgun)

In 1976, the US Fish and Wildlife Service began a controversial effort to ban the use of lead shotgun pellets in waterfowl hunting. It had become evident that the accidental ingestion of spent lead shot by waterfowl was resulting in the lead-poisoning deaths of millions of ducks, geese, and swans in North America. After a lengthy and often bitter debate, a series of lawsuits, and a tangle of legislative wrangling in Congress and state legislatures, the lead shot ban went into effect in 1991. The lead ban has been a significant factor in the resurgence of North American waterfowl populations in recent years.

Although the ban was successful, it wasn't without problems. Ammunition manufacturers initially substituted steel shot for lead, but steel is far less dense than lead, and steel pellets don't travel as far or hit as hard as lead pellets do. Then, in 2000, ENVIRON-Metal, Inc., changed the game with the introduction of HEVI-Shot, a composite of tungsten, nickel, and iron. HEVI-Shot isn't almost as good as lead—it's better. Better for hunters *and* better for the environment. HEVI-Shot shells are available in a wide range of loads for waterfowling and upland shooting. (www.hevishot.com)

LAPUA NATURALIS

Get the Lead Out (of Your Rifle)

Let's face it: A general lead-ammo ban is coming. Some hunters will complain, the NRA will fight it, but it's coming, and it's ultimately going to be good for the environment and good for hunters' health. Fortunately, ammunition manufacturers are moving forward with high-performance, lead-free ammo. Lead-free and reduced-lead bullets and cartridges are available today from companies like Federal Cartridge Company (BallistiClean), Winchester (Super Clean NT, WinClean), Barnes Bullets (X-Bullet, TSX, MPG, and others), Remington (Premier Copper Solid), Hornady (GMX), Nosler (E-Tip), and Lapua (Naturalis).

Lapua is a Finnish ammunition maker renowned for the high quality of its products. It is a world leader in the design and manufacturing of lead-free hunting ammo. Lapua's Naturalis bullet is made from copper with a polymer tip. Naturalis bullets are available from gun shops and sporting goods stores in four popular, medium- to large-game hunting cartridges. Don't wait for the law to ban lead ammo when excellent alternatives are already available. (www.lapua.com)

FISHING SINKERS AND JIGS

Get the Lead Out (of Your Tackle Box)

More than 4,000 tons of lead fishing lures and sinkers are lost or discarded in and around North American fishing waters every year. They're being accidentally ingested by waterfowl as well as by raptors that feed on poisoned waterfowl. Thankfully, the tackle industry has stepped up with nontoxic substitutes for lead sinkers and lures.

Dr. Drop manufactures an innovative line of fishing sinkers made from tungsten composite. This stuff is heavier than lead, so you get your bait down to the fish faster. Their Friction Grip System sinkers are shaped to hold tightly to the line, and their Click and Slide System sinkers are designed to allow the angler to adjust the location of the weight on the line. In addition, Dr. Drop makes traditional bullet and bell sinkers from tungsten composite. (www.drdropsinkers.com)

Loon Outdoors, based in Boise, Idaho, is dedicated to making environmentally friendly products for fly fishers. The company offers two nontoxic lead substitutes, both in the form of soft putty that can be squeezed directly onto the leader. These putties get their weight from tungsten powder. They can be removed from the leader after fishing and replaced in their containers for later reuse. (www.loonoutdoors.com)

A trusted name in fishing sinkers since its founding in 1949, the Water Gremlin Company of White Bear Lake, Minnesota, offers a line of premium round and removable split shot sinkers made from tin. Gremlin Green nontoxic split shot are made in a variety of sizes appropriate for all light-tackle fishing. (www.watergremlin.com)

Jigs, typically joined with a natural or soft plastic bait or bucktail, are among the most reliable and productive lures for bass, panfish, walleye, and other game fish. Northland Fishing Tackle jigs are among the best in the business. Northland offers more than 40 different jig styles in many sizes. All Northland jigs are cast from a nontoxic, bismuth-tin alloy and married to top-quality hooks from manufacturers like Mustad. (www.northlandtackle.com)

BERKLEY RECYCLING

Recycle Your Used Fishing Line

Nearly all monofilament fishing line is made of high-density nylon, a material that in most environments will last for more than 500 years. It's thin, strong, and nearly transparent, and when tossed carelessly into the water or up on the bank, it kills. Birds, sea turtles, seals—even pet dogs and cats—have died after becoming entangled in discarded nylon mono. It's a hazard to swimmers and divers and frequently becomes tangled in boat props. All of this can be prevented by participation in a growing, nationwide effort to get old fishing line out of the environment and into a recycling bin.

Twenty-two states, led by Florida with its remarkably successful Monofilament Recovery and Recycling Program, have established fishing-line collection bins at popular fishing areas. Many fishing tackle retailers have set up collection bins in their stores. Most of the used fishing line eventually ends up at the **Berkley Conservation Institute**, which has recycled more than *10 million miles* of old nylon mono since 1990. If you can't find a collection bin in your area, you can put your used line into an envelope or box and mail it, postage prepaid, to Berkley Recycling, 1900 18th Street, Spirit Lake, IA 51360.

Berkley melts the line down into raw nylon pellets that are then used to make other plastic products, such as fish habitat structures (but not new fishing line).

Keep in mind that braided Dacron line, wire-core line, fluorocarbon line, fly line, and nylon monofilament that is tangled with plant material or other debris *cannot* be recycled by Berkley. Dispose of these materials in the trash, but first coil them up and use shears to snip them into short pieces—otherwise they pose a threat to bald eagles and other birds that frequent landfills. (www.berkley-fishing.com)

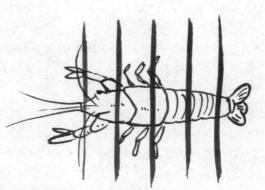

TRAPPER CRAYFISH TRAPS

Invasion of the Alien Crustaceans

Crayfish, crawfish, crawdads—whatever you choose to call them, there are about 400 different species of these pint-size cousins of the lobster in North American waters. Most are innocuous denizens of streams and rivers, and some are raised for the market in aquaculture ponds. In recent years, however, some wild crayfish species have expanded rapidly beyond their native ranges, apparently aided by anglers who purchase live crayfish for bait. Armed with big and notoriously indiscriminate appetites, these alien crustaceans are attacking populations of native fish, invertebrates, and aquatic plants in more than 20 states.

What are we to do? Eat 'em! Crayfish are traditional table fare in the Southeast and have become more popular nationwide with the ever-growing interest in Creole and Cajun cuisines. But first you have to catch them. By far the most efficient way to nab 'em is with a crayfish trap. These are wire cages that are baited (fresh fish parts are best) and left on the stream or lake bottom for anywhere from a few hours to a day or two. The crayfish come into the trap through wire tunnels to eat the bait. After eating their fill, they can't easily find their way out.

Trapper Arne of Payson, Arizona, manufactures and sells some of the very best crayfish traps on the market. There are five different models. The popular Trapper is made from durable, vinyl-covered hardware cloth. Lightweight and portable, the Trapper features black netting on both of the entry funnels to provide cover for nervous crayfish, a hinged side door for easy emptying of the trap, and an "escape stopper" so the crayfish check in but don't check out. (www.trapperarne.com)

10 Things Anglers Can Do to Help Save the Planet

1. **Don't dump live bait.** Dumping nonnative live bait has led to breeding populations of baitfish and crayfish in waters in which they don't belong, upsetting ecosystems that in many cases are already under pressure from habitat degradation. Take your unused live bait home. Kill and freeze it for later use, or put it in the garden for fertilizer.

2. **Don't transfer game fish to other waters.** Fish stocking can spread disease, throw ecosystems out of balance, and destroy native fishes. The decline of the native cutthroat trout of the West, including the extinction of two entire subspecies, is substantially the result of the stocking of rainbow trout. Stocking isn't a DIY project—leave it to the fisheries professionals.

3. **Wash your waders.** Whirling disease protozoans, New Zealand mud snails, and other damaging, invasive species can be transferred from one body of water to another by hitching a ride on dirty wading gear. Clean your gear between uses. While diluted chlorine bleach is effective, it's also polluting. A better way is to wash your wading gear with a mild detergent (such as Ivory) and hot water and then soak your gear for at least 10 minutes in the hottest water you can get from your tap.

4. **Recycle your used fishing line.** Discarded monofilament line tangles up birds and boat propellers alike. Several states, including Florida, Montana, South Carolina, Texas, and others, as well as many private bait and tackle shops across North America, have recycling programs that help to keep used monofilament out of the environment.

5. **Clean and dry your boat.** Proper flushing of bilgewater, removing water weeds from anchors and your outboard's lower unit, and washing down the hull will help to prevent the spread of invasive aquatic plants, such as hydrilla and Eurasian watermilfoil, and invasive animals, such as zebra mussels and spiny water fleas.

6. **Stop using lead sinkers and lures.** Lost lead fishing tackle is toxic, and it kills birds. There are plenty of alternatives.

7. **Replace your old two-stroke outboard** with a four-stroke engine. Two-stroke engines are a major source of water pollution in our lakes. Four-strokes are cleaner and quieter.

8. **Don't discard fish entrails in the water.** That practice can spread diseases to other fish. Besides, it's nasty.

9. **Use a trash bag.** Litter is unsightly and kills sea turtles, birds, and other animals that share the water with us. Pack out your garbage, and try to pick up some of the trash left by slobs who don't. Look especially for discarded fishing line, plastic bags, and six-pack rings, which are particularly hard on wildlife.

10. **Participate in a cleanup day.** Every year, local and state governments and organizations like Trout Unlimited, the Bass Anglers Sportsman Society (BASS), and American Rivers sponsor thousands of volunteer cleanup projects on our lakes and rivers. A few hours of your time just once a year will improve the quality of the water and your fishing experience.

FYI

Catch-and-release angling is not always the best management plan. Some game fish, such as white crappie, bluegill, yellow perch, and smallmouth bass, are prone to overpopulation and stunting. In such situations, the ecosystem may benefit by your killing your limit rather than limiting your kill.

OCEAN KAYAK CAPER ANGLER
'Yak Attack!

Small paddle craft for fishing are older than history, but the last two decades have seen a small revolution driven by the fast-growing popularity of sit-on-top kayaks. The original sit-on-top 'yak was a modified surfboard created in a Malibu backyard in 1971. It worked so well that its inventor, Tim Niemier, went on to found Ocean Kayak, which bloomed in the 1980s and is today the industry leader in sit-on-top kayaks.

For the angler, sit-on-tops have many advantages over more traditional sea kayaks: far greater stability, more accessible storage, easy exit and practical reentry in the event of a capsize, positive flotation, and greater freedom of movement in the cockpit. For anglers, divers, and casual paddlers, a sit-on-top is, well, tops.

Ocean Kayak's Caper Angler represents the best of the breed. Made from superdurable, rotomolded polyethylene, the Caper Angler is a single-seat 'yak specifically outfitted for fishing. Eleven feet in overall length and weighing just 45 pounds, the boat is easy for one person to handle. Features include two flush-mounted rod holders, a small tackle box, paddle keepers, a large bow hatch providing access to a generous storage space, and an open tank well in the stern for additional, easily accessible storage. The boat's superb primary stability comes both from its shouldered, triform hull and from a wide, 31-inch beam. The Caper Angler is quick enough for most trolling, tracks well for such a short boat (there is a modest keel that is most pronounced at the bow and stern), and boasts excellent maneuverability. Equally at home in freshwater and the salt, the Caper Angler is a fine, versatile little fishing boat. (www.ocean kayak.com)

FYI

A good coat of wax, such as Island Girl's Simply Brilliant, on an unpainted fiberglass hull will prevent dirt from adhering. This will improve your fuel efficiency, enhance your boat's performance, and reduce the number of times you'll have to power-wash the hull.

SODABLAST SYSTEMS
Clean and Green

Cleaning fiberglass hulls of old paint and barnacles is one of the dirtiest, most labor-intensive jobs in boating. Traditional techniques, such as sanding and the use of corrosive chemicals, can damage your boat's gelcoat and even the underlying fiberglass laminate. SodaBlast Systems LLC of Houston has a better technology that won't damage your hull *and* is nontoxic.

SodaBlasting uses specially formulated sodium bicarbonate—baking soda—in a stream of compressed air to strip away old paint. It's a proven technology that has been used for several years in such varied applications as graffiti removal from brick walls, cleaning of public monuments, and mold remediation in flood-damaged homes. It's versatile in hull cleaning: SodaBlasting can be used to completely strip old paint right down to the gelcoat, to remove an outer layer of paint and dirt to prepare the hull for repainting, or just to brush away the oxidized outer layer of paint from a hull that has been stored out of the water for a long time.

Your marina operator may have access to SodaBlasting equipment or may have a regular arrangement with one of SodaBlast Systems' factory-trained and certified contractors. Or you can find a contractor yourself at the SodaBlast Systems Web site. (www.sodablastsystems.com)

HONDA BF2D OUTBOARD
Lightweight Engine, Heavyweight Performance

In 1964, Honda developed the first four-stroke outboard engine, a design based on technology similar to that used in most automobile engines. Four-stroke outboards cost more than conventional two-stroke engines—typically about 20 to 25 percent more for engines of comparable power. However, four-strokes are much more fuel efficient, burning from 20 to 80 percent less fuel than comparable two-strokes, so the higher purchase price is really an investment that will save money in the long run. Four-strokes are also far less polluting than two-strokes. Besides using less fuel, they consume about half as much engine oil, reduce hydrocarbon emissions by as much as 90 percent, and don't discharge fuel and lubricating oil into the water.

Among Honda Marine's four-stroke outboards is the BF2D, an offshoot of the BF2, the lightest four-stroke outboard in the world. The BF2D is equipped with a centrifugal clutch, which enables it to be started and smoothly operated at idle without turning the propeller. This is a great feature for fishing and for general boating safety, as a quick turn of the throttle control will instantly take the motor out of gear. Available with either a 15-inch or 20-inch shaft and weighing just 27 or 28 pounds, the BF2D is designed to power canoes, small inflatables, jon boats, yacht tenders, and all manner of small utility boats. The BF2D is operated with a tiller and has 360-degree swivel steering and full-throttle reverse, features that add to its usefulness as a trolling motor and for getting in and out of tight fishing spots. The engine is air-cooled (no water pump) and doesn't require an oil filter. It's equipped with an integrated fuel tank that holds 1 quart of 87-octane gas. (www.hondamarine.com)

FYI

Driving your powerboat through shallow water at high speeds can damage aquatic habitats and erode the shoreline.

Treat all water fewer than 6 feet deep as a no-wake zone.

NO

STINGRAY BOATS
Green Performance

Founded in 1979 by Al Fink, **Stingray Boats** of Hartsville, South Carolina, is today a leading manufacturer of family-oriented runabouts. Famous for boats that combine craftsmanship, performance, and value, Stingray works hard to be a first-class steward of the environment. It is the only US boat manufacturer to employ low-styrene resins in its fiberglass laminates and gelcoats. Stingray boats also feature four-stroke engines, fuel vent surge protectors to eliminate refueling spills, and chlorofluorocarbon-free, ozone-friendly flotation foams. But what really distinguishes Stingrays as the most environmentally friendly boats in their class is their patented "Z-plane" hull. Originally conceived as a way to improve handling, the Z-plane hull design has another, unintended result. By reducing the amount of aerated water around the propeller when the boat is going fast on plane, the hull makes the power plant more efficient—as much as 20 percent more efficient. This means that Stingrays get better fuel efficiency than comparable boats and can get similar performance from smaller engines. Stingray offers a line of open-bow boats and small to medium-size cuddies and cruisers. (www.stingrayboats.com)

FYI The Clean Marina Initiative is a national, incentive-based program that encourages marinas to use environmentally sound operating practices to protect coastal water quality. Find a marina that participates in your state's Clean Marina program, or talk to your marina operator about signing up.

Whole Green Catalog

244

EPAINT EP-ZO
Antifouling, Eco-Friendly

In 1960, the introduction of tributyltin (TBT), an organotin-based antifouling agent, into boat hull paints promised to make hull cleaning easier, but TBT was subsequently banned from use on most small boats because of its toxicity to marine invertebrates. After the ban took effect in 1988, copper-based antifouling agents replaced TBT. But copper in marine environments carries its own toxic baggage, and it additionally promotes corrosion of aluminum hulls.

Enter ePaint. Established in 1991 to market copper-free hull paints earlier developed with funding from the US Navy, the ePaint Company, headquartered in Falmouth, Massachusetts, today offers a diverse line of high-performance, low-toxicity antifouling and release coatings for hull bottoms. EPaint's antifouling coatings are ingenious. In essence, they contain photoactive pigments that, when exposed to sunlight, catalyze dissolved oxygen and water to create a microscopic layer of hydrogen peroxide on the surface of the hull. The hydrogen peroxide makes the hull inhospitable to the

larvae of organisms that foul boat hulls. When released into the water, however, it breaks down again into its component parts—oxygen and water.

EPaint's EP-ZO is a great bottom paint for the recreational marine boater. It has been rated excellent by *Practical Sailor* and *Powerboat Reports* and is a practical, eco-friendly alternative to the toxic bottom paints on the market today. The ePaint Web site has a thorough FAQs section, as well as a handy, interactive paint selector and a paint calculator to identify the ePaint product and quantity best suited to your specific boating needs. (www.epaint.com)

10 Small Ways to Keep a Clean Boat

Boats are dirty—paints and polishes, trash and wastes, fuel and lubricants. Here are 10 things boaters can do to keep the water clean and their boats environmentally friendly.

1. Clean your polyester and nylon sails by rinsing with freshwater. Scrubbing sails with detergents and bleaches will make them look brighter, but it's unnecessary and shortens the life of the sails. And store your sails *dry*; sails stored damp are more likely to get mildew and stains.

2. Eliminate accidental fuel spills. When refueling, use a fuel collar and keep a rag on hand to clean up drips. And resist the urge to top off the tank.

3. Duct-tape an absorbent pad around your oil filter to keep oil from leaking into the bilge. Keep your bilge clean and don't pump or bail oily water overboard.

4. Keep your trash and recyclables on board and ask your guests to do the same. Clearly marked, easily accessible garbage and recycling containers make this so much easier.

5. Remove mildew and stains with a thin paste made from equal amounts of vinegar and borax. Borax (sodium borate) cleans, deodorizes, and removes stains. Vinegar cuts grease, removes stains, and dissolves hard-water deposits. Together, they make a formidable, nontoxic cleaner.

6. Polish brass fittings with a paste made from equal amounts of table salt and vinegar. Use a little cornstarch on a damp cloth for an extrabright shine.

7. Polish stainless steel with a paste made from equal amounts of vinegar and baking soda.

8. Remove stains from fiberglass by scrubbing with a thin paste of baking soda and water. The same cleaner does a good job of cleaning pretty much everything in the head.

9. Clean and deodorize dry carpets and upholstery by sprinkling them with cornstarch or baking soda. Brush lightly to work the powder into the fabric. Wait 5 minutes, then vacuum.

10. Clean windows with a solution made from a half cup of white vinegar, 2 tablespoons of cornstarch, and a half gallon of warm water.

Round Trips

It's no small irony that one of the best ways to appreciate the magnificent diversity of our planet is also contributing to its demise. Travel is truly a double-edged sword. Trust me. I know from experience. I try to tread lightly on the earth, but as a travel writer, my frequent-flier status is the single factor in my carbon footprint that puts me in a league with Hummer drivers and McMansion owners. You can ride your bike instead of your car around town and opt for heavy sweaters in lieu of heating your home, but a single one-way flight across the country puts out 2 tons of carbon dioxide—about what the average American expends during 4 months of driving.

We'd cut a lot of harmful pollutants if we all stopped traveling tomorrow (though we'd eliminate only 5 percent of worldwide carbon emissions), or even if we cut back to only what is essential—an annual business retreat here, a family wedding there. But what about the child who comprehends Darwinian evolution while vacationing in the Galapagos, and then decides to devote her life to protecting wildlife? Or the retired couple who sponsor the construction of an orphanage because they got a peek at life in the slums of Nairobi after a Kenyan safari? Or the midwesterner whose Muslim Turkish tour guide gives a human face to a foreign way of life? Travel provides an education for visitor and resident alike, a reason to preserve natural environments—and a way to make a living for millions of people around the world. If we all stopped traveling tomorrow, forest reserves would be clear-cut for their timber, 10 percent of the world's workers would be out of a job, and the stories in the international section of the newspaper would all seem far less compelling.

There are ways to reduce the greenhouse gases that are a nasty by-product of our travels—flying during the summer instead of the winter whenever possible, for instance. But green travel isn't just about minimizing and offsetting your carbon footprint. It's also about choosing travel companies that are socially and environmentally responsible. Like Journeys Within, a tour operator in Cambodia that builds clean-water wells, distributes microloans, sponsors free English classes, and awards scholarships to underprivileged would-be university students. Or Accor, a huge, worldwide hotel chain that requires all of its 1,200 properties to execute a 65-point environmental checklist. These are companies that understand the importance of being a good neighbor and a good citizen of the earth.

For a long time, the travel industry didn't think vacationers wanted to hear this kind of news—who likes to think about global warming on the one short holiday we get from work each year? But if you don't look at the choices you make on vacation with the same rigor that you do at home, you could cancel out a year's worth of environmental good deeds. More and more, hotels are advertising their good deeds—and often encouraging travelers to take part, through either financial donations or cultural activities. Now that being green is a business advantage, however, it can be hard to tell the real deal from a "greenwasher"—a business that passes off negligible environmental efforts as proof of its supposed eco-sensitivity.

Another popular fallacy has it that ecotourism only takes place deep in the jungle of the Amazon or on the African savanna—destinations with a pristine (or nearly so) natural environment. In fact, it's just as important for city hotels to mind their environment. The Lenox Hotel in Boston is a pioneer in urban ecotourism; it was the first hotel in the United States to institute a linen and towel reuse program. Beach resorts need ecotourism, too, and badly. The Mayakoba complex on Mexico's Yucatan Peninsula, which includes four luxury hotels, aims to avoid the environmental tragedies that have accompanied the rampant development at nearby Cancun.

Environmental concerns can't afford to take a vacation. Choose wisely when you do.

— **Brook Wilkinson**

LINDBLAD EXPEDITIONS
Green Cruise Pioneers

Cruising the deep blue sea is at its greenest on a **Lindblad Expeditions** ship. Founder Lars-Eric Lindblad led the first tourist expeditions to Antarctica and the Galapagos, both popular travel destinations today. Since the natural world is a highlight of every Lindblad trip, it makes sense that the company is doing its part to preserve our environment. In addition to donating money to wildlife projects around the world, Lindblad has become a pioneer in another travel phenomenon, this one called travelers' philanthropy. At the end of each cruise, every guest is invited to make a donation to the Lindblad Expeditions/National Geographic Fund, which supports environmental research, conservation, and education projects in the regions the cruise line visits. Since the company pays for the fund's overhead, 100 percent of donations go directly to the programs. As an added incentive, guests who donate $250 or more receive a $250 travel voucher toward a future booking.

To date, Lindblad has raised more than $6 million for projects such as the eradication of feral pigs on Santiago Island in the Galapagos, radar surveillance of illegal fishing in the Gulf of California, and research on humpback whale communication and behavior off Alaska. Lindblad has also established a foundation in Ecuador that supports local artisans, a project to recycle glass into jewelry and art, and a sort of microgrant fund for grassroots conservationists. (www.expeditions.com)

FYI

These days, most hotels leave a card in every room that explains how guests can reuse their towels and linens. If your hotel doesn't, post the Do Not Disturb sign on the door and remake your bed yourself.

THE TRAVEL FOUNDATION'S INSIDER GUIDES
Acting Local

This UK-based charity funds projects that explore new paths toward sustainable tourism—helping to develop a village-to-village tourist route in Cyprus that would provide work for young people in these rural areas, or reviving the dying craft of lace making in post-tsunami Sri Lanka. Most useful for consumers, however, are the Insider Guides that the **Travel Foundation** publishes online, full of concrete tips on how to be a respectful traveler. In the Dominican Republic, for example, one learns that some animal parks mistreat their residents, but whale watching in Samana Bay is carefully regulated by conservation groups and the navy. In Thailand, where the head is sacred and the feet are not, travelers should never place a hat on the floor or point their feet at monks. (www.thetravelfoundation.org.uk)

RAINFOREST ALLIANCE'S ECO-INDEX
Healing the Rain Forest

This nonprofit organization is best known for its grassroots work with Latin America's agriculture and forestry industries. You may well have purchased a **Rainforest Alliance**–certified banana or SmartWood-tagged building materials. The group's Eco-Index of Sustainable Tourism does much the same for the travel industry, recognizing businesses in Latin American and the Caribbean that are environmentally and socially friendly. You can sign up for a monthly update or just log on as you plan each upcoming trip. Users select their preferred country or type of destination (a city versus an indigenous community), type of accommodation, amenities, activities, and even traveler profile (families, say, or seniors). If you'd rather browse through your options, download *Go Green! A SmartGuide to Sustainable Travel in the Americas*. (www.eco-indextourism.org)

JEAN-MICHEL COUSTEAU FIJI ISLANDS RESORT

Living Well While Doing Good

Traveling with a small carbon footprint doesn't have to mean roughing it in spartan accommodations. Instead, at the Jean-Michel Cousteau Fiji Islands Resort, it's all about enjoying gourmet meals cooked by the Fijian chef with produce from the onsite organic garden and edible landscaping; snorkeling along a coral reef with the resident marine biologist, also a Fijian; and hiking to a roaring waterfall or visiting the town market with local guides. This upscale take on ecotouring comes as no surprise when you consider the resort's pedigree: It was founded by marine explorer and environmentalist Jean-Michel Cousteau (son of Jacques), along with the owner of California's luxurious yet eco-sensitive Post Ranch Inn.

The Cousteau Resort sits on a former coconut plantation, which means that no pristine land was harmed in its construction, and even so, much of the natural vegetation was left intact. The deluxe *bures*, or traditional thatched bungalows, contain all the creature comforts—a king-size bed, complimentary minibar, and Italian-tile bathroom—but only enough electricity to run a few lamps. There are no telephones, no televisions, and especially no noisy air conditioners (floor-to-ceiling louvered windows supply an ample breeze). Behind the scenes, the Cousteau Resort has pioneered an innovative system that uses coconuts and recycled bottles to filter its wastewater, which pools in lagoons found around the property.

Rates include all meals, nonalcoholic beverages, airport transfers, daily activities, and daycare for up to two children age 12 and under. An optional $4 per night donation goes to the Savusavu Community Foundation and other local health, education, poverty, and environmental projects. Rooms from $608 per night, 3-night minimum. (www.fijiresort.com)

Buying Crafts Responsibly

Locally produced crafts make wonderful souvenirs—when they're authentic and legal, that is. Each year, US customs seizes thousands of purchases that Americans try to bring into the country. Some are made from endangered flora and fauna. Others are priceless antiquities not meant to leave their home country. Many don't break any international regulations but are fakes masquerading as the real thing—Native American kachina dolls sold in the Southwest but manufactured in Asia, for example. Here are a few tips to keep in mind while you're shopping:

1. Visit locally owned stores—or even the artisan's own workshop, if possible. The closer you get to the person who made the object, the more confident you can be of its authenticity, the less energy will have been spent to transport it, and the more money will go directly to the artisan. If you're a big shopper, plan your trip around local market days.

2. Engage in a bit of bargaining—it's an expected part of the buying process in many countries—but don't take it too seriously. The difference of a few dollars means little to you, but it could feed a family in the developing world for days.

3. Don't buy anything that you know or suspect is made from an endangered plant or animal. That means no ivory (unless it is more than 100 years old); rare coral, hardwoods, shells, or starfish; tiger, leopard, or jaguar skins; ostrich feathers; or turtle shells. If you're not sure whether something comes from an endangered species, just don't buy it.

4. Be circumspect about any supposed antiquities. A UNESCO convention and US law prohibit the transport of many artifacts and cultural antiquities, including pre-Columbian sculptures and murals from Central and South America, Native American artifacts from Canada, colonial-period objects from Peru, Byzantine-period icons from Cyprus, and Khmer stone sculptures from Cambodia. To make it simple, unless you're a knowledgeable antiquities dealer, stay away from anything that's more than 50 years old. If you buy something that looks old, be sure to get documentation of its origin and age.

5. Look for a fair-trade symbol on a product or in a shop window. This indicates, among other things, that the workers or craftspeople were paid a reasonable wage or price under safe working conditions and that the method of production is environmentally sustainable.

CONSERVATION INTERNATIONAL
Grassroots Intervention

Conservation International is well known for its work to preserve the earth's biodiversity, which it does primarily by funding scientific research and local nongovernmental organizations. Less well known is CI's work in ecotourism, an industry with obvious potential side benefits for rare flora and fauna in the so-called biodiversity hot spots.

Unlike many other Web-based listings of ecotourism options, CI recommends only a handful of projects on its Destinations page. But the few projects featured are always far off the beaten path and generally unlike those you'll find anywhere else—for example, a canopy walkway in Ghana or a network of community-run inns along the Venezuelan Andes. Conservation International has also teamed up with Responsible Travel to build a community-based tourism database. (www.ecotour.org)

FIGHTING FOR HUMAN RIGHTS IN TRAVEL

Trekking porters are mistreated from the Inca Trail to Mount Kilimanjaro. Villagers are displaced to make room for glitzy resorts. Hotel pools deplete a region's meager clean-water resources. Tourism Concern is a UK-based charity with a mission to fight these and other examples of exploitation within the travel industry. Simply by reading their Issues Explained section, travelers can become much more sensitive to how not to do harm on their next trip. For about $50 a year, you can become a Tourism Concern member and receive the quarterly magazine, *Tourism in Focus*, which details the progress of each of their projects. (www.tourismconcern.org.uk)

DEVIL'S THUMB RANCH
How the West Was

Had it not been for the current owners of Devil's Thumb Ranch, this 5,000-acre property in Colorado's Fraser Valley, 65 miles west of Denver, would have gone the way of much of the West—plastered over with high-density housing and a golf course. Instead, it has become an environmentally sensitive wilderness resort, with less than 2 percent of the property developed and the rest reserved for recreation and wildlife.

The lodge and cabins are heated via geothermal energy (as are the pool and Jacuzzi), supplemented by EPA-approved fireplaces that burn wood harvested onsite, mostly from beetle-infested pines. Recycled asphalt from a nearby highway project was used on the few roads found on the ranch. Guests can partake in fly-fishing, hiking, kayaking, horseback riding, and mountain biking in the summer and cross-country skiing, horse-drawn sleigh rides, and snowshoeing in the winter—all without leaving the ranch. There's also a spa and yoga studio, two restaurants serving organic produce and free-range meat, a wine cellar, and even a Civil War–era barn from Indiana that has been repurposed as a meeting center. Of course, the best attractions are the elk, coyotes, moose, foxes, bears, beavers, and other wildlife that still call the ranch home, thanks to preservation efforts. Rooms from $245 per night. (www.devilsthumbranch.com)

THE INTERNATIONAL ECOTOURISM SOCIETY

Ecotourism Pioneer

Way back in 1990, a couple of forward thinkers launched the International Ecotourism Society (TIES), defining the then little-known notion of ecotourism as "responsible travel to natural areas that conserves the environment and improves the well-being of local people." Today that definition is still used around the world and encompasses a much larger phenomenon. Along the way, TIES has instructed tour operators, parks, and regional organizations on how to enhance their offerings to travelers while remaining sensitive to local environments and cultures.

TIES Web site's Travel Choice page lists travel companies that have committed to five criteria: minimizing their impact, increasing

environmental and cultural awareness and respect, providing positive experiences for visitors and hosts, supplying direct benefits for conservation and local people, and raising sensitivity to host countries' political, environmental, and social climates—in short, being good citizens of the earth. Search the directory by region for a tour operator, travel agent, lodge, hotel, or mode of transportation that fits these criteria. Some give discounts to TIES members, who pay $35 per year to support the society. Watch also for TIES's annual online auction each spring, during which you can bid on eco-adventures from Alaska to Australia, with the proceeds benefiting the organization. (www.ecotourism.org)

LONELY PLANET'S PICK & MIX SYSTEM

Waste Not, Want Not

Ever dragged a continent-wide guidebook on a trip, only to use small sections of it in each of the countries you're visiting or to ruin the entire volume by tearing out a few pages to take on the road? Never again. Now you can buy only the chapters you need from Lonely Planet's acclaimed series of travel books. Most chapters cost between $2 and $4— even less if you buy several at once. Your purchases arrive electronically as PDFs. For extra green points, rather than print out the chapters (using recycled paper, of course), just download them onto your

BlackBerry or iPhone or other electronic companion. Doing a grand tour of Eastern Europe? Instead of buying the entire, 988-page tome on the region, choose the chapters for the countries you're visiting—Croatia, Hungary, and the Czech Republic, say. Long weekend in San Diego? Save $20 by downloading the city chapter instead of the whole California guide. Each chapter that you purchase may be downloaded up to five times, so you can store one digital copy at the office (for lunchtime daydreaming), another on your home computer (for weekend planning sessions), and one on your PDA (for the commute). Go to shop www.lonelyplanet.com to pick and mix the chapters for your next trip.

YACHANA LODGE

Saving the Rain Forest

Since the nonprofit Yachana Foundation owns and operates the Yachana Lodge, deep in the heart of the Amazon basin, every dollar you spend there helps support the foundation's projects. These days, the number-one priority is a technical high school Yachana started in 2005. Here in Ecuador's remote jungle, only 15 percent of children complete their secondary education; Yachana's nontraditional classes include sustainable agriculture, forest and wildlife management, and ecotourism. Students get on-the-job training at the lodge, a no-frills but comfortable affair with solar-powered hot water and lights and meals sourced from the school's organic farm. The foundation also operates Yachana Gourmet, which purchases cacao from local farmers at fair-trade prices and manufactures tasty chocolate nibs; this income persuades the farmers to plant sustainable crops like shade-grown cacao rather than clear land for cattle ranching or logging.

Back at the lodge, indigenous guides lead hikes around Yachana's 4,300-acre protected forest, where biologists conduct research daily (and where a new species of glass frog was discovered in 2006). They also lead early-morning bird walks and night hikes. Unlike most other Amazon lodges, though, Yachana encourages guests to learn more about the local culture through tours of the high school, traditional cleansing ceremonies led by a medicine man, visits to a nearby market, cooking classes, and lessons in traditional ceramic bowl making.

Rates include boat transfers to the lodge, plus all meals and activities. Three-night stay, $525 per person. (www.yachana.com)

JUNGLE BAY RESORT & SPA
The Green Caribbean

Jungle Bay's owner likes to think of his resort as an alternative to the Caribbean's traditional "sun-n-sand" model. Indeed, on his island of Dominica, there are almost no beaches. What, then, brings tourists to Jungle Bay? Daily hikes, mountain biking, snorkeling, sea kayaking, yoga classes, and, of course, the spa. If this doesn't sound like the Caribbean to you, just think of it as an offshore territory of Central America. The resort was built using discarded stone from a nearby mining quarry and sustainably harvested wood, with cottages elevated off the ground to minimize their ecological footprint. Almost all of the food served at the restaurant is locally grown and organic.

The biggest kudos, however, go to Jungle Bay's community projects, on an island where 30 percent of the population lives below the poverty line. The resort's microloan program allows local entrepreneurs to borrow up to $4,500 for businesses that support the resort, such as organic farming, local arts production, and tour guiding. And Jungle Bay has donated tens of thousands of dollars to the construction of a home for physically and mentally disabled children. The owner's charitable spirit must be contagious, because his staff voluntarily opted to donate 10 percent of their tips to a community fund that aids environmental and social projects. This isn't the best place in the Caribbean to spread a towel on the sand and bury your head in a book, but it's an ideal option for travelers looking for some authentic culture and exhilarating adventure. From $169 per person. (www.junglebaydominica.com)

Turn off your lights, TV, and air-conditioning or heat every time you leave your hotel room and when you check out.

VOLUNTOURISM
Make a Difference during Your Next Vacation

Gone are the days when we did charity work at home and lay idle by the pool on vacation. Charity and holidays have merged to form voluntourism, or the volunteer vacation. Under this new rubric, a traveler combines work and pleasure, perhaps adding a few days of sightseeing to a week building houses with Habitat for Humanity, or spending an afternoon teaching English after a tour of Southeast Asia. Some trips involve a professional skill, such as dentistry. Others require nothing more than a helpful attitude. Whatever the mix of charity and recreation, the intent is to benefit the people and environment at a given destination while bestowing the traveler with a deeper understanding of, and appreciation for, the local culture.

A poll of volunteer vacationers conducted by *Condé Nast Traveler* magazine and MSNBC found that 91 percent believed their efforts were at least as worthwhile as donating money. It's also a fantastic learning experience for children; the exposure to difficult living situations and environmental calamities can make them lifelong activists. Elsewhere in this chapter you'll find organizations that set up volunteer vacations around the world or can match you to a company that runs such trips.

OFF THE RADAR NEWSLETTER
Hot Tips on Cutting-Edge Travel

Subscribing to this "newsletter for adventurers" is like getting monthly updates from that friend who's always jetting off to places you've never even heard of, buddying up to the locals, and bringing home fantastic photos to prove it. Christina Heyniger is that friend, an adventure-tourism consultant whose trips provide much of the fodder for the newsletter. *Off the Radar* highlights small, owner-operated tour companies—none of which pay for the coverage—that focus on sustainable, environmentally sensitive travel and incorporate local, authentic experiences. A single issue might include advice on how to go trekking in northern Ethiopia or swim with beluga whales in Canada. The Web site's Outtakes section features readers' accounts of their own fascinating adventures, such as a 26-hour bus trip from Vietnam to Laos. (www.traveloffttheradar.com)

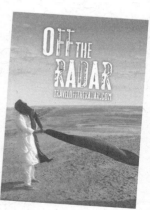

NIHIWATU

Green Surfer's Paradise

Many of the world's most popular beach resorts are just a stone's throw away from desperate poverty and degraded environmental conditions. Few resorts do anything to alleviate the situation, but Nihiwatu is not like most beach resorts. This Indonesian surfing getaway, on the remote island of Sumba, has made measurable improvements in the lives of its neighbors. The resort's nonprofit Sumba Foundation has built and staffed seven medical clinics that serve 15,000 people; handed out 6,000 insecticide-treated mosquito nets to prevent the rampant spread of malaria; built wells that provide clean water for 200 villages; and renovated or rebuilt six schools. The foundation has just installed a biodiesel generator that converts coconuts—bought from local people to the tune of $100,000 per year—into energy for the resort, thus cutting polluting emissions by 75 percent. Meanwhile, the resort's staff is looking out for the local sea turtle population: They buy turtle eggs that local people dig up, keep them safe in an onsite hatchery, and then release the hatchlings out to sea.

Most guests (and more than a few professional surfers) come to Nihiwatu for the world-renowned waves that break just off the resort's beach, but there's plenty else to do: horseback riding, hiking, mountain biking, deep-sea fishing, scuba diving, and yoga, plus weaving lessons with the local ikat craftspeople. Rates include airport transfers, all meals, nonalcoholic beverages, a massage, and a visit to a local village. Rooms from $490 per night, five-night minimum. (www.nihiwatu.com)

POWERMONKEY

This solar charger is light, compact, and powerful—in short, perfect for traveling. It can be juiced up via sunlight, an electrical outlet, or even your laptop's USB port, so you don't have to worry about the inevitable cloudy day. After 6 hours in the sun, the Powermonkey can recharge an iPod to play for 40 hours, a cell phone to run for 96 hours, or a digital camera to take 1,600 photos. Best of all, the entire kit—which comes with tips for most portable electronic devices and adapters to plug into any international socket—is just over $100. It's well worth the investment. (www.power traveller.co.uk)

Flying Green

There's no way around the fact that air travel spews greenhouse gases high into the atmosphere and will continue to do so for the foreseeable future. If you must take to the skies, you can minimize your impact with these practices:

★ Start by flying during the day. A study by the University of Reading, published in *Nature*, revealed that night flights account for only 25 percent of air traffic but 60 to 80 percent of the industry's contribution to global warming. Why? At night a plane's contrails (the clouds of water vapor that form in its wake) trap heat that is emitted from the earth's surface, adding to the greenhouse effect that warms the planet. During the day, however, these white clouds reflect some sunshine back into space, reducing their impact. And flights during the winter are more environmentally destructive.

★ Fly nonstop whenever possible; taking off and landing eat up a lot of jet fuel.

★ Look for airlines and routes that use newer, more fuel-efficient planes such as the Airbus A380 and the Boeing 787 Dreamliner.

★ Pack light: This will save you money now that many airlines are charging for checked luggage. It will also reduce fuel usage.

★ Sit in coach. It's more eco-friendly, since you're taking up a smaller portion of the plane's capacity.

Green Travel Certification Labels

We're all familiar with the star rating systems used for hotels. But have you ever walked into a hotel lobby and seen a plaque with three green leaves on the wall, or sunbathed on a beach that was sporting a blue flag? As more and more travelers come to expect travel companies to go green, a number of certification labels have appeared—but no single certification system has risen above the rest. Here's a cheat sheet to some of the more prevalent labels you might find at eco-friendly travel businesses. Keep in mind that many travel companies have green business models but don't carry a label to prove it, since the certification process can be labor intensive, expensive, or both. You can find directories of members at many of these certifiers' Web sites.

★ **Green Globe:** Perhaps the world's most widely accepted and used certification scheme, Green Globe takes into account a number of criteria—including energy efficiency and conservation, waste management, land use, and involvement of staff and community. The program requires independent audits of members and annual measurement of environmental improvements. Seals are awarded at the gold, silver, and bronze levels. Certification is available for both companies and communities. (www.greenglobe.org)

★ **Leadership in Energy and Environmental Design Green Building Rating System (LEED):** This certification system, developed by the US Green Building Council, takes into account sustainable site development, water savings, energy efficiency, materials selection, and indoor environmental quality. Both existing properties and new builds can apply for the certification, which is awarded on four levels: platinum, gold, silver, or certified. (www.usgbc.org)

★ **Energy Star:** You're probably familiar with this EPA program from its labeling of home appliances. The hotel label is awarded to properties that score high on energy efficiency. (www.energystar.gov)

★ **European Union Eco-Label:** This label, represented by a green flower, certifies that a hotel or campsite limits energy and water consumption, reduces waste production, favors the use of renewable resources and less hazardous substances, and promotes environmental education. What it doesn't tell you is to what extent it achieves each of these goals. (www.eco-label.com)

★ **Sustainable Tourism Eco-Certification Program:** This new system from Sustainable Travel International measures environmental, social, and cultural impacts as well as best practices. After a self-assessment, onsite audit, and committee evaluation, members achieve anywhere from one to five stars. (www.sustainabletravelinternational.org)

★ **Blue Flag:** This program, run by a Danish nonprofit, certifies that beaches live up to standards of high water quality, environmental education and management, and safety. There are thousands of Blue Flag beaches and marinas in Europe, Africa, New Zealand, Canada, and the Caribbean. (www.blueflag.org)

★ **Sustainable Tourism Certification Network of the Americas:** This program, run by the Rainforest Alliance and the International Ecotourism Society, is a certifier of certifiers. Member organizations include the Certification for Sustainable Tourism, which operates in Costa Rica; Green Deal in Guatemala; Green Globe 21; Green Seal in the United States; and Smart Voyager in Ecuador. The eventual aim is to integrate certification programs around the world. A major step toward that goal is the group's unanimously accepted baseline criteria by which all members must abide. (www.rainforest-alliance.org)

Bring your own bath products, or take home the disposable bottles that you opened at the hotel. The housekeeping staff will have to throw out half-used bottles of shampoo and unwrapped bars of soap.

TIAMO RESORTS

The Sun King

When **Tiamo**'s owner decided to run his resort entirely on solar power, he was thinking green—but not that kind of green. It was originally a financial decision (the closest connection to the Bahamian grid was a dozen miles away), but one that has paid dividends to the environment. Tiamo is now among the most eco-friendly resorts in the Caribbean: The 11 bungalows are elevated on stilts to reduce land alteration; construction materials were brought in on shallow boats so that no roads had to be built or marine channels dredged; and the staff uses phosphate-free soaps that don't create algae blooms, which could endanger South Andros Island's large barrier reef. Though the solar panels soak up plenty of rays, the resort requires only as much energy as the average three-bedroom home here in

the United States. That's because there are no TVs, no air-conditioning, not even a commercial ice maker—the staff freezes cubes in trays instead. Low-flow composting toilets (don't worry, they look almost like yours at home) even turn waste into rich peat for the landscaping.

Activities are equally earth conscious: no pollutant-spewing Jet Skis here. Instead, you'll find snorkel equipment, kayaks, sailboats, and a nature concierge team eager to teach guests about Bahamian bush medicine and local lore. Family-style dinners are a casual affair, but the cuisine is plenty sophisticated. Rates include all meals, daily biologist-guided tours, airport transfers, and use of all water toys. Rooms from $315 per night. (www.tiamoresorts.com)

LEAVE NO TRACE

Take Only Pictures, Leave Only Footprints

The **Leave No Trace** (LNT) philosophy was adopted by the National Park Service long before the general public started talking about global warming and carbon offsets. Today, the Leave No Trace Center for Outdoor Ethics teaches kids and adults how to reduce their impact while they hike, camp, picnic, showshoe, run, bike, hunt, paddle, ride horses, fish, ski, climb, or do just about anything else outdoors.

The LNT Web site lists the center's principles—dispose of waste properly, for example—and then details just how to achieve these goals (build a cathole at least 200 feet, or 70 adult steps, from water, trails, and camp for all . . . uh . . . solid human waste). Three Leave No Trace teams travel the country leading hands-on workshops covering these principles. Book them for your next mountain biking or sea-kayaking club meeting and they'll tailor the demonstration to your sport. (www.lnt.org)

GREEN SPOT TRAVEL

Vacation + Philanthropy

This travel agency's mission is to have clients make a tangible impact on a local community even as they visit the most ecologically pristine parts of Central America and stay in luxurious but green hotels. And they're not just talking the talk: Green Spot has funneled much of its profits into opening a used clothing store in rural Costa Rica. Proceeds from the sale of the clothing (much of it donated by clients) pay for computers and environmental education at the town's school. **Green Spot**—run by an American who lived in Costa Rica for 12 years and his Costa Rican wife—customizes trips to suit a variety of travelers, from beachgoers to ziplining adrenaline addicts.

Above all, Green Spot excels in authentic cultural experiences; one favorite is a cooking lesson in a Costa Rican home, shaping tortillas and mashing plantains into *patacones*. The company partners only with hotels and tour companies that themselves show a strong commitment to the environment and the local community; these partners might have designated part of their land as a protected reserve, installed solar energy panels, or hired and trained only local residents. (www.greenspot.travel)

> **FYI**
>
> Be careful not to step on coral while snorkeling or scuba diving. Even a light touch can kill decades' worth of growth.

NATURAL HABITAT ADVENTURES
Where the Wild Things Are

This tour operator was the first travel company in the world to go carbon neutral: Its Boulder, Colorado, home office runs entirely on alternative energy, and it offsets the greenhouse-gas emissions released as a result of its trips by funding renewable energy projects (you're on your own when it comes to your flights, though). Natural Habitat Adventures also designed the planet's first hybrid safari vehicle—a Toyota Highlander with more-rugged suspension, a sliding canvas top, and flip-up photography windows—which doubles a typical safari truck's mileage, and they run a cooking-oil-fueled van in Canada.

"Meaningful encounters with wildlife in its natural surroundings" is the common theme of the company's trips, whether the destination is Africa, Asia, or the Arctic—which may be why the World Wildlife Fund has used Natural Habitat Adventures as its exclusive travel provider since 2006. Many of the company's expedition leaders hold master's degrees or PhDs in botany, ecology, and the like. Its most popular trips are the polar-bear-viewing excursions to Churchill, Manitoba, where Natural Habitat donates time on its tundra buggies to local groups and space on its Churchill-to-Winnipeg charter flights in exchange for donations to local organizations. The company also specializes in family trips to several US national parks as well as to South America and Africa. (www.nathab.com)

LAPA RIOS ECOLODGE
A Jewel in the Jungle

If Costa Rica is the motherland of ecotourism, Lapa Rios is her golden child. This lodge blends a truly green environmental credo with a level of luxury unheard of this deep in the rain forest. First, for the environment: Lapa Rios has protected 1,000 acres of mostly primary rain forest that serves as a wildlife corridor for animals from the Corcovado National Park on Costa Rica's Osa Peninsula, the least developed region in the country. The lodge itself was built using 70 percent renewable materials, initiated the first glass and plastic recycling system in the area, and operates its own solid-waste and sewage-treatment systems. Lapa Rios' owners have also built an elementary school, which guests can visit on one of the numerous guided tours offered each day. Most travelers spend four nights at Lapa Rios, spotting rare wildlife, learning about the medicinal uses of plants and seeds, swimming in the Golfo Dulce, or even playing soccer with a team of Ticos, or local Costa Ricans.

The palm-thatched bungalows are simply appointed, with indoor and outdoor showers, bamboo furnishings, mosquito-netted queen beds, and private decks overlooking the Pacific Ocean—it's no surprise that this place is popular with adventurous honeymooners. From the dining room, guests can climb a spiral staircase 50 feet up to an observation platform from which monkeys and toucans are easily spotted.

Rates include all meals, nonalcoholic drinks, airport transfers, and one guided hike of the hotel's nature reserve. Rooms from $210 per person. (www.laparios.com)

SUSTAINABLE TRAVEL INTERNATIONAL

One-Stop Green Travel Shopping

Sustainable Travel International (STI) runs a number of programs that help travelers fulfill its motto to "leave the world a better place." The site's free monthly Responsible Travel Report includes tips on how to leave a lighter footprint during your travels, and the online Eco-Directory lets users search for hundreds of green travel providers according to the type of trip (archaeology or beaches, for instance) and the destination. Travelers wanting to give back to a place they've just visited can search for projects on STI's Travelers' Philanthropy page. The online Fair Trade Store sells products handcrafted by local artisans. Finally, STI's annual Green Gear and Gift Guide is a great go-to resource for eco-friendly clothes, sports gear, and other products. (www.sustainable travel.com)

VOLUNTOURISM 101

So you'd like to take a volunteer vacation, but you want to make sure your money and time are going to a useful, well-run project. A good place to start is VolunTourism.org, a site that aids organizations developing voluntourism programs and lets travelers find the right one for them. The site's pages will help you figure out if a volunteer vacation fits your needs, identify what you want to get out of the experience, prepare for your trip, and even evaluate your post-trip emotions. If you follow the site's steps, you'll ask yourself the hard questions that will prepare you for the trip, such as "How good are my people skills—do I feel comfortable speaking with anyone, anywhere?" The site also produces weekly webcasts and a quarterly newsletter with additional tips.

A sister site, TheVolunTourist.org, features online forums through which you can compare notes with fellow voluntourists and give first-hand advice on the pros and cons of various trips. Although Volun-Tourism.org doesn't have a user-friendly, searchable database of volunteer programs, it does list a number of organizations judged to do good work. Beyond that, it's your job to search out other options and evaluate their missions and actions with the tools you've been given here.

FYI

Always return your plastic key card when you check out of a hotel. Be sure to mention to the front desk staff that wooden key cards are much more sustainable.

TENUTA DI SPANNOCCHIA

Under the Tuscan Sun

Villas in Italy's Tuscan countryside are a dime a dozen. But if environmental credentials are among your vacation criteria, there's only one place to go: **Tenuta di Spannocchia**. This 1,100-acre working agricultural estate specializes in heirloom produce and nearly extinct animal breeds such as the Cinta Senese pig, all part of a plan to preserve the cultural and agricultural heritage of the region. In fact, you could eat like royalty off the land here: The fields are sown with legumes and grains, grapevines provide fruit for wine, and acres of orchards produce olives and fruit. The turreted *castello* was built in the 12th century by the Spannocchi family, and its rustic apartments and several surrounding farmhouses (once occupied by the *mezzadria* sharecroppers who worked the land) are available for rent by the night or the week.

In addition to touring the famous nearby sites in and around Siena, guests are welcome to take part in the nonprofit Spannocchia Foundation's workshops held onsite, which cover Italian history, art, cuisine, writing, sustainable agriculture, and architecture. The estate has one of Tuscany's first natural wastewater treatment facilities, as well as composting and recycling programs. In order to book a room at Tenuta, you must become a member of the foundation, which costs $45 per person or $70 per family. Rooms from $108 per night, including breakfast; farmhouses from $739 per week. (www.spannocchia.com)

VAIL RESORTS
Skiing Green

Even though climate change has actually lengthened Colorado's ski season in recent years, Vail Resorts—owner of the Vail, Beaver Creek, Breckenridge, Keystone, and Heavenly Mountain Resorts—made a bold move to reduce global warming: The company now offsets all of its electricity use with wind-power credits. Only Whole Foods buys more wind-power credits than does Vail Resorts, which estimates that the move was equivalent to taking 18,000 cars off the road. The company limits idle time for its vehicles to 5 minutes and has replaced its two-stroke snowmobiles with more-efficient four-stroke models. It even serves only local organic dairy products and hormone-free meats in all 40 of its restaurants, and $1 from every season pass, online lift ticket purchase, and hotel night goes to the National Forest Foundation.

But Vail Resorts is not done yet. The $1 billion Ever Vail complex, a residential and commercial pedestrian village at the base of Vail Mountain that will open in 2010, expects to earn LEED (Leadership in Energy and Environmental Design) certification for its sustainable building materials, geothermal heating, graywater use, green roofs, and other eco-friendly measures. Skiing never had it so green. (www.vailresorts.com)

FYI

Thinking about renting a car? Look into public transportation options instead. If you decide to rent, go for economy size. You'll save on rental fees and gas consumption.

JOURNEYS WITHIN
Time Out from the Temples

No one could accuse the Cambodians of having it easy. Since the 1970s, this Southeast Asian land has endured US bombing runs, a coup d'état, the Khmer Rouge genocide, and Vietnamese occupation. In this decade, the country has finally found peace, but it is still struggling to get a toehold in the world economy. As a tourist with Journeys Within, you can help. This tour operator's nonprofit wing, Journeys Within Our Community (JWOC), runs several projects in the areas of health, education, and business development and encourages visitors to lend a hand. When you sign up for Journeys Within's Give and Take Tour, you'll spend half your time sightseeing around Siem Reap—an area that includes Angkor Wat and dozens of other less famous but equally beautiful temples—and the other half volunteering for JWOC. You might help the organization's university scholarship students teach free English classes, lend your financial acumen to their microloan program, write a few articles for JWOC's newsletter, help out at a local orphanage, or collect samples from the clean-water wells they've dug. The tour includes accommodation at the Journeys Within Bed & Breakfast, a private guide, tours and admission fees, and all meals and transportation while you're volunteering. Give and Take Tour, $1,165 per person, double occupancy. (www.journeys-within.com)

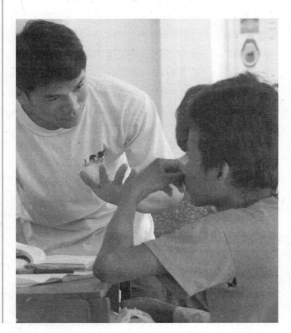

SOLAR CAMPING OVEN: HEAT OF THE SUN

The Tulsi-Hybrid solar cooking oven uses sunshine (or electricity on a cloudy day) to cook meat, veggies, and even cakes and cookies. It's a bulky, heavy contraption that you certainly won't strap onto your backpack, but it works great for car camping and outdoor barbecues. The cooking surface is even big enough to handle a large pizza ($299; www.sunbdcorp.com).

ACCOR

Company with a Conscience

Few Americans know the France-based Accor hotel group, but they're sure to know at least a few of its brands: Motel 6, Sofitel, Ibis, and Novotel, as well as Pullman, Mercure, Suite-hotel, Adagio, All Seasons, Etap Hotel, and Formule 1. Whether you've stayed at a budget Motel 6 or a top-of-the-line Sofitel, what you probably don't know is how important corporate responsibility is to the company; its Earth Guest program includes both environmental and social projects. By the end of this decade, Accor has pledged to reduce the consumption of water and energy in all of its hotels by 10 percent and to install solar panels in at least 200 properties. On this large a scale, simple changes make a big difference: By installing occupancy sensors in about a hundred Motel 6 properties throughout California, Accor is reducing its carbon dioxide emissions by more than 10 million pounds per year.

The company has also trained thousands of its employees to watch for suspicious behavior and other signs of child sex tourism, a sad but persistent phenomenon in which youths from developing countries are lured into pornography or prostitution for the benefit of wealthier tourists. And each hotel has its own pet projects—training more than 100 farmers near Siem Reap, Cambodia, to improve and diversify their produce, for example, and housing women and children in France when the local Red Cross shelters are full. (www.accor.com)

FYI

Before you leave for a trip, unplug your TV and other appliances that drain electricity. If possible, adjust your refrigerator a few degrees warmer.

ECOCLUB

An Insider's Perspective

This Athens, Greece–based international association of affordable ecolodges and tour operators has one of the most thorough lists of green travelers' guidelines we've seen anywhere (everything from unplugging home appliances before the trip to not correcting locals who try to speak English), as well as summaries of its member businesses. Ecoclub's bimonthly free online magazine includes thoughtful interviews with ecotourism pioneers (which are also archived in the country directories for pre-trip reading) and, of course, updates from its members, who operate in more than 80 countries. The club's annual Ecotourism Awards fund innovative projects that can further green the travel industry; one past winner from Rwanda used his prize to teach former gorilla poachers how to be farmers. (www.ecoclub.com)

ecoclub.com

SIERRA DESIGNS RECYCLED SLEEPING BAGS

Sweet Dreams

These his-and-hers bags (the women's model is shorter, with narrower shoulders, wider hips, and more insulation around the torso and toes) are made from over 90 percent green materials—the insulation and shell fabric from used soda bottles, the liner from coconut husks and recycled plastic. In fact, only the zippers and Velcro are on their first time around. The Climashield Green insulation is a continuous filament, so it won't separate or clump while you're tossing and turning. Add in conveniences like a chest pocket for your headlamp and straps to attach the bag to your sleeping pad, and you've got one perfect camping setup. The only downside is the bag's relative heft, which ranges from 2 pounds 13 ounces to 3 pounds 8 ounces, depending on the model. (www.sierradesigns.com)

Earn Your Scientist Badge

Scientists need help. Lots of it. And since 1971, Earthwatch has been connecting researchers in the field with willing volunteers. Researchers from around the world apply to the institute for grants that provide both financial assistance and free labor. Travelers sign on to these field expeditions, which involve no guided touring but plenty of eye-opening firsthand experience in foreign lands and subjects, living, working, and eating as the scientists do. The tasks are dirty and sometimes difficult, the food is far from gourmet, but the science is real and important. You need no prior experience and will be taught how to do fieldwork that might involve uncovering dinosaur bones with a dental pick, counting fish on a coral reef, or interviewing African villagers.

Earthwatch offers expedition opportunities on every continent, with accommodations that run from homestays to hotels, and at lengths of 3 days to 3 weeks. Some of the projects are in areas that are off-limits to regular tourists. Not only does an Earthwatch trip give scientists a helping hand, it enlightens travelers to the problems facing our natural world. And the cost you pay for the trip—a portion of which supports the project you're working on—is generally tax deductible. (www.earthwatch.org)

African Community

When he was 4 years old, Italian Luca Belpietro slept in a tent in his front yard to prove to his father that he was old enough to go on safari. Twenty-five years later, he moved to Kenya permanently to open a safari lodge. Not your average safari lodge, Campi ya Kanzi is owned and managed by a Maasai community. Belpietro set up the lodge so that it would benefit the people of the Kuku Group Ranch on which it is located—and which borders three national parks. By involving the local people in the camp, Belpietro has given them a source of income, a source of empowerment, and a reason to protect the roaming wildlife—more than 60 species of mammals and 400 bird species live inside the ranch. He also created the Maasai Wilderness Conservation Trust, funded through donations and fees charged to guests of the lodge, which pays the salaries of local teachers, nurses, and game scouts and sponsors other community and environmental projects.

Guests can go game-spotting by foot or vehicle, spend a night in the lodge's mobile tented camp, or visit the Maasai village. And since the ranch is two-thirds as large as the Maasai Mara Game Reserve but allows in just 14 tourists as opposed to 5,000, this is one of the most private wildlife experiences in Africa. Rates include all meals, soft drinks, house wine and beer, escorted game drives and walks, cultural visits, laundry service, and airport transfers. From $550 per person. (www.maasai.com)

Patagonia's number-one priority has long been the environment—at times to the detriment of its bottom line. Back in the early 1970s, the company stopped making rock-climbing pitons because they were damaging rock faces. And in 1996, Patagonia switched its entire product line to 100 percent organic cotton. The must-have item of any green traveler's wardrobe has long been a Patagonia fleece, but the latest version is made of Synchilla, a polyester sourced from used garments and recycled soda bottles. These jackets can take a lot of wear and tear, but if you ever get tired of the color, you can complete the cycle by returning it to the company's Common Threads recycling program. (www.patagonia.com)

When building a campfire, use only dead sticks from the ground—don't break off a tree branch for kindling. Don't leave your campsite until the wood or coals are completely out, and be sure to scatter the cool ashes.

OSPREY RESOURCE SERIES OF TRAVEL BAGS

Style and Substance

Long known for making unbeatable mountaineering packs, Osprey has designed a line of bags made mostly from recycled materials—ground-up plastic bottles, to be exact. The backpacks, messenger bags, and shoulder bags range from 71 to 86 percent recycled content and cost about the same as an equivalent bag made from traditional materials. Also noteworthy: The company's Colorado headquarters runs on 100 percent wind power and other renewable energy. (www.ospreypacks.com)

RESPONSIBLETRAVEL.COM

Choose Your Own Adventure

Once you've figured out what type of volunteer vacation is right for you, one good clearinghouse of trip options lives at www.responsibletravel.com. The site lists hundreds of volunteer trips, handpicked by the staff based on environmental, social, and economic criteria, and many include firsthand reviews from past travelers. You can search by type of volunteer work, location, departure date, and length of trip.

BANYAN TREE

A Helping Hand around Asia

This company's Green Imperative Fund supports environmental and community projects near all of its resorts and city hotels throughout Asia. Each guest bill includes $1 to $2 per night for the fund, and every donation is matched by Banyan Tree. This charity has paid for educational scholarships in Thailand, malaria eradication in Indonesia, solar water heaters for a village in China, and a marine conservation laboratory in the Maldives, to name just a few chosen projects. When the Asian tsunami hit 5 years ago, the company helped rebuild 77 houses and repaired 49 boats for Thai villagers who had no other source of income. Banyan Tree has also committed to planting 20,000 trees between 2007 and 2016. None of these good works, however, take away

from the state of bliss guests are likely to experience at the company's resorts, which are particularly famous for their spa facilities—and especially loved by honeymooners.

The company started in 1994, building boutique resorts in parts of Asia that had previously been dominated by big-box hotels. Unlike other chains, the architecture and decor of each Banyan Tree property is meant to blend in with the local styles, though at every resort you'll find sybaritic amenities like individual villas and private pools. (www.banyantree.com)

Never feed wild animals. It makes them reliant on humans, and our foods are often likely to make them sick.

CRUISE SHIPS
Sailing a Blue-Green Sea

Cruise ships have long been accused of having a rather unfriendly attitude toward the planet—they dumped garbage overboard and pumped contaminated bilgewater directly into the ocean. Today, however, many of the cruise lines have been shamed into mending those bad habits, and some are going above and beyond what the law requires. **Disney Cruise Line**, for instance, uses a new hull coating that is both less toxic and more fuel efficient. **Holland America** connects to shore power when docked in Seattle, thus reducing dockside emissions by nearly 65 percent. **Norwegian Cruise Line** donates much of its used cooking oil to an organic farmer who uses it as biodiesel to run his farm equipment. **AdventureSmith Explorations** offsets all of the carbon emissions that result from its cruises. Here are a few questions you can ask to find out if a cruise line is doing more than its share for the environment:

★ Do the ships carry advanced wastewater treatment facilities that go beyond what is required by law?

★ Does the cruise line abide by the United States' strict wastewater dumping regulations, even when traveling near countries that have no regulations?

★ Do the ships use low-sulfur fuel, or any other engine or smokestack technology, to reduce harmful emissions?

★ Does the cruise line support any environmental causes or scientific research?

BICYCLE SHARING PROGRAMS
Two Wheels Trump Four

Riding a bike is one of the world's perfect forms of sightseeing: It's fast enough that you can cover a fair amount of territory in a day, but slow enough that the landscape doesn't blur as you pedal by. It's inexpensive, at least compared to a car rental. You'll blend in with the locals, who in most parts of the world are more avid cyclists than Americans, either for reasons of necessity or fitness. And of course, it's clean and green.

In major tourist centers, it's usually not hard to find a shop that will rent

you a bike for a day—but then you have to figure out where to lock it up, and you can't resort to any other form of transportation. A growing number of cities, primarily in Europe, now offer bike-sharing programs that solve these problems. A company stows a fleet of bikes around the city, which residents and visitors can borrow for 10 minutes, an hour, or a day. When you're done, return the bike to the original location or leave it at another of the company's drop-off points. **Velib**, for example, has 20,000 bikes at nearly 1,500 stations around Paris; you can buy an unlimited day pass for one euro or a week's pass for five euros. There are similar programs in Helsinki, Stockholm, Oslo, Copenhagen, Munich, Frankfurt, Lyon, Vienna, Seville, Pamplona, and Barcelona; in the United States, you'll find them in Washington, DC; Madison, Wisconsin; and Salt Lake City.

STAY SAFELY HYDRATED

You don't buy bottled water at home because you know how quickly that plastic is filling our landfills. Why change your habits on vacation? Instead, pack along an **aluminum SIGG water bottle**. (And don't forget to empty it before you go through security at the airport.) The SIGG's metal construction is 10 to 20 percent lighter than a Nalgene bottle, doesn't affect the taste the way plastic will, and holds up better under wear and tear. The company has been perfecting the design since 1908, and you can choose from 144 exterior patterns and 22 lids. Even if you're traveling where tap water generally isn't safe to drink, many hotels that cater to Western tourists filter what comes out of your room sink, so you can fill up your bottle there each morning—but always check first. And remember to pack a few water purification tablets for emergencies. (www.mysigg.com)

CAR RENTALS
Be Smart *and* Green

Just as with flying, sometimes you simply have to rent a car. When you must, follow these tips to mitigate your environmental effects:

★ **Decline the upgrade.** How many times have you walked up to the car rental counter to pick up a compact and walked out with a sedan? Rental agencies are masterminds of the up-sell—think of the extra room you could have for just a few dollars more per day (sometimes even for free, if they're short on the type of car you want). But think also of all that extra gas you'll be buying. Go for the high-mpg models, which are almost always the smallest available.

★ **Reserve a hybrid.** If you're doing a lot of stop-and-go driving (which is likely when sightseeing), a hybrid is the best choice. Enterprise, Avis-Budget, National, Alamo, and Hertz all carry hybrids in their national fleets, as do smaller agencies such as EV Rental Cars and Fox. Bio-Beetle even rents biodiesel sippers on Maui.

★ **Consider a car-sharing program.** These companies maintain fleets of cars distributed throughout a city—or in the case of Zipcar, over a dozen cities from coast to coast (Enterprise Rent-a-Car recently launched a car-sharing program as well). Say you're visiting San Francisco for a week. You can take public transportation from the airport to your hotel in the middle of the city, but you want to make a few day trips up to Wine Country and out to the beach. Instead of renting a car—which you'll then be tempted to use more than necessary just to amortize the cost—sign up for City CarShare, which has fleet stations all around the Bay Area. The details of each city's plan vary, but you can generally opt for a temporary membership, which includes gas and insurance, and pay only for the miles and hours that you drive.

TRAVELING BY RAIL
Old Standby Makes a Comeback

Riding the rails might seem quaint here in the United States, but elsewhere in the world it's an essential method of transportation—and in Europe and Japan, an ultraquick one. Though not as cheap as they were when you last backpacked around the Continent, Eurail passes are still relatively inexpensive and far more eco-friendly than those no-frill, low-fare airlines (which, by the way, tend to travel between second-tier airports far from the city center). Trains cruise at more than 200 mph, and many offer onboard WiFi. Nearly as fast are the bullet trains in Japan, known as *shinkansen*, which link Tokyo to most of the major cities on Honshu and Kyushu. You can find English schedules and buy rail passes at www.japanrail.com.

Here in the States, travelers can easily navigate the Northeast aboard the Acela Express, which runs from Washington, DC, to Boston via Baltimore, Philadelphia, and New York. When you factor in time to get to the airport, it's quicker to take the train from Washington, DC, to New York, and the journey releases approximately half as much carbon dioxide per passenger mile. More than just a way to get from A to B, trains are a great alternative to road tripping. **Amtrak**'s routes slice and dice the country, passing through scenic areas like the Hudson River Valley, the Sierra Nevada, and the Chihuahuan Desert. **VIA Rail** and **Canadian Pacific** run routes the length of Canada, and **Alaska Railroad** does rail tours of the 49th state. Sightseeing by rail gives you the opportunity to hop on and off, plus much more room (real beds, even) than you could get in a car or plane.

Got kids? Then you have more green power than almost any other person on the planet. In the most potent hat trick of our time, you can make a difference in this world in three very important ways:

★ By nurturing your children's health through the creation of a non-toxic lifestyle for your family

★ By establishing family habits that respect and protect the earth

★ By raising members of the next generation who will accept the charge of keeping the planet green

That's a lot of green power. As a parent, naturally your first concern is to provide for the well-being of your kids. As a parent at the beginning of the 21st century, you have an enormous advantage over parents of past generations in doing this. Sure, your mom and dad and your grandma and grandpa loved you. But they had no idea that everyday foods, toys, clothing, shoes, toothpaste, and bedding were bearing harmful chemicals that could later make you prone to allergies, asthma, chronic diseases, and even cancer. They didn't mean to endanger your health with that plastic baby bottle or teething ring, but the bisphenol A (commonly called BPA) in those plastic items and many others was leaching unhealthy chemicals into your body. A study published in 2008 in the *Journal of the American Medical Association* tells us that BPAs are associated with a slew of health problems, including cardiovascular and respiratory diseases, type 2 diabetes, cancer, and abnormal brain and prostate development.

Our parents and grandparents didn't know that the baby creams, powders, and lotions that they slathered on our tender skin were loaded with chemicals that the Campaign for Safe Cosmetics now tells us are linked to cancer, birth defects, learning disabilities, infertility, and other chronic diseases and problems. And who knew that the preservatives, processed flour, high-calorie sugars and oils, and artificial dyes and flavors in those sweets and treats could poison your body? Really—who knew?

Today, you know these things and so much more, and your kids benefit from that knowledge. This chapter identifies the products and services that will help safeguard your children's health—today and in the future. It's easy to change purchasing habits and protect the health of our children. Here's the kicker: What's good for our kids is almost always good for the environment. By avoiding products that use chemicals known to be harmful to humans, animals, and plants and that require excessive energy consumption and waste in their manufacture, packaging, shipping, distribution, and disposal, we're also protecting the earth. These actions save energy, reduce greenhouse gases, and curtail environmental contamination from toxic chemicals.

Take the common diaper as an example. Today, we can decide to use cloth diapers to reduce landfill waste (conventional disposable diapers hang around for up to 500 years before they decompose!), but not just any cloth diaper: We can choose cloth made of organic *bamboo*. It's a sustainable textile with antibacterial properties that grows without the need of herbicides, pesticides, or harsh bleaches, which are exceptionally tough on baby's bottom and on the land on which they're used. That's the double benefit of raising children green—it's good for them and good for the planet.

The products, tips, and suggestions in this chapter give you practical ways to substitute pure, healthy, and renewable products for products that are toxic, wasteful, nonrecyclable, or energy- and land-depleting. Instead of buying conventional produce, for example, which is typically farmed with pesticides and herbicides that harm the earth and water, you might decide to buy organic fruits and vegetables and organic fabric clothing for your little ones. One simple change like this can make a profound difference. Bottom line: Every time we make this kind of choice as a consumer, we help promote a sustainable environment. We show that we can all meet our present needs without endangering the ability of future generations to meet their needs.

Going green cannot be just a passing fad. If the planet is to survive, our children will have to carry on our determination to preserve it. Organizations noted in this chapter can help us empower our children to take on that task by impressing on them the beauty and the value of pure air, water, and food. The National Wildlife Federation, for example, can hook you up with a list of nature spots within 15 miles of your home through its Green Hour program. The Roots & Shoots network can get your kids involved in community service projects, and an Eco Family Adventure may be just the thing to woo your kids away from their electronic forms of entertainment and turn them on to the joys of the great outdoors.

Sustaining the quality of the air, water, and earth on this planet is not something we can expect other people to do for us. We take on that responsibility every time we—and our children—make a green choice.

—Theresa Foy DiGeronimo

EARTH'S BEST
Baby and Toddler Foods and Juices

Back in 1985, a couple of organic farmers in Vermont realized they couldn't buy any preservative-free baby food to feed their kids—and Earth's Best was born. The brand grew; by 1995, Earth's Best had developed more than 50 product offerings, all certified USDA organic. Since 2000, Earth's Best has been owned by New York–based organic and natural foods company the Hain Celestial Group.

Earth's Best organic infant formulas are blended without the use of growth hormones, steroids, antibiotics, dangerous pesticides, or chemical fertilizers. All food products are organic, whole grain, and Kosher (excluding meat varieties) and made with no genetically engineered ingredients; no added salt, modified starches, or refined sugars; and no artificial flavors, colors, or preservatives.

This brand offers a full pantry of organic foods for your child from birth through toddlerhood. In addition to its organic infant formulas (which contain 17 mg of the omega-3 fatty acid DHA, or docosahexaenoic acid, per 100 calories), the line includes infant cereals and jarred foods in more than 60 varieties, plus infant juices and teething biscuits. The Sesame Street toddler line features breakfast foods such as organic cold cereals, instant oatmeal, and frozen miniwaffles; meals including pasta, soups, whole grain pizza, and new frozen entrées; and snacks of crackers, cookies, and snack bars. (www.earthsbest.com)

ORGANIC MOMS ONLINE

Mothers of Organic (MOO) is an online community about parenting the organic way. Through MOO you'll meet biologists, pediatricians, lunch-lady chefs, gardening farm moms, and parents like you. Sponsored by Organic Valley, this Web site helps parents learn more about the benefits of feeding children organic foods through an educational partnership with Dr. Alan Greene, author of *Raising Baby Green*, and through its online parenting community. (www.organic valley.cop)

ORGANIC VALLEY FOODS
Organic Milk and More

If your kids chug down glasses of milk each day, you're probably concerned about the quality of that milk. For our health, the Organic Valley brand, like other brands of organic milk and foods, is produced without the use of antibiotics, synthetic hormones, or genetically modified organisms. For our environment, organic farming methods return vitality and nutrients to the soil and keep air and water free from pollution caused by pesticides and herbicides.

It is their concern for American farm communities that sets Organic Valley products above others. Started by seven farmers from southwestern Wisconsin in 1988, Organic Valley Family of Farms is now America's largest cooperative of organic farmers and the only national organic dairy co-op to remain independent. The co-op has built eight thriving pools and expanded into 20 states. These 1,266 farm families produce 130 organic products, including milk, cheese, butter, eggs, juice, soy beverages, produce, and meats.

When you buy an Organic Valley product, you're supporting local farmers by buying local products. The co-op farm in your regional area supplies your local stores so that the products are shipped minimal distances and thus are fresh for your family. (www.organicvalley.coop)

Silicone and Rubber, Not Plastic

Most conventional baby bottle nipples and pacifiers contain BPA—that component of polycarbonate plastics linked to health problems such as early puberty, hyperactivity, decreased sperm count, cancer, developmental toxicity, and learning problems. To avoid these products completely, do your shopping at BPAFreeKids (www.bpafree kids.com).

★ **Bottle nipples:** Open your brand-new plastic or glass baby bottle package and immediately throw away the nipple that comes with it. That's right. Since all conventional rubber bottle nipples contain BPA, replace that nipple with a nontoxic silicone variety. Silicone nipples are readily available in most retail stores that sell baby bottles. Or log on to www.bpafreekids.com to find **NurturePure** PureFlo silicone nipples for all bottle types. NurturePure nipples are soft and natural—made from food-grade silicone that is latex free, allergen free, and free of nitrosamines. A package of three sells for $4.99.

★ **Pacifiers:** BPAFreeKids offers top-of-the-line **Natursutten** pacifiers. Made of 100 percent all-natural rubber, this brand is a one-piece pacifier, meaning it has no cracks or joints where dirt and bacteria can hide. Natursutten pacifiers contain no BPA, parabens, PVC, phthalates, artificial colors, allergy-causing substances (like latex), or chemical softeners—yet this rubber is softer than silicone, another non-BPA product. All Natursutten pacifiers are CE certified, which means the product lives up to the European Union directive concerned with safety, health, and environment. Natursutten's orthodontic-style (in two sizes) or round-style (in four sizes) pacifiers cost $7.49. (www.bpafreekids.com)

Better Bottles

The purity of the bottle that holds your baby's nourishment is just as important as the purity of the liquid itself. When shopping for baby bottles, look for products made of glass or polypropylene—these are reportedly safer than plastic baby bottles that contain polycarbonates (the clear, shiny, glassy-looking hard plastic that is in about 95 percent of the bottles on the market). Researchers have found that polycarbonate plastics (recycling symbol #7) can leach bisphenol A (BPA) under certain conditions, including the heating of infant formula and breast milk, and following normal wear as the plastic scratches. BPA is a hormone disrupter that acts like human estrogen. Here are some options to consider when looking for your baby's bottle:

★ **Glass bottles:** Glass bottles do not contain the same potentially harmful chemicals as plastic bottles. Today's glass bottles are made of lightweight tempered safety glass that is easy to clean thoroughly, and of course they are 100 percent recyclable. A 5-ounce glass bottle from **Born-Free** costs about $9 and lasts through a baby's bottle years.

★ **Plastic bottles:** The Institute for Agriculture and Trade Policy (www.iatp.org) says that bottles made of milky, soft, translucent plastic usually contain no polycarbonates. You'll rest easy with BornFree plastic bottles that are made from a honey-colored plastic called PES (polymer) that is free of BPA, phthalates, and PVC. The entire **BornFree** product line of bottles, cups, and accessories is endorsed by the Children's Health Environment Coalition. A single 5-ounce plastic bottle from Born Free costs about $9.50. The starter kit (two bottles with level-1 nipples, a trainer cup, and level-2 nipples) runs $44.99. (www.newbornfree.com)

Grass Wrap

Mother-ease Inc. carries cloth diapers made from bamboo. Sandy's Bamboo Diapers are knit bamboo terry made with bamboo yarns and a polyester knit woven into the base of the fabric for durability. (The fiber content is 85 percent bamboo, 15 percent polyester.) Bamboo fiber is considered a sustainable textile that has antibacterial properties and grows without the need of herbicides and pesticides.

Elastic is added to the waist and leg openings. Depending on size, these diapers run from $13.25 each for extra small to $16.50 for toddler size. (www.motherease.com/cloth-diapers/Home)

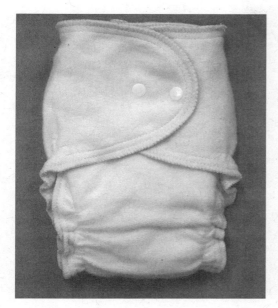

CLOTH DIAPERS
Forget the Bleach

Today's cloth diapers are going green. You can now easily find unbleached organic cotton or even bamboo diapers, and some styles come form-fitted with sewn-in closures. Now that's better than the diapers your grandma used!

Growing Greens one-size diapers, made by **Baby Greens Diaper Company**, are made of 100 percent organic cotton fabric, grown and milled locally and manufactured in the United States. They have a snap-in doubler that can be removed for little ones, then snapped in for older babies. Baby Greens Diaper distributor Karen Amidon cautions that the one-size diaper should not be expected to last from infancy into toddlerhood: "These are made of cotton; they're going to wear out after about a year of use. But they're great for new babies, who speed through different sizes so quickly. The traditional prefolds are much less expensive and are quite fine for older babies."

Whether you use the one-size diapers or traditional prefolds, purchasing Growing Greens diapers is a nice way to wrap your baby in eco-fibers and help our planet. One size fits most children from 7 to 35 pounds. They sell for $16.75 each. While you are purchasing cloth diapers, you might buy Covered Caboose wool cover ($30) to pull over them. This product is Oeko-Tex Standard 100 certified (that means certified organically raised), and the wool is entirely from the United States. (www.green mountaindiapers.com)

FYI

When shopping for baby bottles or pacifiers, check the recycling symbol on the product. Products numbered 3, 6, and 7 may contain harmful chemicals, while those labeled 1, 2, 4, and 5 are considered to be safer.

TEETHING SOOTHERS
Nontoxic Relief

Teething babies aren't exactly "green conscious." Anything that will ease the pain—good or bad, pure or toxic—is going in the mouth. So it's up to us to avoid those cute plastic teething rings and find nontoxic teethers. This is important because of the very function of teethers—babies chew and suck on them, taking in the toxic finish of painted wood teethers or the properties from plastic teethers made with PVC, BPA, phthalates, and allergy-causing substances. Additionally, plastic doesn't biodegrade, and many plastics cannot be recycled.

It's common sense, then, to give your baby a teether made from nontoxic materials. The Bumble Bee teething ring from the **Blue Ridge Eco Shop**, for example, is made of 100 percent organic cotton that can be moistened and tossed in the freezer to provide extra pain relief when chewed. (A cold teething ring temporarily reduces blood flow in the gums and thus eases pain.) The Bumble Bee teether sells for $8. (www.blueridgeecoshop.com)

For hard-surface teethers, try the **Natursutten** teething rings. They're made by the same company that produces the recommended pacifier. These teething rings are filled with purified sterilized water, free of any chemicals. The outer rings are made from Evatane (ethylene vinyl acetate, a material also used for medical products) and are free of silicone and chemical softeners (BPA and phthalates), and they contain no allergy-causing substances, such as the protein known to cause latex allergies. The rings can be refrigerated, and their textured surface massages baby's gums and helps the teeth emerge. Natursutten teethers in apple or fish shapes sell for $8.49. (www.bpafreekids.com)

TERRIFIC TUSH TREATMENT

Gentle on Baby and the Earth

Terrific Tush Treatment is a nongreasy cream for baby's behind. Unlike many other "natural" baby-care body products (even ones labeled "organic"), TerrEssential products are USDA certified organic. They contain only certified organic herbs and essential oils.

Terrific Tush Treatment contains Ayurvedic "skin healing" organic centella (derived from the herb *Centella asiatica*) infused in fragrant organic oils and butters, including cocoa butter. Three ounces sell for $18.95. (www.terressentials.com)

KUSHIES DIAPER LINERS: FLUSHABLE AND BIODEGRADABLE

These diaper liners are a good idea for both cloth and disposable diaper users. The flushable and fully biodegradable product looks like a roll of toilet paper, but you use each piece to line the diaper. When the liner is soiled, remove it and flush it away, for hygienic and convenient disposal of waste. They are *not* recommended for septic tanks. One hundred sheets sell for $8.60. (www.kushies.com)

DISPOSABLE DIAPERS

Clean and Green

Disposables, the diaper of choice for more than 80 percent of North American parents, have taken a hard hit for being non-eco-friendly. And rightfully so, given that approximately 10,000 tons of them end up in landfills each *day*, where they'll sit decomposing for about 500 years!

There are green options: environmentally friendly disposable diapers that work as well as traditional brands. The top pick is Seventh Generation chlorine-free diapers. The folks at Seventh Generation were the first to create biodegradable disposable diapers in the United States. This diaper features unbleached and 100 percent chlorine-free materials, which means the diaper is free of irritating and synthetic chemicals found in the dyes, fragrances, chemical contaminants, and chlorine-bleached paper pulp of conventional disposables. Prices range from 25 cents apiece for size 1 (8 to 14 pounds) to 50 cents apiece for size 6 (35+ pounds). (www.seventhgeneration.com)

Another environmentally friendly disposable diaper that works as well as traditional brands is Tushies, touted as the only gel-free disposable diaper in the world and the only disposable diaper containing cotton. They also contain non-chlorine-bleached, certified-TCF wood-pulp fluff. Join the Tushies "club" and you'll get a break on the cost (although even this discounted rate is slightly more expensive than Seventh Generation diapers), and the diapers will arrive automatically on preselected dates. (www.tushies.com)

RE-RUN MESSENGER

Eco Diaper Bag

Once you decide to "green diaper" your baby with biodegradable disposables or organic cotton cloth diapers, follow through with the purchase of an eco-friendly diaper bag. The Re-Run Messenger from Fleurville is a real find. Not only is it PVC and Teflon free, it's also made out of recycled plastic bottle fabric. Each 13½ x 11¼-inch bag keeps ten 600 ml plastic water bottles out of landfills.

The lightweight bag has an adjustable shoulder strap, a changing pad, a see-through wipe case, and pockets and pouches galore to hold baby's diaper necessities as well as your own iPod or sunglasses. The bag comes in attractive colors and silk-screened with a botanical print. (http://fleurville.com/shop)

ERGOBABY CARRIER
Support and Comfort

Baby carriers are a must-have for busy moms and dads who want to hold their babies close but have their hands free. The ERGObaby carrier will keep your baby comfortable and safe and the earth green.

This carrier has an ergonomic design that supports a correct sitting position for the baby's hip, pelvis, and spine growth. It disperses most of the baby's weight between the hips and thighs, which helps to eliminate compression of the spine. The ERGObaby also balances the baby's weight to the parent's hips and shoulders and alleviates physical stress for the parent.

The ERGObaby carrier (including the linings, infant inserts, and accessories) is made from 100 percent organic cotton that was grown, processed, and manufactured in compliance with organic fiber processing standards, and the dyes are certified under the Oeko-Tex Standard 100 international testing system for textiles.

The backpack and front pouch and infant insert are available in chocolate and forest green for $120. (www.ergobabycarriers.com)

Check Out the Green Clothing Brands

Stop by online retailer Kai Kids (www.kaikids.com) and shop by brand for kids' clothes that are organic and chemical pure. Notable names in this fashion niche include Babysoy, Bamboobino, Bamboosa, Bambu, Bare Organics, BornFree, Butterfly Weed Herbals, Cut 4 Cloth, Dimpleskins, Dress Me Up, Earth Friendly Baby, Echoes in the Attic, Fleurville, Greentainer, Jessica Scott, Jolie Maman, Kid Basix, Klean Kanteen, Little Green Star, Little Soles, Natursutten, Petit Flaneur, Pip Essentials, Ringley, Silikids, South of France, Sweet Memories Quilts, Under the Nile, and Zee Spot.

SPEESEES
Organic Clothing for Kids

Organic baby clothes are "in" and are readily available across the entire retail spectrum. You can locate online specialty shops with a simple search of "organic children's clothing." Or you can stop by your local Wal-Mart or Target superstores, which now stock organic cotton baby clothes. In your search for durable, pure, affordable, and fun kids' clothes, take a close look at speesees.

The name "speesees" reflects the way kids would say or spell "species," and the product line pays homage to animal, plant, and human species. With that fun fact in mind, browse the company's Web site for the basics of a child's wardrobe in sizes newborn to 4T. You can shop by fabric content, such as organic cotton, wool, hemp, or bamboo. For infants, you'll find organic baby bodysuits, clothing sets, T-shirts, pants, blankets, and baby accessories. For older kids, choose from organic T-shirts, shirts, jackets, dresses, and footwear. All products are made with organic materials, low-impact herbal dyes, nickel-free snaps, and pigment prints that are PVC free, and all are produced without formaldehyde or dioxin. (www.speesees.com)

SIMPLE SHOES

Footwear and Footprints

Simple Shoes (Deckers Outdoor Corporation) of Santa Barbara, California, is working hard, as their reps say, "to reduce the ecological footprint left from shoes." Their three lines of 100 percent sustainable shoes for infants and kids prove they've met their goal.

For infant sizes 1 to 3, Simple Shoes has created Weebit, made simply of organic cotton knit uppers and postconsumer paper pulp foot forms. Weebits in a selection of colors sell for $24 each.

For toddlers (sizes 10 to 13) and big kids (sizes 1 to 4), ecoSNEAKS are the best. This very stylish sneaker incorporates a mix of natural and recycled materials (none from animal products or by-products). The uppers are made from hemp; the linings from organic cotton; the outer soles from recycled car tires; the sidewalls, toes, and heel caps from vulcanized rubber; the foot forms from postconsumer paper pulp; and the laces from PET (recycled plastic bottles). A pair of ecoSNEAKS is yours for $40 and is shipped in a postconsumer recycled box.

The Simple Shoes Green Toe line features Green Piggies for kids. Like ecoSNEAKS, these shoes are animal friendly with hemp uppers. They also have natural crepe rubber midsoles, recycled car tire outersoles, coconut buttons, and bamboo linings, all held together with water-based cements. This product does, however, contain latex, making Green Piggies inappropriate for some allergy-sensitive kids. Green Piggies sell for $45.

These are earth-responsible shoes from a forthright company. This caveat on the Web site is honest and fun: "The bottom of these shoes used to be tires that rolled around on an axle that was connected to a car. Given the inherent nature of use like this, some of the shoe bottoms (i.e., tires) are marked up a little. Sure, we buff them out and put them on the bottom of the shoes, but they still show wear. If you get them and you decide you can't deal with the past life of that particular car tire, we'll take them back, as long as they are in new and unworn condition." (www.simpleshoes.com)

LOOP BEDDING LINENS

Stick with Organic Cotton

Our babies grow out of their cribs and into "big people" beds all too quickly. But when the inevitable happens, be sure your youngsters rest their heads on sheets made of organic cotton. The chemicals used in conventional textile manufacturing can remain in sheet fabrics, even after washing, and are classified by the World Health Organization as hazardous. The wastewater from conventional manufacturing also contributes to the pollution of our water. So when looking for bedding for your child's twin or full-size bed, choose organic cotton.

No harmful chemicals are used during the finishing process of **LOOP** 250-thread-count organic sheets; hydrogen peroxide is used for whitening in lieu of chlorine bleach. Even the low-impact dyes are certified organic. In fact, all LOOP products—including duvet covers, pillow shams, woven blankets, and handmade accent pillows—are certified organic and are safe enough for those with acute allergies and chemical sensitivities. They are manufactured either in the United States or abroad under fair-trade guidelines.

Compared to traditional cotton sheets, this bedding is a bit pricey—but because organic fibers grow stronger, they're more durable and longer lasting than conventional cotton when cared for properly. To see for yourself before buying, LOOP will send you fabric swatches for the asking. Prices start at $72.50 for a twin sheet and $77.50 for a full fitted sheet; a standard pillowcase is $20. (www.looporganic.com)

FYI

Here's another reason to buy organic cotton: healthy cows. The folks at **LOOP** bedding explain that the high-protein seed of the cotton plant is used as cattle feed: "Fortunately, organic cottonseed is being sent to organic dairy farms as feed. So when you purchase organic cotton, you are also helping to provide the much-needed chemical-free seed to organic dairy farmers."

PURE-REST CRIB MATTRESS
Green Slumbering

There will be sweet dreams for babies sleeping on the chemical-free, 100 percent natural rubber organic crib mattress from **Pure-Rest Organic Bedding Company**. Their mattresses are NAOMI-compliant. (NAOMI stands for National Association of Organic Mattress Industry.)

Most standard crib mattresses are constructed of polyurethane foam and/or other petrochemical materials and then covered with synthetic fabrics (such as polyester or nylon) and treated with PBDEs (polybrominated diphenyl ethers, which are flame-retardant chemicals added to plastics and foam products to make them difficult to burn and which often include the poisonous boric acid). The off-gases from these substances can be absorbed into the skin and lungs and cause allergic reactions and other health problems.

Pure-Rest's organic crib mattress has a core of 100 percent Sri Lankan natural rubber. The covering is made with quilted organic cotton fabric, organic batting, organically processed wool from organically raised sheep, and European organic cotton fabric. It passes all safety regulations and US Consumer Product Safety Commission guidelines (including the flame-retardancy standards), despite the fact that Pure-Rest uses no PBDEs. It sells for $399. (www.purerest.com or http://ecobaby.com)

AMERICAN BABY CRIB BEDDING
Organic and Stylish

The American Baby Company (ABC) has beautifully soft crib bedding made of organic cotton so your baby can sleep on sheets that are pure—not bleached or dyed. The four-piece organic cotton velour crib set (available in naturally occurring shades of natural and mocha) consists of a crib bumper (four sided, 10 x 162 inches), a reversible comforter (30 x 45 inches), a standard crib sheet, and a standard crib skirt with inverted pleat. The set sells for $129.95. You can purchase the ABC organic cotton velour crib sheet alone for $18.95.

ABC also offers a nice selection of organic bedding, including organic cotton velour changing table covers, a three-piece organic cotton velour cradle set, and an organic cotton sweater-knit blanket. (415-626-3171; www.babyearth.com)

Naturepedic®
Sleep Healthy Grow Healthy ™

NATUREPEDIC CHILD'S BED MATTRESS: ORGANIC COTTON IS THE KEY

Like crib mattresses, nontoxic twin and double mattresses can be found if you look around, and the **Naturepedic** No-Compromise Organic Cotton Ultra mattresses are a good place to start your research. Naturepedic has eliminated from its mattresses those materials (such as vinyl/PVC and polyurethane foam) that are known to off-gas questionable chemicals.

The No-Compromise mattress is filled with organic cotton (a natural and renewable product) so that the mattress contains no products that are bleached, dyed, or grown with synthetic pesticides, herbicides, or chemical fertilizers.

The mattress cover is made of an organic cotton fabric with a clear polyethylene food-grade waterproof coating. The manufacturer assures its customers that "polyethylene is an excellent alternative to the vinyl/PVC and is an environmentally friendly plastic used throughout the food packaging industry for its purity and nontoxic properties."

The No-Compromise Ultra comes with a dust-mite barrier cover and contains no high-allergy materials such as wool or latex, making this bedding hypoallergenic. It exceeds federal and state flammability standards and does so without the use of potentially harmful chemicals. Prices start at $599 for a twin. (www.naturepedic.com)

Toxin-Free Children's Bath Products

Nothing compares to the adorable smell of a child fresh out of the bath—washed, shampooed, powdered, and moisturized. The ingredients in these products, however, are not so adorable. Many baby bath products contain chemicals (particularly dioxane) linked to cancer, birth defects, learning disabilities, infertility, and other chronic diseases, according to the Campaign for Safe Cosmetics (safecosmetics.org). Although children are most vulnerable to these potential adverse effects, the dangerous ingredients do not have to be listed on product labels.

Fortunately, there are many toxin-free products available today. The Environmental Working Group's Skin Deep Cosmetic Safety database keeps a running list of toxic products as well as safe, organic ones. Check out the full list by clicking Baby Care on www.cosmeticsdatabase.com. Here are examples of low-hazard products:

- ★ Body Botanicals herbal baby soap
- ★ Earth Mama Angel baby shampoo and body wash
- ★ Nurture My Body baby lotion
- ★ Seaside Naturals Little Star Dust talc-free all-natural baby powder
- ★ Terressentials organic baby oil

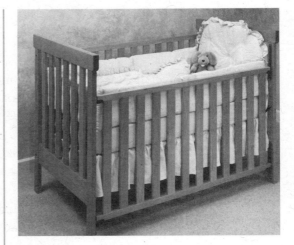

PACIFIC RIM NATURAL CRIBS

Maple Arts and Crafts

This eco-friendly crib by **Pacific Rim Woodworking** is produced entirely in Eugene, Oregon. It is made of Pacific Coast maple harvested from managed Washington and Oregon forests. Each piece is hand-rubbed with a nontoxic finish of tung oil and pure beeswax to highlight the natural beauty of the hardwood.

You'll love the crib's purity as well as its beauty. It is made free of toxic glues, formaldehyde, and particleboard. Completely untreated and raw pieces are available for anyone with environmental sensitivities or allergies.

As a company, Pacific Rim works to have as little negative impact on the environment as possible. The Web site explains how employees strive to use every foot of maple and donate the smallest scraps to local schools, community centers, and low-income families. Even the sawdust gets recycled and composted by a local company.

A finished or unfinished crib starts at $715; add casters for an extra $30 or so.

Find Pacific Rim cribs online at several sites, including www.greenhome.com and www.ourgreenhouse.com. (www.pacificrimwoodworking.com)

GREENHOME BABY BASSINET

A Handmade Nest

The small baby bassinet from **Green Home Environmental Store** in San Francisco is oh-so little, but oh-so green—in use, composition, and company policy.

At 13 x 27 inches, this little bassinet serves triple duty for babies 0 to 3 months old. It is a comfortable nest for your newborn to sleep in, it can be positioned on a bed to fit snugly between two adults (eliminating the worry of rolling over on a sleeping infant), and it's a convenient carrier for a day at the park.

The small baby bassinet is made of handwoven natural corn husks and comes with an organic wool-covered natural rubber mattress. (A separate bassinet lining in natural flannel sells for $45.)

You can buy this bassinet for $158.50 only from the Green Home Environmental Store Web site—another green step. The company eliminates the waste resulting from paper catalogs by processing all orders electronically. "As a result, we're completely virtual," the company says. (www.greenhome.com)

STAINLESS STEEL BOTTLES/SIPPY CUPS
Forget the Plastic

Finally, an earth-friendly alternative to the portable plastic water bottle for toddlers and older kids. The **Klean Kanteen** is made of 100 percent recyclable, high-quality, food-grade stainless steel (no need for a special lining like some other metal bottles). It's completely BPA-free and won't leach chemicals, toxins, or weird flavors into your kid's water, juice, or smoothie. An additional plus: It's durable, so you can reuse the bottle for years. When you are finished with it, it's recyclable.

The bottles come in four sizes (12, 18, 27, and 40 ounces) and range in price from $14.95 to $25.95. For your little one, the 12-ounce Klean Kanteen turns into a sippy cup with the purchase of a sippy spout adapter ($3.95) and sippy spout ($4.95). Both are nonleaching and toxin free. (www.kleankanteen.com)

TOM'S OF MAINE TOOTHPASTE
The Natural Way

Most adults don't swallow their toothpaste. But many kids do. Fortunately, you can buy a toothpaste that is not filled with dyes, preservatives, artificial flavorings, sweeteners, or animal products (as most brands are). The top choice is **Tom's of Maine**. This company pioneered natural hygiene products back in the 1970s and today offers two toothpastes specifically for children. The natural anticavity fluoride paste (which has the American Dental Association seal of approval) uses naturally sourced sodium monofluorophosphate to provide cavity protection and calcium to clean. The natural fluoride-free toothpaste uses calcium and silica to gently clean with no worry of "eating" fluoride.

Tom's of Maine is a true green company, giving 10 percent of all pretax profits to nonprofit organizations and packaging its products in recycled and recyclable materials with soy-based ink. And there's no risk here: If you're not satisfied, Tom's will refund your money. (www.tomsofmaine.com)

FYI

The American Academy of Pediatrics recommends avoiding the use of sunscreens on children younger than 6 months, unless there is no other way to protect them. Instead, the Academy suggests keeping babies this age in the shade under a tree, an umbrella, or the stroller canopy to prevent burns and overheating.

NATURE'S BOUNDARIES
Baby Massage Oil

A light-touch massage provides both parent and child with pleasure, comfort, reassurance, a sense of closeness, and emotional and physical contact. Bring on Little Lamb organic baby oil for massage by **Nature's Boundaries**!

The first of the all-natural ingredients in this oil is organic *Helianthus annuus*—in other words, sunflower seed oil. This oil helps a child's skin retain its natural moisture and provides a protective barrier against infection on baby's skin.

This product received a 9 out of 10 rating on the Best of 2008 Baby Products list prepared by the First Impressions Maternity and Baby Web site. The product review stated: "Wonderfully (yet lightly) scented oil. Works great. However, does contain almond oil." Responding to this comment, Nature's Boundaries quickly changed the formula by removing the almond oil and replacing it with organic avocado oil. As company rep Kathy Cox explained, "Some parents do not want to put almond oil on their babies for fear of triggering nut-type allergies, so we have made the change to ease their fears."

Nature's Boundaries is a Christian-based business that gives 10 percent of its profits to a rehabilitation center for the homeless in Minnesota, and it has signed the Compact for Safe Cosmetics and the Truth in Labeling pledge to assure its customers that its skincare products do not contain harmful or questionable ingredients.

Four ounces of Little Lamb organic oil costs $6.95. (www.naturesboundaries.com)

SUNSCREEN
Natural Blockers

There's a safe and green way to protect our kids from the skin damage caused by the sun's ultraviolet (UV) rays. Most of the health concerns about sunscreens focus on those that use chemical UV absorbers, which absorb rays that come in contact with skin rather than block them. Many of these chemical absorbers act like estrogen in the body; some can cause allergic reactions, and others have been found to break down in as little as 30 minutes when exposed to sunlight. Add this to the fact that these chemical absorbers also contain synthetic dyes and fragrances with hormone-disrupting phthalates, paraben preservatives that also act like estrogen in the body, and urea preservatives that emit formaldehyde as they break down, and it's easy to see that the common sunscreen may be doing your child harm.

So before you head out for a day in the sun with your kids, find a sunscreen formulated with either titanium dioxide or zinc oxide or a combination of both. Titanium dioxide and zinc oxide are minerals that physically block UV rays from reaching your skin. Minerals are considered the best protection against sunburn because they block both UVB rays (which cause sunburns) and UVA rays (which cause skin aging and cancer).

For your kids, you might try **Eco Lani** sunscreen ($15 for 4 fluid ounces; www.lanisimpson.com) or **Avalon Organics** Natural Mineral sunscreen ($9.95 for 3.5 fluid ounces; www.avalonorganics.com). Both use the 100 percent natural, safe-for-kids, UV/UVB blocker titanium dioxide.

Save the Coral Reefs

The same chemicals found in traditional sunscreen that interfere with human hormones were recently found to cause bleaching and death of corals. Seventy-eight million tourists visit areas with coral reefs every year, leaving behind 4,000 to 6,000 tons of sunscreen—and because many sunscreens are petroleum based, they don't break down quickly in water. A study published in *Environmental Health Perspectives* (April 2008) revealed that coral developed viral infections that led to bleaching when exposed to benzophenone- or cinnamate-based sunscreens. The same happened when coral were exposed to paraben preservatives.

ARSENIC TEST
Wood That's Not Good

Most outdoor wooden play sets built before 2004 were treated with chromated copper arsenate (CCA), a wood preservative that contains carcinogenic arsenic that can slowly leach out of the wood. CCA is what gives pressure-treated wood that green tinge, but the color can fade over time, so it's tough to know at a glance if the rungs of that ladder your kids grip with their hands is made of CCA-treated wood. Err on the side of caution and test the wood and soil around the play set for arsenic with a kit from the Environmental Working Group for $25 to $40. (www.ewg.org)

BABY GEAR RECYCLING: PASS IT ALONG!

What's a parent to do with all those outgrown remnants of babyhood? What about that little crib, playpen, car seat, high chair, swing, stroller, or diaper bag? Don't ship them off to the landfill. Instead, send them to **BabyEarth RENEW**, a hassle-free baby gear recycling program. The folks at BabyEarth (an online distributor of environmentally friendly baby products) will take your stuff. If it's in excellent shape, they'll donate it to a family in need. If not, they'll disassemble it and send all usable parts to accredited recycling centers. If you deliver a car seat, for instance, they will ship the fabric to developing countries; the metal, plastic, and foam will be used for construction projects. You pay the cost of shipping your item to BabyEarth; they do the rest.

Send baby gear to BabyEarth, RENEW Recycling Program, 21 Cypress Boulevard, Suite 1120, Round Rock, TX 78665. Want to deliver in person? Visit www.babyearth.com/renew for directions to the BabyEarth flagship store and for drop-off information.

HEALTHY TOYS

Chemical Awareness

HealthyToys.org, a nonprofit created by the the Michigan-based Ecology Center and the Washington Toxics Coalition, has compiled a database of test results for more than 1,200 toys and children's products. Each product tested was given an overall rating of low, medium, or high as well as an individual chemical rating. The tests have found that some toys contain chemicals of concern, including heavy metals such as lead and cadmium.

An independent evaluation of the toys is necessary, says HealthyToys.org, because the presence of toxic chemicals in consumer products is perfectly legal in the United States. The only US law regarding chemicals and toys is the one restricting lead—and that law applies only to paint, not to the lead found in the product's composition. Currently the only standard for chemicals in children's toys is a voluntary industry standard that cannot be legally enforced.

The following are just a few of the 146 products (out of the original 1,200 tested) that were found to have no detectable traces of lead, cadmium, chlorine, arsenic, mercury, antimony, tin, bromine, or chromium in any components tested: DiscoverSounds Guitar by Little Tikes, Alphabet Pal by Leap Frog Enterprises, Classical Stacker by Fisher-Price, James from *Thomas the Tank Engine*, Madame Alexander Holiday Doll by Alexander Doll Co., Pink Bead Necklace by Hannah Montana, and Amazing Animal Hippo by Fisher-Price.

If a toy isn't in the database, visit the Toy Rankings section of the HealthyToys.org Web site and click on the Vote for a Product bar to see if the toy is on the list suggested for testing. If so, cast your vote. If it's not there, nominate your toy for testing. This organization regularly tests the most requested toys. (www.healthytoys.org)

GREENHOUR.ORG

A Cure for Nature Deficit Disorder

"**G**o outside and play!" says every mom across the land. But Junior sits in front of the TV/video game/computer (pick one) and the seasons pass unnoticed.

The **National Wildlife Federation** aims to get kids outside for a leisurely walk through the woods or an afternoon of exploring worms and frogs. This organization has created a new Web site to help parents get kids focused on the outside world. Go to www.greenhour.org, plug in your ZIP code, and you'll find a list of nature spots within 15 miles of your home.

If we want our kids to care about the future of the planet, it's important for them to connect with nature.

MomsRising to the Rescue

HealthyToys.org is a great resource for evaluating the chemical composition of toys. But what if you're standing in the toy aisle, with no access to a computer, and you need some assurance that the toy you're about to buy is safe? MomsRising to the rescue. This grassroots group has teamed up with HealthyToys.org to provide cell phone access to the HealthyToys.org database. Simply text "healthytoys" to 41411 with the name of a particular toy, a type of toy, or a toy manufacturer or retailer to find out whether a toy is safe. MomsRising will respond instantly. (www.momsrising.org/No ToxicToys)

EARTHOPOLY BOARD GAME
Don't Pass Go

EarthOpoly, created and manufactured by Cincinnati-based **Late for the Sky**, is a fun way to encourage kids age 8 and older to think about the planet. As players move around the board, they might get sent outside to play or get hauled off to the dump. They may have to pay $78 to fill up their gas-guzzling automobile, or they may get rewarded for switching to energy-efficient lightbulbs or for using their recycling bin. Players vie for properties ranging from bargains like Concrete Jungle (a collection of urban high-rises) to the more desirable Land of Lakes.

As kids buy up property, they learn more about the earth itself. Buy the property Colorful Coral Reefs, for example, and your deed tells you about these amazing living structures. Property deeds include helpful tips like how to drive to get the most mileage—and produce the least amount of carbon emissions.

EarthOpoly is, of course, earth friendly. The whole game, made of cardboard and printed with soy-based ink, is recyclable, including its plastic tray. Game tokens are charming little pieces of our world: a polished stone imported from South Africa; a little shell exported by Southeast Asians after they've harvested its mollusk as food; a small wooden pyramid, fashioned from scrap wood by a local woodworker; a crystal; a lima bean; a bamboo cylinder.

To counter its own carbon footprint in the making of the game (after all, some of the tokens and the dice had to be imported from around the world), Late for the Sky purchases carbon-offset credits. EarthOpoly sells for $24.95. (800-422-3434; www.lateforthesky.com)

PLAY MART
Recycled Plastic Fun

If your community or school system is purchasing new playground equipment, consider **Play Mart** products. This play equipment is an environmental friend for a number of reasons. The posts, decks, and structural supports are made of 100 percent Recycled Structural Plastic (RSP), Play Mart's brand of plastic lumber—a wood alternative that preserves our pine and redwood forests. The reclaimed plastic comes primarily from milk jugs. The average Play Mart playground set recycles 25,000 milk jugs.

Play Mart is a leading manufacturer of recycled plastic play systems for kids 6 months to 12 years as well as fitness equipment, swings, and site amenities (trash receptacles, benches, picnic tables). The 100-year warranty on the RSP components means these play sets will see several generations of use, but when it is time for the old heave-ho, the RSP components are entirely recyclable.

The Noah's Ark is a good example of a play set for the preschoolers. It accommodates 15 to 20 children on a surface area (including safety zone) of 475 square feet. It's made of 5,687 recycled milk jugs. The small playground systems designed for preschool and elementary kids, including Noah's Ark, Toddler Tunnel Maze, Fire Truck, and Annapolis, sell for between $5,000 and $10,000. Larger playground sets are available, too. (www.playmart.com)

FYI

The Center for Health, Environment, and Justice has created a back-to-school guide to PVC-free school supplies. Check out the guide and the site at www.besafenet.com/pvc/documents.

RECYCLED TIRE SWING
Swingin' Green

Like the tire swing of old hanging by a rope from the tree out back, a handcrafted recycled tire swing from **Abundant Earth** gives a second life to an environmentally dangerous discard.

We've all seen cast-off tires that clog our streams, clutter woods and empty lots, and are just plain ugly. In 2003 alone, the United States generated approximately 290 million scrap tires, according to the Environmental Protection Agency. These old tires are a real threat to our health and our environment: They collect rainwater, which creates a welcoming home for rodents and mosquitoes. They retain heat and when stockpiled in landfills can ignite and burn for months, emitting unhealthy smoke and toxic oils.

Recycled tire swings to the rescue—with an artistic flair. These tire swings are shaped into some fun objects (a motorcycle) and animals (a Tyrannosaurus Rex), all of them ready to suspend from your backyard tree. They are safe, as all hardware is covered to ensure smooth surfaces, and the tires are thoroughly cleaned so that black rubber will not rub off on clothes or hands.

Once the artisans of Abundant Earth get their hands on that old discarded rubber doughnut and work their restorative magic, we all benefit. Each swing comes fully assembled and ready to hang. Most have a 200-pound weight rating (for older kids) and are priced at $119.95. There is also a 250-pound rated version (for even bigger kids and kids at heart) at $165.95. (www.abundantearth.com/store/tireswings.html)

KIWI MAGAZINE: THE INSIDE SCOOP

Offering both a print and an online edition, *Kiwi* magazine covers the world of natural and organic products, nutrition, and wellness. It also offers fun ideas, tips, stories, recipes, fashion, and reviews on kids' media, toys, and games to help your family go green.

Why the name *Kiwi*? The editors named the magazine after this "green" fruit to associate with its delicious as well as nutritious qualities. The humble kiwi contains many phytonutrients, vitamins, and minerals that promote health. The editors say, "It's a unique shade of green. And we are that, too. Our goal is to give you the tools to be as environmentally conscious as possible with realistic advice that fits into your hectic lifestyle."

You can subscribe to the print magazine and receive a copy for free; if you like it, you'll receive six more issues for $11.95. A donation is made to World Vision with each paid subscription. (www.kiwimagonline.com)

BAREFOOT BOOKS
Green Books for Kids

Barefoot Books offers colorful and intriguing books for children. Illustrative of the line is a book-and-CD combo that celebrates the company's values: *Whole World* is a playful adaptation of the famous spiritual song that in this rendition becomes a clarion call for social responsibility. The book includes simple eco-tips for young readers, and the refrain "We've got the whole world in our hands" focuses little minds on what children can do to raise awareness about climate change within the community. The hardcover book is great as a read-along with the CD for any age, and as a read-alone for ages 4 through 9.

Barefoot Books is as green as it gets. This award-winning, independent children's publisher, founded by working moms hoping to nurture the world their children would inherit, produces books that are not sold through big chains because co-founder Nancy Traversy feels they are wasteful in their distribution and return practices. Instead, the books are sold through a network of independent retailers, educators, and other partners, including home sellers.

Barefoot books and marketing materials are printed on recycled or ancient-forest-friendly paper that comes from suppliers who are obliged to replant trees that they have harvested and promise that they do not damage rain forests or other ancient woodlands. The company itself strives to minimize paper usage, has introduced low-energy lighting, encourages low-impact transport, and supports local community activities.

The *Whole World* CD-and-book set sells for $16.99. Visit the Web site for interactive "Go Barefoot, Go Global" content for parents, teachers, and kids. (www.barefoot-books.com)

Barefoot Books
Celebrating Art and Story

Back-to-School Supplies

The typical back-to-school supply list is decidedly ungreen. But there's a one-stop shop for earth-friendly supplies: the online Green Earth Office Supply (www.greenearthofficesupply.com). This company sells environmentally friendly products that meet three minimum standards in manufacture, sale, distribution, use, and disposal. They must (1) minimize the use of resources, (2) create less pollution, and (3) result in less harm to all living creatures.

Here are a few examples of products from Green Earth Office Supply that meet these criteria:

★ **Binders:** These binders are made from brown, unbleached, thick chipboard with approximately 35 percent postconsumer recycled content and no vinyl. Each binder is designed so that the shell can be replaced. The ½-inch size is $4.50; the 3-inch is $7.75. Eco categories: recycled, less toxic, reuse.

★ **Filler paper:** Ampad Envirotech filler paper is 100 percent postconsumer recycled and comes 8½ x 11 inches with college margins. A pack of 200 sheets, three-hole punched, runs $6. Eco category: recycled.

★ **Notebooks:** Ampad Envirotech notebooks are made from 100 percent postconsumer recycled paper and are processed chlorine free. College ruled/margin notebooks are 11 x 8⅞ inches. The one-subject notebook (100 sheets) is $4.35; the three-subject (150 sheets), $6; the five-subject (200 sheets), $8. Eco categories: recycled, less toxic.

★ **Staples:** Because these staples are made from recycled steel, they can be thrown in with recycled paper when recycling. A box of 5,000 staples is $1. Eco category: recycled.

★ **Pens:** All pens sold by Green Earth Office Supply are refillable and reusable. Choose from biodegradable cornstarch pens, recycled newspaper pens, recycled cardboard pens, scrap-wood pens, and recycled rubber tire pens, starting at an affordable 50 cents each, with 10-cent refills. Eco categories: recycled, reuse, long life, animal friendly.

★ **Handheld calculator:** The dual (solar/battery) power calculator has big LCD digits, autopower shutoff to extend battery life, square root and percent keys for schoolwork, and soft-touch rubber keys all for $7. Eco categories: energy friendly, long life.

GREEN BACKPACKS

Multiple Choices

There's no need to buy a new backpack every school year; reusing last year's model is always a green option. But when the old pack is worn out and it's time for something new, choose an eco-friendly, PVC-free product. You can buy backpacks made from recycled car tires (www.vulcanabags.com), made of hemp (www.rawganique.com), or even made from recycled billboards (www.vyandelle.com). But for the latest in high-tech, low-impact backpacks, look into Voltaic solar bags.

All Voltaic bags use PET fabrics (made from recycled soda bottles) that are lightweight, durable, UV resistant, and water resistant.

Embedded on the outside are lightweight, tough, waterproof solar panels that produce 4 watts of power, so 1 hour in direct sun will power more than 3 hours of iPod play time or 1.5 hours of cell phone talk time.

All Voltaic bags include standard adapters for common cell phones and other handheld devices, and all come with a custom battery pack that stores surplus power so it's available when you need it. The battery packs can also be charged using the included AC travel charger or car charger, making them just as useful on the grid as off.

Voltaic offers four solar styles: the Voltaic backpack for $249, a smaller bag called the Converter for $199, the Messenger for $229, and the Generator for $599. The Generator is powerful enough to charge a typical laptop from a day of direct sunlight. (www.voltaicsystems.com)

LUNCH BOXES
Packaging Matters

Green-conscious parents know that organic foods packed in reusable lunch boxes are an everyday must. They also know that the lunch box itself has to be chemical free, especially from lead, PVC, and Teflon. These toxins adhere to kids' hands and their food, and then go into their mouths. So check the box's label for terms such as "lead free" or "lead safe" and "PVC free," "vinyl free," or "phthalates free."

Toxin-free lunch boxes come in a variety of materials. You might like **organic canvas lunch boxes** (www.ecobags.com) or a **Laptop Lunch Bento** box set (www.thesoftlanding.com).

Fleurville (www.fleurville.com) offers a soft insulated bag for little ones, called Lunch Pak, that can be worn as a backpack. This 11 x 8 x 4-inch bag sells for $32. For bigger kids, the insulated **Lunch Buddy** with its waterproof lining is a favorite. This 10 x 7½ x 4-inch bag sells for $28.

ROOTS & SHOOTS
Networking for Kids

Want to excite your kids about their ability to make a positive change in this world? Check out **Roots & Shoots**. This organization for kids is built on humanitarian principles articulated by renowned primatologist and environmentalist Jane Goodall. The Roots & Shoots network connects tens of thousands of young people in almost 100 countries, enabling young people and adults to come together to learn about the issues facing our local and global communities and to take action. This is not a passive club. Members not only identify problems in their communities, they also design, lead, and implement their own community service projects.

If your kids, school system, scout troop, or community program is looking for a way to get involved in helping the planet, this uniquely designed program opens the door with motivation, guidance, and even materials. (www.rootsandshoots.org)

a program of the Jane Goodall Institute

FYI

To identify backpacks made with PVC, scan the materials label for the word "vinyl" or look for a recycling symbol with the number 3 or the letters V or PVC.

GUIDES, GOALS, AND RESOURCES

DrGreene.com
This award-winning Web site invites you to join a community of professionals and parents who have the best answers to all your pregnancy and parenting questions. Note that Dr. Greene also published a book, **Raising Baby Green**, an earth-friendly guide to pregnancy, childbirth, and baby care, in 2007. (Full disclosure: The author of this chapter contributed to Dr. Greene's book). (www.drgreene.com)

Environmental Kids Club
EPA's Environmental Kids Club lets children, parents, and teachers explore the environment and learn how to protect it—through interactive games, pictures, and stories for all ages. (www.epa.gov/kids/index.htm)

Greentimes
This Web site strives to inspire and empower urban high school youth to become curious, successful students and environmentally conscious citizens. (www.greenscreen.org)

Healthy Child Healthy World
This nonprofit organization is dedicated to inspiring parents to protect young children from harmful chemicals. (www.healthychild.org)

Kids Recycle
This site provides students, teachers, school administrators, local recycling coordinators, and community activists with tools developed by their peers to achieve zero waste in their K–12 school systems. (www.kidsrecycle.org/index.php)

Kiwi Green College Report
Fifty US colleges and universities that emphasize green living and learning are highlighted at www.kiwimagonline.com/green-college-report. Plus, hundreds of schools that pledged to go green are listed on the Web site of the Association for the Advancement of Sustainability in Higher Education. (www.aashe.org)

NIEHS Kids' Pages
This site, sponsored by the National Institutes of Health (NIH) and Department of Health and Human Services (DHHS), offers recycling information, resources, games, and activities for children. (www.niehs.nih.gov/kids/recycle.htm)

Playing Clean

In October 1995, Goran Kropp pedaled out of Stockholm hauling a trailer with 200 pounds of food, clothes, and climbing equipment. Over the next 4 months, he cycled more than 7,000 miles across Eastern Europe, Turkey, Iran, Pakistan, India, and Nepal. That was his warmup.

From Kathmandu he shouldered an oppressive load to Everest base-camp. Climbing on his own without supplemental oxygen, he reached the summit on his third attempt. After some R&R in Kathmandu, he saddled up and cycled back home.

A bit player in Jon Krakauer's bestseller *Into Thin Air*—the account of the storm that killed 11 climbers on Everest in May 1996—Kropp was seen by some as just another self-promoting Everest climber. But his own book, *Ultimate High*, makes it clear that this former paratrooper was an experienced, well-prepared mountaineer with a strict climbing aesthetic, a purist who stood in contrast to many of the coddled, high-paying guided climbers who have flocked to Everest in recent years.

Kropp considered porters a luxury; the use of oxygen akin to an athlete taking steroids. "It changes the height of the mountain," he said. He even broke his own trail, refusing to take advantage of the path other climbers had cut through the snow.

After his Everest climb, he helped fund a school in Nepal with 165 students and eight teachers. In 1999 he returned to Everest with his girlfriend, Renata Chlumska. With the help of four Sherpas, they made a trash-collection run, removing 25 discarded oxygen canisters from the mountain before summiting together. Kropp made his living as a professional adventurer, but he also made a point of speaking to kids for free. It seemed the perfect marriage of adventure and activism. But then in September 2002, Kropp fell while rock climbing in Vantage, Washington, and plunged to his death. He was 35 years old.

Kropp was following in the footsteps of bold adventurers like John Muir, Edward Abbey, Bradford Washburn, and Yvon Chouinard—pioneers with a strong wilderness aesthetic and an evangelical need to protect the land they loved. Of course, one doesn't have to cycle to Kathmandu or row from California to Papua New Guinea to make a difference. Take my brother, Marshall, for example: He lives at the end of a dirt road outside of Williamsville, Vermont, and spent two decades publishing *Green Living*, a free environmental magazine. He has a car and electricity and a computer, but he eschews a cell phone and TV and uses fossil fuel minimally. Instead of driving to a large lake to go swimming, he heads to the postage-stamp pond in his backyard, attaches a rope from his ankle to a tree, and swims in place. His wife and daughters may think he's loco—and he is a tad eccentric—but this small act is part of his heartfelt belief that individual accountability is essential to the health of our planet.

Today, you don't have to wear hemp boxer shorts to be aware of the devastating impact of climate change. That's why so many companies in the outdoor recreation industry have been shifting to sustainable materials. Most skateboards, for example, are made of Canadian maple, which takes 50 years to mature. But bamboo is replaced in a tenth of that time. So Bob Burnquist, a Brazilian living in California and one of the world's top skateboarders, has developed a board with his sponsor, Flip, that is made of bamboo, hemp, and maple. Though his goal is to live in harmony with the environment and use his celebrity to help the planet, he points out that one need not go "full, purist radical." Burnquist says, "Connect the coolness factor to the reality of what's possible now."

Take that idea as the aim of this chapter—to inform and inspire sports and recreation enthusiasts interested in taking their green lifestyle outdoors. Think low-impact, human-powered, zero-emission recreation. Clearly there are many larger forces at work over which we have little control. But we can factor in the environment in making our recreational choices.

—Joe Glickman

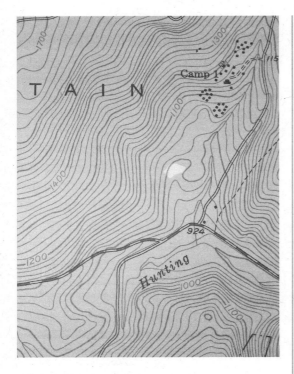

ORIENTEERING
Never Ask Directions

Orienteering sounds like a fancy word for backcountry navigation—and it is—but it's also a structured sport with its own international calendar, including a world championship. It demands precision and quick thinking but precious little equipment, and it impacts the environment hardly at all. Competitors use a compass and a detailed five-color map to navigate—often at a dead run—between checkpoints preset surreptitiously in the woods. Think of an unarmed Daniel Boone on a timed Easter egg hunt and you get the idea.

Invented in Sweden at the turn of the 20th century as a military exercise, the sport is still most popular in Scandinavia. As many as 25,000 people compete in the O-Ringen, an annual 5-day race held in Sweden, where orienteering is practically the national pastime. Billed as "the thinking person's sport," orienteering requires a refined combination of skills: map reading, route finding, woodsmanship, and running. In short, it's high-speed problem solving, which is why a disproportionate number of engineers, computer programmers, and connoisseurs of crossword puzzles are drawn to the sport.

At heart, it's a perfect fit for problem solvers with map addictions. Become fluent at reading a topo map and improve your skills with a compass, and you quickly increase your wilderness IQ. (www.us.orienteering.org)

FYI

Anyone who's logged serious overnight time in an igloo can swear that when the temperature plummets, the igloo is much warmer than a tent. For a how-to introduction or to improve on your igloo-building technique for this essential snow-country skill, check out www.igloobuilding.org.

ALO WAVE SHORTS AND TOP
Go Comfortable, Go Green

Looking for loose-fitting, soft-on-the-skin, two-tone wrinkle-free running shorts made by an eco-conscious company based in Los Angeles in an office powered by solar panels? ALO stands for Air Land Ocean, and their green, low-impact consciousness is as much in evidence in their office (they buy local organic foods, have eliminated water bottles, and are converting their company cars to run on alternative fuels) as in their manufacturing philosophy.

The Wave Shorts have two performance features that marry form and function. The first is a performance fabric called CoolFit, which draws moisture away from your skin and helps keep you cool and comfortable. The second is the antimicrobial treatment that thwarts bacteria and keeps the shorts odor free, which is good news for anyone with the tendency to ease an extra day (or two) out of his or her gym garments before tossing them in the laundry. The Wave Shorts ($32) are a standout on the no-stink front. ALO makes a variety of great running tops, including their Bamboo Short Sleeve Tee ($34). Made of 70 percent lyocell bamboo and 30 percent cotton, it's breathable and wicks away moisture. (www.alosport.com)

**REI ORGANIC CREW SOCKS AND
INJINJI ECO NUBAMBOO QUARTER SOCKS**

X-Hale in Comfort

Ah, the viscerally satisfying feeling of a well-fitting pair of socks. Life's simple pleasures, like a blissful walk in the woods, become even more satisfying when you've just pulled on a pair of REI moisture-wicking, thermo-regulating, no-itch light hiking socks made of an organic merino wool/recycled nylon blend. (Try saying that three times fast.) Their socks are baptized in a chlorine-free, shrink-resistance treatment so the fit survives the wash. The recycled nylon yarn increases durability, and these stretchy suckers have reinforcement in the heel and toes to postpone the holey woes. (www.rei.com)

Injinji Eco NuBamboo Quarter Socks—the sock equivalent of gloves—may look gimmicky, but serious runners swear by them, especially trail runners who are susceptible to blisters. Made of environmentally sustainable NuBamboo fabric (that's bamboo and nylon), these socks feature something Injinji calls AIS technology, which separates your toes with a thin, antifriction membrane that promotes circulation and eliminates blister-causing skin-on-skin contact. Even if you're not a marathon runner, don a pair of the rainbow low-cut crew socks with sandals and you've got the perfect conversation starter. (www.injinji.com)

PATAGONIA WET SUIT

Wetter Is Better

Most neoprene wet suits are made entirely from petroleum-based ingredients, but Patagonia's Regulator wet suit uses just 20 percent, along with recycled polyester, which decreases the dependency on petroleum. The suit features a merino wool lining and kneepads made with silicone instead of environmentally damaging PVC (polyvinyl chloride). The wool lining is treated without chlorine, an extremely polluting chemical that destroys the wool fibers; Patagonia uses a patented Slow Wash process that provides long-term warmth and quick drying. Such a dialed-in wet suit makes sense when you consider that Yvon Chouinard, the company's founder and author of *Let My People Go Surfing: The Education of a Reluctant Businessman*, is a passionate environmentalist with a serious surfing problem. A legendary rock climber, Chouinard decided decades ago to avoid the five C's: commuting, cubicles, and conforming corporate culture. The oft-wet CEO recently opened a surf-dedicated store in Cardiff-by-the-Sea, California. Be sure to check out his eco-friendly wet suits. (www.patagoniawetsuits.com)

SUSTAINABLE SKATEBOARDS

Healthier Boards

Habitat's skateboard deck uses sustainable bamboo, a vegetable-based finish, and nontoxic glue (www.habitatskateboards.com). While bamboo is now used to make bikes, furniture, and even saxophones, the first all-bamboo skateboards were not as durable as a hard maple deck. However, as manufacturers are quick to point out, they've been working with this super-fast-growing, eco-friendly product (with a stronger strength-to-weight ratio than maple) long enough so that "environmentally friendly" no longer means compromised performance. Just make sure you don't leave your board lying around a peckish panda. Manufacturers like Sector 9 (www.sector9.com), Arbor (www.arborsports.com), and Loaded (www.loadedboards.com) all make bamboo boards.

ARBOR SNOWBOARDS
Get on Board

Arbor, a company in Venice, California, that makes snowboards and skateboards out of bamboo and other sustainable materials, is a pioneer of ecologically driven design. Established in 1995, the go-green company started making bamboo boards in 2001. That's when they realized that bamboo is one of the most renewable materials on the earth (one that requires no pesticides or chemical fertilizers), and that adding bamboo to a wood core increases the durability of the boards and makes them lighter, more flexible, and resistant to compression. In addition, by using lighter glasses in the construction of their bamboo-reinforced boards, they're able to use less chemically treated fiberglass and fewer resins. To top things off, last year the company gave 5 percent of profits to the Nature Conservancy's Hawaiian-based efforts. (www.arborsports.com)

ECO HIKING SHOES: GREEN FEET! WHO KNEW?

Several major players in the hiking-shoe game now utilize recycled materials in crafting their wilderness footwear: **Patagonia**, **Keen**, **Simple**, and **Merrell** all manufacture hiking shoes made from hemp and such other recyclable materials as cork or former tractor tires. In addition, an online company called **Wicked Hemp** has come out with the "Wicked Hiker," made from heavy-grade hemp and recycled rubber. The shoelaces, of course, are also hemp. (www.patagonia.com; www.keenfootwear.com; www.simpleshoes.com; www.merrell.com; www.wickedhemp.com)

MARYJANESFARM ORGANIC CHILIMAC
Camping Fare
Like It Ought to Be

The term *organic fast food* sounds like a contradiction in terms, but it makes a bit more sense when you ponder the quixotic life of **MaryJane Butters**. This enterprising woman produces a line of quick-prep instant organic foods that elevates freeze-dried camping fare. Butters grew up in Utah in a self-sufficient Mormon family of seven and worked as a carpenter, waitress, janitor, upholsterer, secretary, milkmaid, wilderness ranger, and environmental activist before she bought a 5-acre farm plot outside of Moscow, Idaho. After years of struggling to make ends meet as an organic farmer, she started *MaryJanesFarm* magazine, and years later she landed a lucrative contract to write *MaryJane's Ideabook, Cookbook, Lifebook: For the Farmgirl in All of Us* (Clarkson Potter), which is as much about her favorite recipes as it is a primer on social responsibility, canning apples, and the history of organic farming in America. (She makes an important distinction between *organic* as a marketing concept and *organic* as a lifestyle.) She grows the meat and produce she sells, plus a biodiesel crop to fuel her car.

Her instant meals are an eco-conscious camper's dream come true. The line features the classic Chilimac and the soup-to-dessert High Attitude Six Pack, which includes six 3-pound "bulk" bags of instant, just-add-water foods. As MaryJane says, "Less weight in your pack means you can eat better, go farther, and stay longer." (www.maryjanesfarm.com)

IBEX ULTIMATE GUIDE SWEATER

Stay Warm, Look Cool

A Kiwi beekeeper named Sir Edmund Hillary wore heavyweight merino wool—the kind that comes from New Zealand sheep—when he climbed Mount Everest in 1953. Now nature's high-tech fabric has been made into a pliable, machine-washable, blessedly nonitchy (it's brushed on the inside) garment with a zip turtleneck for ventilation and a vertical zip breast pocket to hold money, an iPod, or ski wax. Remarkably warm and stylish, it's all you need for cross-country skiing or hiking. It also works well as an insulating layer for downhill skiing or for sitting around in a nippy room. (www.ibex.com)

PRIMUS ETAEXPRESS STOVE

Cook Fast, Burn Less

Roald Amundsen carried a Primus stove when he reached the South Pole in 1911. In 1953, Sir Edmund Hillary and Tenzing Norgay, the first to summit Everest, relied on one. Last year the 110-year-old Swedish company debuted their lightweight, fuel-efficient Primus EtaExpress stove. It weighs just 2.9 ounces and can generate 8,900 Btu per hour. A tight windscreen and pot with built-in heat exchanger mean one canister of fuel lasts up to twice as long as with a traditional stove. (www.primus.se)

Green Hiking Guidelines from Leave No Trace

All responsible hikers and campers know by now that they should "pack it in, pack it out" and "take nothing but pictures." Fair enough: But what exactly does the Leave No Trace (LNT) approach entail?

First, stick to the trail. If the trail is narrow, walk single file and not side by side. The cumulative effect of thousands of boots on the ground can be enormously destructive. Walk through muddy sections and not around them, and don't cut across switchbacks on steep sections, as they are especially prone to erosion.

In wilderness without an established trail, take the opposite approach: Spread out as much as possible. Wherever possible, walk on rock, not dirt; dead vegetation instead of living plants; dry soil instead of mud. In short, think as if you're being tracked and try to avoid detection.

In an established campsite, leave the area just as you found it. Better yet, pack out any trash left by those who were too lazy or inconsiderate to do so. In a pristine area, don't build a fire pit or a ditch around your tent. While your ability to roast marshmallows will be compromised, a campstove leaves no footprint; it also means that you won't have to gather firewood and run any risk of forest fire.

Hard-core proponents of the pack-it-in, pack-it-out ethos insist you should carry out the peels and pits of your fruits and veggies. While I applaud anyone who does so, I'm of the opinion that burying them or tossing them in a crevasse should be okay unless you're in a park with bears and other large predators. When it comes to human waste, bring a trowel and bury your business along with the (unscented) TP at least 200 feet from a water source or trail.

Here are the seven principles of Leave No Trace:

1. Plan ahead and prepare.
2. Travel and camp on durable surfaces.
3. Dispose of waste properly.
4. Leave what you find.
5. Minimize campfire impacts.
6. Respect wildlife.
7. Be considerate of other visitors.

For additional insights, go to www.lnt.org.

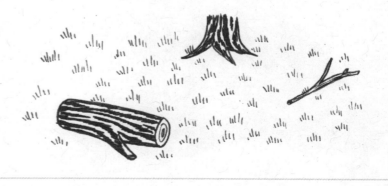

HENNESSY HAMMOCKS

Snoozing without Stakes

A clever low-impact alternative to tent camping is the Hennessy Hammock, an easy-to-set-up shelter that one outdoor publication called "the coolest tent in the world." Although you will have to find two opposing trees, you don't have to bring a sleeping pad or fret about finding level root- and rock-free ground. And you'll never wake up in a puddle after a late-night storm. Their lightest model weighs just 15 ounces and can double as a bivouac sack if you're caught out overnight. The HH features a rain fly and mosquito netting, and it comes with bark-protecting "tree hugger" straps. (www.hennessyhammocks.com)

RECYCLED FLEECE GRIP GLOVES AND BAMBOO GLOVE LINERS

Hands-on Recycling

If you're downhill skiing or doing any winter mountaineering—say, climbing New Hampshire's Mount Washington in February or climbing a frozen waterfall in Ouray, Colorado—a waterproof Gore-Tex glove is mandatory equipment. But for nearly every other late-fall or winter outdoor activity, you can mix and match these two lightweight, quick-drying gloves to keep your hands warm and the environment a bit greener.

Thin, stretchy, and made from that fast-growing, renewable resource that grows without fertilizers or pesticides, the North Face Bamboo Glove (www.thenorthface.com) fits inside shell gloves for added warmth on really chilly days but is also ideal for a run, bike ride, or cross-country ski. REI's Recycled Fleece Glove (www.rei.com/product/773851) is thicker and warmer and features a synthetic leather palm for added grip and durability. Made from recycled Polartec fleece, the gloves have a water-repellent finish, dry quickly, and have an excellent warmth-to-weight ratio.

ECO-FRIENDLY TRAIL COMPANIONS

Osprey (www.ospreypacks.com) offers several eco-friendly backpacks with recycled polyester lining and aluminum hardware. A sign of their commitment to conservation-first ethos is the fact that they sew a label into their larger packs that lists the principles of Leave No Trace. In 2008, Osprey joined forces with other companies in the outdoor industry and the Conservation Alliance in order to lobby Congress to protect 2 million acres of public land across the country. REI (www.rei.com), which has a new ecoSensitive line of clothing, makes a daypack from recycled plastic bottles.

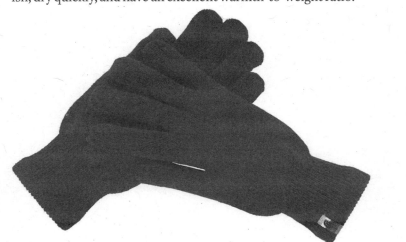

Whole Green Catalog

OUTDOOR EDUCATION SCHOOLS
Follow Your Inner Bear

Paul Rezendes, a master tracker, wilderness photographer, and author of *The Wild Within: Adventures in Nature and Animal Teaching*, said: "Spend enough time outdoors, and you learn total humility." According to Rezendes, spending time in the woods teaches you about the interconnectedness of all living things, and tracking, he says, is an inner journey, "an educational process that opens the door to an animal's life and to our own."

Nicely said, but how do you tap into your inner outdoorsperson? America's most renowned tracker and wilderness survival expert is Tom Brown Jr. Located in Waretown, New Jersey, his Tracker School offers 75 courses (www.trackerschool.com). The Wilderness Awareness School in Duvall, Washington, offers courses in survival skills, outdoor education, and more for kids and adults (www.wildernessawareness.org). For a list of outdoor education schools and clubs across the country, featuring everything from Native American practices to edible plants, go to www.natureskills.com/tracking_schools.html.

MOUNTAINSMITH RECYCLED TOUR LUMBAR PACK
Plastic Made Perfect

Okay, so it's not the most mellifluous name, but it's one worth remembering. This versatile ergonomically designed pack fits snugly around your waist. Made out of 100 percent recycled plastic soda bottles, it's nothing if not durable. It has internal pockets to organize gear like sunglasses, iPod, or passport; two mesh side pouches to keep water bottles handy; and webbing to attach accessories or to strap it to a full-size Mountainsmith recycled backpack for extra volume. The secondary (outside) pocket provides great "stuffability" for a sweater, rain jacket, or loaf of French bread. A square of bungee cord on the pocket lets you pile on even more stuff.

Cinched into the small of your back (near your center of gravity), the pack is ideal for light to medium loads and works great for dayhikes, cross-country skiing, cycling, or as a carry-on bag with 854 cubic inches of space. (www.mountainsmith.com)

GREEN GURU VULCAR MESSENGER BAG
Road Tough for Eco-Transport

The history of rubber took a dramatic turn in 1839 when a diligent inventor from Woburn, Massachusetts, named Charles Goodyear, figured out how to weatherproof the gummy material into a pliable product that didn't melt in the heat or crack in the cold. He called the process *vulcanization*, an homage to the Greek god of fire.

More than a century and a half after Goodyear's breakthrough, a Boulder-based company named Green Guru has taken to recycling old truck and tractor inner tubes into a functional, eco-friendly messenger bag that they've dubbed the Vulcar. This 4.48-pound vulcanized rubber bag may be a bit heavier than those made from other synthetic materials, but it's as durable and spacious as it is good for the environment. At 18 inches wide by 12 inches deep, the Vulcar is large enough to be an all-purpose bag. It's perfect for the bicycle commuter, and it also fits the bill as a gym bag: wide enough to accommodate running shoes and a thick towel or a bulky yoga mat, and sufficiently waterproof inside to endure the soggiest of soggy clothes.

Three large zippered pockets (one outside, two inside) and interior "organizer" sleeves for pens, pencils, and all your electronic gadgets (save a flat-screen TV) mean you can transport a virtual supply closet wherever you go. The overlapping flap is fastened with Velcro and two buckle closures, which keep the contents secure and dry, should you get caught in the rain or have to spend a week on a 72-foot yacht in the Caribbean. (www.greengurugear.com)

BIG AGNES SLEEPING BAGS
Natural Fibers = Green Z's

Big Agnes is a small company in the hip mountain town of Steamboat Springs, Colorado, that offers several sleeping bags, pads, and tents fabricated with up to 100 percent recycled materials. The company's cofounder has used solar power for 15 years; he recently installed a wind turbine to power the offices and warehouse, and he encourages his staff to commute by bike, skateboard, foot, or skis. (www.bigagnes.com)

For a list of other earth-friendly sleeping bags that feature natural fibers like hemp, cotton, coconut husks, and bamboo—all of which reduce our dependency on nonrenewable oil products—go to www.greenyour.com and look under "lifestyle." The site offers sound insights on the most eco-friendly manufacturers and explains ways to detect if a "green" product is really as environmentally sound as advertised. You can also learn about the pros and cons of using a down-filled bag and the lowdown on the ethical treatment of the critters that offer up their woolly coats.

VIBRAM FIVEFINGERS
Run, Walk, Swim (Barefoot) in the Park

The typical human foot has 26 bones, 33 joints, and more than 100 muscles, tendons, and ligaments. Ask anyone who can spell *proprioception* (the sense of orientation of one's limbs in space) and they'll tell you that stimulating the muscles in your feet and lower legs improves your balance, agility, and overall health. In other words, barefoot is best—until you step on a rock, broken glass, or, well, natural fertilizer.

With **Vibram**'s FiveFingers footwear, you get that earth-beneath-your-feet feeling, only with better traction and more protection. These stretchy slip-on sandals provide total freedom of movement. There are three FiveFingers styles, and all are suitable for hiking, climbing, walking, and running as well as for martial arts, yoga, and Pilates. But where they really shine is in canoes and kayaks, filling a need for footwear that fits into the tight spaces of a boat, provides traction on slick rocks, and dries quickly. Named by *Time* magazine as one of the Best Inventions of 2007, they're also so light that you can carry them in a daypack for river crossings. (www.vibramfivefingers.com)

ECO THERMO 6 SLEEPING PAD:
THE WORLD'S FIRST CARBON-NEUTRAL AIR MATTRESS

Spend enough time sleeping (or not sleeping, as the case may be) outdoors, and you'll know that a good pad is worth its weight in z's. Enter the ergonomically obsessed gear geeks from **Pacific Outdoor Equipment**, who log plenty of outdoor hours testing their equipment in the Crazy Mountains of Bozeman, Montana. This small, eco-conscious company specializes in lightweight closed-cell and inflatable sleeping pads. While their lightest tips the scales at 19 ounces, the mummy-shaped Eco Thermo 6 is just 22 ounces and made of water-repellent bamboo fabric and bamboo-based fiber fill, which you inflate the old-fashioned way through a lightweight recycled aluminum valve. More notable, Pacific Outdoor did it all with a neutral carbon footprint—using wind power to offset the carbon emission created in the production of the pads. No wonder the company won the 2007 *Backpacker Magazine*'s Editors' Choice Green Award. (www.pacoutdoor.com)

CROSS-COUNTRY SKIING
Silent Snow, Secret Snow

Cross-country skiing leaves much less of a footprint than the downhill, or Alpine, version that features powered chairlifts and clear-cut trails. For even greener recreation, avoid those Nordic centers with groomed trails and snowmaking machines. Instead, head for the trails in state forests and national parks. In New England, for instance, the Boston Chapter of the Appalachian Mountain Club offers excellent backcountry, cross-country, and telemark skiing trips. (www.amcboston.org)

For a nationwide state-by-state online gateway to self-propelled outdoor winter recreation, check out the directory of roughly 750 US cross-country ski trails at www.a1trails.com/xc_ski/xc_us.html.

ENVIRONMENTAL WRITING SINCE THOREAU
Green Holy Writ

In *American Earth: Environmental Writing Since Thoreau* (Library of America), Bill McKibben, the author of *The End of Nature*, gathered what he deems the essential American writings that have shaped the way we look at the natural world. In his introduction, McKibben states that "environmental writing is America's most distinctive contribution to the world's literature."

McKibben's selection of more than 100 writers includes some of the famed early conservationists like Henry David Thoreau, John Muir, and Walt Whitman. John Steinbeck graces these pages as do contemporary writers like Barry Lopez, Terry Tempest Williams, Barbara Kingsolver, and Paul Hawken. McKibben's introduction to each essay amounts to a running commentary on the progress of the conservation movement in America. And, by the way, the writing is pristine.

FYI

Patagonia's Common Threads Garment Recycling Program enables customers to return certain types of outdoor clothing for recycling. Under this innovative program, an old shirt or vest bearing the Common Threads tag may be transformed into new clothing, staying out of landfills and conserving materials.

Girls' Day Out

Babes in the Back Country is an organization of "powerful, professional, knowledgeable" women that offers year-round outdoor adventures in cross-country and telemark skiing, snowshoeing, avalanche education, and mountaineering as well as mountain biking, yoga, and workshops with titles like "Rejuvenation Retreats" and "Tao of Sports." Founded in 1996 by Leslie Ross, a three-time telemark free-skiing champion, BIB leads members to vertical locales like Arapahoe Basin, Colorado, and Wapta Traverse, British Columbia. The courses are all about fitness and fun, with the underlying aim of building confidence and empowerment in women. (www.babesinthebackcountry.com)

SANUK GOT MY BACK
Barefoot Untechnology

Sanuk is a small surf shoe company in Southern California with a wide-eyed Gumbyish icon: The word means "pursuit of happiness and balance" in Thai. Sanuk's founder, Jeff Kelley, a surfer who began making sandals out of inner tubes and indoor-outdoor carpet, set out to design a supercomfortable shoe/sandal durable enough to tackle the steep steps to his favorite local surf spot. The Got My Back slip-ons feature a flexible, breathable shoe upper wed to a pliable sandal bottom. Somehow he got it just right: Your feet have enough room to wiggle, but you feel perfectly secure on rough surfaces and serious inclines. These funky hybrid dogs are cool, in part because they're as comfortable as bedroom slippers and look as if they'd been swiped from the set of *Gilligan's Island*. Favored by surfers, paddlers, and climbers as pre- and postsport footwear, these addictively comfortable "sidewalk surfers" are so un-cool that the likes of Brad Pitt and Johnny Rotten have worn them. (www.sanuk.com)

BROOKS RUNNING SHOES
Biodegradable Sneaks

Brooks, the running shoe company, has introduced the world's first biodegradable midsole. Called BioMoGo, it's designed to biodegrade 50 times faster than conventional athletic shoes. How? The eco-conscious, aerobically inclined folks at Brooks added a nontoxic natural additive to the MoGo midsole compound that encourages anaerobic microbes to "munch away" when it meets its final resting place. (For the record, traditional midsoles can last up to 1,000 years in a landfill; BioMoGo's decompose in 20 years.) Given this new technology, Brooks says they will save 29.9 million pounds of landfill waste. For you football fans, that's 1,277 football fields covered one shoe deep.

All the paper used by the company is made from wood from well-managed forests. And by using responsible materials like soy-based ink and recycled material for their spring 2009 footwear and apparel catalog, Brooks saved 14,000 pounds of wood (that's 44 trees), 15,989 gallons of water (enough for 1,599 five-minute showers), 4,877 pounds of exhaust emissions (equivalent to driving a compact car 6,372 miles), and 2,646 pounds of solid waste (think 91 thirty-two-gallon cans of garbage). (www.brooksrunning.com)

> **FYI**
>
> Snowshoes are one of the oldest forms of transportation. It is believed that the ancestors of the Inuit and Native Americans migrated from Siberia to North America on wooden snowshoes.

CRESCENT MOON SNOWSHOES
Step Softly, Go Green

When there's enough snow to spill over the top of your boots, walking through the woods is an exercise in futility. The good news: If you can walk, you can snowshoe. Strap on a pair of lightweight snowshoes, venture into a muffled, billowy environment, and you will wax poetic about the virtues of this low-impact, stunningly good cardiovascular workout that nurtures the body, mind, and soul. Although Henry David Thoreau did just fine stepping across a frozen Walden Pond in traditional wood and rawhide snowshoes, if you've ever tried them, you'll be even more appreciative of the high-tech, teardrop-shaped **Crescent Moon** snowshoes, with their snug, quick-in, easy-out bindings.

But this is high-tech done right. While Crescent Moon has made snowshoes for the past dozen years, 2 years ago they revamped their line with materials that contain no PVC, a cheap but toxic material. They use wind-powered energy in their factory and office and recycle nearly everything they use, including coated fabric scraps, aluminum, stainless steel, cardboard, and office materials. The company intends to pursue its goal of being "as green as possible" using aluminum, steel, and other recyclable materials in the construction and design of its snowshoes for the future. They also offer a Take Back Program where you can send in your old Crescent Moon snowshoes to be disassembled and recycled for $12—a price even old Henry David could afford. (www.crescent moonsnowshoes.com)

BAREFOOT HIKERS: WE DON'T NEED NO SHOES!

It sounds like a brain twister: Leave an actual footprint in order to leave less of a footprint. Nevertheless, that's the raison d'être of the 15 or so eco-conscious **Barefoot Hikers** clubs around the country. The Barefoot Hikers are a tough-soled lot who simply enjoy hiking barefoot. The first chapter was started by Richard Frazine, author of *The Barefoot Hiker* (Ten Speed Press), a book with the mother of all subtitles that provides a thorough description of the attractions of this most natural of pastimes: *A Book about Bare Feet and How Their Sensitivity Can Provide Not Only an Unique Dimension of Pleasure, but Also Significant Benefits in Safety, Comfort, and Confidence to Hikers Who Learn to Rely on Them.* (www.barefooters.org/hikers)

PROBAR ORGANIC ENERGY BAR

Carry On Like a Nut

Around the turn of the 21st century, a natural food chef and snowboard fanatic named Art Eggertsen was frolicking on the slopes at Utah's Snowbird Ski Resort when he hit the wall in a big way. He bonked—not literally, but nutritionally. Unable to choke down the frozen energy bar in his pack and unwilling to wait in line to buy an overpriced, greasy cheeseburger midslope, Eggertsen let necessity be the mother of all energy bars. Plenty of tinkering later, ProBar was born. Legions of cyclists, hikers, and skiers would bonk no more.

Made from whole organic raw foods and 100 percent vegan, ProBar is a healthy alternative to the many other nutrition bars containing preservatives and other unrecognizable ingredients. Ponder the healthy fact that ProBar's Sesame Goji bar has raw organic flax, hemp, fennel, cardamom, and fenugreek seed—not to mention something called epazote leaf. Voted the "Best in Food" in 2008 by *Health* magazine, ProBar lists the words *raw*, *nutty*, and *organic* so often on the label that you'd think their target market was squirrels. (www.theprobar.com)

GOLITE SALSA JACKET

Tread Lightly on Terra Firm

Tired of feeling like the pack mules on the mountaineering trips they took around the world, the husband-and-wife team of Kim and Demetri "Coup" Coupounas set out to lighten their loads. In 1998, they began making clothing, backpacking gear, and footwear for adventure racers, backpackers, hikers, trail runners, cross-country skiers, and any outdoor enthusiast who subscribes to the motto "Light Is Right."

Little has changed in that regard, but their mission statement has a new, green wrinkle: "Go lightly on the planet." Consider their 16-ounce synthetic-filled Salsa Jacket, which is made with a 100 percent recycled polyester shell and a 100 percent polyester embossed lining, or their Wisp Wind Shirt, a minuscule 3.2-ounce outer layer that's made of 88 percent recycled material and small enough to stuff into your back pocket.

Headquartered in the outdoors-oriented college town of Boulder, Colorado, they've enlisted the help of Native Energy (www.nativeenergy.com) and Five Winds International (www.fivewinds.com) for a comprehensive environmental footprint analysis. They use renewable energy sources, efficient lighting, and zero waste recycling practices, and they post lots of information on their Web site about going green, including links to "competitors we look up to for their green initiatives." Even better, they are continuing to push to make the company have a net zero footprint. "We are far from having all the answers," Kim Coupounas says, "but we're making progress—day by day, decision by decision." (www.golite.com)

FIVE TEN JET7 ROCK-CLIMBING SHOES
Get High on Recycled Rubber

Shortly after completing his MBA from the University of Michigan, Charles Cole headed to Yosemite National Park, where he notched some edgy first ascents. After a slip on El Capitan, one of the grandest big-wall climbs on the planet, he returned home and aimed to develop a durable, high-friction rubber for climbing and approach shoes (reaching the base of many of these big-wall climbs requires fancy footwork over rocky terrain). Relying on his undergraduate engineering degree and the financial backing of his parents, Cole perfected and patented his Stealth rubber soles, and routes once considered unattainable began to fall.

Located in Redlands, California, this family-owned company makes their Stealth rubber for climbers, paddlers, hikers, and trail runners. The good news for vertical rock jocks is the Jet7, a new sport-climbing and bouldering shoe that features a tough, lightweight upper and Stealth "green" sole made of recycled rubber. This snug-fitting, minimum-stretch, slip-on shoe with the down-turned toe looks a bit like the offspring of a ballet slipper and an inner tube. While you'd probably rather walk around base camp in high heels than in the Jet7, when you're negotiating a wall of rock, the Jet7's supersticky recycled rubber holds firm on minuscule cracks and itsy-bitsy ledges—elevating you to a whole new level. (www.fiveten.com)

RAIL-TRAILS
Postindustrial Connectors

Rail-trails are public auto-free paths based on former railroad rights-of-way. Mostly flat or following a gentle grade, they're ideal for human locomotion, whether it is walking, running, bicycling, in-line skating, cross-country skiing, or wheelchair use. Since the 1960s, more than 13,000 miles of rail-trails have opened up throughout the country, from the 27-mile crushed-stone Aroostook Valley Trail through an area known for its broccoli and potatoes in northern Maine to the 100-mile dirt Maah Daah Hey Trail through the Badlands of North Dakota. Many preserve historic landmarks, while others serve as wildlife conservation corridors, linking isolated parks and establishing greenways in developed areas. They are also great for traffic-free commuting and recreating. Find one in your area and put it to good, green use. (www.railtrails.org)

NUUN HYDRATION TABLETS
Portable Hydration for Those Who Love to Drink

Most seasoned outdoor jocks have sampled enough premade and powdered carb-replacement sports drinks to know that they are unpalatable. The powders are messy, and the ready-to-drink brands are expensive.

Enter Nuun (pronounced "noon") hydration tablets. It's the brainchild of a student and professor from Dartmouth College's Tuck School of Business who set out to create an electrolyte-replacement product free of sugar and carbs that would be easy to use on the move. The product is so tasty and thirst quenching that you're likely to start salivating every time you see one of the small colored disks. They come in a slender plastic tube that fits easily into the back of a bike jersey or the pocket of your running shorts.

There's a fair bit of science behind Nuun, but all you need to know is that one tablet contains the sodium, potassium, calcium, magnesium, and other essential vitamins your body craves after a bout of prolonged exercise. There are 12 tasty, easy-to-use disks in a tube. They come in four flavors—lemon-lime, citrus fruit, triberry, and kona cola (contains caffeine)—in a tube that turns every water fountain into a source of balanced hydration. (www.nuun.com)

CALFEEDESIGN

A Bicycle Made of Panda Food?

The environmental benefits of biking are obvious, but choosing a "green" bike is a much murkier proposition. The materials used in bike frames, such as steel, aluminum, and titanium, must be mined, while carbon fibers are petroleum derived. Materials aren't the only important factor, as longevity counts as well: If you replace your bike every decade or so, that is low-impact transport, right there. Aluminum frames, the most common and affordable, are less durable than steel frames, which are generally heavier. Carbon-fiber and titanium bikes have long life spans but carry a hefty price tag.

So what's the greenest bike on the market? Craig Calfee's *bamboo* frame. Calfee crafts these unusual smoke- and heat-treated bamboo frames for road, mountain, and triathlon bikes. With a lot of handwork and low-volume production, Calfee's creations are not cheap, starting at $2,695, but they're oh so eco-friendly. (www.calfeedesign.com)

SAVING THE WORLD, ONE LIP AT A TIME

How's this for a romantic, eco-friendly tale? A woman who made natural lip balm in her kitchen for her friends met a man who loved her lip balm and, soon after, the woman herself. They were married in 1997, and before you could say organic *Helianthus annuus* (sunflower) seed oil and *Cera alba* (beeswax) three times fast, an organic lip balm company named Eco Lips was born.

Using wind and solar power to run their plant in Cedar Rapids, Iowa, Eco Lips makes lip balms that use only organic (nonhydrogenated) vegetable oils, beeswax, and herbs. They're all vitamin enriched and petroleum free.

Your lips, which have no natural moisturizer, are one of the most sensitive and absorbent parts of your body. Spend enough time outdoors, and you'll quickly learn that protecting your lips from the sun, wind, and cold is essential. Paddlers, skiers, and cyclists are particularly vulnerable to blistering and sunburn due to the wind, cold, and sun. While Eco Lips may not help you find your soul mate, they're doing their best to keep your lips romance ready. (www.ecolips.com)

DISC GOLF

No Clubs, No Pesticides, No Dress Code

Okay, it's not really golf, but it's far greener than the game with clubs, white balls, and jackass pants—and proponents swear it's far more fun. It's the little-known but increasingly popular pastime of disc (aka Frisbee) golf. As with golf, the object is to negotiate a course from beginning to end in the fewest number of throws. Instead of holes, players aim for metal baskets on a pole. The various discs are divided into three basic categories: putters, midrange discs, and drivers. But the similarity pretty much ends there. Disc golf can be played virtually anywhere—fields, campuses, and parks are three popular locales. With LED-equipped discs pioneered by Black Jax Sports, you can even play at night. There are no clubs, course fees, greens, carts, caddies, or dress codes, so it is a cheap, adaptable, sport that tests skills without tarting up the landscape—a good walk unspoiled.

In 2004, the Professional Disc Golf Association reported 1,722 disc golf courses in the United States, with 800 sanctioned events worldwide. Three years later, the number passed 2,500. If you happen to be playing a round in Augusta, Georgia, be sure to stop in at the Disc Golf Hall of Fame and pay homage to "Steady" Ed Headrick, former Wham-O employee and the Father of Disc Golf. An amusing video on the sport can be found at www.youtube.com/watch?v=FFQ8S1LcioQ. (www.discgolf.com)

K2 ECO ETU AND MAIA IN-LINE SKATES
Made with Earth-Friendly Materials

For 15 years, Neil Strauss has skated to work in business attire from 100th Street on the Upper West Side of Manhattan to his Midtown office. He's so efficient on his four-wheel skates that he'd pass a coworker heading into the subway at 96th Street and still beat him to the office. (Writing on the K2 Web site, he said he has come close to being "doored" only once—by a limo-driven passenger named Henry Kissinger.) As long as you watch out for anyone who worked in the Nixon administration, in-line skates are an efficient, healthy way to zip around town. This eco-friendly mode of transportation got greener in January 2009 when K2 unveiled the first sustainable skate to hit the market.

Though the Eco Etu (men's) and Maia (women's) skates feature the stability cuff and soft boot that K2 is known for, they've eliminated PVCs and use a frame built from bamboo, a sustainable material that dampens road vibration. Liners, laces, and embroidery are made from 100 percent recycled plastic, and the mesh from 37 percent recycled material. The skates are also sold in recycled packaging. Check out their eco pad set as well. (www.k2skates.com)

FYI

The 2,178-mile Appalachian Trail is the nation's longest marked footpath. It crosses 6 national parks, and 8 national forests and touches 14 states, from Springer, Georgia, to Katahdin, Maine.

The World's Greenest Machine Gets Greener

Baron Karl von Drais got the bike craze rolling in 1817 when he invented a wooden contraption with two same-size, in-line wheels attached to a frame. It was nearly a half a century before pedals entered the mix. All-metal bicycles with solid rubber tires and comically huge front wheels appeared just after the Civil War, followed by the next innovation: a bicycle with pedals and same-size wheels. A far safer vehicle, it paved the way for the bicycle craze that swept the nation. By the time bike shop owners Orville and Wilbur Wright took flight in the early 1900s, the world's most efficient human-powered mode of transport was here to stay.

How do we love bicycles? Let me count the ways: There are touring bikes (long wheel base, sturdy spokes, gearing to haul loads), mountain bikes (knobby-tired machines, often with front and/or rear shocks to handle rocks and ruts), racing bikes (lightweight, skinny-tired machines with drop handlebars, built strictly for speed), folding bikes (great for travel and/or commuting), tandem bikes (for two), hybrid bikes (with the forgiving gears and upright position of mountain bikes, and thinner tires for smoother riding around town), recumbent bikes (sit-down models with two or three wheels, pedaled with the cyclist's feet out in front as if the rider is sitting on a lounge chair), and electric bikes (bikes with small electric motors).

Anyone who can operate a kickstand understands the virtues of burning calories instead of fossil fuel. For a gas-free vacation, check out www.adventurecyclist.com. They offer a wide variety of cycling-centric maps, such as the Great Divide Mountain Bike Route, a route following the Continental Divide from Canada to Mexico with precious few paved roads. They're also working on strategic partnerships with other national and local bicycle advocates to build mapped and signed bike routes traversing the USA. If you want to ride your mountain bike on a multiday excursion, check out this complete light-is-right gear list: www.adventure cycling.org/features/ultralightpackinglist.cfm.

If a megamile journey isn't for you, cycling around town remains the best way to save on gas, oil changes, brake repairs, tires, car washes, parking fees, and a gym membership. And, of course, it reduces noxious automobile emissions. According to the Web site www.bicyclelife.com, roughly three-quarters of all trips made by car are less than 5 miles. That makes the bicycle a worthy alternative, especially if you're an urban dweller who loathes traffic and hunting for parking spaces. What's the ideal urban bike? A mountain bike with slick tires: It's stable, durable, safe, and effective in coping with deranged cabbies, gaping potholes, and oil slicks.

KAYAKING

Wet, Clean, and Green

More than 70 percent of the world is covered by water, and at birth we are about 78 percent water. In other words, water is in our blood. In its many forms and locations, water is the venue for clean, green outdoor recreation. Certainly there's no shortage of self-propelled watercraft: kayaks and canoes for whitewater, flatwater, oceans, rivers, and lakes; paddleboards; stand-up paddleboards (the latest wrinkle in surfing); windsurfing; kite surfing. The point is that all operate in the same medium and leave no footprint.

Before you buy a kayak, it's a good idea to go to one of the many kayak symposiums around the country to find a kayak that fits your body and is suited to the water in which you will do most of your paddling. For a complete list of symposiums in North America, go to www.rapidmedia.com/home. Surprisingly, it's probably best to choose a boat that initially feels too tippy, as you're likely to grow more stable as you log more water time. Buying a used boat is an excellent idea: You save money, and you're recycling at the same time. Buy the lightest boat you can afford, since you're likely to use it longer, plus it will retain its resale value better than a heavier boat. Odds are your first kayak will be made out of plastic, fiberglass, or wood, while the sleeker and more expensive boats are made out of Kevlar, carbon, or some combination of the two. If you're looking for an entry-level plastic kayak, two companies, Necky (www.neckykayaks.com) and Ocean Kayak (www.oceankayak.com), make boats from 100 percent recycled postindustrial waste.

While paddling a kayak is relatively easy, doing it well consistently is surprisingly hard. That's part of the enduring appeal and why it's called a lifetime sport. The ease of forward propulsion gets you out on the water, and the challenges of mastering the mechanics, balance, and subtleties of reading water keep you there.

PADDLE LIKE A PANDA

These days, with the improvements in light, breathable, waterproof paddling tops and bottoms, not to mention full-on immersion suits, keeping your body warm in cold water is relatively easy (albeit expensive) for hard-core winter paddling enthusiasts. Keeping your digits warm, however, is another, more challenging problem. In the coldest temperatures, kayakers opt for pogies—fleece-lined neoprene overmitts that attach with Velcro onto your paddle. (Canoeists have to wear gloves because they switch their hands on the paddle every time they switch sides.)

Worn alone in warm weather (or under pogies when it's cold), gloves are the way to go, and an eco-friendly choice is Camaro's Seamless Bamboo Paddling Gloves. Grippy, flexible, and waterproof, these durable paddling gloves feature a soft inner lining made of bamboo fibers. Bamboo is sustainable, tends not to stink, and dries quickly.

Similarly, the calf-high Bamboo Water Socks allow you to step into shallow water without getting your feet wet. These snug-fitting water socks are low profile so that you can fit your feet into a narrow cockpit. For added warmth, you can don a thin pair of wool socks underneath. Find the gloves and socks online or at your favorite outdoor gear retailer.

NECKY LOOKSHA 14 RECYCLED KAYAK

Kayaking in the Right Direction

It sounds simple, but ask anyone who knows the difference between a wing paddle and a touring blade, and they'll tell you that the kayak that's best for you will be the boat that's designed for the type of paddling you do. Do you paddle on Lake Michigan or on Lake Tear of the Clouds? The Mighty Missouri or the Roe River (it's in Montana, and at 200 feet long is one of the world's shortest rivers)? Are you paddling on a sandy coast or a rocky one? While location is a critical factor, performance involves several additional factors: the shape of the hull and the size and skill of the paddler. So before you invest in a kayak, consider all of these factors, and you're less likely to have to correct an uninformed mistake.

If you're looking for a sturdy, stable, and environmentally friendly beginner-to-intermediate boat that's versatile for day touring on lakes, rivers, or the ocean, Necky's 14-foot Looksha uses the company's own plastic waste to produce a boat made entirely from recycled material. The 57-pound craft has two hatches for storing gear and a rudder with adjustable foot pedals to keep you headed in the right direction. Necky gives 1 percent of gross sales to the Waterkeeper Alliance. (www.neckykayaks.com)

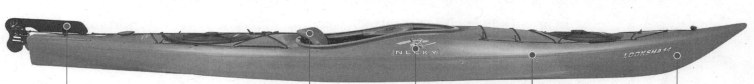

Bungee to Hold
Rudder Down

Ergonomic
High Seat Back

Molded-In
Graphics

Durable 100% Recycled
Plastic Material

High Volume Bow
for a Dry Ride

Doing Well & Good

The premise of eco-conscious investing is simple: If money makes the world go 'round, then greener investments ensure its vitality. Want to see clean energy? Invest in a solar energy start-up. Excited by a new state-of-the-art recycling facility? Buy the municipal bonds that fund it. Angry with Kraft for using genetically modified crops in products? Initiate a shareholder action demanding that it change. Great ideas, all.

But as is often the case with "obvious" good ideas, things aren't so simple. Consider our three examples. All are possible, but there are complications. For the solar start-up, you can only provide the initial financing if you are rich and willing to lose big if the company fails. To directly fund the recycling plant, you don't need to be Daddy Bigbucks, but you do need to be in a high tax bracket and very patient, since bonds for recycling plants are rarely available. And getting a corporation like Kraft to see the light? It's possible, but it won't be easy. Be prepared to roll up your sleeves or join with others to take on the work of organizing what is essentially a grass-roots activist effort.

Such stumbling blocks point to the limitations of investing as a vehicle of social change and underscore a deeper systemic challenge: How can we take advantage of the creativity and drive of capitalism without ruining the planet? Or, more narrowly: How can we make effective green investments when the laws governing our economic playing field have so many brown spots?

Still, there are plenty of things you can do now to green your money. Just be prepared for limitations: There is not a plethora of off-the-shelf, truly eco-friendly investment products available.

For a sense of the difficulty of pure eco-investing, consider investing in a grocery store. What could be more important than getting food to people in an efficient and cost-effective way? But as any environmentalist knows, most food is grown with harmful pesticides, trucked in from many miles away, packaged in plastic containers, and promoted on paper flyers responsible for deforestation. Naturally, a green-minded investor might be drawn to Whole Foods or a similar business, and such companies do make a positive difference. But most of Whole Foods' organic veggies are still transported long distances and produced by large agribusinesses.

Okay, you say, Whole Foods may not be perfect, but it's better than Triple-X Supermarkets, which doesn't offer any organics, irradiates the food, and uses chlorine to clean everything. But before you place an order for Whole Foods stock, understand that even if all its stores were wind powered and the food perfectly harvested, buying Whole Foods stock does not have a direct positive impact in the same way that buying actual organic broccoli does. If your goal is to increase the Whole Foods stock price, you're better off shopping there than buying the stock, since the stock market registers a company's profits or financial health—not its values. Boycotting the stock of a bad company and buying a good one's does not change a company's core financial well-being. While you've probably heard that green investing is like "voting with your dollars," that is rarely true for stocks.

Unfortunately, there has been little straight talk about what socially responsible investing (SRI) can and can't do. Most of what's been written about it is either by those who are against it or by SRI professionals who have something to promote. To eco-empower our money, we need to understand the sacrifices or compromises involved in making environmental changes. Being better informed can help us avoid the mistake of thinking, "Since I have a green stock fund, I'm doing my part."

This chapter is organized around a menu of financial needs: Everyone uses banks, so banking is covered first, followed by a list of safe, environmentally beneficial, high-return personal "investments" to make *before* investing in stocks or bonds. Not all of these suggestions will make sense for everyone, but they can prompt you to consider nonfinancial green options before turning to the markets. For instance, you might see buying a bicycle as an unnecessary expense. But if it allows you to ditch your car, it's a great investment for you, your bank account, and the earth.

After these suggestions, you'll find some commonsense guidelines on your investment portfolio: Time-tested financial research indicates that it's smart to balance your assets in different types of investments. Investment decisions shouldn't be made in isolation but should take into account your whole strategy in seeking an appropriate balance between maximizing returns, minimizing risk, and reflecting your ecological and social concerns.

Last, when you feel financially secure, there's advice on giving your money away. Donating money to effective environmental groups may well be the best thing you can do for the planet. Greening the economy requires activism that addresses root causes. For example, if the true cost of carbon emissions were factored into the price of fuel, then locally grown produce would gain an economic advantage over that grown on factory farms located thousands of miles away. But legislation to that effect will get passed only if nonprofit organizations lobby against the interests of agribusinesses. Those nonprofits need money. Understanding the mechanisms of money, power, and social change will help you maximize the impact of your donations.

—Marshall Glickman

GREENER BANKING
It Pays to Change

When most people think of "greening" their money, they usually mean investing in eco-friendly stocks. But they may still have checking and savings accounts with Citibank or some other sprawling multinational. Such banks fund large, eco-destructive projects—ventures that environmentalists would never knowingly support. From an environmental vantage point, who, what, where, and how your bank loans your money has more impact than which stocks you buy.

You can stop funding big bad projects and increase the capital available to small, planet-friendly businesses like organic farms: Simply switch to an eco-minded bank. For information on a variety of socially focused banks, go to www.communityinvest.org.

Money invested in green jobs creates four times more jobs than similar investments in the oil industry, according to researchers at the University of Massachusetts.

PERMACULTURE CREDIT UNION
Small but Effective

It's hard to find a more grassroots bank purer in green spirit than this Santa Fe–based 30-year-old nonprofit credit union. Permaculture Credit Union (PCU) is guided by the principles of permaculture and run by a volunteer member-elected board of directors (day-to-day operations are handled by a staff of three: CEO, bookkeeper, and member services representative). PCU offers interest-bearing accounts, student loans, and loans to individuals or businesses seeking to fund eco-minded purchases such as fuel-efficient cars and solar-heating units. And PCU's rates on CDs are competitive with national averages. (www.pcuonline.org)

CHITTENDEN BANK'S SOCIALLY RESPONSIBLE BANKING PROGRAM
Committed to Conservation

Chittenden's socially responsible banking division is a $92 million unit within People's United Bank, New England's largest bank. Based in Brattleboro, Vermont, Chittenden has the resources to offer full-service banking and investing options—from online banking to stocks and bonds. The SRB division finances nontraditional Vermont-style eco-businesses, like a furniture maker who creates handcrafted furniture from sustainably harvested trees or a nonprofit that installs geothermal heat. One of Chittenden's strong suits is lending to conservation and agriculture projects. It helps conservation groups preserve forestland and wilderness areas and supports family farmers and organic farmers who promote sustainable agriculture. (www.chittenden.com/socially-responsible.html)

SHOREBANK PACIFIC
They're Eco-Committed

If a new era of environmentally enlightened banking is dawning, ShoreBank Pacific is the shining green star lighting the way. One of several affiliates of the innovative Chicago-based ShoreBank, a socially responsible banking pioneer since the 1970s, ShoreBank Pacific is a full-service, eco-committed bank that offers checking, CDs, money markets, online banking, Web-based bill paying, credit cards, IRA accounts, and business and building loans. Consider Panel-Tech, a company located in an economically depressed former timber town in the Pacific Northwest. ShoreBank Pacific's financing enabled this manufacturer of nontoxic plywood to grow a business that now supports 36 employees with a living wage. Another loan went to Pacific Ethanol, allowing them to expand their facility that produces low-carbon ethanol. ShoreBank Pacific offices are located in Portland, Oregon, and Ilwaco, Washington. (www.eco-bank.com)

FIRST GREEN BANK: JUST LIKE THE NAME SAYS

Opened for business in early 2009, First Green Bank is building its cutting-edge, energy-efficient, and eco-sensitive headquarters in Eustis, Florida. Focused on loaning money to green commercial buildings, First Green offers the usual array of everyday banking options: online banking, money markets, CDs, and IRAs. It is also the only green-dedicated bank to offer a Health ?Savings Account. First Green's "hybrid" CDs and IRAs allow you to lock in rates, but with the flexibility to add to the account or withdraw money. (www.firstgreenbank.com)

First GREEN Bank
in organization

SELF-HELP CREDIT UNION

Big on Sustainable Communities

This nonprofit community-development lender in Durham, North Carolina, provides mortgages and small-business loans to low-income borrowers nationwide. Since its founding in 1980, Self-Help has loaned $5.57 billion to 62,288 families, organizations, and individuals—including Lea Clayton, who used funding to buy a 15-acre organic community-supported-agriculture (CSA) farm. Self-Help offers regular banking services, such as checking and savings accounts and personal loans. (www.self-help.org)

WAINWRIGHT BANK

A Progressive Institution

With $800 million in deposits, Boston-based Wainwright (profiled as the "ultimate" high-purpose company in the 2006 book *The High-Purpose Company*) is one of the premier progressive banks in the country. Though not solely focused on environmental issues, Wainwright Bank has made many an eco-loan, such as providing the nonprofit Silent Spring Institute a line of credit to support work on the links between exposure to environmental toxins and women's health. Wainwright offers an extensive menu of financial products and services, including home equity loans and direct deposit options. If you purchase a hybrid car, Wainwright will take as much as $3/4$ percent off your loan rate. (www.wainwrightbank.com)

INSULATION

Button Up and Save

Insulation is the key to a comfortable and energy-efficient house, holding heat in during winter and out during summer. It is also a good investment. Depending upon how much insulation your house has and where it is located, buttoning up can produce 15 to 40 percent yearly tax-free returns. Adding more insulation to attic floors and basement ceilings will yield the best returns, while wall insulation payoffs are in the 7 to 15 percent range.

Most people assume they have enough insulation because they once noticed some pink stuff in the attic, but most US houses remain underinsulated. In cold regions of the country, few homes have the recommended 2 feet of insulation above the ceiling. Adding even more insulation can do wonders: In frigid parts of Canada and the northern United States, some superinsulated homes use only $200 to $300 worth of fuel a year. Even in warmer climates, increased insulation can produce big savings by eliminating the need for a furnace.

To calculate insulation improvements and potential savings for your house, check out the ZIP Code Insulation Program at www.ornl.gov/~roofs/Zip/ZipHome.html.

AUTOMOBILES
Think Used

Americans spend more on cars than on food. One alternative scenario: Try to avoid owning a car. If that's not realistic, invest in a used, fuel-efficient model. Small, efficient models generally have lower initial prices and lower insurance premiums. Consider your return on investment when gas is $4 per gallon: Let's say you pay $6,500 for your used car; if you drive the average 12,500 miles per year, a 32 mpg model saves over $700 per year over a 22 mpg model. As an investment, that works out to a 10.9 percent *tax-free* annual return—tough to match even in a good market.

For reliable information on fuel-efficient models, go to **Carmax.com** and search for used cars within, say, 100 miles of your ZIP code. Or you can search by EPA gas mileage. A recent search turned up more than 200 such used cars for sale. Or try **Edmunds.com** for data on the 10 most efficient cars.

CREDIT CARDS
Beware This Debtor's Prison

Some 10 percent of US families have an unpaid credit card balance of $9,000 or more. At an average 17 percent yearly interest charge, that's costing them $986 a year in finance fees. Fortunes have been built *earning* 17 percent interest, so what is the point of *paying out* that interest rate? To get out of such debt, first cut back on new, optional purchases (that's the green part). Next, use those savings to pay off card debt. If you have money in a savings account or in the market, cash out and pay off Visa or Mastercard first. Why earn 5 percent or even 16 percent and pay taxes on that—while you're shelling out 17 percent that was earned with after-tax dollars? For information on low-interest credit cards, see such sites as **Credit Cards.com** or **ASAPCreditCard.com**.

ASSET ALLOCATION
Keeping Your Balance

A healthy ecosystem is a diverse, interconnected community. Similarly, a healthy investment portfolio holds types of investments that thrive in different economic climates. And like the ecosystem, it needs to stay balanced.

For investors, there are three types of economic weather: hot or inflationary, when prices and interest rates tend to be rising; cold or deflationary, when prices and interest rates tend to be falling; and temperate, when prices and interest rates are stable. Balmy economic times are best for businesses, and that's when stocks prosper. But economic weather is variable, so it makes sense to own bonds or fixed-income investments for stability and appreciation during deflationary or uncertain times, plus commodities for protection against inflation.

Deciding how much of each type of investment to have, and when to buy each, is more art than science and depends on your stomach for volatility. This table shows simple guidelines for asset allocation, assuming you have a long-term investing horizon (ideally of 10-plus years) *and* you've already taken care of such essentials as maintaining 6 months of expenses in a money market or savings account that is safe and liquid. Funds earmarked for a house, a business, or tuition payments should be in investments that guarantee principal.

Your Risk Tolerance	% Stocks	% Bonds	% Commodities
Negative numbers make you sweat	25	65	10
Prefer safety	40	50	10
Moderate	60	20	20
Aggressive	70	15	15
Unflappable in bear markets	80	10	10

But *do* keep your holdings in stocks, bonds, and commodities in balance; **TDAmeritrade.com** offers a service that for a modest fee allows you to automatically keep your investment in the proportions you choose. If you don't have that option with your investment account, rebalance your investments whenever one type grows or shrinks to more than 25 percent off its ideal weighting. Regardless of your environmental interests, asset allocation is smart investing. Research shows that 93 percent of the return of an investment depends on how well that overall asset group is doing. So you could spend your whole life researching stocks to find undervalued superstars to earn a 13.5 percent average return, while the investor who simply bought an index fund over the same period would get 12.55 percent. Put your investments on automatic pilot and focus your attention on more important things—like saving the planet.

**HOUSE PRICE ESTIMATOR:
SMALLER IS SMARTER**

While the average family shrinks in number, Americans have been building bigger houses. Meanwhile, compact houses are way easier on the wallet and the environment: They take fewer resources to build, maintain, heat, and cool. They're easier to clean and cost less to insure. The National Association of Home Builders (NAHB) "house price estimator" allows you to plug in details about your house with and without extra features, then see how those "improvements" affect resale value. Even before the real estate bubble popped, it was easy to see that adding rooms wasn't a good investment. (www.nahb.com)

FYI

It is flagrantly bad for the environment when a CEO buys a mansion—plus it hurts shareholders! A recent study shows that the return on investment of companies whose CEOs live in houses larger than 10,000 square feet lag the overall market by 7 percent.

HOUSE FANS
Fan-tastic Savings

Most Americans want their homes to be 78 degrees in the winter and 68 in the summer. Reverse those numbers and our national cooling tab wouldn't run up to $25 billion a year or nearly $100 per person. In such places as Florida, Arizona, and Southern California, it's common for air-conditioning bills to reach $500 annually. Those numbers can be reduced by 50 to 75 percent—with accompanying reductions of the roughly 3,500 pounds of carbon dioxide and 31 pounds of sulfur dioxide that each household's cooling adds to the atmosphere.

How? Fans are great investments. Whole-house fans can save 28 to 40 percent on air-conditioning costs. For more information on fans and other ways to save money (and the environment) by improving home energy efficiency, see the US Department of Energy Web site at www.eere.energy.gov/consumer. For comprehensive information on green products that improve home efficiency, visit www.buildinggreen.com.

HOT-WATER HEATERS
Ways to Save on Water Use *and* Cost

When buying large appliances, look beyond purchase price to operating cost. Hot-water heaters consume a lot of energy, costing from $160 to $390 a year (depending upon whether electric or gas) to operate. Two easy investments are low-flow showerheads and faucet aerators that save hot water without affecting water pressure; they can pay for themselves quickly.

Most hot-water heaters are installed by building contractors who profit by selling cheap appliances, regardless of long-term efficiency. Stuck with an inefficient electric unit? Replace it with an efficient gas model—even if the electric one is still working. An efficient gas-powered replacement can pay for itself in 2 to 3 years. Even more efficient is a tankless heater that works on demand. These units cost slightly more than the storage variety but can save 20 percent per year in fuel and should last 50 percent longer. To compare types, models, and life-cycle costs of water heaters, see the American Council for an Energy-Efficient Economy's Web site at www.aceee.org/consumerguide/waterheating.htm.

ACEEE
American Council for an Energy-Efficient Economy

EFFICIENT HEATING
Going Up in Smoke?

For most homes, heating is energy expense numero uno, accounting for two-thirds of yearly energy bills in colder climates. A more efficient source of heat can make a significant impact on your cash flow and the environment. So replacing an antiquated boiler or furnace is a smart investment, often yielding as much as 25 percent in cost savings per year. Regular maintenance and replacing outdated burners can also be big winners. To find out if it makes sense for you and your return on investment, go to www.aceee.org.

LANDSCAPING
Nature as Money Saver

Everyone loves a shady tree in the summer and avoids open fields on blustery winter days. But most people forget to use these natural principles to create a more comfortable, energy-efficient home. Energy-saving landscaping is our most overlooked form of energy conservation. Studies show that strategic landscaping can trim heating costs by as much as 30 percent, cut air-conditioning bills by 50 percent, and prune water bills by 40 percent—reaping annual savings of $300 to $750. The key is to work with nature instead of against it: Trees can block northerly winds, while an open southern exposure can help sun-warm a house. Basics on energy-saving landscaping are available from many state university extension service Web sites (e.g., University of Minnesota, North Carolina State University, University of Vermont) and at www.green builder.com/sourcebook/Land scapingEnergy.html.

BUYING IN BULK
Shop Carefully for the Right Items

Although the advice to buy in bulk for discounts isn't exactly late-breaking news for consumers, it is still an underdeveloped practice. To hone it to a system, make a list of nonperishables that you and your family use regularly. Include everything from pasta to dental floss. Don't put anything on the list unless you really like and use it—then buy it by the case. Once you get the case home, mark the date on the last box to see whether the product gets used enough to justify future bulk purchases. Of course, this strategy depends on having ample storage space at home. When an item on your list goes on sale at more than 10 percent off, buy a year's worth. If groceries are 30 percent off, it even makes sense to dip into savings to buy 'em up. You'll also save the costs of repeated shopping trips. The average household can save $600 a year with this strategy.

INCOME INVESTMENTS
Doing It the Green Way

Income investments provide a safe and stable source of cash flow—the ballast of a portfolio. Often, this means buying US government bonds. But for most green investors, that isn't good enough. Depending upon the accounting, some 21 to 51 percent of the US government budget goes to military spending, while only a small percentage supports green initiatives. But loaning money to Uncle Sam is not our only option. Eco-investors can earn a secure return lending money to eco-projects or green businesses. Unfortunately, there are not many options for doing this—and there's nothing that's *both* truly green and truly convenient.

The easiest option for safe eco-friendly income is to buy a certificate of deposit (CD) at a green bank. They will give you a competitive rate of return and use your money for loans to eco-businesses or other nonprofits. And with CDs, your principal is guaranteed by federal insurance up to $100,000. However, buying a bank CD is awkward for maintaining asset balance, and CDs do not offer the recession or deflation protection that bonds or bond funds do (bonds go up in value when interest rates go down; US government bonds were one of the few investments to do well in the market meltdown of 2008). There is no such thing as an eco-focused bond mutual fund, but stretch your definition of "green," and you'll find a smattering of socially responsible bond funds. They don't invest in US government bonds that fund military spending, they deliver better returns than CDs, and their flexibility makes it easy to fit them into an overall investment strategy.

ORMAT TECHNOLOGIES INC.

Turning Natural Sources of Heat into Energy

Ormat (ORA) has established itself as a large-scale geothermal player, with 11 geothermal plants around the world that produce enough power for almost 400,000 homes. Those numbers should increase, since Ormat's clean-energy offerings fit well with the Obama administration's goals for renewable energy. Geothermal power is clean and quiet and doesn't harm wildlife, and in the right location the energy supply is virtually limitless.

From 2006 to 2008, there was a 183 percent increase in investment for geothermal facilities (including research bankrolled by Google). Over the past 5 years, Ormat's earnings per share increased more than 15 percent per year, and analysts predict a 20 percent per annum increase for the next 5 years. (www.ormat.com)

A Light Green Investment

The Parnassus bond fund (PRFIX) has been the best long-term performer of all the SRI fixed-income funds. PRFIX charges the lowest fees of its SRI compatriots (the bond market is so competitive, higher fees inevitably hurt returns) and, unlike most bond funds, the Parnassus fund typically invests 20 percent in convertible bonds (bonds that are linked to stock prices and can increase in value if the stock of the company issuing the bond does well).

Only a small percentage of the corporate bonds currently held are green or greenish (Burlington Northern Santa Fe and Goldman Sachs have adapted green investment initiatives). Roughly 60 percent of their holdings are US government bonds, 22 percent of which are straight treasuries and the balance issued by government agencies. (www.parnassus.com)

UNIVERSAL DISPLAY CORPORATION: SHEDDING NEW LIGHT ON CONSERVATION

Imagine lighting materials so sophisticated that they could make lightbulbs obsolete. Universal Display Corporation (PANL) engages in the research, development, and commercialization of organic light-emitting diode (OLED) technologies. OLEDs could allow you to light up a whole room with a screen that also shows videos. Or they could be used to create a computer monitor or TV screen so flexible that you could roll it up and put it away. OLEDs use less energy than any other technology, and without toxic components.

Universal Display Corporation is one of the only pure plays for investors hoping to take advantage of the OLED revolution, though there is reason to be skeptical: It has been a "story stock" since it first became a public company in 1996—meaning it's never actually earned a profit. What keeps it going is investor faith in the huge potential of OLEDs and the fact that PANL sips rather than guzzles cash. As a research and licensing firm, its overhead and operating costs are much smaller than a manufacturer's costs. PANL diehards are realistically hopeful: OLED technology is making its way into consumer devices in volume—which is reflected in revenues. (www. universaldisplay.com)

FYI

According to *Business Week*, the three most generous donors to environmental causes were Intel founders George and Betty Moore, investor Robert Wilson, and media mogul Ted Turner.

THE CRA QUALIFIED INVESTMENT FUND: A SOLID ECO TRACK RECORD

Managed by a firm that specializes in fixed-income community-development investing, the CRA Qualified Investment Fund (CRATX) is the country's largest SRI bond fund and is consistently among the top performers in this niche. Although most of the fund is invested in US government agency assets such as GNMA bonds, this Morningstar four-star-rated fund also invests in energy-efficient and eco-friendly bonds—difficult for ordinary investors to buy. CRA fund has invested in taxable municipal bonds funding recycling facilities and an asset-backed security that funded a Florida organic farm. (www.ccmfixedincome.com)

PEER-TO-PEER LENDING

Be Your Own Bank

Looking for a better return than a bank CD while making a direct connection to the borrower? Like the idea of funding solar panels while earning more than 13 percent for the loan? Check out peer-to-peer (P2P) lending sites such as Prosper.com or LendingClub.com.

P2P lending is the result of e-Bay–like online tools that connect individual borrowers to individual lenders. It cuts out the middleman and gives anyone a chance to access credit and capital from those with disposable funds. For example, a recent Minnesota-based Prosper.com borrower was looking to expand his organic food delivery service. While most borrowers repay their loans, be prepared to lose some or even all of what you invest; most experienced P2P lenders lend only small amounts to any given borrower. If you want to support borrowers in undeveloped countries, consider MicroPlace.com, which connects you to low-income borrowers around the world. (www.prosper.com; www.lendingclub.com; www.microplace.com)

PORTFOLIO 21

A Green Mutual with International Reach

With just a third of its holdings in US companies, Portfolio 21 is one of only a half dozen SRI funds that invest globally. Of this group, it's the only one that concentrates on sustainability—plus it has the best track record of the bunch. Portfolio 21 uses strict environmental screens, but it doesn't initiate shareholder actions—not an option for the foreign investment portion of its portfolio. The largest concentration of its portfolio is in information technology stocks. (www.portfolio21.com)

PORTFOLIO 21
INVESTMENTS

SHAREHOLDER ACTIVISM

Pressuring Corporate Policies

Shareholder activism is the muscle in socially responsible investing. Large shareholders can talk to management directly about progressive changes, threatening to sell their stock or create bad publicity if management doesn't respond. Shareholders can also initiate management directives for other shareholders to vote on. Socially conscious investors have pressured General Electric to clean up PCBs in the Hudson River, and they have persuaded Whole Foods to label store-brand products when they contain genetically modified ingredients.

Until recently, anyone with $1,000 of stock held for at least 1 year could initiate a shareholder action that would reach the annual voting ballot. Technically, that's still true, but the Securities and Exchange Commission recently made it more difficult to add items to annual meeting agendas. According to the highly regarded SRI mutual fund company Pax World, "between December 1, 2006, and April 30, 2007, the SEC staff issued 405 'No Action' letters permitting companies to exclude shareholder proposals from their proxy ballots. These No Action letters represented 75 percent of all the shareholder proposals tracked during the period in question." Accordingly, ordinary investors should consider investing in those mutual funds that take shareholder activism seriously.

> **FYI**
>
> To invest in governments with a green outlook that won't fund missile launchers and aircraft carriers, consider government bonds from Switzerland, Sweden, Norway, and Finland—ranked as the greenest countries in 2008.

VANGUARD GNMA AND TAX-FREE FUNDS
Make Housing, Not War

Vanguard funds are not marketed as socially responsible, but this mutual fund giant has grown by keeping investors' best interests in mind. Vanguard charges the lowest fees around—especially important when investing in bonds; over the long haul, the fund manager with the lowest fee will almost inevitably produce the best returns. Vanguard's GNMA fund outperforms not only all SRI bond funds but pretty much all bond funds. Of course, returns aren't the only things that matter, but GNMA bonds are basically benign, supporting housing, not weapons. In fact, the bulk of SRI bond funds, including the others mentioned here, are filled with GNMA bonds.

For tax-free investors, the management fee difference is even greater. Over 10 years, Vanguard tax-frees offer at least a 7.5 percent over-all return advantage—that's $750 on a $10,000 investment. The bonds in Vanguard tax-free funds aren't all that different from other SRI tax-free funds; in some cases, they're even better. (www.vanguard.com)

FYI

The economic value of environmentally related goods and services—everything from waste assimilation to climate—is about $44 trillion per year, according to an estimate by University of Vermont ecological economist Robert Costanza.

TAX-FREE BOND FUNDS
Social Consciousness for High Rollers

Those in higher income brackets may benefit from tax-free municipal bonds, which offer lower absolute yields than taxable bonds but give better returns *after* taxes are factored in. When you buy a new issue of a bond, your money goes directly to the entity raising the money. If you buy bonds from a city funding a new recycling facility, you've helped underwrite an eco-facility. That said, green-focused new bond issues are unusual, so finding one requires patience. Also, municipal bonds come in minimums of $5,000, and buying in small lots means you'll end up paying a premium. Most tax-free investors settle for a tax-free socially conscious bond fund. None is specifically eco-focused.

Calvert versus Vanguard: Tax-Free Bond Fund Face-Off

While not exactly green, most municipal bonds support socially responsible activities that help keep a state going. Only a handful of tax-free mutual funds are marketed as socially responsible, so it might be best to choose the top-notch, inexpensive Vanguard tax-free funds, then use your savings to donate to environmental groups.

Name	Symbol	Upfront Sales Load	Annual Fees	Performance: Morningstar Rating and 5-Year Return*	Percent of Funds in General Obligations Bonds/ Transportation/Health
Calvert National Municipal Intermediate Fund	CINMX	2.75%	0.97%	2 stars; 3.02%	21% - 5% - 5%
Vanguard Intermediate Term Tax-Exempt	VWITX	0%	0.15%	4 stars; 3.81%	30% - 9% - 7%
Calvert Tax-Free Reserves Long-Term Portfolio	CTTLX	3.75%	0.90%	3 stars; 3.45%	29% - 0% - 9%
Vanguard Long-Term Tax-Exempt	VWLTX	0%	0.15%	5 stars; 4.18%	6% - 11% - 15%

*As of September 5, 2008

DOMINI SOCIAL EQUITY FUND WITH A SOCIAL CONSCIENCE

Domini initially established itself as a big player in socially responsible investing circles with the development and marketing of the Domini Social Index, a kinder, gentler version of the S&P 500. Domini developed a large following, attracting over a billion dollars in assets, as its tech-heavy portfolio outperformed its more famous index cousin. But the tech bust in 2000 left the Domini index lagging, and in 2006, the fund technically stopped being an index fund. Still, Domini is broadly diversified, so its returns tend to resemble the stock market averages—minus the management fees, which are higher than those of your typical index fund.

Part of what Domini offers is a proactive approach to shareholder activism, making it an SRI leader. Although not strictly a green-focused fund, Domini has launched a number of eco-initiatives, such as engaging Kimberly-Clark in dialogue over its forestry practices—whereupon the company issued a new policy expressing preference for fiber certified by the eco-friendly Forest Stewardship Council. (www.domini.com)

REAL ESTATE INVESTMENT
Not Necessarily Dirty Words

For many environmentalists, "real estate development" conjures images of unneeded shopping malls and condos that wreck wetlands. However, progressive real estate development is possible: Heating, cooling, and powering buildings accounts for almost half of our nation's overall energy use. So it's easy to see that *how* houses are built or renovated, and *where* a home or office is sited, can have big environmental impacts. There are two ways to invest in real estate: Buy property and manage it yourself, or let others do it for you.

GREEN CENTURY EQUITY FUND: A GREEN *AND* ACTIVIST MUTUAL

The Green Century Equity mutual fund now offers what Domini does not: adherence to the Domini index. The Green Century Equity fund has always been a proxy for the Domini Social Index, and unlike the Domini fund itself, Green Century didn't abandon its cause. Ironically, this loyalty has been repaid by higher returns for its investors than Domini's, in part because Green Century takes lower management fees. Any profits from management fees support the environmental nonprofits that sponsor the fund. Green Century is also an activist fund: It pressed Chevron to issue a report on potential environmental damage from the company's expanding oil sands operations. (www.greencentury.com)

A Guide to Shareholder Activism

The hardest part of shareholder activism is getting enough votes to influence company policies. To initiate an action, work with a nonprofit organization that knows the ropes and already has a network. The most experienced shareholder activist organization is the Interfaith Center on Corporate Responsibility. ICCR can help get your resolution on the ballot, then spread the word by publishing it in their journal and on their Web site.

Tim Smith, director of ICCR for almost 30 years, notes, "Even if a resolution doesn't pass—and most don't—it can still have considerable influence." Why? Because corporate management wants smooth annual meetings and fears negative publicity.

Pay attention to resolutions on annual proxy statements. In addition to casting a ballot, you can write to the CEO, expressing your concerns. If you attend the annual meeting, raise issues during shareholder question time. First, do your homework and have a good grasp of the issue. And don't assume that someone else will speak up.

Shareholder Activism Web Sites for Green Investors

Web Site	Description
www.iccr.org	Since 1971, the Interfaith Center on Corporate Responsibility has been the leading organizer of progressive shareholder initiatives.
www.coopamerica.org/ socialinvesting/ shareholderaction/	This section of Green America's Web site is devoted to shareholder advocacy news.
www.fundvotes.com	Fund Votes tracks mutual fund proxy voting in the United States and Canada. This is an invaluable resource for finding a stock mutual fund that engages in shareholder activism.
www.asyousow.org	As You Sow's Corporate Social Responsibility Program (CSRP) uses shareholder advocacy and the financial markets to catalyze positive change in publicly held companies.

Investing Web Sites Worth Visiting

★ **www.coopamerica.org** or **www.greenamericatoday.org:** In January 2009, the nonprofit, member-supported Co-Op America changed its name to Green America. Its mission remains the same: to harness economic power so our spending and investing make the world a better place. The site covers green and social justice issues, from advice about eco-cleaning products to corporate boycotts. The social investing section includes everything from financial planning advice to an extensive mutual fund chart.

★ **www.corpwatch.org:** This Web site is brought to you by the folks who blew the whistle on working conditions in Nike's Vietnam factory—which led to Nike changing its corporate practices. The nonprofit CorpWatch.org provides news, analysis, research tools, and action alerts for corporate activity worldwide. In addition to reporting on environmental crimes, it covers human rights violations, fraud, and corruption. CorpWatch began investigating Enron in 1998—3 years before the company's collapse.

★ **www.socialfunds.com:** Since this site is owned by a likable neighbor [full disclosure], I like to tell people about SocialFunds.com, but it's fair to say this is a top resource for socially concerned and green investors. With more than 10,000 pages of articles related to social investing, SocialFunds.com offers an inexhaustible supply of news on everything from shareholder actions to sustainability reports. One section allows investors to order free prospectuses for SRI mutual funds.

★ **www.ceres.org:** This is a national network of investors, environmental organizations, and other public interest groups working with companies and investors to address such challenges as global climate change.

STOCK SCREENING

Good for You, Harmless to Corporations

Most investors associate ethical investing with "stock screening," avoiding bad companies and buying shares in good ones. Intuitively, this seems like the right thing to do, but not buying a stock isn't like not buying a product, since it does not actually influence the company's profitability—and it is profits that drive stock prices. If we sold our Exxon stock after the *Valdez* disaster but other motorists kept buying their gas, our stock sale was meaningless to Exxon. Screening, however, can be an expression of your ethics and principles, but don't expect selling a stock to influence corporate profits or behavior.

WILDERHILL CLEAN ENERGY PORTFOLIO

Invest in a Cleaner Future

The **Wilderhill Clean Energy Portfolio** (PBW) is an exchange-traded fund (ETF) with a portfolio of companies that are in the business of conservation and cleaner and renewable energy, with almost two-thirds of its holdings in green industrial and information technology companies. The fund includes both fledgling alternative technology companies as well as well-established utilities. As a diversified basket of stocks within the green energy field, PBW offers a no-brainer way to invest in eco-technologies, since you don't need to know the particulars of any one company. It's still important to check whether the fund is reasonably valued. (www.invescopowershares.com)

WHOLE FOODS
Marketing Organics to the Millions

After years working at food co-ops, CEO John Mackey opened his first health food store in 1978. An ovo-vegan who practices yoga, he understands his customers because he is one of them. Whole Foods (WFMI) is familiar to anyone with an appetite and a yen for organic produce, and as Peter Lynch famously advised, it pays to invest in what you understand. Whole Foods knows how to sell organic foods and related products.

Of course, Whole Foods has its critics; for example, the company has used tough tactics when competing with nonprofit food co-ops. Still, as *Plenty* magazine reported, "in 2006, the company made the largest renewable-energy credit purchase in US history, becoming the only Fortune 500 company to offset all of its electricity usage." It's also the first grocery chain to set standards for humane treatment of animals. (www.wholefoodsmarket.com)

BURLINGTON NORTHERN SANTA FE
All Aboard for Energy Savings

Why would a 21st-century green investor buy a railroad stock like Burlington Northern Santa Fe (BNI)? After deregulation in 1980, railroads invested in efficiency. As *Money* magazine's analyst Michael Sivy says: "Railroads are far more energy-efficient than their competition. Locomotives today get 80 percent more mileage from a gallon of diesel than they did in 1980. As a result, trains consume far less fuel than trucks do to move the same amount of freight. The Environmental Protection Agency calculates that for distances of more than 1,000 miles, using trains rather than trucks alone reduces fuel consumption and greenhouse gas emissions by 65 percent." Eco-cool—but is it smart? Warren Buffett sees BNI as a savvy company with a protected franchise that is well positioned to earn premium profits as fuel prices rise. (www.bnsf.com)

WINSLOW GREEN GROWTH FUND
Small Can Be Beautiful

At times the Winslow Green Growth Fund has produced eye-popping returns, but like the small company stocks it invests in, it can be volatile. Seek elsewhere if you're after a smooth ride. At this writing, it has lost slightly more than half its value in the recent downturn. But it will likely soar again, as the cutting-edge companies it invests in bounce back. It has thorough environmental screens but doesn't initiate shareholder resolutions. (www.winslowgreen.com)

Fund Name	Management Fees	Symbol	Type	5-Year Annual Return*	Benchmark Index (5 Year)	Shareholder Activism**
TIAA-CREF	0.45%	TRSCX	growth	-4.37	-4.77	B+
Green Century Equity	0.95%	GCEQX	growth	-6.16	-4.77	A
Portfolio 21	1.52%	PORTX	global growth	-1.19	-1.29	C
Domini Social Equity	1.20%	DSEFX	growth	-6.93	-4.77	A
Winslow Green Growth Fund	1.31%	WGGFX	aggressive growth	-9.73	-5.24	C

*As of March 31, 2009   **Assessment provided by Jackie Cook, founder of www.fundvotes.com

TIAA-CREF SOCIAL CHOICE EQUITY FUND: DOING THE RIGHT THING

Run by the nonprofit teachers union, yet available to anyone with $2,500 to invest, TIAA-CREF Social Choice Equity Fund is a broad social index fund. It isn't as serious about shareholder activism as Green Century or Domini, but it has taken shareholder actions that support eco-issues. With  the lowest fee of any SRI fund, this index fund outperforms the other green domestic funds. (www.tiaa-cref.org)

FYI

Buy a reusable water bottle and stop buying bottled water in plastic containers. Annual cost savings: $500

COMMODITIES
Not Just Pork Bellies

In the popular imagination, investing in commodities means speculating in pork bellies or crude oil futures, gambles that can take one from rags to riches—or from riches to rags. But commodities have recently become available as a nonleveraged investment offering protection against inflation: You can now buy exchange-traded funds (ETFs) on the stock market that allow you to purchase a commodity such as oil or gold. Owning commodities, as a complement to stocks and bonds, provides better and less volatile returns for your overall investment portfolio.

What is green about buying a commodity ETF? If buying oil tends to drive up gasoline prices, then green investors can claim to be doing their part when buying a commodity ETF. The recent spike in oil prices has done something an army of environmentalists could not: It got the American public driving less, conserving gas, and looking for transportation alternatives. During the market meltdown of 2008 and 2009, gold (GLD) held up the best. Investors turn to gold in times of financial uncertainty.

Selected Commodity Exchange-Traded Funds

Fund Name	Type	Symbol	Management Fee
Goldman Sachs Commodity Index (GSCI) Total Return Index ETN	diverse commodity	GSP	0.75%
iShares GSCI Commodity-Indexed Trust ETF	diverse commodity	GSG	0.75%
Goldman Sachs Crude Oil Total Return ETN	oil	OIL	0.75%
United States Oil Fund	oil	USO	0.50%
SPDR Gold Shares	gold	GLD	0.40%

REAL ESTATE INVESTMENT TRUSTS
The REIT Stuff

The easy way to hire a pro manager is to buy shares in a real estate investment trust (REIT). REITs are publicly traded stocks that invest in commercial properties, apartment buildings, nursing homes, and office complexes. Investors pool their money and hope the real estate manager's expertise and access to capital will pay off. Management fees are relatively low, since real estate trusts invest multimillions at a time. And unlike property you purchase directly, a REIT is totally liquid. It can also be added to in increments as small as the REIT's share price. To maintain their special tax benefits, REITs must pass on 95 percent of each year's operating profits in regular dividend payments. The typical REIT offers a much higher yield than the average stock, plus the chance at appreciation.

REITs can head south like any other stock if properties depreciate or rental income dries up. REIT prices tend to fluctuate along with the whole market, so they don't work as an inflation hedge the way owning real estate outright does. Avoid REITs that put up strip malls. Be patient, and find one that favors more enlightened projects.

Does Socially Responsible Investing = Poor Returns?

When most socially conscious *growth* funds have lagged behind market averages, the *Wall Street Journal*, *Money*, and *Forbes* have run headlines like "It's Not Easy Being Green," portraying concerned investors as good-hearted saps condemned to inferior returns. But a few years earlier, those same publications ran headlines like "Doing Well by Doing Good," suggesting that superior investing returns resulted from ethical screens—an idea originally popularized by *Good Money* publisher Dr. Ritchie Lowry. Lowry thought social screening improved investing performance because ethical companies were less likely to be sued and tended to be fiscally conservative. Research has not supported either claim: Social screens have little or no impact on investing results.

GUIDESTAR

RESEARCHING CHARITIES

The Info Is Out There

The $150 billion nonprofit "industry" doesn't get regular media coverage. Fake charities and embezzlement make the front pages, but ineffective bureaucracy and poorly focused management receive scant media coverage. Still, thanks to the Internet, it is possible to find comprehensive information on even small groups. First, check out a group's IRS Form 990 and annual report, available on the Web at sites such as www.guidestar.org. The Action Without Borders Web site, www.idealist.org, also links to sites of over 57,000 charities. IRS Form 990 lists expenditures for programs, fund-raising, and administration and highlights major uses of capital. Every charity that takes in more than $25,000 (except church groups) must file a 990 annually. Attachments to the 990 disclose the salaries of the five highest-paid staff members as well as board members' compensation. A sense of proportion is important: The head of the Sierra Club Foundation pulls in $240,000-plus a year, modest for a $90 million organization. But that salary would be a red flag in a group with just $1 or $2 million.

By law, nonprofits must mail the past 3 years of tax filings to anyone who requests them, and most groups will send potential donors a free copy. Getting a sense of how each group handles fund-raising and program expenses will let you compare apples to apples. The more an organization relies on volunteers, the lower its expenses. Professional fund-raisers typically take at least 40 percent of the haul, and sometimes as much as 85 percent. Note deficits and operating reserves. Note how often the board of directors meets and whether it's paid or volunteer. Large boards tend to be ineffective. If a board is small, are all the members from the same company or, worse, the same family?

Serving on a board yourself will give you insights into the group's effectiveness. Volunteering can also clue you in to how well a charity is run. Ask tough questions; you have a right to know your donations are being well spent.

Evaluating the Evaluators

★ **Charity Navigator** is a large database that covers more than 5,000 of the country's most popular charities. After you register (free), you type in a nonprofit name and get a capsulate evaluation with a four-star rating system. It provides clear spending ratios, a color graph of spending, and information on what the CEO earns. Its star rating system can be slightly confusing. Critics say Charity Navigator puts too much emphasis on a charity's financial stability and growth potential rather than its less tangible attributes. (www.charitynavigator.org)

★ **GuideStar** covers more than one million charities. For info on less-well-known nonprofits, this is the site to turn to. The downside of GuideStar's database: It doesn't offer detailed analysis of charities but is more a self-service research tool. Sign up for a free account and get access to a charity's IRS Form 990 tax forms. Reading a 990 is pretty straightforward, although it can confuse a novice.

Many of GuideStar's more sophisticated options aren't free, and many are expensive. If you're willing to drop $1,000 a year for their platinum membership, you'll get financial statistics, industry analysis, and much more. (www.guidestar.org)

★ **American Institute of Philanthropy (AIP)** isn't afraid to flunk a charity and seems to relish going after those that underperform. AIP has a stellar reputation among journalists and members of Congress for holding charities accountable after 9/11 and Hurricane Katrina. AIP researchers dig deeper, uncovering accounting irregularities other evaluators miss.

Unfortunately, the AIP Web site gives a simple letter grade but little more information, and its style could charitably be called clunky. For more detailed info, send in $3 for the triannual Charity Rating Guide, which covers more than 500 national charities. (www.charitywatch.org)

FURTHER READING FOR GREEN INVESTORS

Profit from the Peak: The End of Oil and the Greatest Investment Event of the Century by Brian Hicks and Chris Nelder (Wiley, 2008). How to navigate the end of the oil-based economy and explore investment angles for energy alternatives poised to perform in the future.

Green Investing: A Guide to Making Money through Environment-Friendly Stocks by Jack Uldrich (Adams Media, 2008). Profiles 100 of the leading green firms and suggests a model portfolio.

Clean Money: Picking Winners in the Green Tech Boom by John Rubino (Wiley, 2008). The essential guide to green investing for anyone interested in the environmental technology sector. Rubino, an experienced financial writer and investor, offers a balanced look at the opportunities and perils ahead.

Unconventional Success: A Fundamental Approach to Personal Investment (Free Press, 2005). David Swensen gives clear and interesting explanations guiding ordinary investors to a well-balanced portfolio.

One Up on Wall Street: How to Use What You Already Know to Make Money in the Market, by Peter Lynch (Penguin, 1989). Lynch is famous for guiding Fidelity's Magellan fund from 1977 to 1990 to an eye-popping 29.2 percent average annual return.

As Green As Real Estate Gets

Although no real estate investment trust markets itself as socially responsible, a few will please green investors. In 2006, Gary Pivo, a professor of urban planning and natural resources at the University of Arizona, identified seven publicly traded REITs recognized by the Environmental Protection Agency's Energy Star Program for their energy-efficient buildings. Of these, two remain viable investment options: Brandywine Realty (BDN; www.brandywinerealty.com) and Parkway Properties (PKY; www.pky.com). At this writing, the real estate market is still struggling, so investigate carefully before investing.

DONATING APPRECIATED ASSETS
They're Not like Cash

The IRS rules governing deductions taken for assets that have appreciated in value are different from those that cover gifts of cash. Knowing those rules can help you to stretch the impact of your donations. Stocks, bonds, mutual funds, and real estate that have appreciated in value make great charitable gifts because you can write off their current market value and sidestep capital gains taxes. So if you have $5,000 worth of Google stock that cost you $1,000, you could give the shares to a charity and take the full $5,000 deduction, without paying taxes on your $4,000 profit. Two caveats: The asset must be considered a long-term gain—that is, held for at least 18 months. And you must give the shares to the charity and have them sell the shares. Otherwise the gain, and the IRS levy, will be yours.

Deductions of gifts of appreciated property are limited to 30 percent of your adjusted gross income for public charities and 20 percent for private foundations. Any excess write-offs can be carried forward for 5 years. If you can't afford to give away fully appreciated property but want part of it to benefit a charity, sell the asset to the charity at a below-market price.

YOUR OWN GIFT FUND
A "Poor Man's" Foundation

You once had to be rich to establish the equivalent of your own foundation. Now donor-advised or gift funds are shrewd ways for generous souls with a modest lifestyle to make donations. You can create your own charitable gift fund with as little as $5,000 (subsequent contributions can be as low as $250) and get better benefits. Since gift funds are considered public charities, you get advantages that private foundations don't: You can write off more of your donations against your income; you don't have to give away a minimum of 5 percent every year; you don't have to keep books and file foundation tax returns. You can name your gift fund account whatever you'd like, so your recipients will know their benefactor.

One sizable gift will allow you to write off expenses and contributions beyond the standard deduction, yet you don't have to give away all the money in that year; you can make your donations whenever you please, though the donations must be at least $100. When you use appreciated assets for gifts, your tax savings are even better. In addition to write-offs, you also get to bypass the capital gains tax you otherwise would have owed.

For years **Fidelity**, which pioneered charitable gift trusts, was the only game around, but now it has competition from brokerage houses eager to earn management fees from the funds they manage for you.

Sponsor	Web Site	Assets under Management*	Minimum Initial Donation	Minimum Subsequent Donation
Fidelity Charitable	www.charitablegift.org	$3.5 billion	$5,000	$1,000 for individuals, $5,000 for companies
Schwab Charitable	www.schwabcharitable.org	$1.1 billion	$10,000	$500
Renaissance Charitable Gift Fund	www.rcgf.org	$52 million	$5,000	$250
T. Rowe Price Charitable Giving Program	www.programforgiving.org	$38 million	$10,000	$500
American Endowment	www.aefonline.org	$118 million	$10,000	$1,000
Johnson Charitable	www.johnsoninv.com	$23 million	$1,000	$1,000

*2006 data

DONATIONS AND TAXES

Within certain limitations, the more you give to non-profits, the less you send to the IRS. If you want tax write-offs, stick to 501(c)(3) registered organizations, which the IRS recognizes as legitimate recipients of tax-deductible donations. Donations to political lobbying groups such as the Sierra Club cannot be deducted, but you may still get write-offs by earmarking checks to their educational or restoration programs.

Any single donation of $250 or more requires a receipt from the charity at the time of the gift. Simply saving your canceled check for these larger deductions isn't enough for the IRS.

Cash gifts made to public charities—charitable organizations that receive support from a variety of sources—can be written off up to 50 percent of the donor's adjusted gross income. Any amount over the 50 percent limit can be carried forward and deducted for 5 years. *Cash* doesn't mean the literal green stuff, which cannot be tracked and verified.

Don't rely on charities themselves for tax advice. Most are stretched so thin that they can't hire a tax expert to keep up with the latest rules. Instead, check with a tax accountant or the IRS.

Green Charities

Here are some of the greenest charities out there. They will certainly put your donations to good eco-use.

The Nature Conservancy

With over $5 billion in assets, the Nature Conservancy (TNC) is the third largest nonprofit in the United States, where it has protected some 17 million acres.
Annual revenue: $1.3 billion (2007)
Revenue to programs: 79.5 percent
Members: More than 1 million
Focus: Buying land to keep it wild and development free
www.nature.org

Sierra Club

Sierra has been effective at stopping environmentally damaging dam projects and has earned an A rating from the American Institute of Philanthropy. It is a 501(c)(4) organization, and it spends substantial revenue on political lobbying, so not every donation is tax deductible; donations to Sierra Club Foundation are deductible.
Annual revenue: $90 million
Revenue to programs: 61 percent
Members: 1.3 million
Focus: Land acquisition, preservation, recreation, political lobbying on eco-issues
www.sierraclub.org

Environmental Defense Fund

The Environmental Defense Fund (EDF) blends sound science and good business sense to find solutions to global environmental problems. It campaigned successfully to ban DDT worldwide. EDF scores high marks with most charity watchdogs.
Annual revenue: $85 million
Revenue to programs: 80.1 percent
Members: 500,000
Focus: Systemic environmental problems
www.edf.org

Greenpeace International

Greenpeace became a global name brand with its tradition of seafaring expeditions and direct confrontation; it was instrumental in effecting a moratorium on commercial whaling in 1986. Greenpeace is a 501(c)(4) organization that spends substantial revenue on political lobbying, so not every donation is tax deductible; donations to Greenpeace Fund are deductible.
Annual revenue: $308 million
Revenue to programs: 81 percent
Members: 2.9 million
Focus: Environmental policy change
www.greenpeace.org/international

Rainforest Action Network

Combining grassroots activism, street theater, and civil disobedience, Rainforest Action Network (RAN) has won campaigns against corporations that profit from rain forest destruction.
Annual revenue: $3.6 million
Revenue to programs: 82.7 percent
Members: 14,000
Focus: Saving rain forests
www.ran.org

National Resources Defense Council

If there's an environmental issue before Congress or the courts, chances are the National Resources Defense Council (NRDC) is involved; it's been a litigator in countless lawsuits, many against the US government.
Annual revenue: $87 million
Revenue to programs: 78.4 percent
Members: 1.2 million
Focus: Environmental policy and law
www.nrdc.org

Natural Healing

Herbal supplements are everywhere these days, along with homeopathics, essential oils, and other natural remedies. Stroll through the aisles of any health food store, natural foods grocery, supermarket, big chain pharmacy, or mom-and-pop drugstore and you'll see shelves full of supplements whose "natural remedy" claims vie for your attention.

But popping supplements is not what herbal *medicine* is about—or any other form of natural medicine, such as naturopathy, traditional Chinese medicine, homeopathy, or Ayurveda (traditional Indian medicine), for that matter. Western medicine focuses largely on how to fix what goes wrong with us, that is, disease and injuries. Natural medicine—*green* medicine, if you will—focuses more on how to keep your body healthy. And the benefits of doing so extend well beyond the obvious to increased energy, peace of mind, and longevity.

Green medicine starts with a healthy lifestyle. That means eating at least five daily servings (ideally nine) of fresh, locally grown, mostly organic fruits and vegetables. Try to eat low on the food chain—choose vegetable proteins more often than animal proteins because they're healthier and because it takes less energy to bring fruits, vegetables, whole grains, and legumes to your table than it does to bring beef, pork, lamb, and chicken. Add three small servings of wild fish a week—salmon, herring, sardines, mackerel, and black cod are rich in heart-healthy fats. Toss in a brisk 30-minute walk or other activity most days of the week. Finally, practice stress-relieving activities, such as meditation or yoga, to calm your mind and blunt the effects of stress.

Herbs help support a healthy lifestyle in countless ways. The herbs known as adaptogens help your body counter the toxic consequences of stress. American ginseng, eleuthero, cordyceps, and rhodiola, for example, when taken regularly over time, enhance your energy. Others, such as astragalus, jiaogulan, or reishi strengthen the immune system. Herbs called nervines (chamomile, passionflower, hawthorn, and lemon balm, among others) help relax you without the downsides of pharmaceuticals. Study these underappreciated herb groups, discover their broad range of health-giving actions, and learn how they can meet your needs.

A lifetime of eating unwisely, being inactive, and letting stress run you ragged can result in chronic or even acute disease. Unrelenting stress and a nutrition-poor diet can trigger diseases with devastating consequences, including type 2 diabetes, heart disease, osteoarthritis, dementia, and cancer. Once these chronic conditions take hold, you can still fight back with herbal medicines if you're in the hands of a qualified practitioner, such as a botanically trained MD or a licensed naturopath. Another strategy is to find a credentialed herbalist who's experienced in your condition and who will work with your MD to create a treatment plan that combines herbs with pharmaceuticals. You may be able to use fewer pharmaceuticals, which are necessary for treating some acute and chronic conditions, even though their eco-unfriendly practices may be a less appealing choice than earth-friendly herbs.

Some of the medicines in this chapter, such as vitamins and tonic herbs, are meant to be taken regularly to support your health. Others are gentle remedies for specific problems, which taken as directed and with the advice of a qualified health consultant might help you avoid taking pharmaceutical drugs—and avoid some of their potential side effects.

An additional benefit: Most of the products mentioned in this chapter come from companies that make a significant effort to promote green principles. These firms get a green star for aggressively helping to protect our health and the environment via organic farming, sustainable harvesting, energy-saving practices, recycling, investment in indigenous communities, and other eco-friendly policies.

—Sara Altshul

To make a good cup of medicinal tea, steep a tea bag or two in 8 ounces of just-boiled water, covered, for at least 10 minutes. Covering the cup prevents the herb's essential oils from dissipating in the steam.

ARNICA
Homeopathic Helper

Arnica (*Arnica montana*) is famous for its ability to prevent or lessen bruising and swelling due to trauma. It comes from the alpine plant known as leopard's bane, which mountain climbers have used for centuries to recover from bruises. What makes arnica particularly effective is its power to soothe the emotional shock that follows a fall, bump, crash, or hammer thwack to the thumb.

As with some other homeopathic remedies, arnica is formulated according to the "law of infinitesimals," based on the premise that substances treat health problems most effectively when they're extremely diluted. Homeopathic practitioners believe that these remedies stimulate the healing response.

To use arnica, dissolve five pellets under your tongue as soon as possible following an injury; then use five pellets three or four times a day for the next day or two. A pack of three vials should cost under $10.

Boiron, the world's largest supplier of homeopathic drugs, is a 75-year-old French company committed to preserving the environment. Its divisions around the world encourage recycling, limit waste and pollution, and promote environmental awareness. Its network of 120 botanist-harvesters use organic or sustainably harvested botanicals whenever possible. (www.boironusa.com)

TEA TREE OIL: LIQUID FIRST AID

The essential oil of this Australian evergreen (*Melaleuca alternifolia*), which grows exclusively in New South Wales, may have an overwhelming aroma, but it's powerful stuff. Think of it as a first-aid kit in a bottle. It contains more than 100 different compounds, many of which are proven to kill various disease-provoking microbes, including *Candida albicans*, *E. coli*, *Pseudomonas aeruginosa*, and *Staphylococcus aureus* (the bug that causes MRSA, the potentially devastating antibiotic-resistant staph infection). It's been successfully used to treat acne (in a 5 percent solution), impetigo, boils, warts, topical infections, ringworm, first- and second-degree burns, and nail fungus.

Note: Tea tree oil is for external use only, although there are products specially formulated as oral rinses for treating gingivitis and other oral infections. Keep tea tree oil out of the reach of children—it's toxic when ingested even in tiny amounts.

To use tea tree oil, dab it on the affected area two or three times a day. Try Erbaviva's tea tree oil, which is steam-distilled from organic plant material and costs $12 for ⅓ ounce. (www.erbaviva.com)

ASPEN ARTHRO-BLEND
Powerful Pain Reliever

This tincture, or liquid herbal extract, blends tree bark extracts from European aspen (*Populus tremula*) and ash (*Fraxinus excelsior*) with goldenrod (*Solidago virgaurea*), a mixture of ingredients long used by herbalists to relieve arthritis and joint pain. In European studies, this combination has proved to be as powerful a pain reliever as nonsteroidal anti-inflammatory drugs (NSAIDs)—without the side effects. This formula is cold processed with organic and wild harvested herbs in distilled water and organic alcohol. A 60-day supply, available from Vital Botanicals, costs about $60. Follow label directions. (www.vitalbotanicals.com)

BUTTERBUR
Banish Migraines

Butterbur (*Petasites hybridus*) has a history of medicinal use stretching back to the 1st century, when the Greek physician-botanist Dioscorides used it to treat skin ulcers. We now know that butterbur contains compounds that seem to prevent the blood vessel inflammation that may trigger migraines. Neurologists at Albert Einstein College of Medicine in New York who studied 245 migraine sufferers discovered that 70 percent of those who took butterbur extract for 4 months had 48 percent fewer episodes than those who took a placebo. Butterbur is a prophylactic: It helps prevent migraines when taken over time, but it won't relieve a migraine once it strikes. Take 150 mg a day of Petadolex, the extract used in most of the studies, available for about $70 for three bottles each containing fifty 50 mg softgels. (www.migraine aid.com)

COQ10
Statin and Migraine Partner

This supplement is an antioxidant called *ubiquinone*, found naturally in human cells, that boosts energy, lowers blood pressure, and may lower glucose in people with type 2 diabetes. Since taking statin drug therapy to lower cholesterol also lowers levels of CoQ10, many experts recommend that you take this supplement if you take statins.

What's more, when European researchers tested CoQ10 against a placebo in a group of 42 people with chronic migraines, they discovered that by the third month of treatment, 50 percent of those who'd taken 100 mg of CoQ10 three times a day had fewer episodes, fewer headache days, and fewer headaches with nausea compared to 14 percent who'd taken a placebo. Try Nature's Bounty brand, which costs about $24 for thirty 200 mg capsules. (www.naturesbounty.com)

FYI

Vitamin A is available as the "preformed" kind called retinol, which is found in animal products such as liver and whole milk. Additionally, our bodies convert beta-carotene and other carotenoids—the plant pigments found in dark green, yellow, orange, and red fruits—into retinol. Preformed A can be toxic at high levels; at 10,000 iu, the risk of hip fractures and some birth defects increases.

BLACK COHOSH
Hot Flash Chiller

A gift from Native Americans to American colonists, black cohosh (*Actaea racemosa* or *Cimicifuga racemosa*) was a traditional treatment for women's reproductive problems until the 1800s, when (like many herbal and natural cures of the day) it became popularized beyond its capabilities and was touted as a panacea for all kinds of illnesses. By the turn of the 20th century, it was one of the most prescribed herbs in the United States.

Fast-forward to the present. Black cohosh, one of the best researched of all herbal medicines, is a proven treatment for menopausal symptoms, including hot flashes, night sweats, sleep disturbances, nervousness, mood swings, and mild depression. The most frequently studied black cohosh preparation is Remifemin, exclusively imported from Germany by Enzymatic Therapy.

Researchers are still learning how black cohosh works. In one recent study, scientists at the Columbia University Medical Center in New York City discovered that it affects a part of the brain that regulates body temperature, which might be how it eases menopausal hot flashes and excessive sweating. Experts recommend that women take it at the onset of symptoms. Scientists have disproven theories that the herb has estrogenic effects, contains estrogenlike compounds, or should be avoided by women with estrogen-positive tumors. In fact, a 2008 study conducted by the University of Philadelphia School of Medicine showed that women who took black cohosh during menopause had a 60 percent lower chance of developing breast cancer than women who didn't use the herb.

Made exclusively from organically grown German black cohosh, Remifemin costs about $24 for a 30-day supply. Remifemin Good Night, which contains the sleep-promoting herbs valerian, lemon balm, and hops, costs about $13 for 21 pills. (www.enzymatic therapy.com)

ST. JOHN'S WORT
Help for Mild Depression

This plant's bright yellow flowers bloom in late June, around the day dedicated to John the Baptist. Healers have used it since at least 500 BC for wounds, and it later became a treatment for melancholy and madness. St. John's wort (*Hypericum perforatum*), or SJW, contains a chem lab's worth of psychoactive and antiviral substances.

Ongoing research since 1994 has produced more than 100 studies on SJW's ability to ease mild to moderate depression. Recently, a Cochrane review of studies confirmed that it works—potentially as well as many pharmaceutical antidepressants do. Cochrane researchers reviewed 29 trials that included 5,489 patients with symptoms of depression. In the studies that compared SJW to prescription antidepressants, SJW was considered as effective as the drugs, and fewer patients dropped out of trials due to adverse effects.

Note: Because of the way SJW is metabolized in the body, it affects the way some prescription medications are metabolized and may diminish or increase their effects. Consult your physician or pharmacist before taking SJW if you take other drugs.

Perika, distributed in the United States by Nature's Way, is made by Dr. Willmar Schwabe Pharmaceuticals, a world leader in plant-based research for more than 100 years. Perika costs about $15 for 60 tablets. (www.natures way.com)

FYI

New Chapter, Country Life, and Enzymatic Therapy are companies that make whole-food–based, organic vitamins. All three lines are widely available at natural food stores and online.

ZYFLAMEND
Super Inflammation Fighter

This 10-herb formula was created to combat the effects of inflammation, which is now recognized as a potential trigger for degenerative chronic diseases such as arthritis, heart disease, type 2 diabetes, and forms of cancer.

A Columbia University study found that Zyflamend suppresses prostate cancer cell growth and makes prostate cancer cells self-destruct. What's more, the study confirms that Zyflamend has COX-1 and COX-2 anti-inflammatory effects, although its anticancer effects against prostate cancer were independent of COX-2 inhibition.

Formulated by New Chapter, Inc., a 29-year-old Vermont company founded by herbal-ist Paul Schulick, Zyflamend contains 10 COX-2 inhibiting herbs: turmeric, ginger, holy basil, green tea, hu zhang, Chinese gold-thread, barberry, oregano, rosemary, and *Scutellaria baicalensis*. Using a process they dubbed "supercritical extraction," the company extracts herbs at low temperature without using toxic industrial chemical solvents. The delicate, volatile, and potentially active constituents of the herbs are left undisturbed. Zyflamend costs about $20 for 180 capsules. (www.newchapter.com)

Paging Dr. Green

As part of your overall commitment to health, consider seeking counsel from a "green medicine" practitioner. A properly qualified practitioner can help keep you healthy and offer course-correcting therapies, which might include acupuncture, massage, herbal therapies, or other natural treatments to help keep a minor problem from becoming something more serious.

Of course, life-threatening diseases or trauma can befall anyone, no matter how healthy or green their lifestyle. But you're likely to be stronger and better able to conquer whatever comes if you've taken good care of yourself than if you haven't.

SAW PALMETTO
Help for Prostates

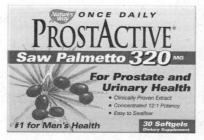

The berries of this fan palm tree (*Serenoa repens*) that grows throughout the South have been studied for 25 years as a treatment for benign prostatic hyperplasia (BPH), a problem that commonly affects middle-aged men. Most studies show that saw palmetto improves urine flow, relieves the urge to urinate at night by 73 percent, and reduces swelling of the prostate—which reduces the need for prostate surgery.

ProstActive, by Nature's Way, contains the extract used in European studies. Take one softgel capsule daily with a meal. It costs about $13 for a 1-month supply. (www.naturesway.com)

TURMERIC
Yellow Super Herb

Turmeric (*Curcuma longa*) is a member of the ginger family and, like its spicy cousin, is a root (more accurately, a rhizome) that does more than merely enhance food's color and flavor. Its principal compound, a yellow pigment called *curcumin*, is under investigation for its potential effectiveness against chronic diseases, including cancer. It's caused such excitement that one prominent researcher dubbed it "curecumin."

Turmeric has a 2,500-year-long history in Ayurveda, the traditional medical system of India, where healers use it to treat digestive woes, wounds, arthritis, and skin problems. In the 1990s, researchers seeking alternative cancer treatments discovered curcumin's apparent ability to slow the spread of cancer cells.

Curcumin blunts the action of several inflammation-promoting substances, including the enzyme COX-2 (cyclooxygenase-2), which has been linked to inflammation that causes osteoarthritis pain and stiffness. But since curcumin is a COX-2 inhibitor 50 to 100 times weaker than prescription COX-2 drugs such as Vioxx, it lacks the harmful heart effects that prompted the FDA to withdraw Vioxx from the market.

In test-tube and animal studies, curcumin appears to make cancer cells self-destruct. And studies conducted on small groups of cancer patients suggest that taking curcumin may inhibit the growth of gastrointestinal cancers, including pancreatic cancer.

Try Turmeric Force by New Chapter (60 capsules for about $28) or turmeric tincture by Herbalist & Alchemist (2 ounces for about $21). Follow label directions. (www.newchapter.com; www.herbalist-alchemist.com)

RAIN FOREST REMEDY

Deep in the Peruvian rain forest, shamans of the Ashaninka tribe call this high-climbing vine *saventaro*, or "power plant." Named for the hooklike claws that grow along its vines, cat's claw (*Uncaria tomentosa*) has been used for centuries as a remedy for painful joints, stomach ulcers, inflammation, dysentery, and fevers.

For the past 40 years, Western scientists have studied cat's claw for its potential to treat inflammation, rheumatoid arthritis, allergies, and even cancer, and also as an immune system strengthener. Its potent blend of phytochemicals, including tannins, sterols, and quinovic acid glycosides, have proven to reduce inflammation and combat certain viruses.

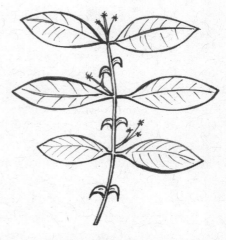

If you're considering taking cat's claw for its ability to ease pain and relieve inflammation, consider that by doing so you can preserve a little piece of the Amazon rain forest. Under Enzymatic Therapy's Better World program, cat's claw is exclusively harvested in the rain forest by Ashaninka Indians, who use sustainable forestry management practices. The harvesters are paid a higher than average wage and rewarded with bonuses, and their community receives funding for education and health care. Saventaro costs about $16 for 30 capsules. (www.enzymatic therapy.com)

GLUCOSAMINE AND CHONDROITIN
Build Strong Joints

The reputation of this well-researched supplement took a hit in 2006, when results were published from the Glucosamine/Chondroitin Arthritis Intervention Trial (GAIT), funded by the National Institutes of Health and involving 1,583 arthritis patients. News reports headlined that glucosamine with chondroitin had failed to ease mild arthritis pain. But those reports downplayed two key results: The combo did relieve moderate to severe pain, and the COX-2 inhibitor, celecoxib (Celebrex), against which they were tested, failed to work.

Glucosamine is a natural sugar found in cartilage, the tissue that cushions joints. It helps keep joints healthy and pain free by decreasing enzyme production that breaks down cartilage and by decreasing nitric oxide production, which leads to cartilage cell death. Glucosamine also helps promote the growth of cells that contribute to cartilage building.

Chondroitin, like glucosamine, is a naturally occurring sugar. It attracts fluid to cartilage, which helps it absorb shock and floods cartilage cells with much-needed nutrients.

Glucosamine and chondroitin have been proven to prevent the progression of osteoarthritis and can decrease the need for anti-inflammatory drugs, which have potentially dangerous side effects. At the end of the GAIT studies, x-rays of people who took the supplement showed healthier cartilage compared to people who took a placebo, and after 5 years people who took glucosamine and chondroitin needed 73 percent fewer joint replacements than did people who took a placebo. Because it improves cartilage structure, "failure to recommend glucosamine/chondroitin for osteoarthritis may one day be considered medical malpractice," says Jason Theodosakis, MD, a clinical assistant professor at the University of Arizona College of Medicine in Tucson and a member of the oversight steering committee for the GAIT study.

Choose supplements that contain at least 1,500 mg glucosamine sulfate or hydrochloride (HCL) and 800 mg to 1,200 mg chondroitin sulfate. Take consistently every day. Avosoy, a supplement formulated by Theodosakis, uses 100 percent shellfish-free pure glucosamine and cow-free, USP grade chondroitin; a month's supply costs about $50, or $32.50 a bottle for 12 bottles (a 1-year supply). (www.drtheos.com)

ELEUTHERO
Type A Helper

If you're a burn-the-candle-at-both-ends type, you might consider taking this herb regularly. Eleuthero (*Eleutherococcus senticosus*) has been used for centuries in China and Russia, where it's a remedy for restoring vigor, increasing longevity, enhancing overall health, and stimulating appetite and memory. According to the American Cancer Society, Russians and Ukrainians were given the herb to counter the effects of radiation poisoning after the Chernobyl nuclear reactor disaster. It's still widely used in Russia to help people adapt to stressful conditions, as well as to enhance productivity.

At one time this herb's common name was Siberian ginseng, but now it's called eleuthero to distinguish it from American and Asian ginseng. It has distinctly separate chemical components.

Eleuthero helps people with fatigue-related problems because it improves their ability to sleep restfully. It's used by athletes to increase endurance. In general it improves cognitive function and improves alertness for anyone who is stressed or working long hours. When you take it long term, eleuthero can improve memory and promote feelings of well-being. In a study of elderly people, it helped to restore some aspects of sociability.

Herb Pharm's eleuthero extract is made from the roots of *E. senticosus* shrubs sustainably harvested in their native habitat. One ounce costs about $12. (http://herb-pharm.com)

Ward Off Colds

Designed to help strengthen children's immune systems and make it easier for them to ward off winter colds and flu, **Children's Winter Health Compound**'s safe, effective formula contains nine organically cultivated or sustainably harvested herbs, all chosen for their gentleness and immune-enhancing ability. The serving size is 1 drop per 4 pounds of a child's body weight (e.g., 10 drops for a 40-pound child). Give two to five servings per day mixed in water or juice. About $7 per 1-ounce bottle.

Quick Guide to Green Practitioners

FYI

It may take glucosamine and chondroitin supplements up to 6 months to work, and even longer for cartilage health to improve. To choose the best product, make sure that the amounts of glucosamine and chondroitin are listed separately. Avoid liquid products and steer clear of bargain brands.

An increasing number of medical schools across the country are graduating physicians who've received at least some exposure to—even extensive training in—complementary and alternative medicine philosophies and techniques.

★ A pioneer program was developed by Andrew Weil, MD, at the University of Arizona, whose Program in Integrative Medicine (PIM) trains physicians to combine the best principles of Western medicine with those of alternative and complementary disciplines. Scores of PIM graduates are now practicing all over the country. To find one, visit http://integrativemedicine.arizona.edu/about/

★ The American College for Advancement in Medicine (ACAM) is a not-for-profit association that for 25 years has been educating physicians and other health care professionals about complementary, alternative, and integrative medicine (CAIM). To find member docs, visit www.acamnet.org.

★ American Holistic Medical Association, founded in 1978, promotes holistic and integrative medicine by licensed health care providers. You can find member practitioners on its Web site, but note that not all the listed members are MDs. Check out practitioners' qualifications carefully to make sure they meet your needs. (www.holisticmedicine.org)

★ Licensed naturopaths (NDs) are physicians who graduate from a 4-year graduate-level naturopathic medical school. They study the same basic sciences as MDs, but they also learn holistic and nontoxic approaches, with a strong emphasis on promoting wellness and preventing disease. In addition to meeting the standard medical curriculum, a naturopathic physician is required to complete 4 years of training in clinical nutrition, acupuncture, homeopathic medicine, botanical medicine, psychology, and counseling (to encourage people to make lifestyle changes to improve health), after which he or she takes rigorous professional board exams in order to be licensed by a state or jurisdiction as a primary care general practice physician. Naturopaths are currently licensed to practice in 16 states, Puerto Rico, and the Virgin Islands. Visit www.naturopathic.org for more information and to find an ND near you.

★ Traditional Chinese medicine (TCM), an ancient healing system, has a distinctly different philosophy based on the Taoist concept of balance, yin and yang. Practitioners believe that imbalanced yin and yang lead to the blockage and stagnation of qi (pronounced "chi"), the body's invisible life force, which runs throughout the body on invisible pathways known as meridians. TCM practitioners use acupuncture, herbal medicine, massage, food therapy, and other techniques to restore balance. Learn more and find licensed practitioners at www.accufinder.com.

★ Ayurveda, which means "the science of life," originated in India more than 5,000 years ago. Practitioners use herbal medicine, yoga, nutrition, massage, and meditation to preserve health and treat disease. Currently there's no certification or licensing process for Ayurvedic physicians in this country, although professional organizations, such as the National Ayurvedic Medical Association, are developing licensing requirements. Make sure to ask about a practitioner's training and experience. (www.ayurveda-nama.org)

TIP: An excellent source of traditional Ayurvedic herbal products is Himalaya Herbal Healthcare, a family-owned company since 1930. The company grows its own herbs organically and follows eco-friendly practices. Find their products in most health food stores or online. (www.himalayausa.com)

ECHINACEA

The Immunity Herb

Echinacea (*E. angustifolia, E. purpurea, E. pallida*) is renowned for stopping a cold in its tracks—but does it actually work? Seems as soon as one study says it does, another comes along saying it doesn't.

Confusion about echinacea shines a light on the way herb news is usually reported in the United States (they'll either cure or kill you) and ignores a reality: Botanicals contain complex chemicals whose subtle synergies we may never fully unravel. Herbs are complicated and variable. The potency of their medicinal constituents depends on when and where they're harvested, which part of what species of the plant is used, which solvents extract the so-called active ingredients, and the delicate interplay of plant chemicals. So it shouldn't be a surprise that echinacea studies have produced contradictory and confusing results. Many herbalists, including David Winston, arguably America's leading herbal educator, say that some studies have used doses too low to be effective. Other studies tested potentially impotent echinacea preparations, such as dried powdered root or freeze-dried leaf juice. Winston and other clinical herbalists familiar with echinacea recommend using products made only from the fresh root of *E. angustifolia*, *E. purpurea*, or *E. pallida* or the fresh flower cone of *E. purpurea*.

Even after scores of studies, we still don't know what makes echinacea effective. As Winston writes in *Herbal Therapy and Supplements: A Scientific and Traditional Approach*: "No single active ingredient has been identified as being responsible for echinacea's medicinal value. Its numerous constituents all contribute to its activity." Where does that leave us? "Echinacea helps the immune system mount a more robust response to infection," says Kevin Spelman, PhD, a botanical researcher at the University of North Carolina. In Germany, echinacea is officially approved for treating colds, flu, and upper respiratory infections. Researchers at the University of Connecticut School of Pharmacy who recently analyzed 14 clinical trials discovered that taking echinacea at the first sign of symptoms decreases your chances of developing a cold by 58 percent and can shorten a cold's duration by about a day and a half. Studies also confirm that it can be an effective treatment for ear infections, sinusitis, tonsillitis, bronchitis, and laryngitis. Used topically, it enhances wound healing.

Avoid "standardized" echinacea supplements. Excellent choices include **Herbalist & Alchemist** Echinacea Purpurea tincture, made from organically grown fresh root and flowers—2 ounces costs about $20; and **Vital Botanicals** Echinacea Angustifolia tincture, made from organically grown fresh root, 1.69 ounce for $18. (www.herbalist-alchemist.com; www.vital botanicals.com)

At the first twinge of cold symptoms, take a teaspoon of tincture in a little water every 1 to 2 hours for the first day. Don't stop even if you feel better. On the second and third days, take 1 teaspoon three times a day. For minor wounds, bug bites, or burns, dab straight echinacea tincture directly on the affected area.

UMCKA COLD CARE: TASTY COLD RELIEF

This cherry-flavored syrup contains an extract from a South African geranium (*Pelargonium sidoides*, or *umckaloabo* in Zulu), a traditional remedy in that country for colds and infections. The special Umcka formula was recently put to a randomized double-blind, placebo-controlled trial. Participants included 124 adults with acute bronchitis who were treated either with Umcka or a placebo for 7 days. Within the first 4 days, 68.8 percent of the Umcka-treated group reported feeling better, compared to only one-third of the placebo group. Take 1 teaspoon four or five times a day at the first sign of cold symptoms. Umcka Cold Care, by **Nature's Way**, is widely available for about $15 for a 4-ounce bottle.

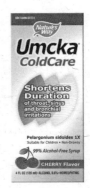

FYI

When you take echinacea in water, hold it in your mouth for a few moments before swallowing. Traditional herbalists say this helps stimulate the herb's immune-enhancing benefits. Good echinacea tincture makes your mouth tingle slightly.

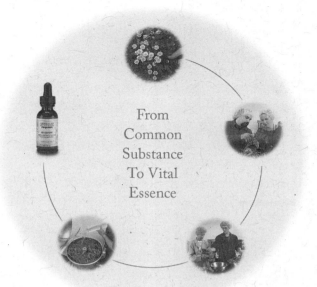

From
Common
Substance
To Vital
Essence

AMERICAN GINSENG
Improve Immunity, Balance Mood

Herbal educator David Winston calls American ginseng (*Panax quinquefolius*) an appropriate treatment for "overworked, overstressed Americans" and recommends it for people with mild depression, chronic fatigue syndrome, fibromyalgia, stress-induced asthma, and age-related memory loss. Mayo Clinic researchers recently put American ginseng's energy-boosting reputation to the test in a study of 282 people suffering from cancer-related fatigue. Results were promising: Twenty-five percent of those who took 1,000 mg or 2,000 mg a day for 8 weeks reported that fatigue interfered less with activities such as grocery shopping, housework, and socializing, compared to people who took a placebo or 750 mg dosage. In a test that measures pep, energy, and tiredness, those who took 1,000 mg a day felt better than those who took the higher dose—and they also felt nearly twice as well in general as did people who took 2,000 mg.

American ginseng's ability to deter colds was recently studied at the University of Connecticut. Forty-three people were given ginseng or a placebo for 4 months. Of those who took American ginseng, 32 percent caught colds, compared to 62 percent who became ill while taking a placebo. In a University of Alberta study, 323 people took ginseng or a placebo for 4 months. Ginseng takers had 25 percent fewer colds and less severe cold symptoms than did placebo takers. University of Connecticut researchers noted that ginseng seems to activate the immune system to clear the virus before it can replicate and cause the tissue destruction that produces cold symptoms.

Note that too much ginseng can cause overstimulation—and some people are sensitive to its effects. Discontinue use if you experience insomnia, nervousness, or elevated blood pressure.

American ginseng is a slow-growing plant that's expensive to harvest and endangered in the wild. For that reason, bargain and other American ginseng supplements may not be fully potent. Choose a brand such as Herbalist & Alchemist American ginseng, made from fresh, certified organic root and costing about $46 for 2 ounces. Follow label directions. (www.herbalist-alchemist.com)

SINGER'S SAVING GRACE
Vocalists Take Comfort

Developed over 20 years ago for performers at the famed Santa Fe Opera, Singer's Saving Grace, a spray made by Herbs Etc., comes to the aid of singers and others who use their voices professionally. It moistens and lubricates throat tissues and helps relieve sore throats.

Created by noted herbalist Daniel Gagnon, the formula contains yerba mansa (*Anemopsis californica*), which treats mucous membrane inflammation, swollen gums, and sore throat; stoneroot (*Collinsonia canadensis*), known by traditional American herbalists as a treatment for "minister's sore throat"; licorice (*Glycyrrhiza glabra*), used in China for sore throats; jack-in-the-pulpit (*Arisaema triphyllum*), a traditional sore throat remedy; propolis, the resinlike substance bees make, which kills oral bacteria; echinacea, which is antiviral; ginger (*Zingiber officinale*), an anti-inflammatory; and osha (*Ligusticum porteri*), an antiviral expectorant. Spray two or three times directly into the mouth every 1 to 4 hours. It costs $12 for a 1-ounce bottle. (www.herbsetc.com)

Make Your Herbal Medicines

Herbal tinctures are liquid medicines that rely on alcohol to extract medicinal compounds from fresh or dried herbs. Making your own can be surprisingly easy, inexpensive, and satisfying. Unless you grow herbs in your garden, it's probably easiest to purchase them directly from **Blessed Herbs**, a company that sells organic and wild, sustainably harvested varieties.

You'll need:

Organically grown fresh or dried herbs
Cutting board, knife, and grinder
Vodka, 80 or 100 proof
Clean glass jars with lids
Labels
Wire mesh strainer
Unbleached coffee filters
2- to 4-cup glass measuring cup
Cheesecloth or muslin
Funnel
Clean dark glass (amber or cobalt blue) medicine bottles with dropper tops

★ Chop the herbs with a knife or grind them until fine in a clean coffee grinder. Place 1 part dried herb to 2 parts or more of vodka in a jar, making sure that 1 to 3 inches of liquid cover the herbs. Close tightly and label with herb name and date. Place the jar in a warm, dark place and steep for at least 4 weeks—the longer the better. Shake the bottle daily and add more vodka if necessary to keep the herb material completely covered in liquid.

★ After a month (or longer), pour the tincture through a wire mesh strainer lined with a coffee filter and strain into the measuring cup. Place the herbs remaining in the strainer in a piece of cheesecloth or muslin, then twist and squeeze to extract every last drop. (Used herbs are wonderful added to your compost heap.)

★ Using a funnel, pour the tincture directly into dark glass dropper bottles and label.

Resources

Bulk dried herbs: www.blessedherbs.com
Medicine bottles: www.nutritionsurplus.com
Making Plant Medicines by Richo Cech, available at www.horizonherbs.com

---

CINNAMON

Tasty Sugar Balancer

A key ingredient in foods ranging from cookies to curry, cinnamon (*Cinnamomum verum*) made headlines a few years ago when studies showed that it could lower triglycerides, LDL cholesterol (the unhealthy kind), and total cholesterol and could also improve glycemic control in people with type 2 diabetes. In the studies, a daily dose of cinnamon lowered participants' glucose by 18 to 29 percent, their triglycerides by 23 to 30 percent, their LDL by 7 to 27 percent, and their total cholesterol by 12 to 26 percent—pretty impressive results for such an easy intervention. According to Richard A. Anderson, PhD, the USDA research chemist who coauthored those studies, effects like this could help prevent or alleviate type 2 diabetes as well as its consequences, such as heart disease and kidney problems.

But that's just the latest research on cinnamon. Traditionally, it's a reliably effective antidiarrhea, antinausea, and antivomiting treatment, partic-

ularly for the kinds of digestive illnesses you can pick up when traveling—such as Montezuma's revenge.

To lower cholesterol, sprinkle ¼ to ½ teaspoon on foods twice a day. Frontier sells USDA-certified organic cinnamon, available in the spice section of natural food stores and some supermarkets. For stomach bugs, try Cinnamon Force, from **New Chapter**, made with a special solvent-free process that protects the environment. Sixty capsules (a 1-month supply) sell for about $20.

STEVIA

No-Calorie Sweetener

This herbal sweetener, made from the leaves of a South American shrub (*Stevia rebaudiana*), is 250 to 300 times sweeter than sugar, though it contains no calories or carbohydrates. Tribal people of Paraguay introduced it to Spanish conquistadores in the 16th century. Though stevia is considered a good option for people with diabetes and others who can't tolerate sugar—and was found in one small Danish study to lower blood glucose levels in type 2 diabetes—its use as a sweetener was never popular, perhaps because stevia has a bitter aftertaste similar to licorice that many people find unappealing.

NuNaturals is a 20-year-old company committed to saving energy, recycling, and using environmentally friendly products as well as recycled paper and shipping materials. Their all-natural process removes stevia's bitter-tasting components. Packets of stevia powder or a 4-ounce jar run about $10. (www.nunaturals.com)

WEEDY DIGESTIVE TEA

Dandelion (*Taraxacum officinale*) is a gentle remedy for heartburn and other digestive complaints that also acts as a mild diuretic. In one study, dandelion tea stimulated the growth of 14 strains of good-for-you bacteria, which could be why it eases mild indigestion. It may also be helpful for restoring normal balance of bacteria in the bowel after you've been on antibiotic therapy. Traditional Medicinals, which has been committed to organic agriculture for 30 years and is the world's largest solar-powered tea factory, makes a delicious organic roasted dandelion root tea. A box of 16 tea bags sells for about $6. (www.traditionalmedicinals.com)

CHAMOMILE

Sweet Tummy Soother

The tiny, daisy-shaped flowers of German chamomile (*Matricaria recutita*) have a distinctive, delicate, sweet apple flavor and aroma. Chamomile's triple action makes it the classic remedy for easing digestive problems, including stomach cramps, indigestion, diarrhea, gas, and colic. First, its mild sedative properties relax you and blunt stress-related reactions that make digestive muscles tense. Second, it contains compounds that curb muscle contractions, especially in the smooth muscles of the intestines. Third, it contains a compound called *azulene* that kills staphylococcus and streptococcus infections, which comes in mighty handy when you've picked up a nasty case of stomach flu.

Herbalists often recommend a strong cuppa chamomile to ease mild insomnia. It's useful for nursing mothers of colicky babies—safe, soothing chamomile passes through breast milk to the baby and can ease junior's tummy cramps and teething pain.

Choose organic chamomile tea. Make sure the chamomile is fragrant, an indicator of freshness. Brew as you would a regular tea and let it steep, covered, for about 10 to 15 minutes; squeeze the tea bag for best results. Adults can drink up to 4 cups a day. Children ages 5 to 18 can have 2 cups a day in divided doses. For children to age 5, offer ½ cup a day in divided doses. Avoid chamomile if you're allergic to ragweed, to which chamomile is closely related. Traditional Medicinals organic chamomile tea runs about $5 for 16 tea bags. (www.traditionalmedicinals.com)

CORDYCEPS

Energizer Bunny Mushroom

Cordyceps (*Cordyceps sinensis*) is actually a mushroom parasite of the *Thiarodes* genus of ghost moth caterpillar. It sounds scary, but don't worry—the cordyceps product you buy will probably have been grown on soybeans or rice or in fermentation tanks. In fact, if you do come across authentic wild cordyceps, don't buy it—even if you could cough up the money for its astronomical price tag. It's endangered in the wild, and because it fetches so much money, harvesters in the Himalayan foothills tear up alpine meadows searching for it.

Cordyceps has a reputation for boosting libido. In a 2004 Chinese study, taking 1 gram of cordyceps daily improved sexual performance for 65 percent of the men who participated. It also seems to enhance athletic performance; Olympic swimmers and runners from China have attributed their success to its use. Unlike other herbs, whose effects build after weeks of use, cordyceps acts quickly. Most people feel energized after just one dose.

Clinical herbalists in the United States use it in formulas for people with kidney problems and to alleviate chronic lung problems such as bronchitis. It's useful for chronic fatigue and for normalizing immune function; herbalists recommend it as a treatment for allergic asthma and allergic rhinitis.

Buy cordyceps online from Fungi Perfecti, a company founded by America's leading mushroom expert and educator, Paul Stamets. Capsules contain 615 mg of freeze-dried, organically grown and cultivated cordyceps mycelium (the medicinal part of mushrooms, roughly equivalent to a plant's roots). Sixty capsules cost about $27. (www.fungi.com)

GINGER
Root of Healing

Pregnancy, boat rides, car trips, chemotherapy, and surgery have one thing in common: They can trigger miserable bouts of nausea, retching, and vomiting. Ginger (*Zingiber officinale*), the same spicy stuff used to season Asian dishes and baked goods, is a safe, proven remedy for easing the problem.

When it comes to motion sickness, ginger has been shown to be as effective as Dramamine. Morning sickness yields to ginger so effectively that many obstetricians now routinely recommend it to expectant mothers. And ginger has gotten good marks for easing the nausea and vomiting that often follow chemotherapy treatments and surgery. Researchers aren't entirely sure how ginger defeats nausea, but they suspect its compounds may block gastrointestinal feedback mechanisms.

Beyond that, ginger has two powerful anti-inflammatory effects. It inhibits one type of inflammation similarly to the way NSAID drugs work. It also performs similarly to the way one of the new allergy drugs on the market, Singulair, does. By using ginger, you get the effects of an anti-inflammatory like ibuprofen as well as a leukotriene inhibitor like Singulair, with the bonus of no side effects.

Try Gingerforce, by **New Chapter**, a company whose pure organic ginger comes from its own biodynamic farm in Costa Rica. For morning or motion sickness, take a 150 mg capsule of Gingerforce four times a day (it's a concentrated product) or up to eight 500 mg to 600 mg ginger root capsules a day. Sixty capsules cost about $20. Or try a spoonful of New Chapter's delicious Ginger Honey Syrup (4 ounces costs about $10) in seltzer or tea four times a day. (www.newchapter.com)

Take vitamins with meals; it improves their absorption and lessens the chances for stomach upset.

PEPPERMINT
Minty Digestion Aid

This refreshing herbal remedy is serious medicine for digestive distress. Because peppermint (*Mentha piperita*) calms stomach muscles and stimulates the flow of bile, which helps you digest fats, it's well suited for easing the discomfort caused by rich foods. It's also useful for relieving flatulence. Try the organic peppermint tea from **Traditional Medicinals**. A box of 16 tea bags is about $5. Steep the tea, covered, for 15 minutes, and drink a cup after dinner and before bedtime. (www.traditional medicinals.com)

In Europe, where peppermint oil capsules are a standard remedy for irritable bowel syndrome symptoms such as constipation or diarrhea, a German review of peppermint oil studies concluded that peppermint oil capsules are a good irritable bowel treatment. Try Peptogest from **Progena**, an enteric-coated peppermint oil; about $12 for 90 capsules. (www.progena.com)

Homeopathy: The Less-Is-More Medicine

Of all the natural healing systems, the one that may be hardest for people to get their heads around is the concept of homeopathy. It requires a huge leap of faith to believe that an infinitesimal amount of a substance that causes illness in a healthy person can cure that illness (known as the "law of similars") or to believe that a remedy that in normal doses is a proven treatment will also work when dispensed as an infinitesimal amount (the "law of infinitesimals"). In short, homeopathy challenges pretty much everything we know about the way remedies work.

Making it more unconventional is the way homeopaths practice: During your first visit, a homeopath spends up to 2 hours with you, taking a medical history that goes way beyond physical ailments to include your hopes, fears, dreams—even what temperatures make you most comfortable. Such an approach makes it extremely difficult to study homeopathy scientifically.

To learn more or to find a qualified practitioner, visit http://nationalcenterforhomeopathy.org.

FRANKINCENSE

Mystical Aromatic

Frankincense (*Boswellia carteri*) has been burned during religious ceremonies for thousands of years. What would High Mass on Sunday be without it? With so many historical references to its spiritually uplifting abilities, who can be surprised that researchers are studying this resin to see whether it might have properties that could be developed into an antianxiety drug. Scientists at Tel-Aviv University and Johns Hopkins School of Medicine recently discovered that frankincense made mice less fearful, and their discovery has interesting implications: Frankincense apparently activates a channel in the brain that plays a role in regulating emotions.

Frankincense essential oil costs $18 for ⅙ ounce. Use it in an aromatherapy diffuser. (www.erbaviva.com)

LICORICE

Candy for Digestion

You know it as the chewy black candy with the love-it-or-hate-it flavor. But the great Greek and Roman physicians of ancient times, first Hippocrates and later Pliny the Elder, regarded licorice (*Glycyrrhiza glabra*) as one of the few reliable remedies to ease asthma and coughs. Today Western herbalists often use it—usually in multiherb formulas—for treating ulcers, irritable bowel syndrome, and similar problems because it soothes irritated mucous membranes, and also for coughs and bronchial conditions. Its mild anti-inflammatory action is similar to cortisone, and it's been used as a component of women's herbal formulas because it contains hormonelike compounds.

Used topically, licorice can heal shingles and herpes lesions. In the hands of a professional herbalist, this is one of the most useful of all botanical medicines. Two ounces of **Herbalist & Alchemist** licorice tincture costs about $21. Follow your practitioner's dosage advice. (www.herbalist-alchemist.com)

DEEP SLEEP OFF TO DREAMLAND

It takes a master herbalist to create a sleep supplement this effective. The herbs used in the Deep Sleep formula come from fresh plants, because they retain a broader spectrum of their active compounds, says Daniel Gagnon, **Herbs Etc.**'s veteran herbalist. This supergreen company, whose laboratory is also a certified organic manufacturing facility, exclusively uses herbs grown on family-owned certified organic farms throughout the United States. Gagnon blends California poppy (*Eschscholzia californica*), valerian (*Valeriana officinalis*), passionflower (*Passiflora incarnata*), chamomile (*Matricaria recutita*), lemon balm (*Melissa officinalis*), milky oat seed (*Avena sativa*), and orange peel (which enhances the function of the other herbs and improves the tincture's flavor). All affect different aspects of the sleep cycle and can help calm an overactive mind. The formula is available in tincture or softgels from about $6 to $25. (www.herbsetc.com)

KAVA

The Peaceful Relaxer

South Pacific Island natives have used the roots of the kava plant (*Piper methysticum*), a black pepper cousin, as a traditional ceremonial beverage for hundreds of years. As an herbal medicine, kava relieves mild anxiety—including that accompanying menopause—without affecting alertness. It was proven to be as effective for anxiety relief as certain prescription antidepressants and tranquilizers, but without their side effects or dependency problems.

For more than 100 years, kava was a prescription medicine in Germany. But in 1999, when reports began surfacing about its potential for causing liver damage, kava sales were banned in many European countries, though never in the United States. When those reports were closely examined, it turned out that kava's role in causing liver damage was unclear. Today leading herbalists say that taking kava is safe if:

★ You don't have liver problems.

★ You don't take prescription or recreational drugs that might be toxic to the liver.

★ You use kava supplements that are made from pure kava root (kava stem contains a liver-toxic alkaloid).

★ You don't exceed the recommended dosage or use it continuously for longer than 4 to 6 weeks.

Herb Pharm, founded 30 years ago by Ed Smith and Sara Katz, offers a Pharma Kava supplement, made with organically grown and naturally processed kava, available at health food stores and online for about $23 for 60 capsules. Herb Pharm's Herbaculture Intern Program teaches students how to grow medicinal herbs, and the company uses green practices throughout its operations. (http://herb-pharm.com)

LAVENDER
Sweetly Scented Relief

With its frosty green spiky leaves and tall stalks of fragrant blue blossoms, the sweetly aromatic lavender (*Lavandula officinalis*) has been grown in herb gardens since at least the Middle Ages. French chemist René-Maurice Gattefossé popularized its medicinal properties nearly a century ago, after he badly burned his hand, then plunged it into a vat of lavender oil. When his hand healed quickly, Gattefossé pursued his study of what he called *aromatherapie*, the healing art that harnesses the essential oils of aromatic plants. Recent studies have validated what he discovered so long ago about lavender's relaxing and pain-relieving capabilities. Anesthesiologists at New York University Medical Center swabbed lavender or a nonscented oil on the oxygen masks of people who'd just undergone a gastric banding procedure for obesity. The patients who whiffed lavender needed 55 percent less morphine than those who inhaled a placebo.

In other studies, researchers at Chiba University Graduate School of Medicine in Japan discovered that lavender aromatherapy lowers blood levels of the stress hormone cortisol. And psychologists at Wesleyan University in Connecticut learned that inhaling lavender helped sedate and promote deep sleep in a study of 31 people. Finally, three small studies published several years ago in the *British Medical Journal* suggested that inhaling lavender oil could help ease behavioral problems common in people with dementia—not because its aroma is soothing, but because the essential oil contains terpenes, which are components of many essential oils that are rapidly absorbed through the lungs and could directly affect the nervous system.

Erbaviva, a certified organic company in Topanga, California, makes two different lavender oils—high terpene and wild lavender. Since its founding in 1996, the company has been part of a project that helps fund the Pwo Karen hill tribe of northern Thailand and Burma. The project runs a health clinic for the hill tribe children and assists villagers to transition from slash-and-burn agricultural practices to permanent, sustainable farming. Erbaviva buys its fabric packaging and basketry through this project, which directly benefits the tribe.

Erbaviva's products are made by hand; bottled products are packaged in recyclable amber glass, protecting the essential oils from ambient light and preserving their therapeutic integrity. High-terpene lavender essential oil is $15 for 1/3 ounce; wild lavender oil is $21 for 1/3 ounce. (www.erbaviva.com)

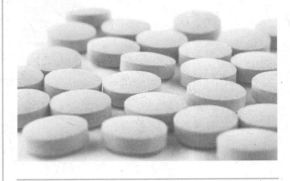
Adaptogens: Herbal Tonics 101

Here's a term you may not have heard unless you're a devotee of herbal medicine: *Adaptogen* refers to herbs that help you cope with stress in its many forms—environmental, emotional, and physical. Adaptogens are nontoxic herbs that increase resistance to stress. Simply put, they help your body cope with a range of harmful influences, abetting your ability to normalize your body's reaction to these influences.

Western herbalists believe the active compounds in adaptogens have specific effects on endocrine and immune systems via actions we may not yet fully understand. "Herbalists know that if they use good-quality adaptogenic herbs, prepare well-made extracts from these herbs, and use adequate doses, the results will be significant therapeutic benefits," says David Winston, author of *Adaptogens: Herbs for Strength, Stamina, and Stress Relief.*

Adaptogenic herbs include American ginseng, Asian ginseng, cordyceps, eleuthero, licorice, and rhodiola.

ASIAN GINSENG
The Man Root

Asian ginseng (*Panax ginseng*) is an adaptogen, an herb that helps the body adapt to the toxic effects of stress. The Chinese have used ginseng for more than 4,000 years. Its Chinese name, *ren shen*, means "man root," a nod to its reputation for boosting virility and potency.

In *Adaptogens: Herbs for Strength, Stamina, and Stress Relief*, David Winston says that Western herbalists consider Asian ginseng the most stimulating of adaptogenic herbs. This makes it a good treatment choice for people who are chronically weak or exhausted. Winston also uses Asian ginseng, often in a formula with other Asian herbs, for what Chinese healers call "disturbed *shen*"— roughly, an unsettled emotional state.

Recent studies suggest other uses for Asian ginseng. One, conducted at the University of Toronto and published in 2008, showed that when people with mild type 2 diabetes took 2 grams of Korean red ginseng three times a day for 12 weeks (along with their diabetes medication), they achieved better insulin control and lowered blood glucose levels beyond those attained by people who took meds and a placebo.

There are many forms and varieties of Asian ginseng. In Asian markets across America you can find dried roots of various ages and qualities. Red ginseng is steam-cured. Wild ginseng is virtually extinct, but the herb is widely cultivated in China and North and South Korea.

Ginseng may cause nervousness or insomnia, especially in type A individuals. Red ginseng is considered especially stimulating and is often reserved for use by the elderly. Check with your physician before using Asian ginseng if taking prescription drugs, especially the anticoagulant warfarin or antidepressants called monoamine oxidase inhibitors, or if you have diabetes.

Herbalist & Alchemist makes a Korean red ginseng tincture that sells for about $28 for a 2-ounce bottle. **Herb Pharm**'s Chinese ginseng tincture is made from ginseng root grown, harvested, and processed in China according to traditional methods; the company uses only medical-grade ginseng roots that haven't been fumigated, irradiated, or sulfured. A 4-ounce bottle sells for about $55. The dose is from 60 to 100 drops three times a day. (www.herbalist-alchemist.com; http://herb-pharm.com)

STRESS RELIEF FROM SIBERIA

The Siberian herb *Rhodiola rosea* has a 2,000-year history of easing stress and boosting mood. Now a UCLA researcher suggests it may also ease the infernal drip of discomforting thoughts. In his study, 10 people diagnosed with generalized anxiety disorder took rhodiola for 10 weeks. Five people experienced at least a 50 percent reduction in symptoms such as exaggerated worry and tension, headaches, fatigue, sweating, nausea, and hot flashes.

Though that study isn't conclusive because rhodiola's effects weren't compared to a placebo, other studies support the findings. For example, a placebo-controlled study of 89 people with depression, which often coexists with anxiety, published in 2008 by researchers in Sweden and Armenia, showed that symptoms of those who took rhodiola lessened significantly.

The rhodiola extract used in the UCLA study was Rhodax, widely available for about $14 for 60 capsules. Or try **Herbalist & Alchemist**'s rhodiola tincture. Follow label directions.

GINKGO
Need Help Remembering?

Ginkgo (*Ginkgo biloba*) trees line many city streets because they're handsome and tolerate urban pollution well. But ginkgo is probably best known as a memory enhancer. Four hundred or so research papers have been published about ginkgo's powers, making it one of the most researched herbs in the world. Herbal medicine experts have concluded that it has a positive effect on neural function and can improve memory with consistent use, though you need to take it for at least 8 weeks before you notice any benefit. In a 2006 study, it was as effective as donepezil (Aricept) for treating mild to moderate Alzheimer's disease. It's also been proven to ease tinnitus (ringing in the ears), vertigo, and anxiety.

Ginkgo contains ginkgolides and bilobalides. The ginkgolides protect nerves and increase circulation, among other subtle functions; bilobalides may stimulate the regeneration of damaged nerve cells. What's more, ginkgo contains potent antioxidants known as flavonoids and flavonols, which protect against cell damage. For a ginkgo supplement to be effective, it must be standardized to contain 24 percent flavonoid glycosides and 6 percent terpenoids.

Ginkgold, by **Nature's Way**, is the German extract that's been used in the clinical trials. It's widely available for about $21. Take two to four 60 mg tablets each day, divided into two or three doses.

MAITAKE
Powerful Mushroom Medicine

Thanks to the many natural food markets and gourmet supermarkets springing up across the country, you may have come across the ruffly looking maitake mushroom (*Grifola frondosa*), aka hen of the woods, in the produce section. Sliced and sautéed, it's a delectable treat with a concentrated mushroom flavor. But used as medicine, maitake has amazing potential to balance a hypersensitive immune system—and thus ease allergies or autoimmune problems. It's also useful for people who have immune deficiencies caused by cancer or chronic fatigue syndrome. If you're undergoing chemotherapy, consider consulting a skilled clinical herbalist to discuss maitake therapy for reducing side effects and enhancing the treatment. Sixty capsules of freeze-dried maitake extract from **Fungi Perfecti** cost about $27. (www.fungi.com)

FYI

If you're grinding your own flaxseed, buzz a handful of uncooked, dry white or brown rice through your coffee grinder first to remove the coffee odor. Use this trick for grinding spices, too, and you'll only need one grinder.

FLAXSEED
The Tiny Powerhouse

For something so small, flaxseed packs a sizable health punch. The seeds contain alpha linolenic acid (ALA), an omega-3 fat that helps reduce inflammation levels implicated in asthma, osteoarthritis, migraine headaches, osteoporosis, and other problems. Recent studies have suggested that ALA might ease hot flashes and could even protect against breast and prostate cancers. A rich source of lignans, antioxidant compounds found in whole grains and legumes, flaxseed has proven to work as well as hormone replacement therapy for easing mild menopausal symptoms in one study.

Because it's rich in fiber, adding flaxseed to your foods can help lower cholesterol and protect against heart disease and colon cancer. To reap its benefits, buy fresh flaxseed and refrigerate in an airtight container; freshly grind as much as you need in a clean coffee grinder. You can store ground flaxseed up to 30 days in the fridge, but most experts suggest using it as soon as you grind it.

Or try **Barlean**'s Forti-Flax ground flaxseed. It's certified organic, free of pesticides and herbicides, and made with select flaxseed from North America. Barlean's uses a special cold-milling process that the company says liberates vitamins, minerals, amino acids, lignans, and phytonutrients without damaging delicate omega-3 fatty acids. A 16-ounce container costs about $8. (www.barleans.com)

RELIEF FROM A LEAF?

Olive oil's health benefits are undisputed—diets rich in the gold-green fluid, which is the healthy Mediterranean diet's keystone, help inhibit inflammation, mildly lower cholesterol, and ward off heart disease. But less is known about another olive product—the leaves of the olive tree (*Olea europaea*). Do they have medicinal value? Perhaps.

In a recent Swiss study, researchers used 20 pairs of identical twins with elevated blood pressure to see whether olive leaf supplements could lower BP. Half the twins were given either 500 mg or 1,000 mg of olive leaf extract; the other half were given a placebo. After 8 weeks, the group who took a daily dose of 1,000 mg reduced their systolic pressure (the "top" BP number) by 11 and their diastolic pressure (the "bottom number") by 5 mmHg. Try **Barlean**'s Olive Leaf Extract. (www.barleans.com)

Those All-Important Vitamins and Minerals

Here is a primer on vitamins and minerals—what they are, what they can do for you, and how much you should take.

★ **Vitamin A: Not enough veggies?** Unless you have five to nine servings of fresh, organic fruits and veggies every day—especially dark leafy greens and yellow and orange veggies—you may not be getting adequate vitamin A, which prevents night blindness and enhances immunity by stimulating the production and activity of white blood cells, keeping epithelial tissues (which line your body's interior surfaces) healthy, regulating cell growth and division. If your produce consumption is spotty, consider taking a vitamin supplement that contains an organic, whole-foods source of vitamin A (look for the words beta-carotene or mixed carotenoids on the label). Aim for 2,300 international units (iu) per day.

★ **Vitamin B$_6$: Nerve cell helper.** B$_6$ enables normal nervous cell communication. Researchers suspect that vitamins B$_6$, B$_{12}$, and folic acid may protect you against heart disease and cancer by reducing levels of the amino acid homocysteine. Do not exceed 100 mg a day of vitamin B6; high levels are associated with nerve damage.

★ **Vitamin B$_{12}$: Over 50?** B$_{12}$ helps maintain healthy nerve cells and red blood cells and is essential to making DNA. People over 50 often have trouble absorbing enough B$_{12}$ from food sources, so experts advise taking a multivitamin that contains B$_{12}$. In fact, some people diagnosed with dementia or Alzheimer's disease actually have a reversible B$_{12}$ deficiency, according to nutritionists at Harvard's School of Public Health.

★ **Folate: Guard against anemia.** Folate, a B vitamin, helps produce and maintain new cells and prevents changes to DNA that could lead to cancer. Both adults and children need folate to make normal red blood cells and prevent anemia. Folate occurs naturally in foods; its synthetic form is folic acid. Pregnant women should take 600 mg a day to lessen the chances of having a baby born with spina bifida or anencephaly.

★ **Vitamin C: Guard against colds.** This vitamin helps your body make collagen, the tissue needed for building and maintaining bones, teeth, gums, and blood vessels. A recent review of vitamin C studies shows that 200 mg a day shortens colds by 8 percent in adults and by 13.6 percent in children. Most experts suggest adults take 250 mg to 500 mg a day.

★ **Vitamin D: The sunshine vitamin.** Research on this vitamin is one of the hottest areas in nutritional science these days. Its ability to preserve strong, healthy bones and prevent rickets is well known, but additional discoveries about vitamin D's abilities to prevent disease are emerging on what seems like a daily basis.

Sunshine helps your body form vitamin D, but people with dark skin, who wear sunscreen, or who live in northern areas (above the line from San Francisco to Philadelphia) may not absorb enough sunlight to make vitamin D, especially in winter. A 1998 study concluded that nearly 60 percent of the people admitted to a Boston hospital were vitamin D deficient.

Some leading nutrition experts recommend taking supplements and eating vitamin D fortified foods to get a minimum of 5,000 iu and suggest that the official DRI, 400 iu per day, be revised to reflect recent research.

★ **Vitamin E: Free-radical shield.** This antioxidant protects your cells against free radicals that contribute to the development of heart disease and cancer. Vitamin E also enhances immune function and is a factor in DNA repair. According to vitamin experts, most people don't get enough vitamin E from their diets. Taking 600 iu every other day helps prevent blood clots; just 33 iu a day may reduce your risk of dying from various chronic diseases by about 50 percent. Listed amounts are for the natural form of vitamin E, d-alpha-tocopherol, the kind experts recommend.

★ **Calcium: Keeps bones strong.** Calcium helps build and maintain the strength of your bones and teeth and is vital for muscle contraction, blood vessel contraction and expansion, hormone and enzyme secretion, and for sending messages through the nervous system. If you don't eat calcium-rich foods such as dairy products, dark leafy greens, or beans, and if you don't take calcium supplements, your body will compensate by pulling what it needs from your bones. Adults need 1,000 mg a day; people over 50 need 1,200 mg a day.

★ **Magnesium: Manage chronic conditions.** This mineral helps maintain normal muscle and nerve function, steadies heart rhythm, supports a healthy immune system, and keeps bones strong. It may also help people manage chronic conditions such as hypertension, diabetes, and heart disease. ConsumerLab.com investigated magnesium supplements and found two with high lead levels. Chose carefully. Aim for 400 mg a day.

FISH OIL
Heart's Best Friend

Fish oil contains omega-3 fatty acids—healthy fats that are considered one reason why the Mediterranean fish-rich diet is so healthy. Fish oil lowers the risk of irregular heart rhythms and blood levels of triglycerides, a type of cholesterol that when high leads to plaque growth in arteries. The American Heart Association recommends that people with elevated triglycerides take 2,000 mg to 4,000 mg combined EPA and DHA. If you have heart disease, the recommendation is 1,000 mg of EPA and DHA.

Choose products from **Nordic Naturals**, a leader in sustainable fishery practices. The company uses a special process to remove environmental toxins and heavy metals. It engages in companywide eco-friendly practices and is certified by the Monterey Bay Area Green Business Program. Its Ultimate Omega costs about $27 for 60 capsules. (www.nordicnaturals.com)

YOUR LIVER'S LOVER

For more than 2,000 years, healers have relied on milk thistle (*Silybum marianum*), a cousin of the artichoke, as medicine for liver problems. The most widely researched liver-protective herb in the world, it's been shown to improve survival in people with cirrhosis. Using it may even reverse liver damage, as long as patients abstain from alcohol.

Studies have shown that silymarin, milk thistle's main compound, safely detoxifies the liver after it's been exposed to chemical pollutants and can treat nonalcoholic fatty liver disease, a common obesity-related condition that contributes to diabetes. What's more, silymarin's antioxidant activity may help reverse the molecular activity that triggers chronic liver inflammation—which is among the suspected causes of insulin resistance, says Kevin Spelman, PhD, a research scientist at the University of North Carolina.

Iraqi researchers recently found that when people with type 2 diabetes who had blood sugar control problems took 200 mg of silymarin a day for 120 days with their diabetes drug, their fasting blood sugar dropped by 20 percent. Mayo Clinic doctors give milk thistle a green light for its safety and ability to protect the liver.

Milk thistle is worth a try for helping lower blood sugar, but some supplements came up short in recent tests by ConsumerLab.com, an independent testing facility. Thisilyn, by **Nature's Way**, was approved for use and is available at health food stores. Take 200 mg a day, the amount used in the recent study. Thisilyn costs about $19 for 100 capsules.

HAWTHORN
The Heart Tonic

The flowers, ripe berries, and leaves of this ornamental tree (*Crataegus monogyna, C. laevigata*) have been used since the 17th century for heart problems. Modern herbalists consider it a tonic—a "cardiovascular trophorestorative," says David Winston in his book *Herbal Therapies and Supplements: A Scientific and Traditional Approach*. He calls hawthorn safe preventive therapy for preserving a healthy cardiovascular system and a "mild but useful treatment for cardiovascular disease."

In studies, hawthorn has reduced congestive heart failure and abnormal cardiac rhythms, stabilized angina, and mildly lowered blood pressure. Hawthorn is rich in antioxidants that protect cells from damage, as well as compounds called *procyanidins* that strengthen blood vessels.

HeartCare, by **Nature's Way**, the formula used in many of the European studies, is widely available online for about $10 for 120 tablets. A tasty alternative is Hawthorn Solid Extract, a delicious mix of hawthorn and blueberry that's lightly sweetened with apple juice. "Hawthorn is what I refer to as 'food for the heart,' and it's one of my favorite tonics for strengthening the cardiovascular system," says Winston, who developed the solid extract. Use ¼ to ½ teaspoon of Hawthorn Solid in smoothies, stir it into your yogurt or oatmeal, spread it on toast—or eat it right off a spoon. A 3-ounce jar is about $17; 6 ounces cost $30. (www.natures way.com)

Tip: To be effective, hawthorn must be taken daily. Discuss it with your doctor if you're taking digitalis-based medications, hypertensives, nitrates, or beta-blockers.

PYCNOGENOL
Pine Tree Power

Taken as an extract in pill form, pine tree bark has shown promise as a treatment for heart disease, asthma, ADHD, varicose veins, menopause symptoms, arthritis, and even jet lag. The superpotent antioxidants extracted from pine bark are called oligomeric proanthocyanidins, or OPCs. Researchers suspect that OPCs, which are also found in grapes, cocoa, cranberries, and apples, may be why the wine-loving French, whose diets are cholesterol rich, have less heart disease than Americans do.

Researchers recently studied 100 people with osteoarthritis of the knee. Half were given Pycnogenol, and the others were given a placebo. All were allowed to take their arthritis pain medication. After 3 months, those who took Pycnogenol took less pain medication; those in the placebo group needed to take more.

Last year Italian researchers discovered Pycnogenol's ability to relieve jet-lag symptoms by nearly 50 percent, including fatigue, headaches, insomnia, and brain edema (swelling), in both healthy individuals and people with high blood pressure. In the study, conducted in 2007, 133 passengers who took flights that were 7 to 9 hours long were given 50 mg of Pycnogenol three times a day for 7 days, starting 2 days prior to their flight.

The pine trees (*Pinus pinaster* ssp. *atlantica*) that produce Pycnogenol grow along the coast of southwest France. **Horphag**, the Swiss company that harvests and manufactures the extract, maintains its plant in Biolandes, where the manufacturing process is run on steam energy, using bark from trees that are harvested for timber; new trees are planted to replace those harvested. No toxic substances are released or used during the manufacturing process, and the company uses very light containers to reduce its CO_2 emissions. Thirty Pycnogenol capsules cost about $17. (www.pycnogenol.com)

RED YEAST RICE
Naturally Lower Cholesterol

Red yeast rice is rice that's been fermented by the yeast *Monascus purpureus*. The Chinese have used it for centuries to flavor, color, and preserve food—Peking duck would be a pale dish without it—and as an ingredient in rice wine. Traditional Chinese physicians use it medicinally to promote blood circulation and to stimulate digestion.

Red yeast rice's use in the United States has been controversial for a decade because it naturally contains a compound called monacolin K, a by-product of the fermentation process, which is chemically identical to the statin drug lovastatin. The FDA now carefully monitors red yeast rice products to make sure producers are not making drug claims and that levels of lovastatin aren't problematic.

In a study published in 2008 in *Mayo Clinic Proceedings*, (www.mayoclinicproceedings.com) researchers randomly assigned people with high cholesterol to one of two options—taking the cholesterol-lowering statin drug simvastatin or following a 12-week program of healthy eating, exercise, daily fish oil supplement, and red yeast rice supplement. Those on the program lost more weight (almost 5 pounds compared to statin takers, who lost less than a pound) and lowered their LDL cholesterol 42.4 percent, compared to 39.6 percent in the statin group. Triglyceride levels of people who followed the program plummeted 29 percent, compared to 9.3 percent in the statin group.

Though red yeast rice has fewer side effects than statins—it doesn't seem to cause the muscle pain that 10 percent or so of statin takers experience—you still need tests for blood and liver problems twice a year. And David Becker, MD, the Philadelphia cardiologist who conducted the study, says there's no way to tease out which of the program's lifestyle changes are most effective for cholesterol lowering because the program's components may work synergistically. If you'd like to explore taking red yeast rice to lower your high cholesterol, discuss it with your doctor. Cholestene is similar to the red yeast rice used in the study. It costs $14.50 for a 30-day supply.

In these times of growing environmental awareness, the pet care industry is opening up new markets for conscientious consumers and concerned pet owners. More and more products and services are emerging that are essential for pets' health and overall well-being and that come under the banner of being green. To meet the basic criteria of greenness, pet products and services should be pet safe; recyclable, biodegradable, and not harmful to the environment; and produced and delivered in efficient and sustainable ways.

Pet owners' trust in the pet food industry has been severely tested in recent years. Many cats, dogs, equines, and other animals have become ill and even died from contaminated products. The massive pet food recall of 2007 in response to the deaths of thousands of pets and the subsequent $30 million in settlements to aggrieved pet owners was a wake-up call for all pet food manufacturers and consumers.

Most manufactured and highly processed pet foods contain varying amounts of genetically engineered ingredients, especially from commodity crops such as corn and soybeans. There is some evidence from environmental studies and laboratory animal tests that genetically engineered crops and the foods derived from them may not be safe for consumption. Yet in the current lack of sufficient scientifically verifiable data, the United States and other countries around the world continue to permit the planting of millions of acres of genetically engineered crops. This has resulted in the genetic contamination of certain conventional and heirloom crop varieties, and it may eventually pose a serious threat to agricultural sustainability and food safety.

Thankfully, there is a new generation of commercial cat and dog foods emerging—from raw to freeze-dried, canned to dry—that contain organically certified, whole food ingredients properly formulated and balanced. They are being more broadly marketed and sold by local and national supply chain networks, which means they are appearing in increasing numbers on grocery and pet store shelves. Organically certified foods of both animal and plant origin contain more essential nutrients for pets than conventionally grown produce, they cause less environmental harm, and they are pesticide free. This trend in improved pet food formulations and ingredients goes hand in hand with increasing consumer demand for organically produced, minimally processed foods for human consumption.

While pet owners have been sorely tested in the pet products arena, their trust in the veterinary profession is being reaffirmed, as increasing numbers of veterinarians prescribe less-harmful drugs and take a more holistic approach to disease prevention and treatment. This is a hopeful sign that the general thinking on pets and pet care is shifting to a more naturalistic and green approach among pet health providers and pet owners alike.

The first-place award for adaptability to living with us in a sedentary, domestic environment goes to the dog, which has been domesticated for more than 40,000 years. A more distant second place goes to the cat, which has been domesticated for only a few thousand years (and still prefers for the most part to walk on the wild side!). Cats and dogs are now regarded as family members and companion animals, and accordingly, we should make similar efforts to green up their lives, much as we do for our own when it comes to health, nutrition, sanitation, recreation, and overall well-being.

From the perspective of green consumer choices for pets, cats and dogs represent by far the largest market component of the pet industry and are the focus of this chapter. Reducing their environmental paw prints through consumer support of green pet products and services is an enlightened ethical choice that benefits you, your animal companions, and the environment.

—Dr. Michael Fox

PEPPERDOGZ AND PEPPERCATZ RAW FOODS

A Focus on Native Feeding Habits

Pepperdogz and **Peppercatz** have a simple philosophy: "Create products that are as close to a dog's and cat's native feeding and life habits as possible." Launched in 2003, Pepperdogz and Peppercatz premium raw dog and cat foods are made entirely from human-grade ingredients: pasture-raised buffalo, free-run locally grown chicken and turkey, fresh regional fruits and vegetables, and organic supplements. Pepperdogz and Peppercatz foods contain no grains or potatoes, which are used as binding ingredients in many dry kibble diets.

Pepperdogz Kick'n Chicken, Go Go Buffalo, and Perky Turkey and Peppercatz Chicken Lick'n and Turkey Lurky are naturally rich in vitamins, minerals, and essential fatty acids.

Pepperdogz also offers raw grass-fed buffalo knuckle, marrow, and rib bones called Buffalo Mojo and free-range, grain-free training treats in venison and lamb varieties called Meaty Treaty.

These pet foods are manufactured in a state-of-the-art, USDA-approved meat processing plant in Washington State. Ingredients are delivered shortly before each run, and the final product is quick-frozen and stored in a blast freezer—the most effective way of preserving fresh foods. (www.pepperdogz.com)

THE HONEST KITCHEN

Good Stuff, Honestly

The Honest Kitchen produces dehydrated raw diets for pets that are 100 percent human-grade food and free of by-products, fillers, and chemicals of any kind. The foods are actually made in a human food factory in Los Angeles.

Verve is the diet that started it all, the original dehydrated raw dog food made with beef and organic grains. Force is the company's first grain-free dog food, an adult-maintenance food designed for dogs with sensitive stomachs and chronic ailments related to the consumption of glutenous grains. Embark is a grain-free, low-carbohydrate dog food designed for all life stages, including active adults, puppies, pregnancy, and nursing. Thrive is a gluten-free, low-carbohydrate dog food also designed for all life stages. It is ideal for sensitive dogs who need gluten-free food but a little grain to help maintain healthy body weight.

For cats, The Honest Kitchen developed Prowl, a higher protein, grain-free cat food that can stand alone or act as a base for your own homemade cat food diet. (www.thehonestkitchen.com)

EVO DRY CAT FOOD

Complete and Balanced Feline Nutrition

Natura's EVO Cat and Kitten Food supplies the nutritional benefits of a raw food diet in a safe and convenient manner. If you prefer to feed your cat a raw or home-cooked diet but don't always have time to prepare meals, EVO is a good alternative. It can be fed exclusively or used in combination with a raw diet to provide vitamins and minerals that your feline might otherwise be missing.

EVO is made from ground chicken and turkey meat, bones, fat, cartilage, and connective tissue and includes whole, raw fruits and vegetables, and added probiotics and prebiotics. It contains no grains.

EVO Cat and Kitten Food has the highest meat content of any dry cat food; it contains 50 percent protein, 22 percent fat, and only 7 percent carbohydrates, the lowest in the industry. The company also has an excellent line of canned cat food and dry and canned dog food. (www.evopet.com)

ORGANIX CANNED CAT FOOD
Certified Organic

The organic certification process requires that every ingredient in Organix (including those that are not organic) be reviewed by the certifying agency that operates under the USDA National Organic Program. Certified organic ingredients must have no pesticides, no synthetic fertilizers, no antibiotics, no growth hormones, no bioengineering, and no by-products.

This company has several different cat food formulas, and all are certified organic. (www.castorpolluxpet.com)

PUREBITES
Tasty Treats

PureBites are dog treats made with only one ingredient: either 100 percent pure USDA-inspected beef liver, 100 percent pure USDA-inspected chicken, or 10 percent US-made Cheddar cheese. These are excellent products for reward training your dog, and they work as well for travel treats because they do not spoil if kept dry. (www.purebites.com)

FELINE FUTURE INSTINCTS TC
Next Best Thing to a Mouse

In 1995 the Feline Future Cat Food Company, Inc., based in Canada, published and distributed its recipe for homemade, raw-meat cat food. Still one of the most popular raw-meat cat foods today, this helped launch other raw pet food companies. Urged by clients to offer a finished food to assist busy cat lovers, Feline Future developed its powdered premix, called InstinctsTC, containing everything from the original recipe except the raw meat and raw liver.

The cat food resulting from mixing InstinctsTC with raw meat mimics the highly nutritional composition of a mouse. InstinctsTC is rich in minerals, vitamins, omega-3 fatty acids, bioavailable animal source proteins, essential amino acids, fiber, and antioxidants. (www.feline-future.com)

FREEZE-DRIED BEEF AND CHICKEN TREATS

Solid Gold goes to great lengths to produce quality pet foods and supplements. Its founder and owner, Sissy Harrington-McGill, actually served jail time in the early days of the federal government's crackdown on health food claims, when the FDA contended that there was no such thing as a natural dog food (even though natural dog food had been available in Europe for 20 years). In 1974, they seized the entire supply of nutritional yeast that she had imported from Europe for her original Solid Gold Hund-N-Flocken. In spite of 6 months' incarceration, she has prevailed, and her products are now sold worldwide. These freeze-dried treats are fortified with vitamins, grains, and minerals and are enjoyed by dogs and cats alike. (www.solidgoldhealth.com)

PETGUARD ORGANIC CANNED FOOD
Goodness in a Can

PetGuard cat foods are prepared from wholesome ingredients including meat, fish, chicken, vegetables, and fresh-milled whole grains and are correctly balanced with the proper amount of protein, fat, carbohydrates, vitamins, and minerals. What's missing? The excess sodium, magnesium, and other additives that may harm pets. The PetGuard Premium line does not use by-product ingredients.

For Fido, PetGuard offers certified organic canned dog foods in such varieties as turkey, lamb, beef, liver, rabbit, venison, vegetarian, and a puppy formula. (www.petguard.com)

FYI

A new generation of commercial cat and dog foods is appearing on grocery shelves throughout North America. From raw to freeze-dried and canned to dry, these foods contain certified organic, whole-food ingredients properly formulated and balanced. Buy them. Your pet will thank you!

MONZIE'S PREMIX FOR DOGS
Whole Food Diet

When **Sojourner Farms** (Sojos) was founded in 1985, the first product was a premix that customers could blend with meat to create their fresh, homemade pet food.

Sojos attests to the benefits of a whole food diet of high-quality grains and seeds, herbs, nuts, fruits, and vegetables and fresh, healthy selections of meat. With Monzie's Organic Müesli Mix, you simply add meat and water, let it soak, and serve. What people love about the premix concept is that they get to be in control of the quality and variety of the meat their pets eat. Providing an easy-to-use, balanced recipe also saves time and nutritional guesswork. (www.sojos.com)

BIOBAG DISPOSABLE DOG WASTE BAGS
Increase Your Disposal Options

The best solution for disposal of pet waste has always been to separate it from the bag or paper and flush it down the toilet rather than send it to a landfill. Using **BioBags** extends your options: You can toss the waste and the bag in your backyard compost, where both items will decompose naturally; you can bury the waste and bag so that microorganisms will quickly eat both; or you can place the waste and bag at curbside with other yard waste where communities collect biodegradable waste for composting. The company also makes disposable cat litter box liners. (www.biobagusa.com)

PETZLIFE ORAL CARE PRODUCTS
Clean, Healthy Teeth and Gums

PetzLife Oral Care Spray and PetzLife Oral Care Gel remove plaque and tartar on dogs and cats and safely kill bacteria on contact, helping to eliminate bad breath. PetzLife's proprietary blend of grapefruit seed extract and other natural herbs and ingredients produces a safe and effective alternative to scaling. One bottle will last up to 3 months if used as directed (and 6 months if used for maintenance). The product is 100 percent natural and doctor formulated in an FDA-approved facility.

Apply the gel or spray to the largest area of tartar, or simply spray or smear Oral Care on gums and teeth. You will notice your pet licking its lips repeatedly. This helps mix the ingredients with your pet's saliva to coat all surfaces of your pet's teeth and gums. For the first week, use twice daily if there is a heavy tartar buildup and/or red, inflamed gums. Otherwise, one application per day is normally all that is needed for moderate buildup.

Users are amazed at the results—and it's the best, zero-risk alternative to having pets routinely anesthetized for dental work when they develop tartar or scales, often associated with gingivitis and periodontal disease. (www.petzlife.com)

BARK STIX DOG TREATS
Something for Every Canine

Developed by the company's vice president—a professional chef— **Bark Stix** are made from 100 percent organic flours grown by family farmers in the Midwest and Canada. The vegetables are usually organic but not always, so they can't be listed as such. The meats are USDA inspected and sourced from a San Francisco Bay Area supplier to local restaurants and delis.

Dudley's Do Right Training Treats contain organic wheat flour, USDA beef liver, water, carrots, bacon, parsley, and nonaluminum baking powder. They won't leave a greasy mess on hands or pockets and are ideal for small dogs or big dogs on diets. Missie's Wheat Free Munchies were developed specifically for dogs who may have allergic responses. These treats contain USDA chicken liver, organic barley flour, oat flour, water, rolled oats, carrots, parsley, and nonaluminum baking powder.

Fart Busters were developed for pet owners who want to feed their dogs

a grain-free diet (ergo, the name). These treats are made from the bone, skin, meat, heart, and liver of Fulton Valley Farms range chickens, which are raised without the use of antibiotics or animal by-products. Lots of protein, calcium, and other nutrients result from consuming the whole bird, the way nature intended. Cats love this treat, too! (www.barkstix.com)

SMART CAT BOX
A Urine Collection System

This system is arguably the world's most eco-friendly cat litter box. The **Smart Cat Box** uses all-natural, nonabsorbent safflower seed litter. Safflower seed is grown in the United States and is both biodegradable and renewable. Safflower seed litter lasts much longer than scoopable, non-biodegradable clay litter and thus using safflower reduces the volume of litter entering landfills. The urine collection system collects urine in its liquid form for disposal and/or for urinalysis as needed.

The Smart Cat Box is easy to maintain, has no dust, is virtually odor free, stays dry, is all-natural, and contains no sodium bentonite. It's safe for the pet owner, the pet, and the environment. (www.smartcatbox.com)

THE WORLD'S BEST CAT LITTER

This company developed a patented process that turns corn into a natural litter. It clumps better. It controls odors without the need for perfumes or scents. It's flushable and more sanitary, and it's virtually dust free, which helps eliminate tracking. A few cats are allergic to corn, in which case an alternative litter would be advised. (www.worldsbest catlitter.com)

PETAPOTTY
Community-Minded Disposal

The **PETaPOTTY** is an eco-friendly, self-draining toilet system for animals. The top layer of soilless organic or synthetic sod makes a comfortable "rest area" for pets. Liquids drain through the sod layer, pulling unwanted bacteria away from a pet's potty space and into a removable pan. The system's top pallet is sealed to keep the PETaPOTTY and its surrounding area sanitary.

Made of nonporous polyvinyl, the PETaPOTTY is guaranteed for life not to rot, warp, discolor, fade, or retain moisture. It's manufactured with dogs in mind, but customers have taken advantage of the low-maintenance system by training cats, ferrets, and rabbits to use it. (www.petapotty.com)

CAT DANCER PRODUCTS
Irresistible Play Toys

When your cats get the "evening crazies," it's the ideal time to engage in play. **Cat Dancer Products** has some safe, interactive cat toys made in the USA. The original and popular Cat Dancer consists of a spring steel wire with cardboard tassels that mimic flying insects that cats enjoy swatting. This toy can be stuck onto a wall with an adhesive pad so the cat can play with it anytime—day or night.

The Cat Charmer is a 4-foot-long snake of all-natural colored fleece material attached to an unbreakable wand. You shake the wand so the snake moves, and this stimulates your cat's playful prey-chasing and killing behavior. (www.catdancer.com)

RUFF WEAR GOURDO DOG TOY
Perfect for Fetching and Feeding

The Gourdo is a multitasking dog toy made from 30 percent reclaimed rubber content. Use it for playing fetch on land or water (it floats). Fill it with treats as a reward and it will massage Fido's gums. (www.ruffwear.com)

NINA OTTOSSON'S INTERACTIVE DOG PUZZLES
Cutting-Edge Canine Toys

Nina Ottosson's wonderful line of food-find puzzles stimulates dogs' minds and dexterity. Designed and built in Sweden from local wood and fiberboard, the Zoo Active toys are harbingers of a new generation of interactive toys for dogs—and cats—that synthesize human creativity with a deeper understanding of animal behavior and well-being.

Dogs, cats, and other animals can become adept at operating and manipulating interactive devices such as these puzzles, from food-rewarding levers and pulleys to advanced, so-called operant conditioning procedures that animal psychologists have been using for many years to test animals' cognitive and other mental processes. (www.nina-ottosson.com; www.petpdc.com)

KONG ZOOM GROOM
Pet Hair Magnet

It is rare to find grooming tools for pets that are still made in the USA. The **KONG** Zoom Groom removes loose hair like a magnet while gently stimulating capillaries and natural oil production for healthy skin and coat. The KONG Zoom Groom is also the perfect bath and shampoo brush.

Zoom Groom brushes work effectively for all cats and dogs and coat types. All ingredients in their natural rubber compound are FDA approved and nontoxic. The compound's exact formula is proprietary, but the company assures pet owners that KONG rubber toys do not contain phthalates or bisphenol A. (www.kongcompany.com)

FYI

For help with cat health and behavioral problems, visit www.fabcats.org. This is the Web site of the Feline Advisory Bureau, a charity organization dedicated to promoting the health and welfare of cats.

pet care

PLANET DOG'S ORBEE-TUFF RECYCLEBALL AND RECYCLEBONE

Regrind and Recycle

The Orbee-Tuff RecycleBALL and RecycleBONE demonstrate this company's imaginative approach to making new toys from old toy leftovers. Planet Dog makes the durable, pliable, chewy, buoyant, and bouncy Orbee-Tuff toys in the United States. The leftover materials—known as "regrind"—from manufacturing these nontoxic, mint-scented Orbee-Tuffs are now recycled into RecycleBALLs and RecycleBONEs.

Due to the recycled content, the color of both toys varies—aptly as a range of deep greens. The packaging is also made from recycled material. Although the toys are extremely durable, some dogs will chew through anything. Should this happen, Planet Dog customers can send their Orbee-Tuff toys back to Planet Dog to be recycled into new RecycleBALLs and RecycleBONEs. (www.planetdog.com)

Planet Dog is proud to donate a percentage of every purchase to the Planet Dog Foundation, their nonprofit grant-making organization, to support canine service programs nationwide. (www.planetdogfoundation.org)

CANINE GENIUS TOYS

Crack the Puzzle, Get the Snack

Made in the USA, Canine Genius's Leos and Mini Leos are of durable, hollow-core construction with open necks and two cross-cut holes that allow you to stuff the toys with treats. Connect two, three, or more Leos or Mini Leos to build customized treat-release puzzles that both exercise and reward your dog's problem-solving skills. Feed dinner from a Leo to entertain your dog, to slow down gulpers, or to help obese dogs lose weight by extending the duration of a meal so they feel more satisfied with less food.

The Mini Leo is scaled down for smaller canine companions (and cats!). Mini Leos also connect together to form customizable puzzles.

Dishwasher-safe Leos and Mini Leos are made from an FDA-approved nontoxic material and can also be used for fetch, tug-of-war, and water sports (they float). (www.caninegenius.com)

Why a Holistic Veterinarian?

What is a holistic veterinarian, and why should you consider one? Holistic vets first advise their clients on proper nutrition and preventive health care maintenance, knowing that dogs and cats with strong immune systems have fewer health problems. Holistic vets do not routinely prescribe special manufactured diets that are often nutritionally inadequate to address canine and feline maladies such as obesity, diabetes, cystitis, and nephritis. Nor do they add insult to injury by routinely prescribing corticosteroid and other potentially fatal anti-inflammatory drugs when animals develop allergic reactions to food and fleas, further impairing the pets' already compromised immune systems and causing diseases such as Cushing's disease, Addison's disease, diabetes, and chronic cystitis.

The best medicine is prevention, and a holistic approach to companion animal health in the 21st century calls for a revision of vaccination protocols, less use of highly processed commercial pet foods, and no overmedicating—especially with so-called preventive medications when there are effective and much cheaper alternatives available that pose far less risk to animals' health and to the environment. Holistic veterinarians do not push annual booster vaccinations for all kinds of diseases or make clients feel guilty if they do not comply. Overvaccinated and over-medicated cats and dogs may develop lifelong health problems.

If you would like to learn more about the holistic approach to animal and pet care, contact a holistic veterinarian in your area. A searchable list may be found online at www.holisticvetlist.com.

UNTANGLER COMBS AND RAKES
Painless Grooming

Combing out a pet's matted and tangled coat can be painful for owner and pet alike. No matter how gentle you try to be, a rigid-tooth comb always seems to pull at the coat and tear out hair by the roots. Untangler combs for dogs and cats take away the pain and the tangles. Special teeth rotate 360 degrees to roll and glide through tangles while gently stimulating your pet's skin. Untanglers decrease hair pull-out and are much gentler to hair than a conventional grooming comb. The rake goes deep and gently into thick, long coats and is especially good for shedding coats. It's like giving your dog or cat a stimulating surface massage. (www.theuntangler.com)

THE COMB N' TRAP FLEA COMB
Fleas Be Gone!

This brilliantly designed comb from Untangler delivers an integrated attack on fleas whenever they are around. The comb's teeth gently turn, trapping and containing fleas in the attached plastic shield. The shield then snaps up for easy cleaning. Use the Comb N' Trap to remove fleas on pets of all sizes, and spare your pet those toxic flea powders and soaps. (www.theuntangler.com)

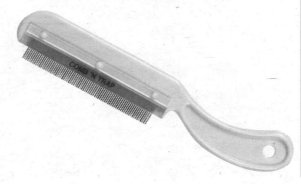

FYI

Pets eat all kinds of things they're not supposed to. If you suspect your animal companion may have been poisoned, call 800-213-6680 or go to www.petpoison helpline.com.

NUHEMP BOTANICALS GROOMING PRODUCTS
Organically Clean

NuHemp premium grooming products blend science-based nutrients, plant extracts, and essential/botanical oils to clean and leave your pet's hair healthy, shiny, and bright—never stripped—without the use of harsh, synthetic chemicals. NuHemp Botanicals are formulated with certified organic ingredients and enriched with the moisturizing, rejuvenating, and antiseptic properties of hemp seed oil. Shampoos include Omega Sudz, a moisturizing shampoo with oatmeal; Omega Zapp, with herbs and essential oils that rid a dog's coat of strong odors such as skunk; and Omega Therapy, a tree-tar shampoo with oatmeal that addresses itching and skin problems. (www.nuhemp.com)

ADDITIONAL RESOURCES

Here are some other sources of information that you may find helpful in creating a greener lifestyle for your animal companions:

Dog Body, Dog Mind, and Cat Body, Cat Mind by M. W. Fox (Lyons Press, 2007)

The Nature of Animal Healing: The Path to Your Pet's Health, Happiness, and Longevity by M. Goldstein (Ballantine Books, 1999)

Natural Remedies Dogs and Cats Wish You Knew by V. Harris (Ulysses Press, 2008)

Eco Dog: Healthy Living for Your Pet by C. Marshall and J. Deskevitch (Chronicle Books, 2008)

Foods Pets Die For: Shocking Facts About Pet Foods A. Martin (Sage Press, 2003)

Natural Health Bible for Dogs and Cats: Your A–Z Guide to Over 200 Conditions, Herbs, Vitamins, and Supplements by S. Messonier (Three Rivers Press, 2001)

Dr. Pitcairn's Complete Guide to Natural Health for Dogs and Cats by R. H. Pitcairn and Susan Hubbard Pitcairn (Rodale, 2006)

Veterinary Herbal Medicine by S. G. Wynn and B. J. Fougere (Mosby, 2007)

MOOSEDREAMS DOG SHAMPOO AND CONDITIONER
Calm and Clean

All dogs need to be bathed occasionally—some more often than others—such as when they have an oily or odoriferous coat, which is most often a result of poor nutrition. Moosedreams Lavender Farms Full Moon Dog Shampoo and Full Moon Conditioner are ideal for the job. The shampoo and conditioner are certified vegan and pH balanced for pets. A base of aloe juice and vitamin B5 leaves coats clean and skin soft.

The shampoo also includes essential oil of lavender to calm and relax a nervous or excited pet. Lavender is an excellent flea and tick repellant, and the lavender and aloe soothe itching skin caused by allergic reactions to flea bites. Essential oil of lemongrass leaves your dog smelling wonderfully fresh and is a natural antibacterial and antifungal. Tea tree oil is one of nature's best antiseptics. It relieves skin irritations and conditions the skin and coat. Essential oil of peppermint leaves a cooling and refreshing scent that keeps doggie odors at bay.

The conditioner contains wheat protein; and vitamin B_5 to add gloss, body, and luster to your pet's coat; and castor seed oil, which is rich in fatty acids and moisturizes and lubricates the skin. (www.moosedreamslavender.com)

PLANET DOG SHAMMY TOWEL: A THOROUGHLY GREEN DRYING TOOL

For drying your cat or dog thoroughly after bathing or for wiping down a damp pet coming in from the rain, this rugged and compact chamois is a wonderful piece of material. The Shammy is made from 100 percent viscose (containing recycled wood chips), making it a fast-drying towel that absorbs more than 10 times its weight. Wring to release water, or machine wash and air-dry. (www.planetdog.com)

WAGGING GREEN DOG COLLARS AND LEASHES
Made from Bamboo

Wagging Green Company is making waves in the pet fashion world with bamboo collars and leashes. Bamboo fiber is a wonderful choice for pet products because it's naturally antibacterial, which means no more smelly collar. Bamboo also dries faster than any other natural fiber and is hypoallergenic and thermoregulating. It's as strong as nylon webbing but feels as soft as silk.

All Wagging Green products are hand-sewn in Florida by women working from their homes. Having the goods sewn locally allows the company to closely monitor quality, create custom designs when requested, and support the local economy.

Each design tells a story about an important environmental issue. For example, Fresh in the City is a design that supports the reduction of greenhouse gas emissions in urban areas. No wonder: Wagging Green gives 5 percent of its profits from this design to companies that are working toward improving air quality. (www.wagginggreen.com)

RUFF WEAR K-9 OVERCOAT AND TRACK JACKET

All-Weather Protective Outerwear

Ruff Wear has unveiled an eco-sensitive line of high-performance dog gear using recycled and sustainable materials that protect dogs from the elements.

The K-9 Overcoat is made with a recycled fleece insulating liner enclosed in a durable, recycled polyester shell. The K-9 Overcoat reduces the loss of core body heat and protects dogs from wind, rain, snow, brush, and burrs. The integrated chest panel with adjustable side release buckles keeps the coat securely in place even during vigorous activities.

The Track Jacket is a lightweight safety jacket in blaze orange with reflective trim for maximum visibility during hunting season and in low-light conditions. The water-resistant shell and polyester mesh lining protect in inclement weather.

Ruff Wear is committed to preserving wild lands and waterways, providing important habitat for wildlife and recreational opportunities. Ruff Wear partners with the Conservation Alliance and works with regional grassroots organizations to give back to the special places so important to canines and humans. (www.ruffwear.com)

RUFFWEAR

For Dogs On The Go

FYI

For legal issues relating to animal cruelty, contact your local Humane Society, animal control center, or the police. For information about major issues on this topic, and to support the legal rights of animals, contact the Animal Legal Defense Fund at www.aldf.org.

ORGANIC COTTON LEASHES AND COLLARS: COTTON IS KING

Made in the USA with certified 100 percent organic cotton grown in Africa, these machine-washable leashes and collars are treated only with metal-free, low-salt, earth-friendly dyes. They sport solid brass clips.

Westminster Pet is committed to preserving the environment and to supporting the African people. Organic farming encourages the preservation of Africa's natural resources by avoiding chemical-based pesticides and fertilizers. Additionally, Westminster Pet donates 10 percent of the profits from the sale of these products to FORGE, a nonprofit program that creates educational and empowerment opportunities for African refugees. (www.westminsterpet.com)

RUFF WEAR DOG BOOTS

All-Terrain, All-Season Paw Wear

The Bark'n Boots Grip Trex features an upper inspired by human shoes and a high-performance Vibram sole. Dogs need boots when out on rough terrain and when there is ice and salt on the roads. Many kinds of dog boots just don't stay on, but this design is one of the best. (www.ruffwear.com)

A PET-SAFE DE-ICER

Safe Paw is a 100 percent salt-free ice melter that is safe for children, pets, surfaces, and the environment. It contains a patented dual-effect compound made of a crystalline amide derivative core infused with special glycols. It generates no heat and therefore won't cause either external burns to paws or eyes or internal burns, even when pets lick their paws or eat Safe Paw pellets directly. These components are nonpoisoning and 100 percent safe if ingested. (www.safepaw.com)

RUFF WEAR MT. BACHELOR PAD

A Dog's Home Away from Home

This versatile sleeping pad made of recycled polyester fleece and a PVC-free recycled polycloth base, is available in a larger size for big dogs who need a soft place to lie down, especially when old age and arthritis creep into their bones and joints. Use it at home or in the car to protect carpeting and upholstery, or pack this easy-to-carry pad on a camping trip. The larger size means more moisture blocking and insulating comfort for your larger canine companion and more protection for home and automobile interiors. (www.ruffwear.com)

RUFF WEAR WEB MASTER DOG HARNESS

Connects Dog and Human

The Web Master Harness is a well-designed improvement on the common harness, a leash-attachment alternative to a collar that allows better distribution of a dog's pulling force to prevent choking. The Web Master was originally designed to assist search-and-rescue organizations; the harness design allows humans to lift a dog onto a chairlift, or a truck or out of harm's way. Dogs that slip out of traditional harnesses will find it difficult to escape the Web Master. (www.ruffwear.com)

Choose a "Recycled" Pet

Rather than buying a puppy or kitten directly from a commercial breeder or pet store stocked with puppy mill and kitten mill animals of dubious genetic integrity and viability, go to your local animal shelter or go online to find a furry friend to adopt.

Purebred animals are often noted for their lack of "hybrid vigor" and higher incidence of genetic and developmental abnormalities, hereditary diseases, and behavioral problems ranging from extreme shyness to unpredictable aggression and hyperactivity syndrome.

The mothers of commercially bred or "mill" purebred pups and kittens are often chronically stressed during pregnancy, and other environmental influences (especially the quality of food and quality of human contact provided during pregnancy) can cause changes in their nervous, endocrine, and other body systems. Chronic health problems result for the offspring, and this in part accounts for high veterinary bills.

Additional stress is placed on the offspring when they are shipped out shortly after being weaned from their mothers. Yet more stress may occur in their immune systems after being wormed and given a cocktail of vaccinations. Such treatments can ironically lead to lifelong sickness and suffering.

Going to the local shelter and adopting a cat or dog—kitten or puppy, purebred or mixed—is one way to go green and feel good, taking in the living discards of a sometimes inhumane, disposable society. Recycled animals waiting for adoption all too often end up being euthanized after 7 to 10 days to make room for more incoming animals without homes. We can all help change for the better by supporting our local Humane Societies.

THE CATBIB

Saves the Birds

The CatBib simply and effectively stops cats from catching wild birds, which is a boon for local wildlife conservation. It was invented in 1998 by a bird-feeding cat lover in Springfield, Oregon. When her cats were locked indoors, they showed their displeasure by fighting, clawing screens, meowing continuously, and spraying throughout the house. She invented the CatBib so she could let her cats outdoors *and* stop their bird killing.

The CatBib is made of neoprene, a soft, flexible material, comfortable for a cat but with enough structure to act like a wall between cat and bird. Simply attach the bib to the cat's collar with a hook and loop; remove it when the cat is indoors. The CatBib works by gently interfering with the precise timing and coordination a cat needs for successful bird catching. It doesn't interfere with any of the cat's other activities. A cat wearing a CatBib can still run, jump, climb trees, eat, sleep, scratch, and groom. (www.catgoods.com)

FYI

If you are planning to get a purebred puppy such as a schnauzer, boxer, or Doberman Pinscher, for dog's sake tell the breeder not to cut off the pup's tail. And don't have its ears cropped. Such mutilations can lead to long-term health and behavioral problems.

FENCE 'EM IN, FENCE 'EM OUT

Since 1990, the **Cat Fence-In** has been keeping thousands of cats safe in their yards. It relieves feline stress, arbitrary in-house urinating, boredom, and depression. Made of black polypropylene netting that attaches to any fence, Cat Fence-In protects kitty from unfriendly dogs, misguided humans, cars, and diseases spread by wandering cats. When a cat sees the netting between himself and where he is going to jump, he will not jump. When a cat climbs up a fence and comes in contact with the net barrier, he goes no further.

Being a nonelectric deterrent, it will not harm people or cats. The netting is flexible, with no sharp or jagged edges, and cats can't get tangled in the small, ³⁄₄-inch mesh. The black netting barrier is almost invisible and will not obstruct a neighbor's view. Plus it's easy to install.

This company also makes tree guards that encircle the trunk, preventing cats from climbing up and getting stuck or from ambushing birds in the branches. (www.catfencein.com)

ORANGE PET POWER TKO

A Friend to All Pets

Orange Pet Power TKO uses food-grade d-limonene, an extract from orange peels, to destroy pet stains or odors—including cat and skunk spray—on any surface. Dilute this safe, natural cleaner at 1 ounce per gallon of water and use it to bathe your dog, or apply it as a spritz or with a sponge to repel fleas and other biting insects.

Orange Pet Power TKO contains no synthetic chemicals and may also be used for general housecleaning. Use it instead of cleaning products containing dangerous toxins and you will create a healthy environment for your family, your pets, and the planet. (www.tkoorange.com)

OMEGA PAW RIPPLE BOARD SCRATCH 'N MASSAGE BED

Total Fun and Comfort

The Ripple Board Scratch 'n Massage Bed gives cats a place to sleep, scratch, and massage their paws. This bed is treated with organic catnip oil and has organic catnip flakes laminated in the layers of the board. The bed is made from 98 percent postconsumer waste and diverted materials and is 100 percent recyclable. It's made in Canada. (www.omegapaw.com)

NATURAL PET STAIN AND ODOR REMOVER: A SAFER ALTERNATIVE

Simple Solution offers an eco-sensitive alternative to the harsh chemicals found in traditional household cleaners. This stain and odor remover is made with renewable corn-based ethanol, plant-based mild cleansers, and biocultures and enzymes that digest the organic wastes that cause stains and odors. The ginger-eucalyptus blend of natural fragrance oils not only releases a pleasant aroma but actually works with the cleaning agents to remove pet odor. A customized nozzle allows for targeted saturation of carpet fibers and padding, ensuring that the solution gets to the problem area beneath the surface so pets will not return and resoil the area. (www.simplesolution.com)

OMEGA PAW RIPPLE BOARD SCRATCH BOX

Good for Scratching and the Earth

When cats dig their claws into this catnip-treated cardboard scratcher, they release the aroma of organic catnip oil and flakes and get a soothing paw massage. The Ripple Board Scratch Box is made from 98 percent recycled material and is 100 percent recyclable. The scratch box may also be used as a refill in other Omega Paw products. (www.omegapaw.com)

MOOSEDREAMS TABBY CATNIP SPRAY AND PILLOWS

Sweet Dreams!

Moosedreams Lavender Farms' homegrown Full Tilt Tabby catnip spray contains organic essential oil of catnip. Use it to refresh old toys, scratching posts, or any place your cat is allowed to play. Catnip acts as a mild hallucinogen and an aphrodisiac when sniffed and as a sedative when eaten. It affects about 50 percent of cats to differing degrees. Catnip's active essential oil is nepetalactone, which is much more effective than DEET at repelling mosquitoes and cockroaches.

The catnip pillows are full of farm-grown organic catnip, and when chewed on or rolled on, they release catnip essential oil. Cats will play with and even fall asleep on their catnip pillows. (www.moosedreamslavender.com)

FYI

Regardless of manufacturers' claims, avoid cat foods that are high in cereals, and steer toward feeding your cat a moist cat food.

MOOSEDREAMS GET OUTTA MY HAIR FLEA POWDER

The Name Says It All

Herbs are versatile members of the plant world. Many herbs emit powerfully aromatic and volatile oils that repel or kill insects such as fleas and ticks. Insect pests never become tolerant of botanical repellents and insecticides. In contrast, the ingredients and formulations of synthetic chemical repellents and insecticides must constantly be revised and increased because insects develop immunities to them.

Four very effective herbal insect repellents are found in **Moosedreams Lavender Farms**' Get Outta My Hair powder: lavender, rosemary, lemongrass, and pennyroyal. Please note that pennyroyal has been known to induce abortion, so do not use it on pregnant animals. (www.moosedreamslavender.com)

PERMA-GUARD PET AND ANIMAL PROTECTOR

An All-Purpose Earthen Product

Perma-Guard, a food-grade form of diatomaceous earth, contains fossilized microorganisms that desiccate fleas and their larvae, lice, ticks, and bedbugs. It may be applied as a dry dust rubbed into your pet's fur, sprinkled in your pet's home or kennel, or mixed as a solution for application on lawns. It is an effective, nonchemical insecticide, and it is entirely safe. (www.perma-guard.com)

FLEABUSTERS

Gentle Yet Effective

This brand name is recommended by many veterinarians because it is the least hazardous of all antiflea products for use in the home environment. **Fleabusters** Rx for Fleas Plus has both federal and state EPA clearance and registration. This borate powder is milled extremely fine (so that light applications can be brushed into carpeting) and is statically charged (so that it clings to carpet fibers). The powder attaches to flea larvae and kills them through desiccation. A few microscopic crystals are all that's necessary to kill larvae.

Fleabusters Rx for Fleas Plus is 33 percent less toxic than pure boric acid powder products and much safer than most liquid pesticide alternatives. Because the powder is so fine, it only requires a small amount applied everywhere to be effective. When the product is used properly, exposure to people and pets is minimal. (www.fleabusters.com)

GEORGE'S ALWAYS ACTIVE ALOE

A Breakthrough with Aloe Vera

Aloe vera juices are renowned for their anti-inflammatory properties; they help heal gastrointestinal/digestive problems, various skin conditions, and even gingivitis and certain types of cancer in animal patients. **George's** Always Active Aloe is processed via the company's unique methods to remove the juice's bitter taste and greenish hue and to remove starch and sugars without diminishing the essential properties of the aloe vera plant. The finished product requires no refrigeration. Available as an oral liquid to be taken internally or as a gel for surface application, George's Always Active Aloe has no added water, no preservatives, and no chemicals of any kind. The finished product looks and tastes like spring water. (www.georgesaloe.com)

NORDIC NATURALS FISH OIL SUPPLEMENT

In Harmony with Nature

Nordic Naturals omega-3 fish oil supplements are manufactured in Norway, where they actually exceed the highest manufacturing standards for purity and freshness. Nordic Naturals offers a complete line of award-winning products specially formulated for canines, felines, and humans.

Nordic Naturals' policy is to use nonendangered fish, such as arctic cod harvested in Arctic Norway and anchovies and sardines from the Norwegian Sea and the South Pacific. Sardines and anchovies are ideal fish for long-term sustainability because they have short reproductive cycles. Nordic Naturals works only with fishermen who utilize 100 percent of their catch for human or animal consumption. The company's dedication to the environment continues through their comprehensive recycling and green-use program. (www.nordicnaturals.com)

MISSING LINK FELINE

Supplemental Nutrition for Cats

Missing Link Feline Formula targets special nutritional needs that commercial pet foods may not fill. This all-in-one superfood supplement offers the cat-perfect ratio of omega-3 essential fatty acids, dietary fiber, phyto (plant) nutrients, and naturally occurring antioxidants, trace vitamins, and minerals—in short, what cats need to stay healthy. There are no fillers, preservatives, or artificial colorings or flavors. Additional formulas for cats' special needs are supplied by this company only through your veterinarian. (www.missinglinkproducts.com)

MISSING LINK CANINE

Supplemental Nutrition for Dogs

Missing Link Canine Formula ensures your canine companion receives vital nutrients such as omega-3, omega-6, and omega-9 essential fatty acids, dietary fiber, and phyto (plant) nutrients that promote optimal health and well-being. This all-in-one superfood supplement contains no fillers, preservatives, or artificial colors or flavors. A higher-strength formula is available through your veterinarian for dogs in recovery and needing detoxification. (www.missinglinkproducts.com)

KARMA ORGANIC DRY DOG FOOD

Soul Food

This is the first in a line of organic products being developed by Natura Pet Foods, which also markets high-quality cat and dog foods (albeit not certified organic) under the brand names Innova, Evo, Health Wise, and California Natural. Karma is certified 95 percent organic. This baked kibble's high-quality, all-organic ingredients include free-range chicken, grains, raw fruits and vegetables, plus vitamins and minerals.

Karma's ingredients are produced without the use of conventional pesticides, synthetic fertilizers, sewage sludge, GMO grains, or irradiation. Combine these principles with the packaging made from 100 percent recyclable material, and you can see why Karma organic dog food stands out in the crowded pet food market. (www.karmaorganic.com)

GRIZZLY SALMON OIL

Omega-3 Fatty Acids from Fish

The condition of your dog or cat's skin and coat is influenced by the balance of fatty acids in its diet. Grizzly Salmon Oil supplies a daily supplement rich in EPA and DHA—the right omega-3 fatty acids. These omega-3s help counteract negative effects of allergic dermatitis by producing specific eicosanoids, which are known to reduce and control skin inflammations. Your pet can metabolize the nutrients in fish oil immediately.

Grizzly Salmon Oil is gently extracted in a state-of-the-art production plant that handles nothing but high-quality, salmon-based products. Only wild salmon oil is used, since the oil from farmed salmon is of lower quality and is contaminated with dioxins and other harmful chemicals. (www.grizzlypetproducts.com)

DRY DOG FOOD: ORGANIC TO THE CORE

This company's dry dog food contains a spectrum of nutritious ingredients, including organic free-range chicken, organic grains, organic vegetables and fruits, proteinated minerals, omega-3 and omega-6 fatty acids, and natural antioxidants. There are no synthetic preservatives or coloring agents.

Natural Planet Organics dog food is formulated to meet the nutritional levels established by the Association of American Feed Control Officials (AAFCO) for all life stages. (www.naturalplanetorganics.com)

FOR ENTHUSIASTIC DRINKERS

George's Anti-Splash Water Bowls are made in California, and they come with a safe, lead-free glaze. Crafted with a subtle rim around the top, the heavy-duty ceramic water bowl comes in different sizes and is ideal for dogs who splash as they drink. (http://georgesf.com)

THE ORIGINAL
COLLAPSIBLE FOOD AND WATER BOWL

For a handy, lightweight eco-sensitive feeder on the trail or in the car, look to Ruff Wear's Trail Runner. This bowl collapses into a packet that fits into your pocket yet expands to feed and water even large breeds. (www.ruffwear.com)

PETMATE FRESH-FLOW FOUNTAIN:
KEEPS 'EM HYDRATED

This water delivery system, available in various sizes for pets, could be a lifesaver for many cats who never drink sufficient water. The electrically operated fountain has two replaceable charcoal filters and a silent-running aerator to provide pets with purified, aerated, cool drinking water whenever they wish. It's made from 25 percent recycled materials and is available from Doskocil Manufacturing Company. (888-367-5624; www.petmate.com)

ANXIETY WRAP
Reduces Thunderstorm Jitters

The Anxiety Wrap's most popular use is to reduce and even end thunderstorm fear in dogs. One reason it is so popular for treating storm fear is because there is no training involved. Simply put the Anxiety Wrap on the dog and witness how the wrap has an almost immediate calming effect on most dogs. (www.anxiety wrap.com)

THE POWER OF PROTEIN

Raw Advantage raw pet foods use only hormone-free, chemical-free, and pesticide-free ingredients, such as organic ground turkey with bone, organic ground chicken with bone, organic beef, and all-organic grains, herbs, and vegetables. Some products include ground duck, which is not a certified organic meat, but it meets National Organic Producer standards for acceptable growth and production procedures.

All Raw Advantage meat products are fresh frozen at the farm and are handled with at least the same level of care given to food for human consumption. (www.rawadvantagepetfood.com)

WHINER DINER DOUBLE FEEDER
To Each His Own

The Whiner Diner Double Feeders are handcrafted out of reclaimed wooden wine crates from European and Californian vineyards, so no two feeders are alike. Each wine box double feeder is coated with a protective furniture finish and includes two stainless steel bowls and nonskid bottoms. (www.muttropolis.com)

AROMA DOG AND AROMA CAT
Essential Oil Therapies

Chill-Out is a powerful blend of chamomile, lavender, and sweet marjoram that calms and quiets pet nervousness. This is the company's most popular product, and it is effective in taking the edge off stress-induced emotional reactions such as hyperactivity, separation anxiety, sleeplessness, thunderstorm fears, destructive nervousness, vet visit anxiety, and nighttime pacing. You simply mist the air thoroughly with Chill-Out, dispensing it around the dog or on the pet bedding, then stand back and watch nature work.

Aroma Cat products include Purrfect Ears, a blend of witch hazel and lavender hydrosols that soothe and clean waxy ears harboring ear mites. Soak a cotton cloth and wipe ears clean.

Immewnity Chest Especially for Cats combines hydrosols of eucalyptus, melissa, and lavender to open up breathing passages and stimulate the immune system. Cats are extremely prone to upper respiratory infections, and this inhalant preparation can both heal and give immediate relief. This product is also good for dogs. (www.aromadog.com)

NUHEMP'S OMEGA SAUCES
A Tasty Condiment

NuHemp's Omega sauces contain highly nutritious omega-3 and omega-6 essential fatty acids and other phytonutrients so important to the health of canine dog coats, joints, digestion, and immune systems. Simply pour one of NuHemp's Omega sauces onto your dog's regular food like a tasty condiment. Flavors include chicken, bacon, peanut butter, and liver and cheese. The unflavored Omega Sauce PLUS with Nutraceuticals provides additional benefits for older dogs with arthritic and other joint problems. (www.nuhemp.com)

Spay/Neuter Services: A Good Idea for Your Pet

Having your animal companion spayed or neutered is part of being a green and responsible pet owner. This procedure is almost always mandatory if you adopt an animal from a shelter.

Most dogs and cats should be surgically sterilized under general anesthesia at around 5 to 6 months of age. The operations involve removal of both ovaries and the uterus in females and removal of the testicles in males. Vasectomies can be performed, but they are not advisable.

There are many reasons to advocate spaying and neutering. A visit to your local animal shelter will show you that pet overpopulation is not a myth. There are birth control pills for dogs, but they are not safe. Vasectomizing male dogs and cats won't stop them from wanting to go out to find mates, marking with their urine in the house, and getting into fights with rival males. Spaying/neutering your pet is a wiser alternative.

Spaying females eliminates the chance of their developing cystic ovaries, ovarian cancer, and diseases of the uterus. The chances of developing breast cancer are greatly reduced. Females repeatedly coming into heat can become quite stressed, wanting to go out and find a mate. Fights may erupt between other animals within the same home.

Castrating dogs and tomcats eliminates the possibility of testicular cancer, and it greatly reduces the likelihood of prostate disease. The operation generally makes them more easygoing and less likely to engage in dominance fights with other males over female dogs.

Some purists contend that it is not natural to sterilize pets. But cats and dogs are no longer living natural lives; they are not roaming wild and free. Sterilization helps them adapt better to the sedentary domestic environment where most of them are kept.

Many communities host low-cost spay/neuter programs to help reduce pet overpopulation. Many veterinarians collaborate in community "spay days," offering reduced fees for neutering pets as a public service. You can also contact SPAY/USA, the national low-cost pet sterilization service, at 800-248-7729 to find out about the 7,000 veterinarians and individual organizations in their nationwide network providing affordable spay/neuter services to those who might not otherwise spay or neuter their pets. (www.spayusa.org)

Green Creativity

Artists face special challenges when it comes to going green. They are almost always forced to work with some kind of chemically based, potentially hazardous substance. Paints, glues, solvents, dyes—there are literally thousands of art products on the market that contain carcinogens and other toxins, are manufactured in less than eco-responsible manners, and are disposed of in ways that contaminate land and water supplies.

So what do you do?

There are two choices: You can pack away all of your art supplies, go out into a field, and start drawing in the dirt with a stick. Or you can take baby steps toward not only greening what you do but also changing the art industry.

Here's how: Pay more attention to what you're buying. Learn the proper ways to handle and dispose of your art supplies. Support the companies that produce green, safe, eco-friendly products.

The term "chain of custody" refers to how responsibly a product is made from start to finish. This is one way to hold manufacturers accountable for their products. For example, in making paper from a tree, start by looking at the source forest. Was the tree harvested in an eco-responsible, sustainable manner? How was the wood transported to the factory? Then look at how the product itself is processed: What kinds of energy sources were used? Is the manufacturer using water or wind power?

Then consider the product itself. What is it made of, how is it used, and how does it get disposed of? The next steps are up to the artist-consumer. If you are an oil painter, for example, how are you handling the issue of ventilation? What are you doing with your leftover paints and solvents? Nearly every artist has at some point washed brushes in the sink, regardless of the type of paint they used. Sadly, many art schools don't teach students how to dispose of chemicals responsibly. But some manufacturers are themselves addressing these challenges. For instance, Golden Artist Paints (www.goldenpaints.com) has a great formula for removing acrylic paint solids from your wastewater. They're doing what they can to keep artists informed, and many other manufacturers will be happy to answer questions about proper disposal of their products.

Maybe you are a mixed-media artist or sculptor or crafter working with recycled materials or repurposing materials, like the artists at Eco-Artware.com. How are you putting those materials together—with glues, solvents, or fixatives that release volatile organic compounds (VOCs)? How about replacing such products with something that is safer for you and safer for the environment?

Artists and crafters often feel that the freedom they enjoy in creating makes them immune to the potential hazards, or that changing their ways is too difficult. Some are loyal to the products they use. But going green doesn't mean you have to change everything overnight. Just take baby steps.

—Kim Hall and Louise Buyo

EXOTIC PAPER COMPANY

Poo Sheets

Based in England, this small, independently run manufacturer produces papers made from such unlikely materials as grass, stamps, coffee, straw, human hair, and currency as well as handmade papers from wildflower seeds, lavender, and petals. Their signature papers, however, are Ellie Poo paper and Rhino Poo paper—made (as the names suggest) from the dung of elephants and rhinos.

By purchasing Poo paper, consumers support the work of the Millennium Foundation in Sri Lanka, which gives elephants a home after they've outlived their usefulness as labor animals, and the Elephant Family, a group committed to saving the endangered Asian elephant. Exotic Paper Company also works in partnership with Save the Rhino International, and a portion of the profit on Rhino Poo paper is donated to that organization.

All of the company's paper comes from 100 percent recycled resources and is manufactured in the United Kingdom by traditional methods (without bleach or detergents) in a 110-year-old steam-powered paper mill.

Many of Exotic Paper's products are suitable for craft projects, such as its colored papers, card stock, and radiant board. The latter is a high-quality construction paper that comes in white, yellow, orange, red, purple, light blue, dark blue, light green, dark green, and black.

The Exotic Paper Company is approved by the National Association of Paper Merchants and is a member of the British Association of Fair Trade Shops. (www.elliepoopaper.co.uk)

RENEWABLY SOURCED

Legion Paper Company produces hundreds of different papers using highly renewable plants. Their papers made from cotton linters (waste cotton from the textile industry) result in stronger interwoven sheets than most tree-made papers. Their hand-made mulberry paper is made from kozo fibers from mulberry plants. Papers are dried by solar power, and the company's digital imaging division uses energy supplied by wind power. (www.legionpaper.com)

How to Choose Green Paper

Paper is associated with water pollution, deforestation, and the destruction of unique ecosystems. As developing countries catch up to Western levels of demand, the world's paper consumption is expected to increase by 50 percent by 2010. To counteract this troubling forecast, many companies are seeking alternatives to standard bleached paper. Here are some options:

★ **Recycled paper.** The benefits of recycling paper are obvious: conserving forests, saving landfill space, and minimizing land and water pollution. Recycling also creates jobs, saves energy, and generates fewer greenhouse gases than virgin paper production. New de-inking systems, now widespread in the industry, have made the process greener and safer than ever by reducing noxious solvents and detergents.

When purchasing recycled paper, look for these labels:

★ **Postconsumer waste (PCW):** Postconsumer waste originates from consumer-generated paper that has been recycled from the end of the material stream, such as newspapers or cardboard. The higher the percentage of postconsumer content, the more efficient the reuse of paper.

★ **Recycled:** This indicates that a paper contains some percentage of recycled material, including both pre- and postconsumer content. Buying greener paper may seem as easy as reaching for a product labeled "100 percent recycled," but it isn't. Recycled material may include virgin paper scraps and fibers left over from manufacturing. In contrast, 100 percent PCW paper is made only from postconsumer waste.

Bleach—Look for the following Chlorine Free Products Association certifications:

★ **Totally chlorine free (TCF):** Virgin (nonrecycled) paper that is unbleached or processed without the use of chlorine or chlorine derivatives.

★ **Processed chlorine free (PCF):** Recycled paper in which the recycled content is not further bleached with chlorine or chlorine derivatives; any virgin material portion of the paper must be TCF. This is the best choice.

★ **Elemental chlorine free (ECF):** Paper bleached with a chlorine derivative such as chlorine dioxide. ECF processing reduces emissions compared to chlorine gas but still produces toxic by-products. PCF and TCF are preferable.

Other labels to look for:

★ **Green Seal** places its eco-label on paper that meets international standards and certifies paper products only when manufacturers submit to inspections.

★ **Forest Stewardship Council (FSC)** label confirms that the pulp used to make paper originates from well-managed forests with intact, healthy ecosystems.

Many watercolor and gouache paints can be reactivated with water; some, like those by M. Graham & Company, won't dry on the palette if you keep a lid on it.

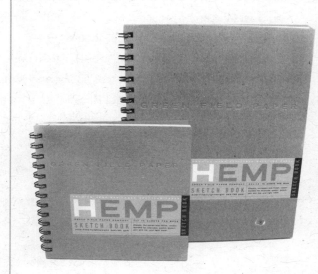

HEMP IS HIP

Since 1992, **Green Field Paper Company** has specialized in making tree-free paper products. The paper in its hemp sketchbooks contains 25 percent hemp (grown in North America) and 75 percent postconsumer waste. The hemp paper is machine made in a process that is acid free and chlorine bleach free, resulting in sheets with a natural white color with small flecks, an elegant finish, and archival quality.

Green Field also offers loose sheets of drawing paper made from hemp that are suitable for pen and ink, watercolor, pencil, and charcoal. The sheets are even ink-jet printer compatible.

Green Field offsets 100 percent of its company's electricity usage by purchasing wind-energy credits for its mills and office facility; the company also uses solar infrastructure, microhydro turbines, and geothermal heating. (www.greenfieldpaper.com)

PAPER ROCKS!

Of all the tree-free papers, Rock Mineral Rich paper is one of the coolest because it doesn't require plant material of any kind. That alone saves approximately 23 trees from being harvested for every metric ton of paper manufactured. In fact, the company sidesteps most of the environmental concerns associated with paper production.

This paper is made mostly from calcium carbonate mixed with a small proportion of nontoxic resin. Overall, the procedure used to make this paper has low emission of harmful gases, and no water is used during the process. And the paper is biodegradable—it reverts back to rock.

Although calcium carbonate is not a renewable resource, it can be recycled hundreds of times without diminishing in quality—unlike wood pulp, which can be recycled into paper only a limited number of times before it must be made into cardboard.

In many ways, "rock paper" is better than paper made from wood fibers. It is stronger, does not tear easily, and is much more durable and water resistant. Yet Rock Mineral Rich paper looks, feels, and prints like traditional wood-pulp paper. It is available in presentation paper, photo paper, double-sided photo paper (both matte and glossy), and greeting card stock. (www.rock-paper.com)

STRATHMORE WINDPOWER PAPER
On the Wind

A full line of recycled and acid-free fine art paper products is now available from Strathmore Artist Papers, including its Windpower sketch pad line. Not only is the medium-weight, lightly textured paper appropriate for any dry medium, it contains 30 percent post-consumer fiber and is manufactured at a paper mill that purchased 100 percent wind renewable energy certificate products toward the production of the paper. Windpower paper products are certified through the Green-e Marketplace Program, administered by the nonprofit Center for Resource Solutions in San Francisco, assuring customers that Strathmore purchases certified renewable energy.

Wind turbines are emission free and use only about 5 percent of the land on which they are sited. That means the land can be used for other purposes, including farming. And because wind turbines do not release greenhouse gases, they do not contribute to global warming.

Strathmore Windpower sketch pads are available in five sizes, with microperforated sheets that are easy to tear out. (www.strathmoreartist.com)

DERWENT GRAPHIC PENCILS
Pencils from Parks

These professional drafting pencils have been an artists' staple since the Cumberland Pencil Company started manufacturing them in 1832. The company, located in England's Lake District National Park, has received multiple awards over the years for its environmental efforts. In 2002, the company received a Queen's Award for Enterprise for developing a solvent-free, UV paint application system for its pencils, ending the lacquering process and improving the air quality around the park.

Derwent Graphic Pencils can be purchased as singles or in sets, with leads ranging from technical (for drafting and precise lines), to graphic (for realistic renderings), to soft sketch (for expressive drawing). (www.pencils.co.uk)

FABER-CASTELL PENCILS
Good Old Writers

This German-based global art-supply manufacturer is renowned for its high-quality pencils and its commitment to the environment. An early advocate of sustainable wood and reforestation, Faber-Castell uses reforested wood in more than 80 percent of its pencils. It was the first company to develop an eco-friendly water-based varnish. In 2006, when the company celebrated its 245th anniversary, Faber-Castell received an award for good corporate governance from the Sustainable Economics Forum.

In factories based in such countries as India and Brazil, the company leads the way in environmentally responsible manufacturing. In the early 1980s, Faber-Castell began its pioneering sustainable forestry project for its Brazilian subsidiary; today the company maintains its own 27,000-acre tree plantation on land that is otherwise not adaptable to agriculture. It produces 1.5 million pencils—and plants about 2.5 million trees—every year. (www.fabercastell.com)

Beware Bamboo

Many paper companies tout tropical bamboo as a tree-free alternative to standard bleached paper. Problem is, it isn't.

Turning the plant into paper isn't an eco-friendly process. The cellulose fibers of bamboo can be broken down only by an extremely caustic process that requires a large amount of harsh chemicals such as soda ash (sodium carbonate) or lye. When these substances are dumped, they contaminate fields and inhibit long-term soil fertility.

Basically, domestically sourced recycled materials are a cleaner and more sustainable choice than bamboo because recycled paper is recovered from the local waste stream. Nothing new is being planted, watered, or grown to make recycled paper.

GENERAL PENCIL COMPANY
Made in the USA

This company has been manufacturing pencils in the United States since 1889. Today their pencils are made from sustainable California incense cedar. Keeping the company domestic helps General Pencil reduce transportation and overall impact on the environment. Cedar left over after pencil manufacturing is recycled, so there is no waste. (www.generalpencil.com)

EARTH PIGMENTS COMPANY
Mixing Your Own

Want to mix your own strong, permanent colors and avoid the chemical additives used by most manufacturers to extend a paint's shelf life? Earth Pigments Company produces finely ground pigments that are environmentally benign, nontoxic, and easy to use for fine art and craft paints (both water and oil based). They contain no cadmium, mercury, tin, arsenic, radium, lead, or other hazardous materials. The Earth Pigment Company receives its pigments from the Société des Ocres de France, a European company that mines the last remaining ocher quarry in the world. The company offers a beautiful range of colors, more than 40 different pigments. Earth pigments are permanent and provide a strong color that cannot be matched by synthetic pigments. Create your own oils, watercolors, temperas, pastels, gesso, caseins, and more.

Earth Pigments Company also carries many other ingredients necessary to make paint, such as oils, water-based mediums, and topcoats. (www.earthpigments.com)

UTRECHT ARTISTS' ACRYLICS
Untroubled Acrylics

Although acrylic paints lack the harsh solvents used frequently in oil paints, until the mid-1980s, nearly all of them incorporated formaldehyde to prevent mold. As the paint dried, the formaldehyde released potential carcinogens into the air. While the concentration of formaldehyde was less than one-tenth of 1 percent of the formaldehyde shown to cause lesions and cancer, it was still potentially harmful, particularly to children and pets. For that reason, manufacturers like Utrecht Art Supplies have replaced formaldehyde with other preservatives that don't release potential carcinogens. (www.utrechtart.com)

M. GRAHAM & CO. OIL PAINT
Alternative Oils

It's great when products that are the safest, greenest, and most eco-friendly end up being among the best on the market.

M. Graham & Company paints have a reputation among professional oil painters for the purity and intensity of their pigments and for overall quality. Unlike most oil paints, which use linseed oil (a nontoxic but highly flammable vegetable oil) as a binder, M. Graham oil paints contain walnut oil—salad-grade walnut oil, to be precise—that does not yellow or crack over time. Better yet, the cadmium pigments used in the paints are non-soluble, which means the metals won't be absorbed into skin. And the cobalt blue is safe enough to meet federal standards for food packaging. Of course, you still don't want to ingest it, and if you get it on your skin, remove it before eating, drinking, or touching children or pets.

These paints contain no added solvents. If you use walnut oil as a brush cleaner and walnut alkyd in place of solvents, you're in the safest, greenest place possible when it comes to oil paint. The company even voluntarily prints California's Proposition 65 labels on all packaging to warn buyers that cadmiums and cobalts of any form are potentially dangerous. (www.mgraham.com)

GAMBLIN ARTISTS OIL COLORS
FLAKE WHITE REPLACEMENT
Losing the Lead

As the name suggests, lead white oil paint, also known as flake white, contains lead. If ingested, lead can cause anemia, peripheral nerve damage, kidney damage, and more. Lead builds up in your system over time, increasing the damage the more you are exposed to it.

The problem is, lead white paint, which dates to ancient Egypt, is a favorite among artists for its ropelike stroke and warm tone. It's particularly great for underpainting because of its transparent nature. What to do?

Try Gamblin Artists Oil Colors Flake White Replacement—the first true lead-free replacement for the toxic staple. The replacement's pigment is created from a blend of titanium dioxide and zinc oxide—much better for you, and much better for your paintings, as traditional lead white can crack over time because it dries too fast, particularly in comparison to the replacement paint. Flake White Replacement is made exclusively by Gamblin Artist's Oil Colors. (www.gamblincolors.com)

ARTEMIS NATURAL DYE WATERCOLORS
Flower Power

These professional-grade watercolors are eco-friendly and completely natural, with no synthetic materials or heavy metals. The downside: They're harder to find than some other brands, and they're comparatively expensive, due to the complicated, time-consuming process of extracting natural pigment from such sources as indigo, buckthorn berries, lac, mignonette, coreopsis, and catechu.

Although these watercolors can be handled safely, they aren't suitable for use by children: Certain yellow and red shades, such as those that contain madder, are extracted from toxic plants and carry the warning "could be poisonous." (www.mercurius-usa.com)

M. GRAHAM & CO. HONEY WATERCOLORS AND GOUACHE

A Honey of a Paint

Watercolors and gouache are among the safest and greenest paints, primarily because they are water based. They are typically made using pigment; a natural gum arabic or sugar-based product, like corn syrup, as a binder; and usually a few chemical additives that extend the paint's shelf life. The chemical toxins released as the paints dry are relatively minimal.

From the 16th to the 18th centuries, most watercolors were made with honey, which absorbs natural moisture from the air and prevents the paint's hardening on the palette. Today most manufacturers use corn syrup because it's cheaper, but M. Graham & Company follows the old-master formulas and uses pure honey for its watercolor and gouache lines. Result? A high-quality product with better overall flow and indefinite shelf life without chemical additives. The cadmium pigments are nonsoluble, so they won't get absorbed into your system, and the cobalt blue pigment is safe enough to be used in packaging for food products.

M. Graham's colors are intensely pigmented, resulting in some of the best, safest, greenest paints on the market. (www. mgraham.com)

M. GRAHAM & Co.

IN GOOD COMPANY

How many people does it take to run one of the highest-quality art supply manufacturing facilities in the United States? Eight, plus one really cool cat. M. Graham & Company produces some of the best paint products on the market, using natural bases and binders and nonsoluble cadmium pigments—all with a staff of eight. Their manufacturing facility uses just about as much power as a small house. And they are one of the few companies that make material safety data sheets (MSDSs) readily available on their Web site, next to the products themselves. (www.mgraham.com)

Keeping good company with M. Graham is Gamblin Artists Oil Colors. Besides taking great strides to provide high-quality, safer paint mediums, solvents, and pigments, Gamblin demonstrates eco-responsibility in every facet of its business: by reusing packaging material; using wind power for their Portland, Oregon, factory; and encouraging employees to bike or walk to work. In 2007, employees biked or walked more than 20,000 miles, saving gasoline and reducing emissions. (www.gamblincolors.com)

Old Medium, New Tricks

Egg tempera, a combination of finely ground dry pigment, egg yolk, and water, has been around for hundreds of years. If natural, earth-friendly pigments (such as those offered by Earth Pigments) are chosen, artists can mix their own nontoxic tempera with relative ease. Just follow artist-author Koo Schadler's instructions when handling the dry pigments.

Her book *Egg Tempera Painting: A Comprehensive Guide to Painting in Egg Tempera* covers everything, from a detailed description of how to make egg tempera and gesso panels to a survey of the ways egg tempera can be applied—using brushes, sponges, glazing, scumbling, and more—all in a beginner-friendly style. The book explains the history of the medium and contains an appendix of extra information on pigments, brushes, and recommended reading. (www.kooschadler.com)

The Trouble with VOCs

Volatile organic compounds (VOCs) are chemicals that evaporate easily at room temperature and are emitted as gases from certain solids or liquids. The term *organic* means the compounds contain carbon. Organic chemicals are ingredients in thousands of products. Common examples of VOC sources are benzene, chloride, formaldehyde, ethylene glycol, and methylene. Paints, dyes, varnishes, solvents, glues and adhesives, permanent markers, ink, and photographic solutions all emit VOCs. And while some VOCs can be distinguished by their smell, others give off no scent. Both types can be harmful to your health and the environment.

VOCs are the primary source of indoor pollution. Studies published by the Environmental Protection Agency have found a dozen common organic pollutants to be present at levels two to five times higher *inside* homes than outside. When you use products that contain organic chemicals, you expose yourself to high pollutant levels. Worse yet, those chemicals linger in the air long after you have stopped using the product.

Acute health effects like eye, nose, or throat irritation; headaches; nausea or vomiting; dizziness; and asthma attacks may signal the presence of a high level of VOCs. Over time, prolonged exposure to the compounds causes cancer, liver damage, kidney damage, and nerve damage. Some art-supply manufacturers have moved away from products that release VOCs, but if you have questions about VOCs in any art or craft product and can't find answers on the product label or the company Web site, contact the manufacturer or distributor directly.

Go Nuts

For a truly solvent-free studio, exchange turpentine and mineral spirits for walnut oil. *Walnut oil?* That's right. A natural vegetable product, walnut oil can be used both as a brush cleaner and as a painting medium, all without releasing harmful fumes or causing disposal problems. When used as a medium, it can create rich, fluid glazes.

The walnut oil produced by M. Graham & Company is a suitable alternative to chemical mediums and solvents. When added to thin your paint, it slows drying times (slower than linseed oil), enhances flow, and increases sheen. And unlike linseed oil, it doesn't yellow or crack over time.

Walnut/alkyd medium, another alternative, has a faster drying time than walnut oil. Use it to thin color, create beautiful glazes, and accelerate drying time while still eliminating toxic solvents. (www.mgraham.com)

Lead-Free Glaze

Robert Gamblin, founder of Gamblin Artists Oil Colors, worked for 2 years to formulate a replacement for Megilp, a silky, gel-like painting medium used for glazing that is also unfortunately toxic. Gamblin's product, Neo Megilp, offers the same smooth texture and produces luminous possibilities—without the lead and the turpentine. And its archival properties can't be beat. (www.gamblincolors.com)

TORRIT GREY OIL PAINT

The Color of Recycling

If you've ever tried to mix your own oil paint using dry pigment, you know about the tiny pigment particles that can create a small dust cloud that is bad to breathe. Now think about a major paint manufacturer, and multiply that cloud by the number of paints mixed every day of every year. While dust masks may give workers some protection, air-ventilation systems send pigment particles out into the environment. But one company came up with an ingenious solution: **Gamblin** Artists Oil Colors captures the particles of all colors in its air-filtration system and mixes them annually into a unique paint color called Torrit Grey. As company founder Robert Gamblin says, "Pigment dust should not go into the earth, water, or landfill, but into paint."

Torrit Grey is of the same quality as any other Gamblin oil paint, but its color is never the same from year to year because the pigment-dust mix varies. Gamblin distributes complimentary 37 ml tubes of Torrit Grey each year through the end of April, in honor of Earth Day, at participating art supply stores. In 2007, more than 10,000 tubes went out. The company now labels the tubes with the year so that artists can collect different paint editions. And each fall, artists can enter Gamblin's competition to create works using only white, black, and that year's edition of Torrit Grey paint. (www.gamblincolors.com)

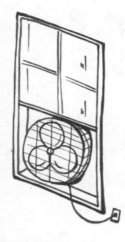

FYI

If you are using art materials without proper ventilation, you're probably breathing in volatile organic compounds or other toxins. "Proper ventilation" does not mean just opening a window; it usually means having some kind of mechanical exhaust system.

SAVANNAH COLLEGE OF ART AND DESIGN

School for Green

Most art schools and universities offer little training on safety measures for using art products. But some, such as **Savannah College of Art and Design** in Georgia, offer solvent-free painting in their courses and studios. And since it's the solvents mixed with the paints that really cause problems—with toxins being released into the air as they dry—these solvent-free studios are some of the safest art facilities around. (www.scad.edu)

Weaker Is Better

Oil painters tend to be traditionalists through and through when it comes to paints and solvents. But for those who seek safer alternatives to traditional solvents, there are worthy alternatives on the market.

If you are unfamiliar with the potential dangers of oil painting, here's a bit of background: Oil paint, in itself, is not inherently dangerous. However, when artists start adding solvents or other chemically based additives to adjust drying times or texture, safety and health problems can arise.

Basically, a solvent is a liquid used to a dissolve a solid material. In watercolors, the solvent is water, so it's harmless, but in oil painting, the solvent needs to be stronger in order to dissolve the pigment particles suspended in the oil base of the paint. The most common solvents used by oil painters are turpentine, mineral spirits, and odorless mineral spirits.

Not only are oil solvents extremely flammable, but as they dry, they release their "spirits" into the air. The faster these spirits evaporate, the more an artist is exposed to toxins that can cause problems like headaches, lung irritation, and worse. So what's the answer? Slow the rate of evaporation and get rid of some of the chemicals. And let's take away the flammability factor while we're at it; no sense in blowing up the studio.

An alternative? **Gamsol** odorless mineral spirits are weaker than other turpentine-based solvents or mineral spirits and evaporate up to five times slower. Yet as a medium or clean-up measure, its performance is remarkably similar. Plus it has a flashpoint of 145 degrees, compared to 95 degrees for turpentine, 105 degrees for mineral spirits, and 125 degrees for other types of odorless mineral spirits. Note: No mineral spirit–based solvent is totally safe for the environment, so don't wash Gamsol down the drain after cleaning brushes.

Keep your solvent or oil in a lidded jar that is properly labeled. Once you've cleaned your brushes, let the jar sit for a day or two; excess sludge should settle to the bottom of the jar so that you can pour the remaining oil or solvent into a separate jar. Always dispose of the unused materials properly.

THE ARTIST'S COMPLETE HEALTH AND SAFETY GUIDE
The Word Is Green

In 1990, artist and industrial hygienist Monona Rossol wrote a comprehensive book on safety and health for artists. Now in its third edition and with 408 pages, *The Artist's Complete Health and Safety Guide* (Allworth Press, 2001) has been completely revised and expanded with new features about safety and ventilation equipment. There is also an updated discussion on the toxins and pollutants associated with specific media. (www.allworth.com)

UTRECHT LINEN CANVAS: LINEN VERSUS COTTON

It's an age-old debate: Which is a better painting surface, cotton or linen? There are arguments for both materials, but here's one fact that might hit home for eco-conscious artists: Cotton cultivation typically requires pesticides and fertilizers, but the Belgian linen imported by **Utrecht Art Supplies** uses no pesticides or fertilizers and is a completely renewable source. (www.utrechtart.com)

How to Read Labels

Everything you need to know about an art material may not be on its label because manufacturers are not legally required to list all ingredients. Be extra cautious when buying or using creative materials made outside of the United States, because other countries have different standards that may not take into account the special vulnerability of children, pregnant women, the elderly, and people with health problems or illnesses. And never transfer art materials out of their original containers because you'll lose valuable safety information. Read the labels on your supplies carefully and cautiously. If you have questions about a product's content, request an item's material safety data sheet (MSDS).

The following are seals, labels, or wording that you may find on art material labels.

★ **ACMI seals.** AP or CL seals indicate that the Arts and Creative Materials Institute (ACMI), a trade group for art supply manufacturers, has had a toxicologist review the list of ingredients in a product. This organization certifies more than 60,000 creative materials. An entire list of certified products can be found on the Web site www.acminet.org. Note that ACMI certification does not guarantee that a product is free of toxic substances or contaminants, even when the word "nontoxic" appears on the seal. Only a handful of substances specifically banned by the Federal Hazardous Substances Act (FHSA) are prohibited.

ACMI's AP (Approved Product) seal indicates that, in the opinion of the toxicologist, the product does not contain "sufficient quantities" of a material that is toxic to humans, with toxicity defined according to standards mentioned above. A CL (Cautionary Label) means that a product contains hazardous ingredients but is labeled in compliance with federal law. Art supplies bearing the CL label should never be given to children.

★ **Proposition 65 label.** This label reads: "WARNING: This product contains chemicals known to the State of California to cause cancer and birth defects or other reproductive harm." California's Proposition 65 obligates manufacturers to put this label on products that contain even very small amounts of chemicals found on the state's list of cancer-causing, reproductively toxic, and other chronically hazardous chemicals. California's standards are currently more stringent than those used by the National Toxicology Program, and the state is required to update its list at least once a year. For the complete listing of substances, see www.oehha.ca.gov/prop65/prop65_list/Newlist.html.

★ **Conforms to ASTM D-4236 label.** This signifies that a product has been labeled in accordance with the standards of the American Society for Testing and Materials. *Note*: The ASTM label does not mean that a product is *safe*; it means only that the product has been labeled properly.

★ **Natural.** Many toxic substances exist in nature: turpentine (made from pine resin), mold, and hemlock among them. Before using these natural products, check the hazards.

★ **Water-based.** Many people reach for water-based products as the safest option for art supplies. However, water-based products are safe only if they do not contain solvents, additives, or other toxic ingredients.

★ **Use with adequate ventilation.** Products labeled with this wording should be used in areas with appropriate, constant airflow. This may mean simply opening a window or turning on an exhaust fan—but in many cases, products so labeled should not be used unless a special exhaust system is in place. Refer to the MSDS to be sure.

★ **Nontoxic.** This is probably the most controversial term of all. Substances that are *harmful* (as legally defined by the National Toxicology Program) are required to carry a "toxic" label. Unfortunately, most substances used in art supplies have never been adequately tested and are labeled "nontoxic" by default. Some products are considered nontoxic only if used within a predetermined time frame, without considering long hours of constant use. *Note:* "Nontoxic" labels are granted to harmful products used in a very specific, limited way. Mixing or experimenting with these substances—as artists are wont to do—may create an unforeseen toxic reaction.

★ **Organic.** Although some art-supply manufacturers use organically grown ingredients (for example, Stockmar's Modeling Beeswax), the term *organic* in chemistry applies to substances containing carbon, including petroleum.

★ **Low-odor.** These are art supplies that have been formulated to produce fewer fumes. Many art supplies, from markers and pens to paint thinner and clear coatings, now carry this label.

Decoding a Material Safety Data Sheet

A material safety data sheet (MSDS) is a complex document prepared by a manufacturer to provide basic information on a chemical's physical properties and related health effects. Typically, it's intended for use in an industrial workplace, where a worker is given information about the substances he or she will be exposed to on the job. However, an MSDS can be a useful resource to artists and consumers concerned about the contents of or the risks associated with a specific product. It spells out rules on using, storing, and handling substances safely, as well as what to do in the event of an emergency such as a fire or a spill.

Unfortunately, MSDS information may be incomplete or out of date. The sheets also do not carry details about the effects of exposure to low levels of chemicals over a long period of time. Nevertheless, if you constantly handle art supplies or are exposed to them daily, it is worth requesting an MSDS from the manufacturers of those supplies. To help you decipher the sometimes complex and technical terminology of an MSDS, here's a description of the nine most commonly featured sections and their key terms:

Section 1: PRODUCT IDENTIFICATION. This identifies the name of the manufacturer and the product. Sometimes substances are referred to by their trade names, especially if the substance is a combination of several chemicals.

Section 2: HAZARDOUS INGREDIENTS. This lists hazardous ingredients along with their exposure limits. Information should be given on what quantity of the ingredient causes ill effects: This amount may be stated as a TLV (threshold limit value, the maximum amount of a product that anyone can be exposed to in an 8-hour workday), a PEL (permissible exposure limit, the exposure limit set by law by the Occupational Safety and Health Administration), or an LD50 (lethal dose concentration that kills 50 percent of test animals). Remember that this information is only for an individual ingredient, not for an entire mixture.

Section 3: PHYSICAL DATA. This describes the physical properties of a product.
★ **Boiling point:** The temperature at which the liquid boils at sea level. In general, a low boiling point means the substance will be a gas at room temperature.
★ **Vapor pressure:** This tells you how easily a liquid will evaporate. Solids have no vapor pressure; they don't evaporate. Liquids that evaporate easily, like solvents, have higher vapor pressures. They build up in the air quickly.
★ **Vapor density:** Vapors that are heavier than air will collect in low places or sink to the floor, where they may create fire or health hazards.
★ **Evaporation rate:** Fast-evaporating solvents quickly release hazardous vapors into the air.
★ **Appearance and odor:** Knowing that a product releases an odor may help you identify a leak. However, odor is not always reliable. Gasoline, for example, has a distinct smell even when a small quantity is present. On the other hand, carbon monoxide has no odor, even at lethal levels.

Section 4: FIRE AND EXPLOSION HAZARD. This section addresses:
★ **Flash point:** The lowest temperature at which vapor will burst into flames.
★ **Flammable limits:** The lowest concentration and the highest concentration of vapor or gas that will burst into flames.
★ **Extinguishing media:** What materials to use to put out a fire.

Section 5: HEALTH HAZARDS. This provides a combined estimate of the total hazard of the product, including the effects of short-term (acute) and long-term (chronic) overexposure in terms of signs, symptoms, and disease. Data for chronic overexposure often are not listed at all.

Section 6: REACTIVITY. This describes how the substance will react under different circumstances.

Section 7: SPILL AND DISPOSAL PROCEDURES. This describes methods for cleanup and disposal of hazardous materials.

Section 8: PROTECTIVE MEASURES. This describes the equipment and ventilation procedures that should be used when working with the substance.

Section 9: SPECIAL PRECAUTIONS. Precautions not listed elsewhere in the MSDS are described in this section, including cleaning or disposing of contaminated clothes, handling procedures, storage information, label statements, etc.

LYPTUS EASELS

Take an Eco-Friendly Stand

The Lyptus easel collection is made by Jack Richeson & Company from Lyptus, a proprietary brand of tropical hardwood. Lyptus is a hybrid of two eucalyptus species and is said to be as hard as oak. The trees are grown on environmentally friendly plantations in South America that mix eucalyptus trees with native tropical forests, ensuring a natural ecosystem.

The trees have been an important component in reforesting the damaged rain forests in Brazil. They are a renewable resource, with seedlings sprouting from the stumps of previously harvested trees. The grain resembles that of cherry or mahogany, and thus the easels are as handsome as stands made from those hardwoods. About as dense as maple and heavier than mahogany, the Lyptus boards are straight, flat, and supersmooth.

Jack Richeson & Company currently offers 12 different full-sized Lyptus wood easels and three Lyptus tabletop easels. (www.richeson art.com)

AMPERSAND HARDBOARD PANELS

True Board

Ampersand, based in Austin, Texas, produces true hardboard art panels that have the highest tensile rating on the market, and their manufacturing process is almost totally green. To bind the pulp, the company uses aspen wood from sustainable US forests to make completely biodegradable boards without formaldehyde or manmade resins. Even the water used to purify the panels ends up cleaner than it was when the process started. Aspen is more pH neutral than other woods, so it doesn't emit acids when you gesso or paint. The museum-grade board is totally archival and should last at least 200 years.

Ampersand produces six different surfaces: uncoated Hardbord (suitable when primed for oil or acrylics), Gessobord (suitable for acrylics), Aquabord (best for watercolors), Pastelbord (for pastels and acrylics), Claybord (for mixed media and egg tempera), and Scratchbord. (www.ampersandart.com)

www.gilmanbrothers.com

BIODEGRADABLE FOAM BOARD

Easily Board

Most foam boards, which are indispensable to artists and crafters, can take from 80 to 450 years to biodegrade. But in July 2008, the Gilman Brothers Company in Connecticut announced two new boards that biodegrade 100 percent in just 1 to 5 years: Insite Biodegradable, a traditional paper-faced board, and Duraplast Biodegradable, which is plastic coated and recyclable. (www.gilmanbrothers.com)

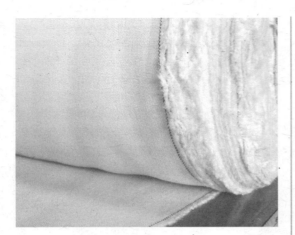

NEAR SEA NATURALS HEMP CANVAS
Make a Joyful Stroke

Artists seeking a greener canvas can add natural light hemp canvas to the list. Hemp canvas—used by van Gogh, Rembrandt, and many other old masters—is especially well suited for oil paintings and can be used for acrylics. Natural light hemp canvas has a thinner, finer feel that lends a beautiful appearance to paintings. One of the best places to find natural light hemp canvas is **Near Sea Naturals**, which specializes in sustainable natural fabrics. (www.nearseanaturals.com)

ebeehoney.com:
Mind Your Beeswax

This company produces some of the best 100 percent beeswax products. This surprisingly versatile substance can be used for literally hundreds of purposes, often replacing materials such as paraffin wax, a petroleum by-product. Projects include encaustic painting supplies; strengthening threads used in sewing, making candles, and toiletries; and polishing wood products, such as handcrafted furniture and children's toys. (www.ebeehoney.com)

SOYSILK FIBER
Smooth as Silk

South West Trading Company distributes Soysilk fiber—derived from soybean proteins—for spinning, knitting, crocheting, and weaving. Soy, a renewable, natural, and earth-friendly resource, produces fibers that are stronger than wool, cotton, or silk and that have the luster of silk and the warmth of cashmere. Soy fiber has the same moisture absorption as cotton, but with better moisture transmission. So because soy fiber wicks away moisture, it makes fabrics that are both comfortable and sanitary. Particularly important, soy fiber holds dye well, has good sunlight resistance, and, in general, takes a long time to fade.

Southwest Trading offers several types of Soysilk yarns: Phoenix, a worsted-weight ribbon style, and Oasis, a sport-weight yarn. Both are available in 16 rich colors. The Infinity line features a fine, lace-weight yarn that comes in natural and white. (www.soysilk.com)

THE OLD FASHIONED MILK PAINT COMPANY: GOT MILK?

The Old Fashioned Milk Paint Company produces one of the best natural milk paint lines around. The paint comes as a dry powder in 20 historical colors to mix with water. There is also a base to which you can add your own water-soluble pigments, or you can blend the existing colors to create a custom color. Unlike many "milk paints" sold in home-improvement stores—which usually have a latex or oil base—this paint is truly biodegradable, nontoxic, and VOC free. The paint will take about 6 months or so to cure, after which it never fades and is weatherproof. It's great for children's furniture, craft projects, and historically accurate finishes. The bad news: Once you mix the paint, it lasts about a day, so mix only as much as you can use.

For sealers, you might want to try the company's clear-coat sealer. Or apply Hope's 100 percent tung oil or Daddy Van's beeswax, both of which are green, nontoxic solutions. (www.milkpaint.com)

Safe Soy

Paraffin, a petroleum by-product, is the wax most commonly used in the candle industry. It may also be hazardous to your health: The American Lung Association has issued a warning about poor indoor air quality resulting from burning paraffin candles. The state of California has identified at least seven toxic compounds in paraffin wax, including the carcinogen benzene. Other dangers: Many commercial candles contain petroleum-based synthetic fragrances and lead-core wicks that are quite toxic.

There is a safe alternative. Soy wax is a great choice for homemade candles. While some other natural waxes are equally safe, soy wax is the least expensive because it's the most common. It is simple to use and can be cleaned up with just soap and water. The process is pretty fast, too. A candle can be made in under half an hour.

For the safest candles, replace fragrance oils with essential oils (natural oils that are extracted mainly from botanical sources). And be sure to use lead-free cotton wicks.

Mill Creek Soy Wax Candle Supply is a great place to start shopping. You can find prepackaged soy kits with all the components and detailed instructions. (www.mcsoywax.com)

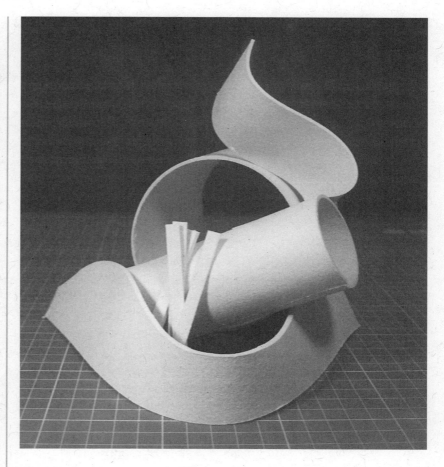

TASKBOARD

The Multitasker

Taskboard is a truly amazing art and craft product with endless possibilities. A wonderful alternative to foam board and other generally less environmentally responsible materials, Taskboard is an unbleached, natural wood product derived from sustainable forests. It is biodegradable and easy to cut into exact pieces.

Although flat in its original form, Taskboard can be formed into shapes: Soak it in water, mold it to form, and let it dry overnight. Once dry, it will hold any curves. White glue is strong enough to hold pieces together, but hot glue or solvent-based glue will work, too.

Since Taskboard can be sanded like wood, joints can be sanded after the glue dries to achieve invisible joints. And it can be colored with any water- or solvent-based paint, stain, or finish.

Due to its incredible versatility, Taskboard can be used in many creative ways, from making architectural models to constructing school craft projects. (www.taskboard.com)

FYI

Picking out art supplies for your kids isn't as simple as you might think. A good place to start: Check out the list of art supplies banned in schools in California because they contain potentially hazardous components at www.oehha.ca.gov/prop65/prop65_list/Newlist.html.

COOKBOOK FOR PAINTERS?

The Natural Paint Book by Lynn Edwards and Julia Lawless (Rodale, 2005) may be geared to home decoration, but the information on earth-friendly decorative solutions can be applied just as readily to crafts and fine art. The first half of the 192-page how-to book is devoted to 20-plus recipes for mixing natural paints and finishes (such as casein, oil paint, and egg paint) using natural ingredients. The second half deals with application of the paint to various surfaces using simple tools—sponges, paint rollers, newspaper, and so on—to create effects such as color washing, marbling, and stippling. At the end of the book is a valuable list of suppliers. (www.rodalestore.com)

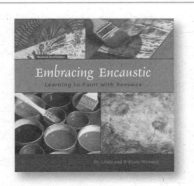

ENCAUSTIC REMARKS

Encaustic painting is one of the greenest painting forms around. It mixes pure beeswax with pigment. Encaustic painting involves using heat sources to melt, form, and finish layers of colored beeswax. In *Embracing Encaustic: Learning to Paint with Beeswax* (Hive Publishing, 2008), authors Linda and William Womack walk you through the process, detailing the tools you'll need, telling you how to mix encaustic paint, and explaining basic techniques. (www.embracingencaustic.com)

GREENPIX PHOTO MATTE
Picture-Perfect Paper

For people who don't want to sacrifice high standards but want to go green when printing digital images, **Red River Paper**'s GreenPix Photo Matte is the perfect choice for ink-jet photo paper. Made from 100 percent postconsumer recycled content, GreenPix is among the most environmentally friendly options available. Its base paper is made in a chlorine-free process and carries certification from the Forest Stewardship Council.

To maintain photo quality, Red River coats GreenPix with an inkjet-receptive layer that helps trap ink for sharp detail and brilliant color. Multiple sizes are available, including three sizes for greeting cards. Red River even offers recycled envelopes. (www.redriverpaper.com)

DIGITAL CAMERAS
Black and White and Green All Over

Digital photography is definitely greener than traditional film processing: no film, no chemicals, little waste. But the biggest players in digital photography, including **Canon**, **Fujifilm**, and **Nikon**, have gone further by changing the process of making their cameras and products.

In the late 1990s, Nikon, for example, invented eco-glass to replace traditional glass, which used both lead and arsenic. In 2007, the company used 950 tons of eco-glass in the manufacture of its digital cameras. In addition, Nikon has implemented high-efficiency production equipment to reduce energy consumption. In 2006, they met the standard of the European Union RoHS directive, which prohibits the sale of products containing hexavalent chrome, lead, cadmium, mercury, PBB, and PBDE in European markets. (www.nikon.com)

SILVERGRAIN PHOTOGRAPHY SUPPLIES

Fixing the Darkroom

Darkroom processing uses many toxic chemicals, so it's encouraging to see that Silvergrain, a US brand of photo-processing supplies, has moved in a greener, safer direction by promoting high-quality, low-toxicity products.

Silvergrain products maintain a low toxicity by using fewer harmful chemicals and smaller quantities of these chemicals. These products are free of known carcinogens and mutagens, Metol, hydroquinone, borates and phosphates, nonbiodegradable organic compounds, acetic acid, perfume, and dye. Although Silvergrain designed its line with demanding fine art photographers in mind, professional labs, photography teachers, and students can all benefit from the greater safety of their products.

Technical charts and details about Silvergrain can be found online at Digital Truth. (www.digitaltruth.com; www.silvergrain.com)

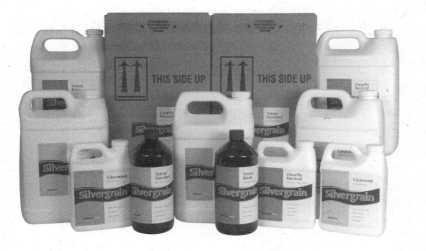

MSDS at Your Fingertips

Blick Art Materials makes it easy for artists to find safety information about art materials because it offers downloadable material safety data sheets (MSDSs) for almost every product it sells. (www.dickblick.com)

FYI

The EPA offers a free downloadable booklet entitled *Environmental Health and Safety in the Arts: A Guide for K-12 Schools, Colleges and Artisans*. The publication provides guidelines for management and disposal of art supplies in classrooms and studios. (www.epa.gov/region02/cap; click on K-12 Schools)

GREEN GRAPHIC DESIGN

It's All in the Book

Of all of the arts, probably the last place you'd think about in terms of finding green solutions is the field of graphic design. After all, it's all business-oriented, bottom-line, cost-savvy stuff, right? Sure, if you're a professional graphic designer, you might be able to incorporate some recycled or tree-free papers without having clients balk or increasing your expenses too much. You might even be able to find some nontoxic inks.

But what if you encouraged your clients to think greener themselves? That's what author, graphic designer, and part-owner of the Celery Design Collaborative Brian Dougherty posits in his book *Green Graphic Design* (Allworth Press, 2009). Dougherty goes beyond theory and presents the kind of organizational and practical solutions that he and his partners use to move forward with this kind of thinking.

The book includes innovative materials, presentation solutions, and ways to encourage clients to select greener solutions, such as using a Sustainability Scorecard. Clients are challenged to achieve their sales goals while maximizing their points on the scorecard, which rates materials according to their environmental impact in three categories: source (where it comes from), energy impacts (the type and amount of energy used to make it), and destiny (whether or not it's reusable or recyclable or will decompose). (www.allworth.com)

ECO-ARTWARE.COM

Art Market

The mantra of green is often "Reduce, reuse, recycle," and there may be no better place to see the effects of this than in the work of artists working with repurposed material. To support artists creating these types of innovative, decorative, and functional works, there's no better (or more fun) place to shop online than Eco-Artware.com.

At Eco-Artware.com, you can find hundreds of handcrafted gifts made from repurposed materials. How about a nice set of dining chairs crafted from former traffic signs? Or a tote bag woven from recycled juice packs? Or maybe a bowl made from vinyl records, and a set of record label coasters to match?

Founded by Reena Kazmaan in 1999, Eco-Artware.com has been featured in such publications as *Time*, *Good Housekeeping*, and the *Wall Street Journal*. The online store features original work by more than 25 artists who are committed to sustainable living and repurposing materials. Many of the handmade items cost less than $100. You can also request custom items and find resources for craft projects, gift wrap ideas, and recycling tips. (www.eco-artware.com)

Old-World Quality

Stockmar is among the best art supply manufacturers in the world, leading the way in commitment to quality materials, consumer safety, and environmental responsibility. This German company has three lines—the Stockmar and Lyra brands, which are suitable for use by children and are created with Waldorf schools in mind, and the Artemis brand, which includes professional-grade products made for practicing artists who demand high quality but do not want to compromise their values.

Stockmar has adopted the parameters of the food provision ordinance, which has more stringent regulations than the toy industry. Strict internal quality control—an independent institute review of all raw materials and manufacturing—and the Stockmar seal, "Constant Raw Material Control," represent this high standard.

Stockmar has been distributing its art supplies in the United States for 20 years and is properly labeled for the American market. (Imported art supplies are not typically required to comply with any labeling standards.) On Stockmar labels you will find ACMI seals and ASTM D-4236 compliance. (www.mercurius-usa.com)

LYRA FERBY COLORED PENCILS

The Triangle Triumphs

The fat, triangular shape of the Lyra Ferby colored pencil's barrel allows young children to grip it properly and is less tiring for small hands. Each pencil yields brilliant color, and the pigment applies smoothly on paper. Twelve pencils are sold as a set, and sets come in several different color schemes. Lyra Ferby colored pencils for children meet all of the safety requirements that Stockmar imposes on itself for art materials. These pencils are appropriate for kids ages 4 through 9. (www.mercurius-usa.com)

SOY CRAYON ROCKS

Crayons Rock!

When Barbara Lee DaBoll invented her soy Crayon Rocks and began selling them in 2006, going green wasn't her primary goal. As a special education teacher, she wanted to help children with writing disorders improve their muscle strength, tripod grip, and eye-hand coordination.

After much trial and error, DaBoll was inspired by a pebble in her garden, and today Crayon Rocks still mimic that shape. The crayons can be held only one way, compelling the user to hold the rock as if holding a traditional drawing instrument.

Here's the eco-friendly part: Crayon Rocks are made from soy wax instead of paraffin wax, the petroleum by-product used in nearly all other crayons. And in place of conventional chemically based dyes, Crayon Rocks use mineral powders, which are nontoxic.

Crayon Rocks are molded by hand and usually sell out as fast as the company can make them. But if you'd like to try to get your hands on these colorful mark makers, visit www.crayonrocks.net.

STOCKMAR WATERCOLORS

Color Me Green

These watercolors are ideal for children and are a favorite art supply in many schools. Produced from gum arabic and light-resistant pigments, they are brilliant in color, nontoxic, and free of heavy metals, dangerous chemicals, or additives. They are perfect for wet-on-wet and transparent painting. If mixed with white paint, they become opaque. (www.stockmar.de)

STOCKMAR MODELING BEESWAX

Model Medium

Beeswax is popular with both children and adults. It is a wonderful modeling material because it stays clean when handled, it doesn't crumble, and its color doesn't bleed. Beeswax does not contain any PVC plasticizers to soften it; instead, it is softened and made pliable by the warmth of your hands. Modeling beeswax comes in sets of multiple colors: transparent, carmine red, vermilion, orange, gold yellow, lemon yellow, yellow green, green, blue, pale blue, red violet, red brown, black, pink, and beeswax color. (www.mercurius-usa.com)

FYI

Seeking cheap supplies for your projects? In Portland, Oregon, a store called SCRAP (School and Community Reuse Action Project) sells stuff that can no longer be used for its original purpose but may have value to artists and crafters. To donate materials or to learn more, visit www.scrapaction.org.

Michael Robbins is the former editor-in-chief of *Audubon* magazine. Author of *Brooklyn: A State of Mind*, *The Hiking Companion*, and other books, he has written articles for such publications as *New York*, *Discover*, *Mother Jones*, *Plenty*, and *Popular Science*. Winner of a National Magazine Award, he is currently a magazine editor for the Weider History Group and lives in Brooklyn, New York, and Leesburg, Virginia.

Wendy Palitz is an experienced art director who has worked for such magazines as *New York*, *Savvy*, *Self*, *Travel Holiday*, *Victoria*, and *Brooklyn Bridge*. She has designed award-winning books on a wide range of subjects including cooking, travel, gardening, landscaping, travel, and wildlife. But never in her career has she art directed a book like the *Whole Green Catalog*. Currently, she is an art director for the Weider History Group and lives in Brooklyn, New York, and Leesburg, Virginia.

Renée Loux ("Cleaning House," "Ready to Wear," "Natural Beauty") has been a trendsetter and eco-barometer in the burgeoning environmental movement for more than a decade. Dubbed the "Queen of Green" and often called a green guru, Loux is an author, eco-consultant, TV personality, chef, restaurateur, and columnist for *Women's Health* magazine. She authored the definitive guide to green lifestyle, *Easy Green Living* (Rodale), and Gourmand Award–winning *The Balanced Plate* (Rodale) and *Living Cuisine* (Avery). She also hosts Fine Living channel's *It's Easy Being Green*. As a frequent green-expert TV guest, eco-advisor, board member, and product tester, Loux understands the rapidly growing eco-market, the science behind it, and consumer trends for greener living. Renée lives on the beach in Maui, Hawaii, in a house powered by solar energy. Visit her at www.reneeloux.com.

Kerry Trueman ("Eating Well") is an environmental activist who has written about edible landscaping and organic gardening for the *Financial Times*. She served as food editor for lime.com before becoming a sustainability blogger for Participant Media's takepart.com. Trueman currently writes about wholesome foods, low-impact living, and sustainable agriculture for the Huffington Post, AlterNet, the Green Fork, Air America, and Open Left. She is cofounder of EatingLiberally.org, an Internet roots organization that promotes sustainable agriculture and progressive politics. Her most recent project is Retrovore.com, a Web site for farmers, gardeners, and eaters who favor conservation over consumption.

Brian Clark Howard ("Green Power") has been an environmental journalist since 2001, and he has a master's degree in journalism from Columbia University. He served five years as managing editor of *E/The Environmental Magazine* and is now a Web editor for The Daily Green, one of the Web's premier destinations for all things relating to the green lifestyle. He has written extensively on energy, home design, and consumer issues, and he is coeditor and coauthor of the book *Green Living* (Plume). Howard has written for *Men's Health*, MSN, Yahoo, *Plenty*, *The Green Guide*, AlterNet, and elsewhere and is very active in online social media. He was a finalist for the 2004 Reuters-IUCN Environmental Media Awards.

Tim Snyder ("Smarter Shelter") learned some early lessons in sustainable living from his grandfather, who managed a wealthy landowner's farm and estate. He was amazed at the abundance of food that his grandfather harvested from the orchards and vegetable gardens on the property. After Snyder graduated from Amherst College with a degree in English and environmental studies, he began a journalism career that has focused on home design and construction, remodeling, and green building. His work has been featured in *Time*, *Men's Health*, *Modern Maturity*, *This Old House*, and *Fine Homebuilding* magazines.

Jim Motavalli ("In Motion," "Closing the Circle") has written extensively about green autos and recycling for such publications as the *Boston Globe*, *Popular Mechanics*, *Men's Journal*, *Salon*, and *Grist*. He writes on environmental topics for the *New York Times*, Bnet.com (CBS), Mother Nature Network, and TheDailyGreen.com (Hearst). He is author or editor of six books, including *Forward Drive: The Race to Build Clean Cars for the Future* (Sierra Club), *Feeling the Heat: Dispatches from the Frontlines of Climate Change*

(Routledge), and *Naked in the Woods: Joseph Knowles and the Legacy of Frontier Fakery* (Da Capo). He is also a senior writer for *E/The Environmental Magazine* and a contributor to the Environmental Defense Fund publications.

Scott Meyer ("Growing Greens") was editor of *Organic Gardening* magazine and Organic Gardening.com from 2002 to 2009. Prior to that, he held a variety of positions with the brand, including product reviewer and Web site producer. He has appeared as an organic gardening expert in many media outlets, including the *Today* show, *Good Morning America*, and the *Wall Street Journal*. His writing has also appeared in *Men's Health*, *Mountain Bike*, and other magazines. Scott is the author of *Totally Roses* (Chronicle) and three other books. He tends his organic garden and lives with his family in Bucks County, Pennsylvania.

Kristi Wiedemann ("Bringing It Home") is a sustainability specialist and nationally published writer who has traveled the globe analyzing the supply chains of consumer products. For nearly a decade, Ms. Wiedemann's work has focused on exploring the impacts of everyday products and services on health and the environment, and on educating the public about safer and greener alternatives. She received her master of science degree from Tufts School of Nutrition with a major in agriculture, food, and the environment, and her bachelor of science degree in environmental and forest biology from the SUNY College of Environmental Science and Forestry.

Robert McGarvey ("Working Green") is a frequent contributor to many national publications, including *Reader's Digest*, *Playboy*, the *New York Times*, and the *Harvard Business Review*. He has reviewed office equipment and design for many years as a frequent columnist for *Entrepreneur* magazine and has interviewed leading green experts at a range of international corporations. McGarvey is also the author of several books, including *How to Dotcom* (Entrepreneur Press).

Ted Samson ("Eco-Technology") is a senior analyst for InfoWorld, a leading business-technology Web destination for information technology decision makers and enthusiasts. He authors a popular Web blog titled "Sustainable IT," in which he delivers in-depth coverage and analysis of all topics pertaining to green IT, from energy-efficient, environmentally friendly computers and laptops to data centers. Samson telecommutes from his home office in Sacramento, California.

Jeff Serena ("Greater Outdoors") started his career writing environmental impact reports for the State University of New York and the University of California. He served as editor at Ragged Mountain Press, acquiring books about the outdoors. He later joined the Globe Pequot Press, heading up the Falcon imprint, the largest line of outdoor recreation books in the world. An accomplished angler and canoeist, he has worked as a fishing guide in Colorado and was an instructor in the Orvis fly-fishing schools. Jeff is also an amateur naturalist with interests in bird-watching and organic gardening.

Brook Wilkinson ("Round Trips") always seeks to satisfy both her inner adventurer and environmentalist. As *Condé Nast Traveler*'s consumer news correspondent, she has written the magazine's World Savers Awards, which recognizes environmentally and socially responsible travel companies, for the past seven years. These assignments show the power of travel to preserve the earth and protect its inhabitants, from the construction of a medical clinic by an Indonesian resort to scientific research supported by an Amazonian ecolodge. Wilkinson has spoken at ecotourism conferences, and she writes a weekly responsible-travel column for *Condé Nast Traveler*'s blog.

Theresa Foy DiGeronimo ("Next Generation") is a veteran writer in the field of parenting. Many of her 60 nonfiction books and numerous magazine articles have focused on her adventures raising her own three children from pregnancy and childbirth through toilet training, disciplining, schooling, athletics, and college. DiGeronimo's collaboration on the book *Raising Baby Green* (Jossey-Bass) with renowned author and pediatrician Alan Greene, MD, sparked her interest in raising children who respect and nurture the world around them. Her current work with Marisa Weiss, MD, on the book *Think Pink, Live Green* continues her focus on healthy, green living for the sake of personal and environmental well-being.

Joe Glickman ("Playing Clean") is a Brooklyn-based freelance writer. His articles have appeared in *Outside*, *Men's Journal*, *National Geographic Adventure*, *Backpacker*, *Condé Nast Traveler*, and the *Los Angeles Times Sunday Magazine*. He wrote two dozen "Weekend Warrior" columns for the *New York Times*, and he is the author of six books, including *To the Top* (Northword Press), and *The Kayak Companion* (Storey Publishing). A two-time member of the US national marathon kayak team, Glickman has cycled across America, paddled solo from Montana to Chicago, and scaled the highest point in each of the 50 states.

Marshall Glickman ("Doing Well and Good") graduated from college and went to Wall Street with a plan: work for three years or until saving $100,000, then quit and do more rewarding work. He reached his goal at age 24 with $135,000 saved, and he moved to Vermont. In 1990, he started *Green Living: A Practical Journal for Friends of the Environment* and served as its editor and publisher until 2005. He has written about socially responsible investing for many publications and is the author of *The Mindful Money Guide: Creating Harmony Between Your Values and Your Finances* (Ballantine).

Sara Altshul ("Natural Healing") has covered natural medicine for almost 20 years. She was *Prevention* magazine's alternative medicine editor for six years, and in 2001, she was invited to testify as an expert before the White House Commission on Complementary and Alternative Medicine Policy. The coauthor of *New Choices in Natural Healing for Women* (Rodale) and *A Woman's Book of Healing Herbs* (Rodale), Altshul's freelance articles have appeared in leading health magazines.

Michael W. Fox ("Green Pet Care"), a veterinarian who also has doctoral degrees in medicine and animal behavior/ethology from London University, England, has been a pioneer advocate for integrative holistic medicine for animals with an emphasis on emotional well-being, healthful environments, and good nutrition. He is author of more than 40 books on animal behavior, environmental and animal health issues, bioethics, sustainable agriculture, and the risks and costs of genetically engineered crops and foods. Dr. Fox is a member of the British Veterinary Association and Honor Roll Member of the American Veterinary Medical Association.

Kim Hall and Louise Buyo ("Sustainable Arts") are the editors of *Art Calendar*, the business magazine for visual artists. In *Art Calendar*'s annual green issue, Ms. Hall and Ms. Buyo encourage artists to approach art making with a greater knowledge of the health and environmental implications of their materials, while informing them about alternative supplies and safer studio practices. Educated in art, residential design, and arts management, Ms. Hall has experimented with a variety of art mediums throughout her career. In addition, she has written frequently about groundbreaking innovations in green and sustainable design and construction. Ms. Buyo, a former art consultant and curatorial assistant at the Harn Museum of Art, has a background in art history and anthropology. She researches contemporary artistic trends and writes on a variety of topics.

Joel Holland, illustrator, resides in Brooklyn, New York, and has worked for numerous publishers, advertising agencies, magazines, and friends. He has also worked in a cereal manufacturing plant and as a model for several book jackets. In addition, he makes his own beer. After working on this project, he has since changed all the lightbulbs in his home.

(All illustrations are by Joel Holland, unless otherwise noted.)

Cleaning House (Housekeeping)

p. 3: The Caldrea Company, Minneapolis, MN
p. 4, upper right: Seventh Generation; middle left: The Caldrea Company, Minneapolis, MN; bottom: Method Products, Inc.
p. 6, upper right: Bon Ami Co; lower left: Citra Solv
p. 7, right: Earth Friendly Products (ECOS.com); left: Method Products, Inc.
p. 8: ©iStockphoto.com/Arndt Design
p. 9, top: The Caldrea Company, Minneapolis, MN; bottom: courtesy of Purelight
p. 10, top: courtesy of Slim-Line; middle: courtesy of Ecover Lime Scale Remover
p. 11, top: Earth Friendly Products (ECOS.com); bottom: Method Products, Inc.
p. 12: Seventh Generation
p. 13, top: courtesy of Kiss My Face; bottom: courtesy of Dr. Bronners Soaps
p. 14, top: The Caldrea Company, Minneapolis, MN; bottom: Earth Friendly Products (ECOS.com)
p. 15, top: Method Products, Inc.; bottom: courtesy of Twist
p. 16, top right: courtesy of Williams Sonoma; bottom left: courtesy of Twist
p. 18, top left: courtesy of Aura Cacia; top right: Seventh Generation; bottom: The Caldrea Company, Minneapolis, MN
p. 19, upper left: The Caldrea Company, Minneapolis, MN; upper right: courtesy of BioBagUSA; bottom: Heritage Bag Company, Carrollton, TX
p. 20, top left: Earth Friendly Products (ECOS.com); bottom right: Method Products, Inc.
p. 21: The Caldrea Company, Minneapolis, MN
p. 22, top: The Caldrea Company, Minneapolis, MN; middle: courtesy of BioKleen Bac Out
p. 23, top right: courtesy of Nellie's Dryer Balls; bottom left : Method Products, Inc.
p. 24, top: ©iStockphoto.com/Marc Dietric; middle: ©iStockphoto.com/Elena Elisseeva; middle right: courtesy of Whitney-Design; bottom: Seventh Generation
p. 25, top: courtesy of The Great American Hanger Company

Eating Well (Food)

p. 27: courtesy of French Rabbit Wines
p. 28, top right: Eat Well guide; middle left: Food &Water Watch; bottom: ©iStockphoto.com/Ying Yang
p. 29, top left and middle right: courtesy Equal Exchange
p. 30, top left: John Scheepers Kitchen Garden Seeds; bottom: photo courtesy of Applegate Farms
p. 31, top right: ©iStockphoto.com/Ufuk ZIVANA; middle left: courtesy of The Field Roast Grain Meat Company; bottom: ©iStockphoto.com/Mykola Velychko
p. 32, bottom: Teeccino Coffee
p. 33, top: Matthew Monroe © 2005; bottom: courtesy of French Rabbit Wines
p. 34, top: courtesy of Wolavers Certified Organic Ales; bottom: Sigg
p. 35, top: Lundberg Family Farms; middle: Annie's Homegrown; bottom: Excalibur Food Dehydrators.
p. 36: ©Rancho Gordo
p. 37, top right: Simply Organic® Spices; bottom left: courtesy of Zingerman's Bake House; bottom right: Nature's Path
p. 38, middle: Eat Well Guide
p. 39, top: courtesy of Spectrum Organics; middle: ©iStockphoto.com/www.kevinmillerphoto.com.
p. 40, top: ©2009 Organic Valley Family of Farms; middle right: courtesy of Clif Bar
p. 41, top: Newman's Own Organics; middle: courtesy of Vita Mix; bottom: www.kuhnrikon.com
p. 42: courtesy of Solar Ovens
p. 43, top: courtesy of Tribest Corporation; bottom: courtesy of Diamond Organics, Wegmans Food Markets, Inc., and Local Harvest

Green Power (Energy)

p. 45: courtesy of the Hunter Fan Company
p. 46, top left: www.Smart Home USA.com; middle right:
Photo courtesy of p3international; bottom left: Energy, Inc. (The Earth Detective)
p. 47, top: Advanced Lumonics, LLC / Earth LED.com
p. 48, lower right: courtesy of Earthmate; bottom left: courtesy of Satco
p. 49: courtesy of Osram Sylvania Inc. and Paul Kevin Picone/PIC Corp.
p. 50, top right: courtesy of RBA Lighting; middle left: courtesy of Philips
p. 51, top left: courtesy of Cooper Lighting; bottom right: courtesy of Real Goods
p. 52, top: courtesy of Real Goods; bottom: photograph courtesy of Rinnai America Corporation
p. 54, top left: courtesy of Lux; top right: courtesy of Comfort Channel; bottom right: courtesy of Lehman's
p. 55: courtesy of the Hunter Fan Company
p. 56, top: courtesy of Renewable Devices
p. 57, top left: courtesy of General Electric; lower right: courtesy of Sharp
p. 58, left: courtesy of Helix Wind Corp.; lower right: courtesy of okSolar
p. 59, left: courtesy of Southwest Windpower; bottom right: Harman Home Heating

Smarter Shelter (Homebuilding)

p. 61: photo courtesy of LP Building Products
p. 62, bottom left: Envision Prefab www: Envision Prefab.com; lower right: logo courtesy of ICFA
p. 63: photo courtesy of LP Building Products
p. 64, left: courtesy of The Murus Company, Inc.; right: courtesy of Bonded Logic
p. 65, left: courtesy of Spray Tech Foam Insulation; bottom right: ©iStockphoto.com /Zoom Studio
p. 66, upper left: ©Solar Direct; right: courtesy of Energy Peak
p. 67, top: courtesy of Serious Materials; right: photo courtesy of LP Building Products
p. 68, right: courtesy of Stanley Tools; lower left: photo courtesy of Armstrong Floors; lower right: courtesy of Goodwin Heart Pine
p. 69, left: logo courtesy of Energy Star; mid-right: courtesy of Milwaukee; lower right: McStain Home Studio, Colorado.
p. 70, bottom left: www.Calibamboo.com,Calibamboo Fossilized Java Flooring; top right: Ice Stone, Photography by Brett Drury Architectural Photography
p. 71, bottom right: Photo courtesy of The Grothouse Lumber Co.; top right: photo courtesy of Climate Master, Inc.
p. 72: ©iStockphoto.com/Jill Chen.
p. 73: ©iStockphoto.com/Tom DeBruyne
p. 74, bottom center: courtesy of Rain Harvest Systems; right: courtesy of Philips Lighting Company

Ready to Wear (Clothing)

p. 77: David Everson
p. 79, lower left: Loomstate; top center: Good Society/Sling & Stones
p. 80, upper left: logo courtesy of Levi Strauss; lower left: courtesy of Linda Loudermilk; right: courtesy of denimtherapy.com
p. 81, upper left: courtesy of Edun; lower right: courtesy of Loyale
p. 82, left: courtesy of H&M; lower right: Thayer Allyson Gowdy
p. 83, right: Graeme Mitchell; middle left: logo courtesy of Lara Miller; middle bottom: courtesy of Deborah Lindquist
p. 84, upper right and lower left: Karyn Craven
p. 85: courtesy of Viridus Luxe
p. 86, bottom left: courtesy of Hess Natur; top right: Danelle Manthey
p. 87, upper right: courtesy of H&M; lower right: courtesy of www.rawganique.com
p. 88, bottom left: courtesy of Bagir Group Ltd; top right: courtesy of Bamford & Sons; bottom right: Organic by John Patrick
p. 89, left: Swanson Studios, 2008; right: courtesy of Dockers
p. 90, top left: courtesy of Topo Ranch; top right: courtesy of Threads for Thought; lower left: Thayer Allyson Gowdy
p. 91, top left: courtesy of Loomstate; lower right: Swanson Studios, 2008
p. 92, top left: Karyn Craven; bottom left: courtesy of Loyale; lower right: Swanson Studios, 2008
p. 93, mid-page: courtesy of Grace & Cello; lower right: courtesy of Form and Fauna
p. 94, right: www.rawganique.com; lower left: courtesy of Cosabella
p. 95, right: courtesy of Blue Canoe Organic; left: courtesy of Enamore Ltd.

In Motion (Transportation)

p. 97: courtesy of Zipcar
p. 98: courtesy of Nissan
p. 99, top left: ©2009 Toyota Motors Sales, U.S.A., Inc.; top right: courtesy of ScanGuage.com; bottom right: courtesy of Ultra Motor A2b
p. 100, top left: EVTAMERICA-F.Pruna; top right: courtesy of Chevrolet; bottom left: courtesy of BMW NA
p. 101, lower left and inset: courtesy of Dahon
p. 102, lower left: courtesy of Ford Motor Company; top right: courtesy of Honda
p. 103, middle left: courtesy of BMW; middle bottom: courtesy of Novica.com; top right: courtesy of Honda
p. 104: courtesy of Nissan
p. 105, top left: ©2009 Wheego Electric Cars, Inc.; right: ©2009 Tesla Motors, Inc.
p. 106, bottom left: SmartUsa; top right: ©2009 Tesla Motors, Inc.; lower right: Volkswagen of America, Inc.
p. 107, top left: courtesy of Vespa; right: courtesy of Ford Motor Company
p. 108: courtesy of Zipcar
p. 109: Courtesy of Honda
p. 110, top left: courtesy of Porsche; bottom: Jim Motavalli photo
p. 111, top left: illustration courtesy of Wikimedia; bottom right: courtesy of Growth Energy
p. 112, left: courtesy of Gary Beckwith; right: ©iStockphoto.com/Terraxplorer
p. 113, top left: courtesy of ecarcenter.org; bottom right: ACEEE's Green Book Online®, www.greenercars.org
p. 114: ©iStockphoto.com/John Simmons
p. 115, top left photos: courtesy of Monte Gisborne/ President, Tamarack Lake Electric Boat Company; bottom right: ©iStockphoto.com/Emanuele Ferrari

Growing Greens (Gardening)

p. 117: HawsWateringCans.Com
p. 118: ©iStockphoto.com/Orlando Rosu
p. 119, bottom left: courtesy of Peaceful Valley Farm & Garden Supply Catalog; bottom right: ©iStockphoto.com/Eduard Vulcan
p. 121, bottom left: ComposTumbler; top right: John Scheeper Kitchen Garden Seeds
p. 122, top left: Seed Savers Exchange; middle left: IP Woody's Creative Woodworks; bottom right: courtesy of Burpee.com
p. 123, top left: Renee's Garden Seed; bottom right: HawsWateringCans.Com
p. 124, top left: Gardener's Supply Company; middle: ©iStockphoto.com/Robyn Mackenzie; bottom right: courtesy of Arbico Organics
p. 125: ©iStockphoto.com/YingYang
p. 126, top right: ©iStockphoto.com/Julián Rovagnati; bottom left: Cross Country Nurseries
p. 127, middle left: Keep It Simple, Inc; bottom right: Joseph Berger, Bugwood.org
p. 128, top left: Territorial Seed; middle: ©iStockphoto.com/Stephanie Phillips
p. 129, top: ©Bat Conservation International, www.batcon.org; bottom left: Randall Roden; bottom right: Planet Natural
p. 130: EarthBox®
p. 131, top left: Spear & Jackson; middle right: Kinsman Company; bottom right: Seeds of Change
p. 132: Photo Courtesy of Lee Valley Tools
p. 133, left: Forestfarm; top right: DripWorks, Inc; bottom right: Johnny's Selected Seeds
p. 134, bottom left: Clean Air Gardening; top right: The Espoma Company
p. 135, left: ©iStockphoto.com/ Nicole S. Young; bottom right: Isthmus Handyman

Bringing It Home (Appliances, Home Furnishings, Bed & Bath)

p. 137: bambu, LLC

p. 138: LG Electronics

p. 139, upper right: courtesy of Omega Products, Inc.; lower left: courtesy Electrolux

p. 140, upper right: courtesy of Kenmore; lower left: courtesy of Honeywell International, Inc.

p. 141: courtesy of Pycnogel®

p. 142, upper right: Haier America; lower left: Fisher & Paykel Appliances

p. 143, upper right: courtesy of Air-n-Water; lower left: courtesy of Honeywell International, Inc.

p. 144, upper left: courtesy of Panasonic; lower right: Model HHP 1500 Mica Panel Heater by Delonghi— www.delonghiusa.com

p. 145, lower right: courtesy of Miele, Inc.

p. 146, upper right: photos courtesy of Twin Oaks Hammocks; lower left: courtesy of Sun Ovens; lower right: SohoDecor.com

p. 147, upper right: courtesy of Crate and Barrel; lower left: courtesy of EcoDesigns

p. 148 mid-right: Outdoor Rugs Only.com; lower left: Fair Trade Certified Logo

p. 149 lower left: The Joinery; lower right: The Boston Lounge

p. 150, upper left: Furniture by Viesso; lower right: courtesy of Urban Woods

p. 151, mid-left: Photo courtesy of Viva Terra, www.vivaterra.com; lower right: courtesy of Recycline Inc.

p. 152, top right: bambu, LLC; mid-left: photo courtesy of www.eartheasy.com; lower right: Emerson Creek Pottery

p. 153, upper right: Photograph by Cassandra Ott, courtesy of Riverside Design Group; mid-left: The Green Glass Company

p. 154, upper left: Photo provided by Lifekind, ® Inc.; lower right: In2green.com ECO Throw Branches Hickory

p. 155, upper left: courtesy of Pillow Dreams Project; center: ©iStockphoto.com/Maria Toutoudaki

p. 156, upper left: courtesy of Flor, Inc.; mid-right: courtesy of Ecorug.com; lower right: RealGoods.com

p. 157, upper left: courtesy of Earthshade; mid-right: Photo by Andrea Marini

Closing the Circle (Recycling)

p. 159: ©iStockphoto.com/Carmen Martínez Banús

p. 160, left: logo courtesy of Freecycle; bottom right: logo courtesy of Earth 911

p. 161, top left: Jim Motavalli photo; middle right: ©2006-2009 Recyclelogos.org., all rights reserved

p. 162: Photo by Daniel Kinsbursky

p. 163, top: logo courtesy of AAA Great Battery Round Up; lower left: ©iStockphoto.com/studiovitra

p. 164, top: ©iStockphoto.com/René Mansi; bottom right: courtesy of www.nexcyclecalifornia.com

p. 165, top: ©iStockphoto.com/ Brian Powell; bottom right: Sarah Nelson, reusablebags.com

p. 166, lower left: courtesy of BMRA; top right: logo courtesy of www. thethriftshopper.com™; bottom right: logo courtesy of Carpet America Recovery Effort

p. 167: ©iStockphoto.com/Stain Studio

p. 168, top: ©iStockphoto.com/Felix Möckel; bottom: courtesy of Trex® decking

p. 169, bottom left: Photo courtesy of Fetzer vineyards; bottom right: courtesy of cleanairgardening.com

p. 170, top: ©iStockphoto.com/Marcus Lindström

p. 171, top: ©iStockphoto.com/Ron Hohenhaus; bottom left: American Flags Express Inc., www.FlagsExpress.com

p. 172, top: ©iStockphoto.com/Nicholas Monu; bottom: ©iStockphoto.com/pixelery.com

p. 173, top left: ©Kim Baker 2008; middle right: courtesy of Green With Envy

Working Green (Workplace)

p. 175: courtesy of Staples, Inc.

p. 176, top left: courtesy of Xerox Corporation; bottom right: Michael Young / YAM Brand

p. 177, mid-left: courtesy of J2 Global Communications, Inc.; bottom left: www.GrassRootsStore.com

p. 178: logo courtesy of GreenPrint

p. 179, upper left: courtesy of Natural Territory; bottom right: courtesy of Staples, Inc.

p. 180, top left: courtesy of Grassroot Store; top right: courtesy of Bits Limited; lower left: courtesy of Green Office

p. 181, top right: courtesy Blue Max™ Light Therapy Lamps; lower left: courtesy of ECO-Heater, Inc.

p. 182, top right: ©iStockphoto.com/Le Do

p. 183, middle left: courtesy of Greenhome Products; lower right: courtesy of Epic Furniture Polish

p. 184, top left: courtesy Greenline Paper; middle right: Photo courtesy of House of Doolittle; bottom photo: Herman Miller, Inc.

p. 185, middle left: The natural printing logo is a trademark of midi natural enterprises; bottom left: courtesy of Cottage Home, www.cottagehome maine.com; top middle: courtesy Atpine

p. 186, top left: courtesy of Texas Instruments; lower middle: courtesy of Olympus Imaging America, Inc.; middle right: courtesy of Office Depot

p. 187: ©iStockphoto.com/Jostein Hauge

p. 188, top left: ©iStockphoto.com/Andrew Johnson; bottom left: courtesy of Zebra Pen Corp.; upper right: www.resourcerevival.com; lower right: with permission from Voltaic Systems

p. 189, upper left: courtesy of Natural Territory; lower left: Photo Courtesy of Patrick W. Robbins; middle right: private collection; lower right: courtesy of Robert McGarvey

Natural Beauty (Beauty Aids)

p. 191: ©iStockphoto.com/Alan Lemire

p. 192, right: 302 Professional Skincare; left: courtesy of Jurlique

p. 193: courtesy of Juice Beauty

p. 194, top left: courtesy of Jurlique; bottom: ©iStockphoto.com/Peter Witkop; right: courtesy of GRN

p. 195, left: courtesy of Dr. Hauschka; right: Spa Technologies Intl., Inc.

p. 196, left: courtesy of REN; right: courtesy of Desert Essence

p. 197, left: courtesy of Pharmacopia; right: courtesy of Red Flower

p. 198, left: courtesy of Pangea Organics

p. 199, left: courtesy of Astara; right: courtesy of Naturally Fresh Deodorant Crystal

p. 200, top left: courtesy of Simply Divine Botanicals; bottom right: courtesy of Colorescience

p. 201, left: Skinceuticals Ultimate UV Defense SPF 30 at skinceuticals.com; top right: courtesy of MyChelle Dermaceuticals; bottom right: courtesy of Gigi Organic

p. 202, top: courtesy of Burt's Bees; bottom right: Preserve www.preserveproducts.com

p. 203, top left: Preserve www.preserveproducts.com; right: Kevin Bubben Moyer

p. 204, top left: PeaceKeeper Cause-Metics; top right: courtesy of Dr. Hauschka Skin Care; bottom right: courtesy of SpaRitual

p. 205, bottom left: Seventh Generation; middle right: Bodywise UK (Ltd)/Natracare LLC

p. 206, left: courtesy of GladRags; bottom right: courtesy of The Body Shop

p. 207, middle left: John Masters Organics Dry Hair Nourishment & Defrizzer; bottom right: Tela Beauty Organics by Phillip Pelusi Alex Milligan www.alexandermilligan.com

p. 208, bottom left: Bubinga wooden bristle brush (photograph courtesy of Dustin Haines); top right: courtesy of Intelligent Nutrients

p. 209: courtesy of Giovanni Cosmetics

p. 210, left: courtesy of Mineral Fusion; bottom right: courtesy of Perfect Organics

p. 211, top left: NVEY ECO Organic Makeup; top right: Josie Maran Cosmetics; bottom right: courtesy of Jane Iredale Mineral Cosmetics

p. 212, left: Suki Advanced Organic Skincare; right: courtesy of Eminence Organic

p. 213, top left: courtesy of Jane Iredale Liquid Minerals; bottom right: courtesy of Clairsonic

Eco-Technology (Electronics)

p. 215: Courtesy of Vers Audio

p. 217, top left: Courtesy of Belkin International, Inc.; bottom: courtesy of Hymini.com

p. 218, middle: courtesy of Dell Inc.; top right: courtesy of Apple

p. 220, bottom: courtesy of USBcell; middle right: courtesy of Solio

p. 221, bottom left: courtesy of HP; middle right: courtesy of Canon USA. All rights reserved.

p. 222, top left: Eton; bottom right: courtesy of Anycom.com

p. 223, top left: courtesy of Iqua.com Bluetooth; right: courtesy of Lenovo.com

p. 225, top left: courtesy of www.usa.philips.com; bottom right: courtesy of plxkiwi.com

p. 226, bottom left: ©iStockphoto.com/Jonathan Brizendine; middle right: courtesy of Samsung

p. 227: courtesy of http://michaelbluejay.com/Saving Electricity

p. 228: logo courtesy of Staples.com/Eco Easy

p. 229, top right: courtesy of Berkeley Institute of the Environment

Greater Outdoors (Outdoors)

p. 231: ©iStockphoto.com/Plainview

p. 232, top: courtesy of wildwingsorganic.com; middle: Photo courtesy Rubicon International

p. 233, bottom right: Photo courtesy Nikon Inc.

p. 234, top: courtesy of Ebird.com; bottom: courtesy of Sibleyguides.com

p. 236: Photo courtesy Echo, Inc.

p. 237, top: Photo courtesy Youngstown Equipment Company; bottom: Photo courtesy Tasco Corporation

p. 238, top: Photo courtesy of Jeff Serena; right: Photo courtesy Stihl USA; bottom: ©iStockphoto.com/ Eric Isselée

p. 239, top: Photo courtesy Corona Clipper, Inc.; bottom: Photo courtesy Ames True Temper®

p. 240, top left: Photo courtesy ENVIRON-Metal, Inc.; bottom left: Photo courtesy Nammo Lapua; right: Photo courtesy Loon Outdoors

p. 241, bottom left: Courtesy Berkley Recycling

p. 243, bottom: Photo courtesy Ocean Kayak; top: courtesy of Sodablast Systems LLC

p. 244, bottom: Photo courtesy Honda Marine; top: courtesy Stingray Boats

p. 245: Photo courtesy ePaint Company

Round Trips (Travel)

p. 247: ©iStockphoto.com/Geoffrey Holman

p. 248, left: Photo courtesy of Lindblad Expeditions; middle right: Sage Photo & Video Art for Artisans' World Marketplace; lower right: logo courtesy of Rainforest Alliance Certified

p. 249: ©iStockphoto.com/pederk.

p. 250, top: ©iStockphoto.com/Fenykepez; lower right: Devils Thumb Ranch

p. 251, left: The International Ecotourism Society (TIES); right: Frank Sanchez; bottom left: logo courtesy of Lonely Planet

p. 252, left: Todd Anderson; right: courtesy of Xola Consulting

p. 253, left: courtesy of Nihiwatu Resort Sumba; bottom: courtesy of Powertraveller.co.uk

p. 254: ©iStockphoto.com/Howard Oates

p. 255, left: Courtesy of Tiamo Resorts; upper right: Green Spot Travel

p. 256, left: © Glen Delman; right: Lapa Rios Eco Lodge

p. 257, right: Spannocchia Foundation

p. 258, left: Jack Affleck/Vail Resorts (photo taken at Vail); bottom right: Courtesy of Journeys Within Our Community

p. 259, mid-right: courtesy of ECOCLUB®; lower right: courtesy of Tim DeFrisco—Sierra Designs Deja Vu sleeping bag

p. 260, left: Charles H. Whitfield; bottom left: iStockphoto.com/Chris Fourie; right middle: courtesy of Patagonia

p. 261, mid-right: courtesy of Osprey Packs; upper right: courtesy of responsibletravel.com; bottom: Photo courtesy of Banyan Tree Hotels & Resort

p. 262, bottom left: Gordon Thorne; upper right: courtesy of Michael Robbins; bottom right: Sigg

p. 263, left: courtesy of Bio-Beetle ECO Rental Cars; middle: ©iStockphoto.com/Christopher Conrad; bottom: ©iStockphoto.com/www.reddotstudio.ch

Next Generation (Parenting)

p. 265: Speesees Peacock Booties, www.speesees.com

p. 266, bottom right: Play Mart, Inc.—The Leader in Recycled Plastic Play Systems

p. 267, top: Used with Permission: Organic Valley Family of Farms; bottom: Used with Permission: The Hain-Celestial Group

p. 268, top: courtesy of Natursutten, Denmark; bottom: Photo used with permission from Mother-ease Inc.

p. 269, top: www.greenmountaindiapers.com; bottom: courtesy of Blue Ridge Eco Shop, Charlottesville, Va., www.BlueRidgeEcoShop.com

p. 270, top: courtesy of TerrEssentials; middle right: Used with Permission: Fleurville, Inc.; bottom left: courtesy of Kushies.com

p. 271, top: Used with Permission: ERGObaby; bottom: cocoa lap tee by speecees.com

p. 272: courtesy of "Weebit" by Simple Shoes

p. 273, top right and bottom right: Naturepedic.com

p. 274, top: courtesy of Pacific Rim; bottom: courtesy of Green Home

p. 275, top left: © Stickeen Photography; bottom right: ©iStockphoto.com/Eric Isselée

p. 276, top: courtesy of Avalon Organics; bottom: ©iStockphoto.com/TIM MCCAIG

p. 277, top: courtesy of Healthy Toys; middle right: courtesy of The Natural Wildlife Federation; bottom center: ©iStockphoto.com/Carlos Alvarez

p. 278, top: courtesy of Playmart, Inc.; bottom: Used with Permission: Late for the Sky Production Co.

p. 279, bottom right: Image reprinted with kind permission from Barefoot Books

p. 280, top: with permission from Voltaic Systems; bottom: courtesy of Green Earth Office Supply

p. 281, middle left: Used with Permission: Fleurville, Inc.; bottom: courtesy of The Jane Goodall Institute

Playing Clean (Sports and Recreation)

p. 283: courtesy of Crescent Moon

p. 284, top left: courtesy of Michael Robbins; bottom right: courtesy of ALO

p. 285, top left: courtesy of Injinji; top right: courtesy of Patagonia; bottom: courtesy of Habitat

p. 286, bottom left: courtesy of Merrell; top center: courtesy of Arbor

p. 287, top left: courtesy of Ibex; bottom left: courtesy of Primus

p. 288, top left: courtesy of Hennessy Hammocks; bottom left: courtesy of REI; middle right: courtesy of Osprey Packs

p. 289, bottom left: courtesy of Mountain Smith; top right: courtesy of Green Guru

p. 290, top left: courtesy of Vibram Five Fingers; bottom right: courtesy of Big Agnes

p. 291, left: ©iStockphoto.com/Stephen Strathdee; bottom right: courtesy of Sanuk

p. 292, left: courtesy of Brooks; center and bottom right: courtesy of Crescent Moon

p. 293: courtesy of ProBar

p. 294, middle left: courtesy of Five Ten; top right: courtesy of Nuun

p. 295, left, courtesy of Calfee Design; top right: courtesy of Disc Golf; bottom: courtesy of Eco Lips

p. 296, lower left: courtesy of K2 Skates; top right: Photo courtesy of Patrick W. Robbins

p. 297: courtesy of Necky® Kayaks

Doing Well and Good (Money)

p. 299: ©iStockphoto.com/PeskyMonkey

p. 300: ©iStockphoto.com/Skip O'Donnell

p. 301, bottom right: courtesy of ShoreBank; middle left: Chittenden Bank, a division of Peoples United Bank; top right: courtesy of Permaculture Credit Union

p. 302, middle left: logo First Green Bank; bottom left: ©iStockphoto.com/Matteo De Stefano; middle right: courtesy of Vicky Vaughn Shea

p. 303: ©iStockphoto.com/Tomasz Pietryszek

p. 304, top left: ©iStockphoto.com/Marcela Barsse; middle right: courtesy of the Hunter Fan Company; bottom: ACEEE logo

p. 305, bottom: ©iStockphoto.com/John Woodcock

p. 306, top left: courtesy of Ormat Technologies Inc.; middle right: courtesy of Parnassus Investments

p. 307, top right: logo courtesy of Portfolio 21

p. 308, top right: ©iStockphoto.com/pixhook

p. 309: by permission of the copyright holder, Domini Social Investments LLC

p. 310, middle right: ©iStockphoto.com/blackred

p. 311, top left: ©iStockphoto.com/Victor Melniciuc; middle right: courtesy of BNSF

p. 312: logo courtesy of TIAA-CREF

p. 313: courtesy of Guidestar

p. 314: ©iStockphoto.com/James McQuillan

p. 315, bottom right: logo courtesy of Sierra Club

Natural Healing (Medicine)

p. 317: ©iStockphoto.com/Anna Subotina

p. 318, bottom left: courtesy of Boiron; bottom right: courtesy of Vital Botanicals

p. 319, middle right: courtesy of migraineaid.com; bottom right: courtesy of Enzymatictherapy

p. 320, middle right: courtesy of New Chapter, Inc.; bottom left: ©iStockphoto.com/Liane Matrisch

p. 321, middle top: courtesy of Nature's Way; bottom left: ©iStockphoto.com/Floortje

p. 322, middle left: courtesy of Dr. Theo's; bottom: ©iStockphoto.com/Monika Adamczyk, middle right: courtesy of Herb Pharm

p. 324, middle right: courtesy of Nature's Way; bottom: ©iStockphoto.com/Cory Docken

p. 325, top left: courtesy of Herbalist & Alchemist; bottom right: courtesy of Herbs Etc.

p. 326, middle right: courtesy of New Chapter; bottom right: courtesy of NuNaturals

p. 327, upper left: ©iStockphoto.com/Anna Subotina; bottom: Courtesy of Traditional Medicinals; middle right: Courtesy of Fungi Perfecti, © Paul Stamets

p. 328: ©iStockphoto.com/Anna Yu

p. 329, top left: courtesy of www.erbaviva.com; bottom right: courtesy of Herb Pharm

p. 330, bottom left: ©iStockphoto.com/Elena Elisseeva; top right: ©iStockphoto.com/JordeAngjelovi

p. 331, top right: courtesy of Herbalist & Alchemist; bottom middle: courtesy of Nature's Way

p. 332, top left: courtesy of Fungi Perfecti, © Paul Stamets; top right and bottom: courtesy of Barleans

p. 334, middle: Photograph courtesy of Nordic Naturals; top right: courtesy of Nature's Way

p. 335: courtesy of Pycnogenol®

Green Pet Care (Pet Care)

p. 337: courtesy of Planet Dog

p. 338, lower left: The Honest Kitchen, Inc.; upper right: courtesy of Evo

p. 339, upper left: Castor & Pollux Pet Works®; mid-left: PureTreats Inc.; mid-bottom: courtesy of PetGuard

p. 340, mid-left: Maggie Johnson/Sojourner Farms; mid-right: courtesy of Petzlife; lower right: Courtesy of Bark Stix

p. 341, upper left: Sara Maguire; mid-bottom: Petapotty.com

p. 342, mid-left: Cat Dancer Products ©2009; upper right: courtesy of Ruff Wear, Inc.; lower left: KONG Company 2009; lower right: courtesy of Pet PDC

p. 343, mid-left: courtesy of Planet Dog; bottom left: Canine Genius

p. 344, mid and lower left: courtesy of The Untangler; mid-right: Courtesy of Nu Hemp

p. 345, upper left: courtesy of Moosedreams Lavender Farms; lower right: photo courtesy of Wagging Green Inc.

p. 346, upper and lower left: courtesy of Ruff Wear, Inc.; mid-right: ©iStockphoto.com/jclegg photograph; lower right: courtesy of Ruff Wear, Inc.

p. 347, upper left: courtesy of Gaia Enterprises, Inc.; upper right and lower left: courtesy of Ruff Wear, Inc.

p. 348, upper left: Diane Henry Studio; mid-right: Doug Wournell—Keystroke Design; lower right: Omega Paw Inc. / Darryl Hodgins

p. 349, upper left: Omega Paw Inc. / Darryl Hodgins; lower right: courtesy of Moosedreams Lavender Farms

p. 350, mid-left: courtesy of Fleabusters; upper right: courtesy of George's Always Active Aloe; lower right: Photographs courtesy of Nordic Naturals

p. 351, upper left: courtesy of Designing Health Inc., Makers of the Missing Link; mid-right: Grizzly Salmon Oil logo; bottom: ©iStockphoto/Eric Isselée

p. 352, upper left: courtesy of Georgesf.com; mid left: Courtesy of Ruff Wear, Inc.; lower left: courtesy of PetMate; upper right: Anxiety wrap; lower right: photo courtesy of Muttropolis.com

p. 353, lower left: Courtesy of NuHemp; lower right: logo courtesy of SPAY USA®

Green Creativity (Arts and Crafts)

p. 355: courtesy of M. Graham & Company (water color tubes)

p. 356, lower left: courtesy of Exotic Paper; upper right: courtesy of Legion Paper, Inc.

p. 357: GreenField Paper Company, www.greenfield paper.com

p. 358, top right: ©iStockphoto.com/ooyoo; middle left: courtesy of Rock Mineral Rich Paper; bottom: Cumberland Pencil Company, www.pencils.co.uk

p. 359, mid-page: Faber-Castell; lower right: Earth Pigments Company, www.earthpigments

p. 360, mid-left: courtesy of Utrecht Art Supplies, www.utrecht.com; upper right: Gamblin/Logo; lower right: Artemis Acquacolours

p. 361, upper left: M Graham & Company; bottom: ©iStockphoto.com/Mayumi Terao; top right: M. Graham Signature Logo; middle right: Gamblin/Logo

p. 362, mid-right: courtesy of M. Graham & Company (walnut oil)

p. 363, upper left: Gamblin/Torrit Grey; lower right: Image by Wayne C. Moore. Image courtesy of SCAD.

p. 364, mid-left: Gamblin/Gamsol; upper right: *The Artists Complete Health and Safety Guide* by Monona Rossol, published by Allworth Press, 2002. Used by permission. www.allworth.com; lower right: Utrecht Art Supplies, www.utrechtart.com

p. 367, lower left: Image courtesy of Jack Richeson & Co. Fine Art Materials, www.richesonart.com; upper right: Ampersand Products; lower right: Courtesy the Gilman Brothers Company

p. 368, upper left: photo by Peter Norby.com; lower left: eBeeHoney.com; upper right: Phoenix Phan © 2008 SWTC designed by Joan Sommerville, Styling by Lena Walker Smith; mid-right: Michael Lafferty

p. 369, upper right: Taskboard Photo by Ena Nyari

p. 370, upper left: Image courtesy Rodale; lower left: Cover of *Embracing Encaustic: Learning to Paint with Beeswax*. Linda Womack; mid-right: Red River Paper, www.redriverpaper.com; lower right: photo courtesy Nikon Inc.

p. 371, mid-left: Silvergrain Group Photo by Freestyle Photographic; upper right: Blick Art Materials, www.dickblick.com; lower right: *Green Graphic Design* by Brian Dougherty with Celery Design Collaborative, published by Allworth Press, 2008. Used by permission www.allworth.com.

p. 372, upper left: image courtesy of Eco-Artware.com; lower left: Lyra Ferby; mid-right: Stockmar Logo

p. 373, mid-left: Alex Thach; upper right: Stockmar Modeling Beeswax; bottom: courtesy of Stockmar Aquarell Watercolors

Looking for even more of the best things for you and the earth?

Find more FYIs, expert advice, up-to-the-minute reviews, and everything green under the sun online at:

wholegreenearthcatalog.com